Microsoft®
Office 2000
Enhanced Edition

INTERACTIVE COMPUTING SERIES

Kenneth C. Laudon
Kenneth Rosenblatt

with Robin Pickering

Azimuth Interactive, Inc.

InformationTechnology

McGraw-Hill
Irwin

Boston   Burr Ridge, IL   Dubuque, IA   Madison, WI   New York   San Francisco   St. Louis
Bangkok   Bogotá   Caracas   Kuala Lumpur   Lisbon   London   Madrid   Mexico City
Milan   Montreal   New Delhi   Santiago   Seoul   Singapore   Sydney   Taipei   Toronto

McGraw-Hill Higher Education

A Division of The **McGraw-Hill** Companies

2 3 4 5 6 7 8 9 0 QPD/QPD 9 0 9 8 7 6 5 4 3 2 1

ISBN 0-07-250017-4

Publisher: *George Werthman*
Sponsoring editor: *Jodi McPherson*
Associate editor: *Steve Schuetz*
Developmental editor: *Craig S. Leonard*
Senior marketing manager: *Jeff Parr*
Senior project manager: *Jean Hamilton*
Senior production supervisor: *Michael R. McCormick*
Freelance design coordinator: *Pam Verros*
Cover illustration: *Kip Henrie*
Supplement coordinator: *Marc Mattson*
Compositor: *Azimuth Interactive, Inc.*
Typeface: *10/12 Sabon*
Printer: *Quebecor Printing Book Group/Dubuque*

Library of Congress Catalog Card Number: 99-63491

www.mhhe.com

Microsoft®
Office 2000
Enhanced Edition

INTERACTIVE COMPUTING SERIES

Kenneth C. Laudon
Kenneth Rosenblatt

with Robin Pickering

Azimuth Interactive, Inc.

InformationTechnology

At McGraw-Hill Higher Education, we publish instructional materials targeted at the higher education market. In an effort to expand the tools of higher learning, we publish texts, lab manuals, study guides, testing materials, software, and multimedia products.

At McGraw-Hill/Irwin (a division of McGraw-Hill Higher Education), we realize technology will continue to create new mediums for professors and students to manage resources and communicate information with one another. We strive to provide the most flexible and complete teaching and learning tools available and offer solutions to the changing world of teaching and learning.

McGraw-Hill/Irwin is dedicated to providing the tools necessary for today's instructors and students to navigate the world of Information Technology successfully.

Seminar Series – McGraw-Hill/Irwin's Technology Connection seminar series offered across the country every year, demonstrates the latest technology products and encourages collaboration among teaching professionals.

Osborne/McGraw-Hill – A division of the McGraw-Hill Companies known for its best-selling Internet titles *Harley Hahn's Internet & Web Yellow Pages* and the *Internet Complete Reference*, offers an additional resource for certification and has strategic publishing relationships with corporations such as Corel Corporation and America Online. For more information, visit Osborne at www.osborne.com.

Digital Solutions – McGraw-Hill/Irwin is committed to publishing Digital Solutions. Taking your course online doesn't have to be a solitary venture. Nor does it have to be a difficult one. We offer several solutions, which will let you enjoy all the benefits of having course material online. For more information, visit www.mhhe.com/solutions/index.mhtml.

Packaging Options – For more about our discount options, contact your local McGraw-Hill/Irwin Sales representative at 1-800-338-3987, or visit our Web site at www.mhhe.com/it.

Preface

Interactive Computing Series

Goals/Philosophy

The *Interactive Computing Series* provides you with an illustrated interactive environment for learning software skills using Microsoft Office. The Interactive Computing Series is composed of both text and multimedia interactive CD-ROMs. The text and the CD-ROMs are closely coordinated. *It's up to you. You can choose how you want to learn.*

Approach

The *Interactive Computing Series* is the visual interactive way to develop and apply software skills. This skills-based approach coupled with its highly visual, two-page spread design allows the student to focus on a single skill without having to turn the page. A running case study is provided through the text, reinforcing the skills and giving a real-world focus to the learning process.

About the Book

The Interactive Computing Series offers *two levels* of instruction. Each level builds upon the previous level.

Brief lab manual – covers the basics of the application, contains two to four chapters.
Introductory lab manual – includes the material in the Brief textbook plus two to four additional chapters.

Each lesson is organized around **Skills**, **Concepts**, and **Steps (Do It!)**.

Each lesson is divided into a number of Skills. Each **Skill** is first explained at the top of the page.
Each **Concept** is a concise description of why the skill is useful and where it is commonly used.
Each **Step (Do It!)** contains the instructions on how to complete the skill.

About the CD-ROM

The CD-ROM provides a unique interactive environment for students where they learn to use software faster and remember it better. The CD-ROM is organized in a similar approach as the text: The **Skill** is defined, the **Concept** is explained in rich multimedia, and the student performs **Steps (Do It!)** within sections called Interactivities. There are at least 45 Interactivities per CD-ROM. Some of the features of the CD-ROM are:

Simulated Environment – The Interactive Computing CD-ROM places students in a simulated controlled environment where they can practice and perform the skills of the application software.
Interactive Exercises – The student is asked to demonstrate command of a specific software skill. The student's actions are followed by a digital "TeacherWizard" that provides feedback.
SmartQuizzes – Provide performance-based assessment of the student at the end of each lesson.

Using the Book

In the book, each skill is described in a two-page graphical spread (Figure 1). The left side of the two-page spread describes the skill, the concept, and the steps needed to perform the skill. The right side of the spread uses screen shots to show you how the screen should look at key stages.

Figure 1

Skill: Each lesson is divided into a number of specific skills

Concept: A concise description of why the skill is useful and where it is commonly used

Running case: A real-world case ties the skill and the concept to a practical situation

Do It!: Step-by-step directions show you how to use the skill

Lesson 2 • Managing Files with Windows Explorer

Using the Recycle Bin

Concept

The Recycle Bin is a storage place for files that have been deleted. Files that you no longer need should be deleted in order to save disk space and maximize the efficiency of your computer. If you decide that you need a file again, or have accidentally deleted a file, you can rescue it from the Recycle Bin. If you know you will never need a file again, you can delete the file permanently.

Do It!

Send the Copy of Alice and To Be Deleted folders to the Recycle Bin. Then rescue To Be Deleted from the Recycle Bin. Finally, delete both items from your hard drive permanently.

1. Open Windows Explorer from the Start menu.

2. Expand the necessary icons, and then click the My Student Files folder in the left panel to select it.

3. Click the Copy of Alice folder in the right panel, then click the Delete button ⊠ on the Standard Buttons toolbar. The Confirm Folder Delete dialog box (**Figure 2-22**) will appear, asking if you are sure you want to move the folder to the Recycle Bin.

4. Click [Yes]. The dialog box will close and the folder will be moved to the Recycle Bin. Notice the change in the Recycle Bin icon when it is not empty.

5. Click the Close button ⊠ to exit Windows Explorer.

6. Click and drag the To Be Deleted shortcut from the desktop to the Recycle Bin. When the Recycle Bin becomes highlighted, release the mouse button. The shortcut is deposited in the Recycle Bin.

7. Double-click the Recycle Bin icon. The Recycle Bin window will open. **Figure 2-23** shows the inside of the Recycle Bin displaying all the files and folder you have sent there.

8. Drag the To Be Deleted shortcut from the Recycle Bin window to an empty space on the desktop. The shortcut appears on the desktop and is now an accessible item that can be used. Items still in the Recycle Bin cannot be opened.

9. Right-click the To Be Deleted shortcut and choose the Delete command from the pop-up menu to send the folder back into the Recycle Bin.

10. Click [Yes] to confirm the operation.

11. Click the Empty Recycle Bin button [Empty Recycle Bin] (if not visible click File, then click Empty Recycle Bin). The Confirm Multiple File Delete dialog box will appear.

12. Click [Yes] to delete the folders from your hard drive permanently.

13. Click ⊠ to shut the Recycle Bin window. Note that you also can empty the Recycle Bin by right-clicking it and then choosing the Empty Recycle Bin command.

WN 2.20

End-of-Lesson Features

In the book, the learning in each lesson is reinforced at the end by a quiz and a skills review called Interactivity, which provides step-by-step exercises and real-world problems for the students to solve independently.

Figure 1 (cont'd)

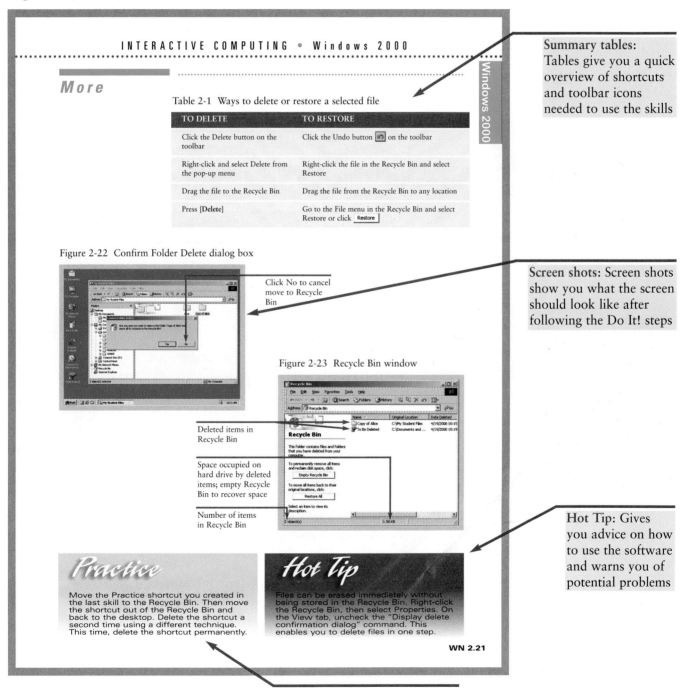

INTERACTIVE COMPUTING • Windows 2000

Summary tables: Tables give you a quick overview of shortcuts and toolbar icons needed to use the skills

Screen shots: Screen shots show you what the screen should look like after following the Do It! steps

Hot Tip: Gives you advice on how to use the software and warns you of potential problems

Practice: Allows you to practice the skill with a built-in exercise or directs you to a student file

Table 2-1 Ways to delete or restore a selected file

TO DELETE	TO RESTORE
Click the Delete button on the toolbar	Click the Undo button on the toolbar
Right-click and select Delete from the pop-up menu	Right-click the file in the Recycle Bin and select Restore
Drag the file to the Recycle Bin	Drag the file from the Recycle Bin to any location
Press [Delete]	Go to the File menu in the Recycle Bin and select Restore or click Restore

Figure 2-22 Confirm Folder Delete dialog box

Click No to cancel move to Recycle Bin

Figure 2-23 Recycle Bin window

Deleted items in Recycle Bin

Space occupied on hard drive by deleted items; empty Recycle Bin to recover space

Number of items in Recycle Bin

Practice

Move the Practice shortcut you created in the last skill to the Recycle Bin. Then move the shortcut out of the Recycle Bin and back to the desktop. Delete the shortcut a second time using a different technique. This time, delete the shortcut permanently.

Hot Tip

Files can be erased immediately without being stored in the Recycle Bin. Right-click the Recycle Bin, then select Properties. On the View tab, uncheck the "Display delete confirmation dialog" command. This enables you to delete files in one step.

WN 2.21

Using the Interactive CD-ROM

The Interactive Computing multimedia CD-ROM provides an unparalleled learning environment in which you can learn software skills faster and better than in books alone. The CD-ROM creates a unique interactive environment in which you can learn to use software faster and remember it better. The CD-ROM uses the same lessons, skills, concepts, and Do It! steps as found in the book, but presents the material using voice, video, animation, and precise simulation of the software you are learning. A typical CD-ROM contents screen shows the major elements of a lesson (see Figure 2 below).

Skills list: A list of skills allows you to jump directly to any skill you want to learn or review, including interactive sessions with the TeacherWizard

Figure 2

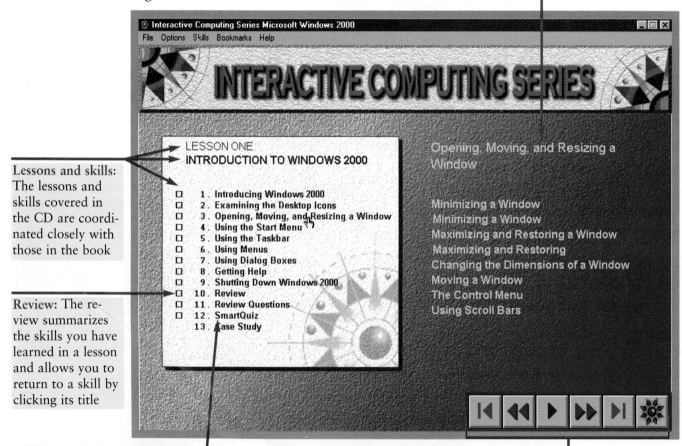

Lessons and skills: The lessons and skills covered in the CD are coordinated closely with those in the book

Review: The review summarizes the skills you have learned in a lesson and allows you to return to a skill by clicking its title

Review Questions and SmartQuiz: Review Questions test your knowledge of the concepts covered in the lesson; SmartQuiz tests your ability to accomplish tasks in a simulated software environment

User controls: Precise and simple user controls permit you to start, stop, pause, jump forward or backward one sentence, or jump forward or backward an entire skill. A single navigation star takes you back to the lesson's table of contents

Unique Features of the CD-ROM:
TeacherWizard™ and SmartQuiz™

Interactive Computing: Software Skills offers many leading-edge features on the CD currently found in no other learning product on the market. One such feature is *interactive exercises* in which you are asked to demonstrate your command of a software skill in a precisely simulated software environment. Your actions are followed closely by a digital TeacherWizard that guides you with additional information if you make a mistake. When you complete the action called for by the TeacherWizard correctly, you are congratulated and prompted to continue the lesson. If you make a mistake, the TeacherWizard gently lets you know: "No, that's not the right icon. Click on the Folder icon on the left side of the top toolbar to open a file." No matter how many mistakes you make, the TeacherWizard is there to help you.

Another leading-edge feature is the end-of-lesson SmartQuiz. Unlike the multiple-choice and matching questions found in the book quiz, the SmartQuiz puts you in a simulated digital software world and asks you to show your mastery of skills while actually working with the software (Figure 3).

Figure 3

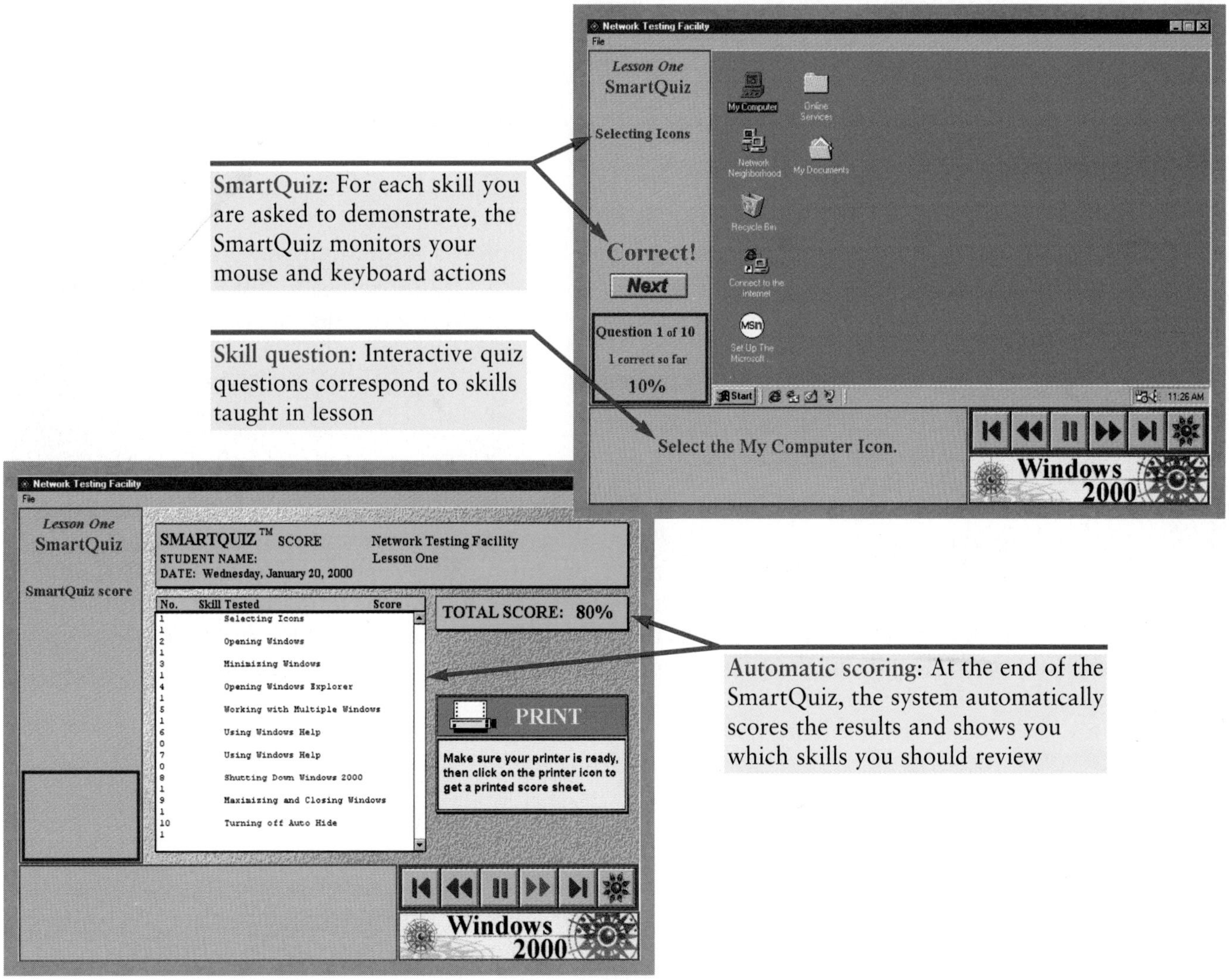

SmartQuiz: For each skill you are asked to demonstrate, the SmartQuiz monitors your mouse and keyboard actions

Skill question: Interactive quiz questions correspond to skills taught in lesson

Automatic scoring: At the end of the SmartQuiz, the system automatically scores the results and shows you which skills you should review

Teaching Resources

The following is a list of supplemental material available with the Interactive Computing Series:

Skills Assessment

McGraw-Hill/Irwin offers two innovative systems, ATLAS and SimNet, which take testing beyond the basics with pre- and post-assessment capabilities.

ATLAS (Active Testing and Learning Assessment Software) – available for the *Interactive Computing Series* – is our live-in-the-application Skills Assessment tool. ATLAS allows students to perform tasks while working live within the Office applications environment. ATLAS is Web-enabled and customizable to meet the needs of your course. ATLAS is available for Office 2000.

SimNet (Simulated Network Assessment Product) – available for the *Interactive Computing Series* – permits you to test the actual software skills students learn about the Microsoft Office applications in a simulated environment. SimNet is Web-enabled and is available for Office 97 and Office 2000.

Instructor's Resource Kits

The Instructor's Resource Kit provides professors with all of the ancillary material needed to teach a course. McGraw-Hill/Irwin is dedicated to providing instructors with the most effective instruction resources available. Many of these resources are available at our Information Technology Supersite www.mhhe.com/it. Our Instructor's Kits are available on CD-ROM and contain the following:

Diploma by Brownstone – is the most flexible, powerful, and easy-to-use computerized testing system available in higher education. The diploma system allows professors to create an Exam as a printed version, as a LAN-based Online version, and as an Internet version. Diploma includes grade book features, which automate the entire testing process.

Instructor's Manual – Includes:
–Solutions to all lessons and end-of-unit material
–Teaching Tips
–Teaching Strategies
–Additional exercises

PowerPoint Slides – NEW to the Interactive Computing Series, all of the figures from the application textbooks are available in PowerPoint slides for presentation purposes.

Student Data Files – To use the Interactive Computing Series, students must have Student Data Files to complete practice and test sessions. The instructor and students using this text in classes are granted the right to post the student files on any network or stand-alone computer, or to distribute the files on individual diskettes. The student files may be downloaded from our IT Supersite at www.mhhe.com/it.

Series Web Site – Available at www.mhhe.com/cit/apps/laudon.

Digital Solutions

Pageout Lite – is designed if you're just beginning to explore Web site options. Pageout Lite is great for posting your own material online. You may choose one of three templates, type in your material, and Pageout Lite instantly converts it to HTML.

Pageout – is our Course Web site Development Center. Pageout offers a Syllabus page, Web site address, Online Learning Center Content, online exercises and quizzes, gradebook, discussion board, an area for students to build their own Web pages, and all the features of Pageout Lite. For more information please visit the Pageout Web site at www.mhla.net/pageout.

OLC/Series Web Sites - Online Learning Centers (OLCs)/Series Sites are accessible through our Supersite at www.mhhe.com/it. Our Online Learning Centers/Series Sites provide pedagogical features and supplements for our titles online. Students can point and click their way to key terms, learning objectives, chapter overviews, PowerPoint slides, exercises, and web links.

The McGraw-Hill Learning Architecture (MHLA) - is a complete course delivery system. MHLA gives professors ownership in the way digital content is presented to the class through online quizzing, student collaboration, course administration, and content management. For a walk-through of MHLA visit the MHLA Web site at www.mhla.net.

Packaging Options - For more about our discount options, contact your local Irwin/McGraw-Hill Sales representative at 1-800-338-3987 or visit our Web site at www.mhhe.com/it.

Visit www.mhhe.com/it
THE ONLY SITE WITH ALL YOUR CIT AND MIS NEEDS.

Acknowledgments

The Interactive Computing Series is a cooperative effort of many individuals, each contributing to an overall team effort. The Interactive Computing team is composed of instructional designers, writers, multimedia designers, graphic artists, and programmers. Our goal is to provide you and your instructor with the most powerful and enjoyable learning environment using both traditional text and new interactive multimedia techniques. Interactive Computing is tested rigorously in both CD and text formats prior to publication.

Our special thanks to George Werthman, our Publisher; Craig Leonard, our Developmental Editor; and Jeffrey Parr, Marketing Director for Computer Information Systems. They have provided exceptional market awareness and understanding, along with enthusiasm and support for the project, and have inspired us all to work closely together. In addition, Steven Schuetz provided valuable technical review of our interactive versions, and Charles Pelto contributed superb quality assurance.

The Azimuth team members who contributed to the textbooks and CD-ROM multimedia program are:

Ken Rosenblatt (Editorial Director, Writer)
Russell Polo (Technical Director)
Steven D. Pileggi (Multimedia Project Director)
Robin Pickering (Developmental Editor, Writer)
Stefon Westry (Multimedia Designer)
Chris Hahnenberger (Multimedia Designer)
Joseph S. Gina (Multimedia Designer)
Irene Pileggi (Multimedia Designer)
Dan Langan (Multimedia Designer)

Contents

Office 2000 Enhanced Edition

Contents *continued*

Contents continued

Contents *continued*

Contents continued

LESSON

1

INTRODUCTION TO WINDOWS 2000

Windows 2000 is an **operating system** that controls the basic functions of your computer, such as loading and running programs, saving data, and displaying information on the screen. Operating system software is different from application software, such as a word processor or spreadsheet program, which you apply to letter writing or calculating data. Instead, operating system software provides the **user interface** — the visual display on the screen that you use to operate the computer by choosing which programs to run and how to organize your work. Windows 2000 offers a **graphical user interface** or **GUI** (pronounced "gooey") that presents you with pictorial representations of computer functions and data.

It is through these pictures, or icons, that you interact with the computer. **Data files** are represented by icons that look like pieces of paper and can be organized into groups called **folders**, which look like manila folders. The **My Computer** icon, represented by a small desktop PC, allows you to organize these files and folders. Other icons allow you to run programs such as a word processor, a Web browser, or Windows' built-in file manager, **Windows Explorer**.

Windows 2000 is a powerful operating system that allows you to perform a variety of high-level tasks. Windows 2000 is actually the successor to the Windows NT 4.0 operating system, but it looks, acts, and responds in much the same manner as Windows 98. For instance, the GUI is very similar, using many of the same icons as Windows 98. It also includes integrated Web features. Thus, Windows 2000 gives you the ease of use of Windows 98, with the power, stability, and security previously provided by Windows NT. This makes Windows 2000 an ideal tool for operating a business whether it is run on a laptop computer, a desktop system, or a large business server.

Windows 2000 is easy to use and can be customized with the preferences and options that you desire. Built-in programs called **Accessories** can be used to help you with day-to-day tasks. **Help** offers fast tutorial and troubleshooting advice. This book will teach you about the basic elements of Windows 2000 and how to use them. You will learn file management, advanced Windows functions, Internet skills, and some of the other special features of Windows 2000.

Examining the Desktop Icons

Concept

The screen you see when Windows 2000 completes the StartUp procedure is called the desktop. Do not be surprised if your desktop does not look exactly like the one pictured in **Figure 1-1** as computer setups vary from machine to machine. (Throughout this book the appearance of your desktop and windows will depend on the software installed and the configuration of various settings of your computer.) Like the desk at which you are sitting, the Windows desktop is the workspace on which all actions are performed. On the left side of your screen you will see small pictures called icons. Icons are pictorial representations of a task, program, folder, or file. Each icon represents an application or utility that you can start. You use the mouse — a hand-controlled input device that, when connected to the computer and moved along a clean, flat surface, will move the graphical pointer around the screen — to double-click an icon to open an application or a file. The buttons on the mouse are used to give commands, and there are four basic ways you can use the mouse: **pointing, clicking, double-clicking,** and **dragging.**

Do It!

Use the mouse to move the pointer $\&$ around the desktop to explore the desktop icons.

1 Using the mouse, move the pointer over various areas of the desktop to get a feel for how the pointer moves in relation to the motion of the mouse. Positioning the pointer over an item is called pointing.

2 Locate the My Computer icon on the desktop; it resembles a desktop PC. Place the pointer on the icon and click the left mouse button once (throughout this book, the term click will always refer to pressing and releasing the left mouse button once quickly; other types of clicks will be specified as necessary). This will highlight the icon, indicating that it has been selected. Click a blank area of the screen to undo this selection. Note that primary mouse functions are done using the left button.

3 Double-clicking is done to open a program, file, or window. Open the My Computer window by placing the pointer on the My Computer icon and clicking the left mouse button twice quickly. The My Computer window, shown in **Figure 1-2,** will appear on the desktop.

4 To close the window you have just opened, position the pointer over the Close button ☒ in the upper-right corner and click the left mouse button.

5 Icons are not fixed on the desktop and can be moved by dragging. Move the pointer to the My Computer icon, then click and hold down the button. You have grabbed the icon.

6 With the mouse button held down, move the icon by dragging it to the center of your desktop. A faint image of the icon will appear to indicate the current position of the icon on the desktop. Let go of the mouse button to drop the icon into position. Then return the icon to its original position.

More

Windows 2000 allows you to change the way you work with icons so that the interface behaves more like a Web page. To make this change, click on the word Tools on the Menu bar in the My Computer window. This will cause a list of commands, called a menu, to appear. Click the Folder Options command on the Tools menu to open the Folder Options dialog box. Whenever you see an ellipsis (three dots) following a command, it indicates that the command will open a dialog box revealing options for the execution of the command. The dialog box will open to a tab named General. In the bottom section of this dialog box, the default option is Double-click to open an item (single-click to select). This is the traditional way of interacting with Windows icons. If you select the first option in the section, Single-click to open an item (point to select), the operating system will switch to a Web-like environment where pointing and clicking are concerned.

Figure 1-1 The Windows desktop

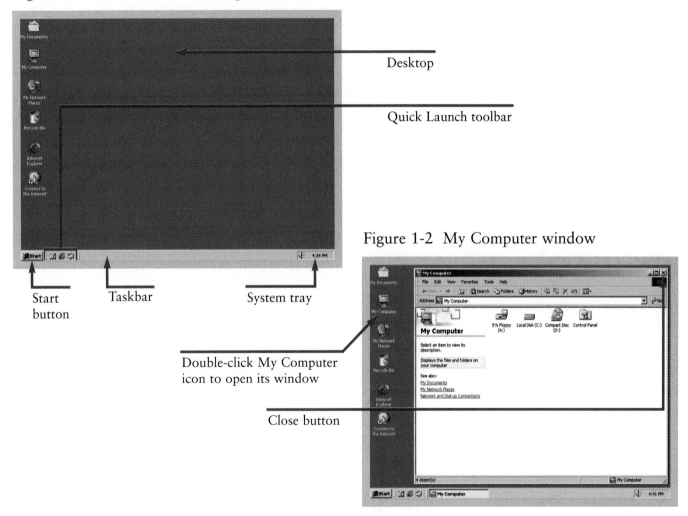

Desktop

Quick Launch toolbar

Figure 1-2 My Computer window

Start
button

Taskbar

System tray

Double-click My Computer
icon to open its window

Close button

Opening, Moving, and Resizing a Window

Concept

As you saw in the previous Skill, icons are pictorial representations of different items on your computer, the most common of which are folders, files, and applications. When you double-click an icon to open it, its contents are revealed in a window or on-screen frame. It is in this window that you interact with a program or utility. Windows are flexible and can be moved, resized, reshaped, and even hidden.

Do It!

Open the My Computer window, then resize, move, minimize, and close it.

1. Double-click the My Computer icon. The My Computer window will open, as shown in **Figure 1-3**.

2. You cannot resize or move a window that is maximized or fills the entire desktop. Look at the three sizing buttons at the right end of the window's title bar, the band at the top of the window that contains the name of the application. The middle button's appearance will change depending on the window's state. If the Restore button ⬚ is visible, click it so the window will no longer be maximized. Once the window is restored to its previous size, the button will change to the Maximize button ⬚. A summary of the sizing buttons can be found in **Table 1-1**.

3. Position the mouse pointer on the right edge of the window. This will change the pointer to a double arrow ↔ that is used to resize an object. In Windows 2000, the appearance of the mouse pointer changes to reflect its function during various tasks.

4. Click and hold the left mouse button, drag the edge of the window towards the center of the screen, and then let go of the mouse button to drop the side of the window into place. As you drag the mouse, the border of the window will move with the double arrow, toolbar buttons will disappear (don't worry; their respective commands can still be accessed through menus), and scroll bars (see More below) may appear. This action may be repeated on any of the window's four sides or at any corner. Resizing from the corner will alter both the height and the width of the window.

5. Windows can be dragged and dropped just as icons can. Move the pointer over the title bar of the My Computer window, and then click and hold the left mouse button to grab the window.

6. With the mouse button depressed, drag the window to another area of the desktop.

Figure 1-3 Components of a window

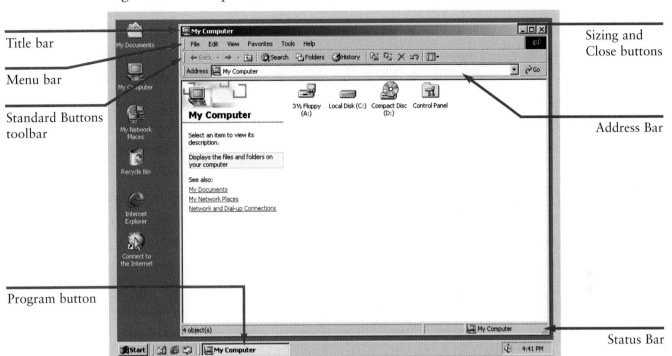

Title bar

Menu bar

Standard Buttons
toolbar

Program button

Sizing and
Close buttons

Address Bar

Status Bar

Table 1-1 Sizing buttons

SIZING BUTTON		USE
Maximize		Enlarges the window so that it fills the entire screen, with the taskbar remaining visible
Restore		Returns the window to its previous size
Minimize		Shrinks the window so it only appears as a program button on the taskbar
Close		Closes a window or program

Opening, Moving, and Resizing (continued)

Do It!

7 Click the Minimize button 🔲. The My Computer window will disappear from the desktop and be reduced to a program button on the taskbar, as shown in **Figure 1-4**.

8 Click the My Computer program button to restore the window to its previous size.

9 Click File on the menu bar. The File menu will appear as shown in **Figure 1-5**.

10 Position the pointer over the last command, Close, to highlight it, and then click the mouse button. The Close command will be executed, just as it would if you clicked the Close button 🆇, and the window will disappear from the desktop.

More

When a window is too small to display all of its information, scroll bars (**Figure 1-6**) will appear on the right and/or bottom edges of the window. Scroll bars are context-sensitive objects and only appear when the situation is appropriate. The scroll bars are used to slide information inside the window so you can see additional contents of the window. If you need to scroll slowly, or only a short distance, click a scroll bar arrow located at the end of the scroll bar. The scroll bar box indicates where you are located in the window. Clicking above or below the scroll bar box moves the display in large increments. Dragging the scroll bar box allows you to control the slide of the window's information precisely.

In the above Skill, you clicked the My Computer program button to unhide the window and make it active. An active window is identified by its highlighted title bar and will be the frontmost window on your desktop if more than one program is running. You also can click the program button of a visible window to minimize it. Right-clicking a program button, clicking it with the right mouse button, will cause a pop-up menu to appear with commands that mirror those of the sizing buttons. These commands also can be found by clicking the Control icon, the icon at the left edge of the title bar representing the application, or by right-clicking the title bar. Right-clicking will usually cause a context-sensitive menu to appear. This menu will contain commands that relate to the task you are performing. Double-clicking the title bar will restore or maximize a window.

Figure 1-4 Minimized My Computer window

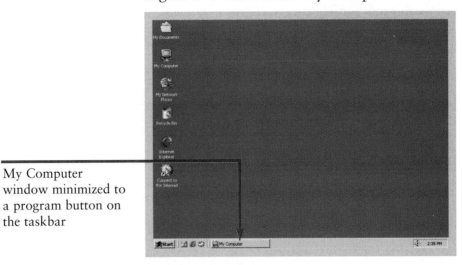

My Computer
window minimized to
a program button on
the taskbar

Figure 1-5 Working with the File menu

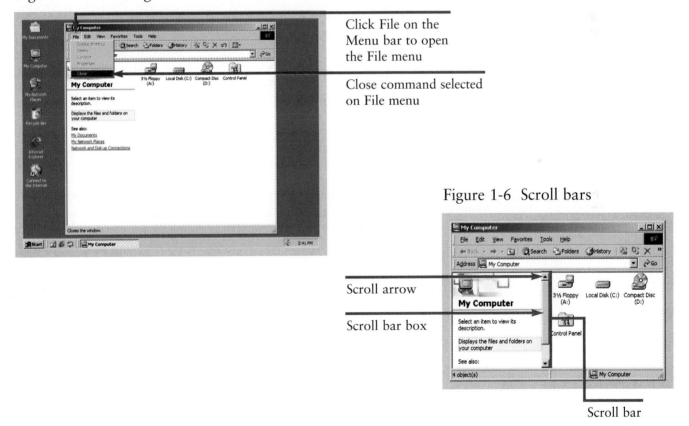

Click File on the
Menu bar to open
the File menu

Close command selected
on File menu

Figure 1-6 Scroll bars

Scroll arrow

Scroll bar box

Scroll bar

Practice

Open and maximize the My Documents window. Then restore the window and drag its right border outward. Close the window when you are done.

Hot Tip

Clicking the Show Desktop button  minimizes all open windows. Clicking the button again opens all of the previously visible windows.

Using the Start Menu

Concept

The Start button [Start], located on the left side of the taskbar, provides a quick and easy way to open and organize the applications found on your computer. Clicking the Start button opens a special menu called the Start menu, shown expanded in **Figure 1-7**, that contains left-to-right lists of program groups. Items with an arrow ▶ next to them contain submenus. Pointing to an item highlights it, and a simple click will then open the program you wish to use.

Do It!

Use the Start button to access the Start menu and start Windows Explorer, a file management utility that will be discussed in detail in Lesson 2 (if you do not see an item that is named in this Skill, click the double arrow at the bottom of the menu).

1 Click the Start button [Start] on the taskbar, usually located at the bottom of your desktop. The Start menu will open. Do not be surprised if your Start menu does not match **Figure 1-7** exactly. The appearance of your Start menu depends on the software installed and the shortcuts created on your computer.

2 Position the pointer over Programs (notice the little arrow) to bring up the Programs menu. The Programs menu contains a list of shortcuts to some of the applications found on your hard drive, as well as folders that hold groups of related shortcuts to other frequently used programs and utilities.

3 Guide the pointer to Accessories, which is likely located at the top of the Programs menu. The Accessories menu will appear alongside the Programs menu.

4 Move the mouse pointer over to the Accessories menu and click the program named Windows Explorer to launch it. **Figure 1-8** displays an open Windows Explorer, with the My Documents folder selected. Notice that a program button displaying the name of the folder selected in Windows Explorer has appeared on the taskbar.

5 Click the Close button [X] on the title bar to exit Windows Explorer.

More

Items on the Start menu and its submenus are really shortcuts to the actual folders and files that they represent.

The Documents menu contains a list of the files that have been opened most recently so that you can access your most recently and most often used data quickly.

On the Settings menu you will find folders that contain utilities for altering your computer's software and hardware settings. The way you interact with your desktop, the folders on it, the taskbar, and printers can all be altered through icons on the Settings menu.

One of the keys to using a computer is being able to locate the data you need. The Search menu offers you multiple ways in which to find information. You can search for files or folders on your computer, content on the World Wide Web, and people in locally stored address books and Internet directories.

Figure 1-7 Start menu

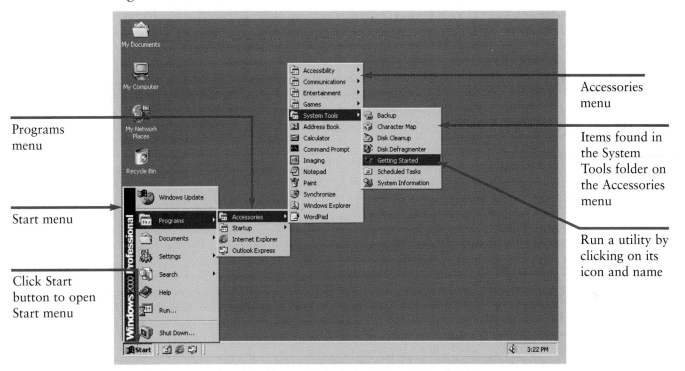

Accessories menu

Items found in the System Tools folder on the Accessories menu

Run a utility by clicking on its icon and name

Programs menu

Start menu

Click Start button to open Start menu

Figure 1-8 Windows Explorer

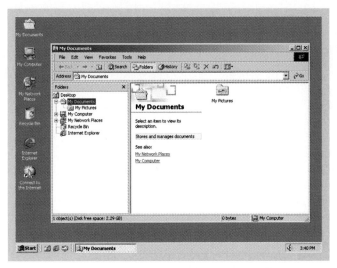

Practice

Use the Start button to open the Printers folder on the Settings menu. If your computer is hooked up to a printer or printers, the name(s) will appear in this window. Close the window from the title bar.

Hot Tip

The Start menu right-click pop-up menu has commands for quickly opening Windows Explorer and the Search feature.

Using the Taskbar

Concept

The taskbar is your guide to the applications running on your system. Each open application creates its own program button on the taskbar, so switching between programs is as simple as the click of a button. While the taskbar is usually found at the bottom of the desktop, it is fixed in neither size nor location.

Do It!

Use the taskbar to open two applications and switch between them. Then, move and resize the taskbar.

1 Click the Start button to open the Start menu, highlight Programs, highlight Accessories, and then select Windows Explorer.

2 Click the Start button, highlight Programs, highlight Accessories, and then select **Calculator**. The calculator will open and two windows will be on your desktop with their respective program buttons on the taskbar, as shown in **Figure 1-9**.

3 Click the Windows Explorer program button, which is labeled **My Documents**. The Windows Explorer window will become active, moving to the foreground of the desktop. Notice that its title bar is now blue, and its program button is indented.

4 Click the Calculator button to make the Calculator window active.

5 Position the mouse pointer on the top edge of the taskbar. The pointer will change to a vertical double arrow when it is in the correct spot.

6 Press and hold the mouse button and drag the top of the taskbar up, until it is three times its original height. The taskbar can be enlarged to up to half of your desktop.

7 Click a blank space on the taskbar, and then hold the mouse button down while dragging the taskbar to the right edge of your desktop, as shown in **Figure 1-10**. The taskbar can be placed on the top, bottom, left, or right of the desktop.

8 Drag the taskbar back to its original place on the desktop and then resize it so it is one program button high.

9 Click each application's Close button to remove the windows from the desktop.

More

Additional taskbar settings can be found in the **Taskbar Properties** dialog box, accessed by highlighting **Settings** on the Start menu and then clicking the **Taskbar & Start Menu** command on the Settings menu. When you open this dialog box you will see five options on the **General** tab. Those with a check mark are turned on. The **Always on top** option prevents any window from obscuring the taskbar. With **Auto hide** turned on, the taskbar will drop out of sight when it is not in use. Move the pointer to the bottom of the desktop to make it reappear. The relative size of your Start menu items is controlled with the **Show small icons in Start menu**. You can turn the taskbar clock on or off with the **Show Clock** command. The **Use Personalized Menus** command permits Windows to hide the menu items that you do not use frequently. When you do need to access a hidden item, click on the double arrow at the bottom of the menu to expand it to its full size.

Figure 1-9 Two open applications

Inactive application window

Active application window

Active program button

Inactive program button

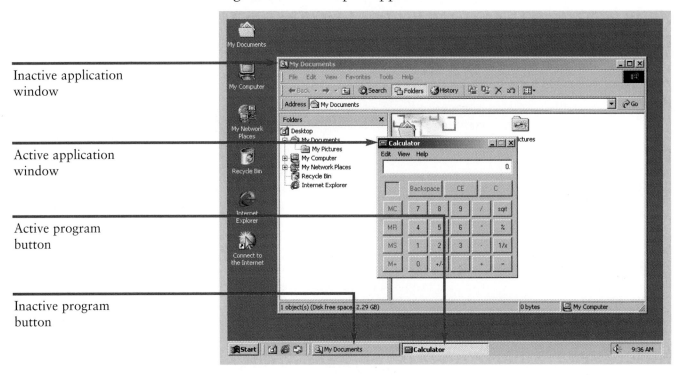

Figure 1-10 Resized and moved taskbar

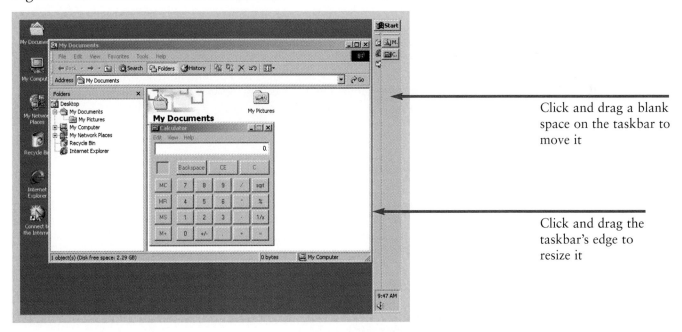

Click and drag a blank space on the taskbar to move it

Click and drag the taskbar's edge to resize it

Practice

Turn on the Auto hide taskbar option. Then open Windows Explorer, My Computer, and Calculator. Practice moving among the open windows. If you do not like the Auto hide option, turn it off again.

Hot Tip

You can move between open applications by holding [Alt] and then pressing [Tab]. Press [Tab] again to cycle through the list of all running applications. Release the [Alt] key when the correct icon is selected. Right-click the taskbar for more options.

Using Menus

Concept

A menu is a list of related operations, also known as commands, that you use to perform specific tasks. The menus that are available to you in any particular window are listed on the Menu bar, which is situated just below the window's title bar. Each Windows program has its own selection of menus, though many are similar. To access a menu, simply click on its menu title on the Menu bar. Some menu commands have shortcut buttons that allow you to execute them by clicking on a toolbar button. You will also find that many commands have keyboard shortcuts. If you prefer the keyboard to the mouse, Windows also provides a way to open all menus and choose any command without clicking.

Do It!

Examine and use a typical menu in the My Computer window.

1. Double-click the My Computer icon to open its window.

2. Click View on the Menu bar to open the View menu, shown in **Figure 1-11**.

3. You will notice that in addition to commands, several symbols appear on the menu. A right-pointing triangle after a command indicates that the command has a submenu. Point to the Toolbars command with the mouse to reveal the Toolbars submenu.

4. Move the mouse pointer down to the Status Bar command. The Toolbars submenu closes. The check mark to the left of the Status Bar command indicates that the feature is currently turned on. A bullet next to a command tells you which command in a set is currently active. Only one command in a set such as the icon view commands may be active at a time.

5. Open the Toolbars submenu again. Then click the Standard Buttons command, which is turned on, to turn it off. The menu closes and the Standard Buttons toolbar disappears, as shown in **Figure 1-12**.

6. You also can use the keyboard to open a menu and execute a command. One letter in each menu title is underlined. Pressing this letter while pressing the [Alt] key will open the corresponding menu. With the My Computer window active, press [Alt], then press [V] to open the View menu.

7. Each command on a menu also has an underlined letter. Pressing this letter on the keyboard initiates the command. Press [T] to open the Toolbars submenu. Then press [S] to execute the Standard Buttons command from the submenu, turning the Standard Buttons toolbar back on.

More

Some commands have keyboard shortcuts that you can use to avoid opening menus altogether. You can learn many of these shortcuts simply by seeing them listed on a menu. For example, if you open the Edit menu in the My Computer window, you will see that the Select All command is followed by [Ctrl]+[A]. This means that you can use the Select All command by holding down the [Ctrl] key and pressing [A].

Figure 1-11 View menu

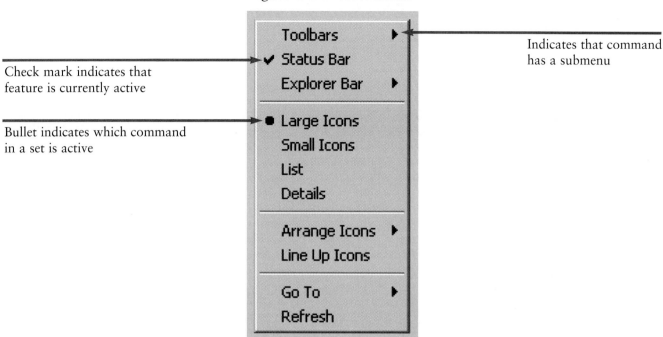

Check mark indicates that
feature is currently active

Bullet indicates which command
in a set is active

Indicates that command
has a submenu

Figure 1-12 My Computer window without Standard Buttons

Practice

Open the My Computer window by double-clicking its icon. Then use the Close command on the File menu to close the window.

Hot Tip

Once a menu has been opened, you can use the arrow keys to move from command to command (up and down arrows) or from menu to menu (left and right arrows). Press [Enter] to execute a highlighted command.

Using Dialog Boxes

Concept

Some commands require additional information before Windows will perform the operations that accompany them. In these cases, a dialog box will appear. Dialog boxes allow you to customize a command's options according to your needs or preferences. Commands that include a dialog box are followed on a menu by three dots, called an ellipsis.

Do It!

Open the WordPad application, and then use the Print command to access and examine the Print dialog box.

1 Click **Start**, highlight Programs, then highlight Accessories, and then click WordPad. WordPad, Windows 2000's built-in word processor, will open.

2 To add text to a WordPad document, you can simply begin typing. Type Your Name's dialog box practice. Your document should look like **Figure 1-13**.

3 Open the File menu and click on the Print command. The Print dialog box will appear, as shown in **Figure 1-14**. The Print dialog box contains a number of common dialog box features, each connected to a specific printing option. Refer to the figure to gain an understanding of how each of these features works.

4 Click the Cancel button **Cancel** . The dialog box closes without executing the Print command.

5 Close the WordPad window. Windows will ask you if you want to save changes to the document. Click **No** .

More

Dialog boxes contain their own help tool. In the upper-right corner of a dialog box, you will find a button marked with a question mark. If you click on this button, a question mark will be attached to your mouse pointer. When you click on any dialog box feature with this pointer, a ScreenTip (**Figure 1-15**) will appear that explains the feature. Click the mouse button again to erase the ScreenTip and restore the pointer to its normal state.

Figure 1-15 Example of a dialog box ScreenTip

If you have selected more than one copy, specifies whether you want the copies to be collated.

Figure 1-13 WordPad document

Click Save button to save a WordPad document

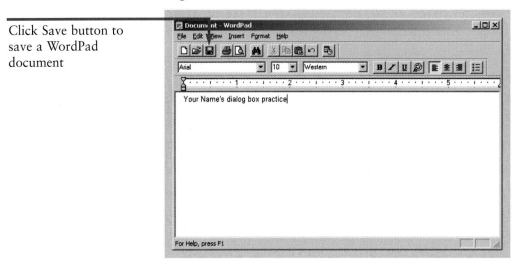

Figure 1-14 Dialog box features

Click tabs to access additional options

Click to get help on dialog box items

Click check box to activate associated option

Use text box to enter a value

Radio buttons allow you to select one option in a set

Click to execute command

Click up or down arrow to change value in spin box

Click to perform operation without closing dialog box

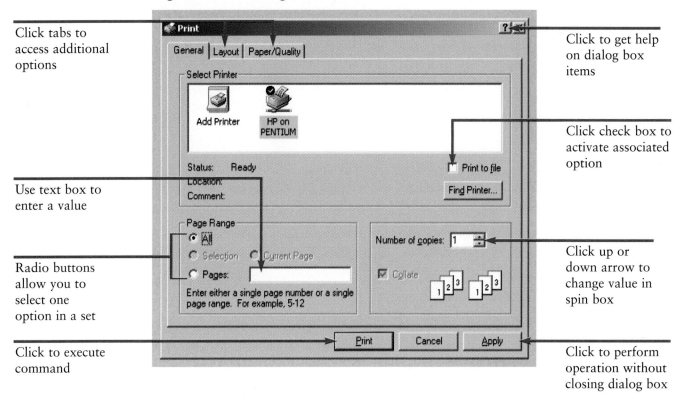

Practice

Find three other WordPad commands that use dialog boxes. View the features of each dialog box.

Hot Tip

When a dialog box has more than one option, you can use the [Tab] key to cycle through the options.

Getting Help

Concept

You might find that you need a little assistance along the way as you explore Windows 2000. The Help files provide you with an extensive list of topics that provide aid, troubleshooting advice, and tips and tricks. You can use Help while you work, and even print topics when it is inconvenient to use Help on the fly.

Do It!

Use the Windows 2000 Help facility to learn about working with programs and word processing.

1 Click Start, then click Help on the Start menu. The Windows Help window will open with the Contents tab displayed, as shown in **Figure 1-16**. Each of the major help topics covered is listed next to a book icon.

2 Position the pointer over Working with Programs in the Contents topics list. When you move the mouse pointer over the topic, the pointer will change to a hand, and the topic will be highlighted in blue and underlined, much like a Web page hyperlink.

3 Click Working with Programs. A list of subtopics will appear below it.

4 Click Start a Program. The help topic, including instructions, notes, and links to related topics, is loaded into the right half of the window for you to read (**Figure 1-17**).

5 Click the Index tab to bring it to the front of the left pane. The Index tab allows you to search the help files by keyword.

6 Type word processing. As you type, the list of topics will scroll to match your entry.

7 Click the subtopic WordPad to select it below the main topic word processing. Then click the Display button [Display]. Read the help text on Using WordPad that appears in the right frame.

8 Click ☒ to exit Help.

More

The Windows 2000 Help facility is written in HTML (Hypertext Markup Language). This is the same language used to create Web pages. Help's interface is similar to that of the Windows 2000 system windows, such as My Computer, and the Web pages you view with a Web browser. Across the top of the Help window are five buttons. Clicking the Hide button shrinks the Help window to only its right frame, giving you more room to view other open windows. The Hide button changes to the Show button when the window is shrunk. The Back button takes you back to the topic you just viewed, while the Forward button takes you to the place you were before you clicked Back. The Options button offers you menu commands for the buttons, as well as others such as a print command and a stop command to interrupt long searches. The Web Help button gives you quick access to help on the Internet.

Figure 1-16 Windows Help facility

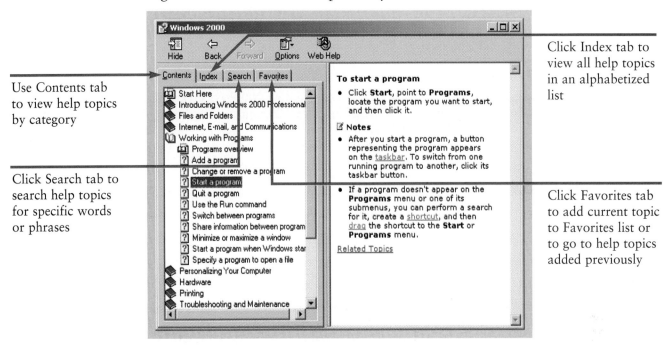

Use Contents tab to view help topics by category

Click Search tab to search help topics for specific words or phrases

Click Index tab to view all help topics in an alphabetized list

Click Favorites tab to add current topic to Favorites list or to go to help topics added previously

Figure 1-17 Help on WordPad

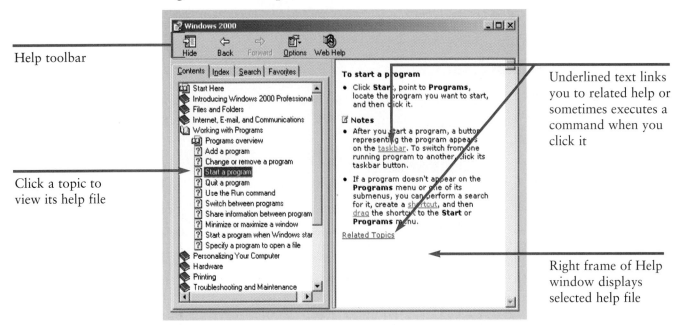

Help toolbar

Click a topic to view its help file

Underlined text links you to related help or sometimes executes a command when you click it

Right frame of Help window displays selected help file

Get help on **printing a document** using both the Contents tab and the Index tab. Close the Help facility when you are done.

Hot Tip

The **Glossary** and **Reference** help topics on the Contents tab are very useful for getting help on specific Windows 2000 features that are not covered by the other general help topics.

Shutting Down Windows 2000

Concept

It is important to **shut down** Windows 2000 properly. Failure to do so can result in loss of unsaved data. When you go through the shutdown procedure, Windows 2000 checks all open files to see if any unsaved files exist. If any are found, you will be given the opportunity to save them. It also uses the shutdown procedure to copy to your hard disk the data it has logged while your system was running.

Do It!

Shut down your computer to end your Windows 2000 session.

1 Click the Start button to open the Start menu.

2 Click **Shut Down**. A dialog box (**Figure 1-18**) will appear on your desktop.

3 A drop-down list in the center of the dialog box allows you to choose whether you want to log off the current user, shut down, or restart the computer (see **Table 1-2**). If the drop-down list box is set to **Shut down**, leave it as is. If not, click the arrow at the right end of the box, and then click Shut Down on the list that appears.

4 Click the OK button ⬚OK⬚. Windows will go through its shutdown procedure.

5 Turn off your computer when you see the message that reads: It is now safe to turn off your computer (**Figure 1-19**).

More

Table 1-2 Shutdown options

SHUTDOWN OPTIONS	RESULT
Log off User	Ends the current session, but leaves the computer running so that another user may log on
Shut down	Prepares the computer to be turned off
Restart	Ends the current session, shuts down Windows 2000, and then starts Windows again

Figure 1-18 Shut Down Windows dialog box

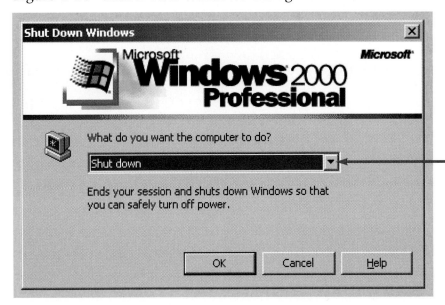

Click to select
another shut-
down option

Figure 1-19 Shut down confirmation

Make sure all files and applications on your
computer are closed, and then restart your
computer.

Hot Tip

You also can access the **Log Off** and **Shut
Down** commands by pressing
[Ctrl]+[Alt]+[Delete] on the keyboard to
open the **Windows Security** dialog box.

Shortcuts

Function	Button/Mouse	Menu	Keyboard
Close window	⊠	Click Control icon, then click Close	[Alt]+[F4]
Maximize window	▢	Click Control icon, then click Maximize	
Minimize window	▬ Or click program button on taskbar	Click Control icon, then click Minimize	
Restore window	▣	Click Control icon, then click Restore	
Change active window	Click window, if visible, or click program button on taskbar		[Alt]+[Tab]
Get Help on a specific item in a dialog box	?		[F1]

Identify Key Features

Name the items indicated by callouts in **Figure 1-20**.

Figure 1-20 Components of the Windows 2000 interface

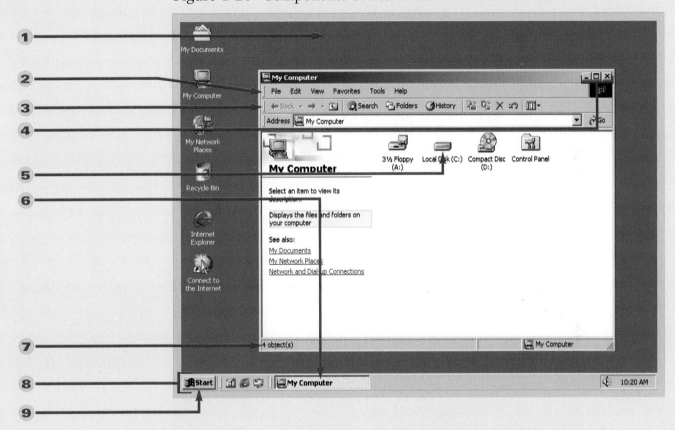

Select the Best Answer

10. Traditional way of opening a file, program, or window

11. Returns a maximized window to its previous size

12. Appears when a window is too small to display its information

13. Where you provide additional information before a command is carried out

14. Organizes the help files in major categories represented by book icons

15. Where program buttons appear

16. Used to manipulate the pointer on the screen

17. Minimizes all open windows

18. Contains a list of related commands

a. Scroll bar

b. Menu

c. Show Desktop button

d. Double-clicking

e. Restore button

f. Contents tab

g. Taskbar

h. Dialog box

i. Mouse

Quiz (continued)

Complete the Statement

19. All of the following are basic ways you can use a mouse except:

    a. Clicking

    b. Dragging

    c. Keying

    d. Pointing

20. You can move a window:

    a. When it is maximized

    b. By dragging its title bar

    c. When it is minimized

    d. By using the double-arrow pointer

21. To open a context-sensitive pop-up menu:

    a. Click the mouse

    b. Click the Start button

    c. Double-click an icon

    d. Right-click the mouse

22. To scroll through a window in large increments:

    a. Click above or below the scroll bar box

    b. Click a scroll bar arrow

    c. Click the scroll bar box

    d. Right-click the Control icon

23. To locate a help file by means of a scrolling list that matches a topic you enter, use the:

    a. Contents tab

    b. Index tab

    c. Find tab

    d. Explorer tab

24. To reposition the taskbar:

    a. Open the Taskbar Properties dialog box

    b. Select it and press the arrow keys

    c. Drag it to a new location

    d. Right-click it and choose the Move command

25. A standard menu contains a list of:

    a. Related commands

    b. Shutdown options

    c. Help topics

    d. Icons

26. Windows 2000's pictorial representation of a computer's functions and data is called:

    a. An IBI or "ibbey" (Icon Based Interface)

    b. A LUI or "louie" (Local User Interface)

    c. A HUI or "huey" (HTML Unified Interface)

    d. A GUI or "gooey" (Graphical User Interface)

27. An ellipsis after a command indicates that:

    a. Windows is still working

    b. The command is not available

    c. The command has a keyboard shortcut

    d. The command uses a dialog box

28. To open a menu, click on its title on the:

    a. Menu bar

    b. View menu

    c. Standard Buttons toolbar

    d. Keyboard

Interactivity

Test Your Skills

1. Start Windows 2000 and work with the desktop icons:

    a. If it is not already running, turn on your computer.

    b. Use the mouse to point to the **My Computer** icon.

    c. Move the **My Documents** folder icon to the center of the desktop, and then back to its original position.

    d. Open the My Documents folder icon.

    e. Close the My Documents window.

2. Work with an open window:

    a. Open the My Computer window.

    b. Move the window so that its title bar touches the top of the screen.

    c. Maximize the window.

    d. Restore the window.

    e. Use the mouse to resize the window until it is shaped like a square.

3. Run multiple programs and use the taskbar:

    a. Open **Windows Explorer** and **Calculator** from the Start menu.

    b. In turn, make each of the three open windows the active window.

    c. Minimize all open windows.

    d. Move the taskbar to the top of the desktop.

    e. Make the taskbar twice its original size.

    f. Return the taskbar to its original location and size.

    g. Close all open windows and applications

4. Use the Windows 2000 Help facility and then shut down Windows:

    a. Open **Windows Help**.

    b. Use the **Contents** tab to read about **What's New in Windows 2000**.

    c. Use the **Index** tab to get help on **printing help topics**.

    d. Close the Help facility.

    e. **Shut down** Windows 2000 properly and turn off your computer.

Interactivity (continued)

Problem Solving

1. Using the skills you learned in Lesson 1 and your knowledge of the Windows 2000 operating system, arrange your desktop so that it resembles the one shown in **Figure 1-21**. Remember that computers can be configured in a number of different ways, and settings can be changed over time. Therefore, your setup, and the icons made available by it, may prevent you from replicating the figure exactly. Do not delete icons without consulting your instructor first.

Figure 1-21 Example of a Windows 2000 desktop

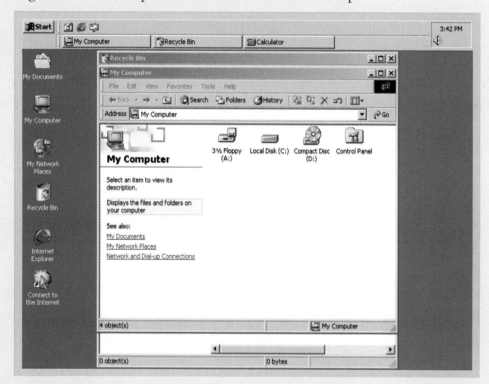

2. You have noticed an item on your Accessories menu named Notepad, but you are not sure what its function is. Use both the Contents and Index tabs in Windows 2000's Help facility to find out as much as you can about Notepad. Then use the Help facility to find out how to store the Notepad help topics you found on the Favorites tab. Once you have learned this procedure, add the most informative Notepad help topic to the Favorites tab.

3. You are working on a project that requires you to use two applications at the same time, Windows Explorer and Notepad. Open each application from the Start menu. Then resize and arrange the two open windows so that you can view them side by side on the desktop.

4. You are new to the Windows operating system, but you have used another operating system with a graphical user interface. You have decided to set up your desktop so that it resembles this system. Move all of your desktop icons to the right side of the desktop. Then move the taskbar so that it is anchored to the left side of the screen instead of to the bottom of it.

L E S S O N

2

MANAGING FILES WITH WINDOWS EXPLORER

A file is a text document, picture, or any other collection of information that is stored under its own unique name. A **folder**, much like a paper folder, is a collection of files that also can house other folders. Your computer stores electronic files and folders as you might store paper ones in a filing cabinet. To make finding files and folders easier, you should group them in an organized and logical manner. The manner in which your files and folders are arranged is called a **file hierarchy**.

A file hierarchy, as shown in **Figure 2-1**, is similar to a family tree. The parent, child, and grandchild branches are represented by disk drives and folders. A file hierarchy depicts all the drives, applications, folders, and files on your computer. Placing similar files into well-named folders is the best way to create a meaningful file hierarchy. By viewing the higher levels of your file hierarchy, you will be able to get a sense of where files are stored without having to open each particular folder.

My Computer and **Windows Explorer** are both file management tools. File management can be complex and even tricky at first. The key to understanding file management is being able to visualize and organize the placement of your files. Having to search through the entire file hierarchy every time you wish to locate an item can become time-consuming and frustrating. Learning how to manage your files effectively, by understanding My Computer and Windows Explorer, will help you to get the most out of your computer. My Computer and Windows Explorer are similar in function and in use. After a brief examination of My Computer we will concentrate on Windows Explorer, the more versatile file organizer.

Managing your files will often involve more than just organizing them. In this lesson, you will learn how to use the **Recycle Bin** to delete files and folders correctly. This will save you space on your hard drive and prevent you from disposing of important work accidentally. The lesson also introduces the **Search** command, which can help you locate a file when you lose track of it.

Viewing Folders with My Computer

Concept

My Computer is a tool that shows you the organization of the drives and configuration of folders on your computer. You can use My Computer to navigate through your system's files. Opening an icon in the My Computer window, usually for a drive or a folder, will show you that particular icon's contents. My Computer allows you to view the contents of your computer four different ways: by Large Icons, by Small Icons, in List form, or with Details. Once you open a drive or folder from the My Computer window, a fifth viewing option, Thumbnails, becomes available. How you view the contents of a drive or folder will depend on the information you require.

Do It!

To get a better understanding of file management, explore your C: drive by viewing its contents with the different View options.

1. Open the My Computer window by double-clicking its icon on the desktop (usually located in the upper-left corner of the screen).

2. To toggle between views, you need to make sure the Standard Buttons toolbar is visible. Open the View menu and guide the pointer onto the Toolbar command. If there is no check mark beside the Standard Buttons command, point to it and click the left mouse button.

3. The My Computer window displays icons that represent your computer's disk drives and system control folders. Double-click the C: drive icon ⬛ Local Disk (C:) to view the folders and files on your hard drive (your C: drive may have a different label than the one shown here). Figure 2-2 shows the C: drive window in Large Icons view. This view takes up window space, but offers a clear view of a window's contents. By default, Windows 2000 enables Web content in folders, meaning the folders are presented like Web pages with frames and graphics. Evidence of this appears on the left side of the window, where the selected drive is named and a pie chart graphic depicts the drive's storage capacity in percentages of free and used space.

4. To view the items as Small Icons, click the Views button on the right end of the Standard Buttons toolbar ⬛▾. A menu will appear, shown in Figure 2-3, allowing you to select your choice of views. The bullet marks the current view, Large Icons.

5. Click Small Icons on the Views button menu. The icons will become smaller, and they will be arranged alphabetically in rows. This view is useful when you have many icons to fit into one window.

Figure 2-1 Sample file hierarchy

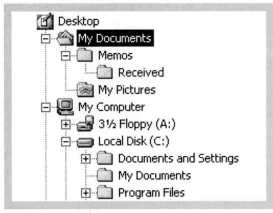

Figure 2-2 C: drive in Large Icons view

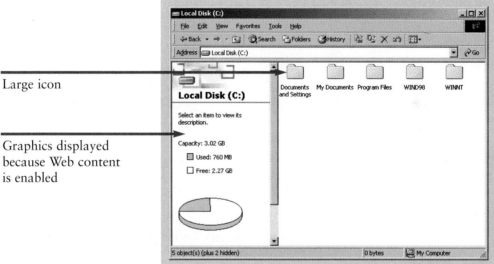

Large icon

Graphics displayed
because Web content
is enabled

Figure 2-3 Views button menu

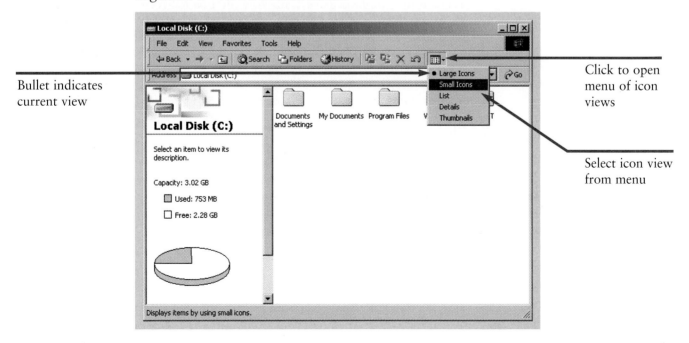

Bullet indicates
current view

Click to open
menu of icon
views

Select icon view
from menu

Viewing Folders with My Computer (continued)

Do It!

6 Click ⊞▾ again, then select List. The icons will be put into List view. List view is similar to Small Icons except that icons are organized in columns.

7 Click ⊞▾ again, then select Details. **Figure 2-4** shows Details view, which will tell you the name of an item, its size if it is a file rather than folder, its type, and even the last time you modified it.

8 To return to the top level of the hierarchy, click the Up button ⊞. The Up button steps you up one level in the file structure, while the Back button ⟵ Back returns you to the last file or folder you viewed regardless of its place in the hierarchy.

9 Right-click the title bar of the C: drive window, then select Close from the pop-up menu that appears to remove the window from the desktop.

More

As hard as you try, even with good file organization and file naming, it is impossible to remember what every file on your computer contains. Having Web content enabled in your folders can help relieve some of this frustration. Folders with Web content enabled allow you to see previews of file content, as well as get descriptions of hard drives and system folders. Compatible material includes Web pages, audio files, video files, and most graphic formats. When you select a file that can generate a preview, a small image of the file, called a thumbnail, will appear on the left side of the window, as shown in **Figure 2-5**. **Thumbnails** view allows you to view previews of all image files in a folder rather than file icons. Audio and video previews will contain controls for playing the particular file from the window without having to open another application.

The columns that are shown in Details view for a particular folder are determined by the **Column Settings** dialog box, which can be accessed by selecting the **Choose Columns** command from the View menu. The dialog box provides a list of column headings that are available for viewing and check boxes next to each heading to allow you to activate and deactivate the headings according to your needs and preferences. You also can alter the order in which the column headings appear and specify their individual widths.

You also can customize the appearance of a folder by choosing the **Customize This Folder** command from the View menu. The command activates the **Customize This Folder** wizard, which will guide you through the steps required to choose or edit an HTML template for the active folder, change the folder's background picture and file name appearance, or add a comment to the folder.

The number and type of drives installed in a computer can vary greatly, but the configuration you have seen represented in this book is quite common. The drive designated with the letter A is almost always a 3½-inch floppy disk drive. The drive designated with the letter C is generally the computer's main hard drive. The D designation is usually assigned to the computer's CD-ROM drive. Traditionally, the letter B is reserved for a second floppy drive.

Windows 2000

Figure 2-4 C: drive in Details view

Selected drive, folder, file, or Web address displayed in Address Bar

Click here to arrange window contents by date last modified

Click here to sort window contents by file format

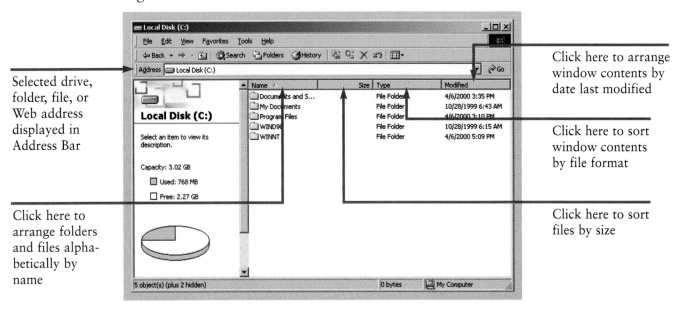

Click here to arrange folders and files alphabetically by name

Click here to sort files by size

Figure 2-5 Preview of a bitmap image file

Details of selected file

Preview of selected file

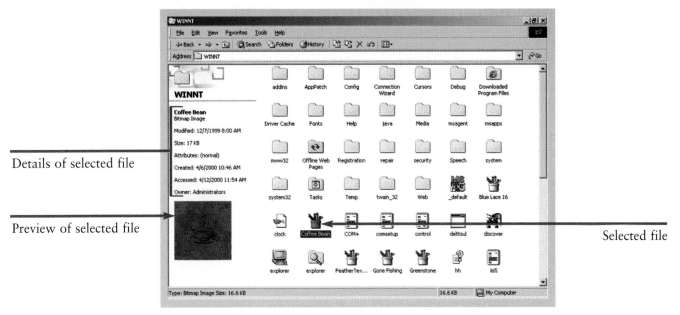

Selected file

Open My Computer, double-click the Control Panel folder, then use the Views button to display the items in each of the available views. Leave the window in the view you like best. Close the window when you are finished.

Hot Tip

The My Computer and Control Panel windows are always displayed as Web pages. The Customize This Folder wizard is not available for these folders.

Using Windows Explorer

Concept

Windows Explorer, found on the Accessories menu in Windows 2000, is similar to My Computer. Both are file management tools that allow you to view the contents of your computer. But Windows Explorer is more powerful and provides you with more options than My Computer. Windows Explorer displays itself as the two-paneled window you see in **Figure 2-6**, allowing you to work with more than one drive, folder, or file at a time. The left panel, which usually consists of the **Folders Explorer Bar**, shows all the folders and disk drives on your computer. The right panel, the contents panel, is a display of the items located within the folder or drive that is selected in the Folders Explorer Bar. This two-paneled window creates a more detailed view of a specific folder and makes for easier file manipulation, especially copying and moving.

Do It!

Use Windows Explorer to examine folders on your computer.

1 Click ![Start], highlight Programs, highlight Accessories, and then click **Windows Explorer** on the Accessories menu. Windows Explorer will open with the contents of your computer shown in the left panel and the My Documents folder selected. If you do not see the Folders Explorer Bar on the left, click the **Folders** button ![Folders] on the Standard Buttons toolbar.

2 Click the plus symbol ![+] next to My Computer in the Folders Explorer Bar (left panel). The ![+] next to an item in this panel indicates that the item can be expanded to reveal its contents. You should now see the same drives and folders you saw previously in the My Computer window listed below My Computer in the left panel. Notice that the ![+] you clicked has now changed to a ![-]. This symbol indicates that a drive or folder is already expanded. Clicking the ![-] collapses a drive or folder's contents back into the parent drive or folder. If a folder contains files but no subfolders, a plus sign will not appear next to it.

3 Click the ![+] next to your C: drive in the Folders Explorer Bar to expand the drive, revealing its top-level contents. The list of items you see in the left panel will differ from computer to computer depending on the files that have been installed and the way they have been configured.

4 Click the WINNT folder in the left panel. Now that the folder is selected, its contents, including subfolders and files, are displayed in the right panel (you may receive a message that explains the contents of the folder — if so, click the **Show Files** link that appears in the message).

5 Double-click the Media folder in the right panel to open the folder. You also could have expanded the WINNT folder in the left panel and then clicked the Media folder there to display its contents in the right panel. Notice that the WINNT folder is now expanded in the Explorer Bar and the Media folder is shown with an open folder icon. The files inside the Media folder are sound files that were installed automatically with Windows 2000.

6 Press [Ctrl]+[A]. All of the items in the right panel will be selected, as shown in **Figure 2-7**. Pressing [Ctrl]+[A] is the keyboard shortcut for the Select All command on the Edit menu.

Figure 2-6 Windows Explorer

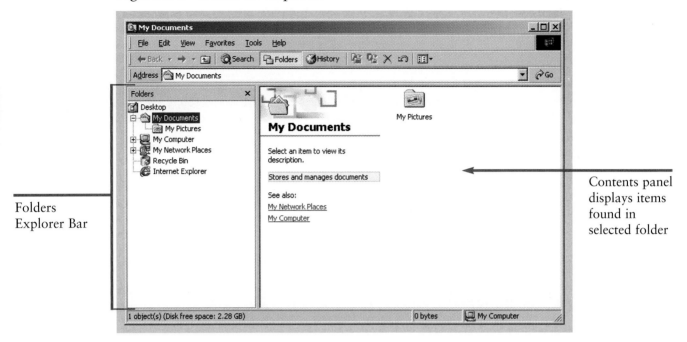

Folders
Explorer Bar

Contents panel
displays items
found in
selected folder

Figure 2-7 Media folder with all items selected

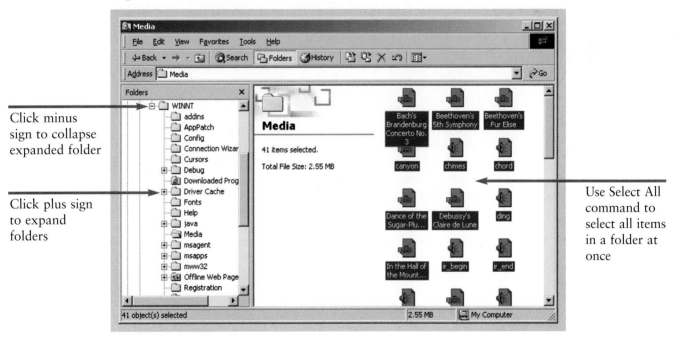

Click minus
sign to collapse
expanded folder

Click plus sign
to expand
folders

Use Select All
command to
select all items
in a folder at
once

Using Windows Explorer (continued)

Do It!

7 Switch to Small Icons view and then press [End] on the keyboard. The last file in the Windows folder will be selected. Since this is a sound file, audio controls appear in the window, allowing you to play the sound directly from Windows Explorer.

8 Press [Home] to select the first item listed in the Media folder.

9 Press [R] to select the first item in the folder that begins with the letter R. This is useful if you know the name of a file or folder and want to jump to it quickly.

10 Press [R] again to move to the next item in the list that begins with the letter R. Continuing to press [R] will cycle you through all the items in the folder that begin with R. Stop when you return to the first R item in the list.

11 With the first file that begins with R selected (most likely this will be recycle), hold [Ctrl] then click the file named chord. Holding the Control key down while you click allows you to select multiple, nonconsecutive files or folders.

12 Click the recycle sound file icon again to select it and deselect the chord file.

13 Hold [Shift], then click the first file listed. All of the files between the two you clicked will be highlighted, as shown in **Figure 2-8**. Holding the Shift key while you click allows you to select all of the items between the first and last selected.

14 Click a blank area to the right of the file names in the right panel to deselect all of the currently selected items. Leave Windows Explorer open for use in the next Skill.

More

Windows Explorer is a unique tool. As you saw in the Skill above, its two-paneled structure allows you to view all the folders on a specified drive while working within a particular folder. One of the more powerful features of Windows Explorer is the left panel. The left panel, called the Explorer Bar, can be set to view one of four folders. By default, Windows Explorer opens in Folders view, which allows you to view any folders, files, or utilities found on your computer or your network. The Search Explorer Bar, shown in **Figure 2-9**, allows you to activate Windows 2000's Search facility and locate files or folders directly in the Windows Explorer window. The Search Bar also contains a link that permits you to load an Internet search engine into Windows Explorer's left panel. If you would like to see a list of the locations you have visited recently, including local and network drives and Web sites, select the History Explorer Bar. Clicking the address or name of the place you want to view will load the site into the contents panel. You can choose to view items in the History Explorer Bar by date, site name, frequency of visits, or order visited today. The Favorites Explorer Bar allows you to store the places you visit most frequently so you can access them with a simple click. This feature is especially helpful with Web sites, which often have long, cumbersome addresses that are difficult to remember. You can close the active Explorer Bar by clicking the close button on its title bar, or by selecting the None command from the Explorer Bar submenu on the View menu.

Figure 2-8 Selecting multiple folders

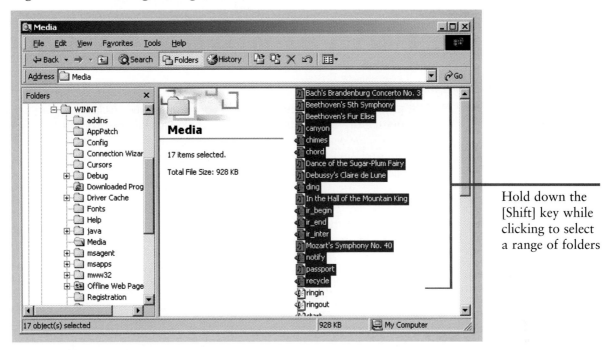

Hold down the [Shift] key while clicking to select a range of folders

Figure 2-9 Search Explorer Bar

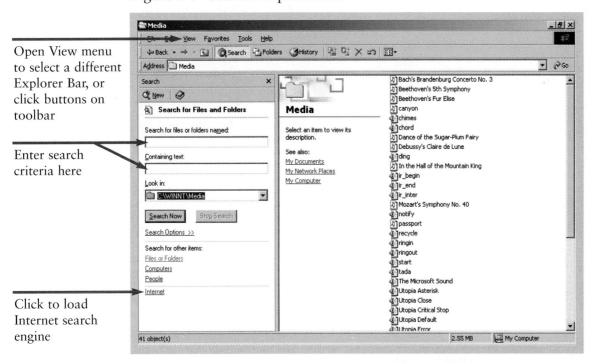

Open View menu to select a different Explorer Bar, or click buttons on toolbar

Enter search criteria here

Click to load Internet search engine

Practice

Expand the WINNT folder and select the Fonts folder in the Folders Explorer Bar. The files for all of the fonts installed on your computer will appear in the contents panel. Use the keyboard to select the font called **Verdana**.

Hot Tip

You can resize the panels of Windows Explorer. Place the pointer on the bar that divides the window (it will change to ↔), then drag to the left or right to resize the bar.

Creating New Folders and Files

Concept

Creating folders is necessary when you want to store related files in a single location on a drive. Creating, naming, and placing folders properly in your hierarchy makes your work easier and more efficient. While most files are created in the program with which they will be used, you also can make new, blank files right in the folder where they will be stored.

Do It!

Create a new folder on your C: drive, and then create another folder within that folder. Finally, create two new files in the folder that you made.

1. Expand the C: drive, and then click its icon in the left panel of Windows Explorer to view the items on your main hard drive in the contents panel on the right.

2. Click File on the menu bar. The File menu will open.

3. Guide the pointer to New, then click Folder on the submenu that appears. A folder with the default name New Folder will appear in the contents panel with its name highlighted, ready to be changed.

4. Type My Student Files, then press [Enter] to give the folder a unique name so you can find it again. Notice that the new folder also appears in the left panel.

5. Click the new folder's icon in the left panel of Windows Explorer to select it and reveal its contents. The right panel should be blank since this folder is empty.

6. Click File, point to New, then select Folder to create a new folder within your My Student Files folder.

7. Type Alice, then press [Enter] to name the new folder. The folder will be in the contents panel and a plus will appear next to My Student Files (**Figure 2-10**) in the left panel to indicate that at least one folder is nested within the parent folder.

8. Click the plus ⊞ next to the My Student Files folder in the Folders Explorer Bar to expand the folder and reveal the Alice folder nested inside.

9. Click File, select New, and then click WordPad Document on the menu that appears. A new file with the default name New WordPad Document will appear.

10. Type Letter to rename the new file. Press [Enter] to confirm the file name. Creating a new file this way makes a blank document with a specific file format in the location you specify.

11. Repeat the above step to create a WordPad document named To Do List. Your window should look similar to the one shown in **Figure 2-11**.

Figure 2-10 Creating a new folder

Name of selected folder

Alice folder created inside
My Student Files folder

Plus sign indicates that folder
may now be expanded to
reveal nested folders

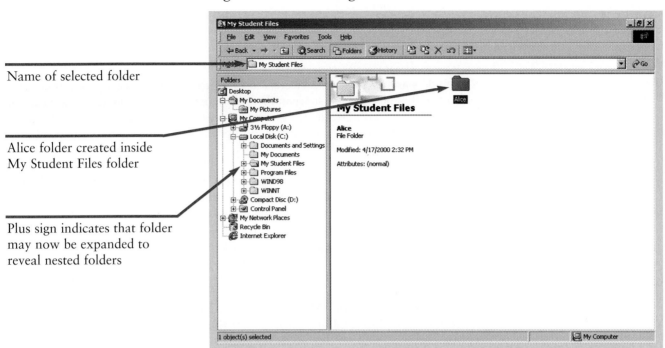

Figure 2-11 File hierarchy including new folder and files

New files in My Student
Files folder

Parent folder

Child folder nested
inside parent folder

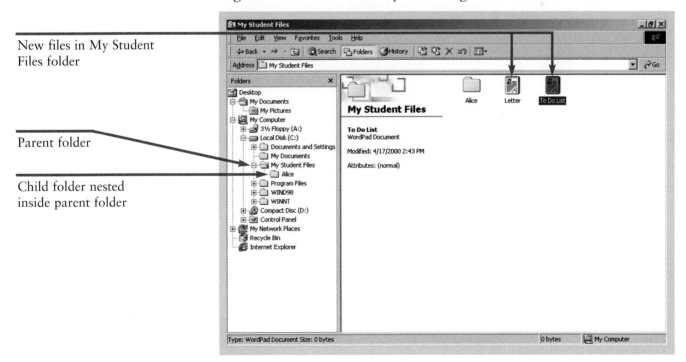

Creating New Folders and Files (continued)

More

New folders and files also can be created by right-clicking. Once a parent folder is selected, right-click a blank space in the right panel. A pop-up menu will appear, as shown in **Figure 2-12**. Highlight the New command on this shortcut menu and a submenu will appear. By choosing the appropriate command from the submenu, you can make a folder or file just as you would using the File menu.

If you right-click a file or folder, you will be given a different pop-up menu. **Figure 2-13** shows the menu that appears when you right-click on a file. The Open command opens the file with the application associated with the file's extension (such as .txt for a text file or .wav for a sound file). The Open with... command allows you to choose a different application with which to open the file. The Print command lets you create a hard copy of the file without having to open the application with which it was created first. You also can use commands on the pop-up menu to cut, copy, delete, or create a shortcut to the file or folder you right-clicked. The Rename command allows you to change the name of the file or folder. Selecting a file or folder, pausing, and then clicking it again will also let you rename an item, as will selecting it and pressing [F2].

The pop-up menu that appears when you right-click a folder differs slightly from the file menu. It includes commands for opening the folder in Windows Explorer and setting network sharing options.

You can set options for each folder on your computer that control the way the folders appear and the way in which you interact with them. To do this, select a folder, open the Tools menu from the Menu bar, and then click the Folder Options command. The Folder Options dialog box, shown opened to the General tab in **Figure 2-14**, will appear. On the General tab, the Active Desktop section lets you determine whether Web content will be enabled on the desktop. The Web View section controls whether Web content is enabled in folders. The Browse Folders section is responsible for whether each folder you open appears in the same window or in a separate window. Finally, you can use the Click items as follows section to set your icon selecting and opening preferences: select by pointing/open by single-clicking (Web style) or select by single-clicking/open by double-clicking (traditional Windows style).

The View tab in the Folder Options dialog box contains advanced folder settings such as the option to display entire file paths in the Address Bar and the option to hide file extensions for known file types. The File Types tab is where associations between file types (extensions) and applications are set. The Offline Files tab allows you to make network files accessible when you are not connected to your network.

Figure 2-12 Right-click pop-up menu and submenu

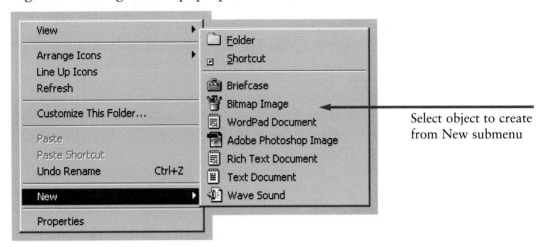

Select object to create
from New submenu

Figure 2-13 Right-clicking a file

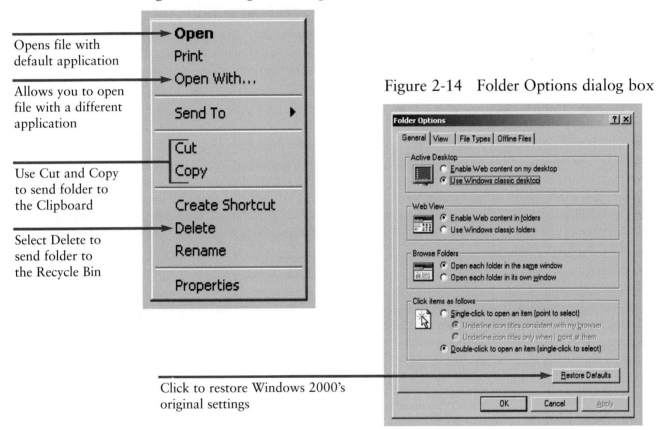

Opens file with
default application

Allows you to open
file with a different
application

Use Cut and Copy
to send folder to
the Clipboard

Select Delete to
send folder to
the Recycle Bin

Figure 2-14   Folder Options dialog box

Click to restore Windows 2000's
original settings

Create a folder inside the My Documents
folder called **Practice**. Then create a new
WordPad file called **Prac2-3** inside this
folder.

Hot Tip

Folder and file names can be up to 215
characters long so you can name your data
accurately. The only characters you are not
allowed to use are \ / : * ? " < > |.

 # Moving and Copying Files and Folders

Concept

There are times when you will want to **move** or **copy** folders or files. Moving an item to group it with other files or folders that contain similar data can increase the overall efficiency of your work. Moving a folder changes its location and alters your file hierarchy accordingly. Copying a file or folder can be done to place a duplicate in another place on your system.

Do It!

Move the Letter and To Do List files into the Alice folder, and then make a copy of the Alice folder inside the My Student Files folder.

1. Open Windows Explorer using the Start menu if it is not already open.

2. Click your **My Student Files** folder in the left panel to select it (expand My Computer and the C: drive if necessary). The contents of the My Student Files folder, the Alice folder, Letter, and To Do List, will appear in the contents panel.

3. Click the ⊞ next to the My Student Files folder so you can see the Alice folder in the left panel of Windows Explorer.

4. Hold down [Ctrl], while you click Letter and To Do List to select both files.

5. Drag the selected files from the right panel to the Alice folder in the left panel to move them. When you begin to drag, a faint outline of the files will follow the pointer. In certain areas, the pointer may become a circle with a line through it, indicating that you cannot drop your files at that particular location. You will know that the files are in the correct position when the Alice folder is highlighted, as shown in **Figure 2-15**. As soon as this occurs, release the mouse button to drop the files into the folder.

6. Click the Alice folder in the right panel to select it.

7. Click **Edit** to open the Edit menu, then select the Copy command to place a copy of the Alice folder on the **Clipboard**. The Clipboard is a temporary storage area in your computer's memory that holds copied or cut items until they are replaced on the Clipboard by another item or the computer is shut down.

8. Click Edit, then select Paste from the menu. A copy of the Alice folder will appear in the My Student Files folder as shown in **Figure 2-16**.

More

There are many ways to move and copy items in Windows 2000. Dragging and dropping files and folders from panel to panel in the Windows Explorer is one of the easiest ways to manage the information stored on your computer. Moving and copying also can be accomplished by dragging almost any item from your desktop to another system window or vice versa. You also can move and copy with toolbar buttons. First, select the item you wish to move or copy. Then, click either the Move To 🔲 or Copy To 🔲 button on the Standard Buttons toolbar. In both cases, the Browse for Folder dialog box will appear, allowing you to choose a destination for the item to be moved or copied. Moving or cutting an item removes it from its original location. Copying leaves the original item in its original location.

Figure 2-15 Moving files

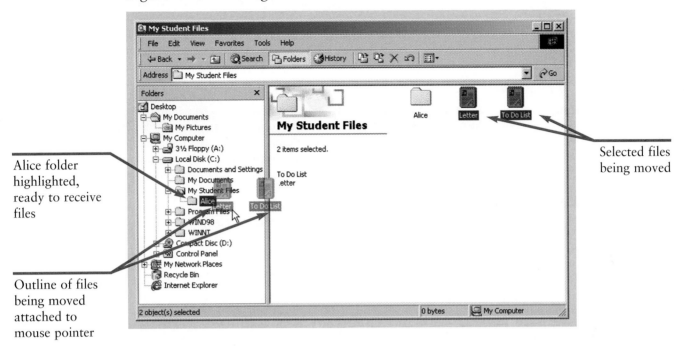

Alice folder highlighted, ready to receive files

Outline of files being moved attached to mouse pointer

Selected files being moved

Figure 2-16 Copying a folder

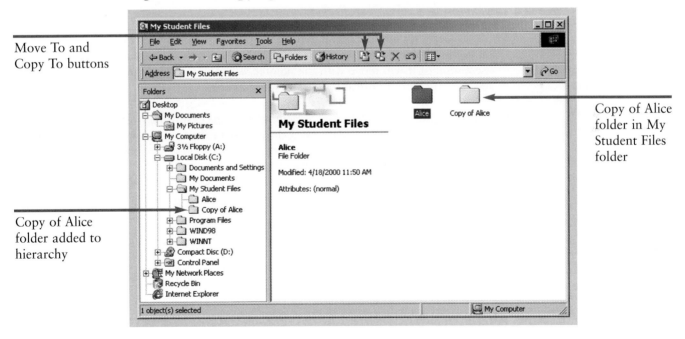

Move To and Copy To buttons

Copy of Alice folder added to hierarchy

Copy of Alice folder in My Student Files folder

Practice

Make a copy of Prac2-3 in the My Documents folder. Rename the copied file **Prac2-4**. Then move Prac2-4 back to the Practice folder using the Cut command.

Hot Tip

Windows 2000 will not allow you to place two files with the same name in the same folder. If you attempt to do so, you will be asked if you want to overwrite the first file with the second. You may have files with the same name in different folders.

Creating Shortcuts

Concept

Shortcuts are icons that give you direct access to frequently used items so that you do not have to open applications or folders in order to work with the item. Shortcuts can be created for programs, folders, files, Internet addresses, or even devices like printers. You can place shortcuts directly on the desktop or Start menu, or anywhere else you find convenient.

Do It!

Create a shortcut to the My Student Files folder on the desktop, rename it, and then change its icon.

1 Open Windows Explorer if it is not already running on your desktop.

2 If the Explorer window is maximized, click the Restore button so you can see a few inches of the desktop. You may have to resize the window so more of the desktop is visible.

3 Expand the appropriate icons so that the My Student Files folder is visible in the Folders Explorer Bar (left panel) of Windows Explorer. Place the mouse pointer over the folder's icon.

4 Right-drag (drag while holding down the right mouse button) the My Student Files folder to a blank space on your desktop. As the folder is dragged, a dimmed representation of it will move with the pointer. When you release the mouse button, you will see the pop-up menu shown in **Figure 2-17**.

5 Click Create Shortcut(s) Here. A new folder named Shortcut to My Student Files will be created. The small arrow in the corner of the icon denotes that the folder is a shortcut, allowing you to access the My Student Files folder from the desktop without actually storing the folder on the desktop.

6 Right-click the Shortcut to My Student Files folder. A pop-up menu with commands relating to the folder will appear.

7 Click Rename. The folder's name will be highlighted so you can edit it.

8 Type To Be Deleted, then press [Enter] to rename the folder. **Figure 2-18** displays the shortcut with its new name.

Figure 2-17 Right-dragging to create a shortcut

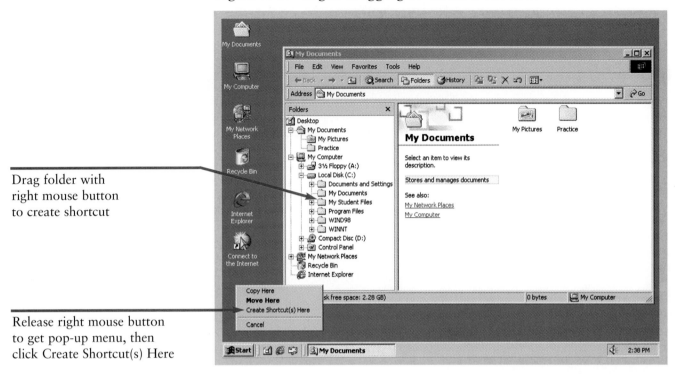

Drag folder with
right mouse button
to create shortcut

Release right mouse button
to get pop-up menu, then
click Create Shortcut(s) Here

Figure 2-18 Renamed shortcut folder on desktop

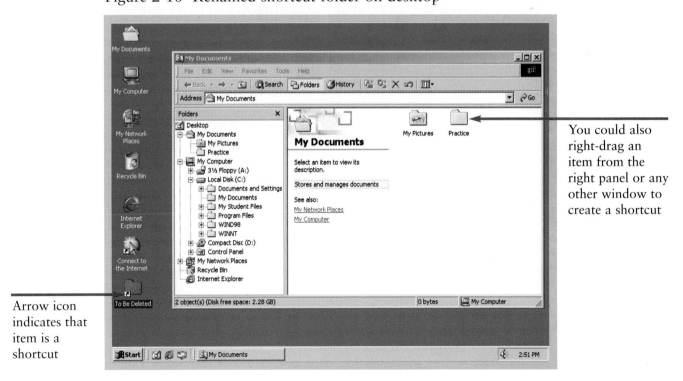

You could also
right-drag an
item from the
right panel or any
other window to
create a shortcut

Arrow icon
indicates that
item is a
shortcut

Creating Shortcuts (continued)

Do It!

9 Right-click the To Be Deleted folder, then select Properties from the pop-up menu. A dialog box (**Figure 2-19**) titled To Be Deleted Properties will open to the Shortcut tab. This tab contains data relating to the selected folder's shortcut properties.

10 Click the Change Icon button [Change Icon...]. **Figure 2-20** shows the Change Icon dialog box that will open.

11 Click and drag the horizontal scroll bar box to the right until the tree icon ⵷ is visible.

12 Click the tree to select it.

13 Click [OK]. The Change Icon dialog box will close, returning you to the To Be Deleted Properties dialog box. The preview icon in the upper-left corner of the Shortcut tab will change to reflect your selection.

14 Click [OK]. The To Be Deleted Properties dialog box will close and the folder icon will be replaced with the tree icon, as shown in **Figure 2-21**.

More

Shortcuts can be made for many items stored on your computer, including files, folders, and drives that you access over a network. For example, you can make a shortcut to a frequently used folder that you access over a network for quick access to those files. Shortcuts do not have to be placed on the desktop either. You can create a folder of shortcuts to your favorite programs and place it on your C: drive, or even the Start menu.

As you have seen, many tasks can be accomplished using drag-and-drop techniques. One of the more powerful Windows 2000 features allows you to drag files to program icons. Doing so will open the file with the program whose icon you drop it on, assuming the file and application are compatible. For example, you can create a shortcut to your word processing program and place it on the desktop. Then, you can drag word processing files to that shortcut to open them. This also works with printers.

In the above exercise you changed the name and icon for the shortcut you created without altering the folder to which the shortcut points. While a shortcut points to a specific item, that object can be renamed without affecting the shortcut. However, target objects that are moved to another folder or drive will cause the shortcut to malfunction. If a target item is moved, Windows 2000 has the ability to find it, or you can specify the new path manually. Since shortcuts are icons that point to the actual file, folder, or program that they represent, deleting a shortcut will not affect the target item.

You also can create a shortcut by right-clicking an item and then choosing Create Shortcut from the pop-up menu that appears. The shortcut will be created in the same folder as the original item. You can then move the shortcut to the desired location. If you drag a shortcut to the Start button, the Start menu will open. You can drop the shortcut on the Start menu or any of its submenus.

Figure 2-19 Properties dialog box

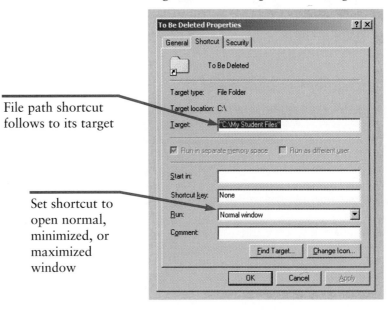

File path shortcut follows to its target

Set shortcut to open normal, minimized, or maximized window

Figure 2-20 Changing an icon

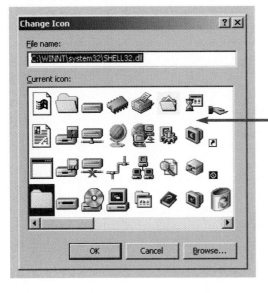

Select an icon to replace the current one

Figure 2-21 Desktop shortcut with new icon

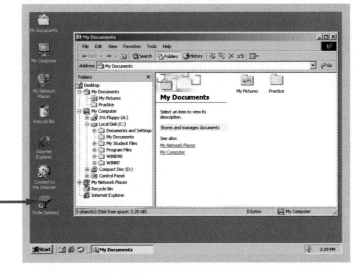

Renamed shortcut with tree icon

Practice

Place a shortcut to the Practice folder on your desktop.

Hot Tip

You do not have to be working in Windows Explorer in order to create a shortcut. You can also create shortcuts from the My Computer window or any standard folder window.

Using the Recycle Bin

Concept

The Recycle Bin is a storage place for files that have been deleted. Files that you no longer need should be deleted in order to save disk space and maximize the efficiency of your computer. If you decide that you need a file again, or have accidentally deleted a file, you can rescue it from the Recycle Bin. If you know you will never need a file again, you can delete the file permanently.

Do It!

Send the Copy of Alice and To Be Deleted folders to the Recycle Bin. Then rescue To Be Deleted from the Recycle Bin. Finally, delete both items from your hard drive permanently.

1 Open Windows Explorer from the Start menu.

2 Expand the necessary icons, and then click the My Student Files folder in the left panel to select it.

3 Click the Copy of Alice folder in the right panel, then click the Delete button ☒ on the Standard Buttons toolbar. The Confirm Folder Delete dialog box (**Figure 2-22**) will appear, asking if you are sure you want to move the folder to the Recycle Bin.

4 Click [Yes]. The dialog box will close and the folder will be moved to the Recycle Bin. Notice the change in the Recycle Bin icon 🗑 when it is not empty.

5 Click the Close button ☒ to exit Windows Explorer.

6 Click and drag the To Be Deleted shortcut from the desktop to the Recycle Bin 🗑. When the Recycle Bin becomes highlighted, release the mouse button. The shortcut is deposited in the Recycle Bin.

7 Double-click the Recycle Bin icon. The Recycle Bin window will open. **Figure 2-23** shows the inside of the Recycle Bin displaying all the files and folder you have sent there.

8 Drag the To Be Deleted shortcut from the Recycle Bin window to an empty space on the desktop. The shortcut appears on the desktop and is now an accessible item that can be used. Items still in the Recycle Bin cannot be opened.

9 Right-click the To Be Deleted shortcut and choose the Delete command from the pop-up menu to send the folder back into the Recycle Bin.

10 Click [Yes] to confirm the operation.

11 Click the Empty Recycle Bin button [Empty Recycle Bin] (if not visible click File, then click Empty Recycle Bin). The Confirm Multiple File Delete dialog box will appear.

12 Click [Yes] to delete the folders from your hard drive permanently.

13 Click ☒ to shut the Recycle Bin window. Note that you also can empty the Recycle Bin by right-clicking it and then choosing the Empty Recycle Bin command.

More

Table 2-1 Ways to delete or restore a selected file

TO DELETE	TO RESTORE
Click the Delete button on the toolbar	Click the Undo button 🔙 on the toolbar
Right-click and select Delete from the pop-up menu	Right-click the file in the Recycle Bin and select Restore
Drag the file to the Recycle Bin	Drag the file from the Recycle Bin to any location
Press [Delete]	Go to the File menu in the Recycle Bin and select Restore or click Restore

Figure 2-22 Confirm Folder Delete dialog box

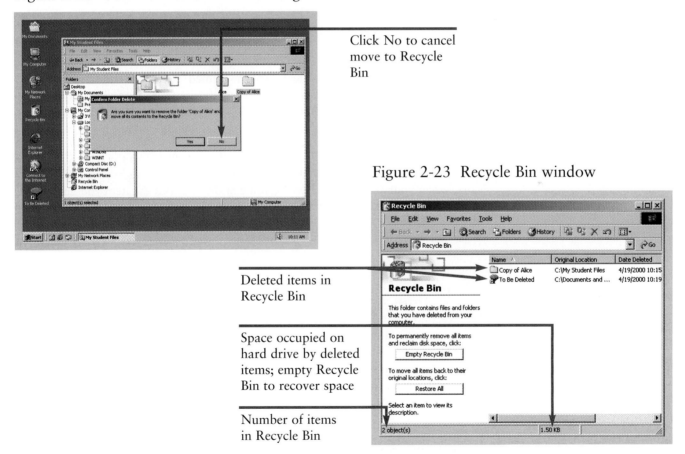

Click No to cancel move to Recycle Bin

Figure 2-23 Recycle Bin window

Deleted items in Recycle Bin

Space occupied on hard drive by deleted items; empty Recycle Bin to recover space

Number of items in Recycle Bin

Practice

Move the Practice shortcut you created in the last skill to the Recycle Bin. Then move the shortcut out of the Recycle Bin and back to the desktop. Delete the shortcut a second time using a different technique. This time, delete the shortcut permanently.

Hot Tip

Files can be erased immediately without being stored in the Recycle Bin. Right-click the Recycle Bin, then select Properties. On the View tab, uncheck the "Display delete confirmation dialog" command. This enables you to delete files in one step.

Searching for Files or Folders

Concept

Managing your files effectively includes knowing how to locate an item when you need it. The Search command on the Start menu is a tool that allows you to search your computer for files and folders when you do not know exactly where they are stored. You also can access the Search facility when working in Windows Explorer or My Computer by clicking the Search button [🔍 Search] to activate the Search Explorer Bar.

Do It!

Use the Search command to locate the Discover Windows 2000 tour.

1 Click [🏳 Start], highlight Search, and then click For Files or Folders. The Search Results window, shown maximized in **Figure 2-24**, will open. The left side of the window contains the Search Explorer Bar. Near the top of the Explorer Bar is a text box in which you can enter the name, or a portion of the name, of the file or folder you wish to locate.

2 Type discover in the Search for files or folders named: text box. The Look in box should show your main hard drive. If not, click the arrow at the right edge of the box and select your main hard drive from the drop-down list.

3 Click the Search Now button [Search Now]. Windows will begin to search your computer's hard drive for any files or folders named discover. When the search is complete, the results will be displayed in the lower portion of the right panel (**Figure 2-25**). When your search is successful, you can open or run the item you have found by double-clicking it directly in the Search Results window. In this particular case, the item you have found is actually a shortcut and you would be prompted to insert your Windows 2000 CD-ROM in order to run the tour.

4 Close the Search Results window.

More

When you do not know the exact name of the file or folder you are looking for, you can use the wildcard character * in your search request. For example, if you search for all files or folders named J*, the search will return all files and folders whose names begin with the letter J. You also can use the Search Explorer Bar's Search Options feature when you do not know the file or folder name, or when you need to refine your search. When you click the Search Options link, the Search Options box opens in the Explorer Bar. The box contains four options: Date, Type, Size, and Advanced Options. Click the check box next to an option to use it. The Search Options box will expand to accommodate controls for the option you selected. For example, the Date option (**Figure 2-26**) allows you to search for files or folders that were last modified, created, or last accessed on a particular date or in a specific time frame. Setting such criteria can help narrow your search down to the items that will most likely satisfy your request.

Figure 2-24 Search Results window

Enter name of desired file or folder

Click to select location to be searched

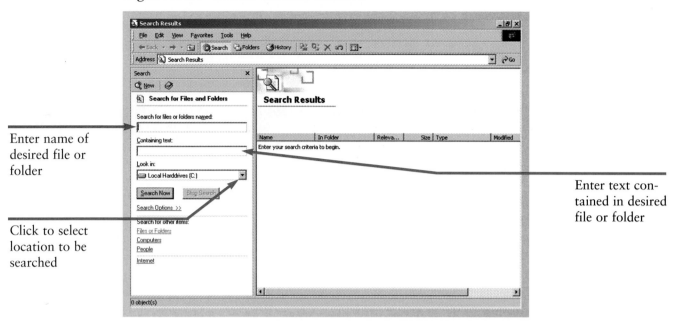

Enter text contained in desired file or folder

Figure 2-25 Results of search for discover

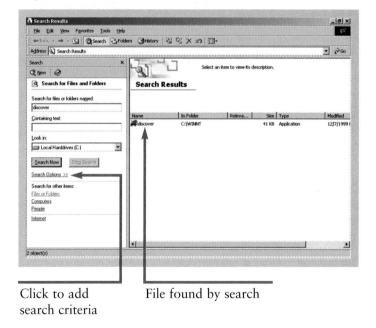

Click to add search criteria

File found by search

Figure 2-26 Date Search option

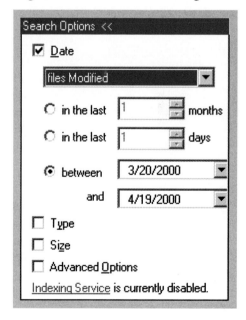

Practice

Use the Search command to locate your computer's Desktop folder.

Hot Tip

The Search menu and Search Explorer Bar also provide direct links to facilities for Web page and people directory searches. You can even search for other computers located on your network.

Shortcuts

Function	Button/Mouse	Menu	Keyboard
Large Icons view	Click button, then click Large Icons	Click View, then click Large Icons	[Alt]+[V], [G]
Small Icons view	Click button, then click Small Icons	Click View, then click Small Icons	[Alt]+[V], [M]
List view	Click button, then click List	Click View, then click List	[Alt]+[V], [L]
Details view	Click button, then click Details	Click View, then click Details	[Alt]+[V], [D]
Thumbnails view	Click button, then click Thumbnails	Click View, then click Thumbnails	[Alt]+[V], [H]
Move up one level in file hierarchy		Click View, then highlight Go To, then click Up One Level	[Alt]+[V], [O], [U]
Move selected item to another folder		Click Edit, then click Move To Folder	[Alt]+[E], [V]
Copy selected item to another folder		Click Edit, then click Copy To Folder	[Alt]+[E], [F]
Cut selection to Clipboard		Click Edit, then click Cut	[Ctrl]+[X]
Copy selection to Clipboard		Click Edit, then click Copy	[Ctrl]+[C]
Paste selection from Clipboard		Click Edit, then click Paste	[Ctrl]+[V]
Delete selection		Click File, then click Delete	[Delete]
Undo last action		Click Edit, then click Undo	[Ctrl]+[Z]
Back	⇐ Back	Click View, then highlight Go To, then click Back	[Alt]+[Left Arrow]
Forward	⇒	Click View, then highlight Go To, then click Forward	[Alt]+[Right Arrow]

Identify Key Features

Identify the names and functions of the items indicated by callouts in **Figure 2-27**.

Figure 2-27 Standard Buttons toolbar

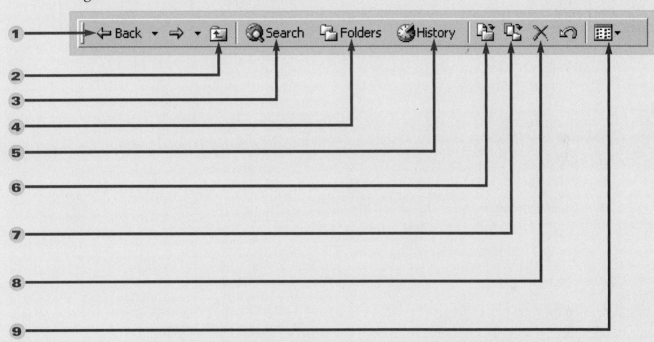

1
2
3
4
5
6
7
8
9

Select the Best Answer

10. Right side of the Windows Explorer window

11. One of the Explorer Bars

12. Allows you to relocate a selected file or folder

13. Storage place for deleted items

14. Its keyboard shortcut is [Ctrl]+[A]

15. An icon that gives you direct access to a frequently used item

16. Tool that allows you to view, open, and organize the contents of your hard drive

a. My Computer

b. Shortcut

c. Contents panel

d. Select All command

e. Folders

f. Move To button

g. Recycle Bin

Quiz (continued)

Complete the Statement

17. A small arrow attached to the bottom-left corner of an icon signifies:

    a. A selected icon

    b. An expanded folder

    c. A shortcut

    d. A restored file

18. The temporary storage device that holds cut and copied items is called the:

    a. Recycle Bin

    b. Explorer window

    c. My Computer window

    d. Clipboard

19. Clicking the Views button:

    a. Automatically puts the icons in List view

    b. Automatically puts the icons in Large Icons view

    c. Opens the Views drop-down menu

    d. Cycles to the next view on the Views menu

20. To view information about the icons listed in a window, put the icons in:

    a. Details view

    b. List view

    c. The Recycle Bin

    d. The Windows folder

21. A plus sign next to a folder or drive in the Folders Explorer Bar indicates that it can be

    a. Collapsed

    b. Expanded

    c. Moved

    d. Deleted

22. A file in the Recycle Bin:

    a. Has been deleted permanently

    b. Can be opened by double-clicking it

    c. Can be restored by dragging it to a new location

    d. Must be copied and pasted to be restored

23. To find a folder by searching for its file type or file size, click the:

    a. Name & Location tab

    b. Search Options link

    c. Find Now button

    d. Find Now tab

24. The powerful two-paneled tool that allows you to work with more than one drive, file, or folder is:

    a. My Computer

    b. Windows Explorer

    c. The Recycle Bin

    d. The Create Shortcut dialog box

Interactivity

Test Your Skills

1. View the folders and files on your hard drive:

   a. Use **My Computer** to display the contents of your hard drive (C:).

   b. Put the contents of your hard drive in **Small Icons** view.

   c. Change to **List** view using the Menu bar.

   d. Return to the top level of the file hierarchy.

   e. Close the My Computer window without using the Close button.

2. Use **Windows Explorer** to view and select items on your hard drive:

   a. Open Windows Explorer.

   b. Expand **My Computer**, your C: drive, and then the **Program Files** folder.

   c. Select the **Internet Explorer** folder so that its contents are displayed in the right panel.

   d. Select all of the items in the contents panel.

   e. Select the PLUGINS folder in the contents panel without using the mouse.

   f. Select every other item in the contents panel.

   g. Select the last four items in the contents panel.

3. Create a new folder and a new file, then copy the file to another folder:

   a. Create a new folder on your C: drive (not in the Internet Explorer folder) called **TYS**.

   b. Make a copy of the folder.

   c. Create a new WordPad document called TYS2 in the original TYS folder.

   d. Place a copy of the TYS2 WordPad document in the My Documents folder.

4. Create a shortcut and practice using the **Recycle Bin**:

   a. Place a shortcut to the original TYS folder on your desktop.

   b. Send the **Copy of TYS** folder to the Recycle Bin without dragging it.

   c. Drag the **Copy of TYS2** WordPad document that you placed in the My Documents folder to the Recycle Bin.

   d. Empty the Recycle Bin.

Interactivity (continued)

5. Create a new shortcut and then use the Search feature to locate it on your hard drive:

a. Place a shortcut to your C: drive on the desktop.

b. Practice using the Search feature by locating the shortcut you just created.

c. Open the shortcut from the Search Results window.

d. Close all windows and delete the shortcut you created in step a.

Problem Solving

1. You have been running a successful guitar instruction business for several years now. Since your business continues to grow, you have decided to start managing it with a computer running Windows 2000. The first step of this project is to set up your hard drive with a system of useful folders. Start with a main folder called Business. Within the Business folder you should place a folder for each day of the week that you teach, Monday through Friday. Eventually, each of these folders will contain a folder for each student who has a lesson on that day. For now, each day-of-the-week folder should hold a new WordPad document called [Insert day] Schedule. Back inside the Business folder, create one WordPad document with the name Student List and another called Master Schedule. Finally, place a shortcut to Master Schedule inside each day-of-the-week folder.

2. Your supervisor has asked you to be in charge of the New Media department's new multimedia software and documentation. Create a folder on your C: drive named New Media. Create two folders inside the New Media folder named Programs and Documentation. Open the Documentation folder and place a new WordPad document named Tech Support inside the folder. Copy the document to your My Documents folder. Then rename the Programs folder you created Software.

3. Before you install Windows 2000 throughout your office, you want to review the software's end user license agreement, but you are not sure where to find it. Use Windows 2000's Search facility to look for a file named eula on your local hard disk. If you find it successfully, double-click the file in the Search Results window to open it. Then close the file and create a shortcut to it on your desktop.

L E S S O N

3

WORKING WITH INTERNET EXPLORER

Microsoft **Internet Explorer** is a software application that gives you the tools you need to take full advantage of the **World Wide Web**. Its integration with the Windows 2000 operating system makes it easy to browse the Web whether you want to find a local take-out restaurant, e-mail your sister to tell her about your new job, or find a message board relating to mandolins.

One of the most used facets of the Internet is the World Wide Web. It has increasingly become a key element of business, culture, community, and politics. You have already seen the browser window, as it is the same one used for My Computer and the Windows Explorer. The function of a browser is just that: it lets you browse, or surf, and view the pages that make up the Web. The World Wide Web is like a long hypertext document consisting of millions of pages that contain text, pictures, movies, and sounds. Among these pages you can find everything from information on NASA's latest launch to samples from your favorite musical artist's new CD.

When using Internet Explorer, most Web browsing can be done through a series of mouse clicks. Web pages are made up of **hypermedia**, which are words and pictures that are linked to other places on the Web and will transport you there when they are clicked. Internet Explorer also has toolbars that contain buttons to help you move through all the interesting material you will encounter on your journey across the Web.

As you wander around the Web, you will encounter pages that you will want to return to later. To go to any page, all you need to do is remember the address (each Web page has its own), and then enter it into the text box provided on Internet Explorer's Address Bar. If you will want to visit a page often, there is even a way to create direct links, or shortcuts, to your favorite Web sites. This is a good idea if a site's content changes frequently, such as that of a news service. The nature of the Web allows for frequent updating of a page's data. As you go through this book, keep in mind that a page's look or contents may have changed since the authors visited it. Some references may no longer be accurate when compared with what you view on your computer.

Introduction to the Internet

Concept

The **Internet** is an extended world-wide computer network that is composed of numerous smaller networks. In the late 1960s, the U.S. Defense Department's Advanced Research Projects Agency (ARPA) created a network of computers designed to withstand severe localized damage, such as that of a nuclear attack. Each computer on the ARPA network was connected to every other machine in such a way as to form a web. Each chunk of data sent from one machine to another was formatted as a packet, which also contained the address of where the packet originated and where it was headed. The web configuration and packet format enabled data to be rerouted if a node along its path in the network should be rendered inoperable. The packet-switching technology developed for ARPAnet became the foundation of today's Internet.

In the early 1980s, the National Science Foundation founded NSFnet, five super-computing centers connected together on a network. Soon, other government agencies and educational institutions connected to NSFnet as well, adding information and infrastructure upon which an ever-larger network began to grow.

As more scientists, students, and computer enthusiasts became familiar with the Internet, more people began to log on from a variety of locations. **Figure 3-1** illustrates the phenomenal growth of Internet use. Soon, new software was developed to facilitate access to the Internet. Along with **e-mail** and **newsgroups**, two major uses of the Internet, the **World Wide Web** began to rise in popularity in the first half of the 1990s. The **WWW** is made possible by hypermedia and hypertext, objects such as pictures or lines of text that, when clicked, instruct the browser to go to another location on the Web. This allows for a nonlinear presentation of information, making the WWW, in effect, one huge hypermedia document made up of millions of individual files, each with its own address on the Web. The address at which a document is located on the Internet is called a **Uniform Resource Locator** or **URL**. A URL consists of three parts: the protocol (such as http or ftp), the location of the server on the Internet (domain), and sometimes the path to the requested data on the server's drive.

The Web works on a **client–server** model (**Figure 3-2**). The server, which is the computer containing the requested data, sends information to the client, the computer that receives it. The transfer of data between server and client follows a standardized protocol, or information exchange process. The Web standard is **HTTP** (**HyperText Transfer Protocol**), which allows all kinds of computers to understand and reliably translate hypertext Web files. Internet Explorer is a Web browser, which, like all Web software, conforms to HTTP standards. Web browsers are programs that allow a computer to translate the hypertext and display it. All Web browsers can read the text of all Web pages because these pages are written with a platform-independent language called **hypertext markup language**, or **HTML**. HTML documents consist of the text that will appear on the page, formatting instructions, and references to other files such as graphics that will be displayed on the page. The World Wide Web has become the most popular feature of the Internet, providing access to an almost unimaginable diversity of information.

Figure 3-1 The growth of the Internet

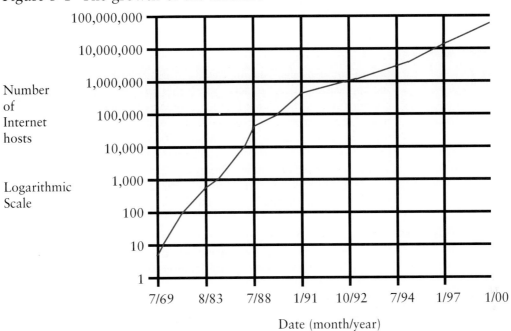

Number of Internet hosts

Logarithmic Scale

Date (month/year)

Figure 3-2 Clients and servers on the World Wide Web

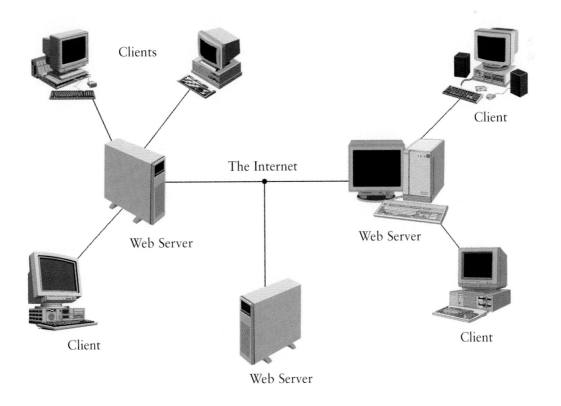

Opening Internet Explorer

Concept

Before you can begin surfing the Web with Internet Explorer (IE), you must open the application. You can accomplish this task in a variety of ways, including using the Start menu, the Quick Launch toolbar, or a desktop icon. This skill assumes that you have a valid Internet connection and that your Web browser has been configured correctly. If this is not the case, begin by double-clicking the Connect to the Internet icon 🌐 on your desktop to launch the Internet Connection Wizard (also available on the Start menu: Programs/Accessories/Communications), which will guide you through the steps necessary to set up your Internet account and browser. Once you have run the Wizard, its shortcut icon will be removed from the desktop.

Do It!

Open Internet Explorer and then guide the pointer over the various parts of the window to become familiar with its interface.

1 Click the Internet Explorer quick launch icon 🅴, located next to the Start button, to open the Internet Explorer window. Assuming that your connection to the Internet is valid, Internet Explorer will open. A page will appear in the browser window, which is shown maximized in **Figure 3-3**. This is called the browser's home page and refers to the document that loads automatically when the application is launched. IE's default home page is the Microsoft Network's (MSN) home page, http://www.msn.com. (In this instance, the term home page refers to the main page of Microsoft's Web site.) Since Windows allows for customization, your browser window may be different than the ones shown, and your startup procedure may vary slightly from the one demonstrated here. For example, you may have to go through a dial-up procedure if you are connecting to the Internet with a modem.

2 Internet Explorer's browser window resembles the standard Windows 2000 system window with which you are already familiar. You will notice the most change in the Standard Buttons toolbar. **Table 3-1** explains some of the features of this toolbar and how they allow you to use IE most effectively.

More

Changing your browser's home page is a relatively simple procedure. Open the Tools menu from Internet Explorer's Menu bar and click the Internet Options command. The Internet Options dialog box will open to the General tab. The top section of the General tab is titled Home page, and it contains a text entry box that holds the Web address for your browser's current home page. This address will be selected automatically when the dialog box opens. You can type any Web address to replace the one that is already there. Then click [OK] to confirm the adjustment and close the dialog box. The next time you open your browser or click on the Home button, the Web page whose address you provided will appear in your browser window.

If you have difficulty remembering the functions of the different toolbar buttons, you can customize the Standard Buttons toolbar so that it displays text labels for all buttons. To do this, right-click the toolbar, and then click the Customize command on the menu that appears. Near the bottom of the Customize Toolbar dialog box is a drop-down list box labeled Text Options that allows you to choose text labels for all buttons, selected buttons, or no text labels. The main part of this dialog box permits you to change which buttons actually appear on the toolbar.

Figure 3-3 Internet Explorer opened to MSN home page

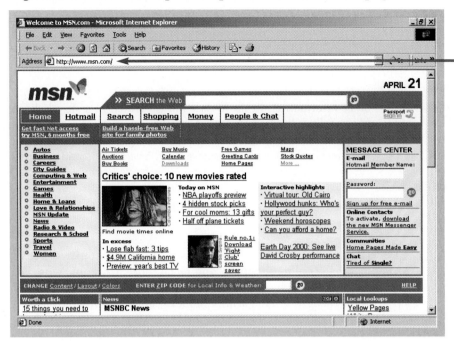

Address (URL)
of current Web
page displayed
in Address Bar
text box

Table 3-1 IE Standard Buttons toolbar

BUTTON	FUNCTION
⊗	Stops the loading of a page into the browser window
🗎	Reloads the current page; especially useful for pages that update frequently
Search Favorites History	Activates the corresponding Explorer Bar in the browser window
🏠	Loads the browser's home page into the browser window; the home page can be set on the General tab of the Internet Options dialog box
📧	Opens a menu of commands related to working with e-mail
🖨	Instructs a printer properly connected to your computer to print a copy of the current page

Practice

Change your browser's home page to the following address:
http://www.theglobe.com.

Hot Tip

To restore your browser's original home page setting, open the Internet Options dialog box from the View menu. Then click the **Use Default** button in the Home page section of the General tab.

Navigating the Web

Concept

Since information on the Web is not presented in a strictly linear fashion, it is possible to follow links in any order you like, examining whatever you wish in more detail. This often is referred to as browsing or surfing. Most Web browsing with Internet Explorer is done using a few basic actions and controls.

Do It!

Practice moving around the Web using hyperlinks, navigation buttons, and the Address Bar.

1 From the MSN home page, you can gain access to news, free e-mail, reference materials, online shopping, and much more. Clickable words and images on the page are called hyperlinks. Position the pointer over the Hotmail link. The pointer will appear as a hand with a pointing finger 🖑 when over the link, indicating that it is an active link. The underlined text also may change color to red.

2 With the pointer still over Hotmail, click the left mouse button. The Microsoft Windows icon at the right end of the Menu bar will animate to indicate that the page you have requested is loading. The page should appear in the browser window momentarily, as shown in **Figure 3-4**.

3 Locate and click the Terms of Service link. You will be transported to a page that explains the terms of service for Hotmail®, Microsoft's free Web-based e-mail service. Notice that since you started following links, the Back button on the Standard Buttons toolbar has become active. Use the scroll bar to read text that is not visible.

4 Click the Back button ⬅Back to go back to the previously viewed page, the main Hotmail page.

5 Click the Forward button ➡. The Terms of Service page reappears in the window. The Forward button only becomes active once the Back button has been clicked, and reverses the Back command.

6 Position the pointer in the Address Bar text box, and then click once. The URL (Uniform Resource Locator) of the current page will be selected.

7 Type http://www.altavista.com to enter this address manually, then press [Enter]. The home page of the AltaVista search engine, shown in **Figure 3-5**, will appear.

8 Click the Home button 🏠 to go back to your browser's home page.

More

The Forward and Back buttons both have small black downward-pointing arrows on their right edges. These arrows indicate that the button has a drop-down menu associated with it. If you click the arrow with the left mouse button, a list of recently visited pages appears below the button with the most recent at the top. Using this list allows you to quickly go back to a previously visited page without having to click the Back button repeatedly. In the same way, the Forward button's drop-down list shows sites that can be visited by clicking the Forward button. Right-clicking the Back or Forward button also will bring up these menus.

Figure 3-4 Microsoft's Hotmail® page

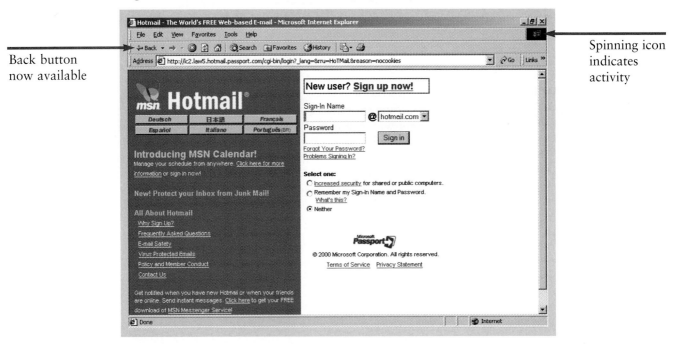

Back button now available

Spinning icon indicates activity

Figure 3-5 Using the Address Bar to enter a URL

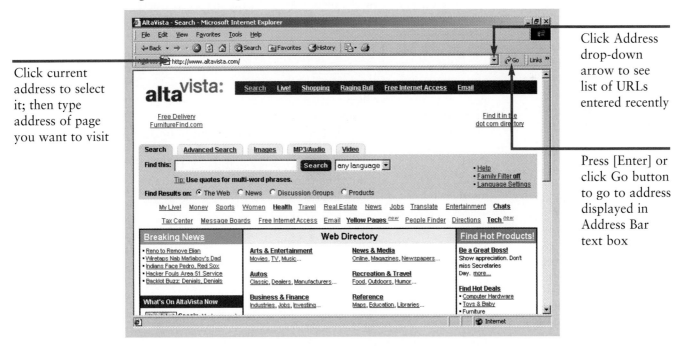

Click current address to select it; then type address of page you want to visit

Click Address drop-down arrow to see list of URLs entered recently

Press [Enter] or click Go button to go to address displayed in Address Bar text box

Visit the Web page found at **http://www.usps.gov**. Then use the tool-bar to return to your browser's home page.

Clicking the History button on the toolbar opens the History Explorer Bar on the left side of the browser window. The History Bar lists all of the pages you have visited recently as hyperlinks so you can revisit them with a single click.

Searching the Internet

Concept

There is an inordinate amount of information on the Internet. Being able to find what you want will help make your experience surfing the Web more productive and enjoyable. With Internet Explorer's **Search Explorer Bar**, you can retrieve and display a list of Web sites related to your topic of interest, and then load the actual Web pages into the same window. This convenience prevents you from having to navigate back to your search page each time you want to follow a different link.

Do It!

Use the Search Explorer Bar to find a Web site that offers used car listings.

1 Click the Search button [Q Search]. The Search Explorer Bar (**Figure 3-6**) will appear in the browser window. Notice that Internet Explorer's Search Bar differs from the one you saw in Windows Explorer. This one is configured for Internet searches rather than for finding files or folders, though a link for searching for files or folders is still provided.

2 The default search category is Find a Web page, and the Find a Web page containing: text-entry box is ready to receive your search query. Type "used cars" (include the quotes). Enclosing the phrase in quotation marks instructs the search engine to treat the words you enter as a single unit and only search for pages that contain used and cars next to each other in that order. If the keywords are not enclosed in quotation marks, the search will return any pages that simply contain either word.

3 Click the Search button [Search]. The MSN search engine lists links to the 10 Web pages that will most likely satisfy your needs, determined by factors such as proximity of the words to each other and to the top of the page. If you point to a link, you will receive a ScreenTip that includes a description of the page and its URL.

4 Click a link from the list of results to visit that page. The site will load in the right panel, while the search engine remains in the left panel so that you can select another link, as shown in **Figure 3-7**.

5 To view the page in the entire window, click the Search button again to hide the Explorer Bar. The current search will remain in the Search Bar until you close Internet Explorer or click the Search button again to begin a new search.

More

Once you click a link in Internet Explorer, the link will change color so that you know you have already visited it. This is very helpful when you are working with a list of links such as that in the Search Explorer Bar. Most searches will return more than 10 results. If the first 10 do not satisfy your needs, you will find a link below them that allows you to view the next set of links that match your search criteria. If you still aren't successful, you can try using a different search engine by clicking the Next button [Q Next ▾] near the top of the Explorer Bar. If you want to choose a specific search engine, click the arrow on the right end of the Next button to open a menu of search engines. Clicking the New button [Q New] reloads the basic Search Explorer Bar (**Figure 3-6**) so you can choose a new category of search. Clicking the Customize button [Customize] allows you to choose which engines and directories will be used for each search category and the order in which they will be activated by the Next button.

Figure 3-6 Internet Explorer's Search Explorer Bar

Select a search category

Enter search words here

Click button to begin search

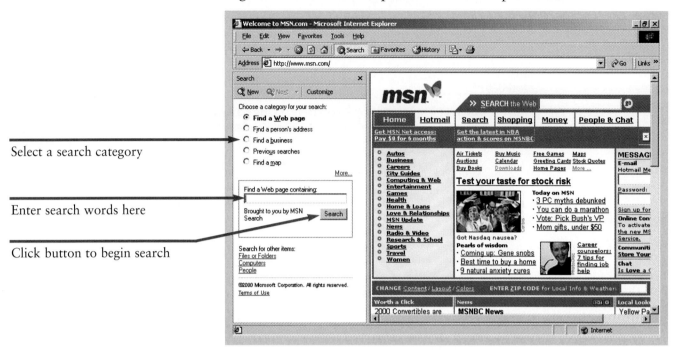

Figure 3-7 Using search results

Click to select a different search engine

Visited link changes color

List of links found as a result of search

Right panel displays selected Web page while search results remain in Explorer Bar

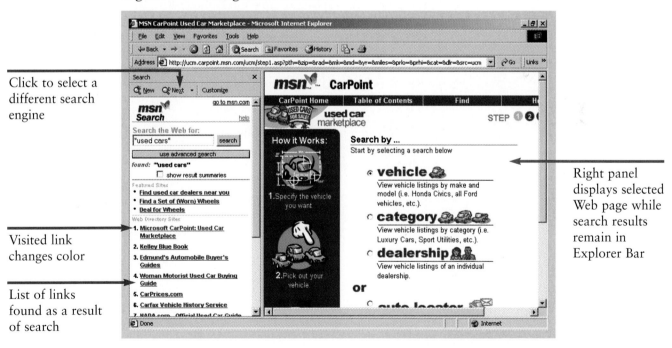

Practice

Use the Search Explorer Bar to find Web pages that will allow you to consult airline flight schedules. Then follow one of the links produced by your search.

Hot Tip

Most search engines are only case sensitive with uppercase letters. For example, a search for **Bugs Bunny** will return sites relating to the cartoon character, while a search on **bugs bunny** will result in a list of sites on insects and rabbits as well.

Creating Favorites

Concept

Internet Explorer allows you to make direct links, or shortcuts, to your favorite Internet sites so that you may revisit them easily without having to remember long URLs. This also is known as bookmarking. The Favorites menu offers several options for adding, organizing, and managing your favorites. Shortcuts to frequently visited sites also may be placed on the Links toolbar, on the desktop, or in a folder on your hard drive.

Do It!

Create a Favorite for a search engine, search for a site that contains a local weather forecast, and then place a shortcut to that site on the Links toolbar.

1 Click the Address text box to select its contents.

2 Type www.excite.com to replace the current URL, then press [Enter]. Internet Explorer automatically adds the protocol http://, and the Excite search engine/Web guide loads into the window.

3 Open the Favorites menu from the Menu bar, then click Add to Favorites. The Add Favorite dialog box will appear, as shown in **Figure 3-8**.

4 Click ⬜ OK ⬜ to create the favorite with the default settings and close the dialog box. The shortcut to the Excite page will be added to your Favorites list.

5 Open the Favorites menu to see that your shortcut is there. Then click the Favorites menu title again to close the menu.

6 Click in Excite's search text-entry box to place an insertion point there.

7 Type +weather +*the name of your city*. This instructs the search engine to look for sites that contain both of the words. If the plus signs had been omitted, sites containing either of the words, but not necessarily both, would be found.

8 Click ⬜ Search ⬜ to initiate the search (if a dialog box appears, click Yes to proceed).

9 Look through the list of matches, using the vertical scroll bar to advance the page as you go. Visit the sites that appear relevant to the original search objective by clicking their hyperlinks. Look for a site with a good local forecast. Use the Back button to return to the search results page to view additional found sites. When you find a site you like, stay there.

10 Assuming your Links toolbar is just visible at the right end of the Address Bar, drag the Links toolbar straight down so that it occupies its own row.

11 Click and hold the IE page icon 🔲 in the Address text box, and then drag it down to the Links toolbar. As you drag, the pointer will appear as an arrow with the shortcut arrow icon attached. A marker will appear in the Links toolbar indicating the place where the new favorite will be created (only when you are between buttons or at the ends of the toolbar). When you release the mouse button, a button for the current site will appear on the Links toolbar (**Figure 3-9**). A favorite also will be added to the Links folder on the Favorites menu.

More

The favorites that you create will not only appear on the Favorites menu in the Internet Explorer window, but everywhere the Favorites folder is accessible. This can include the Start menu and the Favorites menu in any system window. The favorites that you create also will be added to the Favorites Explorer Bar, which can be left open while you browse the Web for quick access to your shortcuts.

Figure 3-8 Add Favorite dialog box

Default favorite name taken from page title

Click to create favorite on different level of Favorites hierarchy

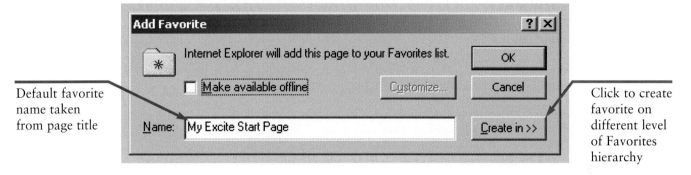

Figure 3-9 Adding a favorite to the Links toolbar

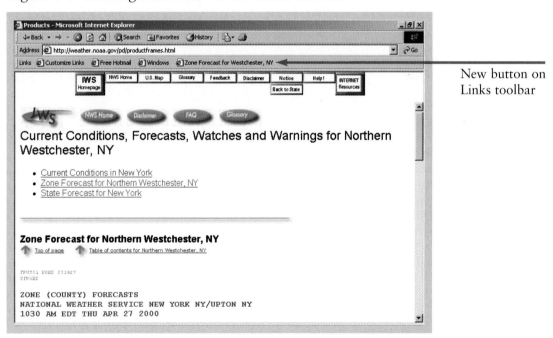

New button on Links toolbar

Practice

Add **www.amazon.com** to your Favorites folder. Then add **www.usps.gov** to your Links toolbar.

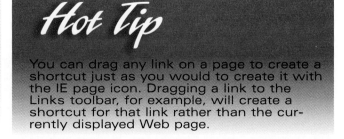

Hot Tip

You can drag any link on a page to create a shortcut just as you would to create it with the IE page icon. Dragging a link to the Links toolbar, for example, will create a shortcut for that link rather than the currently displayed Web page.

Managing Favorites

Concept

Without sufficient attention to organization, a long list of favorites can be difficult to manage. By editing and grouping favorites, you can make them much easier to use. Internet Explorer allows you to create or delete folders on the Favorites menu, redistribute favorites among the folders, and rename favorites and the folders that hold them.

Do It!

Create a new folder that will store your personal favorites, move a favorite into that folder, and then rename the favorite.

1. Click Favorites on the Menu bar, then click the **Organize Favorites** command. The Organize Favorites dialog box will open, as shown in **Figure 3-10**.

2. Click the **Create Folder** button `Create Folder`. A new folder will be created in the Organize Favorites dialog box with its default name selected, ready to be changed.

3. Type Search Engines, then press [Enter]. The name of the folder will change, and the folder will remain selected.

4. Click the favorite you created for the Excite page in the last skill to select it. Notice that its properties are displayed in the bottom-right corner of the dialog box.

5. Click the **Move to Folder** button `Move to Folder...`. The **Browse for Folder** dialog box will open.

6. Click the Search Engines folder you created to select it as the destination folder to which you will move the Excite favorite. When you select the folder, it will be highlighted and appear as an open folder, as shown in **Figure 3-11**.

7. Click the OK button `OK`. The Browse for Folder dialog box closes, and the selected favorite is moved.

8. Click the Search Engine folder to show its contents in the dialog box.

9. Click the Excite favorite to select it.

10. Click the Rename button `Rename`. The favorite's name will be highlighted.

11. Type Excite.com, then press [Enter] to rename the favorite, as shown in **Figure 3-12**. Close the Organize Favorites dialog box.

More

In the previous Skill you created a favorite on the top level of the Favorites hierarchy. The Favorites folder is the default location for creating shortcuts. If you click the Create In button, the dialog box will expand, showing you a pane in which the current Favorites hierarchy is displayed. This pane is similar to the Browse for Folder dialog box pictured in **Figure 3-11**. From this additional pane you can select the folder in which you wish to create the new favorite, thereby eliminating the process of moving it later.

Figure 3-10 Organize Favorites dialog box

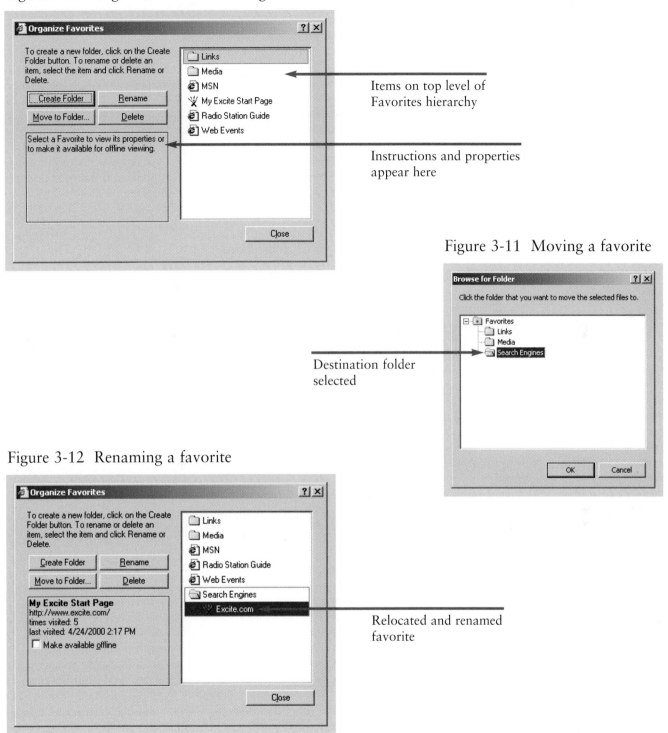

Items on top level of
Favorites hierarchy

Instructions and properties
appear here

Figure 3-11 Moving a favorite

Destination folder
selected

Figure 3-12 Renaming a favorite

Relocated and renamed
favorite

Practice

Create a new Favorites folder called **Online Shopping**. Then move the Amazon.com favorite you created in the previous Practice exercise into this new folder.

Hot Tip

You can use the drag-and-drop technique to move favorites from folder to folder inside the Organize Favorites dialog box. Right-clicking an item will allow you to rename it.

Printing a Web Page

Concept

In general, Web pages are designed primarily for on-screen viewing. However, there may be occasions when you want to print a paper copy of a particular page. In fact, most online shopping sites suggest that you print your transaction page when you have completed a purchase so you can keep it for your records. In addition, many software and hardware manufacturers provide installation instructions online that you can print and then follow as you install new software.

Do It!

Use Internet Explorer's **Print** command to print a paper copy of a Web page.

1 Use the favorite you created earlier to go to www.excite.com.

2 Click File to open the File menu, then click the **Print** command. The Print dialog box, shown in **Figure 3-13**, appears with the **General** tab in front.

3 If your computer is connected to more than one printer, you can select the icon for the printer you wish to use in the **Select Printer** section of the dialog box.

4 When the correct printer is selected, click [Print] to print the Web page with the default settings. Your printer should print one copy of the page, but it might require more than one piece of paper to do so since Web pages are not necessarily designed to fit on standard paper sizes.

More

Even though Web pages are designed for the screen rather than paper, you do have some control over how a page will appear when you print it. Before you print, open the File menu and choose the **Page Setup** command. The Page Setup dialog box will open, as shown in **Figure 3-14**. In the **Paper** section of the dialog box, you can select the size of the paper you are printing on and how it is being fed into the machine. These options are also available on the **Paper Quality** tab in the Print dialog box. In the **Headers and Footers** section, you can specify text that will appear at the top and bottom of the printed page. The **Orientation** section determines whether the page will be printed like a traditional document (**Portrait**), or so that its left to right length is greater than its top to bottom length (**Landscape**). Page orientation also can be controlled from the **Layout** tab in the Print dialog box. Finally, you can set the distance for all four of the page's margins in the **Margins** section.

Some Web pages are divided into separate components known as frames. When you print a page that uses frames, the **Print frames** section of the Print dialog box (**Figure 3-13**) will be active. From here you can choose to print the page exactly as it appears on your screen, print a single frame that you select, or print each frame individually. Just below the Print frames section are two check boxes. The first instructs your printer to print all documents that are linked to the one you are currently printing while the second simply adds a table of these links to the end of the printout. These items are also available on the Print dialog box's **Options** tab.

You can bypass the Print dialog box by clicking on the Print button 🖨 on the Standard Buttons toolbar. Your document will be printed using the current print settings.

Figure 3-13 Print dialog box

Double-click icon to set up another printer on your system

Select a different printer here

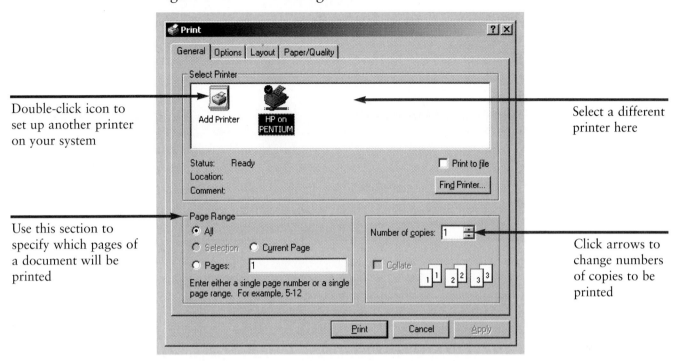

Use this section to specify which pages of a document will be printed

Click arrows to change numbers of copies to be printed

Figure 3-14 Page Setup dialog box

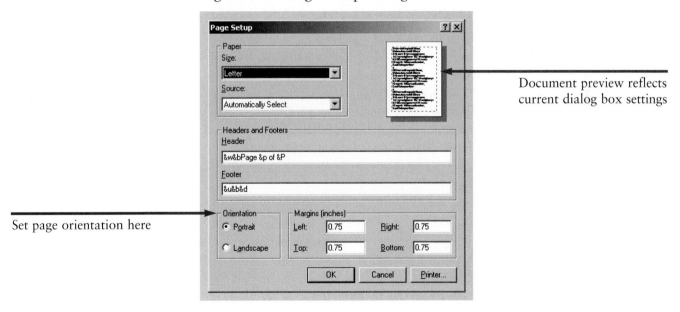

Document preview reflects current dialog box settings

Set page orientation here

Shortcuts

Function	Button/Mouse	Menu	Keyboard
Stop loading page		Click View, then click Stop	[Esc]
Refresh page		Click View, then click Refresh	[F5]
Go to browser's home page		Click View, then highlight Go To, then click Home Page	[Alt]+[Home]
Expand window to full screen view		Click View, then click Full Screen	[F11]
Access mail from IE (start Outlook Express)		Click Tools, then highlight Mail and News	[Alt]+[T], [M]
Print current page		Click File, then click Print (for dialog box)	[Ctrl]+[P] (for dialog box)
Open new browser window		Click File, then highlight New, then click Window	[Ctrl]+[N]
Open new page		Click File, then click Open	[Ctrl]+[O]
Browse back	⇐ Back	Click View, then highlight Go To, then click Back	[Alt]+[Left Arrow]
Browse forward	⇒	Click View, then highlight Go To, then click Forward	[Alt]+[Right Arrow]

Quiz

Identify Key Features

Name and describe the functions of the buttons indicated by callout arrows in **Figure 3-15**.

Figure 3-15 Internet Explorer's Standard Buttons toolbar

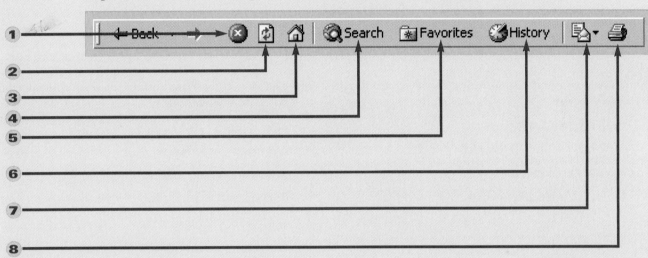

Select the Best Answer

9. Click this to go to your browser's home page C

10. Dialog box that allows you to create shortcuts to pages you visit frequently D

11. Language used to write Web pages H

12. Protocol used to transfer data over the Web F

13. Dialog box that allows you to relocate a favorite I

14. A subset of the Internet that allows users to publish documents on remote servers B

15. An individual component of a Web page that can be printed independently J

16. A Page Setup option E

17. Reloads the current page in the browser window A

18. Allows you to create buttons for your favorites G

a. Refresh button
b. World Wide Web
c. Home button
d. Links toolbar
e. Orientation
f. HTTP
g. Browse for Folder
h. HTML
i. Add Favorite dialog box
j. Frame

Quiz (continued)

Complete the Statement

19. A document's address on the Web is also known as its:

    a. EARL

    b. IRL

    c. URL

    d. HTTP

20. To help you find documents on the Web, you should use:

    a. IE's Search Explorer Bar

    b. Windows 2000's Help facility

    c. Outlook Express

    d. IE's Favorites Explorer Bar

21. All of the following are popular search engines except:

    a. AltaVista

    b. MSN Search

    c. Outlook

    d. Excite

22. The Web runs on a:

    a. Linear platform

    b. Decreasing number of hosts

    c. Government-regulated network

    d. Client–server model

23. You can create a favorite for the current page by dragging and dropping the:

    a. Favorites button

    b. IE page icon

    c. Favorites Explorer Bar

    d. Current URL

24. Clicking on the Print button causes your document to be printed without:

    a. Margins

    b. Headers and Footers

    c. The appearance of the Print dialog box

    d. Frames

25. To change your browser's home page, choose the Internet Options command from the:

    a. Tools menu

    b. File menu

    c. Home Page dialog box

    d. Favorites menu

26. The mouse pointer changes to a hand with a pointing finger to indicate that:

    a. The page you requested has finished loading

    b. The link you are pointing to is a favorite

    c. You must wait until the page finishes loading

    d. You are pointing to an active link

Interactivity

Test Your Skills

1. Open Internet Explorer and practice navigating the Web:

   a. Launch Internet Explorer.

   b. If your browser is not set to open to **www.msn.com**, go there now.

   c. Look for a link to **microsoft.com** and click it to go to Microsoft's home page.

   d. Click the **Privacy Policy** link near the bottom of the page.

   e. Go back to Microsoft's home page.

   f. Return to the Privacy Policy page.

2. Visit a Web page whose address you have entered manually:

   a. Use the **Address Bar** to visit **http://www.cnn.com**.

   b. **Stop** the page before it finishes loading.

   c. **Refresh** the page.

3. Use the **Search Explorer Bar** to find Web sites about your hometown and store them as favorites:

   a. Activate the Search Explorer Bar.

   b. Conduct a search for Web pages that relate to your hometown.

   c. Follow the links generated by the search until you have found two or three that you like.

   d. Add these sites to your **Favorites** list.

4. Create a new Favorites folder and move existing favorites into it:

   a. Open the **Organize Favorites** dialog box.

   b. Create a new folder named [Your Hometown] **Links**.

   c. Move the favorites you created in the previous step into the new folder.

   d. Rename the new folder so that its name is just that of your hometown and doesn't include the word "Links."

Interactivity (continued)

5. Print a Web page with Landscape orientation:

   a. Direct your Web browser to one of the hometown favorites you created above.

   b. Open the Page Setup dialog box from the File menu.

   c. Change the page orientation from Portrait to Landscape, then click OK.

   d. Open the Print dialog box.

   e. Print two copies of the current page.

Problem Solving

1. Search the Web for information on guitars and guitar instruction. Use at least three different search engines to conduct your search. When you find helpful sites, be sure to bookmark them in appropriately named folders. Create at least four different folders to house favorites for the sites you find. Some categories you might use are Guitar Sales, Online Instruction, and Chords and Tablature.

2. As a sales representative, you fit the title of "business traveler" perfectly. Fortunately, the World Wide Web can do wonders for your travel expenses. Various Web sites can now assist you in finding the cheapest air fares and hotel rooms available. Use the skills you have learned in this lesson to find at least three such sites on the Web. Add each site to your Favorites list. Then create a new Favorites folder named Travel Savings and move the favorites you have added into the new folder.

3. As the Director of Human Resources at a large accounting firm, it is important for you to stay on top of the issues that affect the workforce. Chief among these is health insurance. Your approach to this topic is twofold. You like to keep one eye on what the insurance companies are saying about themselves and the other on what the watchdogs are saying about the insurance companies. Use your Web skills to find the Web sites of major health care providers. Store the home pages of these sites in a Favorites folder named Health Care Providers. Then focus your Web search on pages that provide reviews of, or news about, particular health care companies. Organize these pages in a Favorites folder named Health Care Reviews. Print the page that offers the best summary of current health insurance issues.

4. Your department is in the market for a new color laser printer. You have been chosen to research the purchase and recommend a printer to your boss. Use your Web skills to find out as much as you can about four top-of-the-line color laser printers. You should search for the Web sites of companies that actually manufacture and sell the printers as well as independent reviews of printers. When you find a page on a manufacturer's site, save it as a favorite in a folder named Printers. When you find a page that reviews the performance of a particular printer or printers, save it as a favorite in a folder named Printer Reviews. After studying the four candidates you have found, select the printer that you think will best suit your department's needs (a high output rate, low maintenance, network ready, reliable service program). Create a button on the Links toolbar for the Web page of the printer you have chosen.

 Glossary

A

Accessories
Programs built into Windows 2000 that are useful for everyday tasks.

Active Desktop
Gives you the ability to integrate live Web content and animated pictures into your desktop.

Active window
The window you are currently using. When a window is active, its title bar changes color to differentiate it from other open windows and its program button is depressed.

Address Bar
Used for entering a Web address manually; also can be used to view a local folder or drive.

Address Book
Component of Outlook Express that allows you to store contact information.

Appearance tab
In the Display Properties dialog box, lets you customize the appearance of individual system items or apply an appearance scheme.

Attach button
Permits you to e-mail a computer file.

B

Back button
Allows you to return to the Web page or system window you viewed previously.

Background tab
In the Display Properties dialog box, used to apply wallpaper to your desktop.

Bitmap (bmp)
Basic image file format used by Windows.

Browsing
Examining Web pages in the manner of your choice.

C

CD Player
Windows application that lets you play audio CDs.

Check box
A small square box that allows you to turn a dialog box option on or off by clicking it.

Classic Style
A folder option that requires a double-click to open an icon and a single-click to select it.

Click
To press and release a mouse button in one motion; usually refers to the left mouse button.

Client–Server
A computing model in which computers known as clients request and receive data from a central computer with high storage capacity called a server.

Clipboard
A temporary storage area for cut or copied text or graphics. You can paste the contents of the Clipboard into any Windows program, such as WordPad or Microsoft Word. The Clipboard holds the information until it is replaced with another piece of text, or until the computer is shut down.

Close
To quit an application and remove its window from the desktop. The Close button appears in the upper-right corner of a window, on the title bar.

Command
Directive that carries out an application feature or provides options for carrying out a feature.

Command button
In a dialog box, a button that carries out an action. A command button usually has a label that describes its action, such as OK, Cancel, or Help. If the label is followed by an ellipsis, clicking the button displays another dialog box.

Control menu
Contains commands related to resizing, moving, and closing a window.

Control Panel
A utility used for changing computer settings. You can access the various control panels through the Start menu, My Computer, or Windows Explorer.

Copy
To place a duplicate of a file or portion thereof on the Clipboard to be pasted in another location.

Cursor
The blinking vertical line in a document window that indicates where text will appear when you type. Also referred to as the insertion point.

Cut
To remove a file, or a portion of a file, and place it on the Clipboard.

Cut and paste
To remove information from one place and insert it in another using the Clipboard as the temporary storage area.

D

Date/Time Properties dialog box
Allows you to set your system clock and calendar.

Deleted Items folder
Outlook Express folder that functions much like the Windows Recycle Bin.

Desktop
The on-screen area, created using the metaphor of a desk, that provides workspace for your computing tasks.

Dialog box
A box that explains the available command options for you to review or change before executing the command.

Disk Cleanup
Windows utility that removes unnecessary files from your computer, creating more free space.

Disk Defragmenter
Windows utility that rearranges the data on your hard disk so that they can be accessed more efficiently.

Document window
The window within the application window in which a file is viewed and edited. When the document window is maximized, it shares a border and title bar with the application window.

Double-click
To press and release the mouse button twice rapidly; usually refers to the left mouse button.

Drafts folder
In Outlook Express, allows you to store messages that you have not finished composing.

Drag
To hold down the mouse button while moving the mouse.

E

Edit
To add, delete, or modify elements of a file.

E-mail
A method of sending electronic messages from one computer to another over the Internet.

Entire Network icon
Gives you access to the other workgroups that are a part of your network.

F

Favorite

A shortcut to a local, network, or Internet address that you have saved so that you can access the location easily.

Favorites Explorer Bar

Makes your Favorites menu part of the browser window so that it is always available.

Favorites menu

Allows you to store shortcuts to your favorite Web pages and other files for easy access.

File

A document that has been created and saved under a unique file name.

File hierarchy

A logical order for folders and files that resembles how you would organize files and folders in a filing cabinet. Your file hierarchy displays where your folders and files are stored on your computer.

File management

The skill of organizing files and folders.

Folders

Subdivisions of a disk that work like a filing system to help you organize files.

Folders Explorer Bar

Default left panel of Windows Explorer; shows all of the drives and folders available on your computer.

Footer

Text that appears at the bottom of a printed document.

Format

The way information appears on a page. To format means to change the appearance of data without changing their content.

Format Bar

Toolbar that allows you to format text in a WordPad document.

Formatting Toolbar

Allows you to change the characteristics of the text in an e-mail message and insert objects.

Forward button

Allows you to revisit a Web page or system window from which you have browsed back.

Forward command

Used to pass a message you have received to another e-mail address.

Frame

An independent component of a Web page.

Full

A file-sharing setting that allows others to read and edit your shared files.

G

Graphical user interface (GUI)

An environment made up of meaningful symbols, icons, words, and windows that control the basic operation of a computer and the programs it runs.

H

Header

The summary information for an e-mail or newsgroup message. Also, the text that appears along the top of a printed page.

Help button

A button in a Help window that opens a dialog box or a program to provide an answer to your question.

Highlight

When an item is shaded to indicate that it has been selected.

History Explorer Bar

Displays links for all of the drives and folders or Web pages you have visited recently.

Home page

The page to which your browser opens upon launch or clicking the Home button; also can refer to the main page of a particular Web site.

Horizontal scroll bar

Changes your view laterally when all of the information in a file does not fit in the window.

Hypermedia

Text, pictures, and other objects that are linked to files on the Web and will access those files when clicked. Also known as hyperlinks.

HyperText Markup Language (HTML)

Platform-independent computer language used to write Web pages.

HyperText Transfer Protocol (HTTP)

The exchange process used by servers and clients in transferring data over the Web.

I

Icon

Pictorial representation of programs, files, and other screen elements.

Inbox

Holds the e-mail messages you have received in Outlook Express.

Inbox Assistant

Creates filters that route incoming messages to a specific folder based on criteria you supply.

Internet

A worldwide computer network made up of numerous smaller networks.

Internet Connection Wizard

Runs you through the process of setting up an Internet account.

Internet Explorer

Windows 2000's Web browsing application.

K

Keyboard shortcut

A keyboard equivalent of a menu command (e.g., [Ctrl]+[X] for Cut).

L

Landscape orientation

Page setup in which the left-to-right length is greater than the top-to-bottom length.

Launch

To start a program so you can work with it.

Links toolbar

Makes Favorites available as buttons in your browser window.

List box

A drop-down list of items. To choose an item, click the list box drop-down arrow, then click the desired item from the list.

Lurk

To read the messages on a newsgroup without participating in the discussion.

M

Map Network Drive

Command that connects your computer to a remote shared folder as if it were a local drive.

Maximize

To enlarge a window to its maximum size. Maximizing an application window causes it to fill the screen; maximizing a document window causes it to fill the application window.

Menu

A list of related commands in an application.

Menu bar

Lists the names of menus containing application commands. Click a menu name on the Menu bar to display its list of commands.

Minimize

To shrink a window to its minimum size. Minimizing an application window reduces it to a button on the Windows taskbar.

Mouse

A palm-sized, hand-operated input device that you roll on your desk to position the mouse pointer and click to select items and execute commands.

Mouse buttons

The two buttons on the mouse, called the left and right mouse buttons, that you use to make selections and issue commands.

Mouse pointer

The usually arrow-shaped cursor on the screen that you control by guiding the mouse on your desk. You use the mouse pointer to select items, drag objects, choose commands, and start or exit programs. The appearance of the mouse pointer can change depending on the task being executed.

Multitasking

The ability to run several programs on your computer at once and easily switch among them.

My Computer

A tool used to view the files and folders that are available on your computer and how they are arranged. The default icon, a PC, appears on the desktop.

My Network Places

Allows you to view and access the computers that make up your network.

N

Network

Two or more computers linked together to allow for the sharing and exchanging of data.

New Toolbar command

Allows you to create a custom toolbar that can be placed on the taskbar or in its own window.

Newsgroup

An electronic bulletin board on the Internet used to post messages on a specific topic.

O

Operating system

Controls the basic operation of your computer and the programs you run on it. Windows 2000 is an operating system.

Organize Favorites command

Allows you to rename your Favorites and restructure your Favorites hierarchy.

Outbox

Stores e-mail messages you have composed in Outlook Express until you send them.

Outlook Express

E-mail software that comes with Windows 2000.

P

Paint

Windows 2000's built-in drawing program.

Pattern

Used to fill in the area of the desktop that is not covered by wallpaper.

Personalized menus

Feature that permits the Start and Menu bar menus to adapt to your usage by temporarily hiding the commands you use infrequently so the others are more accessible.

Point

To place the mouse pointer over an item on the desktop.

Pop-up menu

The menu that appears when you right-click certain places in the Windows environment.

Portrait orientation

Traditional document setup in which the top-to-bottom length is greater than the left-to-right length.

Post

To send a message to a newsgroup.

Program

A software application that performs specific tasks, such as Microsoft Word or WordPad.

Program button

The button that appears on the taskbar to indicate that an application is open. The active program is represented by an indented button.

Properties

The characteristics of a specific element (such as the mouse, keyboard, or desktop display) that you can change. Properties also can refer to characteristics of a file such as its name, type, size, and location.

R

Radio button

A small circular button in a dialog box that allows you to switch between options.

Read-Only

A file-sharing setting that prevents others from editing your shared files.

Recycle Bin

An icon on the desktop that represents a temporary storage area for deleted files. Files will remain in the Recycle Bin until you empty it, at which time they are permanently removed from your computer.

Reply to All

Allows you to send a direct response to an e-mail message that is also received by each recipient of the original message.

Reply to Author

Allows you to send a direct response to an e-mail message.

Restore

To return a window to its previous size before it was resized (either maximized or minimized). A Restore button usually appears in the upper-right corner of a window, on the title bar.

Right-click

To click the right mouse button; often necessary to access specialized menus and shortcuts. (The designated right and left mouse buttons may be reversed with the Mouse control panel to accommodate user preferences.)

Run

To open an application.

S

Screen saver

A moving or changing image that covers your screen when you are not working.

ScreenTip

A yellow help box that Windows provides to explain a particular feature.

Scroll bar

A graphical device for moving vertically and horizontally through a document with the mouse. Scroll bars are located along the right and bottom edges of the document window.

Scroll bar box

A small grey box located inside a scroll bar that indicates your current position relative to the rest of the document window. You can advance a scroll bar box by dragging it, clicking the scroll bar on either side of it, or clicking the scroll bar arrows.

Search command

Allows you to search for local or network files, other computers on your network, Internet addresses, and more.

Search engine
A Web site that generates Web links based on criteria you provide.

Search Explorer Bar
Permits you to keep an Internet search in the browser window and visit links at the same time. Also allows you to search local and network drives for files and folders.

Select
Highlighting an item to indicate that it is the active object on the screen. Usually done in order to perform some operation on the item.

Selection bar
The unmarked column on the left side of the WordPad document window that allows you to select entire lines or paragraphs of text at once.

Sent Items folder
Folder that automatically stores a copy of each e-mail message you send in Outlook Express.

Set as Wallpaper
Command that allows you to use an image as desktop wallpaper.

Shared folder
A folder that is accessible over a network to computers other than the one on which it is stored.

Shortcut
A link that takes you directly to a particular file, folder, or program without having to pass through each item in its file hierarchy.

Shut down
The process you go through to turn off your computer when you finish working. After you complete this action, it is safe to turn off your computer.

Sound Recorder
Windows application that lets you record and play audio.

Start button
A button on the taskbar that accesses a special menu that you use to start programs, find files, access Windows Help, and more.

Stationery
A picture used to enhance the appearance of an e-mail message.

Surfing
A synonym for browsing.

System Tray
The box at the right edge of the taskbar that houses your system clock and various utility icons.

T

Task Scheduler
Allows you to automate Windows tasks.

Taskbar
A bar, usually located at the bottom of the screen, that contains the Start button, shows which programs are running by displaying their program buttons, and shows the current time.

Taskbar and Start menu command
Allows you to control the behavior and content of the taskbar and the Start menu.

Thumbnails View
Allows you to view previews of all image files in a folder rather than file icons

Title bar
The horizontal bar at the top of a window that displays the name of the document or application that appears in the window.

Toolbar
A graphical bar containing buttons that act as shortcuts for common commands.

Triple-click

In some programs, performing this action is an easy way to select an entire line or block of text.

U

Uniform Resource Locator (URL)

The address of a file on the Internet.

V

Vertical scroll bar

Moves your view up and down through a window, allowing you to view portions of a document that are not currently visible.

W

Wait box

Determines how many idle minutes Windows will wait before initializing a screen saver.

Wallpaper

A picture you apply to your desktop.

Wave (wav)

A Windows sound file.

Web

A subset of the Internet that allows users to publish documents on special computers called servers so that others (clients) can access them.

Web browser

A computer application that allows you to view documents on the World Wide Web.

Web Style

A folder option that allows you to select an icon by pointing to it and open an icon with a single click.

Web tab

In the Display Properties dialog box, used to control Active Desktop content.

Window

A rectangular area on the screen in which you view and work on files.

Windows Explorer

A tool that allows you to view the hierarchy of folders on your computer and all the subfolders and files in a selected folder. Windows Explorer is very useful for moving and copying files among folders.

Windows Media Player

Windows 2000's audio and video player, capable of playing a variety of sound and movie formats including streaming media.

WordPad

Windows 2000's built-in word processing program.

Workgroup

A group of computers that is a subdivision of a network.

L E S S O N

1

INTRODUCTION TO WORD

Microsoft Word 2000 is a word processing software program designed to make the creation of professional-quality documents fast and easy. Unlike a typewriter, Word allows the user to edit, move, and copy text that has been written, providing enormous flexibility in how the finished product will appear.

Among many other features, Microsoft Word will let you:

• Copy, move, and change the appearance of text in a document
• Create documents using ready-made templates
• Automatically add page numbers and footnotes to documents
• Automatically find and correct spelling and grammatical errors
• Insert tables, charts, and pictures in your documents
• Request help while you are using the program
• Search for specific instances of text and formatting in a document
• See how your document will appear on paper before you print it
• Share text and other page elements among documents

Microsoft Word keeps each document (letter, report, or other piece of written work) in the computer's memory while you are working with it. In order to keep a document permanently, you must save it as a file on your computer's storage device (either floppy or hard disk). Word documents can contain just a few words or thousands of words and images.

Case Study:
Sabrina Lee, a graduating senior from Indiana University, is learning to use Microsoft Word to create a cover letter that she will include with her résumé when she sends it to a prospective employer.

Starting Word

Concept

To use the Microsoft Word program, or application, the user must open it. You can use a variety of techniques to launch Word. When you install the program, a short-cut is automatically placed on the Windows Start menu. You also can use My Computer or Windows Explorer to locate Word's executable file.

Do It!

Sabrina wants to open the Microsoft Word application so she can write a cover letter.

1 Make sure the computer, monitor, and any other necessary peripheral devices are turned on. The Windows screen should appear on your monitor, as shown in **Figure 1-1**. Your screen may differ slightly from the one shown.

2 Click the **⊞Start** button on the Windows taskbar at the bottom of your screen. This will bring up the Windows Start menu.

3 Move the mouse pointer ⯈ up the Start menu to the Programs folder. The Programs submenu will appear (see **Figure 1-2**).

4 Position the pointer over Microsoft Word, highlighting it, and click the left mouse button to open the application (if Word is not there, try looking under Microsoft Office on the Programs submenu). Word will open with a blank document in the window.

More

When you started Word, you may have noticed a small window containing the Office Assistant. If the Assistant is not in your Word window, it can be accessed by clicking the Microsoft Word Help button ⓐ found at the right side of the Standard toolbar, or by selecting the Show the Office Assistant command from the Help menu (in case the Assistant has been turned off previously). Part of the Microsoft Office Help facility, the Assistant offers tips, advice, and help on most Word functions. The Assistant has the ability to guess the help topic you desire based on the actions you are performing, and it also can answer queries by accepting full questions rather than being limited to keyword searches. The Assistant will become active when you use a wizard, walking you through the steps, offering advice and suggestions. When the Assistant feels that you need help with a particular feature, it will produce a light bulb in its window, or on the Office Assistant button. Clicking this light bulb will cause a help tip to materialize in the window. Clicking on the Assistant brings up a balloon with various options, Help topics, and a space in which you can type your question.

With your Word or Office 2000 CD-ROM inserted in the appropriate disk drive, you can change the appearance of the Assistant by clicking the Options button in the Assistant's dialog balloon. The Office Assistant dialog box also offers choices for customizing the Assistant's behavior and functionality. To hide the Assistant, choose the Hide the Office Assistant command on the Help menu. If you are working with a freshly installed copy of Word, you will have to click the Start using Microsoft Word option in the Assistant's dialog balloon in order to begin working with the program.

Figure 1-1 Windows screen

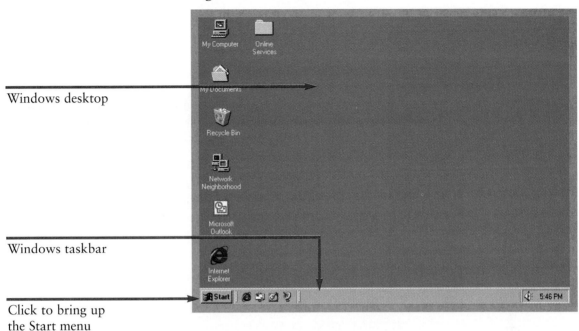

Windows desktop

Windows taskbar

Click to bring up
the Start menu

Figure 1-2 Opening Word from the Start menu

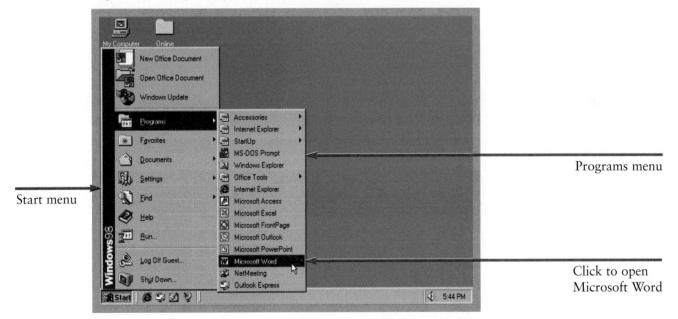

Start menu

Programs menu

Click to open
Microsoft Word

Click File, then click Exit to close Word.
Then open Word again. If you do not see
the Exit command on the File menu, wait a
few moments or click the double arrow at
the bottom of the menu to expand it.

Hot Tip

Each computer can vary in its setup
depending on its hardware and software
configurations. Therefore, your Word
StartUp procedure may be slightly different
from that described above.

Exploring the Word Screen

Concept

When Word is opened, it will present a window with many common Windows features including a title bar, a menu bar, and toolbars. In addition to these, there are many features unique to Word that are designed to make document production fast, flexible, and more convenient.

The Microsoft Word screen, or **application window**, contains the following components, as shown in **Figure 1-3** (Note: the figure displays the screen in a maximized window set to **Normal View**. If your screen does not look like the one in the figure, click View on the menu bar, and then click **Normal** to switch to Normal View.):

The **title bar** shows the name of the application and the name of the active document. A new document is automatically called Document1, Document2, and so on, until it is saved with a new name.

The **menu bar** shows the names of menus containing Word commands. Clicking one of these names will make its menu appear, listing the commands you may choose from. When you open a menu in Word 2000, or in any Office 2000 application, only a few commands will appear at first. These are the commands that have been deemed most popular by the designers of the software. If you do not click one of these commands, the menu will expand to reveal more commands after a few seconds. You can expedite this expansion by clicking on the down-arrow button at the bottom of the menu. As you use Word more and more, the program will sense which commands you use most often. These commands will then be the first to appear when you open a menu.

The **Standard toolbar** contains buttons with icons illustrating commonly used commands. When you position the mouse pointer over a button on a toolbar, the button becomes raised and a small box called a **ScreenTip** will appear below the button naming its function. Using toolbar buttons is faster than pulling down menus. You can position toolbars in any order, and in various screen locations.

The **Formatting toolbar** contains the **Style**, **Font**, and **Size** boxes along with buttons for common formatting commands.

The **horizontal ruler** shows paragraph and document margins and tab settings. In print layout view, the horizontal ruler also shows column widths and a vertical ruler appears.

The **insertion point** is the blinking vertical bar that marks the place where text will appear as it is entered.

The **document window** is the open space in which your document appears. When the mouse pointer enters the document window, it changes from an arrow to an I-beam ⌶ so you can more accurately position it in text.

The positions of the scroll bar boxes in the scroll bars show where the text on the screen is located in relation to the rest of the document. You can move quickly through a document by clicking the scroll bar arrows at either end of the bars to move the scroll box, or you can click and drag the box itself. The horizontal scroll bar also contains the four View buttons. These allow you to view your document in different ways, which you will learn about in Lesson 3.

The left-hand section of the status bar tells you what page and section of your document is currently displayed and the total number of pages. The next section shows the distance (in inches) from the insertion point to the top of the page and its current position given as coordinates of Line and Column number. The remaining portion of the bar is dedicated to showing whether certain options such as Overtype mode or Grammar and Spell Checking are currently active.

Word 2000

Figure 1-3 Components of the Word application window

Title bar
Menu bar
Standard toolbar
Formatting toolbar
Horizontal ruler
Insertion point
Document window
Vertical scroll bar
Office Assistant
Horizontal scroll bar box
Horizontal scroll bar
View buttons
Status bar

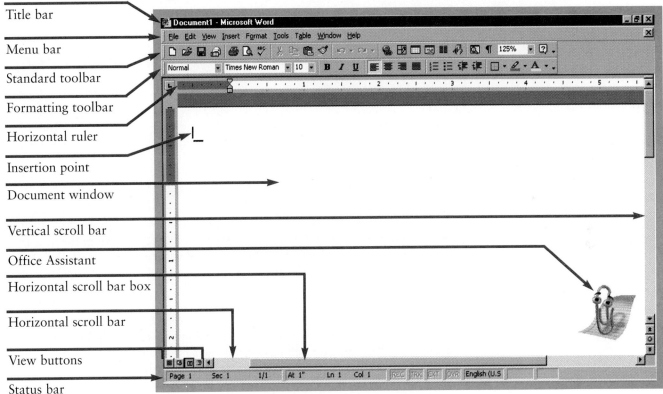

Familiarize yourself with the tools in the toolbar by positioning the mouse pointer over each button and reading its ScreenTip.

Hot Tip

By default, your Standard and Formatting toolbars may be positioned in a single row in the Word window. In the figure above, the toolbars have been positioned in separate rows allowing more buttons to be visible on each at once.

Creating a Document and Entering Text

Concept

Just as a new sheet of paper must be put into a typewriter before you can type, you must create a new document before you can enter information into Microsoft Word.

Do It!

Sabrina wants to open a new document in Microsoft Word and enter text.

1 When you opened Word, a new document should have appeared with **Document1** in the title bar. You also can create a new document once Word is open by clicking the **New Blank Document** button ▢ on the left end of the Standard toolbar.

2 Using the blank document you just opened, type in the following address, pressing **[Enter]** after each line:

> Sabrina Lee
> 12 Oakleigh Ave.
> Indianapolis, IN 46202

The text will appear at the insertion point as you are typing it. When you are finished, your document should resemble **Figure 1-4**.

More

In this example, you pressed **[Enter]** after each line of text to begin a new one because an address consists of short, distinct lines. When writing in a document that does not require abbreviated lines, you do not have to press **[Enter]** to begin a new line, as Word uses a feature known as **Word Wrap** to continue on the next line when you run out of space in the line you are on. If a word is too long to be added to the end of the current line, it is placed at the beginning of the line below, allowing you to type without interruptions or guesswork.

A new document also may be made by clicking **File**, then clicking **New**. As shown in **Figure 1-5**, the New dialog box will appear, giving you several options to create new documents. For now you will learn to use general blank documents. Other kinds of documents and methods of document creation will be covered in Lesson 2.

You may have noticed that some words have wavy red lines beneath them. If **Automatic Spell Checking** is active, Word checks your spelling automatically as you type and in this fashion points out words it does not recognize. These lines will not appear when the document is printed. You will find out more about Word's spell-check options in Lesson 3. You also may have noticed dots appearing in spaces and a ¶ at the end of every paragraph and blank line. These are called nonprinting characters and, as the name implies, they do not affect the final appearance of your document. Nonprinting characters can be turned on and off with the **Show/Hide** button ¶ on the Standard toolbar. A ¶, or **paragraph mark**, is created every time **[Enter]** is pressed.

Figure 1-4 Sabrina's name and address

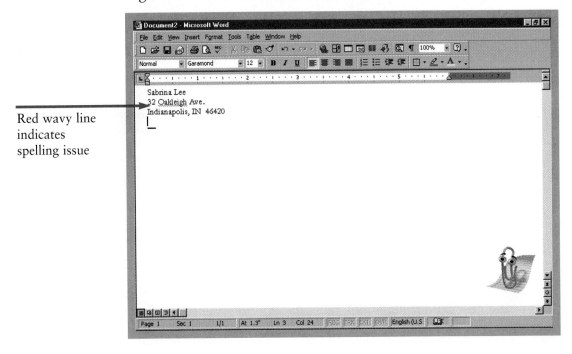

Red wavy line
indicates
spelling issue

Figure 1-5 New dialog box

Click a tab to view the
document types available
in that category

Standard blank document
template

Activate radio button to
edit an existing template

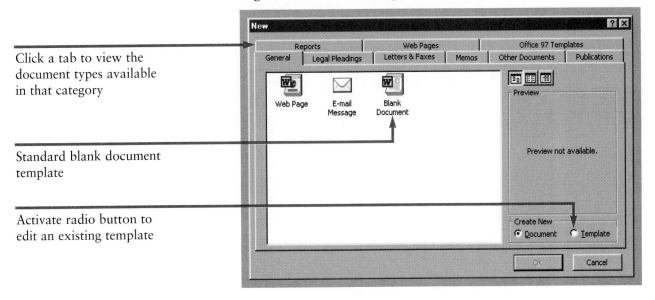

Hot Tip

Some menu commands have shortcut keys
next to them. Pressing these key combinations is the same as using the menu commands. For example, when creating a new
document, the key combination **[Ctrl]+[N]** is
equivalent to the New command.

Saving and Closing a Document

Concept

When using a computer, it is essential to Save documents by giving them unique names and storing them on a floppy disk or hard drive. Otherwise, work will be lost when you exit Word or when the computer is shut down. It is also a good idea to save documents as they are modified so that work will not be lost due to power or computer failures. Closing a document removes it from the screen and "files it away" until it is needed again.

Do It!

Sabrina will save her name and address as a file and then close the file.

1 You should still have Sabrina's address on your screen from the previous Skill. Click File, then click Save As to bring up the Save As dialog box, shown in Figure 1-6. When you are saving a new document for the first time, the Save As dialog box will appear regardless of whether you have chosen the Save command or the Save As command. The Save As dialog box allows you to provide a file with a particular file name, and select the location where the file will be saved. Once a file has been saved, the Save and Save As commands have different purposes. Using the Save command will overwrite the previous version of the file with the new one, without bringing up a dialog box. Using the Save As command will open the Save As dialog box, allowing you to save another version of the file with either a new file name, new storage location, or both.

2 Word will automatically name your document based on its first few words. In this case, the file name (displayed in the File name: box) is not acceptable, so you must type in another in its place. Notice that the default file name is highlighted. This selected text will be replaced as soon as you begin to type.

3 Type the file name Address into the File name: box (remember, the dialog box opens with the File name: box already activated and ready to receive text). If you choose not to add the .doc extension to the end of the file name, Word will do it for you automatically when it saves the file. An extension identifies a file's data type for the computer. The extension .doc identifies a Word file.

4 Word needs to be told where your document should be stored in the computer. The left side of the dialog box contains buttons you can click to access some of the most common save locations directly. This includes the My Documents folder, the desktop, and even Web servers. Click the Save in: box to open a drop-down list of the disk drives and main folders available on your computer. Click the appropriate drive or folder on the list to select a location. You will be saving the file on your student disk, which will most likely be in the drive labeled 3½ Floppy (A:), unless your instructor tells you to save the file in a different drive and folder.

5 Click ⊞ Save to save your document to the selected location.

6 Click File, then click Close. The document will disappear from the screen.

More

If you modify a document and do not save the changes before you close it, Word will ask you if you want to save it in one of two ways. If the Office Assistant is open, it will prompt you to save changes via a button in its balloon. If the Assistant is not open, Word will open a dialog box asking if you wish to save changes. These are equivalent methods of saving a file. If you do not save, any changes you have made since the last time you saved will be lost. You can create a new folder in which to save your document by clicking the Create New Folder button in the Save As dialog box. In addition to using the Close command, a document can be closed by clicking the document Close button at the right end of the menu bar. The application Close button in the Word title bar is grouped with the sizing buttons , called the Minimize and Maximize buttons, respectively. Minimizing the window reduces it to a program button on the taskbar; click on this button to bring the document back into view. Clicking the Maximize button expands the window so that it fills the entire screen. When the Word window is maximized, the Maximize button will be replaced by the Restore button , which reduces the window to its previous size. When you have multiple Word documents open at the same time, each one will have its own application window. This is a change from previous versions of Word in which one application window held multiple document windows. Clicking the Application Window Control icon opens a menu that contains commands equivalent to those executed with the sizing buttons.

Word 2000

Figure 1-6 Save As dialog box

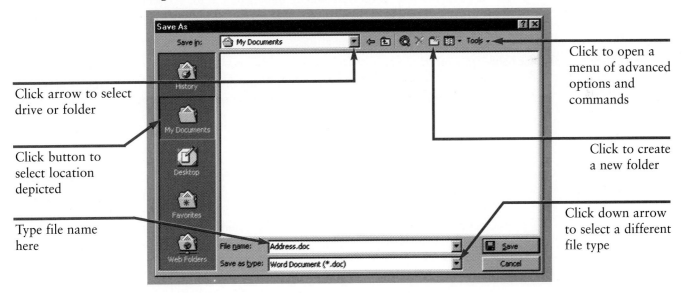

Click arrow to select drive or folder

Click button to select location depicted

Type file name here

Click to open a menu of advanced options and commands

Click to create a new folder

Click down arrow to select a different file type

WD 1.9

Opening an Existing Document

Concept

To view or edit a document that has been saved, you must open it from the location in which it was stored. Furthermore, you must open it with the application in which it was created, or a comparable one.

Do It!

Sabrina needs to open her cover letter so she can continue to work on it. The file is saved under the name Doit1-6.doc.

1 Click **File**, then click **Open**. The Open dialog box will appear, letting you choose which document to open.

2 Click the **Look in:** box to select the drive that contains your document. A list of folders and drives will appear, as shown in **Figure 1-7**. The drives and directories on your screen may be different from those in the figure. Clicking on a drive or folder will list the documents and/or folders it contains in the contents window below the Look in: box. Double-clicking documents or folders in the contents window will open them. Ask your instructor where to locate the student files and select the appropriate drive and folder.

3 Click **Doit1-6** to select it. It will be highlighted in the contents window.

4 Click [🖝 Open ▾] to open the selected file.

More

Word can open word processing documents in a variety of file formats. That is, files created with other programs can be opened and edited by Word. To open a file of a different format from the Open dialog box, just click the **Files of type:** box and select **All Files (*.*)**. This allows all files in the selected folder to appear in the contents window, available for opening.

If you click the arrow on the right edge of the Open button in the Open dialog box, a menu appears that offers three commands for opening a document in addition to the basic Open command. If you select **Open Read-Only**, Word will not allow any permanent changes to be made to the document during that particular work session. You can edit the text on your screen, but you will not be able to save the changes. The **Open as Copy** command creates a new copy of your document, allowing you to keep the old version and edit the new one. The **Open in Browser** command becomes active when you have selected an HTML document in the contents window. Executing this command opens the selected document in your default Web browser rather than in Word. If you double-click a file name or icon in the contents window, the file will open just as if you had selected it and clicked the Open button, as you did in Steps 3 and 4 above.

Word 2000

Figure 1-7 Open dialog box

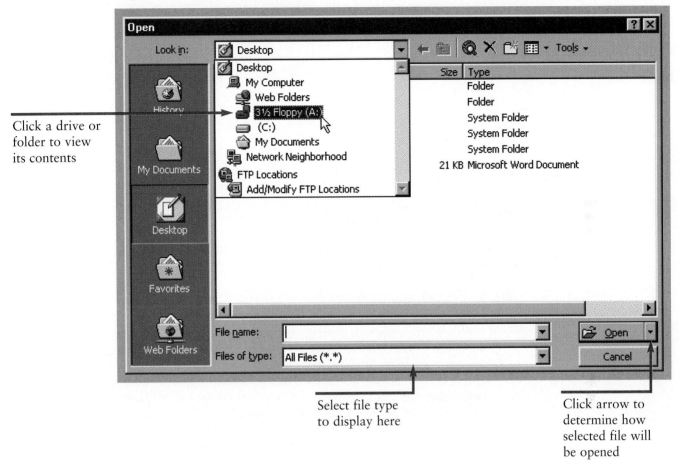

Click a drive or folder to view its contents

Select file type to display here

Click arrow to determine how selected file will be opened

Practice

To practice opening a document, open the student file **Prac1-6**. Leave the file Doit1-6 open, as you will be using it in the next Skill.

Hot Tip

You also can access the Open dialog box by clicking the Open button 📂 on the Standard toolbar.

Deleting and Inserting Text

Concept

One of the fundamental advantages of word processing is the ease it provides in changing content that has been entered previously. Word makes it easy to edit, replace, or delete unwanted text.

Do It!

Sabrina wants to modify her street address by changing Oakleigh Ave. to Oakleigh Avenue.

1 Make sure that Doit1-6 (which was opened in the previous Skill) is still in the active window.

2 Move the insertion point to the immediate right of the period in Ave. in Sabrina's address by moving the mouse pointer there and clicking.

3 Press [Backspace] once to erase the period.

4 Type nue to correct the address. Sabrina's address should resemble the one in the final stage of **Figure 1-8**.

5 Save the file to your student disk as Letter.doc.

More

As you just saw, the [Backspace] key erases the character immediately to the left of the insertion point. To erase the character to the right of the insertion point, press [Delete]. Word inserts text at the insertion point; that is, it moves nearby text to the right instead of typing over it. To type over existing text without moving it, double-click the Overtype button OVR on the status bar to enter Overtype mode. Just remember that any existing text to the right of the insertion point will be deleted as you type. Double-click on the Overtype button again to deactivate Overtype mode. When Overtype mode is not active, the letters OVR on the status bar will be grayed out.

You can move the insertion point one character at a time to the left or right and one line at a time up or down with the **arrow keys** on the keyboard. This is especially helpful when you are moving the insertion point only a short distance. More ways to move the insertion point using the keyboard are shown in **Table 1-1**. If you will be using the [Home], [End], [Pg Up], and [Pg Dn] keys on the numeric keypad, as required for some of the movement techniques in the table, make sure that **Num Lock** is disabled. Some keyboards include separate keys for these functions.

Figure 1-8 Changing Ave. to Avenue in Sabrina's address

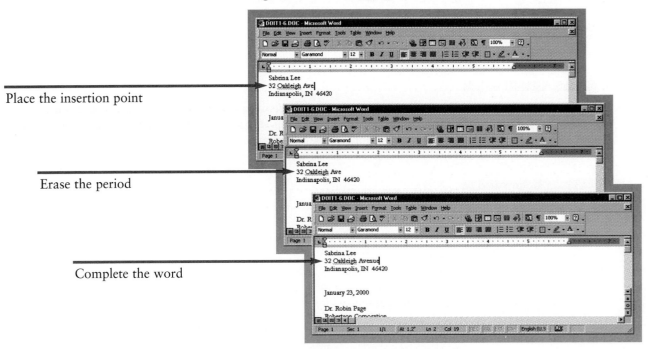

Place the insertion point

Erase the period

Complete the word

Table 1-1 Moving the insertion point with the keyboard

TO MOVE THE INSERTION POINT	PRESS
Left or right one word	[Ctrl]+[←] or [Ctrl]+[→]
Up or down one paragraph	[Ctrl]+[↑] or [Ctrl]+[↓]
Up or down one screen	[Pg Up] or [Pg Dn]
To the beginning or end of a line	[Home] or [End]
To the beginning or end of a document	[Ctrl]+[Home] or [Ctrl]+[End]

Hot Tip figure

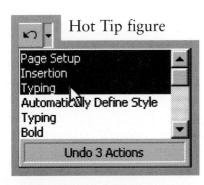

To practice deleting and modifying text, open the student file **Prac1-7**. Save and close the file when you are done.

Hot Tip

Clicking the **Undo** button 🔄 on the Standard toolbar allows you to reverse your last action. Clicking the arrow next to the Undo button opens a menu that lists all of your previous actions, allowing you to undo several actions at once (see figure above).

Formatting Text

Concept

Word allows the user to easily change the font, font size, and alignment of text in a document, as well as many other text and document characteristics. Formatting text serves to improve the presentation of your document. You can format text for both stylistic and organizational purposes.

Do It!

Sabrina wants to make her name bold and change the font size of her document.

1 Make sure that Letter.doc is still in the active window.

2 Select Sabrina's name by clicking before the S in Sabrina and dragging (moving the mouse with the button held down) to the end of her last name. The selected text will be highlighted (white text on a black background).

3 Click the **Bold** button **B** on the **Formatting** toolbar. The letters in her name will become heavier.

4 Deselect the text by clicking once anywhere in the document window.

5 Select the entire document by clicking before the S in Sabrina and dragging down to the last line and releasing the mouse button after the period in **enc.** at the end of the document.

6 Click the **Font Size** arrow `10 ▼` on the Formatting toolbar and then click **11** (see **Figure 1-9**). The text in the document will increase slightly in size. Do not close the document, as you will be using it in the next Skill.

More

There are several text attributes that the Formatting toolbar allows you to change. The **font,** or typeface, refers to the actual shape of each individual letter or number as it appears on the screen or in a printed document. Text **size** is usually measured in **points** (one inch equals 72 points). For example, the text in a newspaper is ordinarily printed in 10 point. Sabrina changed her name to 11 point from Word's default of 10. Other Formatting toolbar options include **Bold B**, **Italic *I***, **Underline U**, and **Highlight**. Another option, **Alignment**, refers to the manner in which text follows the margins of your document (see **Figure 1-10**). Knowing how to format text for maximum effect is an essential skill that will make your documents appear crisp and professional. Notice how the text on this page is used; different fonts and sizes are used for headings and subject matter, and important terms are bold or colored for added emphasis. To format an entire document, as above, you must select it first. You can select an entire document without dragging the mouse pointer over it by clicking **Edit**, and then clicking the **Select All** command. You also can change the color of your font by clicking the **Font Color** button **A ▼**. Click the button itself to apply the current color to the selected text. Clicking the arrow on the right edge of the button opens a color palette from which you can choose a different color.

Figure 1-9 Adjusting font size

Font size drop-down list

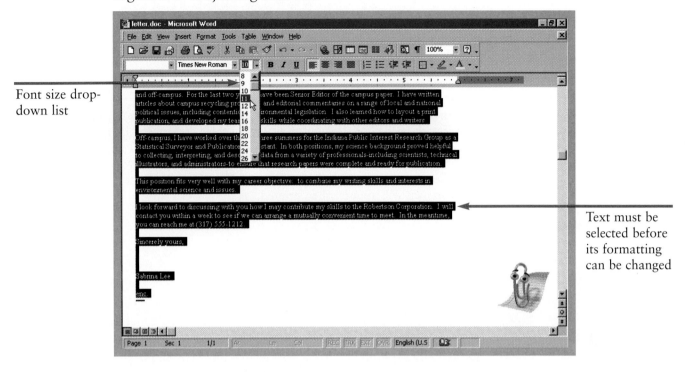

Text must be selected before its formatting can be changed

Figure 1-10 Text alignment

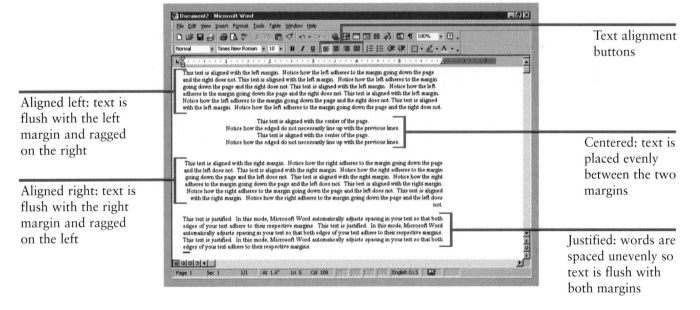

Text alignment buttons

Aligned left: text is flush with the left margin and ragged on the right

Aligned right: text is flush with the right margin and ragged on the left

Centered: text is placed evenly between the two margins

Justified: words are spaced unevenly so text is flush with both margins

To practice formatting text, open the student file **Prac1-8**. Save and close the file when you are done.

Hot Tip

You can align an entire paragraph by clicking anywhere inside the paragraph and then clicking the desired alignment button on the Formatting toolbar.

Previewing and Printing a Document

Concept

While today's offices are becoming more and more electronic, many people still like to work with hard copies (paper printouts) of their documents. If your computer is properly connected to a printer, you can print a paper copy of a document with a click of a button. Or, if you desire more flexibility in printing, Word provides more comprehensive options, including a Print Preview that allows the user to see the document as it will appear when printed.

Do It!

Sabrina wants to print her document.

1 Confirm that your computer is properly connected to a printer (ask your instructor or network administrator if necessary).

2 Click File, then click Print to open the Print dialog box (**Figure 1-11**).

3 Click ⟨ OK ⟩ to print. (Clicking the Print button 🖶 on the Standard toolbar skips the dialog box and prints automatically.)

4 Save and close the document.

More

You also can view your document as it will appear when printed by clicking File, and then clicking Print Preview. The Print Preview screen (Figure 1-12) will appear. A miniature version of your document will be in the window and the mouse pointer will change to the magnification tool 🔍 when it is in the document window. The Standard and Formatting toolbars are replaced with the Print Preview toolbar, and the vertical ruler appears. The Zoom selection box displays how much the document has been shrunk or magnified. To view a particular portion of your document up close, simply click it to display it at 100% of normal size. The mouse pointer will then change to 🔍 and clicking will reverse the magnification. The Print Preview screen is a WYSIWYG (What You See Is What You Get, pronounced "wizzy-wig") display, meaning that what appears on the screen is exactly what will print out on the paper copy. To edit in Print Preview mode, click the Magnifier button 🔍 to change the mouse pointer to an I-beam, then edit and enter text as you normally would. When you are finished editing, click the Magnifier button again to look at other parts of the document. If the document appears correct, you can print it by clicking the Print button at the left end of the Print Preview toolbar. To exit the Print Preview screen and return to your document, click ⟨Close⟩.

Figure 1-11 Print dialog box

Specify the printer you are using here

Additional printer options

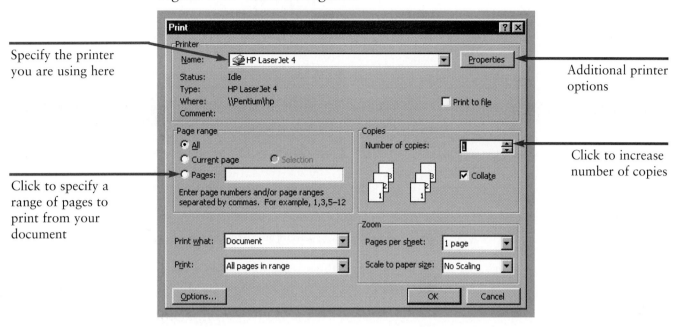

Click to specify a range of pages to print from your document

Click to increase number of copies

Figure 1-12 Print Preview screen

Magnifier toggle button

Print Preview toolbar

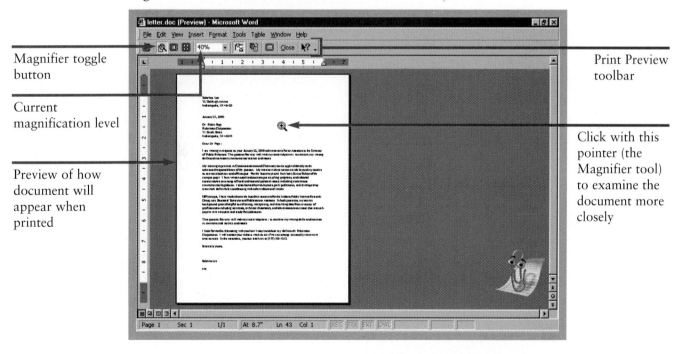

Current magnification level

Preview of how document will appear when printed

Click with this pointer (the Magnifier tool) to examine the document more closely

To practice previewing a document, open the student file **Prac1-9**.

Hot Tip

It is a good idea to do a Print Preview every time you print a document. This will allow you to correct layout errors before you print, saving time and paper.

Shortcuts

Function	Button/Mouse	Menu	Keyboard
Create a new document	🗋	Click File, then click New	[Ctrl]+[N]
Show/Hide nonprinting characters	¶	Click Tools, then click Options, then click the View tab; choose All	[Ctrl]+[Shift]+[*]
Save the active document	🖫	Click File, then click Save	[Ctrl]+[S]
Close the active document	✖ (on menu bar)	Click the control menu icon, then click Close	[Alt]+[F4]
Open a document	📂	Click File, then click Open	[Ctrl]+[O]
Bold selected text	B	Click Format, then click Font; choose Bold	[Ctrl]+[B]
Italicize selected text	I	Click Format, then click Font; choose Italic	[Ctrl]+[I]
Underline selected text	U	Click Format, then click Font; choose Underline	[Ctrl]+[U]
Highlight selected text	🖊		
Print Preview	🔍	Click File, then click Print Preview	
Print the active document	🖨	Click File, then click Print	[Ctrl]+[P]

Identify Key Features

Name the items indicated by callout arrows in **Figure 1-13**.

Figure 1-13 Identifying components of the Word screen

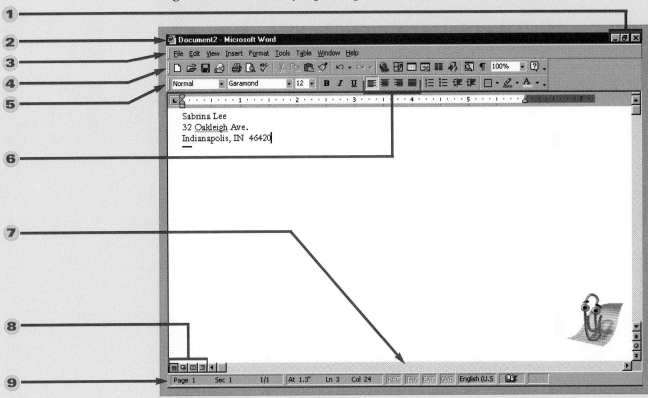

Select the Best Answer

10. The exact location where text appears when entered

11. The shape of letters and numbers

12. Reduces a window to a button on the Windows taskbar

13. The way in which text relates to the left and right margins

14. A window that appears allowing access to specialized commands

15. Allows you to see how your document will appear when printed

16. Offers tips, advice, and help on most Word functions

17. The unit of measurement for font size

a. Office Assistant

b. Alignment

c. Print Preview screen

d. Insertion point

e. Points

f. Dialog box

g. Minimize button

h. Font

Quiz (continued)

Complete the Statement

18. In order to change the formatting of a section of text, you must first:

    a. Click one of the formatting buttons

    b. Save the document

    c. Select the text to be changed

    d. Click the Start button

19. Clicking the 🖫 button:

    a. Ejects the floppy disk

    b. Saves the document

    c. Searches for a file on the hard drive

    d. Selects text

20. Clicking the 🔍 button on the Standard Toolbar:

    a. Searches the document for errors

    b. Magnifies part of the document

    c. Opens the Print Preview window

    d. Brings up the Document Detective window

21. The file extension for Word files is:

    a. .txt

    b. .jpg

    c. .doc

    d. .htm

22. An ellipsis (...) after a command in the command menu means that:

    a. That command has a dialog box

    b. That command is unavailable

    c. The shortcut for that command is the [...] key

    d. The whole name could not fit on the menu

23. The elements of text formatting do NOT include:

    a. Font size

    b. Justification

    c. Style

    d. Delete

24. Text that is justified is:

    a. Carefully edited

    b. Adjusted to meet both margins

    c. Centered

    d. Bold

25. To toggle on and off the mode that allows you to type over existing text instead of displacing it:

    a. Click the Undo button

    b. Double-click the Highlight button

    c. Double-click the Overtype button

    d. Disable Num Lock

Interactivity

Test Your Skills

1. Identify a job that interests you and determine what the employer is looking for:

   a. Go to the classified section of a newspaper or to an online job listing and find a specific listing that you think might suit you.

   b. Think about what skills and experience might be necessary to apply successfully. Determine how your own skills and experiences relate to the qualifications that the job would require.

2. Open Word and write a brief letter applying for the job (open **SkillTest1.doc** to view a sample business letter):

   a. Launch Word using the **Start menu**.

   b. Enter your name and address at the top of the page.

   c. Skip a line and enter today's date.

   d. Skip a line and enter the name (if available) and address of the prospective employer.

   e. Write the letter, beginning with a salutation and continuing with four short paragraphs, one each for your educational background, prior job experience, any other relevant experience, and the reasons for your interest in this particular job.

3. Format the letter text to more effectively present the letter:

   a. Make all the text in the letter 12 pt **Times New Roman**.

   b. Format your name at the top of the letter with **Bold** type.

   c. Align your name and address with the right margin by selecting the appropriate lines and clicking the **Align Right** button on the **Formatting** toolbar.

4. Print the letter, then save and close the document and exit Word:

   a. Use **Print Preview** to examine your letter and then make any changes you think are necessary. Exit Print Preview mode.

   b. After making sure your computer is properly connected to a working printer, click the **Print** button on the **Standard** toolbar to print the letter.

   c. Save the letter to your student disk as **Test 1**.

   d. Close the document and exit Word by clicking the application **Close** button at the right end of the title bar.

5. Open, edit, and save an existing document:

   a. Open Test 1 from your student disk.

   b. Change the color of the document's text to red and **italicize** your name.

   c. Save the changes as a new file on your student disk called **Test 1-Red**.

Interactivity (continued)

Problem Solving

1. Using the skills you learned in Lesson 1, open a new document and write your name, address, and today's date on it as a heading, then add a few sentences about yourself. Adjust the text's formatting so that it matches the example in **Figure 1-14** below. Then conduct a Print Preview to check and print the document. Save it on your student disk as Solved 1.

Figure 1-14 Problem Solving

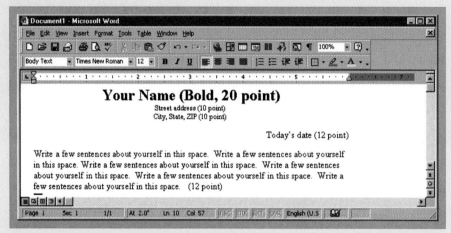

2. As the Assistant Technical Director at VER Recovery Corp., a collection agency, you have been asked to research various word processing programs to determine which is the best for your company. After testing several products, you have decided that the company would benefit most from adopting Microsoft Word 2000. Use a blank Word document to write a memo to your boss that details this decision. Be sure to include your name in the document. When you are done, save this file to your student disk as VER Recovery memo.

3. Due to your outstanding performance as Assistant Technical Director at VER, you have been promoted to Associate Technical Director. As your first act in your new capacity, you have proposed an expansion of the Information Technology department. Your proposal has been approved. Using Word, write a notice for the company bulletin board to announce the good news. Take advantage of Word's formatting features such as bolding, underlining, font sizing, and text alignment to make your document lively. Include your name in the document, and save it to your student disk as VER IT notice.

L E S S O N

2

EDITING DOCUMENTS

O nce text has been entered into a Word document, it may be manipulated and edited to suit the requirements of the user. Text may be selected in several different ways so that particular portions can be modified without affecting the rest of the document. Selected text can be copied, moved, or deleted altogether.

Word has a powerful file search function that allows the user to find documents based on a wide variety of search criteria, and a Help facility that provides many types of information and assistance with various word processing tasks and special features of the application. This Help facility includes the Office Assistant, who acts as a liaison between the user and the help files.

In addition to the general blank document template on which Word bases its standard new document, there are a multitude of other templates for document types that can be created with Word. In addition, programs called wizards guide the user through the steps necessary to create various complex documents.

Case Study:
In this lesson, Sabrina will edit her cover letter and create a résumé to go with it, as well as search for a document and explore Word's Help facility.

Searching for Files

Concept

There are so many locations in a computer's storage devices in which data may be saved that documents are sometimes difficult to locate. Word's Open dialog box contains **powerful search tools** that you can use to locate and open misplaced files. The Find command is particularly helpful when you only remember certain characteristics of a file, as is often the case, such as a portion of its name, text it contains, or the date you last modified it.

Do It!

Sabrina would like to open the Windows Frequently Asked Questions (FAQ) file, but she does not know where it is located.

1 Click the Open button 📂 on the Standard toolbar. The Open dialog box appears.

2 Click the Files of type: drop-down list arrow and select Text Files.

3 Click the Tools button Tools ▾. The Tools menu will open.

4 Click the Find command. The Find dialog box appears, as shown in **Figure 2-1**. The top section of the dialog box shows the search criterion you have chosen so far, which instructs Word to search for the file type Text Files. The second section of the dialog box allows you to provide additional search criteria. Leave the Property: selection box set to File name, and the Condition: selection box set to includes.

5 Click inside the Value: text-entry box to place the insertion point there. Then type faq as the search value.

6 Click the Look in: drop-down list arrow and select your main hard drive (most likely C:) as the search location.

7 Click the Search subfolders check box to activate it. The Find dialog box is now set to search your hard drive and all its subfolders for a text file whose name includes the letters faq.

8 Click the Find Now button Find Now. Word will ask if you want to add the File name property you specified to the search. Click Yes.

9 The Find dialog box closes and the results of your search are displayed in the Open dialog box's Contents window. The file Faq.txt should be selected (see **Figure 2-2**), ready for you to open if you wish. If you do open this file, Word will have to convert it from its text format because it is not a Word document. If you open the file, do not save changes to it when you close it. Also, set the Files of type drop-down list box back to Word Documents.

More

It is worthwhile to examine the list of properties by which you can search for a file in the Find dialog box. You can use everything from the number of words in a document to the date it was created as a search property. Each search property has its own customized list of conditions from which you can choose when setting your search criteria. You can even save a search and run it whenever you need to find the file with which it is associated.

Figure 2-1 Find dialog box

Chosen in
Open dialog box

Click to make your search
sensitive to uppercase and
lowercase letters (does not
apply to File name property)

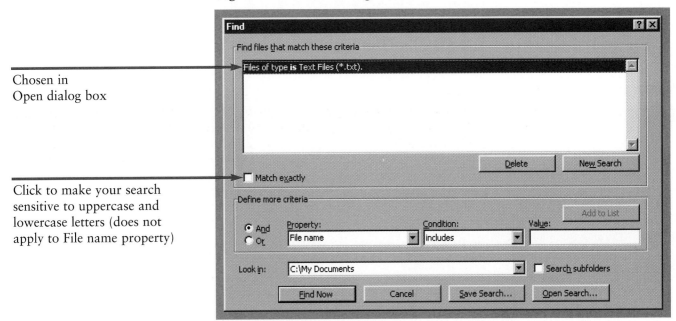

Figure 2-2 Result of file search

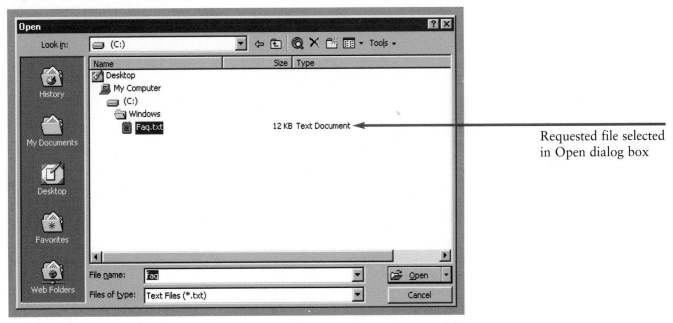

Requested file selected
in Open dialog box

Practice

To practice finding files in Word, open the
student file **Prac2-1**.

Hot Tip

Being as restrictive as possible in your
search criteria will make the search process
faster and reduce the number of unwanted
files found.

Selecting Text and Undoing Actions

Concept

Sections of text must be **selected** before they can be modified. Selected text acts as a single unit that can be moved, modified, or formatted. When text is selected, it appears highlighted on the screen. That is, text that normally appears black on a white screen will be white on a black background. It is important to be careful when working with selected text as it is possible to erase an entire document by pressing a single key. The **Undo** command can be used to correct such errors by reversing previous commands or actions.

Do It!

Sabrina wants to select a paragraph using two different techniques.

1. Open the student file **Doit2-2** and save it to your student disk as **Cover Letter**.

2. Scroll down to the paragraph that begins **My training and experience ...**

3. Select the paragraph by clicking just before the first letter and dragging the mouse pointer to the end of the paragraph. If the Office Assistant is in the way, it will automatically move to another location.

4. Type the letter **X**. The selected text will be replaced by the text you entered.

5. Click the **Undo** button ⟳ on the Standard toolbar to bring back the missing paragraph.

6. Deselect the paragraph by clicking once anywhere in the document window.

7. Now select the same paragraph by **triple-clicking** any portion of it.

More

Once text is selected, it can be replaced by typing in new text; the new entry will take the place of what was selected. When clicking and dragging to select text, the selected area will follow the mouse pointer letter by letter in the first word; subsequent words will be added to the selected area all at once. To select a single line or multiple lines of text, use the **Selection bar**, a column of space on the left edge of the document (see **Figure 2-3**). When the mouse pointer enters this area, it will appear reversed ⟨. Clicking here selects the entire line to the right of the pointer. Dragging up or down will select additional lines. More ways to select text are shown in **Tables 2-1 and 2-2**. Keep in mind that Num Lock must be disabled in order to use the [Home], [End], and arrow keys on the numeric keypad.

You can select large sections of text by placing the insertion point at the beginning, moving to the other end, and pressing [Shift] while you click there.

The Undo command is an essential tool that easily corrects many of the worst mistakes you will make when using Word. The Undo and Redo buttons are grouped on the Standard toolbar. Clicking the **Undo** drop-down list arrow ⟳▾ opens the Undo drop-down list, which lets you undo one or more of several recently completed actions and commands by simply clicking on the item you wish to undo. The Redo command and its drop-down list work in a similar fashion, but instead reverse past Undo commands.

Figure 2-3 Using the Selection bar

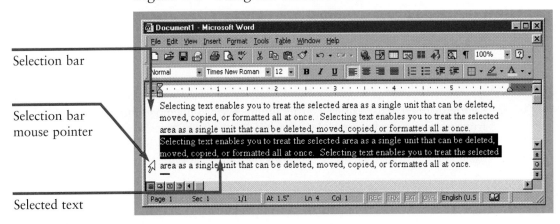

Table 2-1 Mouse selection shortcuts

DESIRED SELECTION	ACTION TO TAKE
A single word	Double-click the word
A sentence	Click the sentence while pressing [Ctrl]
A paragraph	Triple-click the paragraph or double-click next to it in the selection bar
A line of text	Click next to it in the selection bar
A vertical block of text	Click and drag while pressing [Alt]
The entire document	Triple-click in the selection bar

Table 2-2 Keyboard selection shortcuts

DESIRED SELECTION	ACTION TO TAKE
A single character	[Shift]+[←] or [Shift]+[→]
Part of word to left/right of insertion point	[Ctrl]+[Shift]+[←] or [Ctrl]+[Shift]+[→]
Part of ¶ before/after insertion point	[Ctrl]+[Shift]+[↑] or [Ctrl]+[Shift]+[↓]
To the beginning or end of a line	[Shift]+[Home] or [Shift]+[End]
To the beginning or end of a document	[Ctrl]+[Shift]+[Home] or [Ctrl]+[Shift]+[End]
A vertical block of text	[Ctrl]+[Shift]+[F8] (toggle on/off) and arrows
The entire document (Select All)	[Ctrl]+[A]

Practice

To practice selecting text and using the Undo command, open the student file **Prac2-2**.

Hot Tip

When you choose an action to undo from the Undo drop-down list, all actions that took place after the selected action will be undone as well.

Cutting, Copying, and Moving Text

Concept

Sections of text can be moved easily within a Word document, deleted or copied from one place, and reapplied in another. Word offers two ways to move text: the drag-and-drop method, which involves the mouse and will be discussed in the next Skill; and Cut-and-Paste, which utilizes the Office Clipboard.

Do It!

Sabrina wants to move a paragraph in her cover letter using the Cut-and-Paste method.

1 Select the entire paragraph that begins with This position ..., as shown in **Figure 2-4** (the file Cover Letter should still be in the active window).

2 Click the Cut button on the Standard toolbar. The selected text disappears, leaving an extra blank line between the remaining paragraphs.

3 Press [Backspace] once to remove the extra blank line.

4 Place the insertion point to the left of the first letter in the second paragraph in the message section, the one that begins My training and experience ...

5 Click the Paste button on the Standard toolbar. The text you cut earlier reappears at the insertion point.

6 Press [Enter] to add a blank line to separate the paragraphs.

7 Close the file, saving changes when prompted.

More

The Cut, Copy, and Paste commands use the Office Clipboard, a temporary holding area for data. The Office Clipboard can hold up to 12 items simultaneously, unlike the Windows Clipboard, which holds only one. The Cut command removes selected data to the Clipboard, while the Copy command leaves selected data where they are and sends a copy of them to the Clipboard. You can copy text to the Clipboard by selecting it and then clicking the Copy button on the Standard toolbar. The Copy command is also available on the Edit menu. The Paste command inserts data stored in the Clipboard at the insertion point. If you have more than one item stored on the Office Clipboard when you use the Paste command, Word will paste the item that was sent there most recently. To paste an item that you sent to the Clipboard earlier, open the View menu, highlight the Toolbars command, and click Clipboard to activate the Clipboard toolbar. The Clipboard toolbar, shown in **Figure 2-5**, displays each item currently being stored as an icon, allowing you to choose exactly which item or items you want to paste.

The Clipboard also can be used to move data between documents or even between different Office programs. The last item you sent to the Office Clipboard also will be stored on the Windows Clipboard, allowing you to share the data with any Windows program for which they are appropriate. Clearing the Office Clipboard removes the contents of the Windows Clipboard as well. Both Clipboards are erased when you shut down your computer.

Figure 2-4 Selected paragraph

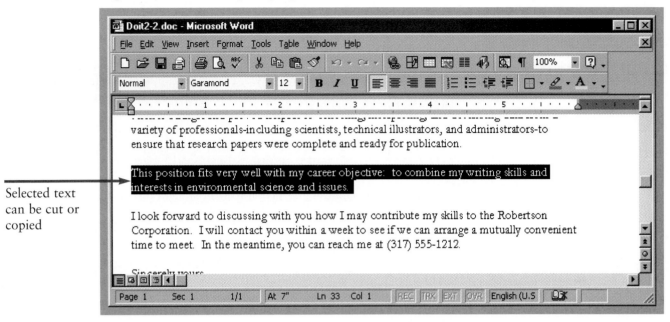

Selected text can be cut or copied

Figure 2-5 Clipboard toolbar

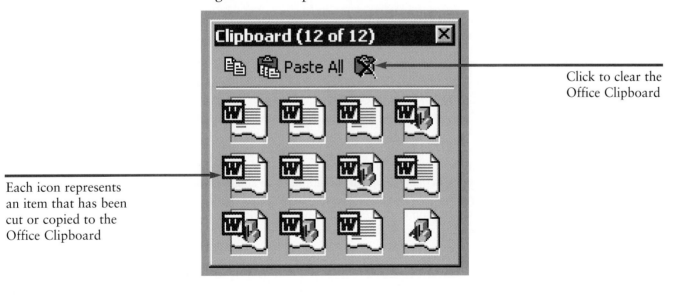

Click to clear the Office Clipboard

Each icon represents an item that has been cut or copied to the Office Clipboard

To practice cutting, copying, and pasting text, open the student file **Prac2-3**. Save the file as **MyPrac2-3** when you have completed the exercise and close the file.

Though pressing [Delete] removes selected text just as using the Cut command does, it does not save it to the Clipboard, and thus the text cannot be reinserted elsewhere.

Copying and Moving Text with the Mouse

Concept

The drag-and-drop method of copying and moving text is quick and convenient for moving text a short distance within a Word document. In many instances it is preferable to using the Clipboard with the Cut, Copy, and Paste commands.

Do It!

Sabrina wants to move a paragraph in her cover letter using the drag-and-drop method.

1. Open the student file Doit2-4 and save it to your student disk as Cover Letter 2.

2. Select the entire paragraph that begins with This position including the blank line beneath it, as shown in Figure 2-6.

3. Click on a portion of the selected area without releasing the mouse button. The mouse pointer will change into the drag-and-drop pointer, indicating that there is text loaded and ready to be inserted.

4. Position the dotted insertion point ⏐ to the left of the first letter in the second paragraph in the message section, the one that begins My training and experience …

5. Release the mouse button. The text will disappear from its previous location and reappear at the insertion point.

More

Dragging and dropping text moves it from its previous location. To copy the text to another area while leaving the original intact, press [Ctrl] before dropping the dragged text. The drag-and-drop pointer will appear with a small plus in a box at the bottom to signify that it will make a copy of the selected text. When the mouse button is released, the selected text will appear in its original place as well as at the insertion point (make sure you release the mouse button before you release the [Ctrl] key). You can drag and drop single words, sentences, paragraphs, and multiple paragraphs so long as they are selected. The ability to drag and drop text is an option that can be turned on and off from the Edit tab of the Options dialog box, which you can access by clicking the Options command on the Tools menu.

Figure 2-6 Moving text with the mouse

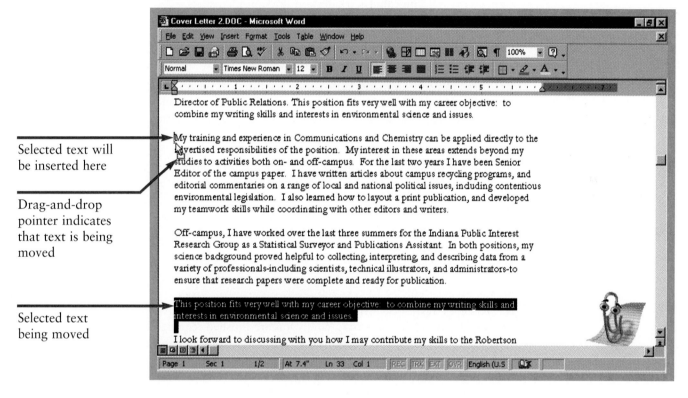

Selected text will be inserted here

Drag-and-drop pointer indicates that text is being moved

Selected text being moved

Practice

To practice copying and moving text using the mouse, open the student file **Prac2-4**. Save the file as **MyPrac2-4** when you have completed the exercise and close the file.

Hot Tip

If you are copying or moving text over a long distance in a document, it might be easier to use the Clipboard instead of the drag-and-drop method. It can be difficult to stop the screen's scrolling accurately when you drag beyond the current screen.

Using the Office Assistant

Concept

The Office Assistant provides several methods for getting help in Word. You can choose from a list of topics that the Assistant suggests based on the most recent functions you have performed. You also can view tips related to your current activity. Or you can ask a question in plain English.

Do It!

Sabrina wants to ask the Office Assistant about using ScreenTips.

1. If the Office Assistant is not visible, activate it by clicking Help, then Show the Office Assistant. Click the Office Assistant. A balloon will pop up with suggested topics related to the actions you have most recently completed.

2. In the text box type **What are ScreenTips?**, then click the Search button [Search]. The Office Assistant peruses the Word Help files and presents a selection of topics (**Figure 2-7**) relating to your question.

3. Position the pointer over the bullet labeled Show or hide toolbar ScreenTips and click. A window will appear, as shown in **Figure 2-8**, displaying the help topic.

4. Click on the blue text that says "ScreenTip." A ScreenTip tip will appear, in this case, to define ScreenTips. Click again to close the ScreenTip.

5. Read the rest of the help topic's explanation. You can leave the window on-screen to refer to while you work. When you are finished reading about ScreenTips, click the Help window's Close button to remove it from the screen.

More

From time to time the Assistant will offer you tips on how to use Word more efficiently. The appearance of a small light bulb, either in the Assistant's window or on the Office Assistant button, indicates that there is a tip to be viewed. To see the tip, just click the light bulb or Office Assistant button if the Assistant is hidden.

The Office Assistant's behavior and appearance can be customized to conform to your needs and preferences. Clicking [Options] opens the Office Assistant dialog box. This dialog box has two tabs: Gallery and Options. The Gallery tab contains different Assistants you can install from your Office or Word CD-ROM, and scrolling through the characters offers you a preview of each one. From the Options tab, shown in **Figure 2-9**, you can control when the Assistant will appear, and what kinds of tips it will provide.

Word 2000

Figure 2-7 ScreenTip help topics

Figure 2-8 Microsoft Word Help window

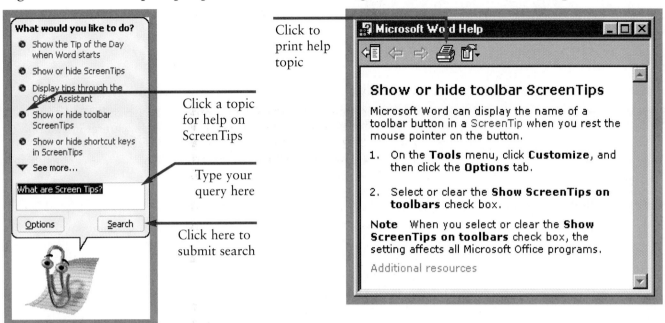

Click to print help topic

Click a topic for help on ScreenTips

Type your query here

Click here to submit search

Figure 2-9 Office Assistant dialog box

Remove this check to disable the Office Assistant

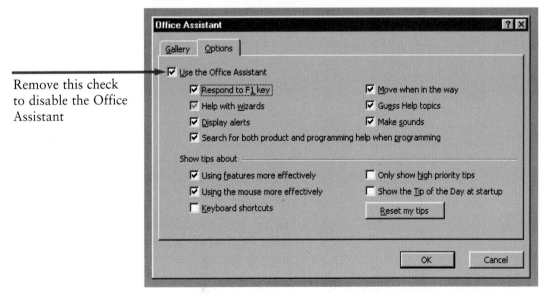

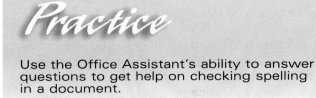

Practice

Use the Office Assistant's ability to answer questions to get help on checking spelling in a document.

Hot Tip

The Office Assistant is common to all Office 2000 applications. Therefore, any of the Assistant's options that you change will affect it in all Office programs.

Other Word Help Features

Concept

Working with new software can be confusing, and, at times, even intimidating. Fortunately, Microsoft Word offers a number of built-in help features in addition to the Office Assistant that you can use when you encounter problems or just have a question about a particular aspect of the program. The **What's This?** command and the **Help tabs** are two such features.

Do It!

Sabrina will use Word's What's This? command to get information about the **Save** command, and the Help tabs to find out more about the **status bar**.

1 Click **Help**, then click **What's This?** The pointer will now appear with a question mark ？ attached to it indicating that help has been activated.

2 Click the **Save** button 🖫 with the modified mouse pointer. A ScreenTip will appear, as shown in **Figure 2-10**, describing the command. Click the mouse to erase the ScreenTip.

3 Click the Office Assistant and select any help topic or tip offered to open a Microsoft Word Help window.

4 Click the **Show** button 🔄. The window will expand to a two-paneled format. The left panel consists of three tabs while the right panel displays help files.

5 Click the **Index** tab to bring it to the front of the window if it is not already there.

6 Click in the text-entry box labeled **Type keywords:**, and then type **status**. Notice that the list box in the middle of the tab scrolls automatically to match your entry.

7 Click the Search button 〔 Search 〕. Word searches its help files for the word status and displays the topics it finds in the list box at the bottom of the tab.

8 Click the help topic titled **Items that appear in the status bar**. The help file is loaded into the right panel, as shown in **Figure 2-11**.

9 Read about the status bar, and then close the Help window.

More

The Index tab organizes Word's help topics alphabetically in one continuous list. If this type of search does not suit your needs, you can search the help files using the **Contents** tab or the **Answer Wizard** tab. The Contents tab is organized like an outline or the table of contents you might find in a book. It begins with broad topics, symbolized by book icons, each of which can be expanded to reveal more specific subtopics. Once you have revealed a general topic's subtopics, you can select a subtopic in the left panel to display it in the right panel, just as on the Index tab. The Answer Wizard tab replicates the Office Assistant, allowing you to request help topics by entering questions in your own words. Once you have clicked the Show button to display the Help tabs in a Help window, the button changes to the Hide button. Click the Hide button to collapse the window back to a single panel.

Figure 2-10 Save button ScreenTip

Save (File menu)

Saves the active file with its current file name, location, and file format.

Figure 2-11 Getting help with the Index tab

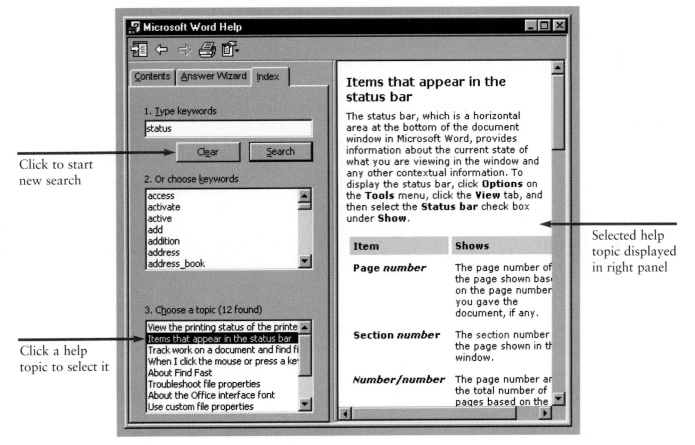

Click to start
new search

Selected help
topic displayed
in right panel

Click a help
topic to select it

Practice

To practice getting help in Word, open the student file **Prac2-6**.

Hot Tip

When working in a dialog box, click the ? button to get help on features in that dialog box. A question mark will be attached to the mouse pointer, just as if you had selected the What's This? command.

Using Templates and Wizards

Concept

When a new document is created, its font and text layout characteristics are based on a collection of previously saved settings. Together, the settings associated with this document are called a template. Word provides templates in many categories, including letters, faxes, brochures and Web pages, and styles, such as contemporary, professional, and elegant. When you opened Word, the new document that appeared was based on the Blank Document template, also known as the Normal template. A wizard is a template that walks the user through the creation of a specific type of document, such as a résumé or newsletter, further automating the process. Templates and wizards serve as a great launching pad for creating items that seem too complicated to start from scratch. Documents created with these tools may be freely edited and changed to meet a user's specifications.

Do It!

Sabrina wants to create a résumé with the Résumé Wizard.

1 Click File, then click New to open the New dialog box.

2 Click the Other Documents tab to bring it to the front of the dialog box. Several icons representing various templates and wizards appear.

3 Click the Résumé Wizard icon. A preview of its output will appear in the Preview box, as shown in **Figure 2-12**.

4 Click `OK` to open the Résumé Wizard. The Résumé Wizard dialog box will appear at the Start step, as shown in **Figure 2-13**. The green square next to Start indicates which step of the wizard you are currently on.

5 Click `Next >` to advance to the Style step.

6 Click the Elegant radio button to select this style of résumé, then click `Next >`.

7 At the Type step, click `Next >` to use the default résumé type, Entry-level, and advance to the next phase in the wizard. The following step allows you to enter your name, address, phone and fax numbers, and e-mail address. Word automatically enters the name of the registered user in the name text box, and any other information that was provided during the install in the other boxes.

8 Enter Sabrina Lee, 32 Oakleigh Ave., Indianapolis, IN 46202 in the name and address text boxes respectively, replacing and deleting any extraneous information that may be entered. Your Résumé Wizard text boxes should resemble those in **Figure 2-14**. Click `Next >`.

Figure 2-12 Templates and wizards in the New dialog box

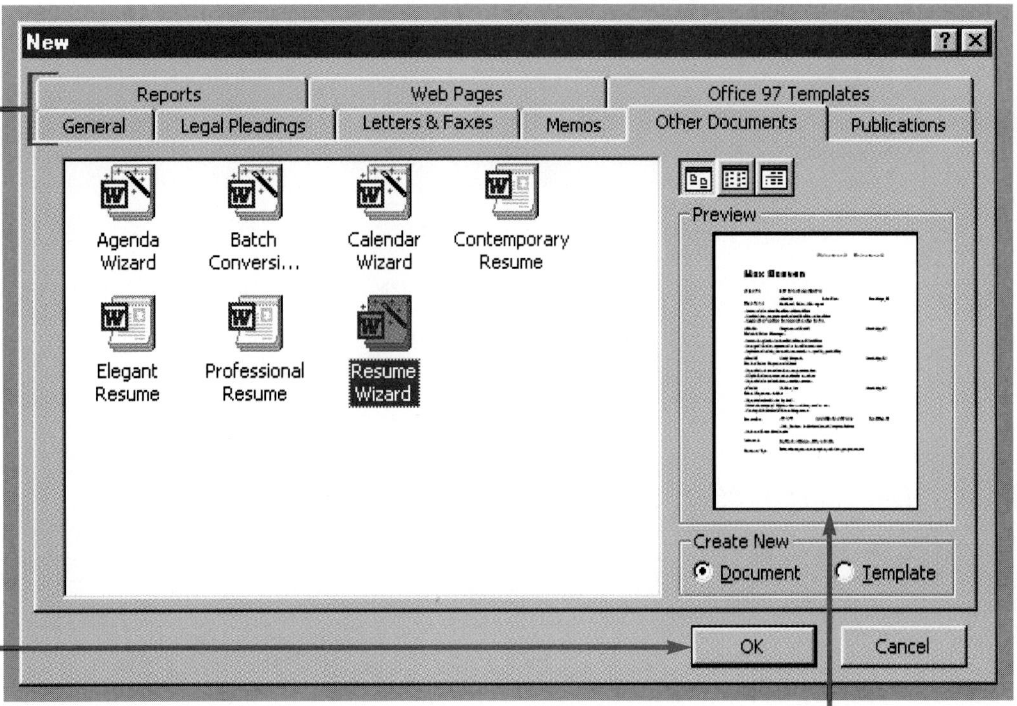

Other tabs containing different types of templates and wizards

Note:
Your installation of Microsoft Word may include a different selection of templates and wizards

Click to open selected template or wizard

Thumbnail sketch of selected template or wizard

Word 2000

Figure 2-13 Résumé Wizard: Start

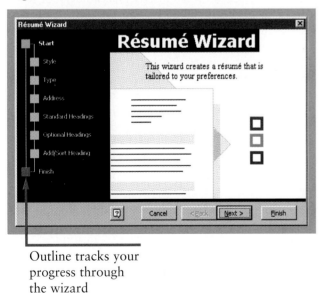

Outline tracks your progress through the wizard

Figure 2-14 Résumé Wizard: Address

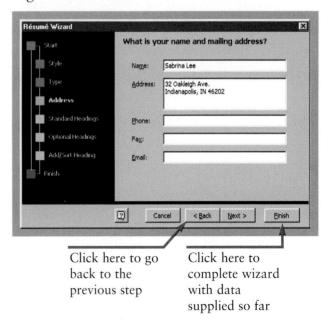

Click here to go back to the previous step

Click here to complete wizard with data supplied so far

Using Templates and Wizards (continued)

Do It!

9. At the Standard Headings step, use the check boxes to select **Objective**, **Education**, **Interests and Activities**, and **Work Experience** as the only headings in your résumé. Click Next > .

10. No additional headings will be included in your résumé; so click Next > to advance the wizard.

11. The Add/Sort Headings step allows you to insert a heading that was not included in the wizard's choices, delete a heading that you decide you do not wish to include on your résumé, or change the order of selected headings. Click **Work experience** to select it, then click Move Up to place it before **Interests and activities** in your résumé, as shown in **Figure 2-15**. Then click Next > .

12. On the outline of the wizard's steps, at the left side of the dialog box, click the box next to **Style** to go back to that step.

13. Click the **Contemporary** radio button to use this style rather than the previously selected Elegant, then click Finish . A résumé will appear in Print Layout view with instructions and space to fill in the rest of the necessary details, and the Assistant will open, as shown in **Figure 2-16**, asking if you would like to do more with your résumé.

14. Click Cancel , then close the document when you are finished viewing it. Close any other open documents as well.

More

Templates vary in the type and amount of formatting information that they contain. Some look like finished documents because Word inserts **Placeholders**, or text used to show you where to correctly place specific kinds of information. To add text to these templates, simply select the text you want to replace and type in your own. Other templates, such as the Professional Report template, contain less preformatting, and instead offer instructions on how to use the template to create the various elements of your document. And wizards, as shown above, automate document production by asking you questions in dialog boxes. By answering these questions, you make the decisions necessary to create the document, and the wizard inserts the information and formats it automatically. Some wizards even include premade examples, in which you need only change certain text variables such as names and addresses to complete the document. Below the Preview box in the New dialog box are two radio buttons that allow you either to create a document based on a template or to directly alter a template's settings. You can create or alter a template and then save the new template to be used for future documents.

Choosing to use a template or wizard does not limit your ability to customize your document. In fact, you can use the elements of a template or wizard to your advantage. Suppose you want to include more than one previous job in the Work Experience section of your résumé. You can simply copy the set of placeholders in the Work Experience section, and then paste additional sets of them below the original as needed.

Figure 2-15 Résumé Wizard: Add/Sort Headings

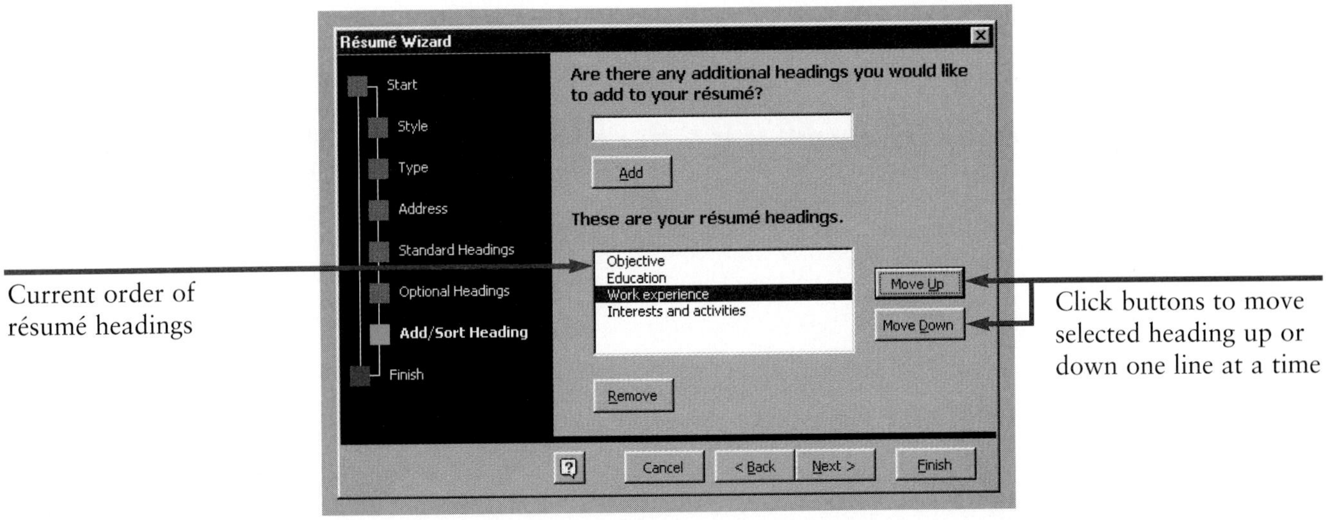

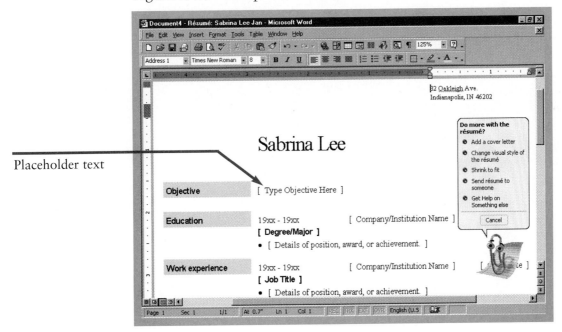

Current order of
résumé headings

Click buttons to move
selected heading up or
down one line at a time

Figure 2-16 Completed résumé

Placeholder text

Practice

To practice using a template to create a
document, open the student file **Prac2-7**.
Close the file when you are done.

Hot Tip

Pressing [Ctrl]+[N] or clicking the New
button creates a document based on the
Normal template automatically. You must
use the New command on the File menu to
access the New dialog box and the
templates and wizards it contains.

Shortcuts

Function	Button/Mouse	Menu	Keyboard
Undo last action	↶	Click Edit, then click Undo	[Ctrl]+[Z]
Redo last undone action	↷	Click Edit, then click Redo	[Ctrl]+[Y]
Cut a selection and place it on the Clipboard	✂	Click Edit, then click Cut	[Ctrl]+[X]
Copy a selection and place the copy on the Clipboard	📋	Click Edit, then click Copy	[Ctrl]+[C]
Paste the contents of the Clipboard into the active document	📋	Click Edit, then click Paste	[Ctrl]+[V]
Call up the Office Assistant	?	Click Help, then Click Microsoft Word Help	[F1]
Get a ScreenTip for an item		Click Help, then click What's This?, then click item	[Shift]+[F1], then click item

Word 2000

Identify Key Features

Name the items indicated in the figures.

Figure 2-17 Features associated with editing

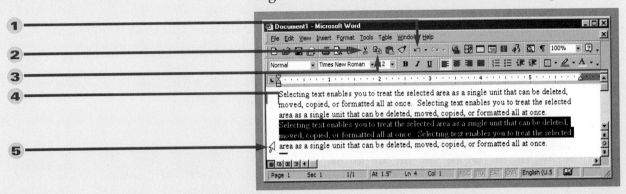

Figure 2-18 Features associated with editing

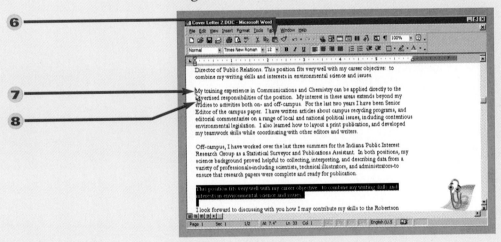

Select the Best Answer

9. An invisible column along the left edge of the text on a page

10. An option that instructs Word to look more thoroughly for a file

11. A menu of recently used commands and actions

12. Observes your work and offers suggestions

13. A program that walks you through the steps of document creation

14. Selects an entire paragraph

15. A temporary storage area for data

16. One of Word's three Help tabs

a. Clipboard

b. Triple-clicking text

c. Search subfolders

d. Index

e. Selection Bar

f. Undo drop-down list

g. Office Assistant

h. Wizard

Complete the Statement

17. The dialog box where Word's file-searching capabilities are used is:

    a. The Find dialog box

    b. The Save dialog box

    c. The Save As dialog box

    d. The Cross-reference dialog box

18. Word bases the formatting of a new document on:

    a. The last document used

    b. The buttons on the Formatting toolbar

    c. The Blank Document template

    d. The Résumé Wizard

19. To copy selected text to another location with the mouse:

    a. Drag and drop the selected text

    b. Double-click the desired location

    c. Print the document and photocopy it

    d. Drag and drop the selected text while pressing [Ctrl]

20. A template differs from a wizard in that:

    a. A template contains no graphic items

    b. A wizard creates the document for you based on answers you give

    c. Documents created with a template cannot be changed

    d. A wizard doesn't allow you to enter information

21. To select the text from the insertion point to the end of the line:

    a. Click the paragraph mark

    b. Press [Ctrl]+[Home]

    c. Click in the Selection bar

    d. Press [Shift]+[End]

22. Double-clicking in the Selection bar:

    a. Opens the New dialog box

    b. Selects the entire document

    c. Selects the adjacent paragraph

    d. Minimizes the document window

23. Pressing [Ctrl] while dragging and dropping text allows you to:

    a. Delete the text

    b. Paste the text

    c. Make a copy of the text

    d. Add the text to the Office Clipboard, but not the Windows Clipboard

24. The 📋 button:

    a. Inserts the last item placed on the Clipboard at the insertion point

    b. Copies selected text to the clipboard

    c. Opens a note pane

    d. Displays the contents of the Clipboard

Interactivity

Test Your Skills

1. Find a file and open it:

   a. Make sure your student files are installed on your hard drive or your student disk is inserted in the appropriate disk drive.

   b. In Word, go to the Open dialog box.

   c. Using the Find command in the Open dialog box, find the student file **SkillTest2**.

   d. Open the file and save it to your student disk as **Test 2**.

2. Select portions of the document and delete them:

   a. Select the last sentence in the second paragraph (the one that begins **He was really great ...**) by clicking it while pressing [**Ctrl**].

   b. Delete the selected sentence.

   c. Select the postscript at the end of the document by triple-clicking it.

   d. Add the text that extends from the selected paragraph to the end of the document to the selection by pressing [**Ctrl**]+[**Shift**]+[**End**].

   e. Delete the selection.

3. Select paragraphs in the document and move them:

   a. Select the third paragraph (the one that begins **On a slightly different note ...**) by double-clicking next to it in the Selection bar.

   b. Drag the selected paragraph to the blank line following the next paragraph and drop it there.

   c. Select the first paragraph by triple-clicking it.

   d. Cut the selected paragraph and send it to the **Clipboard** by using the **Cut** command.

   e. Paste the copy at the end of the final paragraph of the document, before the signature initials.

   f. Save and close the document.

4. Use Word's Help facility:

   a. Ask the Office Assistant about **selecting text**.

   b. Choose the help topic called **Select text and graphics**. Then click the subtopic in the Microsoft Word Help window called **Selecting text and graphics using the keyboard**.

   c. Expand the Help window so that it shows the Help tabs.

   d. Use the **Index** tab to display help topics based on the word **view**. Read the help file titled **Different ways to view a Word document**.

   e. Use the **Contents** tab to read the help files under the heading **Using Shortcut Keys**.

Interactivity (continued)

5. Create a document using a wizard:

    a. Open the New dialog box.

    b. Start the Memo wizard.

    c. Create a Contemporary memo with the title Word 2000 Memo.

    d. Address the memo to your instructor.

    e. When you finish the wizard, add text to the memo that informs your instructor that you have created the document using Word's Memo wizard.

    f. Save the file as TYS2-5.

    g. Preview the document with Print Preview, and then print a copy of the memo.

Problem Solving

1. Using the skills you learned in Lesson 2, use the Résumé Wizard to create a Professional, Entry-level résumé to accompany the letter you wrote at the end of Lesson 1. Be sure to include your current address, career objectives, education, work experience, other relevant experience (include as an additional heading), and interests and activities. When the wizard has created the résumé, use the Cut and Paste commands and the drag-and-drop method to rearrange the order of the résumé headings. Then print out a copy of the finished résumé and save the file to your student disk as Solved2-Resume.

2. You are satisfied with the résumé you created above, but realize that it may not be appropriate for every job opening. Create a new résumé from a blank document (do not use the wizard or a template) but with all of the content from the first résumé. To do this, copy each individual section from Solved2-Resume to the new document, but change the order of the headings. Also, write a new objective for this résumé. Save the new document as Solved2-Resume2.

3. As the owner and CEO of a rapidly expanding financial consulting firm, you are very proud to have had your best recruiting season ever. You have hired six outstanding recent college graduates from this year's recruiting class. Use the Letter wizard to write a letter of congratulations to the head of your recruiting department. Preview and print your letter. Then save it as Solved2-Letter.

4. While at a conference in Chicago, you have been introduced to some startling technological advances in voice-recognition software. Use the Elegant Fax template to create a fax cover letter that you can send to your boss at The Software Train, Inc. The template includes a section in which you can add text so that your fax will only require this one page. Complete the cover letter, including your findings at the conference. Save the document as Solved2-Fax, and print a paper copy.

L E S S O N

3

ADVANCED EDITING

Word allows you to add many different types of formatting to a document. These can be broken down into three major divisions: text-level formatting, paragraph-level formatting, and document-level formatting.

Text-level formatting, which was covered in Lesson 1, refers to all formatting that applies to individual characters in a document, such as size, font, and such options as bold and italics. No matter where text appears, these characteristics can be applied to single letters or entire sections of text.

Paragraph-level formatting covers the characteristics that can be applied to a paragraph or group of paragraphs. These include alignment, indents, line spacing, line numbers, and other aspects that cannot be applied to a single character.

Document-level formatting includes such options as margins and headers and footers, which are items set to appear on every page of a document, including page numbers and the document title.

Once the document has been completed and formatted to meet your needs, Word offers several proofreading aids to assure the quality of the finished product. In addition to a spelling checker that spots misspelled words throughout the document, Word has a feature called AutoCorrect that can actually fix common typing and spelling mistakes automatically, as they are made. Word also contains a built-in thesaurus that makes finding the perfect word both simple and fast. And if you decide to change a word or phrase that occurs in several places in a long document, Word can search your document for all instances of the item and replace them with something you prefer.

Case Study:
In this lesson, Sabrina will add formatting to a research paper that she has written and will add data that has been collected by her research partner, Juan. She and Juan will then proofread the document and make corrections.

 **Setting Up a Page**

Concept

Word gives you control over many aspects of formatting at the document level. These include margins, paper size, and layout. Changing document-level formatting allows you to control how a document will appear both on the screen and when it is printed.

Do It!

Sabrina wants to reduce the left and right margins of a research paper she has been writing.

1 Open the student file **Doit3-1** and save it to your student disk as **Report.doc**.

2 Click **File**, then click **Page Setup**. The Page Setup dialog box appears.

3 Click the **Margins** tab to bring it to the front if it is not already foremost in the dialog box, as shown in **Figure 3-1**.

4 Click the downward-pointing arrow on the side of the **Left** box three times to reduce the Word default setting from 1.25 inches to 1 inch. The Preview box reflects the change you made to the left margin.

5 Triple-click the **Right** box to select it.

6 Type the number 1 to replace the selected value of 1.25. Since **inches** is the default setting for measurement, you do not need to enter its symbol.

7 Click [OK] to apply the changes to the document and close the dialog box. The text of your document may now extend beyond the edge of your screen. You can adjust this by reducing the zoom factor on the Standard toolbar. Do not close the document, as you will be using the same one throughout the next several Skills.

More

The **Margins** tab of the Page Setup dialog box also enables you to adjust the margins at the top and bottom of your pages and the distance from the upper and lower edges of the page of headers and footers, which are items at the top or bottom of a page that remain constant across many pages. Headers and footers can include such information as page numbers, logos, the date, or the title of the document. If your document utilizes facing pages, you can activate the **Mirror margins** option, which adjusts the margins so that the two inner margins and the two outer margins on facing pages are equal to each other. The **Paper Size** tab lets you format a document to fit any size medium (such as legal-size paper or an envelope) that your printer can handle. The **Paper Source** tab tells the printer where to get the right size paper for your document. The Paper Source and Paper Size tabs will offer different options depending upon the current selected printer. The **Page Layout** tab lets you control the vertical alignment of text on each page and allows you to add line numbers to the document.

Figure 3-1 Margins tab of the Page Setup dialog box

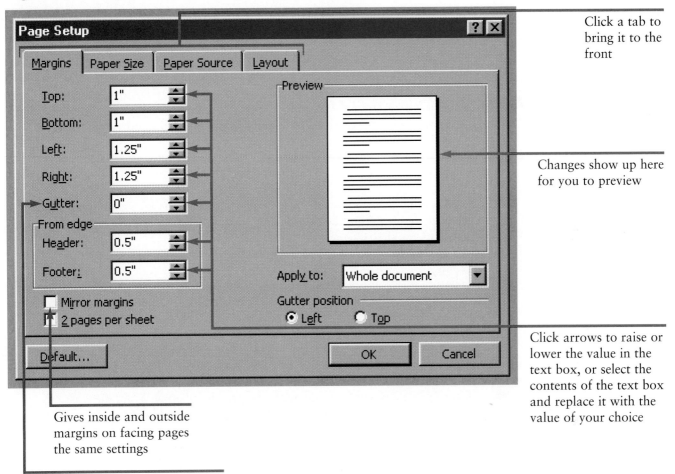

Click a tab to bring it to the front

Changes show up here for you to preview

Click arrows to raise or lower the value in the text box, or select the contents of the text box and replace it with the value of your choice

Gives inside and outside margins on facing pages the same settings

The distance added to the left (or inside, if Mirror margins is selected) margin to allow extra room for binding

Practice

To practice adjusting margins in a document, open the student file **Prac3-1**. Save the file as **MyPrac3-1** when you have completed the exercise and close the file when you are done.

Hot Tip

You can put different kinds of document formatting, such as margins, in one document by changing the setting of the **Apply To** box on the Layout tab of the Page Setup dialog box from Whole Document to This Point Forward.

Inserting Page Numbers

Concept

Word can insert page numbers into documents in a variety of placement locations and styles. Numbers are inserted automatically so you do not have to add a page number to each page individually. You also can add a prefix to each page number to identify chapters or sections, or choose to leave the number off the first page of a document if it is meant to serve as a title page.

Do It!

Sabrina wants to add centered page numbers to the report and view them.

1. Click Insert, then click Page Numbers to bring up its dialog box, as shown in **Figure 3-2**.

2. Click the Alignment box, then click Center to change the horizontal position of each page number from the default right setting to center.

3. Click **Format...** to bring up the Page Number Format dialog box (**Figure 3-3**).

4. Make sure the Number Format box displays Arabic numerals (1, 2, 3 ...) instead of letters or Roman numerals. If it does not, click the box, then click 1,2,3 ... to select Arabic numerals.

5. Click **OK** to leave the Format dialog box and return to the Page Numbers dialog box.

6. Click **OK** to confirm and apply the page numbering. Word automatically shifts to Print Layout View so that the page numbers can be seen.

7. Scroll to the bottom of the page to see the inserted page number.

More

The numbers you added to the document do not appear in Normal View. As you may recall, however, Word allows you to view your document in different ways. For example, the Print Preview screen offers a quick way to see how your document will look when printed, without nonprinting characters but including items not seen in the default Normal View, such as headers, footers, and page numbers. Word's View menu offers other ways of looking at your document. Outline View is helpful when you use Word's outlining features to structure your text with headings and subheadings. Like Print Preview, Print Layout View allows you to see your document as it will appear when printed, including page numbers, but retains the Ruler and the Standard and Formatting toolbars and lacks the Print Preview toolbar and magnifying tool. Web Layout View displays your document as it would appear when viewed with a Web browser. You can quickly move between these different views by using the View buttons at the left end of the horizontal scroll bar (refer to Figure 1-3 on page WD 1.5). The current view is indicated by a depressed button next to the horizontal scroll bar or on the View menu. Other view options include Header and Footer, which displays your headers and footers in an editable text box, and Full Screen, which shows only the document window. The Toolbars submenu on the View menu lets you select which toolbars appear on the screen. The Document Map makes moving from location to location in a document easier by letting you click on headings that are linked to your document.

Figure 3-2 Page Numbers dialog box

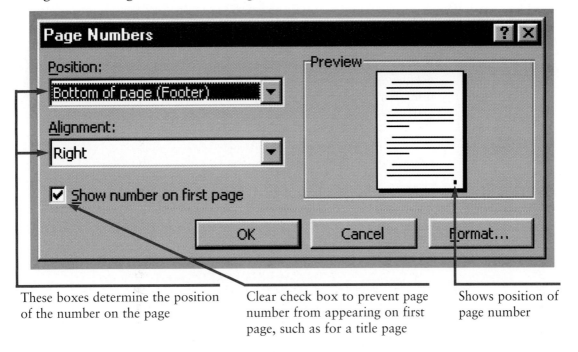

These boxes determine the position of the number on the page

Clear check box to prevent page number from appearing on first page, such as for a title page

Shows position of page number

Figure 3-3 Formatting page numbers

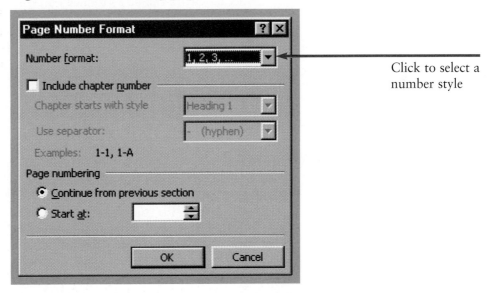

Click to select a number style

Practice

To practice inserting page numbers, open the student file **Prac3-2**. Save the file as **MyPrac3-2** when you have completed the exercise and close the file.

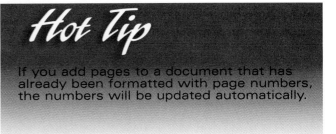

Hot Tip

If you add pages to a document that has already been formatted with page numbers, the numbers will be updated automatically.

 # Inserting Footnotes and Endnotes

Concept

A footnote explains a piece of document text at the bottom of the page on which the text appears. An endnote provides a similar explanation at the end of a document. Both contain two parts: a note reference mark and the note text. Word automates the process of creating and numbering footnotes and endnotes.

Do It!

Sabrina would like to add a footnote to her research paper.

1. Position the insertion point at the end of the first paragraph, after the words their work done. This is where the note reference mark will appear.

2. Click Insert, then click Footnote. The Footnote and Endnote dialog box appears with Footnote (the Word default) selected, as shown in **Figure 3-4**.

3. Click ⌗OK⌗ to insert the footnote using current settings. Word inserts the note reference mark at the insertion point and opens a note pane at the bottom of the window (assuming you are in Normal View).

4. Type the following text:
   These "anytime, anywhere" work environments are sometimes called "virtual offices," because work can be performed outside the traditional physical office setting and work schedule.

5. Click Close to leave the note pane and return to the document window.

6. If you are not already in Print Layout View, click View, then click Print Layout. Scroll to the bottom of the page and view the footnote in its proper place (see **Figure 3-5**). Alternatively, you can position the mouse pointer over the reference mark, and the footnote will appear as a ScreenTip (see **Figure 3-5a**).

More

The note pane is a separate part of the document window where footnote text is entered. All footnotes in each document are accessible through the note pane. In the Footnote dialog box, the **AutoNumber** option is the default setting. With this option selected, Word will automatically renumber the note reference marks if you add or remove some of your footnotes or endnotes, so there will be no break in their continuity. The default formatting for footnote text is 10 point Times New Roman, aligned left. This can be changed just as you would change the formatting of any other text in a document. The Note Options dialog box, accessed by clicking the Options button ⌗ Options... ⌗ in the Footnote and Endnote dialog box, offers further flexibility in number format and note placement.

Like page numbers, footnotes and endnotes do not appear as part of the document in Normal View. You can view and edit a footnote by double-clicking its reference mark in the text, which opens the note pane. Switching to Print Layout View shows the footnotes below a horizontal line at the bottom of a page or endnotes at the end of the document as they will appear on the actual page.

Figure 3-4 Footnote and Endnote dialog box

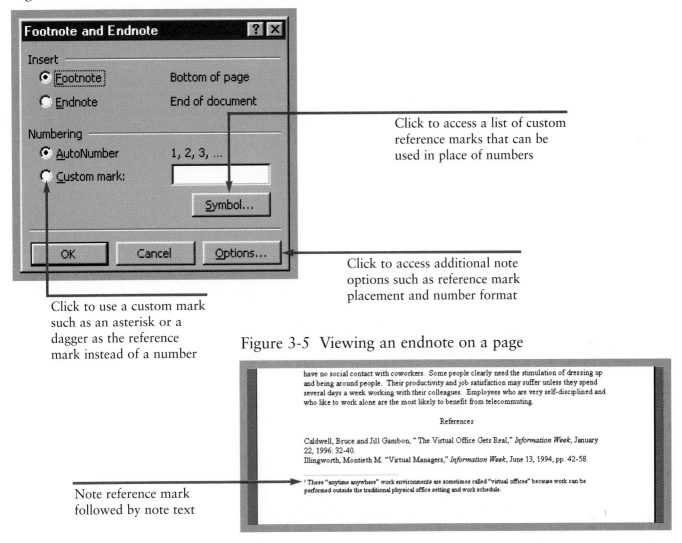

Click to access a list of custom reference marks that can be used in place of numbers

Click to access additional note options such as reference mark placement and number format

Click to use a custom mark such as an asterisk or a dagger as the reference mark instead of a number

Figure 3-5 Viewing an endnote on a page

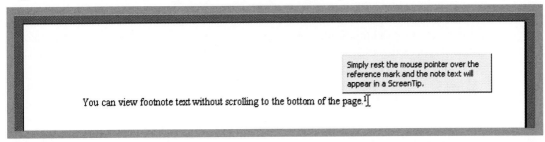

Note reference mark followed by note text

Figure 3-5a Viewing a footnote as a ScreenTip

Practice

To practice inserting Footnotes into a document, open the student file **Prac3-3**. Save and close the file when you are done.

Hot Tip

Make sure you place the insertion point at the precise location where you want a reference mark to appear before you insert a footnote.

WD 3.7

Applying Indents

Concept

Paragraph indents, fixed spaces inside the margins and in front of the first line of a paragraph used to indicate that a new paragraph has begun, may be changed easily using the four indent markers on the ruler, or, for more precise control, the Paragraph dialog box.

Do It!

Sabrina wants to indent the first line of each paragraph in the main text by half an inch and apply a hanging indent to her References section.

1 Select the four paragraphs of main text by clicking before the first word of the first paragraph, scrolling down to the end of the document and holding [Shift] while clicking after the last word of the fourth paragraph. The entire document should be selected between the heading and References sections.

2 Click and drag the First line indent marker in the ruler (see **Figure 3-6**) to the half-inch mark. The first line of each paragraph will move to the right half an inch.

3 Deselect the main text by clicking once anywhere in the document window.

4 Select the entire References section of Sabrina's report, from the word References to the end of the document.

5 Click and drag the Hanging indent marker in the ruler to the half-inch mark (the Left indent marker will move with it). All lines in a paragraph that are not first lines move to the right half an inch. This is called a hanging indent because it leaves the first line hanging by itself at the left margin.

More

All markers on the ruler may be changed by clicking and dragging. The First line indent marker, as seen above, controls the indentation of the first line of selected paragraphs. The Hanging indent marker determines the amount of indentation from the left margin of all lines of a selected paragraph except its first line. The rectangle below the Hanging indent marker is called the Left indent marker and determines the amount of indentation for all lines of a selected paragraph, including the first line. Finally, the Right indent marker at the right end of the ruler regulates the amount of indentation from the right margin for all lines of a selected paragraph. The default settings for all of the indent markers are even with the margins.

You also can indent the first line of paragraphs as you type with the [Tab] key. Each time you press [Tab], the insertion point jumps to the next tab stop. Word's default tab settings are one-half inch. You also can set your own tab stops by clicking the bottom half of the ruler where you want them. After they are set, tab stops can be moved by dragging them along the ruler with the mouse pointer. To remove a tab stop, click and drag it below the ruler. It will vanish when the mouse button is released. Clicking the tab alignment selector at the left end of the ruler selects different tab alignments that can be applied. **Table 3-1** describes various tab alignments and their properties. The tab and indent settings for the current paragraph or selected paragraphs also can be adjusted from the Paragraph dialog box, accessible from the Format menu, and shown in **Figure 3-7**. Any indent changes made with the ruler will show up in the indent settings of the dialog box and vice versa.

Figure 3-6 Horizontal ruler

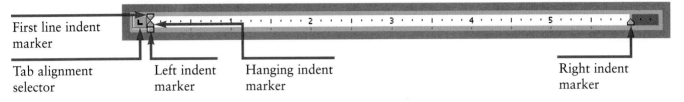

First line indent marker

Tab alignment selector

Left indent marker

Hanging indent marker

Right indent marker

Table 3-1 Alignment of various tabs

TAB ALIGNMENT	PROPERTIES	BUTTON
Left	Text extends from the tab stop to the right	L
Center	Text is centered on the tab stop	⊥
Right	Text extends from the tab stop to the left	⌐
Decimal	The decimal point in the text aligns itself beneath the tab stop; text before the decimal is to the left of the tab stop, text after it is to the right	⊥

Figure 3-7 Adjusting indents from the Paragraph dialog box

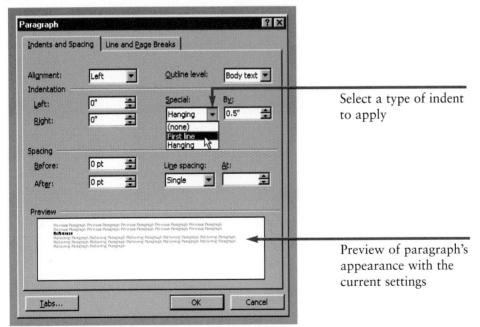

Select a type of indent to apply

Preview of paragraph's appearance with the current settings

Practice

To practice applying indents, open the student file **Prac3-4**. Save and close the file when you are done.

Hot Tip

The formatting of the text or paragraph at the insertion point will automatically be applied to any text or paragraph added after it.

Changing Line Spacing

Concept

The line spacing, or distance between adjacent horizontal lines of text, can be modified from the Paragraph dialog box. Word also allows the user to change the spacing between paragraphs. Many universities and business organizations require written documents to conform to certain standards, which often include spacing considerations. For example, a professor might demand that research papers be double-spaced, except when text is quoted from another source and should then be single-spaced and indented.

Do It!

Sabrina wants to remove the spaces between paragraphs and double-space her report.

1 Delete each of the blank lines between the four paragraphs of the main text by selecting the blank lines and pressing [Delete].

2 Click Edit, then click Select All to select the entire document.

3 Click Format, then click Paragraph to open the Paragraph dialog box.

4 Click the Line Spacing list box, then click Double (see **Figure 3-8**).

5 Click [OK] to accept the changes you have made. All paragraphs in the document are now double-spaced.

More

The Paragraph formatting dialog box has a Preview box that allows you to see how the changes you are making will affect your text. The Word default setting is single spacing. If the spacing interval you want is not available in the Line Spacing list box, the At box allows you to set your spacing at any interval you enter, such as 1.25 or 0.9. The values in the At box are express spacing in terms of numbers of lines. The Before and After boxes refer to the spacing before and after each selected paragraph. This allows you to space paragraphs automatically at any interval without adding blank lines to the document. Values in the Before and After boxes measure spacing in terms of points, the same measurement system used for font sizes. 72 points equal one inch.

Figure 3-8 Adjusting line spacing from the Paragraph dialog box

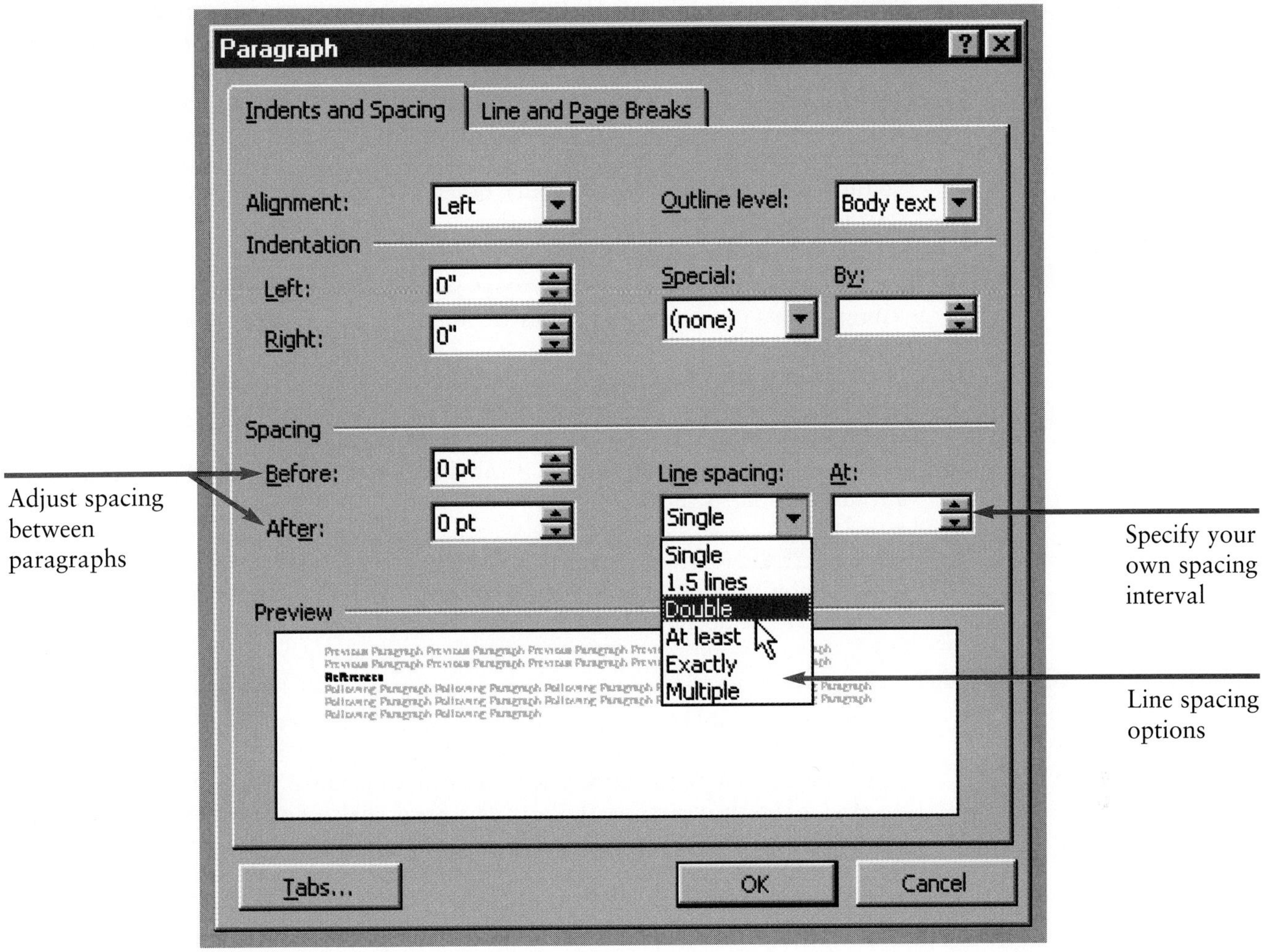

Adjust spacing between paragraphs

Specify your own spacing interval

Line spacing options

Practice

To practice changing line spacing and paragraph spacing, open the student file **Prac3-5**. Save and close the file when you are done.

Hot Tip

When formatting the paragraphs in a document, it is often helpful to show nonprinting characters with the ¶ button.

Inserting Page Breaks

Concept

The dotted horizontal line that divides pages in a document in Normal View (or the clear separation between pages in Print Layout View) is called a Soft page break. It will shift position as lines are added or removed from a document. Likewise, when enough text has been entered to fill a page, Word will create another page. A Hard page break, also known as a **Manual page break**, can be inserted where a page break should always occur, regardless of deletions or additions to previous text. Hard page breaks allow you to define different sections of a document clearly by starting new sections on a separate page.

Do It!

Sabrina wants to put the References section of her report on a separate page.

1 Place the insertion point before the word References at the head of the References section of the report. This will become the first line of the new References page.

2 Click Insert, then click Break. The Break dialog box appears with **Page Break** already selected, as shown in **Figure 3-9**.

3 Click [OK] to insert a page break at the insertion point. The References section will now appear at the top of a new page. Word will automatically renumber the pages of the document to account for the new page.

More

In Normal View, a Hard page break looks the same as a Soft page break, except the words Page Break appear in the center of the solid horizontal line dividing the page. You can remove a Hard page break by clicking next to it in the Selection bar to select it and then pressing [Delete]. The Break dialog box also allows you to add **Section Breaks**. A **section** is just a distinct part of your document that is separated from the rest. For example, chapters in a book can be manipulated as sections. Inserting a section break ends a section and dictates where the next will begin. When you choose the **Next Page** section break option from the Break dialog box, Word breaks the page at the section break and the next section begins at the top of the next page. When you click **Continuous**, Word inserts a section break and starts a new section on the same page. Clicking **Odd Page** or **Even Page** begins the new section on the next odd-numbered page or even-numbered page (see **Figure 3-10**).

Figure 3-9 Break dialog box

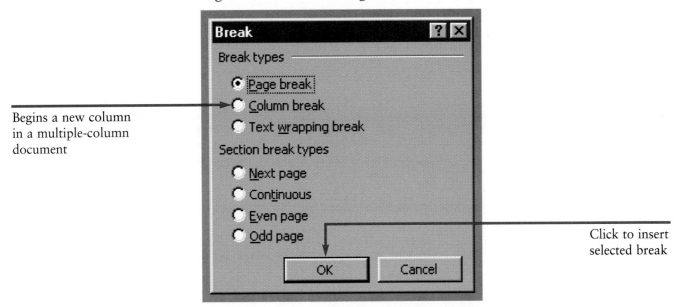

Begins a new column
in a multiple-column
document

Click to insert
selected break

Figure 3-10 Types of section breaks

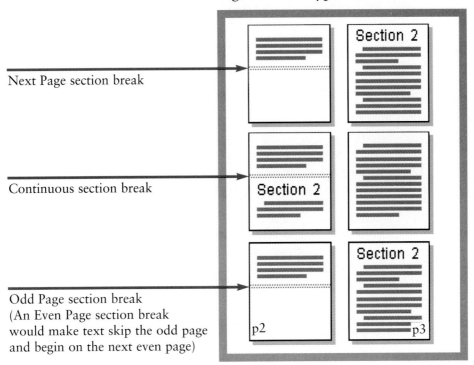

Next Page section break

Continuous section break

Odd Page section break
(An Even Page section break
would make text skip the odd page
and begin on the next even page)

Practice

To practice inserting page and section
breaks, open the student file **Prac3-6**. Save
and close the file when you are done.

Hot Tip

Viewing a page break from Print Layout
View will give you a better idea of how
much space the break leaves behind on the
previous page.

Working with Multiple Documents

Concept

Word, like many other Windows programs, lets the user work with more than one document at a time. You can create a new document or open an existing one without jeopardizing the active document. Document windows can be arranged so that one, two, or all open documents may be seen simultaneously. In addition, text can be copied and moved between open documents by using the Office Clipboard. This can save you from the time-consuming task of having to retype text that you want to use in another document.

Do It!

Sabrina wants to combine text that she and her partner, Juan, have written.

1. Open the student file Doit3-7. This is Juan's contribution to their report. Sabrina's portion, Report.doc will remain open but will be hidden behind the newly opened document.

2. Click Edit, then click Select All to select all of the text in Juan's document.

3. Click the Copy button 📋 on the Standard toolbar to copy Juan's document to the Clipboard.

4. Click Window on the menu bar, then click Report.doc to bring Sabrina's report into view. The Window menu shows all open Word documents, with a check next to the active document.

5. Place the insertion point just before the second paragraph in her report, the one that begins There are both …

6. Click the Paste button 📋 to insert Juan's text into their report. Notice that his text conforms to the documentwide settings that Sabrina set earlier. Its margins change from 1.25 to 1 inch to match the rest of the document. It remains single-spaced, however, as line spacing is formatted at the paragraph level. The text will be revised in the next Skill.

More

There are several ways to move between various open Word documents. The Window menu shows all open Word documents, and on the File menu there is a list of documents that Word has opened recently. The number of recently opened documents displayed here can be altered from the General tab in the Options dialog box, which you can access by clicking the Options command on the Tools menu. There is also a list of recently opened files on the Documents menu available on the Windows Start menu. Clicking one of these file names will open the file, or make it the active document if it is already open. The Clipboard can be used to transfer data between documents in the same way it is used within a single document. Each Word document that is open has its own program button on the Windows taskbar (see **Figure 3-11**). The active document is represented on the taskbar by a depressed button. Clicking these program buttons is perhaps the easiest way to switch among open documents.

Figure 3-11 Working with multiple documents

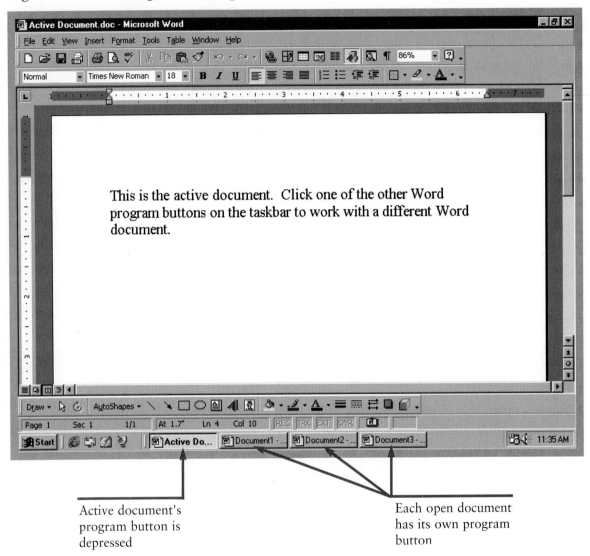

Active document's
program button is
depressed

Each open document
has its own program
button

Using the Format Painter

Concept

The Format Painter makes it possible to copy the formatting settings from selected text to another section of text. This feature allows you to unify the formatting in a document without having to apply each formatting change individually.

Do It!

Sabrina would like to format Juan's text like the rest of her document.

1 Select Sabrina's first paragraph by double-clicking next to it in the Selection bar.

2 Click the Format Painter button ![icon] on the Standard toolbar. The mouse pointer will appear as an I-beam with a paintbrush next to it ![icon] as it moves over areas that have formatting differing from that of the selected text. This indicates that the formatting of the selected text has been copied and is ready to be applied to a new area (see **Figure 3-12**).

3 Click Juan's paragraph (not his references) to automatically format it to match Sabrina's text.

4 Select the three lines of Juan's references by clicking next to the first line in the Selection bar and dragging down to select the other two lines as well.

5 Click and drag the selected text to the very end of the document, releasing the mouse button after moving the dotted insertion point to the right of Sabrina's last reference. With the insertion point just in front of Juan's references, press [Enter] to insert a paragraph mark. Now all references are in their proper place in the References section.

6 Select one of Sabrina's references by double-clicking next to it in the Selection bar.

7 Click the Format Painter button to copy her formatting settings.

8 Select the three lines of Juan's references by clicking next to the first line in the Selection bar and dragging down to select the other two lines as well. Now all of the references follow Sabrina's formatting.

9 Click Window, then click Doit3-7.doc to go back to Juan's document.

10 Click File, then click Close to close Juan's document. Do not save changes.

11 Click File, then Close again to close Sabrina's document. This time, save changes when prompted.

Word 2000

More

To format more than one area with the same selected format settings, double-click the Format Painter button. When you have formatted all the text you need, click the button again to turn off the Format Painter. If you only want to copy the character formatting, don't include the paragraph mark ¶ at the end of the text you are formatting. Remember, the paragraph mark is the place in the text where [Enter] was pressed to go to a new line; it can be displayed by clicking the Show/Hide ¶ button on the Standard toolbar. If the text you have selected to format includes the paragraph mark, the paragraph formatting will be copied too. The collection of all formatting characteristics of a document is referred to as its style. The Style command, available on the Format menu, allows you to apply styles from any of Word's templates to the current document. These styles include the margins, text formatting, indents, and other format options existing in the document style you choose.

Figure 3-12 Copying formatting with the Format Painter

Paragraph from which formatting is being copied

Pointer indicates that formatting is loaded and ready to be applied to another section of text

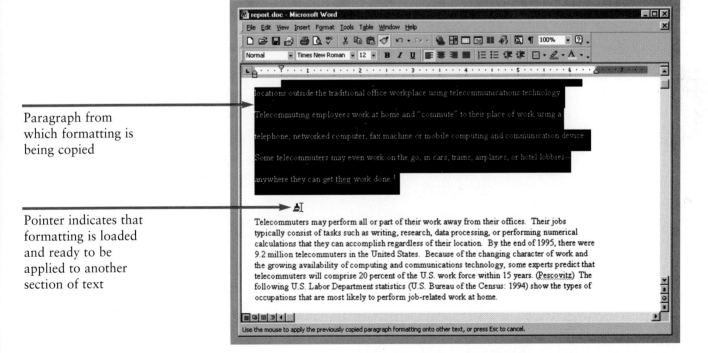

Practice

To practice using the Format Painter, open the student file **Prac3-8**. Save and close the file when you are done.

Hot Tip

To apply copied formatting to multiple locations, double-click the Format Painter button. The Format Painter will remain active until you click its button again or press [Esc].

 # Checking Spelling and Grammar

Concept

Word has the ability to check the spelling and grammar in a document and offer suggestions for how to correct words and phrases that its built-in dictionary does not recognize as correct. Word permits you to check the accuracy of single words, sentences, paragraphs, or the entire document at once. While proofreading your work yourself is still a necessary part of producing professional documents, using Word's automated proofreading features is a good first step. In order to complete this Skill, the Check spelling as you type, Check grammar as you type, and Check grammar with spelling features must be active. These options, which are active by default, can be found by selecting the Options command on the Tools menu and going to the Spelling & Grammar tab in the Options dialog box.

Do It!

Sabrina wants to check a document for spelling and grammar errors.

1 Open the student file Doit3-9 and save it to your student disk as Spelling. This is a sample paragraph with several spelling and grammar errors in it.

2 Right-click (click with the right mouse button) the first word in the paragraph that is underlined with a wavy red line, processer. A pop-up menu appears with several suggested correct spellings. As shown in **Figure 3-13**, move the mouse over the list to select the first choice, processor, and click. Word replaces the misspelled word with the selected alternative.

3 Click Tools, then click Spelling and Grammar. The Spelling and Grammar dialog box will appear, as shown in **Figure 3-14**, with the first error highlighted in red and suggestions for replacing it below.

4 Select the correct word in the Suggestions box, grammar, and click `Change All` to correct all occurrences of this spelling mistake throughout the document. Word then highlights a repeated word.

5 Click `Delete`, which appears in place of the Change button. The second you disappears. Word now detects a grammatical error in the document, noting that the verb provide does not agree with its subject, it.

6 Click `Change` to change the highlighted word to provides, thereby creating agreement between subject and verb and clarifying the meaning of the sentence. Next, the Spelling and Grammar checker highlights a proper name that it does not recognize.

Figure 3-13 Automatic spell checking

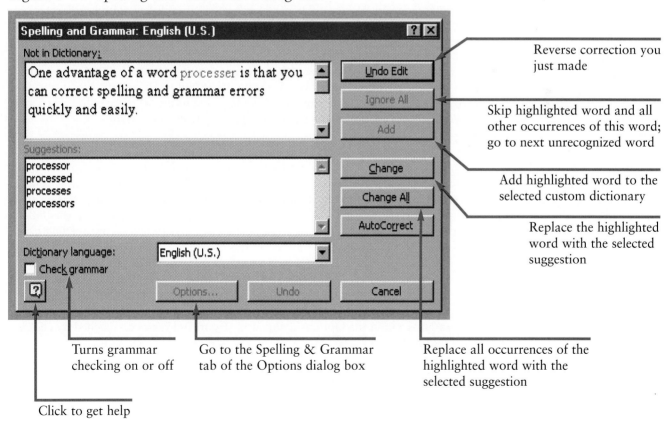

Right-click a flagged word to open pop-up menu of correction choices

Select correct spelling from menu

Figure 3-14 Spelling and Grammar dialog box

Reverse correction you just made

Skip highlighted word and all other occurrences of this word; go to next unrecognized word

Add highlighted word to the selected custom dictionary

Replace the highlighted word with the selected suggestion

Turns grammar checking on or off

Go to the Spelling & Grammar tab of the Options dialog box

Replace all occurrences of the highlighted word with the selected suggestion

Click to get help

Checking Spelling and Grammar (continued)

Do It!

7 Click [Ignore] to ignore the selected word, which, though Word doesn't recognize it, is spelled correctly. Word now highlights a misspelled word.

8 Click [Change]. Word replaces simpley with the correct spelling, simply, and the Spelling and Grammar dialog box disappears, replaced with a small Microsoft Word message box notifying you that no further errors were found and that the check is complete.

9 Click [OK]. The message box disappears.

10 Save and close the document.

More

In the same way that the Change All button in the Spelling dialog box causes Word to correct all further instances of the selected word, the **Ignore All** button instructs Word to skip over all instances of an unrecognized word throughout the document. Word takes capitalization into account when checking spelling, so if it was told to ignore Microwaveable, for example, it would still stop on microwaveable if it were to appear elsewhere in the document. The reason that different copies of Word may recognize different words is that words can be permanently added to Word's **custom dictionary**, a document that is unique to each copy of Microsoft Word. If you click [Add] in the Spelling and Grammar dialog box when the spell checker highlights a word it does not know but that you know is spelled correctly, the word will be added to the custom dictionary and will not be questioned again. You may freely edit the sentence appearing in the **Not in Dictionary** box just as you would edit it in your document; changes you make to the sentence will take effect when the Spelling and Grammar checker goes on to the next error.

Word's **Automatic Spell Checking** feature was mentioned briefly in Lesson 1. As you type, Word can underline with a wavy red line words that it does not recognize. Likewise, it underlines with a wavy green line words or phrases that it believes are grammatically incorrect. Right-clicking a word underlined in red in this fashion brings up a pop-up menu that contains a list of suggested alternatives to the underlined word, the **Ignore All** and **Add** commands, and a shortcut to the Spelling dialog box. Clicking one of the alternate words on the list will change the underlined word to match it. There is also an AutoCorrect option, which you will learn more about in the next Skill. When a word that is underlined with a green wavy line is right-clicked, a similar pop-up menu appears with a list of suggested alternatives, an **Ignore Sentence** option, and a shortcut to the Grammar dialog box. The Spelling & Grammar tab in the Options dialog box (**Figure 3-15**) can be reached by clicking the Options button [Options...] in the Spelling and Grammar dialog box.

The **Recheck Document** button [Recheck Document] on the Spelling & Grammar tab allows you to run a new spell check as if you had not run one previously. Words that you chose to ignore during a previous check will be marked as errors once again. This enables you to correct errors that you might have ignored improperly and to apply new options to the spell-checking procedure. If you have not already checked spelling, this button will be labeled **Check Document**.

Figure 3-15 Spelling & Grammar tab of the Options dialog box

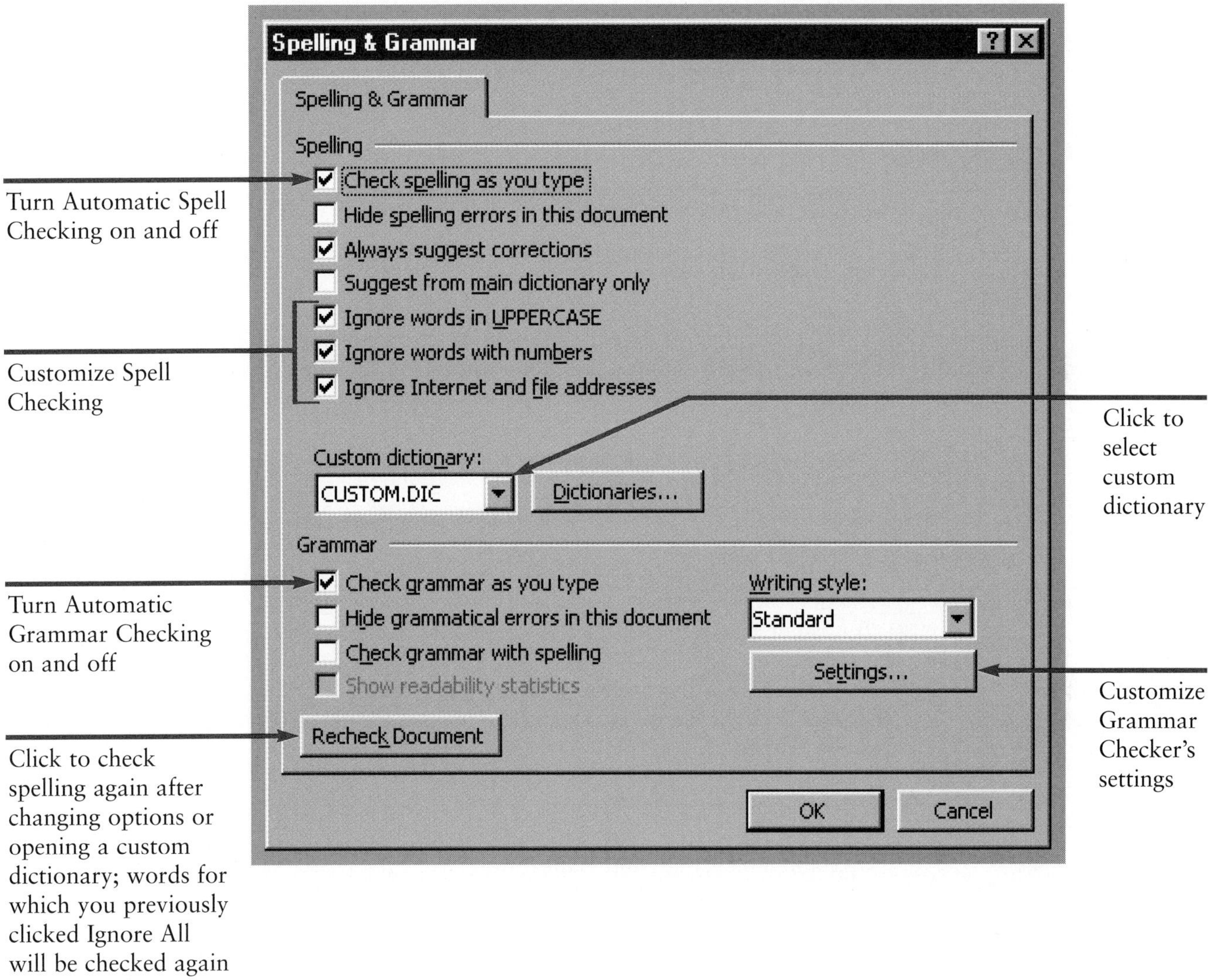

Spelling & Grammar

Spelling & Grammar

Spelling

☑ Check spelling as you type
☐ Hide spelling errors in this document
☑ Always suggest corrections
☐ Suggest from main dictionary only
☑ Ignore words in UPPERCASE
☑ Ignore words with numbers
☑ Ignore Internet and file addresses

Custom dictionary:

CUSTOM.DIC   ▼   Dictionaries...

Grammar

☑ Check grammar as you type
☐ Hide grammatical errors in this document
☐ Check grammar with spelling
☐ Show readability statistics

Writing style:

Standard   ▼

Settings...

Recheck Document

OK   Cancel

Turn Automatic Spell
Checking on and off

Customize Spell
Checking

Click to
select
custom
dictionary

Turn Automatic
Grammar Checking
on and off

Customize
Grammar
Checker's
settings

Click to check
spelling again after
changing options or
opening a custom
dictionary; words for
which you previously
clicked Ignore All
will be checked again

Practice

To practice using the spell checker, open
the student file **Prac3-9**. Save and close
the file when you are done.

Hot Tip

You can create additional custom
dictionaries, but Word comes equipped
with only one.

Using AutoCorrect

Concept

Word's **AutoCorrect** feature corrects specified typing mistakes automatically as they are entered and can be programmed to accommodate a wide variety of errors. For example, it can capitalize the first letter of a sentence automatically. AutoCorrect prevents you from having to fix typing errors that you commit frequently, saving you valuable time. AutoCorrect also allows you to format to convert certain characters and character combinations into symbols that represent them better.

Do It!

Sabrina wants to set AutoCorrect to fix a typing mistake she often makes.

1 Open a new blank document by clicking the New button ⬜ on the Standard toolbar.

2 Click Tools, then **AutoCorrect**. The AutoCorrect dialog box opens to the AutoCorrect tab. An insertion point appears in the **Replace:** box, as shown in **Figure 3-16**.

3 Type the word corect in the Replace: box, misspelling it intentionally.

4 Press [Tab] to move the insertion point to the **With:** box.

5 Type the word correct. Word will now replace corect with correct in any document.

6 If it is not checked, click the **Replace text as you type** check box to activate it.

7 Click ⬜ OK ⬜ to accept the changes you have made and to leave the AutoCorrect dialog box. The blank document that you created in the first step should be in the active window.

8 Type the following sentence exactly as it appears: Word will now corect mistakes i make. Notice that as you typed the sentence, Word fixed the misspelled corect and capitalized the letter i automatically.

Word 2000

Figure 3-16 AutoCorrect dialog box

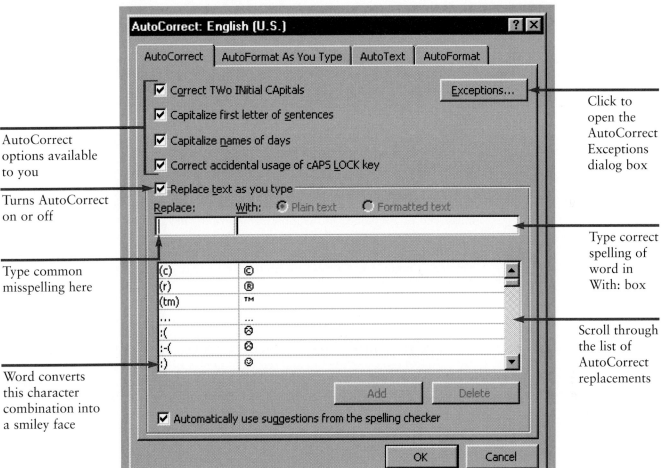

AutoCorrect options available to you

Turns AutoCorrect on or off

Type common misspelling here

Word converts this character combination into a smiley face

Click to open the AutoCorrect Exceptions dialog box

Type correct spelling of word in With: box

Scroll through the list of AutoCorrect replacements

Using AutoCorrect
(continued)

Do It!

9 Press [Space] after the previous sentence, then type the word many (lowercase, as shown) followed by a space. Word recognizes many as the first word of a new sentence, because it is preceded by a period and a space, and therefore capitalizes it.

10 Type misc. mistakes are fixed automatically. Notice that although you typed a period and a space after misc the word mistakes was not capitalized. This is because misc. is on Word's AutoCorrect Exceptions list along with most other common abbreviations.

11 Close the document. Do not save changes.

More

Word's AutoCorrect Exceptions dialog box, shown in **Figure 3-17**, can be accessed by clicking `Exceptions...` in the AutoCorrect dialog box. Word will recognize the period and space after one of the abbreviations on this list as differing from those at the end of a sentence and will not capitalize the next word. To get rid of an AutoCorrect entry that you don't want, select the entry in the AutoCorrect dialog box and click `Delete`. If you are working in a computer lab or similar environment, do not delete any AutoCorrect entries that you did not add yourself.

While AutoCorrect fixes spelling errors in words you have finished typing, Word's **AutoComplete** feature recognizes many words and phrases as you are typing them, predicts the outcome, and offers to complete them for you. For example, if you type **Dear M**, Word will suggest the AutoComplete tip **Dear Mom and Dad**. Simply press [Enter] to accept the tip, and the remaining text will be inserted for you. If Word recognizes that text you are typing matches a word or phrase contained in its list of **AutoText** entries, an AutoComplete tip will appear with Word's guess as to what you wish to type. If the suggestion is incorrect, simply continue typing and the tip will disappear. Use the AutoText tab in the AutoCorrect dialog box (shown in **Figure 3-18**) to add to the list of terms that AutoComplete will recognize. You also can see what AutoText entries are available by clicking `All Entries ▾` on the AutoText toolbar. Clicking one of the AutoText entries inserts it into your document at the insertion point. Some AutoText entries automatically include relevant data. If the insertion point is on the fourth page of a 10-page document and you insert the AutoText entry **Page X of Y** for instance, Word will insert **Page 4 of 10**.

Figure 3-17 AutoCorrect Exceptions dialog box

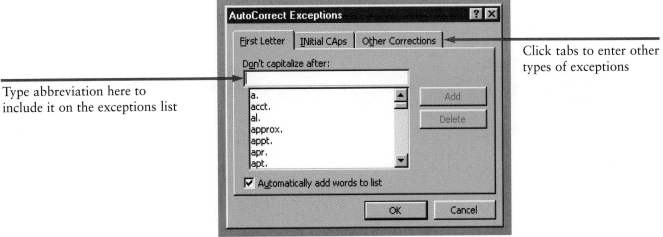

Type abbreviation here to
include it on the exceptions list

Click tabs to enter other
types of exceptions

Figure 3-18 AutoText tab of the AutoCorrect dialog box

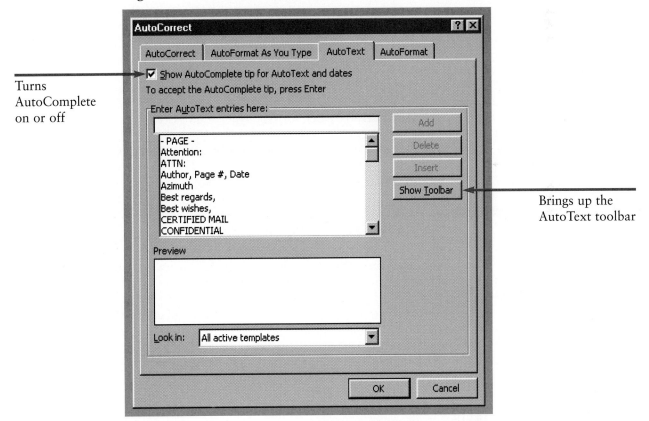

Turns
AutoComplete
on or off

Brings up the
AutoText toolbar

To practice using Word's AutoCorrect feature, open the student file **Prac3-10**. Save
and close the file when you are done.

Hot Tip

The **AutoFormat As You Type** tab in the
AutoCorrect dialog box contains an option
that instructs Word to convert Internet
addresses and network paths into
hyperlinks automatically.

Using the Word Thesaurus

Concept

Word contains a **Thesaurus** facility that can suggest synonyms and antonyms for words that you select.

Do It!

Sabrina wants to find a more descriptive word than the one she used in one of her sentences.

1 Open the student file Doit3-11 and save it as Report2.doc. It is a copy of Sabrina and Juan's report that has been fully checked for spelling.

2 Select the word **hard** in the fifth sentence of the third paragraph of the report, the sentence that begins **Many telecommuters are not locked into a hard 9-to-5 work schedule** . . .

3 Click **Tools**, then click **Thesaurus** on the **Language** submenu. The Thesaurus dialog box appears with the word **hard** displayed in the **Looked Up** box, as shown in **Figure 3-19**.

4 Click the word **inflexible** in the **Replace with Synonym** box to select it.

5 Click **Look Up** to search for synonyms of **inflexible**.

6 Click the word **rigid** in the **Replace with Synonym** box to select it.

7 Click **Replace** to insert **rigid** in place of **hard** in the report.

More

The **Meanings** box in the Thesaurus dialog box shows the various possible meanings of the selected word. Depending on the word, the Meanings box also may have **Antonym** or **Related Words** listed, which will show you opposite meanings and words with similar structure, respectively.

Word also can quickly count and display the number of pages, words, characters, paragraphs, and lines in your document. To activate the **Word Count** dialog box (see **Figure 3-20**) with all the information already calculated for the open document, simply click **Tools**, and then click **Word Count**.

Figure 3-19 Thesaurus dialog box

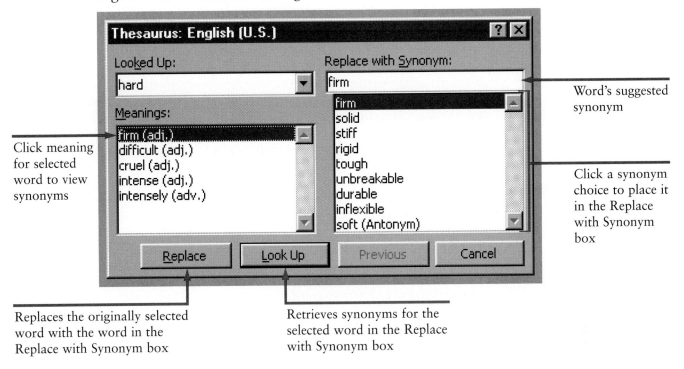

Word's suggested synonym

Click a synonym choice to place it in the Replace with Synonym box

Click meaning for selected word to view synonyms

Replaces the originally selected word with the word in the Replace with Synonym box

Retrieves synonyms for the selected word in the Replace with Synonym box

Word 2000

Figure 3-20 Word Count dialog box

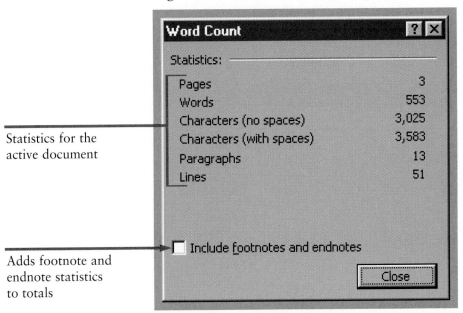

Statistics for the active document

Adds footnote and endnote statistics to totals

Practice

To practice using the Thesaurus, open the student file **Prac3-11**. Save and close the file when you are done.

Hot Tip

Click the **Looked Up** drop-down list arrow in the Thesaurus dialog box to view all words that have been looked up during the current session, with the original selected word at the bottom.

Finding and Replacing Text

Concept

The **Find** command allows you to search a document for individual occurrences of any word, phrase, or other unit of text. The **Replace** command gives you the ability to replace one or all occurrences of a word that you have found. Together, the Find and Replace commands form a powerful editing tool, capable of making multiple documentwide changes in a matter of seconds.

Do It!

Sabrina and Juan have used both per cent and percent in their report and, though both spellings are acceptable, they want to spell the word consistently throughout their document.

1 Place the insertion point at the beginning of the document. Word will search the document from the insertion point forward.

2 Click **Edit**, then click **Replace**. The Find and Replace dialog box appears with the Replace tab in front and the insertion point in the **Find What:** text box, as shown in **Figure 3-21** (click the More button to expand the dialog box if necessary).

3 Type per cent into the Find What: text box.

4 Click in the **Replace With:** text box to move the insertion point there.

5 Type percent as one word in the Replace With: text box.

6 Click [Replace All] to search the document for all instances of **per cent** and replace them with **percent**. A message box appears to display the results. In this case, one replacement was made.

7 Click [OK] to close the message box.

8 Close the Find and Replace dialog box.

9 Save and close the document.

More

You can examine and replace each instance of a word individually instead of automatically by clicking the **Find Next** button instead of **Replace All**. The **Search** drop-down list determines the direction of the search relative to the insertion point; you can search upward or downward through the document or keep the Word default setting of **All**, which checks the entire document including headers, footers, and footnotes. The five check boxes control other Find options, as explained in **Table 3-2**. The **Format** drop-down list contains formatting specifications, such as bold text or a particular indent depth, that Word can search for and replace. The **Special** drop-down list shows special characters that Word can search for, such as paragraph marks, manual page breaks, or a particular letter or digit. The **No Formatting** button removes all formatting criteria from your search parameters.

The **Find** tab of the Find and Replace dialog box is identical to the Replace tab except it lacks the replace function and merely searches your document for the items you specify.

Figure 3-21 Find and Replace dialog box

Enter the word you want to search for and replace here

Enter the replacement word here

Use check boxes to activate search options

Click to determine search direction

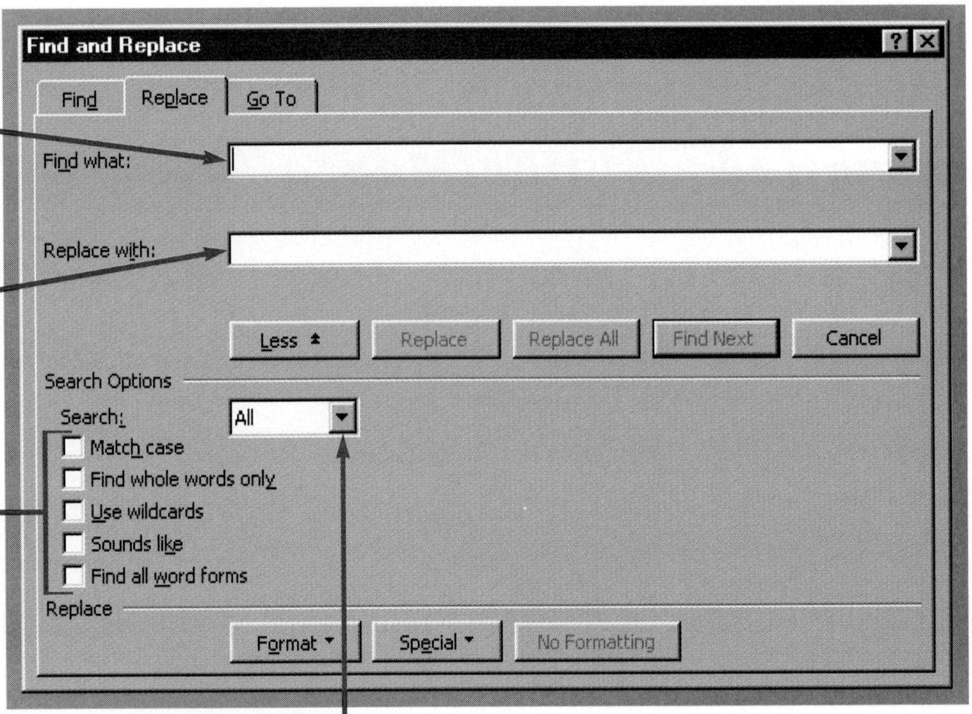

Table 3-2 Find options

OPTION	DESCRIPTION
Match case	Finds only text with uppercase and lowercase letters that match exactly the contents of the Find What: text box
Find whole words only	Disregards larger words that contain the word that is being searched for
Use wildcards	Searches for wildcards, special characters, or special search operators that are in the Find What: box. These can be added from the Special ▾ menu.
Sounds like	Looks for words that sound like the text in the Find What: text box but are spelled differently
Find all word forms	Locates all verb forms of a word, such as Do, Doing, Does, and Did

Practice

To practice finding and replacing text, open the student file **Prac3-12**. Save and close the file when you are done.

Hot Tip

The **Go To** tab in the Find and Replace dialog box provides a quick way to get to a particular place in a long document such as a specific page, footnote, or section.

Shortcuts

Function	Button/Mouse	Menu	Keyboard
Adjust margins		Click File, then click Page Setup, then click the Margins tab	
Indent selected paragraphs	Click and drag indent markers on the horizontal ruler	Click Format, then click Paragraph, then click the Indents and Spacing tab	[Ctrl]+[M] (Normal) [Ctrl]+[T] (Hanging)
Adjust line spacing of selected paragraphs		Click Format, then click Paragraph, then click the Indents and Spacing tab	[Ctrl]+[1] (Single) [Ctrl]+[2] (Double) [Ctrl]+[5] (1.5)
Go to the next window (when working with multiple documents)	Click on the part of the next window that is showing, if the active window is not maximized	Click Window, then click the name of the next document	[Ctrl]+[F6]
Go to the previous window (when working with multiple documents)	Click on the part of the previous window that is showing, if the active window is not maximized	Click Window, then click the name of the previous document	[Ctrl]+[Shift]+[F6]
Check for spelling and grammar errors	☑	Click Tools, then click Spelling	[F7]
Find next misspelling (with Automatic Spell Checking active)	Scroll down in the document to the next word with a wavy red underline		[Alt]+[F7]
Open the Word Thesaurus		Click Tools, then click Language, then Thesaurus	[Shift]+[F7]

Identify Key Features

Name the items indicated by callout arrows in **Figure 3-22**.

Figure 3-22 Identifying formatting and editing concepts

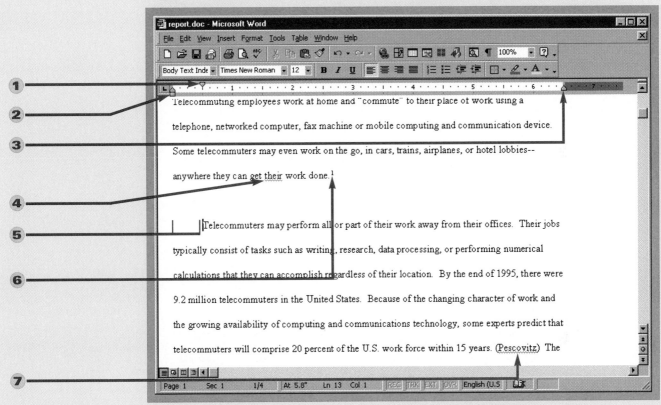

Select the Best Answer

8. Objects that slide along the horizontal ruler and determine text placement

9. A Word feature that fixes common mistakes as they are entered

10. A document where Word places words you "teach" it

11. A line where a new page always begins, regardless of how much space is left on the previous page

12. The place where footnote and endnote text resides

13. The invisible line that marks the boundary between text and the edge of a page

14. Displays the number of words, characters, paragraphs, and lines in your document

a. Hard page break

b. Word Count dialog box

c. AutoCorrect

d. Indent markers

e. Margin

f. Custom dictionary

g. Note pane

Quiz (continued)

Complete the Statement

15. Document-level formatting includes:

    a. Indents

    b. Font

    c. Margins

    d. Footnotes

16. A reference mark is:

    a. A mark in the text referring to a footnote or end-note

    b. Another name for a tab stop

    c. Text that has been highlighted

    d. An encyclopedia buyer

17. When there is no more room on a page and more text is entered, Word automatically creates a:

    a. New document based on the Normal template

    b. Manual page break

    c. Drop-down list

    d. Soft page break

18. AutoCorrect will fix a spelling mistake it recognizes when [Enter] is pressed, a punctuation mark is entered, or when:

    a. The space bar is pressed

    b. The document is saved

    c. Automatic Spell Checking is turned on

    d. The word matches the first five letters of a spelling mistake on AutoCorrect's list of entries

19. Paragraph-level formatting includes:

    a. Page numbers

    b. Headers and footers

    c. Italics

    d. Line spacing

20. The  button:

    a. Adds color to text

    b. Copies formatting from one area to another

    c. Pastes the contents of the Clipboard into the document at the insertion point

    d. Displays or hides the Drawing toolbar

21. One of the ways in which you can copy text from one document to another is to:

    a. Set up File Sharing on the Control Panel

    b. Click while pressing [F11]

    c. Use the Clipboard

    d. Use the Style Gallery

22. To view page numbers, switch to:

    a. Normal View

    b. Print Layout View

    c. Full Screen View

    d. Mirror margins

23. To leave the first line of a paragraph against the margin while indenting the other lines, apply a:

    a. Dangling indent

    b. First line indent

    c. Footer

    d. Hanging indent

Interactivity

Test Your Skills

1. Open a document and format it:

   a. Open the student file **SkillTest3** and save it to your student disk as **Test3**.

   b. Open the **Page Setup** dialog box on the File menu.

   c. Set the left and right margins at **1 inch**.

   d. Insert page numbers at the bottom center of the page.

2. Apply indents to the document, change the line spacing, and insert a footnote:

   a. Select all of the text in the document below the title.

   b. From the **Paragraph** dialog box on the Format menu, apply a **first line** indent of **.5 inch** and change the **line** spacing to double.

   c. Insert a footnote after (p. 43) in the fifth line of the second paragraph of the document reading, **All quotes refer to the revised 1862 edition of the book.**

3. Adjust the alignment and text formatting of the document:

   a. Select all of the text in the document below the title and **justify** it.

   b. Select the title and **center** it.

   c. Add **bold** formatting to the title and the author's name.

4. Open another document and copy text into the original document:

   a. Open the student file **SkillTest3a** and select the paragraph it contains. It is the conclusion to the paper used above.

   b. Copy the selected paragraph to the Clipboard.

   c. Close SkillTest3a, bringing **Test3** back as the active window.

   d. Place the insertion point at the very end of the document.

   e. Paste the copied paragraph onto the end of the paper.

5. Use the **Format Painter** to change the formatting of the inserted paragraph to match the rest of the document:

   a. Select the second-to-last paragraph in the document by triple-clicking it.

   b. Click the Format Painter button to copy the formatting of the selected paragraph.

   c. Drag the I-beam (which now has a paintbrush next to it) across the last paragraph in the document to select it and change its formatting to match that of the previous paragraph.

   d. Click once in the paragraph to deselect it.

Interactivity (continued)

Test Your Skills

6. Check for spelling errors and replace all instances of one word with another:

   a. Click **Tools**, then click **Spelling and Grammar** to run the Spelling and Grammar checker. Clear the Check grammar check box to check only for spelling errors.

   b. Correct the three misspelled words in the document, ignoring names and unusual words.

   c. Click **Edit**, then click **Replace** to open the Replace dialog box.

   d. Use the **Replace All** command to replace all occurrences of **Browne** with the correct name, **Brown**.

   e. Close the document, saving changes if prompted.

7. Add a word to the AutoCorrect **Replace text as you type** list:

   a. Open a new document.

   b. Open the AutoCorrect dialog box.

   c. Use the AutoCorrect tab to instruct Word to replace occurrences of **clcik** with **click**.

   d. Close the dialog box and test your AutoCorrect entry in the blank document.

   e. Return to the AutoCorrect tab and delete clcik from the list.

Problem Solving

1. Using the skills you learned in Lesson 3, open the student file **Problem Solving 3** and save it as **Solved 3**. Change the left and right margins to **1.25"**, apply a hanging indent of **.5"** to the document, and change the spacing to **1.5**. Add page numbers to the upper-left corner of each page, starting on page **1**. Center and boldface the title, and justify the main body text of the document. Insert three footnotes into the paper. The text of the footnotes is contained in the student file **Problem Solving 3a**. Insert the first footnote at the end of the third paragraph, following the word **products**. The second footnote follows the word **inventory** at the end of the fourth paragraph. The final footnote should be placed after the word **line** at the end of the sixth paragraph. Open the Spell checker and correct all misspellings in the document. Finally, add your name to the document and save and close the file.

2. You are applying for a position as a restaurant reviewer for a local magazine. Before your interview, you want to practice your reviewing technique. Review your three favorite restaurants in a three-paragraph, one-page document. Set up the document with **.75"** margins on all sides. After you enter all of your text, insert a Continuous Section break between the first and second, and second and third paragraphs. Then, format the first paragraph with **14**-point, italicized text and a hanging indent. Next, format the second paragraph with a **1.5"** first line indent and **11**-point, Arial text. Finally, format the third paragraph exactly like the first. Add your name to the document and save the document as **Solved 3-Reviews**.

L E S S O N

TABLES AND CHARTS

To present information in a document more accurately, it is often helpful to organize data into a table. Word makes it easy to create and modify tables in its documents, and it has the ability to perform many more complex tasks with data, such as sorting and calculating, that are usually found only in complicated spreadsheet programs.

Word can create blank tables in which data may be entered, or transform existing data directly into table form. Once a table has been made, data can be inserted or deleted quickly to meet your needs, or reorganized to get your point across more effectively.

Sometimes, it may be difficult to glean trends or important facts from a table accurately with so much information in text and number form. A chart can be very helpful by presenting the data as a picture that can be more easily grasped and understood.

Case Study:
Juan has accumulated some data for the report that he and Sabrina are working on, and he would like to organize it as a table that will be inserted into the document. Once the table has been finished, he will create a chart based on it and add the chart to the report.

Creating Tables

Concept

A table consists of information organized into horizontal rows and vertical columns. The intersection of a row and a column is called a cell. A table may be created from scratch or can be assembled from existing text. Tables often utilize row and column headers, which are labels that identify the adjacent data. Data in a table can consist of words, or labels, and numbers, also called values.

Do It!

Juan wants to insert a table into the report he and Sabrina have written.

1 Open the file Report2 from your student disk. This is the copy of Sabrina and Juan's report, which you were working on in the last lesson.

2 Place the insertion point at the end of the second paragraph, after the word home.

3 Insert a Manual page break (there will not be enough room on the page for the table without it). The insertion point will appear just below the new break.

4 Click the Insert Table button 🖩 on the Standard toolbar. A table grid appears, allowing you to choose the number of rows and columns in your table.

5 Move the mouse pointer over the table grid until a 2 * 3 area is selected, as shown in **Figure 4-1**, and click. A table appears in the document at the insertion point with gridlines delineating the rows and columns, and cell markers showing the end of the text in each cell, as shown in **Figure 4-2**. If the cell markers are not showing, you can make them appear by clicking ¶ on the Standard toolbar.

Figure 4-1 Using the Insert Table button

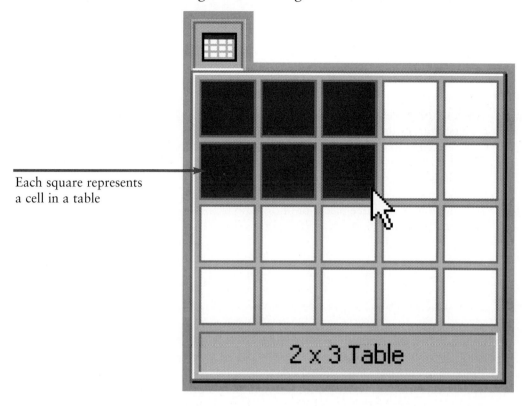

Each square represents
a cell in a table

Figure 4-2 Table inserted in Word document

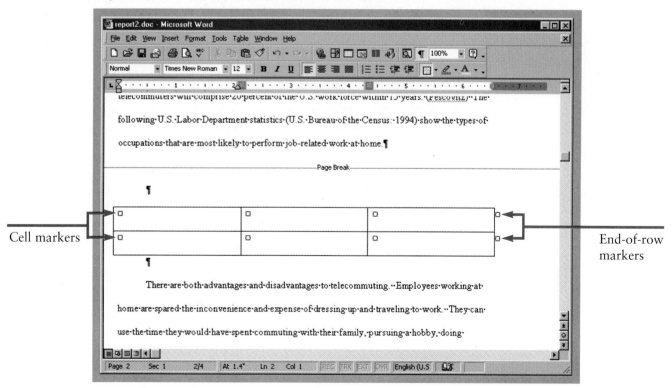

Cell markers

End-of-row
markers

Creating Tables (continued)

Do It!

6 Type the following three pieces of information, pressing [Tab] once after each of the first two headings:

Occupation	Total	Percent at Home

7 Press [Tab] to go to the next row.

8 Type the following three pieces of information, pressing [Tab] once after each of the first two:

Managerial	14.4	5.2

Your table should now resemble the one in **Figure 4-3**.

More

You also can create a table by selecting existing text in your document and clicking the Insert Table button; the cells in the table will be determined by the tabs and paragraphs in the selection. A new table also may be created manually by clicking Table, then clicking Draw Table. The Tables and Borders toolbar (see **Figure 4-4**) will appear, and you can draw a table and its row and column borders using the mouse pointer. If you choose the Insert Table command from the Table menu, you can access the AutoFormat dialog box, which will be explained later in the lesson.

Microsoft Excel is an electronic spreadsheet program that enables you to enter, organize, and analyze data in a tabular structure. An Excel file is called a workbook, and consists of one or more worksheets. The options available to you in Excel for working with data in rows or columns are by far more numerous and more powerful than those available in a Word table. If you wish to insert an existing Excel worksheet into your Word document, you can insert it as a linked object or an embedded object. A linked object will show up in the Word document (its destination file) but will remain linked to its source file. Thus, any changes made to the source file will be reflected in the destination file. If it is inserted as an embedded object, the file will become part of the Word document and can be altered by double-clicking it to open the parent application. This is an excellent example of the way different Microsoft Office applications can be used together productively. For example, if you have an Excel worksheet that is being updated frequently and you would like to insert it into your Word document as a table, insert it as a linked object so that you can be sure that the table will always be up to date. To insert a linked object at the insertion point, click Insert, then click Object, and then click the Create from File tab. Select the file you wish to insert by clicking the Browse button, and activate the Link to file check box (if this box is not checked, the file will be inserted as an embedded object instead). The table will appear in your Word document, and double-clicking it will open an Excel window from which the table can be fully edited. Word's Help facility offers many more tips and methods for fully utilizing these functions.

Figure 4-3 Adding information to a table

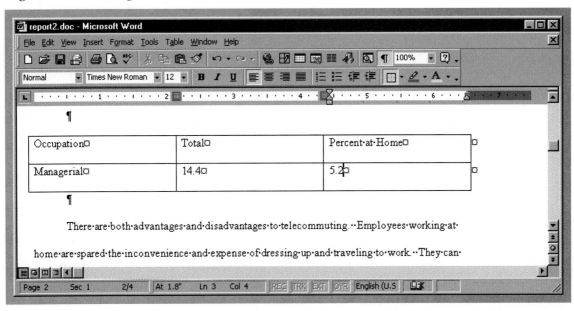

Figure 4-4 Tables and Borders toolbar

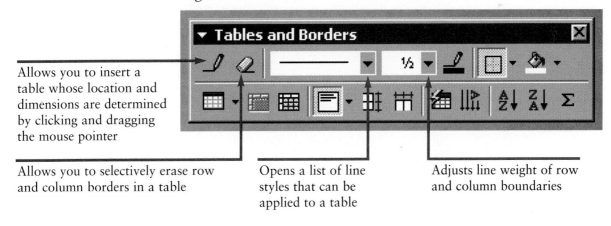

Allows you to insert a
table whose location and
dimensions are determined
by clicking and dragging
the mouse pointer

Allows you to selectively erase row
and column borders in a table

Opens a list of line
styles that can be
applied to a table

Adjusts line weight of row
and column boundaries

Practice

To practice creating tables, open the student file **Prac4-1**. Save and close the file
when you are done.

Hot Tip

You can create a table in Word using
Microsoft Excel by clicking the **Insert
Microsoft Excel Worksheet** button on
the Standard toolbar. This allows you to
use Excel commands within that worksheet as you create your table.

Editing Tables

Concept

A table in a Word document can be edited in much the same way that ordinary text is edited.

Do It!

Juan would like to change the Total heading in his table to Total (in millions) and Percent at Home to Percent Working at Home.

1 Position the insertion point just after the word Total in the table.

2 Type a space, then type (in Millions) to complete the heading.

3 Press [Tab] to move to the next cell to the right. All the information in the cell is selected.

4 Click between the words Percent and at to deselect the cell and position the insertion point there.

5 Type Working and press [Space] to complete the cell edit.

More

As you can see, table editing is very similar to editing text in a paragraph. Text may be centered or aligned to either side of a cell by selecting it and clicking the appropriate formatting button. Also, the Selection bar works in much the same way in a table as it does with text (see **Figure 4-5**). Clicking in the Selection bar next to a row selects the entire row; dragging up or down in the Selection bar adds more rows to the selected area. In addition, there is a miniature selection bar area at the left end of each cell, and clicking it will select the entire cell. A cell also may be selected by triple-clicking it, whereas double-clicking will select an entire word within the cell just as it does in regular text. To select a column, place the mouse pointer over its top border until the mouse pointer changes to a bold downward arrow ↓, then click to select the column. Cells can be made wider or narrower by clicking and dragging their edges: Place the mouse pointer on the gridline that makes up the edge of a cell until it changes to ╫, then click and drag the cell border to the desired distance. If you click and drag the edge of a selected cell, then that cell will be the only one in its column to be affected. To make the whole column's width change, make sure that no cells are selected before you adjust the edges.

The insertion point may be placed anywhere in a table with the mouse pointer. The keyboard may be used in a variety of ways to move through the table and select its contents. **Table 4-1** shows many keyboard movement and selection techniques that will make working with tables much easier. Remember to press [Tab] instead of [Enter] to move to the next cell; pressing [Enter] causes a new line to be created within the cell. When the insertion point is within the boundaries of a table, the ruler will reflect the table's column boundaries (see **Figure 4-5**). Dragging the column boundary markers on the ruler will change the corresponding column widths. When exact precision is required, row and column sizes may be manually entered in the Table Properties dialog box, available on the Table menu.

Table 4-1 Keyboard movement and selection shortcuts

DESIRED ACTION	PRESS THIS
Move to the next or previous cell in a table and select its contents	[Tab] or [Shift]+[Tab]
Move up or down one row	[↑] or [↓]
Move to the first or last cell in a row	[Alt]+[Home] or [Alt]+[End]
Move to the top or bottom cell in a column	[Alt]+[Pg Up] or [Alt]+[Pg Dn]
Select an entire column	[Alt]+Click
Select an entire table	[Alt]+[5] on the numeric keypad (with Num Lock off)

Figure 4-5 Formatting a table using the ruler

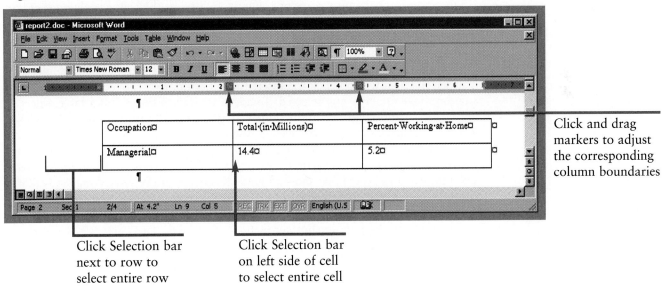

Click and drag markers to adjust the corresponding column boundaries

Click Selection bar next to row to select entire row

Click Selection bar on left side of cell to select entire cell

Practice

To practice editing a table, open the student file **Prac4-2**. Save and close the file when you are done.

Hot Tip

To insert a tab character into a cell to indent its contents, press **[Ctrl]+[Tab]**, as pressing [Tab] alone will simply move the insertion point to the next cell.

Inserting and Deleting Rows, Columns, and Cells

Concept

Word makes it easy to add or delete rows and columns in a table when more or fewer are required.

Do It!

Juan wants to add three rows of new data to the table.

1. Position the insertion point in the last cell in the last row of the table, after the number 5.2.

2. Press [Tab]. The insertion point moves to the first cell of a new row.

3. Type the following nine pieces of information, pressing [Tab] between each:

Professional	15.5	4.9
Sales	13.2	6.2
Service	14.9	3.7

The entered text is automatically formatted to fit into three new rows.

More

To insert additional empty rows or columns, first select the row or column that will be moved down or over to accommodate the new one. Then click the **Insert Rows** button or the **Insert Columns** button, which will appear in place of the Insert Table button on the Standard toolbar when a row or column is selected. The number of new rows or columns created is the same as the number selected. For example, if you select two rows and click the Insert Rows button, two new empty rows will appear above the ones you selected. To add a column to the end of a table, select the end-of-column markers in the same way you would select a column, then click the Insert Columns button. To delete a row or column, select it and then right-click it. The Table shortcut menu (**Figure 4-6**) will appear, offering, among other choices, an option to delete your selection. You also can use this menu to insert additional columns or rows. The Table shortcut menu has many of the same commands that are available on the Table menu, as well as shortcuts to several standard formatting options. To delete an individual cell, right-click it and then choose the **Delete Cells** command from the pop-up shortcut menu that appears. The Delete Cells dialog box, shown in **Figure 4-7**, will open. From this dialog box, you can determine whether the cell is deleted from its column or from its row by shifting the remaining cells up or to the left. You also can use this dialog box to delete an entire row or column. Row and column dimensions also may be adjusted from the **Table Properties** dialog box (**Figure 4-8**), available on both the menu bar Table menu and the Table shortcut menu.

Word 2000

Figure 4-6 Table shortcut menu

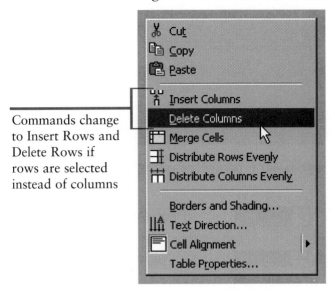

Commands change to Insert Rows and Delete Rows if rows are selected instead of columns

Figure 4-7 Delete Cells dialog box

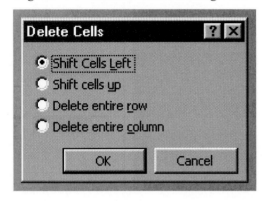

Figure 4-8 Row tab of Table Properties dialog box

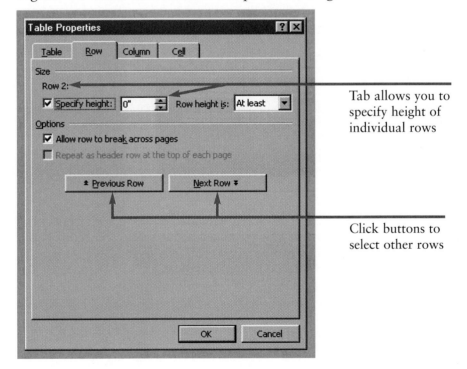

Tab allows you to specify height of individual rows

Click buttons to select other rows

Practice

To practice inserting and deleting rows and columns, open the student file **Prac4-3**. Save and close the file when you are done.

Hot Tip

To easily delete an entire row or column, select it and then either use the cut command or press **[Shift]+[Delete]**. Just pressing [Delete] will leave the cells intact but erase the contents.

Sorting Data in a Table

Concept

Cells in a Word table can be automatically sorted by various criteria without re-typing them or going through tedious cutting and pasting. For example, Word can automatically alphabetize a long table of names or sort a table of orders by shipping date. Sorting allows you to locate specific data in a table quickly.

Do It!

Juan would like his table to list occupations in order of decreasing Working-at-Home percentage.

1 Make sure the insertion point is positioned inside the table.

2 Click Table, then click Sort. The Sort dialog box appears, as shown in **Figure 4-9**.

3 Click the Sort by drop-down list arrow, then click Percent Working at Home. Word automatically reads all your column headings and includes them in the list, with the first heading as the default choice. When Percent Working at Home was chosen, Word analyzed the kind of data in that column and changed the Type list box from text to number.

4 Click the Descending radio button in the Sort By section to make Word sort the table with the largest values first.

5 Click the Header Row radio button in the My List Has section if it is not already selected.

6 Click [OK] to sort the table. The rows are placed in descending order according to their value in the Percent Working at Home column (see **Figure 4-10**).

More

Word allows you to sort by more than one criterion. For example, if you had a table of names with people's first and last names in separate cells, Word could sort them primarily by last name, then by first name. Thus, if several people had the same last name, Word could sort them by first name as well. Word allows up to three levels of sorting in this fashion. You can set secondary sorting criteria on the Sort dialog box by choosing another criterion in the Sort by text box. In the My List Has section, the default setting is Header Row, meaning the first row of your table explains the contents of the cells below, such as the header "Occupation" in Juan's table. If you select No Header Row, Word will make the first row into labels such as Column 1, Column 2, and so on. Also, if No Header Row is chosen but you do in fact have a header row, your column titles will be sorted with the other rows and may not end up at the top of the table.

Since only one row in Juan's table actually needed to be relocated, he could have moved the row manually. An alternative to the sort feature is to select an entire row and then move it with the pointer, the same way you move regular text. Release the dragged text in the row that you want to end up below the selection being moved.

Figure 4-9 Sort dialog box

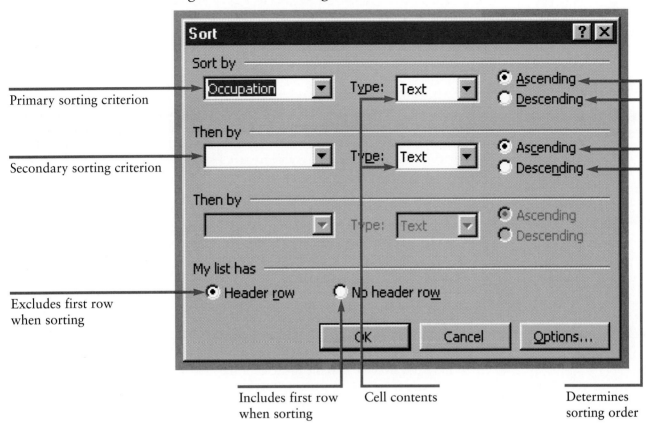

Primary sorting criterion

Secondary sorting criterion

Excludes first row
when sorting

Includes first row
when sorting

Cell contents

Determines
sorting order

Word 2000

Figure 4-10 Sorted table

Occupation	Total (in Millions)	Percent Working at Home
Sales	13.2	6.2
Managerial	14.4	5.2
Professional	15.5	4.9
Service	14.9	3.7

Practice

To practice sorting data in a table, open the student file **Prac4-4**. Save and close the file when you are done.

Hot Tip

You can make Word sort uppercase and lowercase letters differently by clicking the Case Sensitive check box in the Sort Options dialog box, available by clicking Options... in the Sort dialog box.

Calculating Data in a Table

Concept

The Formula command makes it easy to perform calculations with data in a table. Word comes with preprogrammed formulas such as sum, product, and average, but additional formulas may be entered to meet the needs of each user and each table. Using formulas transforms your table from a simple display object into a functional tool. Once you master formulas, you will never have to worry about committing costly mathematical errors.

Do It!

Juan wants Word to automatically average the values in the Percent Working at Home column and insert the average in a new cell.

1 Position the insertion point after the number 3.7 in the last cell of the last row of the table.

2 Press [Tab] to create a new row.

3 Type the word Average into the first cell of the new row.

4 Press [Tab] twice to move the insertion point to the last cell in the row.

5 Click Table, then click Formula. The Formula dialog box appears, as shown in **Figure 4-11**, with the formula =SUM(ABOVE) suggested in the Formula text box.

6 Delete the suggested formula by selecting it and pressing [Delete].

7 Click the Paste function list arrow, then click AVERAGE, as shown in **Figure 4-12**. The AVERAGE formula appears in the Formula text box with the insertion point between parentheses.

8 Type C2:C5, the range of cells you wish to average, inside the parentheses.

Figure 4-11 Formula dialog box

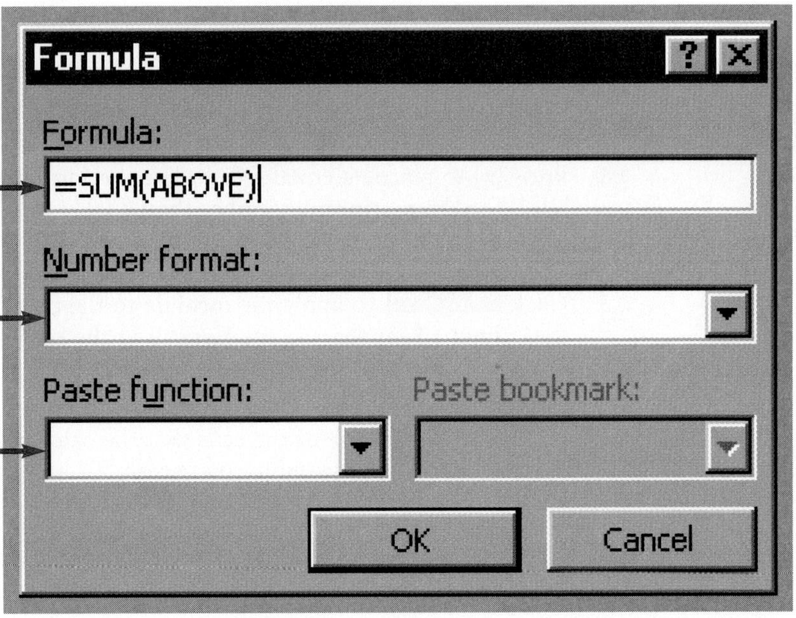

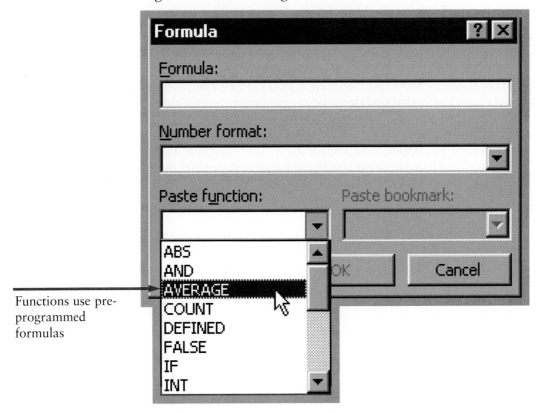

Chosen
formula

Displays results as
percentages, dollar
amounts, etc.

Other formulas you
can select

Figure 4-12 Selecting a function

Functions use pre-
programmed
formulas

Calculating Data in a Table (continued)

Do It!

9 Place the insertion point before the word AVERAGE in the Formula text box.

10 Press [=] to place an equal sign before the formula. The equal sign at the beginning tells Word that a formula, rather than a label or a value, is about to be entered. The formula should now read =AVERAGE(C2:C5).

11 Click [OK] to apply the formula to the column. The average of the values in the column, 5, appears in the last cell of the table, as shown in **Figure 4-13**.

More

Changing data in one of the cells that the calculation is based on does not immediately affect the result seen on the screen. To update the calculation taking the new data into account, triple-click the cell containing the formula to be recalculated and press [F9], which is the Update Fields command.

When entering your own formulas into the Formula dialog box, you will refer to other cells in the table using cell references, which identify a cell by its position as a function of its column letter and row number. For example, the cell reference for the second cell in the third column is C2. (See **Figure 4-14**.) You can use the Word Formula feature in many ways. In **Figure 4-15**, formulas are used to calculate the total monthly spending for three different people as well as the resulting 12-month projected total cost. The formulas shown are the ones that would be entered into the Formula text box when the Formula dialog box is called up with the insertion point in that particular cell. Each formula in the Monthly Total column (Column E) adds the numbers to the left in its respective row to arrive at the total. Likewise, the formulas in Column F multiply by 12 the monthly total for the row that was just calculated to arrive at a projected total for the year. The symbol for multiplication is an asterisk (*); division is represented by a slash (/). As they are in **Figure 4-13**, the formulas will result in an unformatted number. To make the calculated result appear with a dollar sign and two decimal places showing, click the Number Format text box in the Formula dialog box, and then click $#,##0.00;($#,##0.00) on the drop-down list. This will be tacked on to the end of the formula in the Formula text box, which will instruct Word to place the result in the correct format.

Figure 4-13 Appearance of table with average calculated

Occupation	Total (in Millions)	Percent Working at Home
Sales	13.2	6.2
Managerial	14.4	5.2
Professional	15.5	4.9
Service	14.9	3.7
Average		5

Average of the values in the four cells above

Figure 4-14 Cell references

	A	B	C
1	A1	B1	C1
2	A2	B2	C2
3	A3	B3	C3

Cell C2 is in column C, row 2

Figure 4-15 Sample table with formulas in the cells to which they will be applied

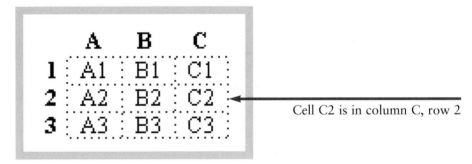

¤	Rent/month¤	Food/month¤	Other/Month¤	Monthly·Total¤	Annual·Total¤
Margot¤	$450¤	$65¤	$340¤	=SUM(LEFT)¤	=E2*12¤
Bart¤	$625¤	$125¤	$385¤	=SUM(LEFT)¤	=E3*12¤
Diane¤	$900¤	$95¤	$290¤	=SUM(LEFT)¤	=E4*12¤

This formula adds all values to the left in its row to get the monthly total

This formula multiplies the contents of cell E4 by 12 to get the annual total

Practice

To practice calculating data in a table, open the student file **Prac4-5**. Save and close the file when you are done.

Hot Tip

Word has several different preset formulas and number formats available to you on the drop-down lists in the Formula dialog box, or you can enter your own into the Formula and Number Format text boxes.

Formatting a Table

Concept

A table's appearance can be changed in many ways. Word's **table formatting** options include, among others, shading, borders, and 3-D effects. You can format individual table elements, or apply an entire set of formatting changes to a table. Both techniques can improve the organization, clarity, and appearance of tables.

Do It!

Juan wants to format his table to improve its appearance.

1. Place the insertion point after the space after the word "Total" and press [Enter].

2. Place the insertion point after the space after the word "Working" and press [Enter].

3. Click and drag the column borders to proportionately match the column widths in the formatted table shown in **Figure 4-16** (your table will not look like this yet).

4. Select columns B and C.

5. Click the Center alignment button on the Formatting toolbar. Word centers the selected columns.

6. Click Table on the menu bar, highlight Select, then click Table to select the entire table. Then press [Ctrl]+[1] (use the number keys above the keyboard, not the numeric keypad) to single-space the text.

7. After deselecting the columns by clicking elsewhere in the table, place the insertion point in the table and click Table, then click Table AutoFormat. The Table AutoFormat dialog box appears with a sample table in its **Preview** box, as shown in **Figure 4-17**.

8. Scroll down in the Formats list box and click Grid8. The Preview box shows the characteristics of this table format.

9. Click the Last Row check box in the Apply special formats to section at the bottom of the Table AutoFormat dialog box. This will visually differentiate your last row from the others, indicating that it contains a different type of information from the other rows.

10. Click [OK] to close the dialog box and apply the specified formatting to your table. It changes from a simple line grid enclosing the data to a clean, professional-looking table (see **Figure 4-16**).

11. Select the entire table as you did in Step 6. Then click the Center button [≡] on the Formatting toolbar to center the table between the left and right margins of the page.

More

You can explore the various formatting options available to you in the Table AutoFormat dialog box by selecting various formats and options and viewing the results in the Preview box. If your table spans more than one page and it has a header row to explain the contents of the columns, you can instruct Word to put the heading at the top of each new page of the table. To do so, place the insertion point in the header (first) row. Click Table, then click Heading Rows Repeat.

Figure 4-16 Formatted table

Occupation	Total (in Millions)	Percent Working at Home
Sales	13.2	6.2
Managerial	14.4	5.2
Professional	15.5	4.9
Service	14.9	3.7
Average		**5**

Figure 4-17 Table AutoFormat dialog box

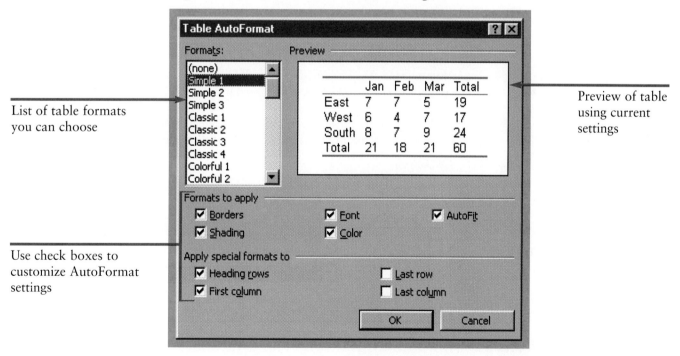

List of table formats you can choose

Use check boxes to customize AutoFormat settings

Preview of table using current settings

Practice

To practice formatting a table, open the student file **Prac4-6**. Save and close the file when you are done.

Hot Tip

Borders applied to a row are moved with it when rows are sorted. Therefore, you should always sort a table before formatting it with Table AutoFormat, or the table could be formatted incorrectly.

Creating a Chart

Concept

Sometimes a table may be more readily understood if it is presented graphically as a chart. Word allows you to create a chart from scratch, or generate it from an existing table.

Do It!

Juan wants to display his table as a chart.

1 Place the insertion point anywhere within the table.

2 Click Table, then highlight Select, and then click Table to select the entire table.

3 Click Insert, then click Object. The Object dialog box appears.

4 Scroll down through the Object Type box and double-click Microsoft Graph 2000 Chart. It opens, turning your table into a Microsoft Graph Datasheet, as shown in **Figure 4-18**. A preliminary chart appears, based on Juan's data and the program's defaults.

5 Click Chart, which now appears as a menu title on the menu bar because the chart is active, then click Chart Options. The Chart Options dialog box appears with the Titles tab on top.

6 Type Home-Based Workers into the Chart title text box. After a brief delay, the title will appear at the top of the preview chart.

7 Press [Tab] to move the insertion point to the Category (X) text box, then type Occupation. After a brief delay, it will appear at the bottom of the preview chart.

8 Click ⬚ OK to create the chart.

9 Close the Datasheet window. The chart you have created appears below Juan's table in a hatched frame, as shown in **Figure 4-19**. Some parts of the chart, especially the labels beneath it, appear cramped and cut off. These will be fixed in the next Skill. Notice that when the chart is selected, positioning the mouse pointer over a column of the chart brings up a ScreenTip displaying both what series the column represents and its exact value.

10 Click the blank area on the right-hand side of the page to deselect the chart.

More

The Chart Type dialog box, available on the Chart menu, has an extensive repertoire of formats you can apply to your charts. The Microsoft Graph application automatically suggests the type of graph or chart that seems to most closely match the format of your data, as all formats are not appropriate for all situations. For example, Juan's table could not be expressed accurately or effectively with a pie chart or radar graph.

Figure 4-18 Chart datasheet created from a table

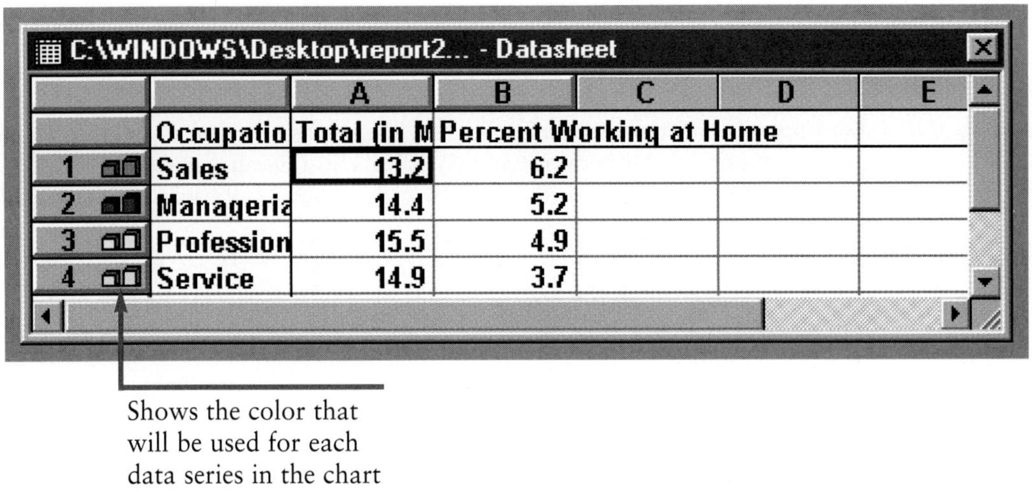

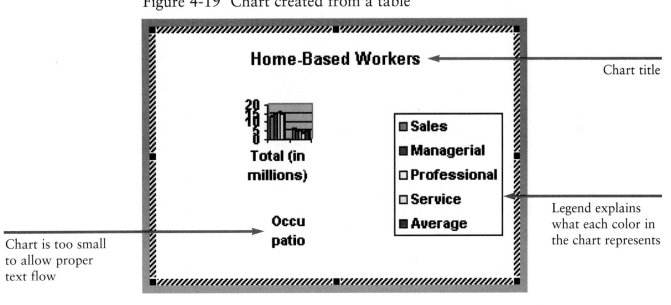

Shows the color that
will be used for each
data series in the chart

Figure 4-19 Chart created from a table

Chart title

Legend explains
what each color in
the chart represents

Chart is too small
to allow proper
text flow

Practice

To practice creating a chart, open the student file **Prac4-7**. Save and close the file when you are done.

Hot Tip

If the proper files have been installed on your computer, you can use the **Help** feature of Microsoft Graph 2000 Chart to find out more about its various capabilities in the same way that you use Word's Help.

Editing a Chart

Concept

Word treats a chart as a graphic object instead of as text, but it still may be modified by accessing the program that created it. You can edit virtually all aspects of a chart including its size, position, and the characteristics of each individual element.

Do It!

Juan is dissatisfied with the appearance of his chart, especially its size and its column labels. He wants to fix these problems and remove the Average column from the chart entirely.

1 Double-click the chart to open **Microsoft Graph**. The Microsoft Graph toolbar will replace the Standard and Formatting toolbars at the top of the screen, and a hatched frame will appear around the chart with sizing handles at its corners and at the midpoint of each side. Close the Datasheet window if it obscures the chart.

2 Click the midpoint sizing handle on the bottom of the chart's frame, drag it downward and release it just below the 4½" mark on the vertical ruler (switch to Print Layout View if you cannot see the vertical ruler). The chart expands vertically, making it possible for more increments to appear along the vertical axis of the chart.

3 Click the midpoint sizing handle on the right side of the frame, then drag the edge of the frame to the right and release it when it is even with the 5½" mark on the horizontal ruler. The chart expands horizontally until it is almost the width of the page, and has room to display the column labels along the bottom without breaking them up awkwardly.

4 Click the **Average** column on the chart. (It is the column farthest to the right.) Dots appear in the corners to indicate that it is selected.

5 Press [**Delete**]. The Average column disappears and the chart is automatically updated, removing its reference from the legend and expanding the other columns slightly to make up for the space left behind by its removal. The chart should now look like the one in **Figure 4-20**.

6 Save and close the document.

More

When working with a chart in a Word document, remember that the chart is a foreign element created by another application. To make changes to the chart itself, you must first double-click it to open its parent application. To alter a chart based on changed data in the table that the chart was created from, you must either alter the datasheet for the table, available on the View menu of the Graph program, or recreate the chart. To act upon the chart as an element of your Word document (that is, move it or copy it to another document), only click it once to select it. A box indicated by sizing handles, not the hatched frame that indicates that its parent application has been opened, will appear around it. Then you may cut the chart and paste it, or move it by dragging it and dropping it to another location within the document. Text added during chart creation, such as the title and category, may be changed by selecting it and entering new text. When selected, a frame will appear around it indicating its selection.

Figure 4-20 Properly modified chart

Graph toolbar

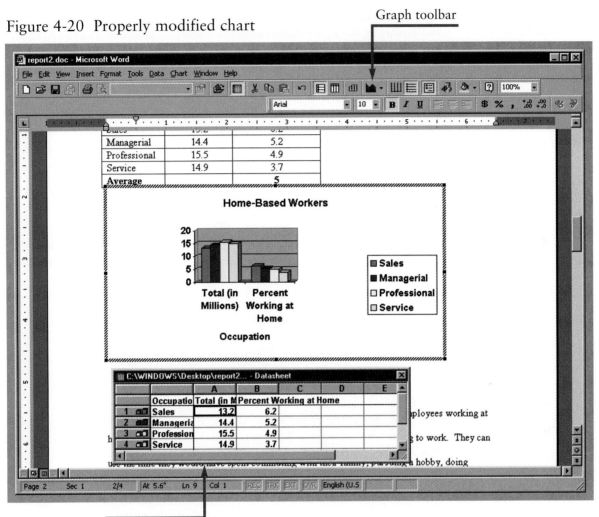

Datasheet will
close when chart
is deselected

Drawing a Table

Concept

As you saw earlier in this lesson, Word allows you to create tables with predefined borders using the Insert Table button. Sometimes, you may want to have more control over the construction of a table. Word makes this possible by letting you draw a table gridline by gridline with the Draw Table tool. Therefore, you can create a table customized precisely for your needs as easily as you can create a standard table.

Do It!

Since Juan and Sabrina's report has involved several steps, Juan wants to create a table to make sure he and Sabrina have completed all the steps required.

1 Click ▫ to open a new blank document.

2 Click the Tables and Borders button ⊞. The Tables and Borders toolbar will appear, floating on the screen. If the toolbar obscures your view of the document window, you can drag it by its title bar to a better location. The document should now be in Print Layout View.

3 Type Sabrina and Juan's Progress Report on the first line of the document and press [Enter].

4 Click the Draw Table button ▱ on the Tables and Borders toolbar. The mouse pointer should look like a pencil when it is over the document.

5 Position the mouse pointer just below the word Sabrina. Then click and drag from that point down and to the right. As you drag, a dashed outline will appear. Release the mouse button when the outline reaches 4 inches on the horizontal ruler and 3 inches on the vertical ruler (see **Figure 4-21**). This rectangle will serve as the outside border of the table.

6 Place the mouse pointer on the top border of the table at the 2-inch mark on the horizontal ruler. Then click and drag straight down to the bottom border, drawing a vertical line in the middle of the table.

7 Place the mouse pointer on the left border of the table at the ½-inch mark on the vertical ruler. Then click and drag straight across to the right border, drawing a horizontal line.

8 Repeat the last step to create horizontal lines in the table every ½ inch. The table should resemble the one shown in **Figure 4-22**.

Figure 4-21 Table border drawn by hand

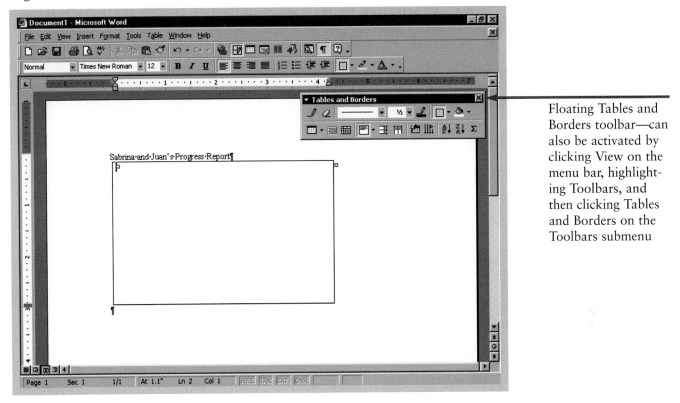

Floating Tables and Borders toolbar—can also be activated by clicking View on the menu bar, highlighting Toolbars, and then clicking Tables and Borders on the Toolbars submenu

Figure 4-22 Table with gridlines drawn

Cell marker

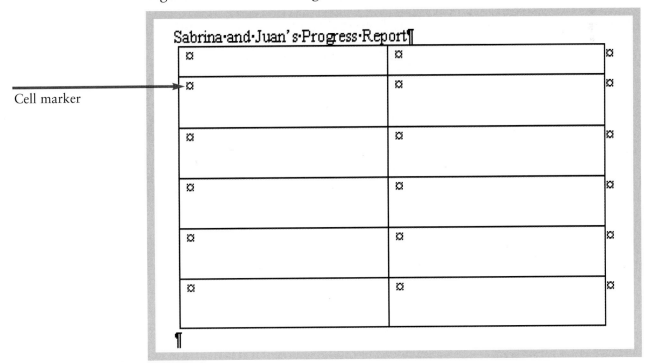

Drawing a Table
(continued)

Do It!

9 Click  to turn off the Draw Table tool.

10 Select the line of text above the table, cut it, and paste it into cell **A1**.

11 Click in the Selection bar next to **Row 1** to select cells A1 and B1.

12 Click the **Merge Cells** button on the Tables and Borders toolbar. Cells A1 and B1 are combined into one cell.

13 With the merged cell still selected, click the **Italic** button. The text in the selected cell is italicized. Click in cell **A2** to place the insertion point there and deselect cell A1. The table should resemble **Figure 4-23**.

14 Type **Task** in cell A2.

15 Press **[Tab]** to move the insertion point to cell **B2**.

16 Type **Completed by** in cell B2.

17 Use the Selection bar to select **Row 2** of the table, and then click the **Underline** button. A line is placed beneath all text in the row.

18 Consult **Figure 4-24** to fill in the rest of the table, then save it as **Progress Table**.

More

You can activate the Draw Table tool to add more gridlines to a table at any time. You also can remove gridlines, thereby eliminating rows and/or columns, by clicking the **Eraser** button on the Tables and Borders toolbar. Simply click on a gridline with the Eraser tool selected to remove the line.

As you have seen, you can apply font formats to text in a table just as you would in a normal document. Most formatting options you have seen applied to text in other scenarios are available in tables as well, including alignment, font, font size, and font color. You can even rotate text in a cell by clicking the **Text Direction** button on the Tables and Borders toolbar.

Figure 4-23 Merged cell with font format applied

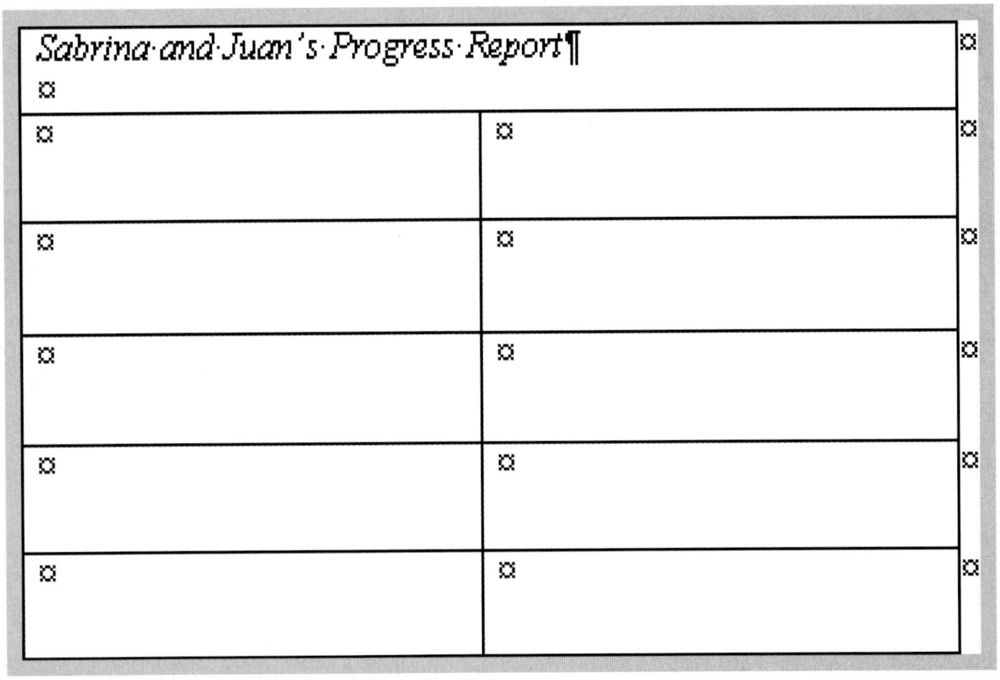

Sabrina·and·Juan's·Progress·Report¶		
¤		
¤	¤	
¤	¤	
¤	¤	
¤	¤	
¤	¤	

Figure 4-24 Completed table

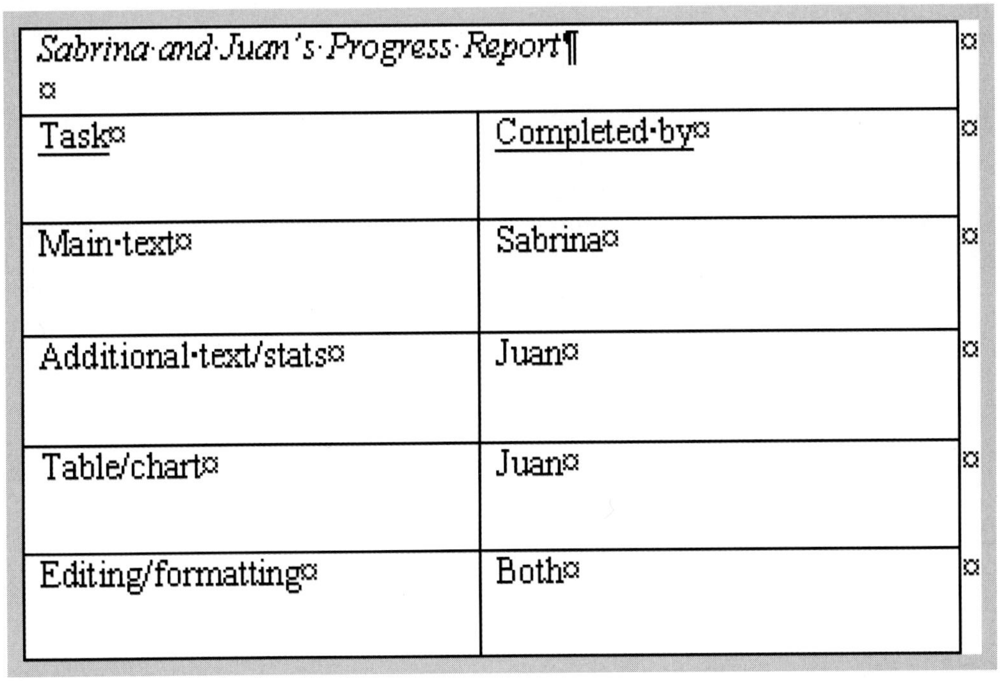

Sabrina·and·Juan's·Progress·Report¶		
¤		
Task¤	Completed·by¤	
Main·text¤	Sabrina¤	
Additional·text/stats¤	Juan¤	
Table/chart¤	Juan¤	
Editing/formatting¤	Both¤	

Practice

Use the Draw Table tool to create a table that will allow you to plot statistics from a survey in which subjects were asked to name their favorite season. Save this table as part of a new document named **Prac4-9**. Close the file when you are done.

Hot Tip

You can transform an existing table into plain text and vice versa by using the Convert command on the Table menu.

Adding Borders and Shading

Concept

Previously in this lesson you enhanced the appearance of a table using the AutoFormat command, which allows you to apply a predetermined set of formats to a table. Although the AutoFormat does offer some options, the degree of control it permits is not great. Just as the Draw Table command gives you greater control over the structure of a table, the Table Properties command opens the door to numerous options for enhancing the appearance of a table.

Do It!

Juan would like to add a customized border and shading to his table.

1 Progress Table should still be the active document. Place the insertion point anywhere within the table, click Table on the menu bar, highlight Select, and then click Table on the submenu. The entire table will be selected.

2 Click Table again, then click Table Properties. The Table Properties dialog box will open to the Table tab.

3 Click the Borders and Shading button Borders and Shading... at the bottom of the tab. The Borders and Shading dialog box opens to the Border tab, shown in **Figure 4-25**.

4 In the Setting section of the tab, click the All option.

5 In the Style box, click the third option, tightly spaced dashes.

6 Click the drop-down arrow at the right edge of the Color box to open a color palette. Then click the blue square.

7 Click the drop-down arrow at the right edge of the Width box to open a list of line weights. Then select the 2¼ pt option.

8 Check the Preview on the right side of the tab to see what the border you have created looks like. Click OK to close the Borders and Shading dialog box.

9 Click OK to close the Tables and Properties dialog box.

10 Click a blank area of the document to deselect the table, which should now appear like the one in **Figure 4-26**.

Figure 4-25 Border tab of Borders and Shading dialog box

Word 2000

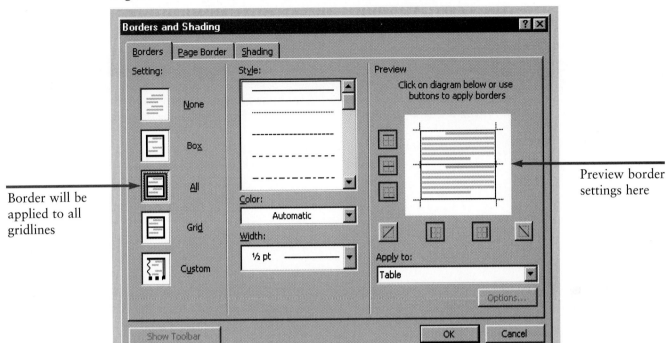

Border will be applied to all gridlines

Preview border settings here

Figure 4-26 Table with border applied

Sabrina and Juan's Progress Report¶ ¤	
Task¤	Completed by¤
Main text¤	Sabrina¤
Additional text/stats¤	Juan¤
Table/chart¤	Juan¤
Editing/formatting¤	Both¤

Adding Borders and Shading (continued)

Do It!

11 Click inside cell A1 to activate the cell.

12 Click the arrow on the right edge of the **Shading Color** button on the Tables and Borders toolbar. The Shading Color palette will appear.

13 Click the **Gray-30%** square (the last square in the first row). Word shades the active cell with the color you selected, as shown in **Figure 4-27**.

14 Click in the Selection bar next to **Row 2** to select the entire row.

15 Shade Row 2 with the color **Red**.

16 Select **Row 4**.

17 Click **Edit,** then click **Repeat Shading Color** to shade the selected row like Row 2. If the Repeat command does not appear right away, leave the Edit menu open for a few seconds until it expands and the command is added.

18 Select **Row 6**.

19 Press the key combination **[Ctrl]+[Y]** on the keyboard, which is a shortcut for the Repeat command.

20 Deselect the table, which should now resemble **Figure 4-28**.

21 Save your changes and close the document.

More

The border options you applied in this Skill also can be accessed from the Tables and Borders toolbar. Likewise, you will find the shading options you applied from the toolbar on the **Shading** tab of the Borders and Shading dialog box. If you choose **More Fill Colors** on the Shading Color palette, you can create custom colors by changing the intensities of a standard color's components. The **Page Border** tab, also in the Borders and Shading dialog box, allows you to add a border to the entire page rather than just to a table.

Figure 4-27 Gray-30% shade applied to cell A1

Sabrina and Juan's Progress Report¶ ¤	
Task¤	Completed·by¤
Main·text¤	Sabrina¤
Additional·text/stats¤	Juan¤
Table/chart¤	Juan¤
Editing/formatting¤	Both¤

Figure 4-28 Red shade applied and repeated

Sabrina and Juan's Progress Report¶ ¤	
Task¤	Completed·by¤
Main·text¤	Sabrina¤
Additional·text/stats¤	Juan¤
Table/chart¤	Juan¤
Editing/formatting¤	Both¤

Practice

Return to the file **Prac4-6**, which includes a table that you AutoFormatted. Change the alternating shaded rows to blue and orange, and the borders around the first and last rows to dashed lines. Save the file as **Prac4-10** and close it when you finish.

Hot Tip

The listing of the Repeat command on the Edit menu will change to include the action that will be repeated when you execute the command. You can only repeat the action you performed most recently.

Shortcuts

Function	Button/Mouse	Menu	Keyboard
Insert a Table	⊞	Click Table, then click Insert Table	
Insert a row above the selected row	Right-click the selected row, then click Insert Rows (or click ⊞⊏)	Click Table, then highlight Insert, then click Rows Above	
Insert a column to the left of the selected column	Right-click the selected column, then click Insert Columns (or click ⊟)	Click Table, then highlight Insert, then click Columns to the Left	
Delete the selected row	Right-click the selected row, then click Delete Rows	Click Table, then click Delete Rows	[Shift]+[Delete]
Delete the selected column	Right-click the selected column, then click Delete Columns	Click Table, then click Delete Columns	[Shift]+[Delete]
Align selected text in a cell or paragraph to the left	▤		[Ctrl]+[L]
Align selected text in a cell or paragraph to the right	▤		[Ctrl]+[R]
Center selected text in a cell or paragraph	▤		[Ctrl]+[E]
Justify selected text in a cell or paragraph	▤		[Ctrl]+[J]
Repeat last action		Click Edit, then click Repeat (action name)	[Ctrl]+[Y]

Identify Key Features

Name the items indicated by callouts in Figure 4-29.

Figure 4-29 Identifying components of a table

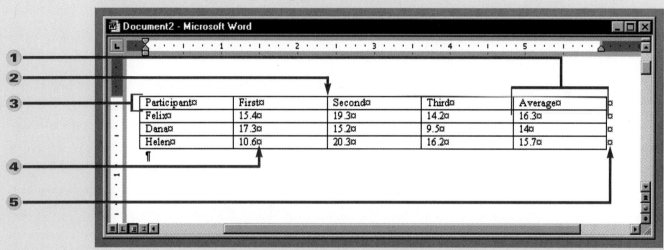

Select the Best Answer

6. Indicates a selected chart		a. Descending
7. An order in which data can be sorted		b. Gridlines
8. Appears when you right-click a table		c. Table shortcut menu
9. Explains the symbols and colors being used in a chart		d. Hatched border
10. Visible boundary between cells in a basic table		e. Legend
11. An existing worksheet that becomes part of a Word document		f. Embedded object
12. What Word uses to calculate data		g. Formatting
13. The basic unit of a table		h. Cell
14. Enhances the information presented in a table		i. Formula
15. Rearranging data in a table by category		j. Chart
16. A graphic representation of a table		k. Sorting

Quiz (continued)

Complete the Statement

17. The Insert Table button:

    a. Creates a table based on the Normal template

    b. Creates a table based on dimensions you choose

    c. Pastes data from the Clipboard into a table

    d. Replaces the desktop with a tabletop

18. To move the insertion point to the next cell in the current row:

    a. Press [End]

    b. Use the right arrow key on the keyboard

    c. Press [Tab]

    d. Double-click the table

19. D14 refers to:

    a. The fourteenth cell in the fourth column

    b. The fourteenth cell in the fourth row

    c. A formula

    d. A document designation for a Word table

20. Paragraphs and table columns both have:

    a. Page numbers

    b. Selection bars

    c. Gridlines

    d. Cell markers

21. The first step in creating a chart from a selected table is:

    a. Clicking the Chart button

    b. Pressing [Ctrl]+[F8]

    c. Clicking Insert, then clicking Chart

    d. Clicking Insert, then clicking Object

22. The Chart legend:

    a. Is about the ChartWizard

    b. Must be created in Excel and inserted into the Word document containing the chart it belongs with

    c. Contains the Color buttons

    d. Explains the meaning of colors used in the chart

23. An equal sign must be written before a formula or Word will:

    a. Read the data as a label and not perform any calculations

    b. Use the wrong data to perform the calculations

    c. Use the right data, but perform the calculations incorrectly

    d. Do nothing

24. You may delete columns by accessing the:

    a. Table menu

    b. Tools menu

    c. Edit menu

    d. Format menu

25. To sort data in a table you should:

    a. Open the Sort dialog box, and use it to sort the data

    b. Cut and paste all of the information you would use to sort the data

    c. Sort it yourself on a piece of scrap paper before entering the data on the computer

    d. You must access a program other than Word

Interactivity

Test Your Skills

1. Open a new document and create a table:

   a. Open a new Word document.

   b. Click **Table**, then click **Insert Table** to open the Insert Table dialog box.

   c. Create a table that is **4 rows by 5 columns**.

2. Add data to the table:

   a. Enter a name into each of the lower three cells in the leftmost column.

   b. Insert a number between **1** and **100** into each of the three cells to the right of each name, for a total of nine cells.

   c. Label the cells in the top row as follows: **Name, March, April, May,** and **Average**.

3. Average the columns and sort the table:

   a. Position the insertion point in the second cell down in the last column, which is cell **E2**.

   b. Click Table, then click **Formula** to open the Formula dialog box.

   c. Enter the formula **=AVERAGE(B2:D2)** into the Formula text box and press **[Enter]**.

   d. Repeat the last three steps for the other two cells in the Average column, making sure that you are using the correct cell references for the appropriate calculation.

   e. Sort the table in the order of **descending** Average.

4. Format the table:

   a. Place the insertion point within the table and click Table, then click **Table AutoFormat**.

   b. Select a table format that you like and check the boxes that you want in the **Formats to apply** section of the dialog box.

   c. Make sure that both the **Heading rows** and **First column** check boxes are checked in the **Apply special formats to** section of the dialog box and press **[Enter]**.

   d. Shade the first row of the table with **Gray-15%** and apply a green **Box** border to the entire table.

   e. Save the document to your student disk as **Test 4**.

5. Create a chart from an existing table:

   a. Select the table you created above.

   b. Create a chart using an appropriate type for the data.

   c. Edit and format the chart as necessary.

   d. Save the document as **Test 4-Chart**.

Interactivity (continued)

Problem Solving

1. Create a table that will allow you to display the high and low temperatures for each of the last five days (use fictional numbers if you do not have these data available). Add a column to the table that will allow you to include the average high and low temperatures for the five-day period, and calculate these averages. Then convert the table into a chart. Finally, add a row to the bottom of the table, merge the cells, and enter your name. Save the file as Solved4-1.

2. Create a table to help calculate the grade point averages of the students you have been tutoring the last two years.

   a. Using the data below, calculate the Grade Point Average for every student, over the two-year period.

   b. Calculate the combined GPA of all the students for each individual semester that you tutored those students.

   c. Calculate the overall GPA, including every student, over the two-year period.

   d. Sort the table by the highest individual GPA over the two years, as found in question a.

   e. AutoFormat the table with a Colorful style, applying special formats to heading rows, the last row, and the first column. Make sure your name is included in the document, and save it as Solved4-2.

Student	Semester 1	Semester 2	Semester 3	Semester 4
Steven	3.6	3.1	4.0	2.7
Sarah	3.3	3.9	3.5	3.0
Donny	2.8	2.3	2.4	3.7
Melanie	3.1	1.4	2.9	2.5
Ray	1.7	2.6	2.0	3.1

3. As the leader of a public relations team, you are responsible for your employees' business expenses. Create a table to calculate information about their expenses over the first half of the year. Format all dollar amounts with dollar signs and two decimal places. (Hint: the table will probably fit best in Landscape page orientation.)

   a. Using the data below, figure out the total each employee spent.

   b. Figure out the total the entire team spent over the six-month period.

   c. Figure out the average amount spent by each employee over the six-month period.

   d. Figure out the average amount spent by the team every month.

   e. Turn the table you created into a chart. Use the default Chart type to create a chart representing the table you created. Make any modifications on the chart you feel are necessary to make it as easy to understand as possible.

   f. Add your name to the document and save it as Solved4-3.

Employees	Jan	Feb	Mar	Apr	May	June
Kit	213	306	176	314	86	103
Pam	143	94	207	77	289	304
Joe	332	256	317	258	112	128

L E S S O N

1

INTRODUCTION TO SPREADSHEET SOFTWARE

Microsoft Excel is a computer application that improves your ability to record data and then extract results from it. With Excel, you can enter text labels and numerical values into an electronic spreadsheet, a grid made up of columns and rows. The computerized worksheets you work with in Excel resemble handwritten ledgers with which you may already be familiar. Being able to use spreadsheet software can help you both professionally and personally. By providing an organized structure in which to work, Excel can increase the efficiency with which you conduct business and track your own affairs. Excel's ability to perform and automate calculations saves time and decreases the possibility of error.

Using Excel, you will learn how to create a spreadsheet employing proper design techniques. You will then explore the application and become familiar with its basic elements and operations. Later on, some of Excel's more advanced features such as formulas, What-If analysis, and macros will broaden your knowledge of how to create and work with a spreadsheet. If you need assistance while using Excel, the program includes an extensive Help facility, as well as the ability to access online support via the World Wide Web.

CASE STUDY

Kay Samoy is the owner of a small but successful company that distributes a wide variety of dog accessories such as treats, furnishings, and toys. She would like to use Excel to track her income, expenses, and profits electronically now that her business is growing. Kay will begin by familiarizing herself with the application. Then she will take the first steps toward creating an effective spreadsheet.

Introducing Excel and Worksheet Design

Concept

Microsoft Excel is an electronic spreadsheet application designed to make the creation and use of professional quality spreadsheets fast and easy. A **spreadsheet** is a table composed of rows and columns that store text and numbers for easy viewing and tabulation. Electronic spreadsheets are very useful for performing rapid and accurate calculations on groups of interrelated numbers. Using Excel, you can

- Organize information rapidly and accurately. With the proper data and formulas, Excel calculates your results automatically.

- Recalculate automatically. Fixing errors in Excel is easy. When you find a mistake and correct the entry, Excel automatically recalculates all related data.

- Keep track of the effect that changing one piece of data has on related numbers. You can postulate changes that may occur in the future and see how they could change the results of your calculations—a feature called **What-If** analysis.

- Display data as graphs or charts. Excel allows you to display numeric data graphically in the form of charts that are automatically updated as the data change. For example, **Figure 1-1** shows the data in a spreadsheet for income and expenditures that also can be displayed in the form of a pie chart. Charts often make relationships among data easier to understand.

The spreadsheet's organization is shaped by its goal or purpose. A well-designed spreadsheet should be accurate and easily understood and should include the four sections visible in **Figure 1-2**: documentation, assumptions, input, and results.

- The first section contains **documentation**, consisting of a complete description of the name of the author, the purpose of the spreadsheet, the date it was created, and the name of the spreadsheet file. Documentation also should specify location of any cell ranges and macros. Ranges are blocks of columns and rows that are useful for performing certain types of calculations and for displaying data. Macros are instructions for automating spreadsheet tasks.

- The second section of a spreadsheet is used to display **assumptions**. Assumptions are variable factors that may change in a worksheet. For example, Kay's profit projections assume that sales will expand by 10 percent each quarter. When her sales numbers are changed, they will affect the amount of profit. It is easier to change documented assumptions than undocumented ones. Assumptions are useful when conducting "What-If" analysis based on calculating the effect of changes in spreadsheet data. For instance, what if sales only grow by 5 percent? You will learn more about What-If analysis in Lesson 2.

- The third section of the spreadsheet stores **input**, the numbers that you enter and manipulate. In **Figure 1-2**, the input section contains data for income and expenditures. Input data are generally arranged in blocks of numbers organized in columns and rows.

- The fourth section is a **results**, or output, section, which displays the results of the calculations made on the input data. Output data are generally placed below and to the right of input data.

More

Microsoft Excel stores each workbook you create as an individual document in the computer's memory. A document, also called a file, can be a single worksheet or may contain many pages of data and graphs. Each file should be given a unique name so it can be easily differentiated from other files. Excel documents are given the file extension **.xls**. A file extension is a three-letter code separated from the file name with a period, called a dot, that tells the computer what application is associated with a particular file. When saving files, you should avoid using periods in file names and never change the .xls extension.

Figure 1-1 A worksheet made with Microsoft Excel

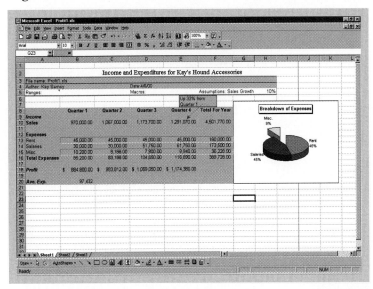

Figure 1-2 Organization of a spreadsheet

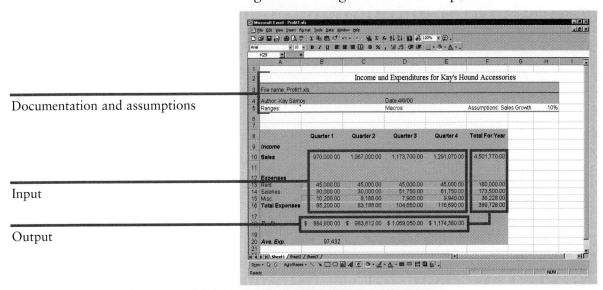

Documentation and assumptions

Input

Output

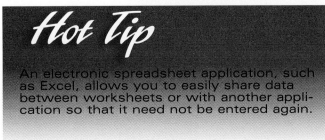

Hot Tip

An electronic spreadsheet application, such as Excel, allows you to easily share data between worksheets or with another application so that it need not be entered again.

 **Starting Excel**

Concept

To use the Microsoft Excel program, or application, the user must first open it. The act of opening an application also can be called running, starting, or launching. In the Windows environment, you can launch a program in a number of ways, including using desktop and Start menu shortcuts, using the Run command, double-clicking executable file icons, and clicking a Windows Quick Launch toolbar button.

Do It!

Kay wants to open the Microsoft Excel application so she can begin to construct a worksheet.

1 Make sure the computer, monitor, and any other necessary peripheral devices are turned on. The Windows desktop should appear on your screen. Your screen may differ slightly from the one shown.

2 Locate the Windows taskbar, usually found at the bottom of your screen. Use the mouse to guide the pointer over the Start button, on the left side of the taskbar, and click [Start]. This will open the Windows Start menu.

3 Move the mouse pointer ⟲ up the Start menu to Programs, highlighting it. The Programs menu will be displayed as shown in **Figure 1-3**.

4 Position the pointer over Microsoft Excel to highlight it, and then click once to open the application. (If Excel is not there, try looking under Microsoft Office on the Start menu.) Excel will open with a blank worksheet in the window as shown in **Figure 1-4**.

More

Each computer can vary in its setup depending on its hardware and software configurations. Therefore, your Excel startup procedure may be slightly different from that described above. The Windows environment allows you to place shortcuts to a program's executable (.exe) file in various places. For example, the Excel listing on the Programs menu is a shortcut. You also can place shortcuts on the desktop, or even on the first level of the Start menu. Because you can customize the Excel program, your screen may not look exactly like the one shown in **Figure 1-4**.

Figure 1-3 Windows desktop and Start menu

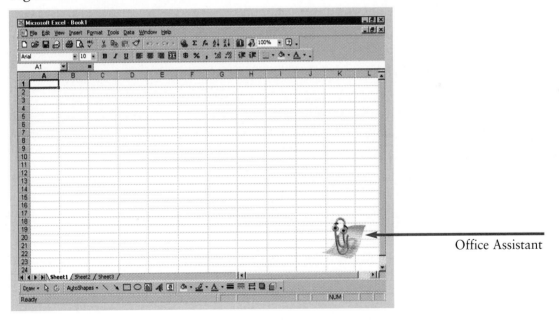

Start menu

Start button

Programs menu

Taskbar

Excel 2000

Figure 1-4 Excel window

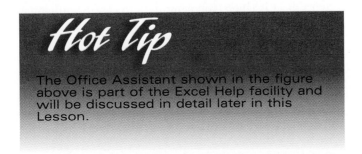

Office Assistant

Hot Tip

The Office Assistant shown in the figure above is part of the Excel Help facility and will be discussed in detail later in this Lesson.

Exploring the Excel Screen

Concept

In order to begin building a spreadsheet, it is necessary to become familiar with the Excel window and worksheet elements.

Do It!

To familiarize herself with the Excel screen, Kay will click on various elements of the window.

1 Click the Maximize button ▣, located at the right side of the title bar, to enlarge the Excel window so that it fills your entire screen. The title bar at the top of the Excel window displays the name of the program and the title of the current worksheet that is open. When Excel opens, it automatically creates a new, empty worksheet file called Book1. The title bar also houses the Minimize ▬, Maximize ▣ or Restore ▣, and Close buttons ✕ used to resize the window. The Minimize button reduces the window to its program button on the taskbar. The Maximize button will appear if the Excel window has not been enlarged to fill the entire screen, and the Restore button, which returns the window to its previous size and location, will appear if the window is maximized. Double-clicking the title bar will also maximize or restore a window.

2 Click File to open the File menu, then guide the pointer over each menu to familiarize yourself with the different commands. The main menu bar is usually displayed right below the title bar. The menu bar contains lists with most of Excel's commands. Each word in the menu bar can be clicked to open a pull-down menu of commands. Or a menu may be opened by pressing the [Alt] key and the underlined letter in the menu name. The menu bar also contains a set of sizing buttons. These controls function in the same manner as the application sizing buttons, only they apply to the active workbook window, not the entire Excel program. You can have more than one workbook window open in the Excel program window.

3 Move the pointer over the New button ▣. A brief description of the button's function, a ScreenTip, will appear in a small rectangle below the button. Guide the pointer over the toolbars, pausing on each button to read its description, as shown in **Figure 1-5**. The two rows of icons beneath the menu bar are called toolbars. Toolbar buttons provide shortcuts to many of Excel's most commonly used commands. You can customize the toolbars to contain the tools that you use most often. The top toolbar in **Figure 1-5** is called the Standard toolbar, and the lower toolbar is called the Formatting toolbar.

4 Click the Select All button, the gray rectangle in the upper-left corner of the worksheet where the row and column headings meet. The entire worksheet becomes highlighted, and the row and column heading buttons will become depressed. The worksheet is where you enter data to create your spreadsheet. A spreadsheet can contain many worksheets, and together multiple worksheets make up a workbook.

More

The Standard toolbar and Formatting toolbar are just two of the many toolbars available in Excel. To view and activate additional toolbars, open the View menu from the menu bar and highlight the Toolbars command. A submenu of toolbar names will appear. Click a toolbar to activate it. Excel toolbars are flexible objects. You can anchor them to any side of the Excel window by clicking and dragging, or float them over the middle of the Excel screen. If all the buttons associated with a particular toolbar do not fit on the toolbar due to window or screen size, a small arrow button will appear at the end of the toolbar. Click on the arrow to reveal a menu of the remaining buttons. In Excel 2000, the default setting for the Standard and Formatting toolbars positions them side by side in one row beneath the menu bar. For this book, these toolbars have been positioned in separate rows so that more buttons are visible on each of them. To change your setup so that these toolbars appear in two rows, click Tools to open the Tools menu, and then click the Customize command. On the Options tab in the Customize dialog box, click the check box labeled Standard and Formatting toolbars share one row to clear the check mark from it. Then close the dialog box.

You may have noticed that the Excel window contains two sets of sizing buttons. The top set, in the window's title bar, controls the Excel application window. The bottom set controls the active Excel document.

Excel 2000

Figure 1-5 Elements of the Excel application window

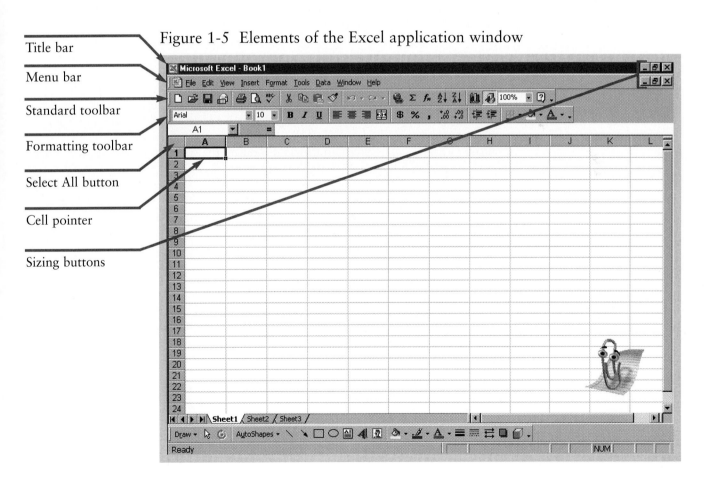

Title bar

Menu bar

Standard toolbar

Formatting toolbar

Select All button

Cell pointer

Sizing buttons

Exploring the Excel Screen (continued)

Do It!

5 Click the letter A that heads the first column. Column A becomes highlighted, as shown in **Figure 1-6**. The columns are designated by letters, from A to Z, then AA to AZ and so on up to IV, altogether making 256 columns.

6 Click the number 1 at the left of the first row. Row 1 becomes highlighted. The rows are labeled numerically down the left side of the worksheet, from 1 to 65,536.

7 Click the intersection of column D and row 7. Cell D7 is now active. Excel designates the active cell on the worksheet by bordering it with a dark rectangle called a cell pointer. Rows intersect with columns forming the grid system. Each intersection of a row and a column is called a cell. Cells are identified by an address composed of the letter and number of the column and row that intersect to form the cell. When a cell is active, you can enter new data into it or edit any data that are already there. You can make another cell active by clicking it, or by moving the cell pointer with the arrow keys found on the keyboard.

8 Click cell H9. Below the second row of icons are the name box and the formula bar. The Name box displays the active cell address, H9, and the formula bar displays the data that you are working on, along with their location on the worksheet. The formula bar is now blank.

9 Double-click cell H9. At the bottom of the Excel screen is the status bar, which changes in response to the task in progress. As **Figure 1-7** shows, "Enter" should now appear in the status bar indicating that you can enter a label, data, or a formula into the cell. The left side of this bar displays a brief description of Excel's current activities. The boxes to the right indicate the status of particular keys, such as the Caps Lock key.

10 Click the down arrow on the vertical scroll bar to move the spreadsheet down one row, hiding row 1. The vertical scroll bar on the far right side of the worksheet window and the horizontal scroll bar on the lower edge of the worksheet window help you move quickly around the worksheet.

11 Below the active worksheet, Excel provides Sheet tabs that you can click to switch to other worksheets in the open workbook. Click the Sheet2 tab. Notice that the cell pointer moved from H9, the active cell on Sheet1, to cell A1, the active cell on Sheet2. Related worksheets can be arranged together in workbooks. Book1 in the title bar actually stands for Workbook 1. Workbooks can contain up to 255 worksheets. Sheet tab scrolling buttons (in the lower-left corner of the window) help you view worksheet tabs not in the window.

Figure 1-6 Selecting a column

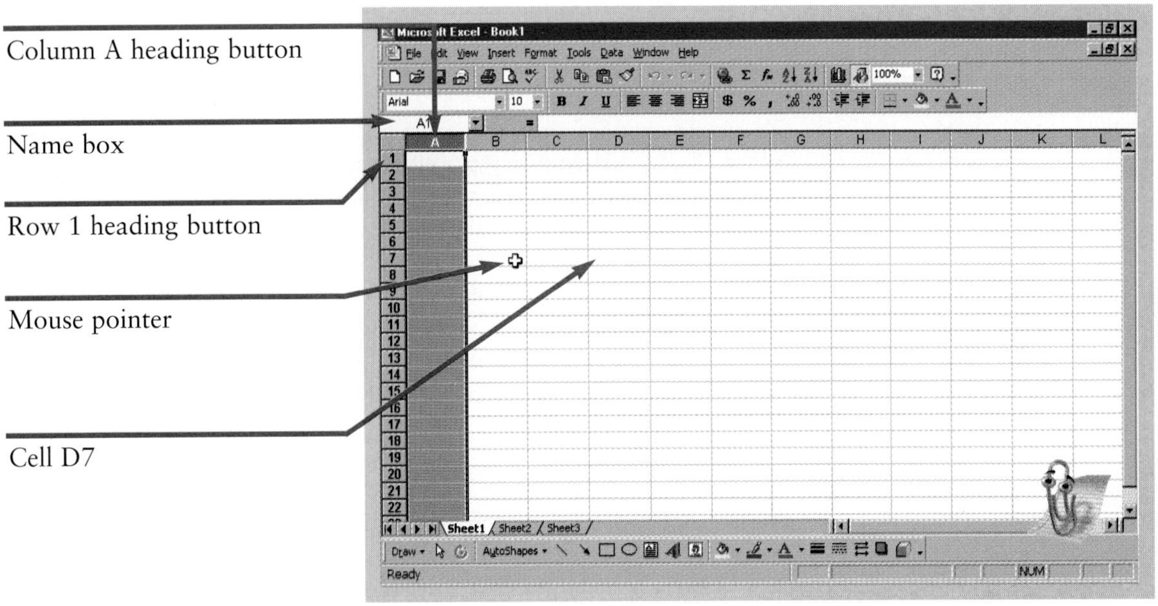

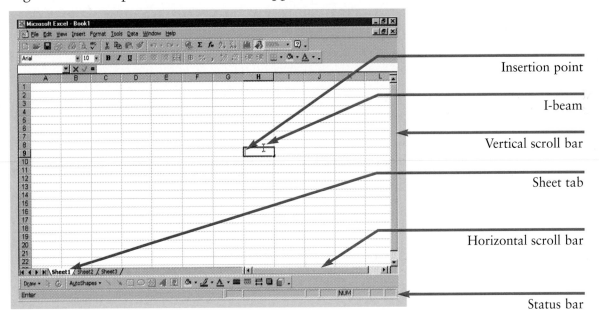

Column A heading button

Name box

Row 1 heading button

Mouse pointer

Cell D7

Excel 2000

Figure 1-7 Components of the Excel application window

Insertion point

I-beam

Vertical scroll bar

Sheet tab

Horizontal scroll bar

Status bar

Practice

To practice what you have learned in this Skill, click the Minimize button on the menu bar to minimize the document window and display it as a small title bar at the bottom of the window. Then click its Maximize button to enlarge the document.

Hot Tip

The document and application control menu icons, at the left end of the menu and title bars respectively, offer menus containing the Close and sizing commands.

Moving Around the Worksheet

Concept

To effectively use Excel, you must be able to maneuver between cells in the workspace. To do this you may use either the mouse or the keyboard, depending on your personal preference or your current activity. For example, if you are entering a large quantity of data quickly into cells that are close together, it may be easier and more efficient to use the keyboard. If you need to select a cell that is far from the active cell, using the mouse would probably be more effective.

Do It!

Kay moves to various points on the Excel worksheet to familiarize herself with Excel's navigation.

1. Using the mouse, move the mouse pointer ✚ to cell **B4** and click the left mouse button. The cell becomes highlighted, marking it as the active cell.

2. Press [←]. The cell pointer moves over one cell to the left to **A4**.

3. Press [↑]. The cell pointer moves up one cell to **A3**.

4. Press the [→], then [↓] to return the cell pointer to cell **B4**.

5. Click once on the arrow at the right end of the horizontal scroll bar. The worksheet will scroll right by one column.

6. Scroll down one row by clicking once on the arrow at the bottom vertical scroll bar.

7. Click the horizontal scroll bar arrow until column **Z** is visible. Notice that the scroll bar box shrinks to allow you a larger movement area, as seen in **Figure 1-8**.

8. Click and hold the mouse button on the horizontal scroll bar box. You have now grabbed the box. Drag the box to the left until you can see column **A**.

Figure 1-8 Getting around the Excel application window

Name box displays selected cell, B4, even though it is not currently visible

Row 4 button bold, indicating that a cell in that row is selected

Column names extend past Z and begin again with AA, AB, etc.

Horizontal scroll bar box

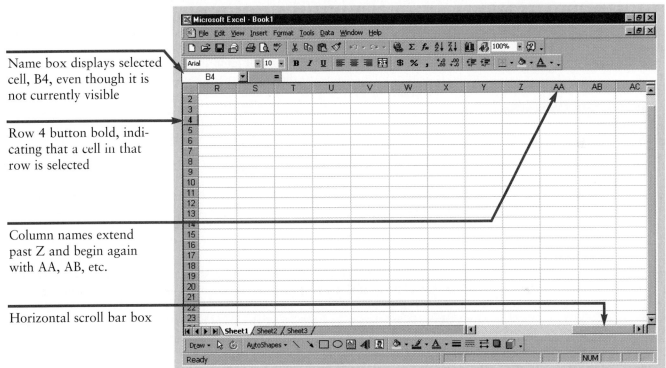

Moving Around the Worksheet (continued)

Do It!

9 Click Edit, then select Go To. The Go To dialog box, shown in **Figure 1-9**, appears. The Go To command is useful when you have to move a great distance across the worksheet.

10 At the bottom of the dialog box there is a text box, the white area with a flashing insertion point, labeled Reference. Type Y95 in the Reference text box.

11 Click [OK]. Excel's cell pointer highlights cell Y95 in the worksheet.

12 Press [Ctrl]+[Home]. The cell pointer will jump to cell A1. The [Ctrl]+[Home] command is helpful for returning to the beginning of a worksheet.

More

At the bottom of the worksheet are three tabs labeled Sheet1, Sheet2, and Sheet3. A workbook is often made up of many worksheets, and each tab corresponds to a different worksheet. Interrelated data can be kept across multiple worksheets of the same workbook for viewing, cross referencing, and calculation. To go to a different worksheet, simply click its tab at the bottom of the window. New worksheets can be added to a workbook by using the Worksheet command on the Insert menu. The new worksheet will appear before the active worksheet.

You can move a worksheet to a different place in the worksheet hierarchy by dragging its tab to the desired place in the row of tabs. The mouse pointer will appear with a blank sheet attached to it ▯ and a small arrow ▼ will indicate where the worksheet will be placed when you release the mouse button. The tab scrolling buttons ◄◄ ◄ ► ►►, located to the left of the sheet tabs, allow you to view tabs that do not fit in the window. Clicking one of the outer buttons moves you to the beginning or end of the list of tabs, while clicking one of the inner buttons will move you through the tabs one at a time.

If you right-click the tab scrolling buttons, a pop-up menu listing all of the tabs in your workbook will appear, allowing you to select a specific tab to jump to. Tabs can be renamed by double-clicking the tab to select its text, and then editing it like normal text. Right-clicking a tab opens a shortcut pop-up menu with commands that allow you to rename, delete, insert, and copy or move a worksheet.

Some of the more common methods of moving around a worksheet are outlined in **Table 1-1**.

Table 1-1 Moving in a worksheet

MOVEMENT	ACTION
Left one cell	Press [←] or [Shift]+[Tab]
Right one cell	Press [→] or [Tab]
Up one cell	Press [↑] or [Shift]+[Enter]
Down one cell	Press [↓] or [Enter] (in default setup)
Left one column or right one column	Click the left arrow or right arrow on the horizontal scroll bar
Up one row or down one row	Click the up arrow or down arrow on the vertical scroll bar.
Up one screen or down one screen	Press [Page Up] or [Page Down]
Left one screen or right one screen	Press [Alt]+[Page Up] or [Alt]+[Page Down]
Go to cell A1	[Ctrl]+[Home]
Go to column A in current row	[Home]

Figure 1-9 Go To dialog box

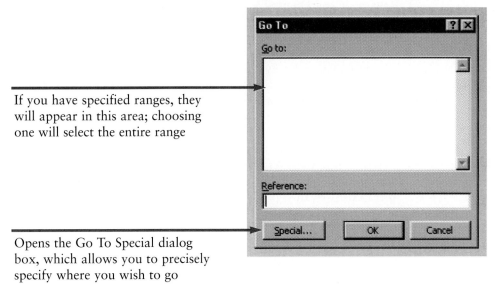

If you have specified ranges, they will appear in this area; choosing one will select the entire range

Opens the Go To Special dialog box, which allows you to precisely specify where you wish to go

Practice

Click cell E12 to make it active, then use the arrow keys to move the cell pointer to cell G7. Open the Go To dialog box and navigate to cell CT2041. Finally, position the cell pointer in cell A1.

Hot Tip

To move across a large area of blank cells press [End]. The word END will appear in the status bar. Then press an arrow key. The cell pointer will jump to the next filled cell in the direction of the arrow key pressed.

Excel 2000

Entering Labels

Concept

Labels are used to annotate and describe the data you place into rows and columns. Properly labeled data make your spreadsheet easy to understand and interpret. Labels can consist of text or numbers and are aligned left so as to differentiate them from data used in calculations. Excel automatically left-justifies labels. Labels should be entered into your spreadsheet first so that your rows and columns are defined before you begin to enter the calculable data.

Do It!

Kay enters the documentation and row labels for her spreadsheet.

1 Click cell **A2** to make it the active cell. The address A2 appears in the name box.

2 Type **Income and Expenditures for Kay's Hound Accessories**, then click the Enter button ☑. The label will appear in the formula bar as you type. Even though the label is longer than the cell width, it will be displayed in its entirety as long as the next cell remains empty.

3 Click cell **A3** and type **File name: Profit1.xls**, then press [Enter]. The label will be entered and the cell pointer will move down one row to cell A4.

4 Type **Author: Kay Samoy**, click cell **D4** and type **Date: 4/6/00**. In cell **A5** type **Ranges:**, in cell **D5** type **Macros:**, and in cell **F5** type **Assumptions: Sales Growth**. These labels are the documentation for your spreadsheet. Documentation describes and titles your spreadsheet. It contains the purpose, file name and author of the spreadsheet, the date it was created, as well as defining any ranges, macros, and assumptions that it may contain.

5 Click cell **A8** to make it the active cell. Type **Income** and then press [Enter]. The next six labels will be the row headings.

6 Type **Sales**, then press [Enter]; skip a cell and in cell **A11** type **Expenditures**, then press [Enter]; in cell **A12** type **Rent**, then press [Enter]; in cell **A13** type **Salaries**, then press [Enter]; in cell **A14** type **Misc.**, then press [Enter]; and in cell **A15** type **Total Expenses**, then press [Enter]. Your worksheet should now look like the one shown in **Figure 1-10**.

More

The Enter button on the formula bar functions in much the same way as the [Enter] key on the keyboard, but after you click the Enter button, the cell pointer remains in the current cell instead of moving to the cell beneath. The Enter button disappears after you use it, but you can bring it back by clicking the text box on the formula bar. The Cancel button ☒ not only removes the contents from a cell, but also restores the cell's previous contents, if there were any.

Excel automatically assumes that a number is a value and aligns it to the right by default. If you wish to use a number as a label, simply type an apostrophe ['] before the number. The data will then be aligned to the left. The apostrophe will be hidden in the cell, but will be shown in the formula bar.

Figure 1-10 Entering labels

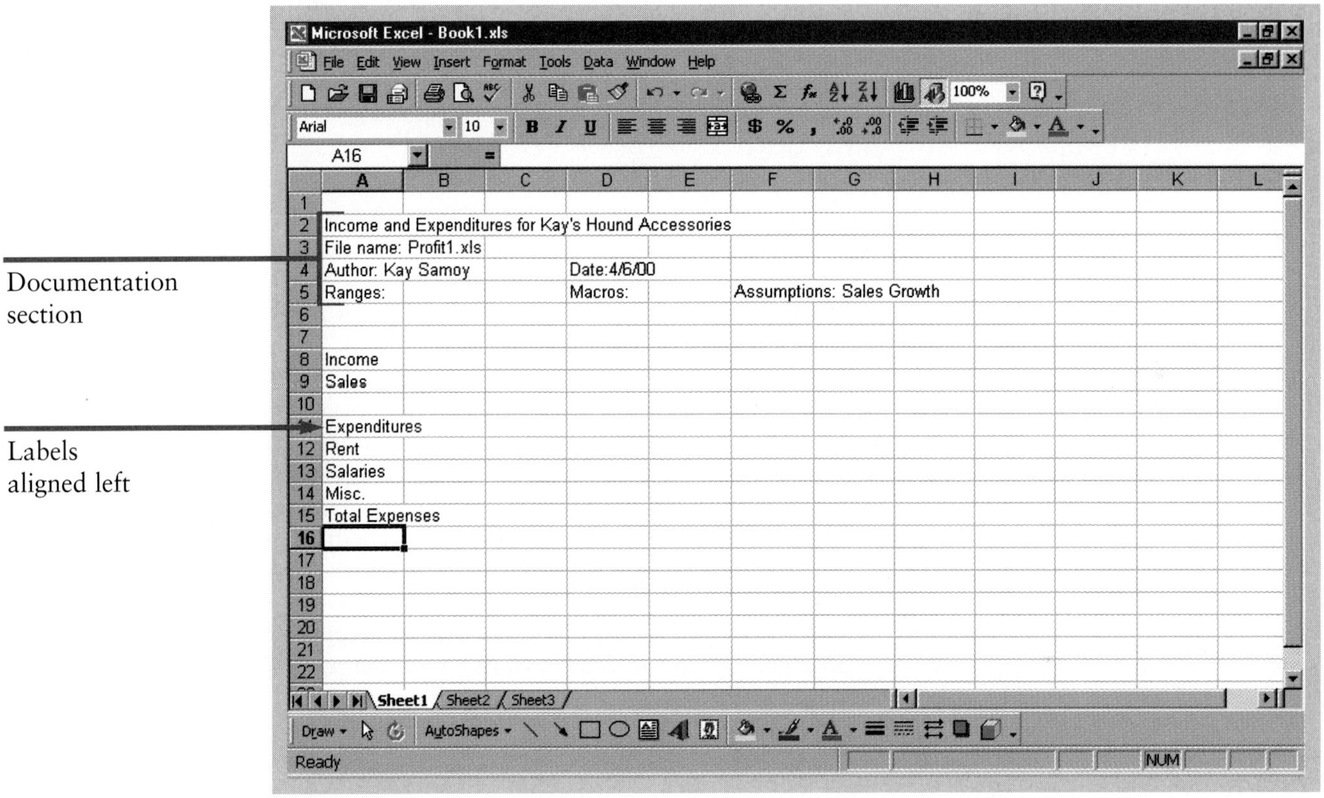

Documentation section

Labels aligned left

Practice

Click the **New** button to open a new workbook. Beginning in cell A2, enter the following cell labels, pressing **[Enter]** after each: your name, today's date, your instructor's name, and the title of this course. Leave the file open for use in the next Skill.

Hot Tip

If you start to enter a label whose first few letters match those of an adjacent cell in the column, Excel will automatically complete the label to match. If you do not wish to accept the suggestion, simply continue typing to overwrite Excel's suggestion.

Saving and Closing a Worksheet

Concept

Saving your work is important; if not saved, work can be lost due to power or computer failure. Once a file has been saved, it can be reopened at any time for editing or viewing. Your workbook can be saved to a hard drive, floppy disk, network drive, or even a Web server. Closing a file removes it from the screen and puts it away for later use. You can close a file while leaving the application open for use with other Excel files. Or, if you are finished using Excel, you can exit the application.

Do It!

Kay wants to save her worksheet under the name Profit1 in a folder titled Kay's Hound Accessories.

1 Click Window, then select Book1.xls from the menu if it is not already active. Book1.xls will become the active document.

2 Click File, then click Save As. Notice that the Save As command is followed by an ellipsis (three dots), indicating that a dialog box will open when the command is executed. The Save As dialog box opens, as shown in **Figure 1-11**. (If you had chosen the Save command, the Save As dialog would have appeared anyway, as this is the first time you will be saving your document.) The file name Book1.xls automatically appears highlighted in the File name: text box, ready to be changed.

3 To give the workbook file a more distinctive name, type **Profit1**. The .xls file extension will automatically be added. As you type the name, Book1.xls will be overwritten. Windows 95, 98, and 2000 support file names of up to 255 characters. The file name can contain uppercase or lowercase letters, numbers, and most symbols.

4 Click the Save in list arrow to choose where to save the file. Excel is programmed to save newly created files in the My Documents folder by default. Click 3½ Floppy (A:) if your student files will be stored on a floppy disk or Maindisk (C:) if your student files are to be stored on your hard drive. Consult your instructor if you have any doubts about this matter.

5 Click the Create New Folder button ⬜. The New Folder dialog box will appear with the folder name New Folder highlighted in the Name: text box, as shown in **Figure 1-12**.

Figure 1-11 Save As dialog box

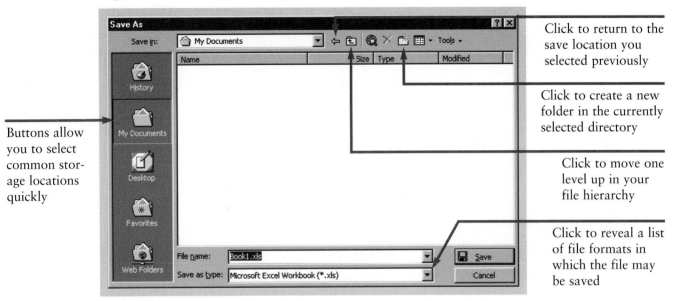

Click to return to the save location you selected previously

Click to create a new folder in the currently selected directory

Buttons allow you to select common storage locations quickly

Click to move one level up in your file hierarchy

Click to reveal a list of file formats in which the file may be saved

Excel 2000

Figure 1-12 New Folder dialog box

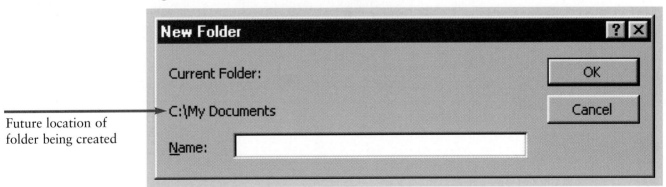

Future location of folder being created

Saving and Closing a Worksheet (continued)

Do It!

6 Type Kay's Hound Accessories. The default name will be replaced with the new text.

7 Click [OK]. The new folder will be created and opened automatically in the Save As dialog box. The contents window will be blank since there are no files or folders in Kay's folder, as shown in **Figure 1-13**.

8 Click [Save] to store the worksheet in Kay's folder. The Save As dialog box will close and the new file name will appear in the Excel window's title bar.

9 Click File, then click Close. The workbook file is removed from the Excel window.

More

You also can use the AutoSave option to have Excel automatically save your file every few minutes. The AutoSave command is found on the Tools menu. If it is not there, you will have to install the AutoSave add-in. Select the Add-Ins command from the Tools menu to open the Add-Ins dialog box. Click the check box next to AutoSave, and then click the OK button. After Excel has set up the AutoSave feature, select it from the Tools menu; the AutoSave dialog box, shown in **Figure 1-14**, will open. You can turn AutoSave on or off with the check box at the top-left of the dialog box, and you can choose the time between saves by entering an interval in the text box labeled minutes. You have the option of saving just the active workbook or all of the open workbooks, and Excel can prompt you before it auto saves if you wish, so as to avoid inadvertently saving unwanted changes.

Understanding the difference between the Save command and the Save As command is an important part of working with most software. When you save a new file for the first time, the two commands function identically: they both open the Save As dialog box, allowing you to choose a name and storage location for the file. Once you have saved a file, the commands serve different purposes. Choosing the Save command will update the original file with any changes you have made, maintaining the same file name and location. Choosing the Save As command will permit you to save a different version of the same file, with a new name, location, or both.

Figure 1-13 Saving a file in a new folder

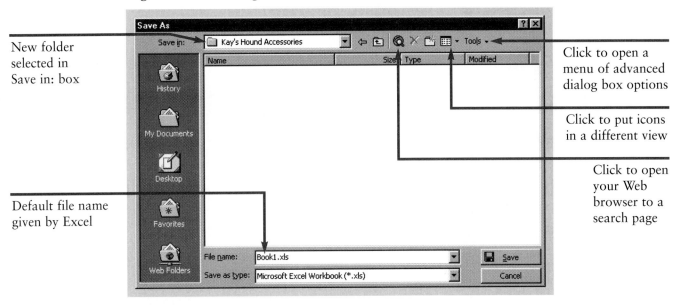

New folder selected in Save in: box

Click to open a menu of advanced dialog box options

Click to put icons in a different view

Click to open your Web browser to a search page

Default file name given by Excel

Excel 2000

Figure 1-14 AutoSave dialog box

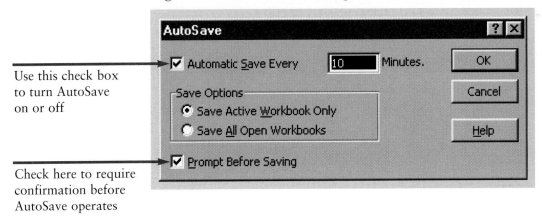

Use this check box to turn AutoSave on or off

Check here to require confirmation before AutoSave operates

Save the workbook you created in the Practice for the previous Skill on your student disk as **Practice1-7** and then close the workbook.

Hot Tip

The Save button 🖫 on the Standard toolbar and the keyboard combination [Ctrl]+[S] are shortcuts to the Save command.

Opening a Worksheet

Concept

In order to work with a saved file, you must first open it. Opening a file requires that you know the file's name and the location in which it is stored.

Do It!

Kay needs to open her file so that she can edit one of the labels.

1 Click File, then click Open. Notice that the Open command is followed by an ellipsis (three dots) indicating that a dialog box will open, as the command requires more information. The Open dialog box will appear as shown in **Figure 1-15**.

2 Earlier you saved the file Profit1 in a folder named Kay's Hound Accessories. Click the Look in drop-down list arrow and select the drive where your student files are stored. Insert your Student Disk into the A: drive and click the 3½ Floppy (A:) if they are stored on a floppy, or click Maindisk (C:) if they are in a folder on your hard disk. A list of the files and folders on the drive will appear in the list box.

3 Click the folder named Kay's Hound Accessories to select it, and then click the Open button 🗁 Open ▾ . The files housed in the folder will appear in the contents window.

4 Double-click the Profit1 file. The Open dialog box disappears and the worksheet will be displayed in the Excel window. Notice that the cell pointer is in the same cell it was in when you last saved the worksheet.

More

If you cannot remember the name of the storage location of a particular file that you need to open, Excel provides a powerful search facility that can help you. Click the Tools button in the Open dialog box and then choose the Find command from the menu that appears as shown in **Figure 1-16**. The Find dialog box, shown in **Figure 1-17**, will open. From the Find dialog box, you can search any drive or folder accessible from your computer for a file. You can conduct your search using a wide variety of properties including file name, the date the file was last modified, or even the name of the person who created it. Each property has its own set of conditions that you can apply to the search. For example, the File name property allows you to find a file whose name includes, begins with, or ends with a specific character or combination of characters. You submit this value in the Value: text-entry box. Use the selection and text-entry boxes at the bottom of the dialog box to set your criteria, and then click the Find Now button to initiate the search. If your search is successful, the file you requested will be selected in the Open dialog box. Once you have run a successful search, you can save it in case you ever need to locate that file again.

The Open button in the Open dialog box includes an arrow on its right edge. Clicking this arrow opens a menu that provides commands for opening a file in a number of different ways. For example, the Open Read-Only command permits you to view a file, but prohibits you from saving changes to it. The Open Copy command creates a copy of the file you are opening and opens the copy instead. The Open in Browser command opens HTML files in your Web browser rather than in Excel.

Figure 1-15 Open dialog box

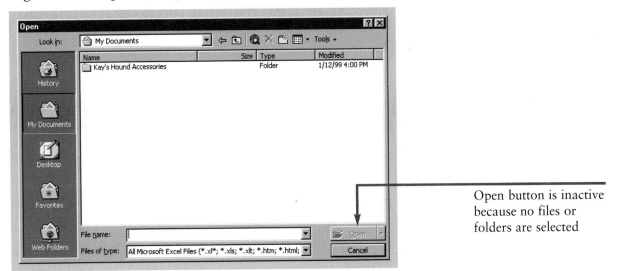

Open button is inactive because no files or folders are selected

Excel 2000

Figure 1-16 Find command

Figure 1-17 Find dialog box

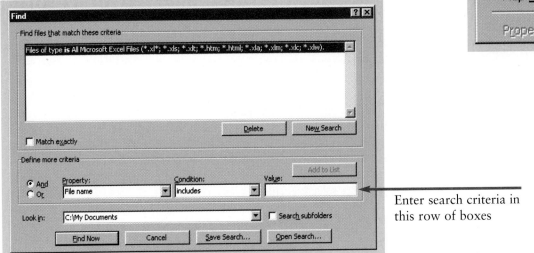

Enter search criteria in this row of boxes

Practice

To practice opening Excel documents, open the student file **Practice-Lesson 1.xls**. Then save it to your student disk as **MyPractice 1**.

Hot Tip

When conducting a file search, activate the Search subfolders check box to ensure that the search includes all folders in a particular location on just the top level of the folder or drive you selected.

Editing a Cell's Information

Concept

Many spreadsheet documents are used over a long period of time and undergo constant updating. Information entered into a cell is not permanent. You can change, or edit, the contents of a cell at any time. Editing the contents of a cell is very similar to editing text in a word processing document.

Do It!

Kay wants to edit cell A11 to change Expenditures to Expenses.

1 Click cell **A11**. The cell pointer moves to cell A11 and Expenditures is displayed in the formula bar.

2 Move the mouse pointer from the worksheet to the formula bar and position it between the n and the d of the word **Expenditures** (the pointer will change from a cross 🔁 to an I-beam ‡) and click. A blinking insertion point will appear, the formula bar buttons will be displayed, and the mode indicator on the status bar will read Edit, as shown in **Figure 1-18**.

3 Click and hold the left mouse button, then drag the I-beam to the right, over the last seven letters of the word **Expenditures**. The rest of the formula bar will become highlighted. Highlighting, or selecting, text allows it to be edited.

4 Type **ses** and then click the **Enter** button ☑. The new text will replace the incorrect label and the spreadsheet will look like **Figure 1-19**.

5 Save your workbook by clicking the **Save** button 💾.

More

Excel provides you with multiple ways to edit a cell's information. You can select the cell you wish to edit and then click the formula bar, as described above. You also may double-click a desired cell, making a flashing insertion point appear. Then you can use the backspace or delete key to remove the character to the left or right of the insertion point respectively, and enter new characters to edit the cell. Or you can double-click a second time to highlight all of the cell's contents and edit the selection. Finally, you can select a cell and then press [F2], again making the insertion point appear in the selected cell.

Figure 1-18 Editing a cell label

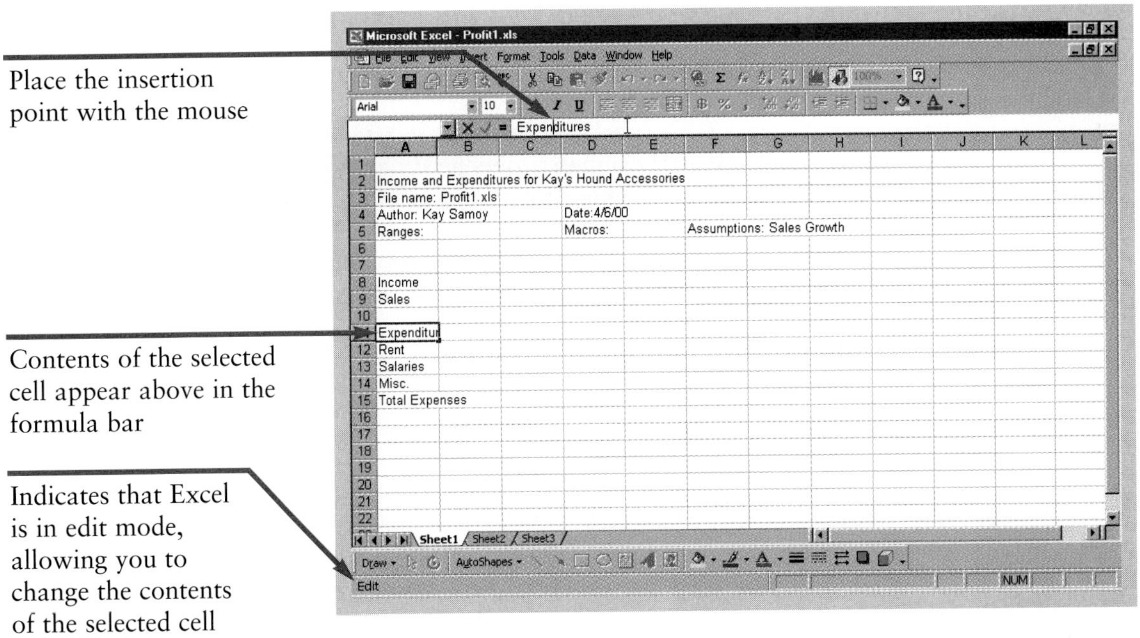

Place the insertion
point with the mouse

Contents of the selected
cell appear above in the
formula bar

Indicates that Excel
is in edit mode,
allowing you to
change the contents
of the selected cell

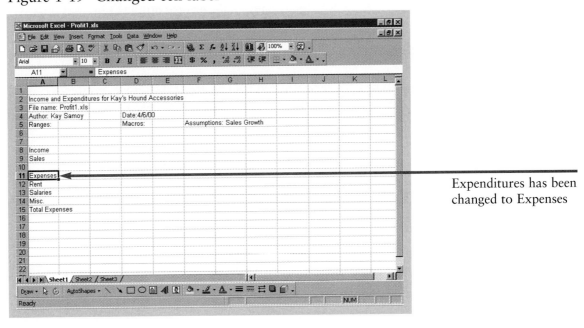

Excel 2000

Figure 1-19 Changed cell label

Expenditures has been
changed to Expenses

Practice

To practice editing cell information,
click the **Prac1-9** worksheet tab in your
MyPractice 1 student file and follow the
instructions.

Hot Tip

The Undo button  on the Standard toolbar will cancel the last action performed.
Clicking the Undo drop-down list arrow
opens a list of recent commands and
actions; clicking one will undo all actions
back to and including the selected one.

Using the Office Assistant

Concept

Even the most experienced computer users need help from time to time. The Office Assistant provides several methods for getting help in Excel. You can choose from a list of topics that the Assistant suggests based on the most recent functions you have performed. You also can view tips related to your current activity. Or you can ask a question in plain English. The Office Assistant will reply with several help topics related to your question.

Do It!

Kay has a question about the Office Assistant. She will use the Office Assistant to get help.

1 If the Office Assistant is not active, click 🔲 on the Standard toolbar. The Assistant and its dialog balloon appear asking what you would like to do. Click the text box that reads Type your question here, and then click Search. The text will be replaced by an insertion point.

2 In the text box, type How do I hide the Office Assistant? and then click ⌈ Search ⌋. A list of topics appears in the balloon, as shown in **Figure 1-20**.

3 Click the first topic, Show, hide, or turn off the Office Assistant. **Figure 1-21** shows the Microsoft Excel Help window that appears.

4 Read the help topic pertaining to the Office Assistant.

5 When you have finished reading about the Office Assistant's capabilities, click the Close ⌈X⌋ button in the upper-right corner of the window.

More

From time to time the Assistant will offer you tips on how to use Excel more efficiently. The appearance of a small light bulb, either next to the Assistant or on the Office Assistant button, indicates that there is a tip to be viewed. To see the tip, click the light bulb in whichever location it appears.

The Office Assistant can be customized. Click the ⌈ Options ⌋ button in its dialog balloon to open the Office Assistant dialog box. This dialog box has two tabs: Gallery and Options. The **Gallery** tab contains different assistant characters you can install, and scrolling through the characters provides you with a preview of each one. From the Options tab, shown in **Figure 1-22**, you can control the Assistant's behavior and capabilities, and decide what kinds of tips it will show. You also can access Office Assistant commands by right-clicking the Assistant itself.

If your computer is properly connected to a printer, you can print the text of any help topic. Simply click the Print button 🖨 at the top of the Help window to open the Print dialog box.

Figure 1-20 Assistant's search results

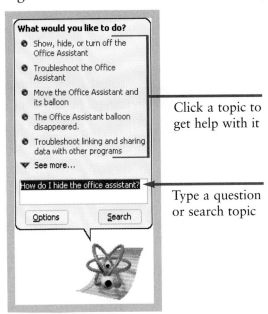

Click a topic to get help with it

Type a question or search topic

Figure 1-21 Help with the Office Assistant

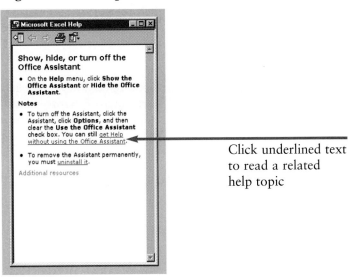

Click underlined text to read a related help topic

Figure 1-22 Office Assistant dialog box

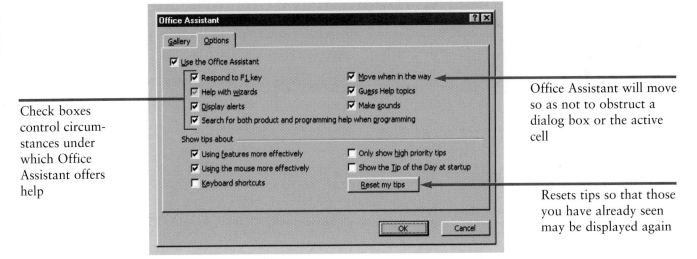

Check boxes control circumstances under which Office Assistant offers help

Office Assistant will move so as not to obstruct a dialog box or the active cell

Resets tips so that those you have already seen may be displayed again

Practice

Use the Office Assistant to learn about moving the Office Assistant and its balloon.

Hot Tip

The Office Assistant is common to all Office 2000 applications. Therefore, any Assistant options you change will affect it in all Office programs.

Other Excel Help Features

Concept

Working with new software can be confusing, and, at times, even intimidating. Fortunately, Microsoft Excel offers a number of built-in help features in addition to the Office Assistant that you can use when you encounter problems or just have a question about a particular aspect of the program. The What's This? command and the Help tabs are two such features.

Do It!

Kay will use the What's This? command to get more information about the Name Box, and the Help tabs to find out more about keyboard shortcuts.

1. Click Help on the menu bar, then click What's This?. A question mark will be added to the mouse pointer ?. With this pointer, you can click many Excel features to receive a ScreenTip that explains them.

2. Click the Name box. A ScreenTip like the one in **Figure 1-23** will appear to explain the item you clicked. Read the tip, and then click the mouse to erase it.

3. Click the Office Assistant (activate the feature from the Help menu first, if necessary). Click any help topic or tip the Assistant is currently offering.

4. When the Help window for that topic appears, click the Show button . The window will expand to a two-paneled format. The left panel consists of three tabs while the right panel is used to display selected help files.

5. Click the Index tab to bring it to the front of the panel if it is not already there.

6. Click in the text-entry box labeled Type keywords:, and then type keyboard. Notice that the list box in the middle of the tab scrolls automatically to match your entry.

7. When you see the word keyboard appear in the list box, double-click it. After a moment, the help topics related to keyboard will be displayed in the box at the bottom of the tab.

8. Find Keyboard shortcuts in the Choose a topic list box (you may have to scroll down) and click it. The Keyboard shortcuts help file will be loaded into the right panel of the window as shown in **Figure 1-24**.

9. Close the Help window when you finish working with it.

More

The Index tab of the Help Topics dialog box is very helpful if you know what the task you are trying to accomplish is called, or if you know the name of the feature that you want to explore. If you are unsure of exactly what you are looking for, the Contents tab may be a better option for you. The Contents tab contains every Help topic that Excel offers, broken down by category, and is useful if you wish to obtain a broad view of the topics available. It is organized like an outline or the table of contents you might find in a book. It begins with general topics, symbolized by book icons, each of which can be expanded to reveal more specific and focused subtopics. Once you have revealed a general topic's subtopics, you can select a subtopic in the left panel to display it in the right panel, just as on the Index tab. The Answer Wizard tab replicates the Office Assistant, allowing you to request help topics by entering questions in your own words. Once you have clicked the Show button to display the Help tabs in a Help window, the button changes to the Hide button. Click the Hide button to collapse the window back to a single panel.

Excel 2000

Figure 1-23 Name box What's This? ScreenTip

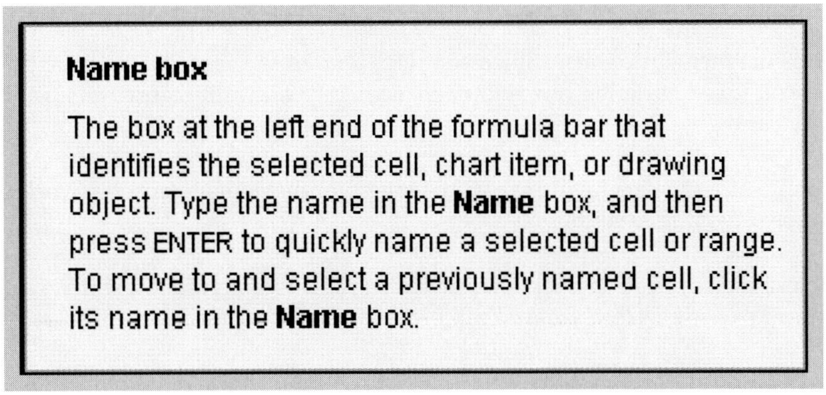

Name box

The box at the left end of the formula bar that identifies the selected cell, chart item, or drawing object. Type the name in the **Name** box, and then press ENTER to quickly name a selected cell or range. To move to and select a previously named cell, click its name in the **Name** box.

Figure 1-24 Using the Help tabs

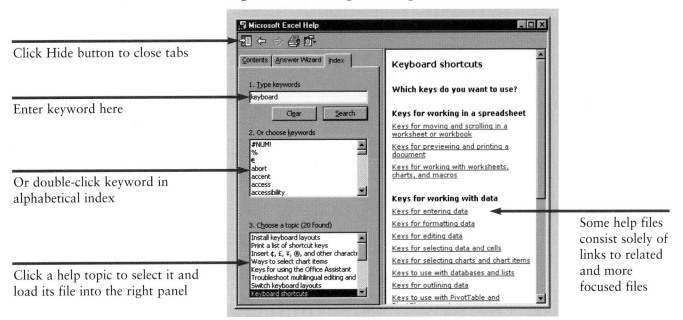

Click Hide button to close tabs

Enter keyword here

Or double-click keyword in alphabetical index

Click a help topic to select it and load its file into the right panel

Some help files consist solely of links to related and more focused files

Practice

Use the Index to find a help topic that discusses shortcut keys that relate to the Office Assistant.

Hot Tip

If your computer is connected to the Internet, you can access Microsoft's Web pages directly from Excel. Open the Help menu and click **Office on the Web** to launch your Web browser and go directly to the Office Web site.

Exiting Excel

Concept

It is important to exit the Excel program properly when you are finished with the day's work session. Closing the application correctly will help you avoid data loss.

Do It!

Kay has finished using Excel for the day and is ready to exit the application.

1. Click File, then click Close. Since you have altered the spreadsheet since the last time you saved, a dialog box will open asking if you want to save changes in Profit1.xls.

2. Click [Yes]. Excel will save the changes you have made and the worksheet will disappear from the window.

3. To close the application click File, then click Exit (see **Figure 1-25**). Excel closes and removes itself from the desktop.

More

There are other ways you can close a file and exit Excel. The easiest method is to use the Close buttons ☒ located in the upper-right corner of the window. The Close button on the menu bar is for the active workbook, and the Close button on the title bar is for the application.

You may open any menu on the menu bar by pressing the [Alt] key followed by the underlined letter in the menu's title. You will notice that menu commands also have a letter in their name underlined; typing the underlined letter will activate its command on the open menu. For example, with the File menu open, typing [c] will close the file and pressing [x] will exit Excel. If you have more than one workbook open in Excel, the program will allow you to save changes to all of them at once before closing.

Figure 1-25 Closing the Excel application

Clicking this Close button will likewise exit the application

Excel 2000

Practice

Open Excel, and then Exit the application by clicking the Close button [X] on the title bar.

Hot Tip

Pressing the [Ctrl] key plus [W] will close your file, while [Alt] + [F4] is the key combination used to exit Excel.

Shortcuts

Function	Button/Mouse	Menu	Keyboard
Create a new file	☐	Click File, then click New	[Ctrl]+[N]
Open a file	☐	Click File, then click Open	[Ctrl]+[O]
Maximize a window	☐	Click Control icon, then click Maximize	
Minimize a window	☐	Click Control icon, then click Minimize	
Restore a window	☐	Click Control icon, then click Restore	
Close a window	☒	Click Control icon, then click Close	[Alt]+[F4] (application) [Ctrl]+[W] (document)
Confirm a cell entry	☑		[Enter], [Tab], Arrow keys
Cancel a cell entry	☒	Click Edit, then click Undo typing	[Ctrl]+[Z]
Search the Web (from the Open dialog box)	☐		
Save a file	☐	Click File, then click Save	[Ctrl]+[S]
Office Assistant	☐	Click Help, then click Microsoft Excel Help	[F1]
What's This?	☐ In a dialog box	Click Help, then click What's This?	[Shift]+[F1]

Identify Key Features

Name the items identified by callouts in **Figure 1-26**.

Figure 1-26 Elements of the Excel screen

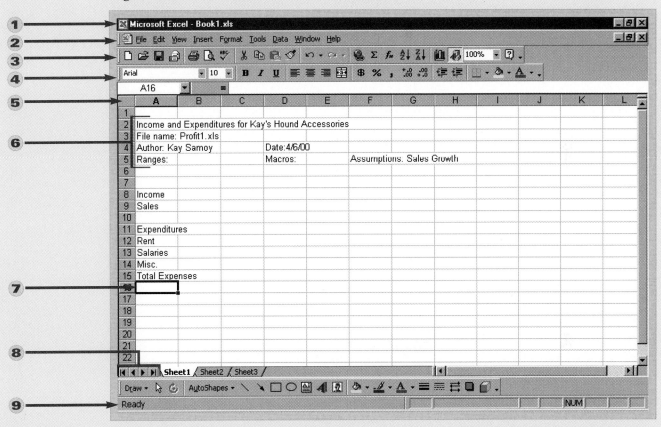

Excel 2000

Select the Best Answer

10. Click this to make the Excel window fill the screen

11. Displays the active cell address

12. Displays a brief description of your current activities in Excel

13. Allows you to choose a name and location for storing a file

14. Saves your file keeping its current name and location

15. Answers your questions and offers guidance as you work

16. Allows you to search for a file from the Open dialog box

17. Location where you can edit the contents of a cell

a. Name box

b. Office Assistant

c. Maximize button

d. Find command

e. Save As command

f. Formula bar

g. Save button

h. Status bar

Quiz (continued)

Complete the Statement

18. To select an entire column, click:

    a. The first cell in the column

    b. Any cell in the column

    c. Its letter column heading

    d. The corresponding row number

19. Text or numbers that describe your data are called:

    a. Annotations

    b. Ranges

    c. Justifications

    d. Labels

20. Pressing [Ctrl]+[Home] will:

    a. Move your view up one screen

    b. Move your view down one screen

    c. Move the cell pointer to cell A1

    d. Move the cell pointer to Column A in the current row

21. All of the following actions will move the cell pointer to another cell except:

    a. Clicking the Enter button

    b. Pressing the Enter key

    c. Pressing the Tab key

    d. Pressing an Arrow key

22. A well-designed spreadsheet does not require:

    a. Documentation

    b. Multiple worksheets

    c. Input

    d. Output

23. All of these are Excel help features except:

    a. The Index tab

    b. The Office Assistant

    c. What's This?

    d. The Help Wizard

24. A file extension:

    a. Allows you to see a hidden file

    b. Lets you edit the information in a cell

    c. Associates a file with a specific application

    d. Is part of Excel's Help facility

25. A workbook can contain:

    a. 16 worksheets

    b. 255 worksheets

    c. 3 worksheets

    d. 65,536 worksheets

26. Excel assumes that numbers entered on the worksheet are:

    a. Values

    b. Labels

    c. Formulas

    d. Apostrophes

Interactivity

Test Your Skills

1. Open the Excel application and document a new spreadsheet:

   a. Use the Start button to launch Microsoft Excel.

   b. Add a documentation section to the blank worksheet using the title **Class Schedule**, your name, and the date.

   c. When you document the file name, use the name **Test 1.xls**.

   d. Include labels for ranges and macros. Your documentation section should occupy Rows 1–4 of the worksheet.

2. Design a worksheet that displays your daily class schedule:

   a. Add labels in Row 6 for the days of the week. Start in cell B6, and skip a column between each day. Friday should be in cell J6.

   b. Add labels in Column A for your class periods. Enter the time of your earliest class in cell A8, and then add a label for each subsequent class period through your last class of the day. Skip a row between each time label.

   c. Enter the names of your classes in the appropriate cells where the day of the week and the time intersect.

3. Get help from the Office Assistant:

   a. Open the Office Assistant's dialog balloon.

   b. Ask the Assistant for information on how to **customize toolbars**.

   c. Choose a topic that the Assistant provides, and then read the information in the Help window.

   d. Close the Help window when you are done, and then close the Office Assistant's window.

4. Save your file and exit Excel:

   a. Save your spreadsheet under the name **Test 1.xls**.

   b. Exit Microsoft Excel.

Interactivity (continued)

Problem Solving

1. Create a new spreadsheet following the design principles you learned in Lesson 1. Design this spreadsheet to log your daily activities. Enter labels for the days of the week just as you did in the previous exercise, but this time add Saturday and Sunday after Friday, and do not leave a blank column between each day. Instead of class periods, add labels down Column A for **Class, Activities, Meals, Studying/Homework, Leisure,** and **Sleep**. Do not skip rows between labels. Save the file as **Solved 1-1.xls**.

2. Due to a recent merger, your accounting firm can now increase the budgets of several departments. You are elated to learn that you will have an additional $10,000 available for your expense account. As a member of the Human Resources department, you know how much this money will help you attract the top candidates for your company's job openings. Use Excel to design a spreadsheet that will detail your strategy for utilizing the new funds over the next year. You do not have to enter any monetary values yet. Simply set up the structure of the worksheet with labels. Save the file as **Solved-HR.xls**.

3. At your urging, the restaurant you manage has just purchased a new computer complete with Office 2000. The owner of the restaurant, who was reluctant to make the purchase, wants you to prove that it was a sound investment. Using Excel, design a spreadsheet that will allow you to keep track of the waitstaff's schedule over one week. Your worksheet should include columns for **Time In** and **Time Out** each day of the week. Save the file as **Solved-Rest.xls**.

L E S S O N

2

MANIPULATING DATA IN A WORKSHEET

O ne of the greatest advantages of using spreadsheet software is that it automates many of the processes that take up so much time when done by hand. In Excel, you can move or copy data from one location in a worksheet to another quickly and easily.

Excel also automates your calculations by using mathematical formulas. If you instruct Excel what operation to perform, and where to get the data, the program will execute the calculations for you. The Paste Function feature prevents you from having to enter complicated formulas that Excel already knows. Once you have entered a formula or a function, you can even paste it into a new location.

Often, businesses like to use the data they have gathered to make projections about their business. In Excel, you can use assumptions to perform calculations under different conditions, altering the results of the worksheet each time. This technique is known as What-If analysis, and takes full advantage of Excel's versatility.

CASE STUDY
In this lesson, Kay will use Excel's Cut, Copy, and Paste features to manipulate the labels in her spreadsheet. She also will fill out the worksheet with values and then use those values to perform calculations using formulas and functions. Then she will change her output by performing a What-If analysis. Finally, Kay will print a copy of her worksheet.

Cutting, Copying, and Pasting Data

Concept

Excel makes it easy to transfer data from cell to cell. Cutting or Copying information places it on the Office Clipboard, a temporary storage place for data. If you have used the Windows operating system or previous versions of Microsoft Excel before, you may be familiar with the Windows Clipboard. The Office Clipboard can hold up to 12 items at once, while the Windows Clipboard holds only one. The two Clipboards are related in the following ways: the last item you sent to the Office Clipboard also can be found on the Windows Clipboard; when you clear the Office Clipboard, the Windows Clipboard is erased as well. Both Clipboards are volatile. That is, they are erased automatically when you shut down your computer. The Paste command inserts the last item you sent to the Clipboard at the insertion point. Cell contents also may be moved by dragging and dropping with the mouse.

Do It!

Kay wants to add the column heading Quarter in four cells, B6, C6, D6, and E6, of her spreadsheet. Then she will cut and paste the column headings from row 6 to row 7.

1 Open Excel by clicking the Start button, then selecting Excel from the Programs menu. The Excel window will appear on your desktop.

2 Click the Open button 📁, then find the folder named Kay's Hound Accessories, and open Profit1.xls. Your workbook will appear in the Excel window.

3 Click cell B6. The cell pointer will appear in cell B6 to indicate it is active.

4 Type Quarter, then click the Enter button ✅ to confirm the entry. The label will appear in cell B6.

5 Click Edit, then click Copy to send a duplicate of the contents of the selected cell to the Clipboard. An animated dashed border appears around the copied selection, as shown in **Figure 2-1**.

6 Press [Tab] to move the cell pointer to cell **C6**. Notice that the animated border remains in cell B6.

7 Click Edit, then click Paste to insert the copied text into the selected cell.

8 Move the mouse pointer to the fill handle, the black square in the lower-right corner of the cell, until it changes to a crosshair ✚, indicating that the selection can be copied elsewhere in the document.

9 Click the left mouse button and drag the fill pointer to cell E6. The cells will appear with a gray border, identifying them as a possible destination for the copied data, and a ScreenTip displaying the text to be copied will appear, as seen in **Figure 2-2**.

10 Release the mouse button. A copy of the selected data will appear in cells D6 and E6.

Figure 2-1 Copying a cell

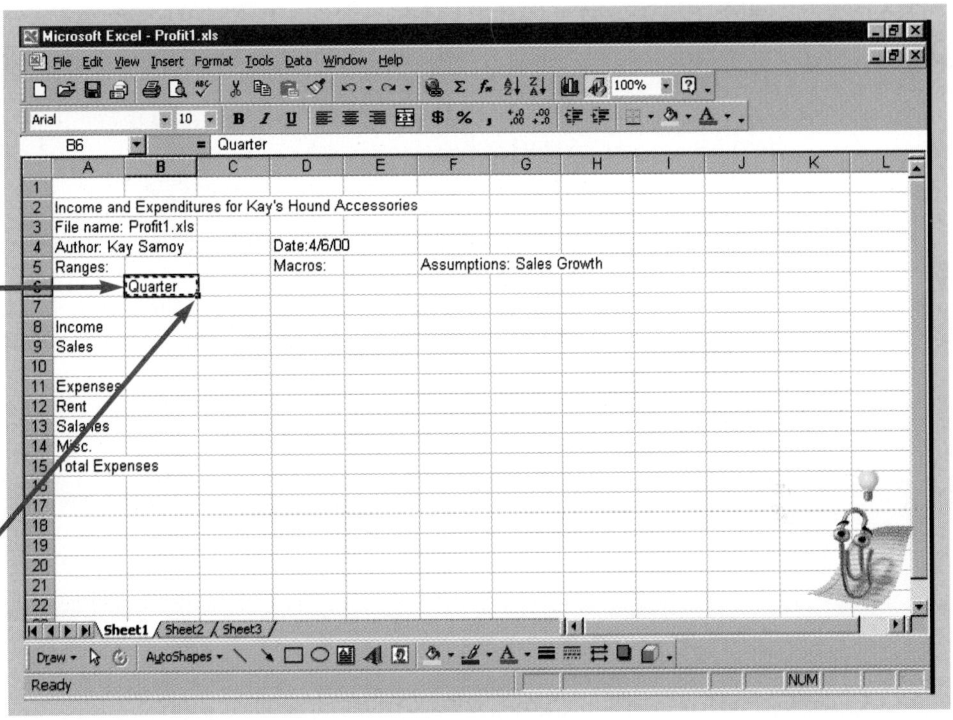

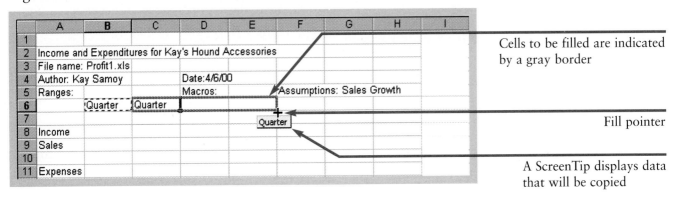

Animated border indicating the cell's information has been sent to the Clipboard

Fill handle

Figure 2-2 Selected destination cells

Cells to be filled are indicated by a gray border

Fill pointer

A ScreenTip displays data that will be copied

Excel 2000

Cutting, Copying, and Pasting Data (continued)

Do It!

11 Double-click cell B6 to put it into edit mode. Edit will appear in the status bar.

12 Place the I-beam after Quarter, press [Space], then type [1]. The label will read Quarter 1.

13 Repeat the previous steps so that cells C6 through E6 read Quarter 2 through 4 respectively. Your worksheet should now resemble the one in **Figure 2-3**.

14 Click cell B6 to select it, then drag the mouse pointer to cell E6 so that all four cells are encompassed in the cell pointer. Cells C6, D6, and E6 will be highlighted.

15 Click the Cut button ✂ on the Standard toolbar. The column headings are surrounded by an animated border.

16 Click cell B7, then drag to cell E7 to select the entire group as the destination cells for the cut information.

17 Click the Paste button 📋. The column headings in row 6 will be pasted into row 7, as shown in **Figure 2-4**.

18 Save your worksheet by clicking the Save button 💾.

More

You can move or copy a cell's contents with the mouse by dragging and dropping. Dragging involves positioning the pointer over an object, clicking the left mouse button to grab the object, and then moving the mouse, and the object, to a new location. When the mouse pointer is over a cell pointer, it will change to an arrow. You can then click and drag the cell pointer to a new location to move the contents of the selected cell or cells without having to use the Clipboard. Releasing the mouse button drops a grabbed object into place. Pressing [Ctrl] while dragging and dropping causes the pointer to change to the copy pointer ▵. When dropped, the contents of the selection will appear in the new location but the original information will remain intact.

If you want to fill a range of cells with copies of a selected cell or cells, move the mouse pointer to the **fill handle**, the square at the bottom-right corner of a cell pointer, until it changes to a crosshair. Then click and drag the mouse pointer in the direction of the columns or rows that you wish to fill; a gray border will appear around the cells that will be filled with copies of your original selection when you release the mouse button. Using the fill handle allows you to make multiple copies of a selected cell's or range's content at the same time, whereas you can only make a single copy of a cell's or range's content using the drag-and-drop method described above.

As stated earlier, you can store up to 12 items on the Office Clipboard. To paste an item other than the one you cut or copied most recently, open the View menu, highlight Toolbars, and click Clipboard on the submenu that appears. The Clipboard toolbar, shown in **Figure 2-5**, will open. The Clipboard toolbar allows you to choose exactly which stored item you want to paste. Point to an icon on the toolbar to receive a ScreenTip that tells you what piece of data the icon represents.

Figure 2-3 Edited cells

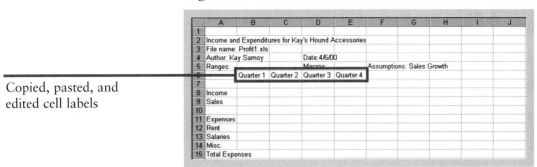

Copied, pasted, and
edited cell labels

Figure 2-4 Cut and pasted cells

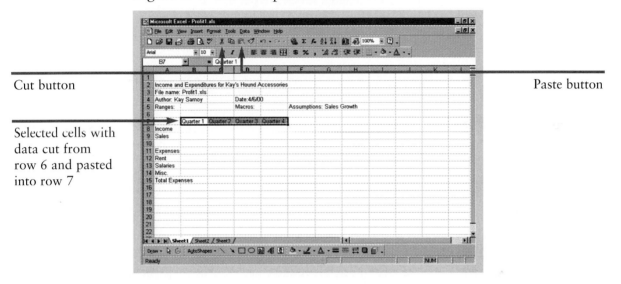

Cut button

Paste button

Selected cells with
data cut from
row 6 and pasted
into row 7

Figure 2-5 Office Clipboard

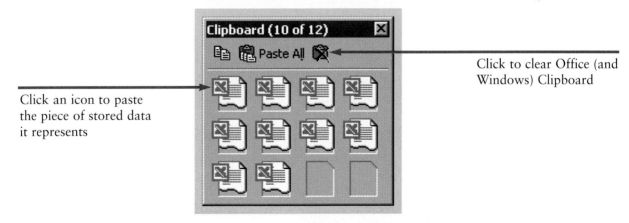

Click to clear Office (and
Windows) Clipboard

Click an icon to paste
the piece of stored data
it represents

Practice

Open the practice file **Practice-Lesson 2.xls**, save it as **MyPractice2**, and then follow the instructions on the **Prac2-1** worksheet in the MyPractice2 workbook. Save the changes you have made when you complete the exercise.

Hot Tip

The Cut and Copy commands both send the selected data to the Clipboard. When you paste data that have been copied, the original data are left intact. However, when you paste data that have been cut, the data are removed from their original location.

Excel 2000

Entering Values

Concept

Values are numbers, formulas, or functions that Excel uses in calculations. They must be entered and confirmed in the same way that labels are.

Do It!

Kay wants to enter sales and expense values into her worksheet.

1 Click cell B9 to make it the active cell.

2 Type 970000, then press [Tab]. The first quarter sales value is entered into the cell and the cell pointer moves to the right to cell C9.

3 Now enter the rest of the Sales values in the row, pressing [Tab] after each: 1000400, 1210305, 1484032.

4 Click cell B12 to activate it.

5 Type 45000 and then click the **Enter** button ☑.

6 Since the rent is the same for each quarter, copy the data in cell B12 and paste it into the other three cells in the row, C12, D12, and E12, by clicking on the fill handle, dragging it to cell E12, and then releasing it. Notice the ScreenTip that shows the data that will be copied.

7 Click cell B13 to activate it and enter the following four values into the Salaries row, pressing [Tab] after each: 30000, 30000, 51750, 61750.

8 Click cell B14 to activate it and enter the following four Misc. values into the row, pressing [Tab] after each: 10200, 8188, 7900, 9940. Your worksheet should now resemble the one shown in **Figure 2-6**.

More

You may have noticed that the values you entered, unlike labels, were aligned to the right when confirmed. Excel aligns values to the right by default and recognizes an entry as a value when it is a number or it is preceded by +, -, =, @, #, or $. Ordinals (1st, 2nd, 3rd, etc.) and other combinations of numbers and letters are recognized as labels. Sometimes you may want to use a number, such as a year, as a label; in this case, you can type an apostrophe (') before it to make Excel recognize it as a label and disregard it when performing calculations. The apostrophe will not be visible in the cell, but will be shown in the formula bar when the cell is selected.

Figure 2-6 Entering values into the worksheet

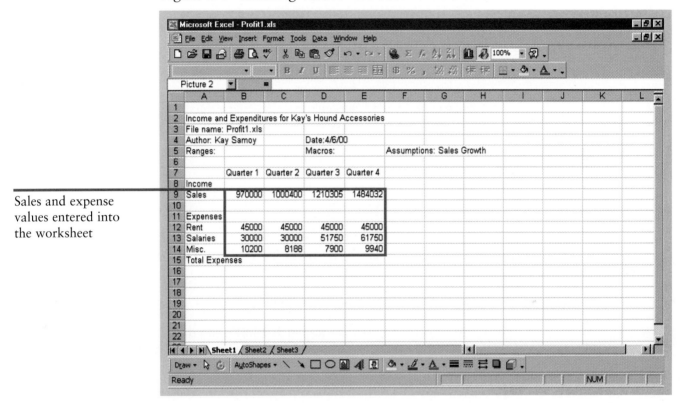

Sales and expense values entered into the worksheet

Excel 2000

Entering Formulas

Concept

Formulas allow Excel to perform calculations such as averages, sums, or products using values that have been entered into the worksheet.

Do It!

Kay would like to calculate the total expenses and profits for each quarter.

1 Click cell B15 to activate it. This is the cell where the formula will be entered, and where the calculated result will appear.

2 Enter the following formula into the active cell: =B12+B13+B14. Notice that part of the label Total Expenses in cell A15 disappeared. You will learn how to widen columns in Lesson 3. The equals sign preceding the cell addresses and arithmetical operators prompts Excel to recognize the information as a formula. This calculation will result in a sum of the values in the three cells referenced in the formula.

3 Click the Enter button. The result, 85200, takes the place of the formula you entered in cell B15, and the formula remains visible in the formula bar, as shown in Figure 2-7.

4 Repeat steps 1–3 to enter similar formulas into cells C15, D15, and E15, substituting C, D, and E respectively for the Bs used above in the formula's cell addresses.

5 Click cell A17 to activate it and enter the label Profit into the cell. Profit is the result of Income, or Sales, minus Total Expenses.

6 Click cell B17 and enter the formula =B9-B15 into the cell, then press [Tab]. Excel subtracts First Quarter Expenses from First Quarter Sales to arrive at 884800, the profit for the First Quarter.

7 Repeat the previous step to enter similar formulas into cells C17, D17, and E17, substituting C, D, and E respectively for the Bs used above in the formula's cell addresses. Your worksheet should now resemble the one shown in Figure 2-8.

8 Save your workbook.

More

As you have seen, Excel formulas use cell addresses and the arithmetic operators; + for addition and − for subtraction. Since the standard computer keyboard does not contain multiplication or division symbols, the asterisk (*) is used for multiplication and the forward slash (/) is used for division to specify the desired calculation. The carat mark (^) is used to express exponentiation. Using cell addresses, called cell referencing, helps Excel keep your calculations accurate by automatically recalculating results whenever the value in a cell referenced in a formula is altered.

Figure 2-7 Entering a formula

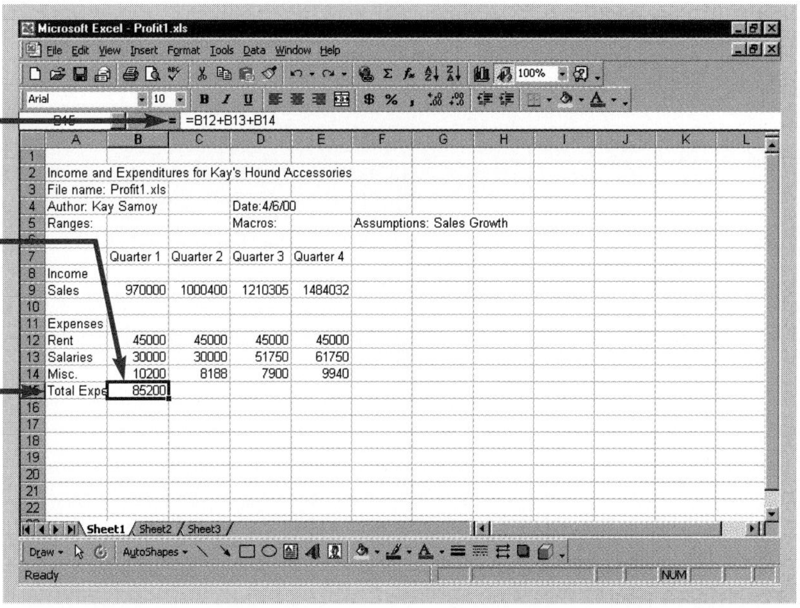

Formula displayed in
the formula bar

Results calculated using
the entered formula

Label in A15
partially covered

Excel 2000

Figure 2-8 Calculating Total Expenses and Profit

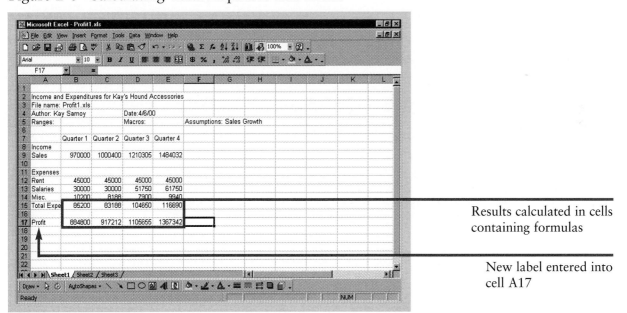

Results calculated in cells
containing formulas

New label entered into
cell A17

Practice

To practice entering formulas, follow the instructions on the **Prac2-3** worksheet of the practice file **MyPractice 2.xls**. Save the changes you have made when you complete the exercise.

Hot Tip

If you select two or more cells that contain values, their sum will appear in the status bar. Right-clicking the sum in the status bar will open a pop-up menu that allows you to select other forms of tabulation.

Using Functions

Concept

Instead of having to create a new formula each time you wish to perform a simple calculation in a worksheet, you can use one of Excel's predefined formulas, called functions. Excel has hundreds of these built-in formulas, covering many of the most common types of calculations performed by spreadsheets.

Do It!

Kay wants to use the SUM function to calculate her Total Expenses.

1 Click cell B15 to make it active.

2 Press [Delete] to clear the previously entered formula. The data disappear allowing the contents of cell A15 to be visible.

3 Click the AutoSum button ⨉. The AutoSum function automatically sets up the formula for adding together the values directly above the active cell. The sum formula (=SUM B12:B14) appears in cell B15 and in the formula bar. The cells being added, called the argument, are indicated with an animated border (**Figure 2-9**). The sum formula contains the notation B12:B14, called a range, which refers to all cells between B12 and B14.

4 Press [Enter] to confirm Excel's assumption and apply the formula to the worksheet. The value 85200 appears in the cell.

5 Click cell F7, then enter the label Total For Year.

6 Click cell F9 to make it the active cell.

7 Click the AutoSum button ⨉. The SUM function appears in the cell followed by the correct range B9:E9. Since there are no values above the active cell, AutoSum uses the values in the cells to the left of the cell pointer.

8 Click the Enter button. The value 4664737 now appears in the cell, as shown in **Figure 2-10**.

9 Save your worksheet.

More

In the example above, you used the AutoSum button to enter the SUM function into Cell B15 in place of the formula =B9+C9+D9+E9. But, unlike AutoSum, most Excel functions require the user to manually enter additional information after the function name. This information, enclosed in parentheses and called the argument, can be cell references or other data that the function needs to produce a result. The function acts upon the argument, as the SUM function above acted on the range of cells enclosed in the parentheses that followed it.

Figure 2-9 Using the AutoSum function

6					
7		Quarter 1	Quarter 2	Quarter 3	Quarter 4
8	Income				
9	Sales	970000	1000400	1210305	1484032
10					
11	Expenses				
12	Rent	45000	45000	45000	45000
13	Salaries	30000	30000	51750	61750
14	Misc.	10200	8188	7900	9940
15	Total Expe	=SUM(B12:B14)		104650	116690
16					
17	Profit	970000	917212	1105655	1367342
18					

Animated border indicating the argument of the formula

SUM formula

Excel 2000

Figure 2-10 Calculating the total expenses for the year

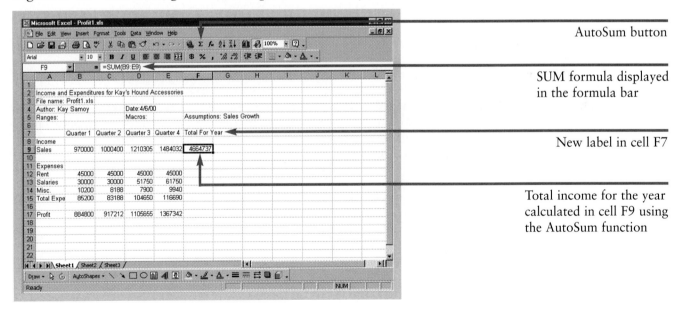

AutoSum button

SUM formula displayed in the formula bar

New label in cell F7

Total income for the year calculated in cell F9 using the AutoSum function

Practice

To practice using functions, follow the instructions on the **Prac2-4** worksheet of the practice file **MyPractice 2.xls**. Save the changes you have made when you complete the exercise.

Hot Tip

Any range of cells may be selected as the argument for an AutoSum. Click the cell in which you wish the result to appear, click the AutoSum button, then select a new argument for the function by clicking and dragging over the desired range.

Using the Paste Function Feature

Concept

To enter a function other than SUM, you can either enter it yourself or use the Paste Function command. The Paste Function command allows you to insert built-in formulas into your worksheet, saving you the trouble of remembering mathematical expressions and the time it takes to type them.

Do It!

Kay would like to use the Paste Function command to calculate the average total quarterly expenses for the year.

1 Click cell B19 to activate it.

2 Click Insert, then click Function. The Paste Function dialog box will open (see Figure 2-11), and an equals sign will appear in the selected cell indicating that a formula is to follow.

3 Click Average in the Function name box to select it. A description of what the Average function does will appear below the function category and name boxes.

4 Click OK. The Paste Function dialog box will disappear, and the Formula Palette will appear with the range B17:B18 listed as the argument in the Number1 text box. Since this is not the correct range of cells, a new range must be specified as the argument.

5 To select the range for the total expenses, click cell B15, then drag to cell E15. An animated border will appear around the selected cells, and as you drag, the Formula Palette will reduce itself to the Number1 text box displaying the selected range. When you release the mouse button, the Formula Palette will reappear in full and the formula =AVERAGE (B15:E15) will appear in the formula bar and in cell B19, as shown in Figure 2-12.

6 Click OK. The Formula Palette closes and cell B19 will display the result 97432.

7 Click cell A19, then label it Ave. Exp. Your worksheet should now resemble the one shown in Figure 2-13.

8 Save your worksheet.

More

When the Paste Function dialog box appears, the default setting for the function category is Most Recently Used. If you have not used the Paste Function command before, this category contains a default list of commonly used functions. Each function on this list also can be found under a more specific category. To find other functions, you can select other categories by clicking on them. The list of function names changes to correspond to the category you have chosen.

You may have noticed that the title of the upper text box on the Formula Palette, Number1, is in bold face whereas the title of the text box beneath it is not. The bold title indicates that data must be entered in the box in order for the function to work. Plain text indicates that entering text is optional.

Figure 2-11 Paste Function dialog box

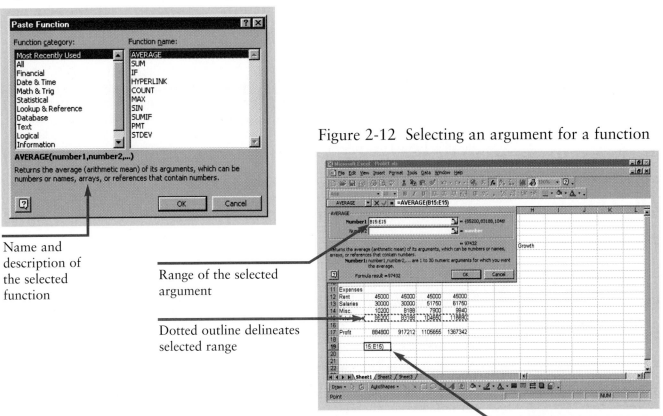

Name and
description of
the selected
function

Figure 2-12 Selecting an argument for a function

Range of the selected
argument

Dotted outline delineates
selected range

Formula is entered into
the active cell with the
selected range inserted
as the argument

Figure 2-13 Pasted function

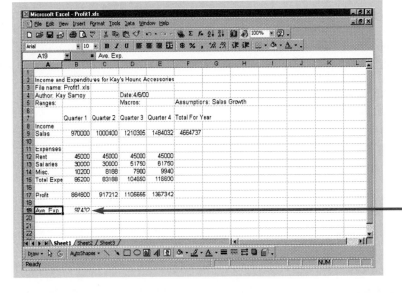

Result of the pasted function

Practice

To practice inserting functions, follow the instructions on the **Prac2-5** worksheet of the practice file **MyPractice 2.xls**. Save the changes you have made when you complete the exercise.

Hot Tip

Instead of using the mouse to select an argument for a function in the Formula Palette, you can enter a range of cells using the keyboard.

Copying and Pasting Formulas

Concept

Formulas can be copied and pasted into other cells just like values or labels. Unless instructed otherwise, Excel considers the cell referred to in an argument to be a relative cell address. This means that if you copy a formula or function into another cell, Excel will substitute new cell references that are in the same position relative to the new formula or function location.

Do It!

To calculate the annual totals for her various expenses, Kay will copy the SUM function from cell F9 and paste it into cells F12, F13, F14, and F15.

1 Click cell **F9** to activate it. The SUM function appears in the formula bar with the argument B9:E9.

2 Click the Copy button 📋 to copy the formula to the Windows Clipboard. An animated border appears around cell F9.

3 Click cell **F12** to select it.

4 Click the Paste button 📋 to insert the copied function into the active cell. The result 180000 appears in cell F12. Notice that Excel has changed the argument in the formula bar from B9:F9 to B12:E12, the range of cell addresses relative to the copied function's position in the worksheet, so that the function will be applied to the row it is in rather than the one it was copied from.

5 Click the fill handle of the cell pointer surrounding cell **F12** and drag down to cell **F15**. A gray border, shown in **Figure 2-14**, will appear around the range as you drag to indicate the target cells.

6 Release the mouse button. The SUM formula will be copied into cells F13, F14, and F15. Check your results against those in **Figure 2-15**.

7 Save the workbook as Profit1.xls.

More

Using relative cell references is similar to giving directions that explain where to go from the present location. Relative cell references follow the same directional instructions regardless of your starting position, such as "the four cells to the left of" or "the three cells above." In the preceding example, the formula told Excel to calculate the average of the values in the four cells to the left of the cell containing the formula. Wherever that formula is pasted, Excel will examine the four cells to the left of the target cell for values. Any cells that are blank, or do not contain values (such as those with labels), will be included in the calculation as zero. If you had attempted to paste the AVERAGE formula used above into a cell in column B, there would not be enough cells to the left of the target cell to fulfill the required argument, and the error message #REF! would have appeared in the cell.

Figure 2-14 Copying a formula using the fill handle

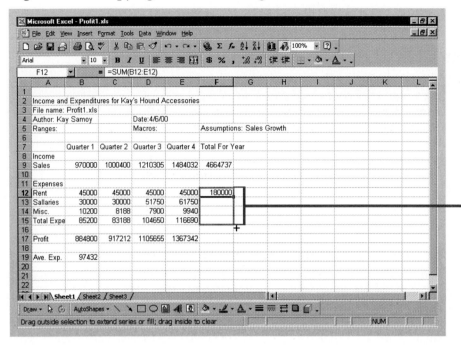

Formula will be pasted into these cells when the fill handle is released

Excel 2000

Figure 2-15 Results of copied formula

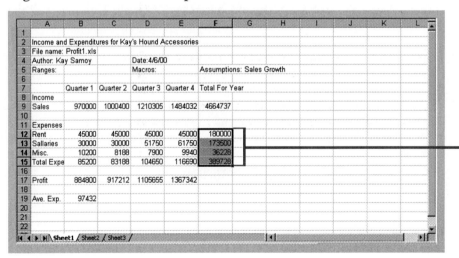

Pasted formulas calculated with appropriate cell references

Practice

To practice copying and pasting formulas, follow the instructions on the **Prac2-6** worksheet of the practice file **MyPractice 2.xls**. Save the changes you have made when you complete the exercise.

Hot Tip

You can select which characteristics of a cell's data you wish to paste by using the **Paste Special** command on the Edit menu. For example, use Paste Special to copy and paste the formula used in a cell, but not the formatting or value it contains.

Using What-If Analysis

Concept

Excel makes it easy for you to change certain conditions in your worksheet, allowing you to see how these changes affect the results of various spreadsheet calculations. This is called What-If analysis and is one of Excel's most useful features. It can be used to produce hypothetical and true projections of your data. Businesses benefit from this type of analysis because they can gain insight into the future with it and act accordingly.

Do It!

Kay wants to see what her sales would have been in Quarters 2, 3, and 4, assuming they grew 10% from the amount shown for the first quarter ($970,000).

1 Select the contents of cells C9, D9, and E9. These are the sales figures for the second, third, and fourth quarters and will be recalculated with the new assumption.

2 Press [Delete] to remove the values from the selected cells. Notice that the values in cells F9 and C15:E15 change. This is due to the fact that Excel automatically recalculates formulas when values in their referenced cells have been altered. The values in cells C9:E9 are now considered to be zero.

3 Click cell I5 to select it.

4 Enter .1 (10% expressed as a decimal) into the active cell. This is the cell that will be referenced in the formula that calculates projected earnings.

5 Click cell C9 to select it. Notice that Excel inserts a zero before the .1 in cell I5 as a place holder.

6 Now you must create a formula to multiply first quarter sales by 110%, which will show the results of a 10% increase. Enter the formula =B9*(1+I5) into the active cell, as shown in **Figure 2-16**. The dollar signs preceding the column letter I and the row number 5 tell Excel not to change the cell address, even if the formula is moved to a new location. This is known as an absolute cell reference.

7 Press [Enter]. The result of the calculation, 1067000, appears in place of the formula in cell C9. Cells F9 and B17 both change to reflect Excel's recalculation of their formulas, which include the cell C9 in their argument.

Figure 2-16 Using absolute cell references to perform What-If analysis

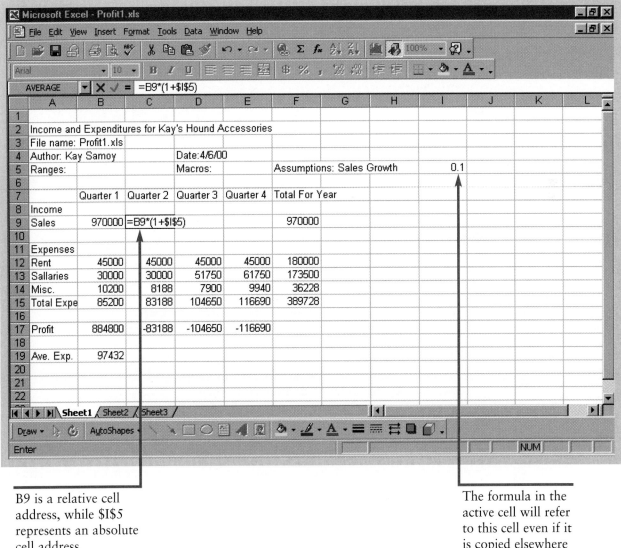

B9 is a relative cell address, while I5 represents an absolute cell address

The formula in the active cell will refer to this cell even if it is copied elsewhere

Using What-If Analysis (continued)

Do It!

8. Click the Copy button to copy the cell's formula to the Clipboard. An animated border appears around cell C9 to indicate that the selection is ready to be copied.

9. Click cell D9 to activate it, then click the Paste button. The pasted formula appears in the formula bar and the result, 1173700, appears in the cell. Notice that the reference to cell B9 has changed to C9, but that the reference to cell I5 remains the same. If the dollar signs had not been included, the copied formula would have replaced the cell reference I5 with J5, an empty cell, and the result would have been wrong.

10. Click cell E9 to activate it, then click the Paste button. As before, the formula is pasted and a new result, 1291070, appears in the cell, as shown in **Figure 2-17**.

11. Press [Enter] to confirm that the correct formula has been pasted into the target cell.

12. Click the Save button to save your work.

More

Formulas can contain several operations. An operation is a single mathematical step in solving an equation, such as adding two numbers or calculating an exponent. When working with formulas that contain multiple operators, such as 12/200+4*8, Excel performs the calculations in the following order:

1. Parentheses
2. Exponents
3. Multiplication and division, from left to right
4. Addition and subtraction, from left to right

Operations inside parentheses are calculated first, in accordance with the rules above. For example, in the calculation 12/200+4*8, the operations would be performed as follows: first, 12 would be divided by 200, then four would be multiplied by 8, and finally the two results would be added together. If the equation was 12/(200+4)*8, then the operations would be calculated like this: first, 200 would be added to 4, then 12 would be divided by the result, and finally the dividend would be multiplied by 8.

Figure 2-17 Copying a formula containing an absolute cell address

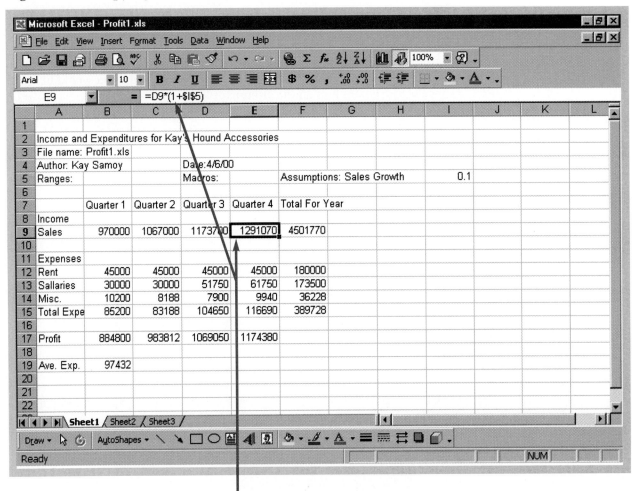

Excel 2000

Though the relative cell address changed from B9 to D9 when the formula was copied, the absolute address for cell I5 remains unchanged

Practice

To practice using absolute cell references and What-If analysis, follow the instructions on the **Prac2-7** worksheet of the practice file **MyPractice 2.xls**. Save the changes you have made when you complete the exercise.

Hot Tip

If you want both the column and row in a cell reference to remain absolute, then a $ must be placed in front of each. Placing a $ before only one part of the reference will make only that part absolute, while the other remains relative.

Previewing and Printing a Worksheet

Concept

Printing your worksheet is useful if you would like to have a paper copy to file, reference, or distribute to others. While offices are becoming more and more electronic, many people still prefer working with paper documents to viewing them on a screen. Excel allows you to view the worksheet as it will appear on the printed page before it is printed so that you can spot errors or items you would like to change before going through the printing process.

Do It!

Kay will display her worksheet in Print Preview mode, then print it.

1 Make sure your computer is properly connected to a working printer. (Ask your instructor.)

2 Click the Print Preview button on the Standard toolbar. The worksheet will be displayed in Print Preview mode, as shown in **Figure 2-18**. The mouse pointer appears as a magnifying glass.

3 Click at the top of the preview page. The worksheet will be magnified so that you may examine it more closely, and the pointer will change to an arrow. Since gridlines are nonprinting items by default, they do not appear in the preview.

4 Click Print... on the Print Preview toolbar. The view will revert to regular mode and the Print dialog box, **Figure 2-19**, will open.

5 Click OK. The Print dialog box will close, a box will appear notifying you of the print job's progress, and the document will be sent to the printer.

More

You can adjust many printing options by selecting the Page Setup command on the File menu. The Page Setup dialog box will open with four tabs: Page, Margins, Header/Footer, and Sheet. The Page tab controls the way in which the printed selection will appear on the page, such as its horizontal or vertical orientation, or by how much or little it is magnified. The Margins tab allows you to adjust the amount of space between printed matter and the edges of the page. The Header/Footer tab allows you to enter items that will appear at the top or bottom of each page, such as page numbers, titles, file names, or the name of the author. The Sheet tab lets you select how your data are presented on the printed page, such as whether or not you want to print gridlines, which parts of the worksheet you wish to print, and whether you want column headings to be repeated across each new page.

Figure 2-18 Previewing your worksheet

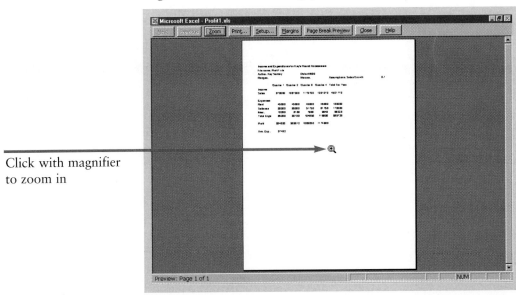

Click with magnifier
to zoom in

Figure 2-19 Print dialog box

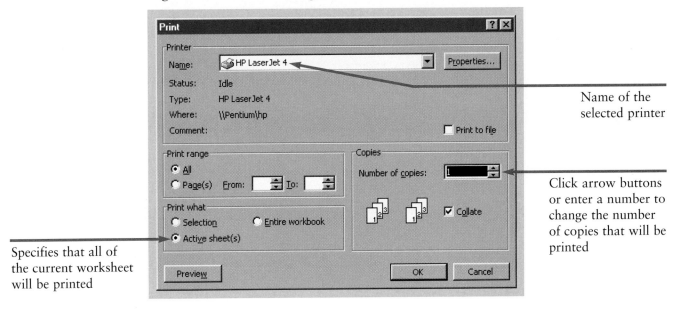

Name of the
selected printer

Click arrow buttons
or enter a number to
change the number
of copies that will be
printed

Specifies that all of
the current worksheet
will be printed

Practice

To practice previewing and printing worksheets, follow the instructions on the
Prac2-8 worksheet of the practice file
MyPractice 2.xls. Close the workbook
when you have completed the exercise.

Hot Tip

If you do not need to conduct a print
preview or adjust the settings in the Print
dialog box, you can print the active worksheet by clicking the Print button 🖨 on
the Standard toolbar.

Shortcuts

Function	Button/Mouse	Menu	Keyboard
Copy data to the Clipboard	📋	Click Edit, then click Copy	[Ctrl]+[C]
Cut data to the Clipboard	✂	Click Edit, then click Cut	[Ctrl]+[X]
Paste data from the Clipboard	📋	Click Edit, then click Paste	[Ctrl]+[V]
AutoSum	Σ		
Paste Function	f∗	Click Insert, then click Function	
Print Preview	🔍	Click File, then click Print Preview	
Print	🖨 (to skip Print dialog box)	Click File, then click Print (for Print dialog box)	[Ctrl]+[P] (for Print dialog box)

Identify Key Features

Name the items indicated by callouts in **Figure 2-20**.

Figure 2-20 Features of an Excel screen and worksheet

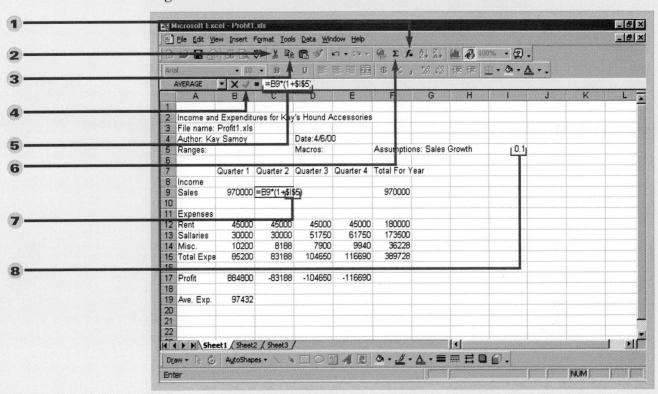

Excel 2000

Select the Best Answer

9. The small square in the lower-right corner of the active cell

10. A temporary storage space for cut or copied information

11. Use this symbol to represent multiplication in a formula

12. Allows you to view a worksheet as it will appear on an actual page

13. Lets you adjust margins or switch the page orientation

14. Offers **AVERAGE** as one of its choices

15. Aligned to the right by default

16. Type this symbol to designate a cell reference as absolute

a. Page Setup dialog box

b. Print Preview

c. Paste Function dialog box

d. Dollar sign

e. Fill handle

f. Clipboard

g. Asterisk

h. Values

Quiz (continued)

Complete the Statement

17. When using the fill handle, cells to be filled are indicated by a:

    a. ScreenTip

    b. Plus sign

    c. Check mark

    d. Gray border

18. Typing an apostrophe before a number instructs Excel to recognize it as a:

    a. Label

    b. Value

    c. Function

    d. Formula

19. None of the following actions will erase the Clipboard except:

    a. Pasting an item

    b. Cutting a new item

    c. Copying a new item

    d. Turning off the computer

20. By default, Excel considers referenced cell addresses to be:

    a. Absolute

    b. Copied from the Clipboard

    c. Relative

    d. AutoSums

21. Changing conditions to see how the results affect spreadsheet calculations is called:

    a. Absolute analysis

    b. Variable analysis

    c. Assumption analysis

    d. What-If analysis

22. To copy cell contents to a new location, drag and drop the cell pointer while pressing:

    a. [Shift]

    b. [Enter]

    c. [Tab]

    d. [Ctrl]

23. An animated border indicates that the cell contents:

    a. Will be deleted

    b. Are the result of a function or formula

    c. Have been sent to the Clipboard

    d. Have been pasted

24. The information enclosed in parentheses in a function is called the:

    a. Quantifier

    b. Argument

    c. Cell reference

    d. AutoSum

Interactivity

Test Your Skills

1. Enter values into your spreadsheet:

   a. Open the file you created in the first lesson, **Solved1-1.xls**.

   b. Fill in values to display how many hours you spend on each activity every day. For example, if you have four hours of class on Monday, enter the number 4 in the cell where the Monday column intersects with the Class row.

   c. If any of the values are repeated during the week, use the copy and paste commands to copy them from one cell to the others.

2. Use the AutoSum function to total the number of hours you spend on each activity during the week.

   a. Create a **Total Hours** label in the same row as the days-of-the-week labels, in the column directly to the right of the Sunday column.

   b. Use AutoSum to enter the total hours you spend in class in the cell where the Total Hours column and the Class row intersect.

   c. Use the fill handle to copy the AutoSum function into the next five cells in the Total Hours column in order to calculate the total hours for the remaining daily activities.

3. Calculate the average time you spend on each activity each week by using the Paste Function command:

   a. Enter the label **Average** in the cell directly to the right of Total Hours.

   b. Select the cell where the Average column intersects with the Class row. Then use the Paste Function command to place the average number of hours spent in class during the week in the active cell.

   c. Place the averages for the five other daily activities in the Average column by using the fill handle.

4. Preview and print the worksheet:

   a. Switch to Print Preview mode.

   b. Zoom in on the right side of the worksheet.

   c. Change the orientation of the page to Landscape.

   d. Print the worksheet.

   e. Return to normal view and save the file as **Test 2.xls**.

Interactivity (continued)

Problem Solving

1. Using the skills you have learned so far, create a spreadsheet that will allow you to track your individual monthly expenses for a year. Divide the year into four quarters, and use category labels such as rent, phone bill, books or supplies, food, entertainment, and so on. Calculate your total expenses for each quarter, as well as your average quarterly expenses. Also include an assumption value of 5 percent to account for going over your allotted budget. Then conduct a What-If analysis to recalculate your total and average expenses based on a 5 percent increase in one of the categories. Save the file as Solved 2.xls.

2. Open the file Solved-HR.xls that you created at the end of Lesson 1. To review, you designed this spreadsheet to detail how you will use the $10,000 increase in your Human Resources expense account to improve recruiting. Now it is time to put the spreadsheet to work. Enter values to fill in the existing structure. Then add a label for a cell in which you can add up the different monetary allotments to demonstrate that you have not surpassed the $10,000 amount. Use a formula or function to calculate this total. Print a copy of the file, and then save it as Solved-HR2.xls.

3. Open the file Solved-Rest.xls that you also created in Lesson 1. Using fictional names and hours, complete the weekly waitstaff schedule that you designed. If your worksheet does not already have one, include a column that will store the total hours for each staff member each day, one for total hours for the week, and one for average hours per day. Using the skills you learned in this lesson, instruct Excel to calculate the data for these columns. When you have finished, print the worksheet and save it as Solved-Rest2.xls.

LESSON

3

FORMATTING WORKSHEET ELEMENTS

As you work with your spreadsheet, you will find that you use certain groups of cells that contain related data repeatedly. Excel allows you to define these groups as ranges, and name them as you see fit. Then, rather than select the range by dragging the mouse over it, you can select the appropriate cells quickly and accurately with the Name box.

Formatting refers to changing the appearance of information in a worksheet without changing its actual content. You can use Excel's many formatting tools to improve the appearance and the effectiveness of your spreadsheet. Text formatting includes font, font size, style, color, and alignment. Labels also can be formatted in a variety of styles, some of which help to express the kind of data they represent. You can format individual cells or ranges of cells. The AutoFormat command permits you to apply a set of predesigned formats to an entire range at once.

Although the structure of an Excel spreadsheet is highly organized, it is also very flexible. You can change the structure by increasing or decreasing column widths and row heights. You also can add and delete rows and columns as necessary. Changes to the structure of your worksheet depend on the data it contains and the formatting you have applied.

CASE STUDY

Kay will continue to develop and organize her spreadsheet by naming her ranges and adding formatting to her data. She also will modify the physical structure of the worksheet in order to improve its layout.

Defining and Naming Ranges

Concept

A **range** is any group of two or more cells, usually contiguous. The range B12 to E12 consists of these two cells, called **anchor cells**, and all cells between them. The data for this range is Kay's rent. Range addresses are defined by citing the first and last cell in the range separated by a colon. The address for the range for Kay's rent is B12:E12. Ranges are named so that they are easy to locate. These names also can be used in formulas. You can name a range using the **Name Box** or the **Define Name** dialog box.

Do It!

Kay wants to define and name all of the ranges in her worksheet that contain data.

1 Open **Profit1.xls**. Click cell **B9**, then drag to cell **F9** to select these cells. The range for Sales is defined as B9:F9, and will be highlighted.

2 Click inside the **Name box** [B9 ▼]. The cell name B9 will become active, indicated by its highlighting.

3 Type **Sales**, then press **[Enter]**. The range B9:F9 is now named Sales, and the range name will appear in the Name box whenever cells B9 to F9 are selected.

4 Repeat this process to name the remaining row labels, being sure to press **[Enter]** after each range name. Name the range B12:E12 **Rent**, the range B13:E13 **Salaries**, the range B14:E14 **Miscellaneous**, the range B15:E15 **Total_Expenses**, and range B17:E17 **Profit**. Be sure to include the underscore (**[Shift]+[-]**) in the name Total_Expenses, as range names cannot contain any spaces. When you click the Name box drop-down arrow your Name box list should now resemble the one shown in **Figure 3-1**.

Figure 3-1 Defining and naming ranges

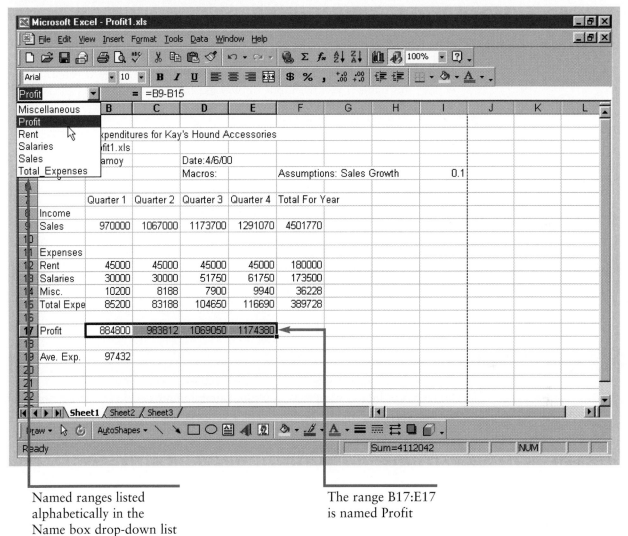

Named ranges listed
alphabetically in the
Name box drop-down list

The range B17:E17
is named Profit

Defining and Naming Ranges (continued)

Do It!

5 Click cell B8, and drag down to cell B17. The range B8:B17 will be selected.

6 Click Insert, highlight Name, then click Define. The Define Name dialog box, shown in **Figure 3-2**, will open with the range name Quarter_1 in the **Names in Workbook:** text box. Excel automatically picks up a column or row label as the default range name if it is adjacent to, or included in, the range selected. You can change this name if you wish, but we will use the defaults for this exercise.

7 Click [OK] to name the range.

8 Click cell C8, then hold [Shift] down and click cell C17. The range C8:C17 will become highlighted. Holding the [Shift] key down highlights all of the cells between the first and the last cells you select.

9 Repeat step six to name this range Quarter_2.

10 Use the Define Name dialog box to name the range D8:D17 Quarter_3, the range E8:E17 Quarter_4, and the range F8:F17 Total_for_Year.

11 Click elsewhere in the worksheet to deselect the range.

12 Click the Save button 🖫 to save the changes you have made to the worksheet.

More

Ranges do not have to be made up of cells that are touching. They can contain nonadjacent blocks of cells, or multiple nonadjoining cells. To create a nonadjacent range, highlight the first group of cells or a single cell that you wish to include, then hold down [Ctrl] while selecting the next cluster of cells. You can select as many noncontiguous cells or ranges as you desire. Clicking anywhere else in the worksheet will deselect the ranges.

Figure 3-2 Define Name dialog box

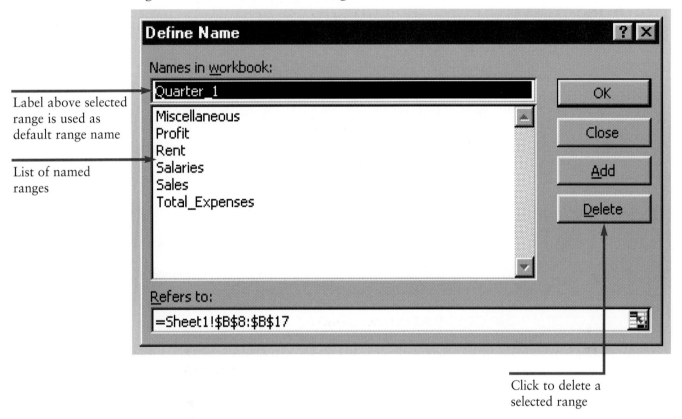

Label above selected range is used as default range name

List of named ranges

Click to delete a selected range

Excel 2000

Practice

Open the practice file **Practice–Lesson 3.xls**, save it as **MyPractice 3,** and then follow the instructions on the **Prac3-1** worksheet. Save the changes you have made when you complete the exercise.

Hot Tip

Use the Name Box drop-down list to quick-ly select a range to be used in a formula or to be formatted.

Formatting Cell Contents

Concept

Formatting enhances the appearance of your worksheet and can make your labels stand out, so they will be easier to read. Formatting options include changing the font (typeface and size), style, and alignment of your text. A cell or range must be selected before formatting can be applied to it.

Do It!

Kay wants to add formatting to various cells to emphasize their contribution to the worksheet.

1. Click the **Name** box drop-down arrow, then click **Profit** on the list of named ranges that appears. If Profit had not been visible, you would have had to use the scroll bar on the right edge of the list to access the rest of the range names it contains.

2. Click **Format**, then click **Cells**. The Format Cells dialog box will open.

3. Click the **Font** tab to bring it to the front of the stack, as shown in **Figure 3-3**.

4. Notice that the current font (**Arial**), font style (**regular**), and size (**10 point**) are highlighted. From the Font style list, select **Bold**. The letters in the Preview box will be made bold so that you may view the results of this change before you apply it.

5. Click [OK]. The dialog box will close and the numbers contained in the range named Profit will appear bold, as shown in **Figure 3-4**.

6. Click cell **A2** to make it active.

7. Click the **Font** box drop-down arrow. A list of the fonts installed on your computer will appear.

8. Drag the scroll bar box on the Font list down until **Times New Roman** is visible, then move the pointer over Times New Roman and click. The typeface of "Income and Expenditures for Kay's Hound Accessories" will change from Arial to Times New Roman.

9. Click the **Font Size** text box. The current point size of 10 will become highlighted, ready to be changed.

10. Type 14, then press [Enter]. The title will increase in size.

11. Select the range A2:K2. These are the columns across which the title will be centered.

12. Click the **Merge and Center** button 🖽, then click elsewhere on the worksheet to deselect the columns. **Figure 3-5** shows the new title placement.

Figure 3-3 Format Cells dialog box

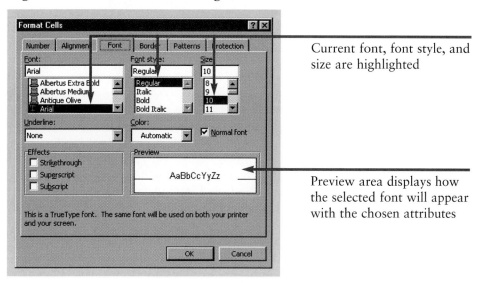

Current font, font style, and size are highlighted

Preview area displays how the selected font will appear with the chosen attributes

Figure 3-4 Bolding cell data

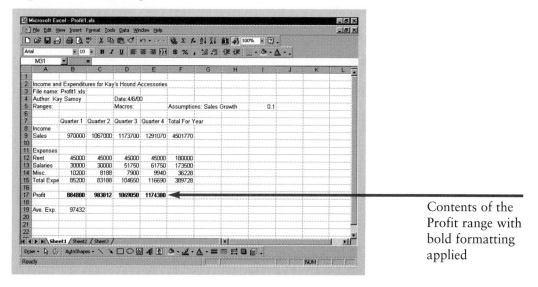

Contents of the Profit range with bold formatting applied

Figure 3-5 Formatted worksheet title

Font Size text box

Font box drop-down arrow

Worksheet title in 14-point Times New Roman and centered across cells A through K

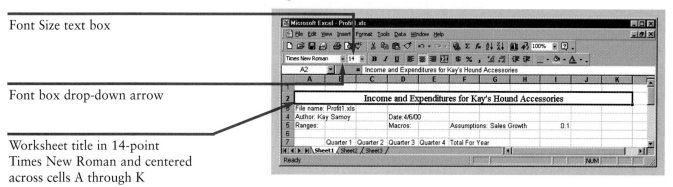

Formatting Cell Contents (continued)

Do It!

13 Select the range B7:F7.

14 Click the Italic button $\boxed{I}$. The column labels will change to italicized type.

15 Click the Underline button $\boxed{U}$. Each column label will be underlined. Notice that the Italic and Underline buttons are indented. An indented button indicates that a particular formatting option is being applied.

16 Select the range A8:A19.

17 Click the right edge, the arrow, of the Font Color button $\boxed{A}$. The Font Color palette, shown in **Figure 3-6**, will open.

18 Select the blue color box in the second row of the palette, then click anywhere on the worksheet to deselect the range. The row labels will change to blue. Your worksheet should appear as the one shown in **Figure 3-7**.

19 Click File, then click Save to save your work.

More

The Font tab in the Format Cells dialog box allows you to change most of the attributes relating to text. The options Font, Font style, and Size each have two boxes attached to them. The lower box is a list box that indexes available fonts, font styles, and font sizes respectively. The upper box is a text box wherein you can enter any of these choices without having to scroll through the list. However, the point size of your font selection is not limited to only those numbers listed, and can be anywhere between 1 and 409.

The Underline option contains a drop-down list with five styles of underlines that can be used. The Color option contains a drop-down palette with 56 color choices. Clicking one of these boxes will turn your text that color. Checking the Normal Font box reverts any changed font formats to the default settings described above. There are three effects you can select: Strikethrough draws a line through text, making it appear as if it has been crossed out; Superscript shrinks the text and raises it above the baseline; Subscript shrinks and drops the text below the baseline. Any alteration to a font formatting characteristic that you make will appear in the preview window in the tab, and none of the changes made will take effect on the worksheet until the OK button is clicked.

Figure 3-6 Font Color palette

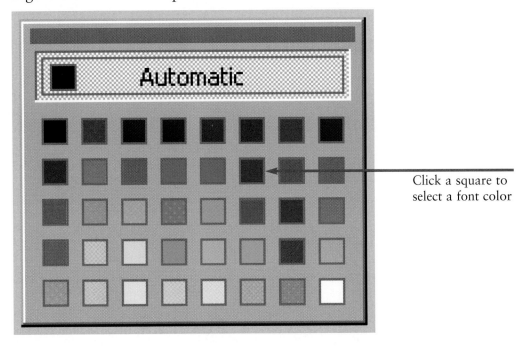

Click a square to
select a font color

Figure 3-7 Formatted cell contents

Italicized and underlined
cell labels

Cell labels with
color applied

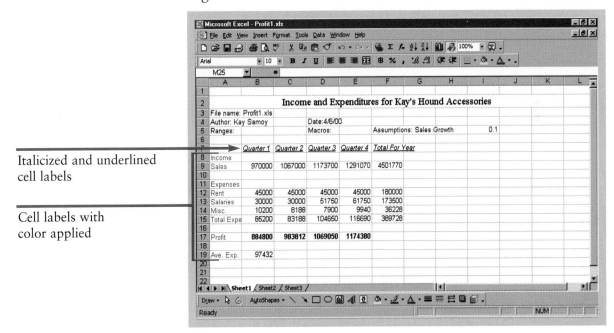

To practice formatting cell labels, follow the
instructions on the **Prac3-2** worksheet of
the practice file **MyPractice 3.xls**. Save the
changes you have made when you complete the exercise.

Hot Tip

Clicking an indented formatting button
removes the applied format and reverts the
button to its normal, flat, state.

Working with Rows and Columns

Concept

There are times when the information you enter into your worksheet will not fit neatly into a cell set with the default height and width. Therefore you may need to adjust the height of a row or, more commonly, the width of a column. The standard column width is 8.43 characters, but can be set anywhere between 0 and 255. **Table 3-1** displays commands you can use to adjust columns.

Do It!

Kay wants to widen some of the columns in her worksheet to accommodate long labels and values.

1 Move the mouse pointer onto the dividing line between the column A and column B heading buttons. The pointer will change from a cross ✛ to a double-arrow ✚ that will allow you to resize the column.

2 Click and hold the left mouse button. The gridline that divides the columns will become dotted and the column width will appear in a ScreenTip.

3 With the mouse button depressed, drag the column boundary to the right until the width reaches 13.00 characters. The entire label "Total Expenses" will be visible. While the "Total Expenses" label was cropped before you resized the column, notice that the label in cell F7, "Total for Year," is fully visible. Excel will display a label that is longer than its cell is wide in its entirety as long as the cell it intrudes upon is empty.

4 Click the column B heading button to select the entire column.

5 While holding [Ctrl], click the column C, D, E, and F heading buttons so that all five columns are selected, as shown in **Figure 3-8**.

6 Click Format, highlight Column, then select Width from the submenu. The Column Width dialog box, **Figure 3-9**, will open.

7 Type 14 in the Column Width text box, then click OK . Columns B through F will increase in width to 14 characters. This width is to accommodate formatting that you will apply to the cell data in a later skill.

8 Save your work.

More

You also can adjust the height of the rows in your worksheet. Row height is measured in points, just as fonts are, and there are 72 points per inch. Dragging the line between two row heading buttons is one way to change a row's height. There is a Row command on the Format menu that allows you to alter height as well. Row height usually does not need to be changed manually, as Excel will adjust row height to fit the largest point size of a cell's label or data.

Table 3-1 Column formatting commands

COMMAND	FUNCTION
Width	Adjust the width to a specified number of characters
AutoFit Selection	Adjust the width to fit the widest cell entry
Hide	Hides a selected column from view
Unhide	Displays a hidden column
Standard Width	Allows you to set a default width size, and resets selected columns to the specified size

Excel 2000

Figure 3-8 Selecting columns to be resized

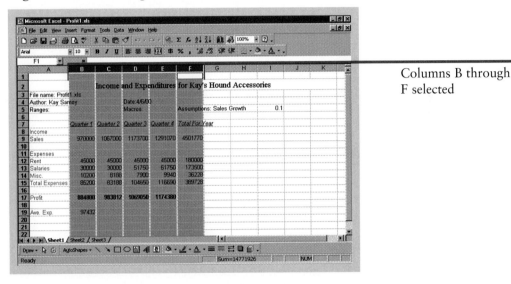

Columns B through
F selected

Figure 3-9 Column Width dialog box

Practice

To practice working with column and row widths, follow the instructions on the **Prac3-3** worksheet of the practice file **MyPractice 3.xls**. Save the changes you have made when you complete the exercise.

Hot Tip

You can resize a column's width to fit the widest entry automatically by double-clicking the right edge of the column heading button.

EX 3.11

Inserting and Deleting Rows and Columns

Concept

In Excel you can add and delete columns or rows to customize your worksheet to your specific needs. For example, you may want to add another column for new inventory products, or perhaps even delete a row that contains expenses that are no longer current.

Do It!

Kay wants to add an additional row between her documentation sections and the main body of her worksheet, and she wants to remove the column between Assumptions and the assumption value.

1. Click cell **A6** to make it active.

2. Click Insert, then click the Cells command. The Insert dialog box, **Figure 3-10**, will open with the **Shift cells down** radio button selected.

3. Click the Entire row radio button. This tells Excel to add a row and shift all of the rows below row 6 down.

4. Click [OK]. A new row will be inserted, the contents of the worksheet will shift down by one row, and your formulas will be updated to reflect the row shift.

5. Click cell **H5** to make it active.

6. Click Edit, then click Delete. The Delete dialog box, similar to Insert, will open with the **Shift Cells Left** radio button selected.

7. Click the Entire column radio button, then click [OK]. Cell H5 will be deleted and the Sales Growth data will move from I5 to H5. Even though the Sales values for Quarters 2 through 4 are based on the absolute address of the assumption, Excel will recalculate the formulas based on the new cell address. Compare your worksheet with that of **Figure 3-11**.

8. Save your workbook.

More

A **dummy column** or **dummy row** is a blank column or row included at the end of a defined range that is used to hold a place or create blank space. A dummy row between a range of values and a cell containing a formula to average them allows Excel to include the added row in the range rather than considering it to be an unrelated value. Then, if a row or column is added to the original range, Excel will recalculate any formulas that include that range to include the change. If you need to add a row or column to a range that does not include a dummy, you must manually adjust your formulas to take into account the new cells and values. If a row or column is inserted into the middle of an existing range, Excel is able to recalculate any formulas that reference that range. It is only when you need to add a row or column to the end of an existing range that is being used in a formula that a dummy row or column becomes necessary.

Figure 3-10 Insert dialog box

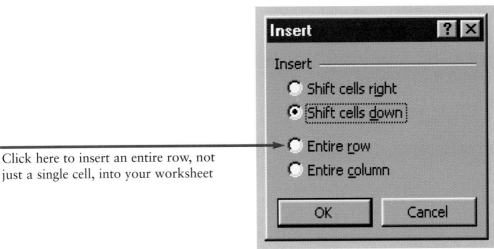

Click here to insert an entire row, not just a single cell, into your worksheet

Excel 2000

Figure 3-11 Worksheet with a row inserted and a cell deleted

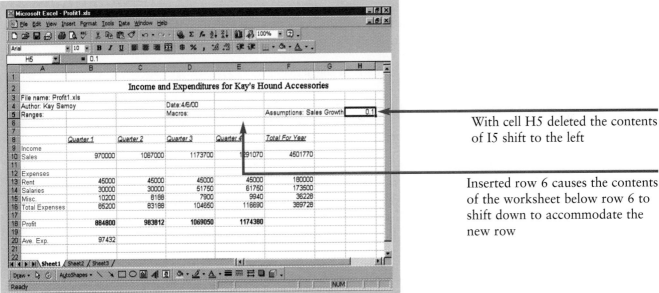

With cell H5 deleted the contents of I5 shift to the left

Inserted row 6 causes the contents of the worksheet below row 6 to shift down to accommodate the new row

EX 3.13

Formatting Cell Values

Concept

Although labels can help identify what kind of data a number represents, you may want to format the values themselves so that their function is more apparent. Common formats include Currency, Percentage, Fraction, and Comma. The format you choose will depend on how the values are to be used, and how you wish them to appear. Cell or range formatting can be applied before or after data are entered.

Do It!

Kay wants to format all of her values with commas so that they will be easier to read, format the Profit range in Currency Style, format her assumption in Percentage Style, and then decrease the number of decimal places in cell B20.

1. Select the range B10:F20.

2. Click the Comma Style button ［,］. All of the cells contained within the selected range will be formatted in the Comma Style, which includes two decimal places.

3. Click the Name box drop-down list arrow, then click Profit on the list of ranges that appears. The range B18:F18 will be highlighted.

4. Click the Currency Style button ［$］. The values entered in the Profit row will appear with dollar signs preceding them and two decimal places to represent cents.

5. Click cell H5 to make it the active cell.

6. Click the Percentage Style button ［%］. The originally entered value of 0.1 will appear as 10%. The result of the formula whose argument references this cell will remain the same.

7. Click cell B20 to activate it.

8. Click the Decrease Decimal button ［.00→.0］ twice. The two decimal places will be erased. **Figure 3-12** displays the worksheet as it should now appear.

9. Save the worksheet.

More

When you applied the Currency, Comma, and Percentage Styles to the worksheet, you used the default settings for each of these buttons. The **Number** tab of the Format Cells dialog box, shown in **Figure 3-13**, can be accessed by selecting the Cells command on the Format menu. It allows you to apply one of 12 different formatting styles to cells. Most of the categories of formatting listed on the Number tab can be customized to suit the specific needs of your worksheet and personal preferences.

The number of decimal place values taken and the appearance of date and time references can be altered, special formats can be defined for use in databases, and custom number formats can be created for advanced users of Excel.

Figure 3-12 Cell values with formatting applied

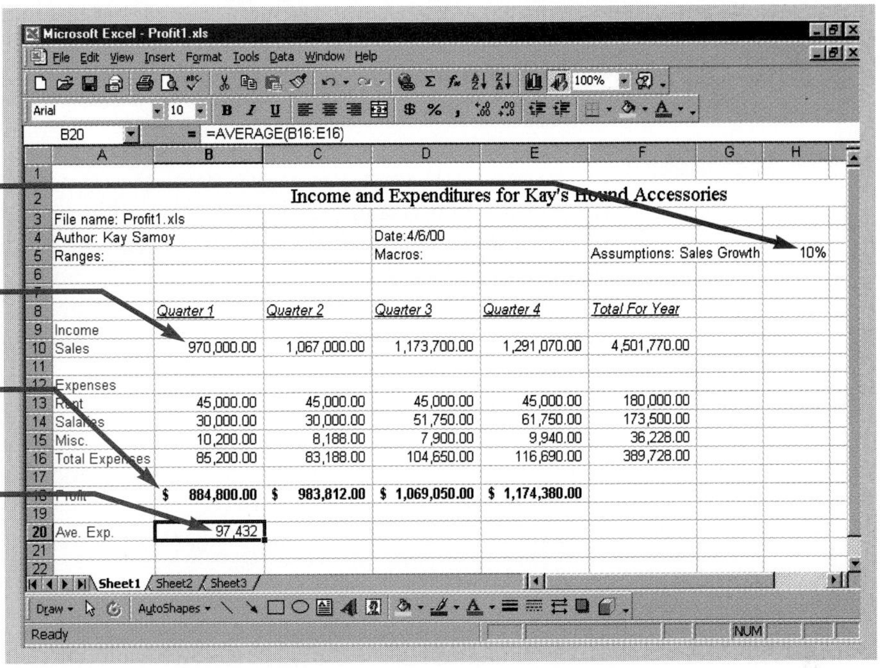

Percentage Style

Comma Style

Currency Style

Decimal places
reduced by two

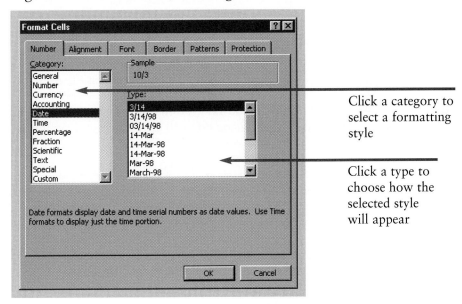

Figure 3-13 Format Cells dialog box

Click a category to
select a formatting
style

Click a type to
choose how the
selected style
will appear

Excel 2000

To practice formatting cell values, follow
the instructions on the **Prac3-5** worksheet
of the practice file **MyPractice 3.xls**. Save
the changes you have made when you
complete the exercise.

Hot Tip

If a cell is too narrow to display a value
correctly, Excel will display number signs
(#####) in place of the data, though the
actual value is unaffected. Making the cell
wide enough to accommodate the data
properly will make the value reappear.

Using AutoFormat

Concept

The AutoFormat command allows you to add one of 16 sets of formatting to selected ranges, creating tables that are easy to read and visually stimulating. Numbers, borders, fonts, patterns, alignment, and the height and width of rows and columns all can be altered using the AutoFormat options. AutoFormat alters the appearance of tables using colors, fonts, and textures.

Do It!

Kay wants to use the AutoFormat function to improve the appearance of her worksheet and set the main body data off from the documentation.

1. Select the range A8:F20 to make this area active.

2. Click Format, then select the AutoFormat command. The AutoFormat dialog box, shown in **Figure 3-14**, will open.

3. Drag the scroll box in the AutoFormat list box down to reveal the lower portion of the AutoFormat list, then select 3D Effects 2.

4. Click ⬚ OK ⬚, then click anywhere in the worksheet to deselect the area. The range A8:F20 will appear as shown in **Figure 3-15**.

5. Select the range A3:H5 to make this group of cells active.

6. Click Format, then select AutoFormat to open the AutoFormat dialog box.

7. Select List 1 from the Table Format list, then click the Options button ⬚ Options >> ⬚. The AutoFormat dialog box will grow to display six format types that you can include or exclude when the AutoFormat is applied.

8. Click Font, Width/Height, and Alignment so they do not display a check in their check boxes. The Sample table will show how the range will look with these options off. These options were turned off so as to preserve the font, size, and placement of the title and the width of the columns.

9. Click ⬚ OK ⬚, then click anywhere in the worksheet to deselect the range. **Figure 3-16** shows the worksheet documentation with the AutoFormatting.

10. Save your workbook.

Figure 3-14 AutoFormat dialog box

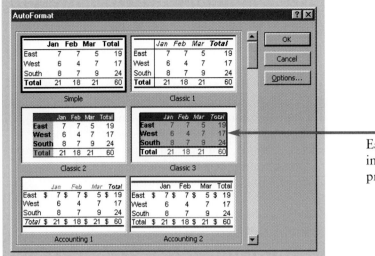

Each AutoFormat style includes a customizable preview

Excel 2000

Figure 3-15 AutoFormatting applied to the selected range

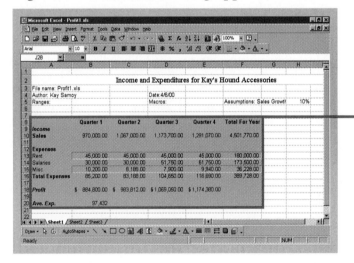

A8:F20 with 3D Effects 2 AutoFormatting applied

Figure 3-16 List 1 AutoFormatting applied

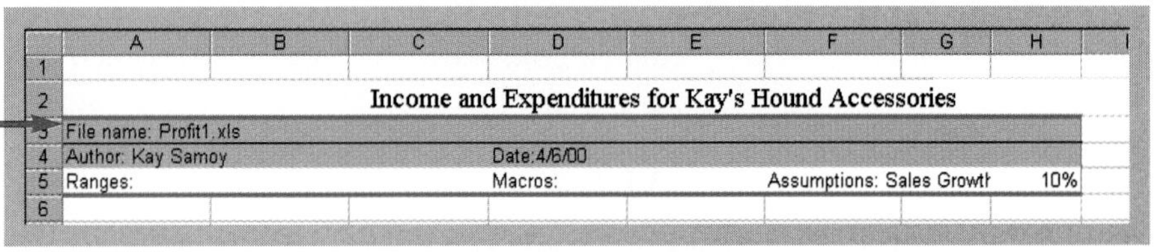

A3:H5 with List 1 AutoFormatting applied with Font, Width/Height, and Alignment left intact

---

Practice

To practice using AutoFormat, follow the instructions on the **Prac3-6** worksheet of the practice file **MyPractice 3.xls**. Save the changes you have made when you complete the exercise.

Hot Tip

The None option on the Table Format list in the AutoFormat dialog box will return a range to its original, unformatted style.

Filling a Range with Labels

Concept

Excel can automatically fill a range with several types of series information. Series information includes numbers, numbers combined with text (such as Quarter 1), dates, and times. Excel can step, or increase, a series by a constant set value, or multiply by a constant factor. For example, you can add all the months of the year to a worksheet by typing only January and then extending the series. The way a series fills will depend on the type of value and the incremental setting.

Do It!

To practice the **AutoFill** feature, Kay will erase the Quarter column headings and then replace them with a series fill.

1 Click cell B8 to select it, then press the [Backspace] key to delete the cell label.

2 Repeat this process for cells C8, D8, and E8. The range B8:E8 will be empty.

3 Click cell B8, then type **Quarter 1**.

4 Move the mouse pointer to the fill handle of the cell pointer surrounding cell B8. It will change to the crosshairs.

5 Drag the pointer to cell E8 with the fill handle. As you drag the pointer, a dimmed border will appear indicating the cells that have been selected, and ScreenTips will appear showing what will be placed in the cell where the mouse pointer currently is, as shown in **Figure 3-17**.

6 Release the mouse button. The range B8:E8 will be filled with Quarter 1 through Quarter 4.

7 Close your workbook without saving changes.

More

In the above example, you used **AutoFill** to enter a series of labels into a range of cells. Along with AutoFill, there are three other series fill types that you can use: Linear, Growth, and Date. These are advanced options and are found in the Series dialog box, shown in **Figure 3-18**, which can be accessed by clicking the Edit menu, selecting Fill, and then clicking Series on the submenu.

A Linear series fill, with the Trend box unchecked, adds the Step value to the value in the cell selected. With Trend checked, the Step value is disregarded and the trend is calculated based on the average of the difference between the values in the selected cells. This average is then used to fill the range by increasing or decreasing the value by a constant amount. If necessary, the original selected cell information is replaced to fit the trend.

A Growth series fill is similar to a Linear series fill, except that instead of adding values together, numbers are multiplied to create a geometric growth trend. A series created based upon dates uses the options in the Date unit list. You can extend selected dates by day, weekday, month, or year. The Stop value can be set so as to fix a value at which the series will end. If the selected range is filled before it reaches the Stop value, it will end at that point.

Figure 3-17 Filling a range with labels

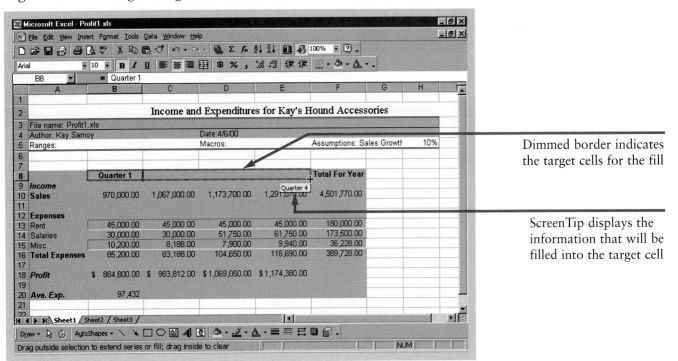

Dimmed border indicates the target cells for the fill

ScreenTip displays the information that will be filled into the target cell

Excel 2000

Figure 3-18 Series dialog box

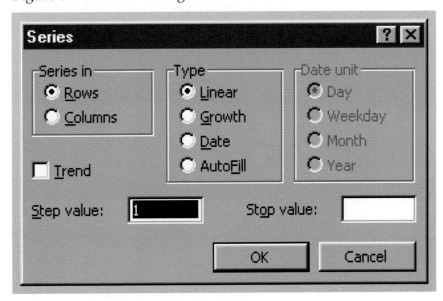

Practice

To practice filling ranges with labels, follow the instructions on the **Prac3-7** worksheet of the practice file **MyPractice 3.xls**. Save the changes you have made when you complete the exercise and close the file.

Hot Tip

If you select a value and then hold the right mouse button while dragging the fill handle, a pop-up menu will appear allowing you to choose the type of series that is inserted into the destination cells.

Formatting Cells and Ranges

Concept

As you have seen, you can format the contents of spreadsheet cells in order to make the spreadsheet more pleasing to the eye and more comprehensible. The AutoFormat command allows you to apply a set of formatting characteristics to the contents of cells or to a cell or range itself. Sometimes, however, you may want to exert more precise control over the appearance of a cell or range than AutoFormat permits. Excel gives you the ability to fill cells and ranges with colors and patterns, and outline them with special borders.

Do It!

Kay wants to experiment with adding a color pattern and a border to the title of her worksheet. She will then undo her experiment.

1 Click cell **A2** to select the merged cell that contains the worksheet's title.

2 Click the arrow on the right edge of the **Fill Color** button ![Fill Color button]. A color palette will open below the button.

3 Click the **Rose** color square in the bottom-left corner of the palette. The palette will close and the merged title cell will be filled with Rose.

4 Click **Format**, then click **Cells**. The Format Cells dialog box will open.

5 Click the **Border** tab to bring it to the front of the dialog box. In the **Presets** section of the tab, click the **Outline** button. In the **Line Style** section, select the dashed line (fourth down in the second column).

6 Click the **Color** selection arrow and choose the **Dark Red** square from the palette that appears. The Border tab should now look like **Figure 3-19**.

7 Click the **Patterns** tab to bring it to the front. Notice that the Rose color square is selected and shown in the **Sample** box because it has already been applied to the active cell.

8 Click the **Pattern** selection arrow. A color palette that includes patterns at the top will open. Click the **Diagonal Stripe** pattern (fourth from the left in the second row). The Pattern tab should now look like **Figure 3-20**.

9 Click ![OK] to apply the border and pattern to the selected cell, and then deselect the cell, which should resemble **Figure 3-21**.

10 Click the arrow on the right edge of the Undo ![Undo button] button and highlight the three Format Cells operations you just performed. Click the mouse to undo the actions.

11 Save and close the workbook.

More

The Font Color, Fill Color, and Borders buttons are all "loaded" with the last option (color or border type) you applied, which is displayed as part of the button's icon. To apply this option again, you do not need to click the button's arrow to open its palette. Simply click on the button itself.

Figure 3-19 Border tab

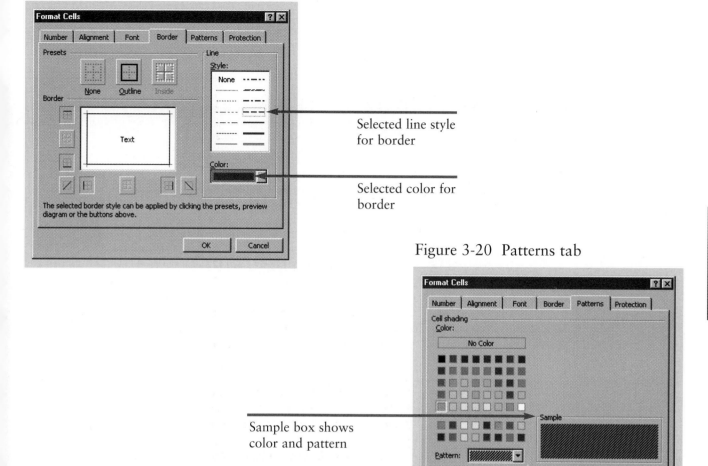

Excel 2000

Figure 3-20 Patterns tab

Figure 3-21 Cell formatted with color, pattern, and border

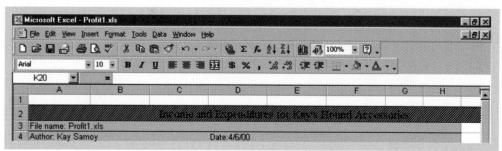

Practice

Open a new workbook. Then fill the range A1:D5 with the color Aqua; add an inside, dotted border to the range; and fill cell B2 with a yellow vertical stripe pattern. Save this exercise as **Prac3-8** and close the file when you are done.

Hot Tip

Color and patterns should be used carefully as overuse and misuse can damage the effectiveness of your spreadsheet, as you may have discovered while completing this Skill.

Shortcuts

Function	Button/Mouse	Menu	Keyboard
Merge cells and center contents	▦		
Merge cells		Click Format, then click Cells, then click Alignment	[Ctrl]+[1]
Make a label bold	**B**	Click Format, then click Cells, then click Font	[Ctrl]+[B]
Italicize a label	*I*	Click Format, then click Cells, then click Font	[Ctrl]+[I]
Underline a label	U	Click Format, then click Cells, then click Font	[Ctrl]+[U]
Add color to a label	A ▾	Click Format, then click Cells, then click Font	[Ctrl]+[1]
Comma Style	,	Click Format, then click Style	
Currency Style	$	Click Format, then click Style	
Percent Style	%	Click Format, then click Style	
Increase or decrease decimal places	.00 or .00		

Identify Key Features

Name the items indicated by callouts in **Figure 3-22.**

Figure 3-22 Formatting features

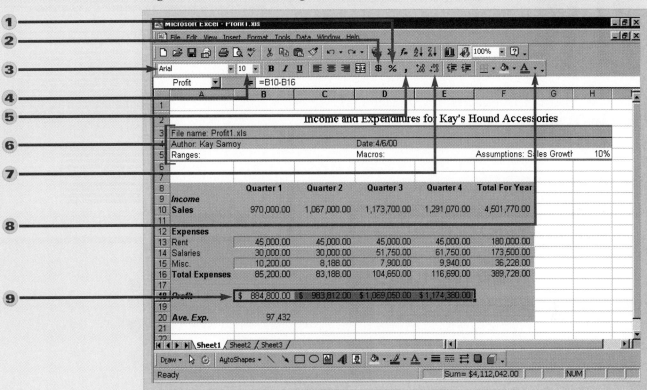

Excel 2000

Select the Best Answer

10. Allows you to select a named range quickly and accurately

11. Contains a tab with options for changing font, font style, and font size

12. Combines the contents of multiple cells into one cell

13. Lets you add a set of predetermined formatting options to a spreadsheet

14. Contains the Bold, Italic, and Underline buttons

15. A group of two or more cells

16. Indicates that a particular formatting style is applied to the current selection

17. A blank column at the end of a defined range

a. Indented button

b. Formatting toolbar

c. Dummy column

d. Format Cells dialog box

e. AutoFormat command

f. Name box

g. Range

h. Merge and Center button

Quiz (continued)

Complete the Statement

18. All of the following are effects available on the Font tab of the Format Cells dialog box except:

    a. Strikethrough

    b. Strikescript

    c. Superscript

    d. Subscript

19. An appropriate way to express a range address is:

    a. B9/E9

    b. B9;E9

    c. B9-E9

    d. B9:E9

20. A range name may not contain:

    a. Uppercase letters

    b. Labels used in the spreadsheet

    c. Spaces

    d. Numbers

21. The Formatting toolbar offers all of the following formatting styles except:

    a. Currency Style

    b. Percentage Style

    c. Fraction Style

    d. Comma Style

22. The standard width of a worksheet column is:

    a. 8.43 characters

    b. 13.00 characters

    c. 13.5 characters

    d. 255 characters

23. All of the following can be done from the Insert menu except:

    a. Insert a blank row

    b. Insert a blank column

    c. Define and name a range

    d. Apply an AutoFormat

24. A 72-point character would be equal to:

    a. 1 inch

    b. 1 foot

    c. 8.43 centimeters

    d. 8.43 inches

25. 3D Effects 2 is a type of:

    a. Cell value

    b. Range name

    c. AutoFormat

    d. Function

26. All of the following are examples of series data you can enter in a worksheet except:

    a. Linear

    b. Growth

    c. Currency

    d. AutoFill

27. The largest font size in points is:

    a. 409

    b. 256

    c. 72

    d. 8.43

Interactivity

Test Your Skills

1. Define and name the ranges in a spreadsheet:

   a. Open the file **Test 2.xls** that you created at the end of the previous lesson.

   b. Define and name the following ranges using the Name box: **Class, Activities, Meals, Studying/Homework, Leisure,** and **Sleep.**

   c. Define and name the following ranges by opening the Define Name dialog box from the Insert menu: **Monday, Tuesday, Wednesday, Thursday, Friday, Saturday, Sunday, Total Hours,** and **Average.**

2. Format cell labels in a spreadsheet:

   a. Change the font of the title of your worksheet to **Times New Roman,** and then change its size to 12 point.

   b. Merge and center the title across the first 10 columns of the worksheet.

   c. Add **bold** formatting to the days-of-the-week labels. *Italicize* and underline the **Total Hours** and **Average** labels.

   d. Change the font color of the daily activities labels in Column A to red, and then make them bold.

3. Adjust the columns and rows in your spreadsheet:

   a. Click and drag the right border of Column A until the column is 18.00 characters wide.

   b. Click and drag the right border of the **Wednesday** column until the entire label "Wednesday" is visible.

   c. Double-click with the mouse to automatically resize the **Total Hours** column so that its label fits.

   d. Add an extra row between the documentation and data sections of your worksheet.

4. Add advanced formatting to your spreadsheet:

   a. Reduce all values in the Average column to three decimal places.

   b. Apply **Comma Style** to all values in the Total Hours column.

   c. Apply the AutoFormat 3D Effects 1 to the documentation section of the worksheet.

   d. Apply the AutoFormat Classic 3 to the data section of your worksheet, but preserve the font and width/height that the worksheet already has.

   e. Add an **outside,** solid blue border to the merged title cell.

   f. Fill the title cell with the color **orange** and the pattern **Thin Horizontal Stripe.**

   g. Save the file as Test 3.xls.

Interactivity (continued)

Problem Solving

1. Utilize the knowledge and skills you have acquired about spreadsheet design to keep yourself on track as you work toward earning a diploma. Using Excel, create a worksheet that displays your graduation requirements and the means by which you are fulfilling them. Include courses you may have already taken, your current courses, and the courses you will need and want to take in the future. Also include data such as the total number of credits you need to graduate and the percentage you have so far. Calculate how many credits you will need to average each academic semester. Then see if your actual numbers are on pace. Finally, be sure to take advantage of Excel's formatting features to enhance the organization and appearance of your spreadsheet. Save the file as **Solved 3-Grad.xls**.

2. Open Solved-HR2.xls, a file you saved at the end of the previous lesson. Define and name all relevant ranges in the worksheet. Format the entire worksheet in a professional manner, using both independent formatting techniques and one instance of the AutoFormat command. Make sure to employ Currency Style where appropriate, and do not allow this formatting to be overwritten by an AutoFormat. Print the worksheet and save the file as **Solved-HR3.xls**.

3. Open Solved-Rest2.xls, the other file you saved at the end of the previous lesson. Delete the column that holds the data for the average hours worked per day by each member of the waitstaff. Delete all of the labels that refer to days of the week in the schedule and replace them using an AutoFill. Apply bold formatting to all column heading labels and make their text green. Italicize all row heading labels and change their font to **11**-point, **Arial Narrow** text. Define all horizontal ranges using the Name box and vertical ranges using menu commands. Save the file as Solved-Rest3.xls and print a hard copy.

4. Replicate the worksheet shown below to the best of your ability.

Then, delete Column B, insert a row between the numbers section and the days section, insert three rows between the days section and the red pattern section, and, finally, delete the extra cells that were added to Column A. Print the resulting worksheet.

L E S S O N

4

INSERTING OBJECTS AND CHARTS

Though the labels and values you enter into a spreadsheet serve as its core, other objects may represent certain data better or simply illustrate it further. Inserting these objects can break up the monotony of row after row of numbers and allow you to explain or highlight aspects of your spreadsheet that might otherwise go unnoticed.

You can insert a number of objects into your worksheet for the purpose of annotating specific information. These include text boxes, shapes such as arrows and connectors, and comments. Text boxes can be any size, but will obscure the portions of the worksheet behind them. Comments are similar to text boxes, but can be hidden from view. All graphics can be formatted and manipulated in a variety of ways.

One very effective way of enhancing your worksheet visually is to add a chart. The Chart Wizard can guide you through the process of creating a graphical representation of a data series that you select from your Excel worksheet. Charts can be moved, resized, and formatted. You can even change a chart's type and characteristics after it has been created. In addition, individual chart elements can be customized for emphasis and clarity.

CASE STUDY
In this lesson, Kay will strengthen her spreadsheet by inserting graphics and creating a chart using the Chart Wizard. Afterward, she will use some of Excel's advanced printing features to print a new copy of her worksheet.

Inserting Text Boxes

Concept

Text also can be inserted into a worksheet within a text box. Creating text boxes allows you to add passages of any size and appearance without the constraints of a cell in the worksheet. A text box is an independent object. Therefore, you can use it to reference data without affecting the data.

Do It!

Kay wants to insert a text box into her worksheet to emphasize the growth in projected Quarter 4 sales.

1. Open **Profit1.xls**. Click **View**, highlight **Toolbars**, then click **Drawing** if it is not already checked. The Drawing toolbar will be visible.

2. Click the **Text Box** button 🖾 on the Drawing toolbar. The pointer will change to the text cursor ↓ when it is in the workspace, allowing you to create a text box.

3. Click in cell **E6**, just below the green line where you want the top-left corner of the text box to appear, then drag down and to the right to cell **F7**, until the box you have created is approximately one cell long by two cells high, like the one shown in **Figure 4-1**. When you release the mouse button, the borders of the box will become dotted and eight small squares called sizing handles will appear. There will be a sizing handle at each corner and one in the center of each side of the text box. A blinking insertion point also will appear in the text box.

4. Type **Up 33% from Quarter 1** to enter it into the text box.

5. Click elsewhere in the worksheet to deselect the text box. Your worksheet should now resemble the one shown in **Figure 4-2**.

6. Save your worksheet.

More

The primary advantage of using text boxes is their flexibility. Text boxes may be easily moved, resized, or reformatted, without affecting the appearance or content of any other part of the worksheet. When text is being entered, a text box acts as a small word processing window. If there is not enough room on a line to fit a word, the text will wrap and continue on the next line. If the text box you have made is not large enough to accommodate the text as you are entering it, then the text will scroll upward, without changing the size or location of the box, to allow the additional text to be entered. The text box will have to be enlarged manually to view all of the text it contains. This can be accomplished through the use of the sizing handles, by clicking and dragging the handle in the desired direction of movement, expanding or reducing the size of the box.

Once a text box has been created, it is not fixed in place, but may be moved anywhere on the worksheet. To move a text box to another part of the worksheet, click the frame of a selected text box (not on a sizing handle) to select its frame, and then drag the text box to the desired destination.

Figure 4-1 Creating a text box

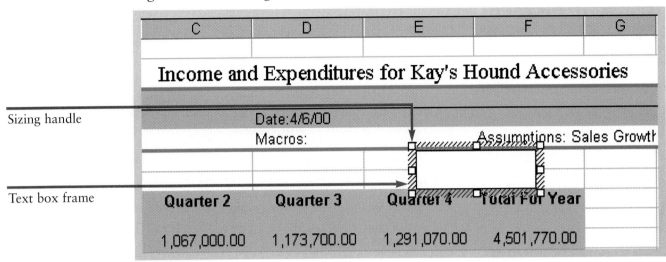

Sizing handle

Text box frame

Figure 4-2 Text box with text

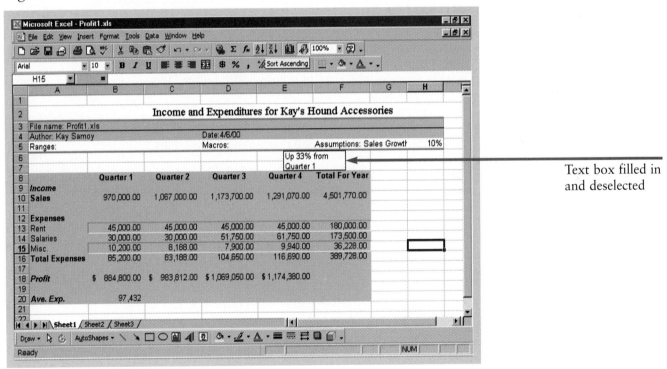

Text box filled in and deselected

Practice

To practice inserting text boxes, open the practice file **Practice–Lesson 4.xls**, save the file as **MyPractice 4.xls**, then follow the instructions on the **Prac4-1** worksheet. Save the changes you have made when you complete the exercise.

Hot Tip

Text boxes are visible by default and hide the portion of the worksheet behind them. Text boxes can overlap each other, however, and their order can be changed by right-clicking one and choosing an option from the Order submenu that appears.

Enhancing Graphics

Concept

Graphic objects that you have inserted, such as lines, text boxes, or pictures, can be modified to alter and improve their appearance.

Do It!

Kay will add a callout arrow and color to the text box that she inserted in the previous Skill.

1 Click the Arrow button ◤ on the Drawing toolbar. It will indent, and the mouse pointer will appear as a thin cross + when it is over the worksheet.

2 Position the pointer just after the **1** in the text box, then click and drag to cell E10, the Sales value for Quarter 4. When the mouse button is released, the line that was being drawn becomes fixed, and an arrowhead appears at the end.

3 Click the text box to select it. Its frame becomes a thick hatched line.

4 Click the text box's frame (but not a sizing handle) to select the frame. It changes from a hatched to a dotted border.

5 Click the arrow on the Fill Color button 🪣 on the Drawing toolbar to open the Fill Color palette.

6 Click the pale blue square in the bottom row of the palette to select it. The text box's background will change to match the selected color.

7 Click the arrow you drew to select it. A sizing handle appears at each end of the arrow to indicate its selection.

8 Click the Line Color drop-down arrow 🖌 to open the Line Color palette, and select the red square in the middle of the first column. The arrow will change to match the color of the selected square.

9 Click elsewhere in the worksheet to deselect the arrow. The text box and arrow should now resemble the ones shown in **Figure 4-3**.

More

The Format menu is context-sensitive, which means that its content changes based on the item that is selected. When a cell is active, the Format menu contains commands for altering a cell, while a selected AutoShape will cause another set of commands to appear on the Format menu. Objects that are inserted into an Excel document, such as lines, AutoShapes, and Clip Art, all have their own formatting dialog boxes with tabs relating to the selected object.

The Format Text Box command, available on the Format menu when a text box is selected, opens the Format Text Box dialog box shown in **Figure 4-4**. This dialog box contains seven tabs with options for altering many aspects of a text box. While many of the controls found in the Format Text Box dialog box have toolbar buttons, the dialog box allows more precise and comprehensive control over such aspects as the size of the text box, the internal margins of the text box, and the orientation of text within a text box.

Figure 4-3 Enhancing worksheet graphics

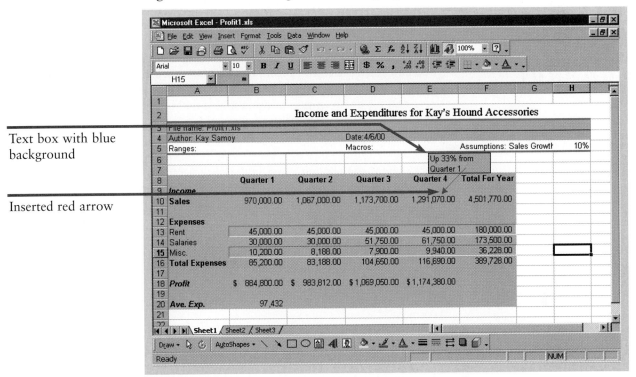

Text box with blue
background

Inserted red arrow

Figure 4-4 Format Text Box dialog box

Click a tab to format
the corresponding
aspect of the selected
text box

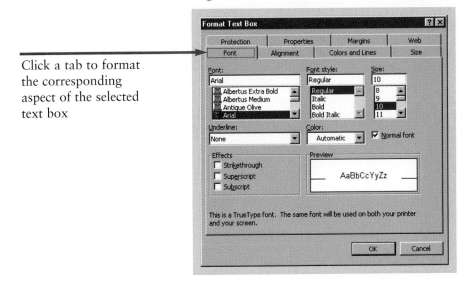

Practice

To practice enhancing graphics, follow the
instructions on the **Prac4-2** worksheet of
the practice file **MyPractice 4.xls**. Save the
changes you have made when you complete the exercise.

Hot Tip

You can open an object's formatting dialog
box by double-clicking it. Double-clicking a
text box's frame will open the dialog box
shown above, but double-clicking in the
text box will only allow you to alter the text
itself.

Adding Comments

Concept

A comment is an electronic note that can be attached to a cell. Comments are hidden from view until the mouse pointer is over a cell that contains one. Comments are useful for documenting information or making notes. If multiple people will be using a spreadsheet, comments can be used as a way to share information.

Do It!

Since there is not enough room in the documentation section of her worksheet to list all of the named ranges, Kay will insert a comment containing the range names.

1 Click cell **A5** to make it active.

2 Click **Insert**, then click **Comment**. An active text box with the name of the designated user and an insertion point, shown in **Figure 4-5**, will appear next to the selected cell. The text box will have an arrow pointing to the cell it references and a red triangle will appear in the upper-right corner of the cell indicating that it contains a comment.

3 Select the contents of the cell by dragging the I-beam over the text in the box.

4 Type **Kay Samoy:** and then press **[Enter]**. This is to indicate that Kay is the author of the comment. Notice that the name that first appeared in the comment box appears in the status bar. This can be changed from the General tab of the Options dialog box available on the Tools menu.

5 Type the following range names, pressing **[Enter]** after each: **Miscellaneous**, **Profit**, **Quarter 1**, **Quarter 2**, **Quarter 3**, **Quarter 4**, **Rent**, **Salaries**, **Sales**, **Total Expenses**. The text will scroll as you type, hiding the first few entries.

6 Drag the midpoint sizing handle of the bottom edge of the comment box down until it is approximately even with row 13. When you release the mouse button, the comment box will expand so that all the text will be visible as shown in **Figure 4-6**.

7 Click elsewhere in the worksheet to deselect cell A5 and hide the comment.

8 Position the pointer over cell A5. The comment will be displayed.

9 Save your workbook.

More

Like cells and text boxes, comment boxes and the text they contain can be formatted. Right-clicking a cell that contains a comment opens a pop-up menu with a command for editing and deleting comments. These commands activate the comment connected to the selected cell. Double-clicking the comment's border will open the Format Comment dialog box, and clicking in the comment box will allow you to manipulate the text itself. The **Reviewing** toolbar, whose buttons are listed in **Table 4-1**, contains commands for displaying and navigating among comments. It can be activated from the Toolbars submenu on the View menu. Once a comment has been opened for editing, you can move it anywhere in the worksheet by clicking and dragging its border; a line always runs from the comment to its parent cell.

Figure 4-5 Adding a comment to a cell

Figure 4-6 Kay's comment

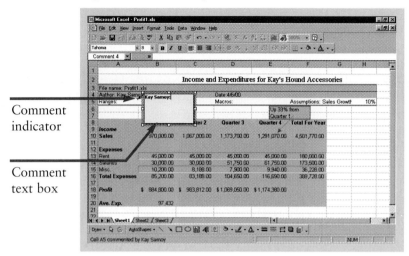

Comment
indicator

Comment
text box

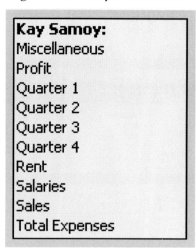

Excel 2000

Table 4-1 Reviewing toolbar buttons

BUTTON	NAME	FUNCTION
	New Comment	Opens a new comment
	Edit Comment	Displays the comment with an insertion point in the comment pane
	Previous Comment	Displays the previous comment
	Next Comment	Displays the next comment
	Show/Hide Comment	Leaves a comment visible even when the mouse pointer is not over the selected parent cell; deselecting this button returns the comment to its default hidden state
	Show/Hide All Comments	Shows or hides all comments on the worksheet
	Delete Comment	Permanently removes a comment and its reference mark in the parent cell

Practice

To practice adding comments, follow the instructions on the **Prac4-3** worksheet of the practice file **MyPractice 4.xls**. Save the changes you have made when you complete the exercise.

Hot Tip

Either the New Comment button or the Edit Comment button will appear on the Reviewing toolbar, depending on whether or not the selected cell already contains a comment.

Creating a Chart

Concept

Charts are graphics that represent values and their relationships. Using charts you can quickly identify trends in data and see the contrasts among values. Excel allows you to portray data easily using a variety of two- and three-dimensional chart styles. These styles give data immediate meaning, unlike data in its raw form, which generally requires studying.

Do It!

Kay wants to show the values for Rent, Salaries, and Miscellaneous expenses as percentages of her total yearly expenses.

1 Select the range F13:F15. These are the values that are required to create the chart.

2 Click the **Chart Wizard** button 🔳 on the Standard toolbar. The Chart Wizard dialog box opens, as shown in **Figure 4-7**, with the Column chart type selected. If the Office Assistant appears, close it by clicking the **No, I do not want help now** option as the Assistant is not necessary for this Skill.

3 Click **Pie** in the Chart type list box. The Chart sub-types will change to show different types of pie charts.

4 Click ❲ Next > ❳. The Wizard will advance to its second step with a pie chart representing the selected data displayed. If you had not already selected cells, you could enter which cells to include in your chart in the **Data range** text box.

5 Click the **Series** tab to bring it to the front of the stack.

6 Click the **Category Labels:** text box to activate it. A flashing insertion point will appear in the text box so you can name the categories for your chart.

7 Click the **Collapse Dialog** button 🔳. The dialog box will shrink so only the Category Labels: text box is shown. Collapsing the dialog box allows you to view more of the worksheet so you can easily select the cells to be inserted as the labels for your chart's categories.

8 Select A13:A15. An animated border will surround the selected range, a ScreenTip will display the size of the selection, and the range will appear in the collapsed dialog box, as shown in **Figure 4-8**.

Figure 4-7 Chart Wizard dialog box: Step 1

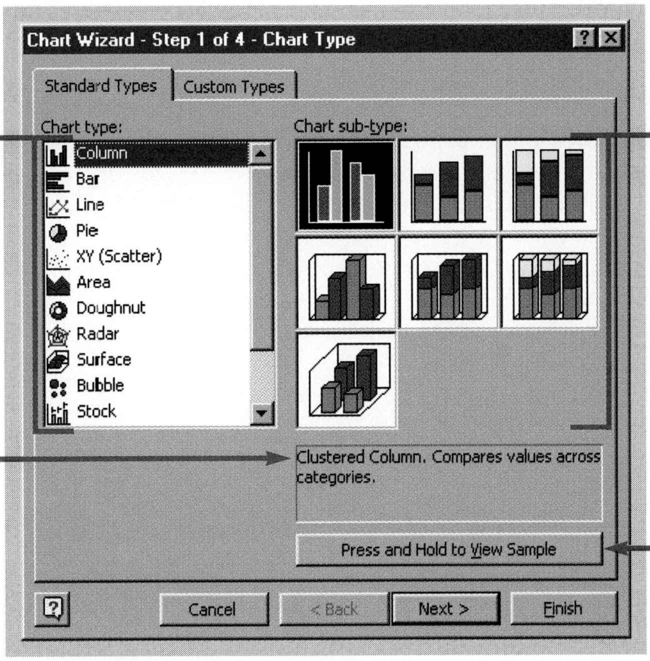

Click here to select a
chart type

Click here to select
a chart sub-type

Name and description
of the selected chart
sub-type

Click here to to preview
the chart sub-type using
data extracted from
your worksheet

Excel 2000

Figure 4-8   Selecting the category labels

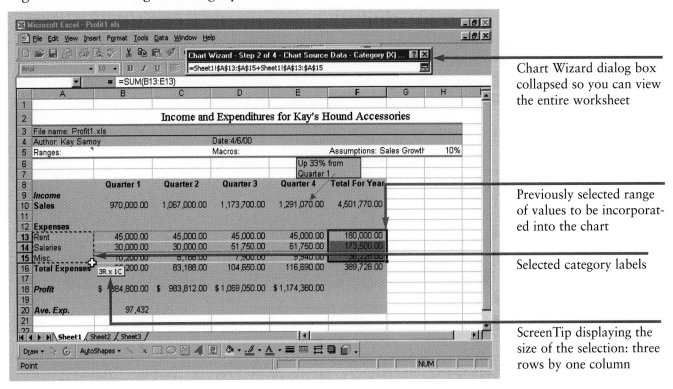

Chart Wizard dialog box
collapsed so you can view
the entire worksheet

Previously selected range
of values to be incorporated into the chart

Selected category labels

ScreenTip displaying the
size of the selection: three
rows by one column

Creating
a Chart (continued)

Do It!

9 Click the Expand Dialog button ⊡ to bring the full dialog box into view.

10 Click ⌊Next >⌋. The third step of the Wizard will be shown.

11 Click the Chart title: text box, then type **Breakdown of Expenses**. The title you have entered will appear in the preview area to the right of the text box. The other text boxes are grayed out since they are not applicable to the chosen chart type.

12 Click the Legend tab to bring it to the front of the stack.

13 Click the Show legend check box to deselect this option, as you will be labeling the chart later.

14 Click the Data Labels tab to bring it to the front of the stack.

15 Click the Show label and percent radio button. Labels and percentages will appear in the preview.

16 Click ⌊Next >⌋ to advance to the last step of the Wizard. As you can see in **Figure 4-9**, the **As object in** radio button is selected, indicating that the chart will appear in the current worksheet as opposed to a new one.

17 Click ⌊Finish⌋. The Chart Wizard dialog box will close, your chart will be displayed in the center of your worksheet, and the Chart toolbar will appear in the Excel window, as shown in **Figure 4-10**.

18 Save your workbook.

More

When the chart is selected, the Data menu is replaced by the Chart menu. The first four commands on the Chart menu open dialog boxes that are similar to the steps of the Chart Wizard. This allows you to alter any of the characteristics of the chart without having to recreate it with the Chart Wizard. The Add Data command lets you append the ranges that are displayed.

Figure 4-9 Chart Wizard dialog box: Step 4

Click to create
chart in its own,
new worksheet

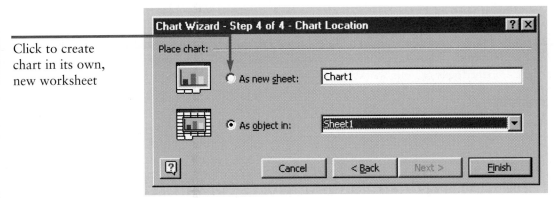

Figure 4-10 Finished chart

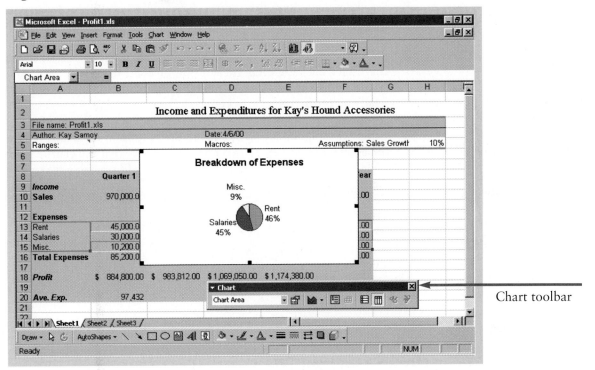

Chart toolbar

Moving and Resizing a Chart

Concept

Once you have created a chart, you can change its size and location in the work-sheet so that it complements your data without obstructing it. While a chart may be the focus of your worksheet, it is still just one part of the overall presentation.

Do It!

Kay wants to move the chart below the main data of her worksheet and then resize it so that its boundaries match those of existing columns and rows.

1. Click the selected chart and drag it down and to the left until the upper-left corner of the dotted border is in cell A21 (see **Figure 4-11**). As you move the mouse, the pointer will change to the movement pointer ✛ and the dotted border will indicate where the chart will appear when the mouse button is released. The worksheet will scroll upward when the mouse pointer is dragged below the document window.

2. Scroll downward until the entire chart can be seen in the document window, if it is not already.

3. Position the mouse pointer over the midpoint sizing handle of the right edge of the chart, then click and drag the edge of the chart to the left until it is even with the boundary between columns C and D. The chart will adjust itself so it remains centered and proportional in its box.

4. Using the midpoint sizing handle on the bottom of the chart, drag the chart edge to the boundary between rows 34 and 35. Notice that the chart elements expand slightly to fill the larger area. Your chart should resemble the one shown in **Figure 4-11**.

5. Save your workbook.

More

Table 4-2 below summarizes different techniques you can use to move and resize charts and other objects.

Table 4-2 Object resizing techniques

ACTION	TO
Press [Shift] while dragging the chart	Constrain a chart's movement to only the horizontal or vertical
Press [Ctrl] while dragging the chart	Copy the chart to another place in the worksheet
Press [Shift] while dragging a corner sizing handle	Constrain a chart's aspect ratio when resizing it
Press [Ctrl] while dragging a sizing handle	Maintain a chart's center point when resizing
Press [Ctrl]+[Shift] while dragging a corner sizing handle	Maintain a chart's center point and aspect ratio when resizing

Figure 4-11 Repositioned and resized chart

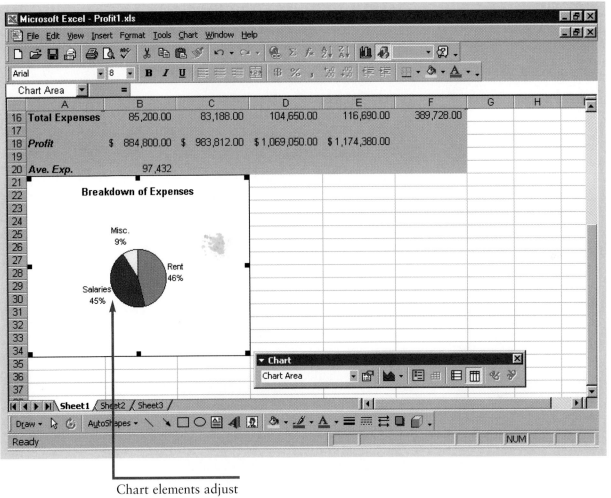

Chart elements adjust
to fit the redefined
chart area

Practice

To practice moving and resizing a chart,
follow the instructions on the **Prac4-5**
worksheet of the practice file **MyPractice
4.xls**. Save the changes you have made
when you complete the exercise.

Hot Tip

As you move the mouse pointer over various elements of the chart, ScreenTips will
appear with a brief explanation of that
item. These ScreenTips may be disabled by
pressing [Alt].

Formatting a Chart

Concept

After a chart has been created, many of its features may be altered. The color and location of chart elements can be changed, and formatting can be applied to text.

Do It!

Kay wants to emphasize that her company has met its goal of keeping miscellaneous expenses under 10 percent of total expenses by isolating the corresponding pie slice in the chart and changing its color. She also would like to format the chart title.

1. Click the pie in your chart to make it active. Three sizing handles will appear indicating its selection.

2. Click the Miscellaneous pie slice to select it.

3. Click and drag the Miscellaneous slice away from the pie so the point of the triangle is even with the former border of the pie. Notice that the slice's label moves to accommodate the slice's new position. (See **Figure 4-13**.)

4. Double-click the Miscellaneous pie slice. The Format Data Point dialog box opens.

5. Click the Patterns tab, shown in **Figure 4-12**, to bring it to front if it is not already there.

6. In the Area section of the tab, click the yellow box in the bottom row, beneath the currently selected color. The sample color, shown in the lower left of the tab, will change to illustrate the newly selected color.

7. Click OK. The dialog box closes, and the chart will appear with the new color applied to the Miscellaneous slice, as seen in **Figure 4-13**.

8. Double-click the chart's title, **Breakdown of Expenses**, to open the Format Chart Title dialog box.

9. On the Patterns tab, click the Shadow check box to activate it.

10. Click OK. The dialog box closes, and the chart's title now appears in a box with a shadow applied to it. Click elsewhere in the worksheet to deselect the chart title; your chart should now resemble the one shown in **Figure 4-13**.

More

Double-clicking any selected element of a chart will open a dialog box that enables you to format and alter the selected chart element. Depending upon what item is selected, the available tabs of this dialog box will provide the appropriate formatting options. Elements also may be selected and their formatting dialog boxes opened using the Chart toolbar, pictured in **Figure 4-14**.

On the Patterns tab of chart element formatting dialog boxes there is a Fill Effects button that lets you apply advanced formatting options such as gradients, textures, patterns, or pictures to the selected element.

Figure 4-12 Format Data Point dialog box

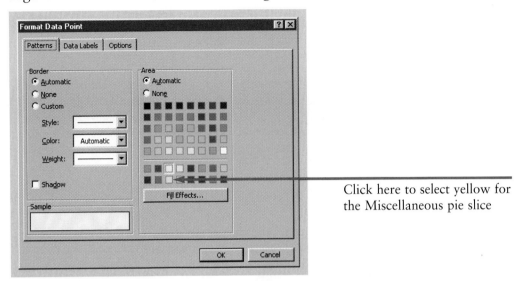

Format Data Point
Patterns
Data Labels
Options
Border
Automatic
None
Custom
Style:
Color:
Automatic
Weight:
Shadow
Sample
Area
Automatic
None
Fill Effects...
OK
Cancel
Click here to select yellow for the Miscellaneous pie slice

Figure 4-13 Formatted chart elements

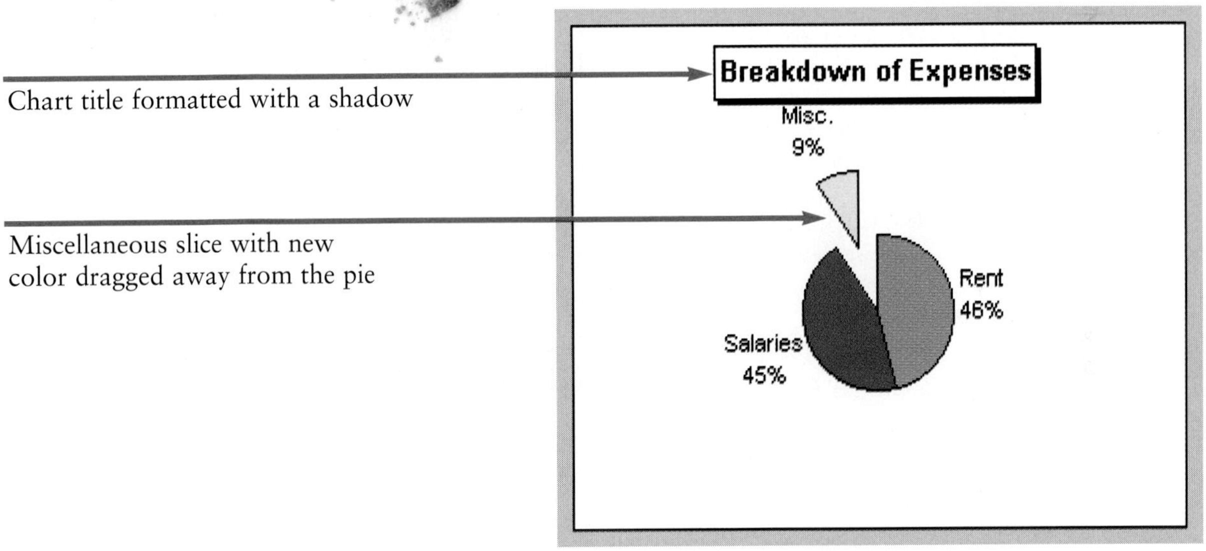

Chart title formatted with a shadow
Miscellaneous slice with new color dragged away from the pie
Breakdown of Expenses
Misc.
9%
Rent
46%
Salaries
45%

Figure 4-14 Chart toolbar

Chart
Chart Area

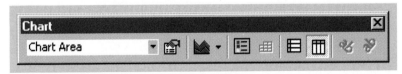

Practice

To practice formatting a chart, follow the instructions on the **Prac4-6** worksheet of the practice file **MyPractice 4.xls**. Save the changes you have made when you complete the exercise.

Hot Tip

Chart titles and labels may be dragged to new locations in the chart area, as can the chart itself.

Changing a Chart's Type

Concept

Excel allows you to change a chart's type while maintaining the same referenced data series. For example, a bar chart can be easily converted to a line graph to more effectively present the data it contains. You also may switch between variants of the same chart type, called sub-types, that will make your chart easier to read.

Do It!

Kay would like to display her pie chart with a 3-D visual effect.

1 With the chart selected, click Chart, then click Chart Type. The Chart Type dialog box opens with the Standard Types tab in front, with the selected chart's type and sub-type selected (if the Standard Types tab is not in front, click it now).

2 Click the second chart sub-type, Pie with a 3-D visual effect. It will become highlighted, and a description of it will appear in the area beneath the Chart sub-types.

3 Click [OK]. The dialog box closes, and your chart appears with the new sub-type applied, as shown in **Figure 4-15**.

4 Click Chart, then click 3-D View. The 3-D View dialog box, shown in **Figure 4-16**, appears with the current elevation of 15 degrees selected.

5 Click [⬆] twice to increase the chart's elevation to 25 degrees. The chart in the preview box will pivot, illustrating the effect that the changes you are making will have on the chart.

6 Click [OK]. The dialog box closes and the chart reflects the changes that you have made, as shown in **Figure 4-17**. Save your changes.

More

Table 4-3 Chart types

CHART TYPE	DESCRIPTION	EXAMPLE
Column	Data changes over time or quantitative comparisons among items	Quarterly income projections
Bar	Similar to a column chart, but horizontal orientation places more value on the X value	Individual sales performance
Line	Trends in data at fixed intervals	Tracking stock trends
Pie	The percentage each value contributes to the whole. Used for a single data series	Budgets, chief exports of a country
XY (Scatter)	Comparative relationships between seemingly dissimilar data	Scientific data analysis
Surface	The range of intersections between two sets of data	Optimal fuel consumption

Figure 4-15 Pie with a 3-D visual effect

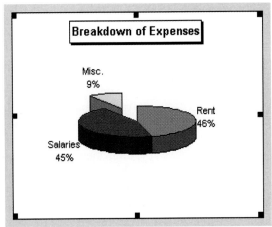

Figure 4-16 3-D View dialog box

Click here to increase or decrease chart elevation below

Click to revert to chart's original elevation and rotation

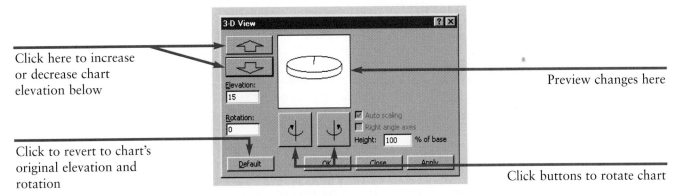

Preview changes here

Click buttons to rotate chart

Figure 4-17 Chart with increased elevation

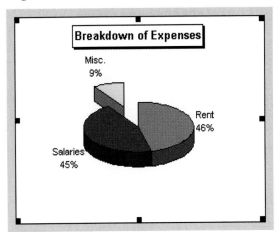

Practice

To practice changing a chart's type, follow the instructions on the **Prac4-7** worksheet of **MyPractice 4.xls**. Save the changes you have made when you complete the exercise.

Hot Tip

The Chart Type drop-down arrow on the Chart toolbar allows you to quickly change the selected chart from one type to another.

Using Advanced Printing Features

Concept

A worksheet, especially one that contains embedded objects such as a chart, may not always fit on a standard printed page using the default printing settings. Excel allows you to preview and change page orientation so as to accommodate different arrangements of data. You also can choose to print specific parts of a spreadsheet such as a chart, a page, the active worksheet, or the entire workbook. As in many programs, you can access these options through the Page Setup dialog box and the Print dialog box. Using these dialog boxes in conjunction with the Print Preview will allow you to get the most out of printing your work.

Do It!

Kay wants to change the page orientation so her entire worksheet will fit onto one printed page.

1. Click outside of the chart to deselect it.

2. Click the Print Preview button ![Print Preview icon]. Your worksheet will be displayed in Print Preview mode. Notice that the status bar reads Preview: Page 1 of 2, and the Next button is active indicating that there is another page.

3. Click in the upper-right corner of the document preview with the magnification pointer. As you can see from **Figure 4-18**, the worksheet will appear magnified in the window with the worksheet title and cell labels cropped, making it apparent that the entire worksheet does not fit on the page.

4. Click ![Setup...] . The Page Setup dialog box will appear as shown in **Figure 4-19**. If necessary, click the Page tab to move it to the front of the dialog box.

5. Click the Landscape radio button in the Orientation section of the dialog box.

6. Click ![OK] . The dialog box will close and you will see that the entire worksheet is now visible on the preview page.

Figure 4-18 Magnified worksheet in Print Preview

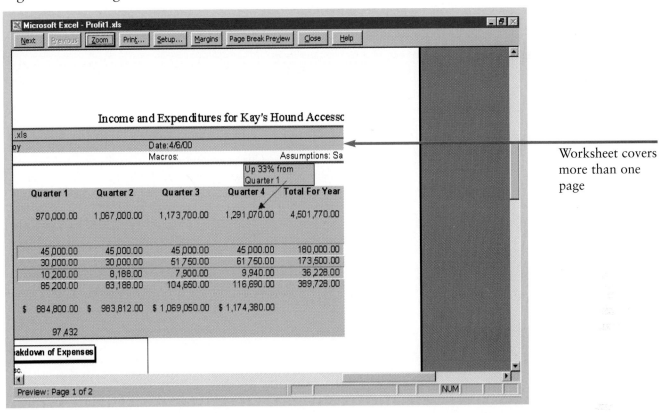

Worksheet covers more than one page

Figure 4-19 Page Setup dialog box

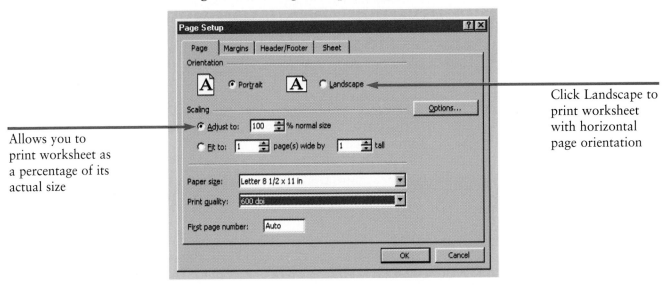

Allows you to print worksheet as a percentage of its actual size

Click Landscape to print worksheet with horizontal page orientation

Using Advanced
Printing Features

(continued)

Do It!

7 Click the preview to zoom out. The entire page will appear horizontally in the window but the status bar will still read Page 1 of 2, as shown in **Figure 4-20** (if this is not the case, exit Print Preview, change the widths of columns A through H to at least 14 characters, and then return to Print Preview and continue).

8 Click Next . A blank page appears. This page contains blank cells that belong to cell A2, which was merged to encompass the range A2:J2 when the title was centered. It is not necessary to print this second page as it only contains blank cells.

9 Click Print... . Print Preview will close, you will be returned to normal view, and the Print dialog box will open.

10 In the Print range section of the dialog box, click the up arrow of the From: text box ⬆ . A 1 will appear selected in the box designating it as the first page to print, and the Page(s) radio button will be selected.

11 Click the up arrow in the To: text box. A 1 will appear selected in the box telling Excel to stop printing after page 1.

12 Click OK . The Print dialog box will close and the document will be sent to the printer.

13 Save your workbook.

More

Excel's print function allows you to select the area or item you wish to print. Therefore, you do not have to send an entire worksheet to the printer if you wish to have a hard copy of a smaller portion. With a chart selected, the Print dialog box will have the Selected Chart radio button active in the Print what area so that only the chart, and not the remaining data of the worksheet, will be printed. Likewise, Print Preview will display just the chart, as this view shows you exactly how the information will be printed with the current settings. If you select a chart, then click the Page Setup command found on the File menu, the Page Setup dialog box will open with a tab labeled Chart. Compare this dialog box shown in **Figure 4-21** to the one shown in **Figure 4-19**. This tab contains options concerning the chart's printed size and print quality.

Figure 4-20 Preview of worksheet in landscape orientation

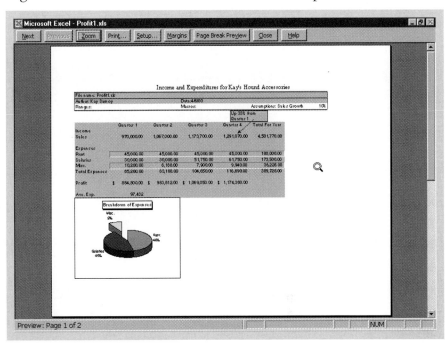

Excel 2000

Figure 4-21 Page Setup dialog box when a chart is selected

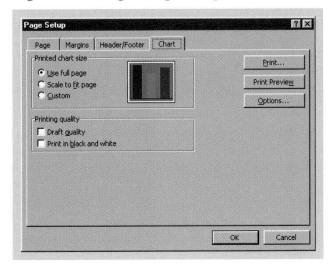

Practice

To practice using advanced printing features, follow the instructions on the **Prac4-8** worksheet of the practice file **MyPractice 4.xls**. Save and close the workbook when you have completed the exercise.

Hot Tip

The Page Break Preview command, found on the View menu, allows you to adjust what portion of the worksheet will fit on one printed page. The data contained in the worksheet will be reduced to fit on the page if you expand the print range.

Shortcuts

Function	Button/Mouse	Menu	Keyboard
Drawing toolbar		Click View, then highlight Toolbars, then click Drawing	
Chart Wizard		Click Insert, then click Chart	
Format chart area (or selected chart object)		Click Format, then click Selected Chart Area (or other object)	[Ctrl]+[1]
Change chart type		Click Chart, then click Chart Type	
Add/remove chart legend		Click Chart, then click Chart Options	
Plot chart data series by row		Click Chart, then click Source Data	
Plot chart data series by column		Click Chart, then click Source Data	

Identify Key Features

Name the items indicated by callouts in **Figure 4-22**.

Figure 4-22 Identify features of the Excel screen

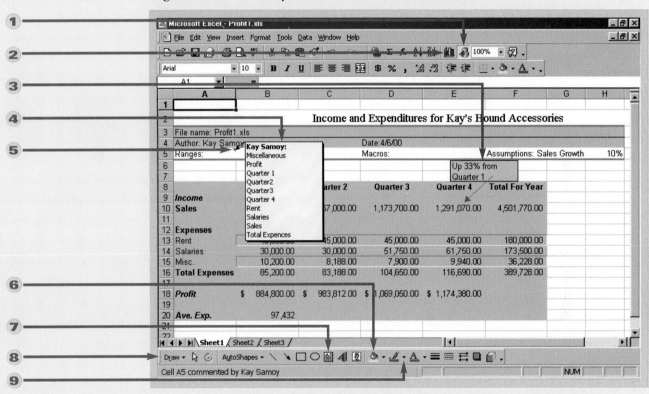

Select the Best Answer

10. Allows you to add text to a worksheet without worrying about cell constraints

11. Reduces the size of a dialog box so that you can easily view the worksheet

12. Appears along with your chart when you complete the Chart Wizard

13. Allows you to format any chart element from a dialog box

14. Indicates that a chart will be printed as opposed to the entire worksheet

15. An electronic note attached to a cell

16. A graphic that represents values and their relationships

17. Horizontal page orientation

18. Allows you to add colors and gradients to chart elements

a. Collapse dialog button

b. Double-clicking

c. Patterns tab

d. Chart toolbar

e. Selected Chart radio button

f. Landscape

g. Text box

h. Comment

i. Chart

Quiz (continued)

Complete the Statement

19. To change the user name that appears on comments, go to the:

    a. Summary tab in the Properties dialog box

    b. Replace dialog box

    c. Define Name dialog box

    d. General tab in the Options dialog box

20. The Arrow tool can be found on the:

    a. Standard toolbar

    b. Formatting toolbar

    c. Drawing toolbar

    d. Shapes toolbar

21. To navigate among comments, use the:

    a. Comment toolbar

    b. Reviewing toolbar

    c. Standard toolbar

    d. Vertical scroll bar

22. All of the following are standard chart types except:

    a. Pie

    b. Doughnut

    c. Line

    d. Volume

23. You can add a title to a chart by using the:

    a. Chart Options dialog box

    b. Source Data dialog box

    c. Format Chart Area dialog box

    d. Chart Type dialog box

24. You may change all of the following chart aspects from the 3-D View dialog box with the exception of:

    a. Elevation

    b. Rotation

    c. Height

    d. Location

25. To maintain a chart's center point when resizing it:

    a. Press [Ctrl] while dragging the chart

    b. Press [Shift] while dragging a sizing handle

    c. Press [Ctrl] while dragging a sizing handle

    d. Press [Tab] while dragging a sizing handle

26. If the text in a text box exceeds the size of the box:

    a. The text box will resize itself

    b. The beginning of the text will be deleted

    c. The text will scroll up

    d. No more text can be added.

27. The small squares in the corners and middle of each side of a comment or chart are called:

    a. Sizing handles

    b. Fill handles

    c. Jug handles

    d. Frames

Interactivity

Test Your Skills

1. Add objects and graphics to a spreadsheet:

   a. Open the file **Test 3.xls** that you created at the end of the previous Lesson.

   b. Add a text box that says **Best day for relaxation and errands** above the day-of-the-week column of your choice.

   c. Use the **Fill Color** palette to add color to the text box.

   d. Draw an **arrow** from the text box to the appropriate day-of-the-week label.

   e. Use the **Line Color** palette to add color to the arrow.

   f. Enter a **comment** that displays the names of all your defined ranges in the cell that contains the Ranges label.

2. Create a chart based on your worksheet data:

   a. Select the **Average** range in your worksheet by using the Name box.

   b. Use the **Chart Wizard** to create a basic pie chart that plots each daily activity as a percentage of the total time you spend on all of your activities during an average day.

   c. In **Step 2** of the Wizard, use the **Series** tab to select the appropriate **Category Labels** for your chart.

   d. In **Step 3**, choose a title for the chart, leave the legend displayed on the right, and show percent data labels.

   e. In **Step 4**, insert the chart into the current worksheet.

3. Move, resize, and format a chart:

   a. Move the chart so that it is centered below the data portion of the worksheet.

   b. Adjust the borders of the chart and the legend so that no chart elements obscure each other. Make any other size and placement adjustments that you think will improve the appearance of the chart.

   c. Change the chart's sub-type to a **3-D Exploded pie**.

   d. Increase the **elevation** of the pie by 30 degrees, and **rotate** it 20 degrees counterclockwise.

   e. Change the color of the largest pie slice in the chart.

   f. Add a shadow to your chart's title and fill the title box with color.

4. Save and print the changes you have made to the spreadsheet:

   a. Save the file as **Test 4.xls**.

   b. Preview the worksheet and use the **Page Setup** dialog box to make it fit on one page if necessary.

   c. Print a copy of the entire worksheet.

   d. Print a copy of just the chart.

Excel 2000

Interactivity (continued)

Problem Solving

1. A friend of yours is considering learning Microsoft Excel. You want to convince your friend that the task is well worthwhile. In order to do this, you plan to show him or her the spreadsheets you have created while learning Excel. First, however, you decide to incorporate the latest techniques you have learned into the spreadsheets so that they are truly impressive. Return to the files Solved 2.xls and Solved 3-Grad.xls, and add at least one text box, one comment, and a chart to each. Use these features to call attention to and further illustrate important data in the worksheets. Be sure to save the additions you make to the files. Save the files as Solved 4.xls and Solved 4-Grad.xls.

2. Open the file Solved-HR3.xls, which you saved at the end of the previous lesson. Using the data you have already entered, create a 3D Pie chart to express graphically the distribution of the $10,000 that has been added to your Human Resources expense account. Also, add a text box that explains that the figures are proposals based on your preferences and projections. Then add two arrows: one that points from the text box to the chart and one that points from the text box to the actual data. Print the worksheet and save the file as Solved-HR4.xls.

3. Open the file Solved-Rest3.xls, which you also saved at the end of the previous lesson. Insert a comment in the worksheet that lists all the ranges that the worksheet contains (if you do not have a cell labeled Ranges, add one and then insert the comment in this cell). Format the comment so that its background is sky blue and its text is red. Then, add data to the worksheet, including appropriate labels and values, that detail the pay scale at the restaurant. For example, include the pay rate earned by an employee with 0–6 months' experience, 7–12 months' experience, 13–18 months' experience, and so on. Finally, use the Chart Wizard to express these data with a Bar chart (use the Clustered Bar sub-type). Save the file as Solved-Rest4.xls and print a copy of just the chart.

4. Use Excel to create the worksheet below. You will need to make formatting changes to the chart once it is created.

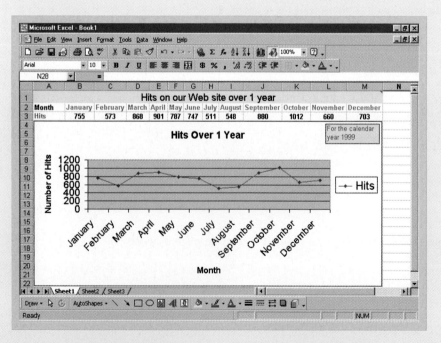

When you are finished, change the chart type to Stacked Column. Format the axis and series labels so that they are easy to read. Decide which chart type presents the data more effectively and keep that chart in the worksheet, changing back to the original if necessary. Save your file as Solved4-Hits.xls.

L E S S O N

1

. . . .

INTRODUCTION TO DATABASES

. . . .

Microsoft Access is a computer application that makes it possible for you to construct powerful systems for organizing information, called databases. An Access database allows you to record, maintain, and edit data, and add to data using simple commands and procedures. The objects you create using the program will facilitate your ability to work with stored information in a number of highly useful ways. Most importantly, because Access provides the opportunity to relate databases to one another, you can share information among objects in a database, or even among separate databases.

Using Access, you will learn how to create a functioning database made up of several components, called database objects, each of which serves a specific purpose. In doing so, you will explore the application and become familiar with its basic elements and operations. Later on, Access's more advanced features, such as table relationships, will augment your ability to work with a database. If you require assistance while using Access, the application includes an extensive Help facility, as well as the possibility to access online support via the World Wide Web.

CASE STUDY
Kyle Dawson is a database consultant who has been hired by Stay Fast, Inc., to design a database that will store information about the company's employees. Stay Fast is a reseller of nuts, bolts, and other fasteners, buying them in bulk from manufacturers and reselling them to retail stores, construction companies, and contractors. A paper system served the company well when it had only 15 employees, but it has grown to 50 employees and wants to convert to an electronic database system before expanding any further. Database consultants like Kyle are often hired to set up a database and to teach employees how to use it. Trained employees of the business can then maintain and expand the database.

Introducing
Database Software

Concept

Microsoft Access is a program that allows you to build computerized databases, which are systems for storing, organizing, and retrieving information. Though you may not realize it, you are probably already familiar with many noncomputerized databases, such as paper records kept in filing cabinets, or your own personal address book. Computer databases can store the same information as traditional paper databases, but they organize it in a more flexible form, storing it in a computerized grid or table.

For example, your address book might have lines for a friend's first and last name, address, phone number, and birthday. In a computerized database, the same information is stored differently. Each column, or field, in a database table contains a specific type of information. So each line from an address book entry, such as your friends' last names, would form a separate column in the table. In turn, all of the lines of information about a friend would make up a single row across the table, called a record (see **Figure 1-1**). A computerized address book would then have the details for each category—name, address, and so on—common to all entries entered down a column, and the complete body of information for any single person entered across a row.

There are many advantages to using computerized databases. One advantage is in the added ease and flexibility of entering and working with data. Just as you can edit text in a word processor or numbers on a spreadsheet, you can easily change data that you enter into a database, adding, deleting, or moving information on screen.

Stored information is, of course, useful only if it can be easily retrieved. One of the greatest advantages of computerized databases is that they offer several ways to retrieve information. For instance, unlike traditional address books, a computerized address database would not limit the user to searching by a person's last name (see **Figure 1-2**). Instead, you could perform searches based on other fields, such as phone number, and even perform searches based on two or more fields at once. For example, you could find all of the people in the database who live in the same state but have different area codes. Furthermore, if the information you seek is spread across separate databases, you can link tables with common data and perform a comprehensive search.

Figure 1-1 Table in an Access database sorted by Last Name

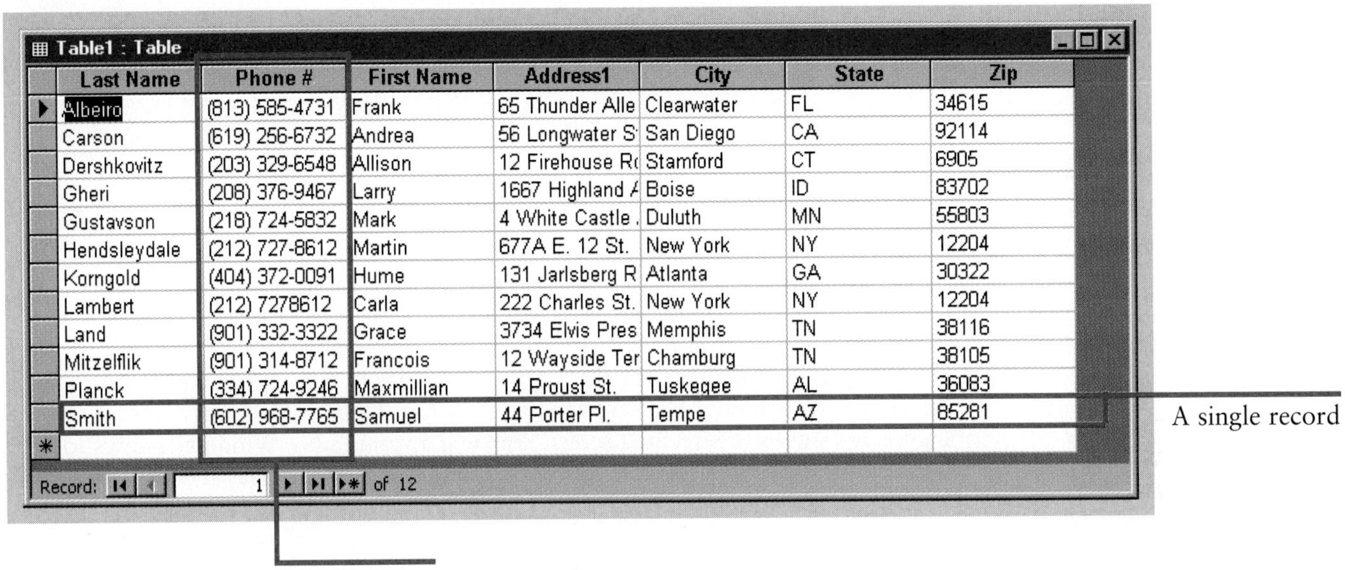

Last Name	Phone #	First Name	Address1	City	State	Zip
Albeiro	(813) 585-4731	Frank	65 Thunder Alle	Clearwater	FL	34615
Carson	(619) 256-6732	Andrea	56 Longwater S	San Diego	CA	92114
Dershkovitz	(203) 329-6548	Allison	12 Firehouse R	Stamford	CT	6905
Gheri	(208) 376-9467	Larry	1667 Highland A	Boise	ID	83702
Gustavson	(218) 724-5832	Mark	4 White Castle .	Duluth	MN	55803
Hendsleydale	(212) 727-8612	Martin	677A E. 12 St.	New York	NY	12204
Korngold	(404) 372-0091	Hume	131 Jarlsberg R	Atlanta	GA	30322
Lambert	(212) 7278612	Carla	222 Charles St.	New York	NY	12204
Land	(901) 332-3322	Grace	3734 Elvis Pres	Memphis	TN	38116
Mitzelflik	(901) 314-8712	Francois	12 Wayside Ter	Chamburg	TN	38105
Planck	(334) 724-9246	Maxmillian	14 Proust St.	Tuskegee	AL	36083
Smith	(602) 968-7765	Samuel	44 Porter Pl.	Tempe	AZ	85281

Record: 1 of 12

A single record

A field

Figure 1-2 Table in an Access database sorted by State

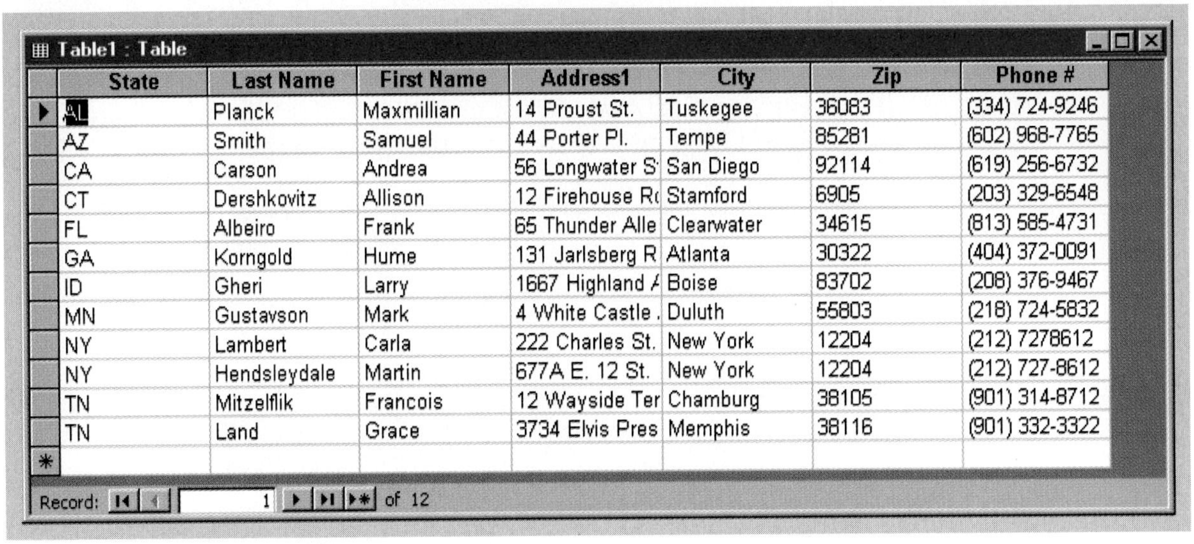

State	Last Name	First Name	Address1	City	Zip	Phone #
AL	Planck	Maxmillian	14 Proust St.	Tuskegee	36083	(334) 724-9246
AZ	Smith	Samuel	44 Porter Pl.	Tempe	85281	(602) 968-7765
CA	Carson	Andrea	56 Longwater S	San Diego	92114	(619) 256-6732
CT	Dershkovitz	Allison	12 Firehouse R	Stamford	6905	(203) 329-6548
FL	Albeiro	Frank	65 Thunder Alle	Clearwater	34615	(813) 585-4731
GA	Korngold	Hume	131 Jarlsberg R	Atlanta	30322	(404) 372-0091
ID	Gheri	Larry	1667 Highland A	Boise	83702	(208) 376-9467
MN	Gustavson	Mark	4 White Castle .	Duluth	55803	(218) 724-5832
NY	Lambert	Carla	222 Charles St.	New York	12204	(212) 7278612
NY	Hendsleydale	Martin	677A E. 12 St.	New York	12204	(212) 727-8612
TN	Mitzelflik	Francois	12 Wayside Ter	Chamburg	38105	(901) 314-8712
TN	Land	Grace	3734 Elvis Pres	Memphis	38116	(901) 332-3322

Record: 1 of 12

Starting Access

Concept

Before you can view or modify a database, you must open the Access application. Unlike other Windows programs, Access does not open with a blank file ready to be used. Instead, it offers you the choice of creating a new database or opening an existing one.

Do It!

In order to open the sample database that he wishes to view, Kyle must first start Access.

1 Click **Start** on the Windows taskbar. The Start menu appears.

2 Move the mouse pointer over the Start menu to Programs, then click Microsoft Access on the submenu that appears, as shown in **Figure 1-3**. Access will open. **Figure 1-4** shows the opening screen that will appear. Since Windows allows for customization, your menus may appear differently than the ones shown, and your startup procedure may vary slightly from the one demonstrated here.

3 Click **OK** to affirm the default option, Open an existing file. The Open dialog box (**Figure 1-5**) appears, allowing you to determine which file is to be opened.

4 Click the Look in: drop-down list arrow, then select the drive containing your Student Files folder from the drop-down list of drives and folders that appears. (Ask your instructor if you cannot locate these files.)

5 Open the Student Files folder. Its contents will be displayed in the main area of the dialog box.

6 Click Do It1-2 to select it, then click **Open**. Access will open the database and display the Database window, shown in **Figure 1-6**.

Figure 1-3 Opening Access from the Start menu

Start button

Programs menu

Start menu

The taskbar

Figure 1-4 Access dialog box

If a database has been
opened before, its file
name may appear here;
simply select it and
click OK to open it

Figure 1-5 Open dialog box

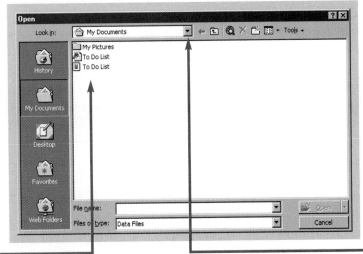

The files and/or folders
that are located in the
selected drive or folder
will appear here

Click here to select the
drive on which your
Student Files reside

Figure 1-6 Database window

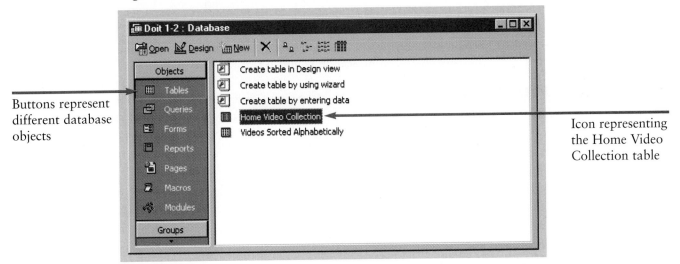

Buttons represent
different database
objects

Icon representing
the Home Video
Collection table

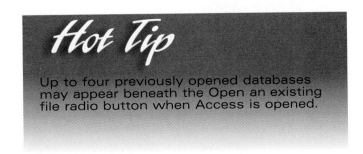

Hot Tip

Up to four previously opened databases
may appear beneath the Open an existing
file radio button when Access is opened.

Opening an Existing Database

Concept

There are several ways Access allows you to find databases on which you were previously working. Some files may be saved in the Access folder, and some may be saved in other folders on your computer.

Do It!

Kyle wants to find a database that was saved in a folder outside of the Access folder.

1 Click the Open button 🗁 . The Open dialog box appears.

2 Click the Look in: drop-down arrow list. Click the C: option, seen in **Figure 1-7**. This option allows you to look in folders in your C: drive, which contains files that have been saved to your computer's hard drive.

3 Double-click the Program Files folder.

4 Double-click the Microsoft Office folder.

5 Double-click the Office folder.

6 Double-click the Samples folder.

7 Double-click the Northwind database to open it. This reveals a list of sample tables to choose from, seen in **Figure 1-8**.

More

Once you have created and saved your own databases using Access, every time you open it you will have the option of opening a database you were working on before.

Access will list the databases you have worked on, starting with the most recent, when you first open Access. Click the database you choose to work on, and click Open. Access will open directly to the database you have chosen.

Figure 1-7 Look in: window in the Open dialog box

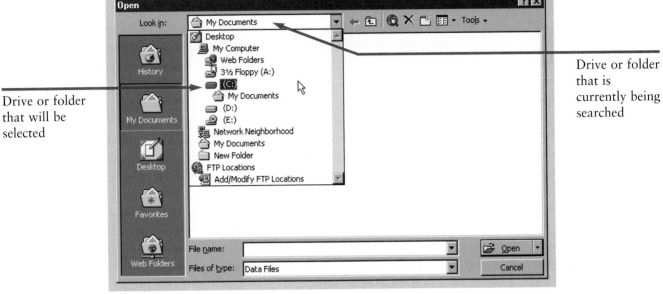

Drive or folder that is currently being searched

Drive or folder that will be selected

Figure 1-8 Access Database window

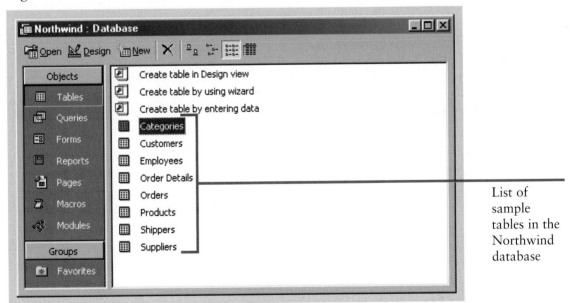

List of sample tables in the Northwind database

Practice

Check out what the other sample databases look like compared to the first one you opened.

Hot Tip

If you click on History in the Open dialog box, it will list the data files you have worked on recently, including the dates and times you worked on them.

Exploring the Access Window

Concept

The Access application window contains the following screen elements (**Figure 1-9**):

- Title bar: contains the application Control menu icon, the name of the application, and the sizing buttons (Minimize, Maximize/Restore, and Close).

- Sizing buttons: located on the title bar and control how you view their window. The Maximize button displays the window at the size of the entire screen, while the Minimize button reduces the window to its program button on the Windows taskbar. The Restore button replaces the Maximize button and makes the window revert to its previous size when clicked.

- Menu bar: contains the names of menus that, when clicked, present lists of commands from which to choose.

- Access application window toolbar: contains graphical buttons that execute specific commands when clicked. The toolbar changes depending on which window is open within the Access application window and the View that is active. For instance, when the Database window is open, the toolbar in the Access application window is the Database toolbar.

- Status bar: appears at the bottom of the screen and displays the activity being undertaken, as well as indicating whether or not certain features are currently active.

When a database is opened, the Database window will appear in the Access window, as shown in **Figure 1-9**. The Database window is the main control center for building and controlling a database. It contains the following Objects bar buttons, each of which relates to a specific database object:

- Tables: give a database its basic structure, storing data and fields in a tabular form.

- Queries: allow you to specify instructions for selecting specific data from one or more tables.

- Forms: electronic data entry sheets that usually contain the fields that comprise a single record; usually make data entry and editing easier by resembling the paper data entry forms that they are designed to replace.

- Reports: used to present processed data in an organized manner.

- Pages: Data Access Pages (DAP), a special type of Web page that allows you to view and work with data that are stored in an Access database on the Internet or on a company intranet.

- Macros: allow you to define and execute a series of actions that automate certain frequently used database tasks.

- Modules: incorporated programs that allow powerful and specialized automation of Access operations.

Figure 1-9 The Access application window

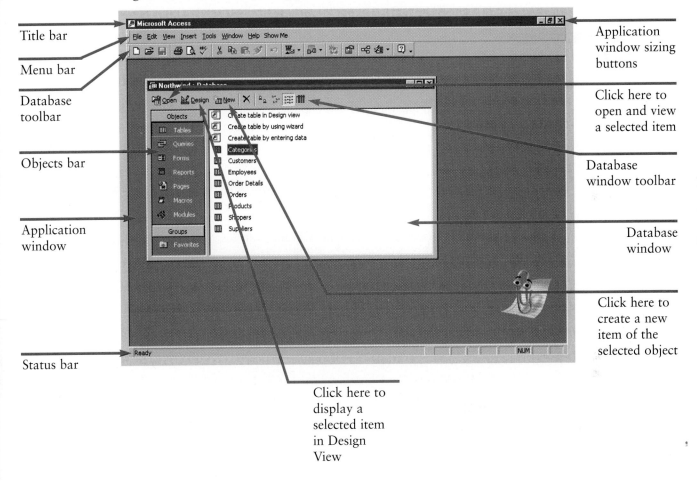

Title bar

Menu bar

Database
toolbar

Objects bar

Application
window

Status bar

Application
window sizing
buttons

Click here to
open and view
a selected item

Database
window toolbar

Database
window

Click here to
create a new
item of the
selected object

Click here to
display a
selected item
in Design
View

Access 2000

Hot Tip

When the mouse pointer is paused over a
button on a toolbar, Access will display a
small box called a ScreenTip that contains
the name of the indicated button.

 # Previewing and Printing a Table

Concept

Once you have entered all of your information in a table, it might be useful to Print the database you have created. Before you print anything, you should check the document in Print Preview. Print Preview will help you make any changes that must be made before you print, with respect to the format of your database.

Do It!

Kyle is satisfied with his document, and he's ready to print it. First, he is going to make sure the format fits his needs in Print Preview.

1 Open the sample table named **Suppliers**.

2 Click File. Click **Print Preview** (see **Figure 1-10**). This is what your table will look like when it is printed.

3 To change the layout of the page, click File, then click **Page Setup**. A dialog box will appear.

4 On the **Margins** tab, double-click in the **Left:** text box and type .75. Follow the same procedure to change the **Right** margin to .75. Then, click the **Page** tab at the top of the dialog box. Click the **Landscape** orientation radio button, as seen in **Figure 1-11**. Then click **OK**.

5 Instead of taking up three pages of printed paper, the table now only takes up two, so you are ready to print. Click File, then click Print. The Print dialog box appears (see **Figure 1-12**).

6 Click OK to accept the default settings and you will print your table. Then click the **Close** button ⊠ in the upper-right corner of the table to close it.

More

As you have seen in this Skill, the Page Setup dialog box can be used to change margins. If part of one page spills over onto a second page, simply changing right and left margins may be all that is needed to fit everything on one page.

If the Page Setup dialog box does not open to the Margins tab, click the Margins tab to bring it to the front of the dialog box.

You also may choose to print only certain pages in a document. By changing the default settings in the Print dialog box, you can print one page of a multiple-page document. You also can print some, but not all, of a multiple-page document.

Figure 1-10 Print Preview window

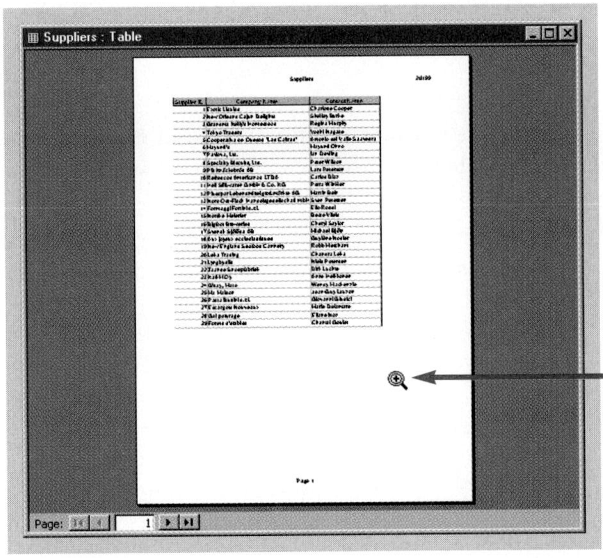

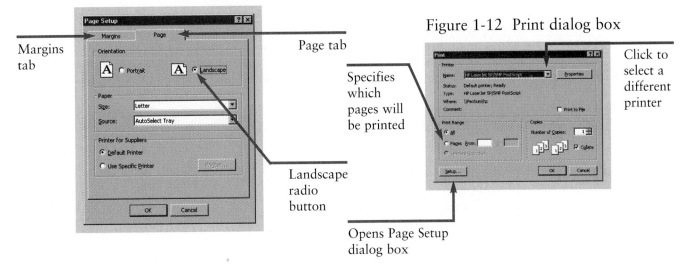

Magnifying tool
allows you a closer
look at your
document

Figure 1-11 Page Setup dialog box

Margins
tab

Page tab

Figure 1-12 Print dialog box

Specifies
which
pages will
be printed

Click to
select a
different
printer

Landscape
radio
button

Opens Page Setup
dialog box

Print a copy of the sample database table, Employees.

Hot Tip

You also may use the Page Setup dialog box to print unusually sized papers. Click the Size drop-down list, and select the size and style of paper on which you are printing.

Getting Help Using the Office Assistant

Concept

The Office Assistant is an animated interface that allows you to access Access's powerful Help features.

Do It!

Kyle will use the Office Assistant to find out more about Access's Help facilities.

1 Click Help, then click Show the Office Assistant. If the Office Assistant is already visible, click the Office Assistant.

2 Type tips with the office assistant into the text entry field, as shown in **Figure 1-13**.

3 Click [Search]. A list of possible help topics appears above the question you entered.

4 Click the second radio button, Display tips and messages through the Office Assistant. **Figure 1-14** shows the Microsoft Access window that will appear.

5 Read the Help topic pertaining to the Office Assistant, clicking a few of the help buttons next to additional topics to find out more.

6 When you have finished reading about some of the Office Assistant's capabilities, click the Close button in the upper-right corner of the dialog box.

7 Click Help again, then click Hide the Office Assistant to hide the Assistant.

More

From time to time the Assistant will offer you tips on how to use Access more efficiently. The appearance of a small light bulb, either in the Assistant's window or on the Office Assistant button, indicates that there is a tip to be viewed. To see the tip, click the light bulb in whichever location it appears.

The Office Assistant can be customized. Click the [Options] button in its dialog balloon to open the Office Assistant dialog box. This dialog box has two tabs: Gallery and Options. The Gallery tab contains eight assistants you can choose from, and scrolling through the characters provides you with a preview of each one. However, you may need to install the additional Assistants from your Access 2000 or Office 2000 CD-ROM before you can actually use them. From the Options tab, shown in **Figure 1-15**, you can alter the Assistant's capabilities and decide what kinds of tips it will show.

Figure 1-13 Office Assistant

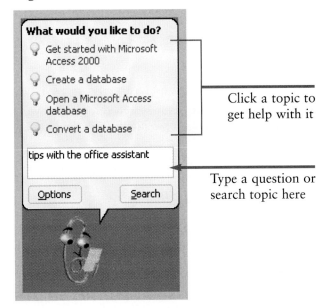

Click a topic to
get help with it

Type a question or
search topic here

Figure 1-14 Help with the Office Assistant

Click to get additional help
with the specified topic

Access 2000

Figure 1-15 Office Assistant dialog box

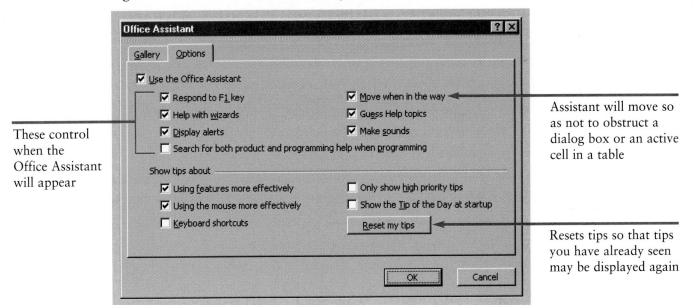

These control
when the
Office Assistant
will appear

Assistant will move so
as not to obstruct a
dialog box or an active
cell in a table

Resets tips so that tips
you have already seen
may be displayed again

Practice

Use the Office Assistant to learn about
moving the Office Assistant and its balloon.

Hot Tip

The Office Assistant is common to all
Office 2000 applications. Therefore, any
Assistant options you change will affect it
in all Office programs.

Getting Help in Access

Concept

Access has more traditional Help facilities that are easily searched if you know what you are looking for. Once you have selected a topic supplied by the Office Assistant, it is not difficult to find the other help features.

Do It!

Kyle wants to use the Index to find out more about ScreenTips.

1. Click Help, then click Show the Office Assistant. Type Ways to get assistance while you work. Then click Search.

2. Position the pointer over the bullet labeled Ways to get assistance while you work and click. A window appears, as shown in **Figure 1-16**. Click the Show button 🔳 in the upper-left corner to access the Index.

3. Click the Index tab to bring it to the front, as shown in **Figure 1-17**.

4. The Index scrolls if you type in the text box, anticipating your selection.

5. Type screentip, and then click Search. The Index will present you with a list of topics. Click on any topic to learn more about it.

6. When you are finished reading, click the Help window's Close button.

More

The Index tab of the Help topics dialog box is very helpful if you know what the task you are trying to accomplish is called, or if you know the name of the feature about which you want to find out more. If you are unsure of exactly what you are looking for, the Contents tab of the Help topics dialog box may be a better option for you. The Contents feature contains every Help topic that Access offers, broken down by category, and is useful if you wish to obtain a broad view of the topics available. The Answer Wizard tab allows you to search for keywords found in Help topics to pinpoint those topics that might be most helpful.

Figure 1-16 Microsoft Access Help topics

Click to access the Index

Clicking an item such as this
opens a large ScreenTip to
more thoroughly explain the
topic

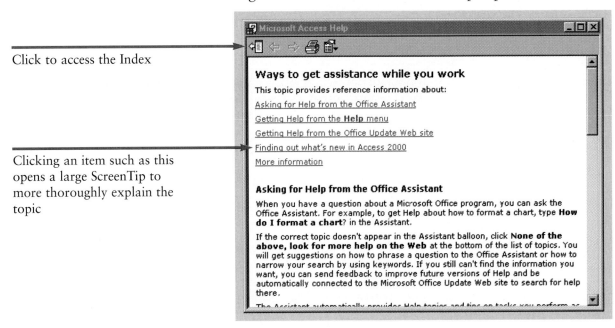

Figure 1-17 Index tab of the Microsoft Access Help feature

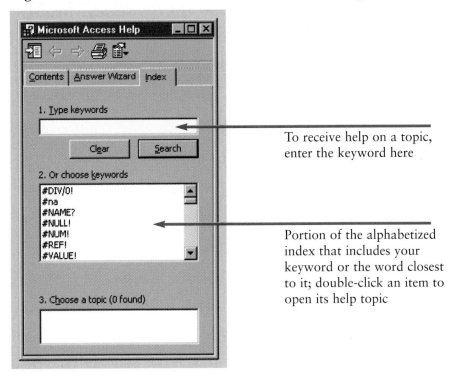

To receive help on a topic,
enter the keyword here

Portion of the alphabetized
index that includes your
keyword or the word closest
to it; double-click an item to
open its help topic

Practice

Use the Index to find a shortcut key that
relates to the Office Assistant.

Hot Tip

If your computer is connected to the
Internet, you can access Microsoft's Web
pages directly from Access. Click the Help
menu, and then click Office on the Web.
Finally, click a topic to go to its Web page.

Closing a File and Exiting Access

Concept

It is important to properly exit the Access program when you are finished with the day's session. Correctly closing the application will help you avoid any data loss.

Do It!

Kyle has finished using Access for the day and is ready to exit the application.

1 Click File, then click Exit (see **Figure 1-18**). Access closes and removes itself from the desktop.

More

There are other ways you can close a file and exit Access. The easiest method is to use the Close buttons ⊠ located in the upper-right corner of the windows. The Close button on the Database window title bar is for the open database, and the Close button on the Access application window title bar is for the application. Also located on the title bar is the Control menu. This menu can be accessed by clicking the Access icon at the left end of the title bar, which is shaped like a key and houses the Restore, Move, Size, Minimize, Maximize, and Close commands.

You may open any menu on the menu bar by pressing [Alt] followed by the underlined letter in the menu's title. You will notice that menu commands also have a letter in their name underlined; typing the underlined letter will activate its command on the open menu. For example, with the File menu open, typing [o] will bring up the Open dialog box to open a database, while pressing [x] will exit Access.

Figure 1-18 Exiting the application

Close command
on the File menu
closes the
Database window

Exit command
on the File menu
closes Access

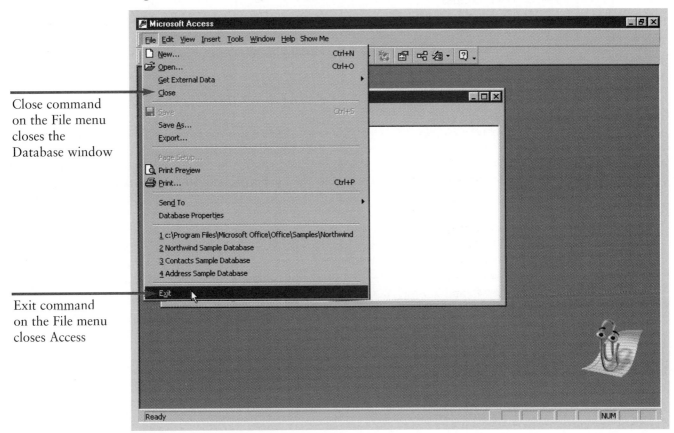

Access 2000

Open Access from the Start menu, close
the Microsoft Access dialog box by clicking
the Close button, then close Access by
using the Control menu.

Hot Tip

Right-clicking anywhere on the title bar will
produce the Control menu, while double-
clicking the title bar will maximize or
restore the window's size.

Shortcuts

Function	Button/Mouse	Menu	Keyboard
Open a database		Click File, then click Open	[Ctrl]+[O]
Minimize a window		Click Control icon, then click Minimize	
Maximize a window		Click Control icon, then click Maximize	
Restore a maximized window		Click Control icon, then click Restore	
Close a window		Click Control icon, then click Close	[Alt]+[F4] (application window only)
Help		Click Help, then click Microsoft Access Help	[F1]
What's This?		Click Help, then click What's This?	[Shift]+[F1]

Identify Key Features

Name the items indicated by callouts in **Figure 1-19**.

Figure 1-19 Components of the Access window

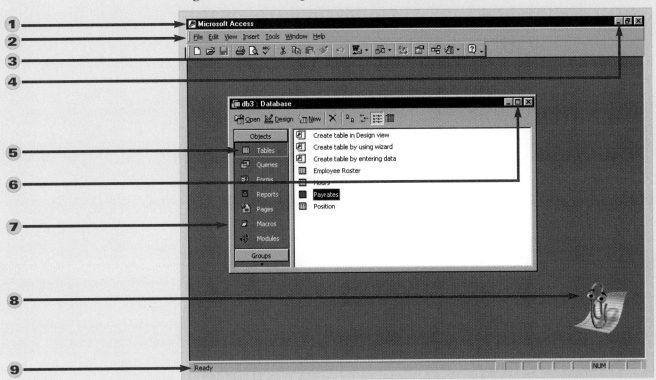

Select the Best Answer

10. Contains a window's Control menu icon

11. Database table element that holds one specific type of information

12. Main control center for working with an Access database

13. Gives a database its basic structure

14. Animated help feature that offers tips and answers questions

15. The Print Preview command is found in this menu

16. Use this to change the view of the table

17. You have to use it to change the page format

a. Page Setup

b. Office Assistant

c. File

d. Field

e. Database window

f. Scroll bar

g. Table

h. Title bar

Quiz (continued)

Complete the Statement

18. A complete set of information contained in one row of a database table is called a:

    a. Field

    b. Form

    c. Record

    d. Column

19. All of the following are Access database objects except:

    a. Table

    b. Field

    c. Form

    d. Report

20. A database object that allows you to automate frequently executed tasks is a:

    a. Query

    b. Wizard

    c. Shortcut

    d. Macro

21. The Index feature lets you search for help topics:

    a. Alphabetically

    b. By asking questions

    c. By category

    d. By keyword

22. Information regarding your current activity in Access appears in the:

    a. Database toolbar

    b. Menu bar

    c. Status bar

    d. Title bar

23. You can use all of the following to exit Access except:

    a. The Database window Close button

    b. The application window Close button

    c. The File menu

    d. The application window Control menu

24. Print Preview mode is best used to:

    a. Edit information in a table

    b. Change the format of your database

    c. See what your table will look like when printed

    d. See what your document will look like in other programs

25. The quickest way to find a specific record in your document is to:

    a. Use the scroll arrows to carefully check the table line by line.

    b. Type the number of the record you are looking for

    c. Click on the scroll bars and quickly scan the table

    d. Minimize the number of records in your table

26. When you first open Access, you have the option of choosing:

    a. A sample database to work on

    b. The most recent databases saved in Access

    c. A comprehensive list of every database ever worked on in Access

    d. Nothing; Access automatically opens a blank database

Interactivity

Test Your Skills

1. Start the Microsoft Access application and browse an existing database:

   a. Use the Start menu to begin using Access.

   b. Open the database file you used earlier, Do It 1-2.

   c. Click each of the object buttons in the Database window to view the titles of the existing objects (some buttons may be empty).

   d. Return to the Tables button when you are done.

2. Use Microsoft Access's Help features:

   a. Ask the Office Assistant for information on designing a database.

   b. View one of the topics provided by the Assistant.

   c. Use the Contents tab to read the Help topics listed under the category Creating and Working with Databases.

   d. Use the Index tab to find information on the Answer Wizard.

   e. Use What's This? to obtain a ScreenTip about the Exit command on the File menu.

3. Print a database table:

   a. Select the Home Video Collection table and view it in Print Preview mode.

   b. Practice making changes in the appearance of the document, by changing the margins in Page Setup.

   c. Print the table, then close it.

4. View different records in a long database table:

   a. Open the Northwind database and then open the Products table.

   b. Find record 53.

   c. Use the vertical scroll arrows to find record 71.

   d. Use the record selector buttons to jump to the last record, then the first record.

   e. Use the horizontal scroll arrows to explore all of the fields in the table.

5. Exit Access:

   a. Use the application window's Close button to exit Access.

   b. If you have altered the database file in any way, do not save the changes.

Interactivity (continued)

Problem Solving

1. Congratulations! You have been hired by Ruloff and DeWitt, a rapidly growing advertising agency that specializes in promoting new products and services. For your first project as a Marketing and Research Assistant, you will compile data on the magazine preferences of a cross section of people. These data will eventually be stored and maintained in an Access database. Your initial assignment is to plan the database on paper following appropriate design principles. First, make a list of the fields that should be included in the database. Create a field for a unique identification number for each record. Also create the following fields: First Name, Last Name, Age, Gender, Occupation, # of Magazines Read Regularly, Favorite Magazine, and Hobbies. Either collect or fabricate data for 25 people and write them down in table format. Next, group the fields to form three different tables. Plan all three tables keeping in mind that you are planning a relational database. The tables must share a common field (most likely the ID#) so that they can be joined later. Make sure you record the fields for each table and the data type for each field. Be sure to name all three tables.

2. For each example of a database given below, write down at least five fields you would expect to find and examples of two possible records.

(a) CD Collection

(b) Address book

(c) Bookstore inventory

(d) Coin collection

(e) Recipe file

(f) Teacher's grade book

(g) Sporting equipment catalog

Skills

L E S S O N

2

CREATING AND ARRANGING A DATABASE

As you have already learned, tables give a database its basic structure. After you create a new database in Access, the next step is to create the tables that store the database's data and fields. Creating a table in Design View allows you the greatest degree of control over the structure and functionality of a table. In Design View you can name fields, select their data types, add descriptive captions, and assign specific properties to the data in each field.

You enter and edit data in a table in Datasheet View. In this view, you also can make structural changes to a table like changing column width and field order. When you enter or edit data in Datasheet View, Access automatically saves the changes for you.

One of the greatest advantages of using database software is that you can arrange and rearrange the data you compile according to specific needs. Access provides a very versatile Find feature to locate specific data. You also can sort data, controlling the order in which records are displayed. Filters allow you to further control data by determining specific items that will be displayed.

You also may select specific data from a database by using a query. A query is a set of instructions that extracts certain pieces of information from tables. You can design, edit, and save a query for future use.

You may create relationships between tables to design queries that involve more than one table. You may link tables with a common field. Linked tables can be queried as if they were one table.

CASE STUDY
In this lesson, Kyle will create a new database, and then design the database's primary table in Design View. He also will enter data in the table, edit it, and then save the table within the database. Finally, Kyle will make modifications to the design of his table in both Design View and Datasheet View.

Kyle also will use the Find feature to locate a specific piece of information, and then he'll apply sorts and filters to his data. Later, he will design simple queries and also design queries by linking tables in a relationship.

Creating a New Database

Concept

In order to start working on a new database, you must first name it and save it.

Do It!

Kyle will now create and save a new database.

1 Open Access by clicking **Start**, then clicking **Microsoft Access** on the Programs menu. The application will open with the Microsoft Access dialog box (**Figure 2-1**), asking whether you wish to create a new database or open an existing one.

2 Click the **Blank Access database** radio button to select it, then click **OK**. The File New Database dialog box appears.

3 Click the **Save in:** drop-down list arrow, then select your student disk or the drive where your Student Files folder is located. (Ask your instructor if you need further assistance.) This is where the new databases will be created.

4 With the Student Files folder showing in the Save in: drop-down list box, click the Create New Folder button **to open the New Folder dialog box.

5 Type **My Access Files**, as shown in **Figure 2-2**. Press **OK**.

6 Once you create the My Access Files folder, its name will appear in the Save in: drop-down list box, and the contents area will appear blank, indicating that the folder is empty. Your File New Database dialog box should now resemble the one shown in **Figure 2-3**.

Figure 2-1 Creating a new database

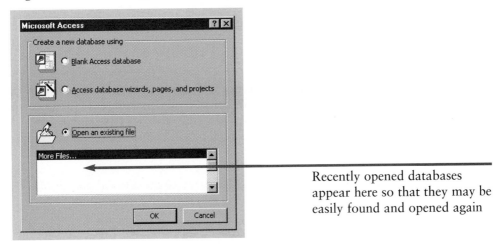

Recently opened databases appear here so that they may be easily found and opened again

Figure 2-2 New Folder dialog box

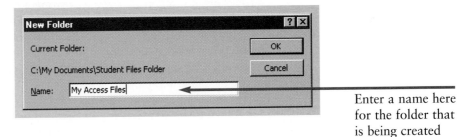

Enter a name here for the folder that is being created

Figure 2-3 File New Database dialog box

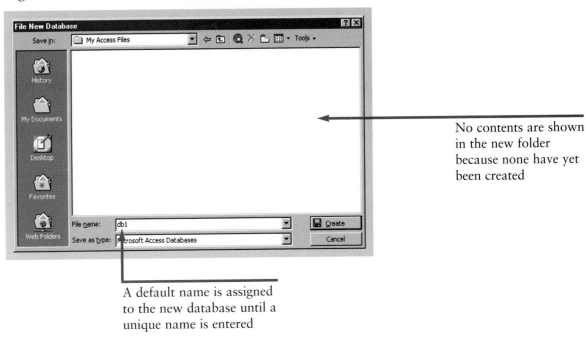

No contents are shown in the new folder because none have yet been created

A default name is assigned to the new database until a unique name is entered

Creating a New Database (continued)

Do It!

7 Triple-click the File name: text box to select the contents of the text box, db1.mdb. Access assigns a default name to all newly created databases that consists of the letters db followed by a number, which is in turn followed by the file extension .mdb. A file extension tells your computer what kind of information a file contains and which applications may open it.

8 Type Employees. The text you enter will replace the selected default name. Access will automatically attach the .mdb file extension if you do not.

9 Click 🔲 Create . The dialog box disappears and a new Database window appears with the file name Employees in its title bar, as shown in **Figure 2-4**.

More

Another option to consider when creating a new database is the Database Wizard. Available on Access's opening screen, just below the Blank Access Database option, the Database Wizard brings up the Databases tab of the New dialog box, shown in **Figure 2-5**, which contains preconstructed database templates. Opening one of these templates activates the Wizard, which walks you through the steps of that database's construction. The Wizard is essentially an interface that asks you questions about the kinds of data your database will contain, as well as the way items in it will be displayed. When you have given it all the information it requests, it will create a database to meet the specifications that it has been given.

Figure 2-4 New Database window

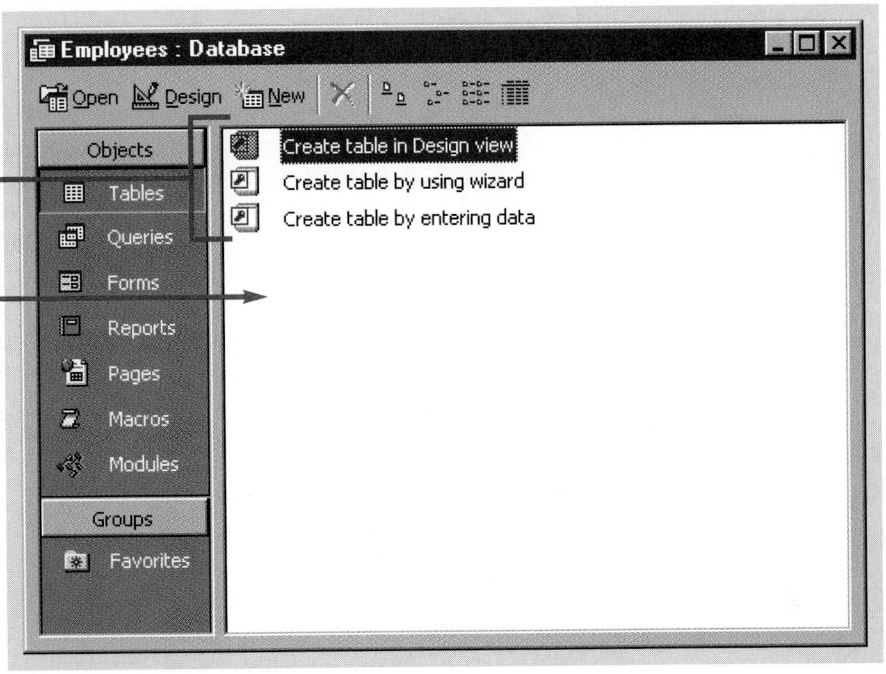

Options for creating
a new table

No tables appear because
none have been created yet

Figure 2-5 Database Wizards

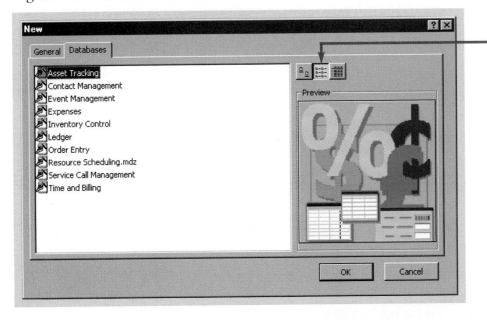

This button is
depressed, indicating
that the Database
Wizards are shown
in List view

Practice

Open a second Access application window by following the start procedures detailed in Lesson 1, and create a new database called **Inventory**. Save it in a new folder named **My Practice Files** in the My Access Files folder you created earlier in this Skill.

Hot Tip

If you are already working in Access and wish to create a new database, use the New button ☐ on the Database toolbar or the corresponding command on the File menu to open the New dialog box.

Creating a Table in Design View

Concept

A table is a collection of data about a specific topic that are organized into columns (called fields) and rows (called records). Using different tables for each topic ensures that data are stored only once, increasing database efficiency and decreasing the chance of mistakes. Creating a table in Design View allows you to define fields and assign properties to them. The Design View window is divided into two parts. The top section is a grid into which you enter the names of your fields, specify the type of data they hold, and enter descriptions that provide information about the field. The bottom section of the Design View window is the Field Properties pane, in which you may further define your fields' attributes.

Do It!

Kyle will use Design View to create a table in the new database.

1 Click [New] on the Employees : Database window toolbar. The New Table dialog box, shown in **Figure 2-6**, and explained in **Table 2-1,** will appear on the screen.

2 Click Design View in the list box on the right side of the dialog box to select it, then click [OK]. The Design View window opens with the insertion point in the first Field Name cell, and the Database toolbar changes to the Table Design toolbar. The status bar also changes, notifying you of Access's current mode.

3 Type Employee Number, then press [Enter]. The Data Type field now contains the highlighted word "Text," as well as a drop-down list arrow that allows you to choose from several data types that will constrain the kind of data that Access will accept as an entry for that field.

4 Press [Enter] to select the default data type, Text, and move the insertion point to the Description field. Although the Number data type would suit the field, it does not allow an entry that has a zero at its beginning, and some employee numbers that will be entered in this field begin with a zero.

5 Type 3-digit number assigned consecutively to each employee as hired. This text will now appear in the status bar when any of the field's values are selected.

6 Double-click the Field Size text box on the General tab in the Field Properties section of the window to select the default field size, 50.

7 Press [3] to replace the default value with the number 3, limiting the maximum number of characters that may be entered into the field (see **Figure 2-7**).

8 Click the cell beneath the Employee Number in the Field Name column. The insertion point will move to the selected cell, and the field indicator arrow ▶ will move down to the second row, designating it as the active row.

9 Type Date Hired, then press [Enter] to move to the Data Type column.

10 Click the Data Type drop-down list arrow [▼], then select Date/Time from the list that appears to replace the default entry "Text." This instructs Access to accept only a date or a time in this field as a valid entry. This also alters the options available for modification on the General tab.

Table 2-1 Table Design options

NEW TABLE OPTION	LETS YOU
Datasheet View	Begin entering and viewing your data right away, while Access automatically configures the table for you
Design View	Set the table's properties before you begin entering data
Table Wizard	Automate the task of table creation by answering questions about the information you wish to include in the database
Import Table	Use a table or object created at another time or in another application in a new database
Link Table	Create tables in the current database that are linked to tables in another file; changing the source table will alter the linked table in the Access database

Figure 2-6 New Table dialog box

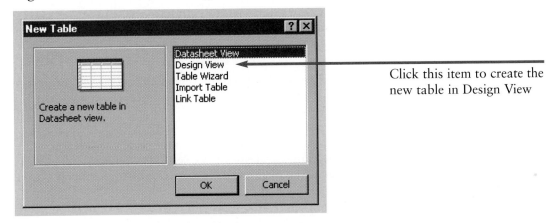

Click this item to create the new table in Design View

Figure 2-7 Creating a table in Design View

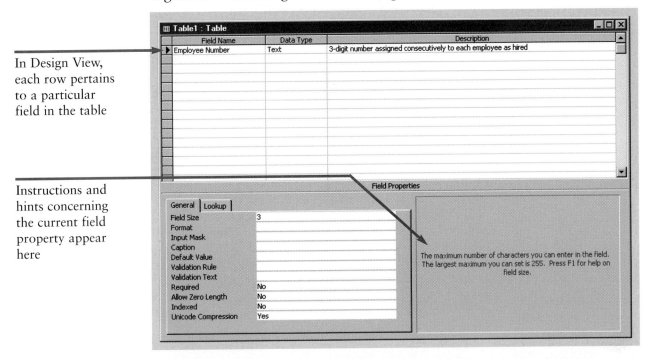

In Design View, each row pertains to a particular field in the table

Instructions and hints concerning the current field property appear here

Access 2000

Creating a Table in Design View (continued)

Do It!

11 Click the Format text box on the General tab. An insertion point and a drop-down list arrow appear.

12 Click the drop-down list arrow in the Format text box and select Short Date from the list that appears, as shown in **Figure 2-8**. Short Date now appears in the Format text box as the selected format.

13 Click the Description cell in the Date Hired row to place the insertion point there, and type Acceptable entry formats are 6/13/98, Jun 13, 98, or June 13, 1998, then press [Enter]. The insertion point moves to the first cell in the next row.

14 Enter the following four field names into the next four rows, leaving the default setting of "Text" in their Data Type fields and leaving their Description fields blank: Last Name, First Name, Street, and City.

15 In the next blank Field Name cell, type State and press [Enter].

16 On the General tab, select the default Field Size of 50 and change it to 2, then press [Enter]. (This limits entries into this field to a two-letter state abbreviation.) The insertion point moves to the Format text box.

17 Type [>] ([Shift]+[.]) to place it in the Format text box. This character instructs Access to make all characters in this field uppercase, so that if someone were to enter ny, for example, it would appear as NY.

18 Click the Default Value text box on the General tab to place the insertion point there, then type NY. Since all of Stay Fast's employees live in New York, it is likely that NY would usually be entered in this field. With this default setting, NY will appear automatically in this field, but may be changed if necessary.

19 Click the Description field in the State row and type Default is NY; 2 character limit; converted to uppercase, then press [Enter].

20 Type Zip Code into the next blank Field Name field, leave the default "Text" data type, and enter the description 10 character limit into the Description field.

21 Change the Field Size (on the General tab) to 10 to allow hyphenated zip codes.

22 Click the Row Selector button next to the Employee Number cell to select the entire row.

23 Click Edit, then click Primary Key. A small key icon will appear to the left of the field icon, as shown in **Figure 2-9**, indicating that the Employee Number field is now the primary key. The primary key field contains data that are common to every table in a database, which in this case will be the Employee Number. Primary key fields must be both unique and constant in order to guarantee a relationship between records in related tables. The three-digit Employee Number makes a good primary key field because it reflects the order in which an employee was hired, and is therefore both unique and constant. Do not close or alter this table, as it will be saved in the next Skill.

More

Notice that when the primary key is set, the Indexed property in the Field Properties area changes from No to Yes (No Duplicates). This prevents duplicate values from being entered in this field. Also, although the Required property does not reflect it, you must enter a value in a primary key field. This condition also can be applied to other fields by changing their Required property from No to Yes.

Database tables need not share the same primary key fields. For example, the Employee Number field may be the primary key field in one table, such as a basic employee roster, but in a related table that lists account managers and the clients for whom they are responsible, an employee's number may be linked to more than one client. In that case, an employee's number could occur more than once in a table and would be disallowed as a primary key. Employee Number would still function as a common field, however, and would allow you to link the two tables. In such a situation, Employee Number is called a foreign key field.

Figure 2-8 Choosing a Date/Time format

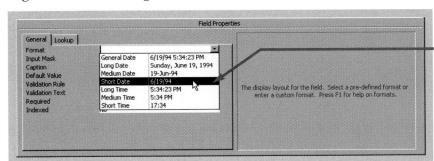

The date or time format is illustrated in the right half of the drop-down list

Figure 2-9 Setting the primary key

The data appearing in the field marked by the primary key symbol appear in every table in the database

New Access 2000 feature that provides a more efficient way to save your table

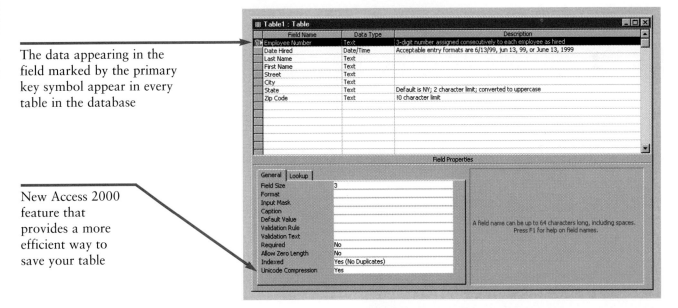

Practice

Create a table in the Inventory database that includes these fields, in order: **Item #, To Be Ordered, Product, Price,** and **Quantity on Hand**. Include appropriate data type formatting and descriptions, and make Item # the primary key field.

Hot Tip

The Lookup tab of the Field Properties section lets you make list boxes or combo list/text boxes out of your fields. This would allow you to create a list box, for example, that would let you choose from a list of cities instead of typing one manually.

Saving and Viewing a Table

Concept

Once a table is created, it must be saved to a disk so that the information can be retrieved later for viewing or editing. If you do not save your work, it will be lost when the application it was created in is exited. It is a good idea to save frequently so as not to lose any data due to computer failure.

Do It!

Kyle will save the table that has been created and then view it in Datasheet View.

1 Click File, then click Save As.... The Save As dialog box, pictured in **Figure 2-10**, opens with the contents of the current database text box selected for editing.

2 Type Employee Roster to replace the default table name, Table1.

3 Click OK. The Save As dialog box closes, the table is saved within the open Employees database, and the table name Employee Roster is displayed in the title bar of the Design View window.

4 Click the View button to go to Datasheet View. The table appears reconfigured with the previously defined field names as column headings, as seen in **Figure 2-11**. These columns intersect with rows to form the field cells into which you will enter data. A single row of this table comprises a record, which is all the data relating to a single item (in this case, each employee).

5 Click the Save button to save your database.

More

The two table views serve different purposes. In Design View, you set up the table's structure so that it can accept data in specific ways. Data do not appear in Design View but can be seen, entered, and edited in Datasheet View, where all of the field formats and restrictions that you set in Design View apply.

Figure 2-11 shows the Datasheet View window with one blank record. To the left of the record is a gray button known as the Record Selector button. The right-pointing arrow on this button indicates which record is currently active. At the bottom of the window is the Specific Record box, which displays the number of the record you are currently working on. The buttons to either side of the Specific Record box are for navigating between records in the table.

Figure 2-10 Save As dialog box for tables

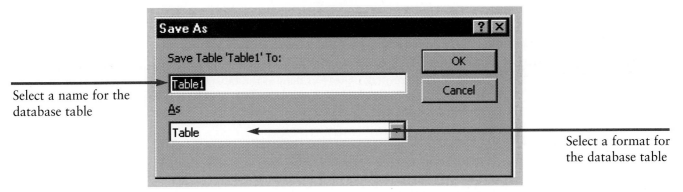

Select a name for the
database table

Select a format for
the database table

Figure 2-11 Appearance of the new table

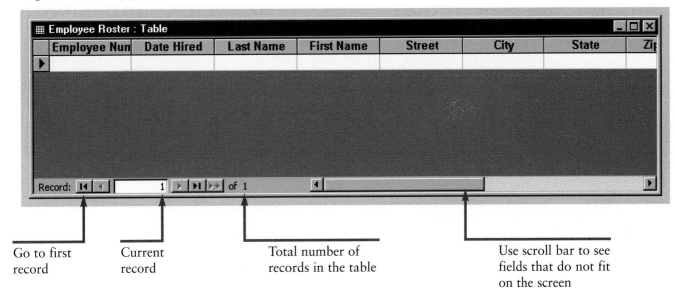

Go to first
record

Current
record

Total number of
records in the table

Use scroll bar to see
fields that do not fit
on the screen

Save the table you created in the previous
Practice, naming it **Orders**. Then, display
the table in **Datasheet View**.

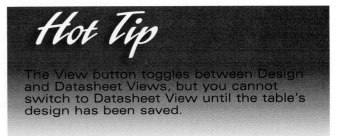

The View button toggles between Design
and Datasheet Views, but you cannot
switch to Datasheet View until the table's
design has been saved.

Entering Data in a Table

Concept

Once a table's fields have been defined, you may start entering data in the form of records. Each record, or row of data in the table, contains the information specific to one item or individual. The more carefully you have planned and designed your table, the easier and quicker this phase of database construction will be.

Do It!

Kyle is now ready to begin entering data into the table he has created.

1 Type 001 into the Employee Number field, then press [Enter]. Notice that as soon as a character is typed, the Record Selector arrow ▶ changes to a pencil ✐ to indicate that the record is being edited (see **Table 2-2**). Also, a second blank record appears beneath the first with an asterisk ✳ in its Record Selector button, which indicates that this is currently the last record in the table. The insertion point moves to the Date Hired field and the description you entered earlier appears in the status bar.

2 Type June 5, 1993 and press [Enter]. The insertion point will move to the Last Name field, and the date you entered will be converted to a shorter form due to the settings in its field properties.

3 Type Busing, press [Enter], type Klaus, press [Enter], and then type 112 Memorial Dr. to place the names and address into their proper fields. The street address you entered does not fit into the Street field in its entirety; the field's width will be adjusted in a later Skill. Likewise, some field names do not fit into their cells. This too will be remedied later on.

4 Type Irvington, then press [Enter] twice, since the correct entry, NY, is already present in the State field. The insertion point moves into the Zip Code field.

5 Type 10533, then press [Enter]. The insertion point moves to the first field of the next record.

6 Enter the following record into the appropriate fields, as you did above: 002, June 5, 1993, Young, Tracy, 665 Boylston St., Elmsford, NY, 10523. Your table should now resemble **Figure 2-12**.

7 Click **Window**, then click **Employees : Database** to activate the Database window and bring it to the front. The menu bar and toolbar also change to reflect the active window.

8 Click the Database window's Close button ☒. Both the Database window and the Table window close.

More

When you closed the Database window, Access did not prompt you to save any changes that you had made. This is because changes made to data are saved as they are entered, while changes to a table's structure or attributes (like those made in Design View) must be manually saved to take effect.

Table 2-2 Record Selectors

ICON	INDICATES
▶	Current record; the record has been saved as it appears
∗	A new record that you can add to
✐	A record that is being edited, but whose changes have not yet been saved
⊘	A record that has been locked by another user and cannot be edited

Figure 2-12 Entering records in a table

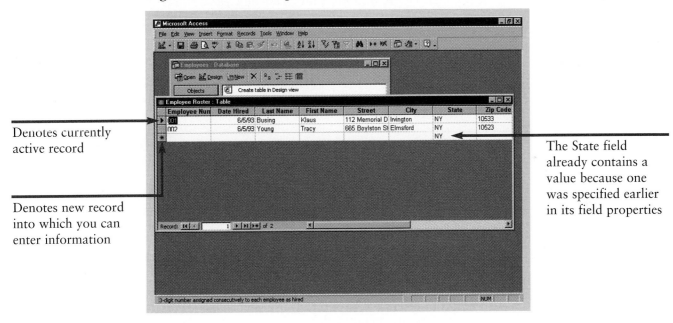

Denotes currently active record

Denotes new record into which you can enter information

The State field already contains a value because one was specified earlier in its field properties

Practice

Obtain a mail-order catalog. Select 10 items and enter their product information into the appropriate fields in your Orders table. Save the table when you are done.

Hot Tip

Pressing [Tab], like pressing [Enter], moves the insertion point to the next field in a record.

Using the Export Command

Concept

The Export command allows you to save a database in a new location. You must first create a blank database into which you can export database objects in order to save it in this new location.

Do It!

Kyle must create a new database so that he can save the database he has created in a new location.

1 Click the New button 🗋 on the Database toolbar to open the New dialog box.

2 Click [OK] to select the default, Database. The File New Database dialog box appears.

3 Locate the My Access Files folder that you created earlier to store your databases and double-click it to open it. It will appear in the Save in: drop-down list box, and its contents will be listed below, as shown in **Figure 2-13**.

4 Triple-click the File name: text box to highlight its contents.

5 Type Employees 2 and click [🖫 Create]. A Database window opens for the new database, Employees 2.

6 Click the Open button 🖼 on the Database toolbar to open the Open dialog box, then select the student file Do It2-5. It is located in the Student Files folder.

7 Click [Open]. The database that opens is the one you created, but with more records added. Since Access can only support one open database window at a time, the new database you created closes.

8 Click File, then click Export.

9 Locate and select the Employees 2 database that you just created in the My Access Files folder, then click Save. The Export dialog box, pictured in **Figure 2-14**, appears with the default table name, Employee Roster, in the Export Employee Roster to: text box.

10 Click [OK]. The data are exported to the target file, the Employees 2 database.

More

Access will only allow you to export one database object at a time. Since the database you were using contained only one object, this was not an issue. However, if you wish to export several objects at once, you must open the target database and then use the Import command on the Get External Data submenu of the File menu. After selecting the database from which you will be importing objects, the Import Objects dialog box will open. Select the objects you wish to import and click OK.

Sometimes you may wish to use a table you have created with different data and for a different purpose. To export just the structure of a table so that you may use it as a template in this fashion, simply click the Definition Only radio button on the Export dialog box when exporting the table.

Figure 2-13 File New Database dialog box

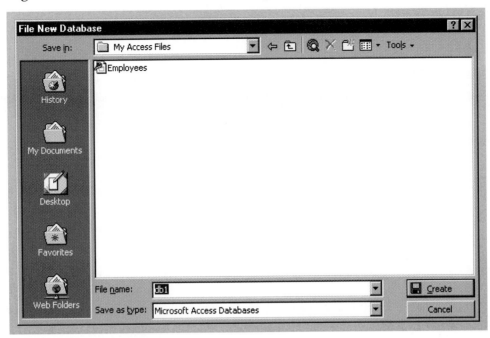

Figure 2-14 Export dialog box

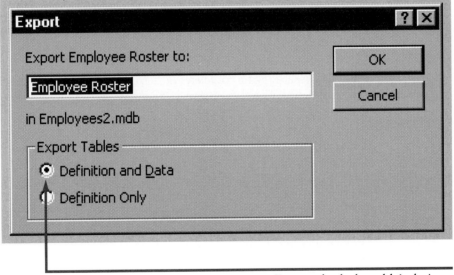

Exports both the table's design
information and the table's data

Practice

To practice exporting database objects, create a new database in your My Practice Files folder called Inventory 2, then export the Orders table to the new database.

Hot Tip

If you wish to open more than one database at a time, you can open it with another copy of the Access application. Open Access as you normally would, whether from an icon on the desktop or from the Start menu, then open the target database.

Access 2000

Editing Information in a Table

Concept

Data that have been entered into a table can be easily modified to reflect changes or correct mistakes.

Do It!

Kyle must open the new database and then fix a typing error that he made when he was adding records to the table.

1 Click the **Open** button 📇 on the Database toolbar to open the Open dialog box, then select the Employees 2 database that you created in the previous Skill, which should be located in the My Access Files folder.

2 Click ⬚Open⬚ to open the selected database and close **Do It2-5** automatically.

3 Double-click the Employee Roster table to open it in Datasheet View. The table opens with records for 50 employees showing.

4 Scroll down to the record for employee 020. Carolyn's last name was misspelled and must be corrected.

5 Move the mouse pointer, which is now an I-beam I, between the ; and the **g**, as shown in **Figure 2-15**, and click once to place the insertion point there.

6 Press [**Backspace**] to delete the semicolon, then press [◄]. The insertion point skips to the left one character.

7 Press [**Backspace**] again to delete the zero, then press [o] to correct the name so that it is spelled Wong, as shown in **Figure 2-16**.

More

The Undo button 🔄 on the toolbar lets you take back changes you have made to a record. Clicking it once undoes the last change made, such as a single keystroke. Clicking it again will undo changes made to the field. Clicking the Undo button a third time will revert the entire record to the form in which it was last saved. It is important that you understand that once you begin editing another record or switch to another window, the changes you have made are saved and the Undo command cannot be used.

Access contains a spell-checking facility, which can be used to search for spelling errors in database objects such as tables, forms, and queries. The Spelling dialog box, accessible by clicking the Spelling button 🔤 or its menu command on the Tools menu, is shown in **Figure 2-17**. It searches for words not contained in its dictionary and brings them to your attention. If the spelling checker stops on a word it does not recognize, but that you know is correct, you may click ⬚Add⬚ to add the selected word to Access's custom dictionary, a document containing all words that are added in this fashion. On future occasions when running the spelling checker, Access will no longer stop on these words. If you do not wish to add the selected word to the custom dictionary, click ⬚Ignore⬚ to go to the next word without changing it, or ⬚Ignore All⬚ to ignore all instances of the word in the document. Access's spelling checker also allows you to skip entire fields, such as a name or street field, that are sure to contain many words that it will not recognize.

Figure 2-15 Employee Roster table with all records entered

Employee Num	Date Hired	Last Name	First Name	Street	City	State	10!
013	8/21/94	Lee	Mike	72 Charles St	Dobbs Ferry	NY	10!
014	8/23/94	Abdo	Muhammad	112 Atlantic Ave	Scarsdale	NY	10!
015	9/24/94	Reynolds	Ken	25 Flute Pl	Scarsdale	NY	10!
016	9/25/94	Collins	Elmer	17 Cornell Ave	Elmsford	NY	10!
017	12/17/94	Harris	Lorna	43 Lindy Dr	Hartsdale	NY	10!
018	3/4/95	Nowak	Jasmine	39 Davis Ave	Briarcliff Manor	NY	10!
019	4/19/95	Rosafort	Lyle	1 Upland Ln	Elmsford	NY	10!
020	4/25/95	WOn;g	Carolyn	12 Spiff St	Valhalla	NY	10!
021	6/3/95	Johnson	John	345 White Ave	Scarsdale	NY	10!
022	6/6/95	Wolff	Henryk	204 Hamilton R	Chappaqua	NY	10!

Record: 20 of 50

Place the I-beam here to correct the mistake

Figure 2-16 Editing information in a table

Employee Num	Date Hired	Last Name	First Name	Street	City	State	10!
013	8/21/94	Lee	Mike	72 Charles St	Dobbs Ferry	NY	10!
014	8/23/94	Abdo	Muhammad	112 Atlantic Ave	Scarsdale	NY	10!
015	9/24/94	Reynolds	Ken	25 Flute Pl	Scarsdale	NY	10!
016	9/25/94	Collins	Elmer	17 Cornell Ave	Elmsford	NY	10!
017	12/17/94	Harris	Lorna	43 Lindy Dr	Hartsdale	NY	10!
018	3/4/95	Nowak	Jasmine	39 Davis Ave	Briarcliff Manor	NY	10!
019	4/19/95	Rosafort	Lyle	1 Upland Ln	Elmsford	NY	10!
020	4/25/95	Wong	Carolyn	12 Spiff St	Valhalla	NY	10!
021	6/3/95	Johnson	John	345 White Ave	Scarsdale	NY	10!
022	6/6/95	Wolff	Henryk	204 Hamilton R	Chappaqua	NY	10!

Record: 20 of 50

Correct spelling of Carolyn's last name

Access 2000

Figure 2-17 Spelling dialog box

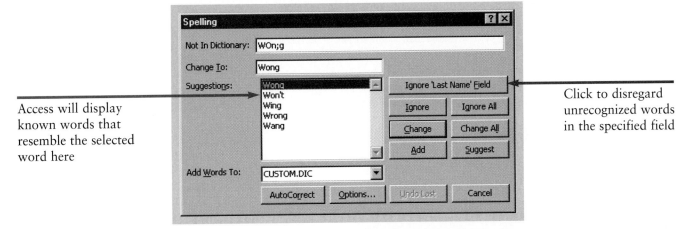

Access will display known words that resemble the selected word here

Click to disregard unrecognized words in the specified field

Practice

Change two of the quantities in the To Be Ordered field. Then, spell check your table for any typing errors you may have made. Finally, fix any mistakes that are found.

Hot Tip

If you need to delete an entire record, first click in any of its fields, then use either the Delete Record command on the Edit menu, or the corresponding button ⊠ on the toolbar. Once you delete a record, it cannot be retrieved.

Manipulating Column Widths

Concept

By default, fields in a table are displayed in a cell that is approximately one inch wide, regardless of its content. Sometimes, this can be too wide, wasting space on the screen. In other cases, a cell may be too narrow, obscuring some of the field data. You can adjust the width of columns so as to reduce wasted screen space and maximize the amount of data that can be seen on the screen at one time.

Do It!

Kyle would like to adjust the width of several of his columns so that they present their data more effectively in his table.

1 Move the mouse pointer to the border between the Employee Number and Date Hired field names. The pointer will change to the resizing pointer ✛, indicating that the boundary can be moved.

2 Using the resizing pointer, click and drag the column boundary to the right until the entire field name, Employee Number, is visible. A black vertical line indicates where the new boundary will appear when the mouse button is released.

3 Click the Date Hired field selector button (the gray box in which the words Date Hired appear) to select the entire column.

4 Click the Zip Code field selector button while pressing [Shift]. All columns from Date Hired to Zip Code will be selected, as shown in **Figure 2-18**. You may have to use the horizontal scroll bar to see the Zip Code field.

5 Click Format, then click Column Width. The Column Width dialog box, shown in **Figure 2-19**, appears with the column width selected.

6 Click Best Fit. Each of the selected columns expands or contracts so that it is just wide enough to contain the largest field in the column.

7 Click once anywhere in the table to deselect the highlighted columns. Your table should look like the one in **Figure 2-20**.

More

You may determine the width of columns in several ways. The Column Width dialog box lets you automatically adjust the width of the selected column(s) by using the Best Fit button, or you can manually enter a column width into the Column Width text box. Once a column's width has been changed, you can revert to the default column width by checking the Standard Width check box.

The height of a table's rows may be adjusted in much the same way that its columns are. The Row Height dialog box, available on the Format menu, lets you manually set the height of all rows in a table, or revert to the standard height. The standard height is based on the font size being used in the table. You also may adjust the height of a table's rows by clicking the border between row selector buttons and dragging up or down. The pointer will change to a vertical resizing pointer, and a horizontal black line will indicate where the new boundary will appear when the mouse button is released. Though you may make a row any height you wish, all rows in a table will have the same height.

Figure 2-18 Selecting multiple columns

Several columns may be
selected at the same time
so that they may be
acted upon as a unit

Figure 2-19 Column Width dialog box

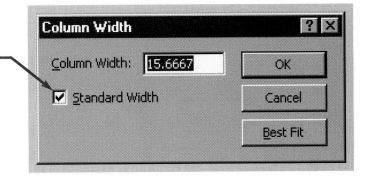

Applies the default column width
(approximately one screen inch)
to the selected columns

Access 2000

Figure 2-20 Table with adjusted column widths

Employee Number	Date Hired	Last Name	First Name	Street	City	State	Zip Code
001	6/5/93	Busing	Klaus	112 Memorial Dr	Irvington	NY	10533
002	6/5/93	Young	Tracy	665 Boylston St	Elmsford	NY	10523
003	6/8/93	Ivanova	Harriet	264 Huntington Ave	Ardsley	NY	10502
004	6/12/93	Watanabe	Hiroshi	2268 Newbury St	Dobbs Ferry	NY	10522
005	6/15/93	Sugarfoot	Frank	1620 Commonwealth Ave	Armonk	NY	10504
006	12/11/93	Silverman	Samantha	429 Washington St	Scarsdale	NY	10583
007	12/11/93	Martin	David	14 Temple St	Irvington	NY	10533
008	12/17/93	Geddes	Leroy	1561 Tremont St	Ardsley	NY	10502
009	4/2/94	Chandler	Kevin	554 Cambridge St	Irvington	NY	10533
010	6/23/94	Kim	Josephine	99 Columbus Ave	White Plains	NY	10601
011	8/13/94	Gluggman	Richard	22 Clarendon St	Dobbs Ferry	NY	10522
012	8/21/94	Kaplan	Chris	112 Massachusetts Ave	White Plains	NY	10601
013	8/21/94	Lee	Mike	72 Charles St	Dobbs Ferry	NY	10522
014	8/23/94	Abdo	Muhammad	112 Atlantic Ave	Scarsdale	NY	10583
015	9/24/94	Reynolds	Ken	25 Flute Pl	Scarsdale	NY	10583
016	9/25/94	Collins	Elmer	17 Cornell Ave	Elmsford	NY	10523
017	12/17/94	Harris	Lorna	43 Lindy Dr	Hartsdale	NY	10530

Record: 1 of 50

Columns are just as
wide as the widest
item they contain

Practice

Adjust all of the columns so that they are
the optimum width for the data they contain.

Hot Tip

Double-clicking the boundary between field
selector buttons with the resizing pointer
will automatically adjust the width of the
column on the left to its optimum width,
just as the Best Fit button adjusts the
width of all selected columns.

Editing and Arranging Fields

Concept

At times, you may wish to change the names of fields to more accurately describe the information they contain or to better fit them into an appropriate column width. Access not only lets you easily rename fields, but also allows you to move and reposition them.

Do It!

Kyle will rename some of his fields so that they take up less space, and will move the First Name field so that it comes before Last Name.

1 Place the insertion point in the Employee Number column, then click Format, followed by Rename Column. The field name will appear highlighted, with a blinking insertion point positioned at its beginning.

2 Type Employee # to replace the previous name, then press [Enter] to save the change.

3 Follow the previous steps to change the Date Hired field name to Hired and to change Zip Code to Zip.

4 Double-click the right edges of the Employee #, Hired, and Zip field selector buttons with the resizing pointer to automatically fit the columns into the least amount of space without obscuring any of their contents.

5 Click the First Name field selector button to select the entire column.

6 Click and drag the First Name field selector button to the left until a vertical black line appears between the Hired and Last Name fields, then release the mouse button. The entire column moves to the new location, effectively causing the First Name and Last Name fields to trade positions. Your table should now look like the one shown in **Figure 2-21**.

More

The Format menu contains commands that affect the way in which table elements appear on the screen. The Font command brings up the Font dialog box, which controls such text aspects as font and font size, style, color, and effects. The Hide Columns command does just what it says, allowing you to hide a column from view while still letting you include its contents as sorting and filtering criteria. The Unhide Columns command opens a dialog box, shown in **Figure 2-22**, that displays a check box for each of your fields; checking a box will make its corresponding column visible, while unchecking the box will hide the column from view. Finally, the Freeze Columns command lets you freeze one or more columns on a datasheet so that they become the leftmost columns of your table. These columns will be visible at all times, no matter where you scroll. This is especially useful in very wide tables, where it may be difficult to match up data in two columns that are too far apart to be viewed simultaneously.

Figure 2-21 Renamed and rearranged fields in a table

Employee #	Hired	First Name	Last Name	Street	City	State	Zip
001	6/5/93	Klaus	Busing	112 Memorial Dr	Irvington	NY	10533
002	6/5/93	Tracy	Young	665 Boylston St	Elmsford	NY	10523
003	6/8/93	Harriet	Ivanova	264 Huntington Ave	Ardsley	NY	10502
004	6/12/93	Hiroshi	Watanabe	2268 Newbury St	Dobbs Ferry	NY	10522
005	6/15/93	Frank	Sugarfoot	1620 Commonwealth Ave	Armonk	NY	10504
006	12/11/93	Samantha	Silverman	429 Washington St	Scarsdale	NY	10583
007	12/11/93	David	Martin	14 Temple St	Irvington	NY	10533
008	12/17/93	Leroy	Geddes	1561 Tremont St	Ardsley	NY	10502
009	4/2/94	Kevin	Chandler	554 Cambridge St	Irvington	NY	10533
010	6/23/94	Josephine	Kim	99 Columbus Ave	White Plains	NY	10601
011	8/13/94	Richard	Gluggman	22 Clarendon St	Dobbs Ferry	NY	10522
012	8/21/94	Chris	Kaplan	112 Massachusetts Ave	White Plains	NY	10601
013	8/21/94	Mike	Lee	72 Charles St	Dobbs Ferry	NY	10522
014	8/23/94	Muhammad	Abdo	112 Atlantic Ave	Scarsdale	NY	10583
015	9/24/94	Ken	Reynolds	25 Flute Pl	Scarsdale	NY	10583
016	9/25/94	Elmer	Collins	17 Cornell Ave	Elmsford	NY	10523
017	12/17/94	Lorna	Harris	43 Lindy Dr	Hartsdale	NY	10530

Record: 1 of 50

Figure 2-22 Unhide Columns dialog box

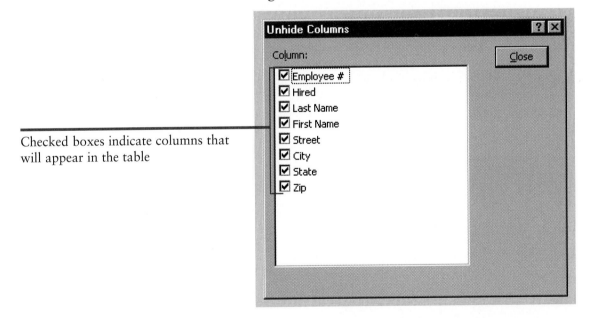

Checked boxes indicate columns that will appear in the table

Unhide Columns

Column:
- ☑ Employee #
- ☑ Hired
- ☑ Last Name
- ☑ First Name
- ☑ Street
- ☑ City
- ☑ State
- ☑ Zip

Close

Practice

Rename the To Be Ordered column so it reads Number Needed. Then, move the Number Needed column so that it is the last in the table.

Hot Tip

Double-clicking a field selector button selects it for modification, just as it does when using the Rename Column command on the Format menu.

Adding a Field

Concept

Once a table has been created, fields may still be added or removed at any time. While fields may be added in Datasheet View, Design View offers much more control over the properties of your fields.

Do It!

Kyle wants to add a new field to his table, and to set its properties so as to restrict the data that may be entered into the field.

1. Click the View button ![icon] on the Table Datasheet toolbar to toggle to Design View.

2. Click the empty cell below the Zip field to place the insertion point there.

3. Type Gender, then press [Enter]. The Data Type field becomes selected.

4. Double-click the Field Size text box on the General tab of the Field Properties section to select the default value of 50.

5. Type [1], then press [Enter]. The insertion point moves to the Format field property.

6. Type [>] ([Shift]+[.]). Access will make all contents of this field appear in uppercase.

7. Click in the Validation Rule text box to place the insertion point there.

8. Type ="M" Or "F" to set the validation rule. When you set a validation rule, Access checks all entries in the field against the rule. Entries that do not fall within the bounds of the rule are not accepted.

9. Click in the Validation Text text box to place the insertion point there, then type You may enter only M or F. This is the error message that will be displayed if a value other than M or F is entered into this field. Your table should resemble the one shown in **Figure 2-23**.

10. Click the Save button ![icon] to save the design changes you have made. A dialog box, shown in **Figure 2-24** will appear asking whether you want to test existing data under the new rule.

11. Since this is a new field and there are no existing data, click [No]. The dialog box disappears, and the table is saved with the changes you have made.

12. Click the Close buttons on the Design View and Database windows to close the file.

More

In the example above, the new field was added to the end of the table. New fields also may be inserted into the middle of a table by using the Rows command on the Insert menu in Design View. A new row will be added above the row in which the insertion point currently resides. New fields also may be added in Datasheet View using the Columns command on the Insert menu, but Datasheet View does not offer the kind of control over field properties that is available in Design View. Commands are available on the Edit menu in both views to delete selected fields.

Figure 2-23 Adding a field to a table in Design View

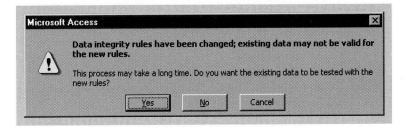

The validation text appears if the validation rule is not met

Figure 2-24 Microsoft Access warning dialog box

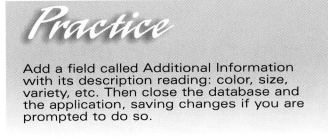

Practice

Add a field called Additional Information with its description reading: color, size, variety, etc. Then close the database and the application, saving changes if you are prompted to do so.

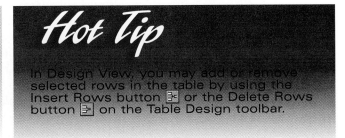

Hot Tip

In Design View, you may add or remove selected rows in the table by using the Insert Rows button or the Delete Rows button on the Table Design toolbar.

Importing Database Objects

Concept

You may easily import objects from other databases into an open database. This is useful if you are creating a new database but want to use some of the objects you have already created for another database.

Do It!

Kyle wants to create a new database and then import several objects into it from another database.

1 Click the New button to open the New dialog box.

2 Click [OK] to accept the default, **Database**. The File New Database dialog box will open.

3 Create a new database called **Employees 3** and save it in the My Access Files folder within your Student Files folder. When it has been created, the dialog box will close and the Database window will appear on the screen.

4 Click **File**, then select **Import** from the **Get External Data** submenu. The Import dialog box will open, as shown in **Figure 2-25**.

5 Locate and select the student file **Do It2-10**, which should be located in your Student Files folder.

6 Click [Import]. The Import Objects dialog box, shown in **Figure 2-26**, appears with the selected database's window showing. This will let you choose the objects that you wish to import.

7 Click [Select All] to select all the tables listed, then click [OK]. Access will import the selected tables into the Employees 3 database and close the Import Objects dialog box.

More

The Office Links submenu of the Tools menu offers commands that can link your database to other Microsoft Office files. A common use for the Merge It with MS Word command on this submenu is the creation of Mail Merge documents using Microsoft Word as the editor and an Access database as the datasheet. This could enable you to create a form letter in Word, for example, and to print out as many copies as you wish, each personalized with information drawn from the Access employees table that you have created, with names, addresses, and other information automatically inserted into their proper places in each letter.

You also may use Microsoft Word to view a datasheet by using the Publish It with MS Word command on the Office Links submenu. This allows you to create Word documents containing partial or whole database objects. Using this command will open Word and display the selected database as an rtf (Rich Text Format) file, which is a text format that maintains formatting information.

Access offers a similar link to Excel, using the Analyze It with MS Excel command, that lets you open databases as Excel files so that Excel's analytical, computational, and display features may be fully utilized.

Figure 2-25 Import dialog box

Objects may be import-
ed from any of these
databases

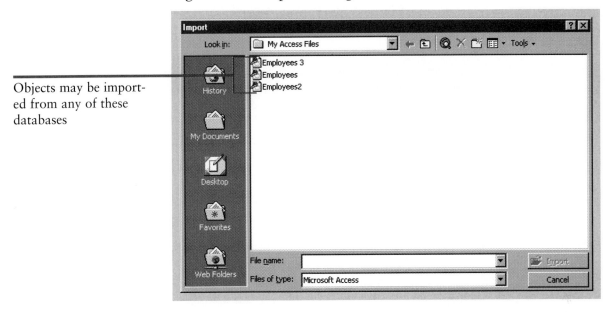

Access 2000

Figure 2-26 Import Objects dialog box

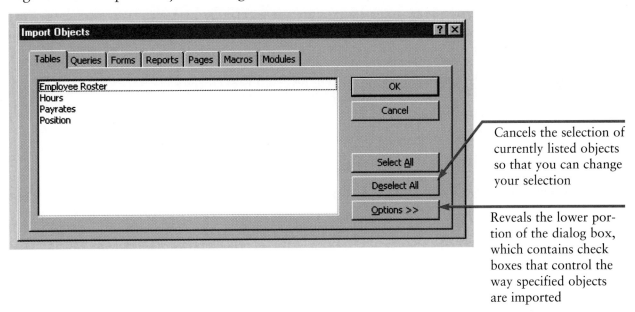

Cancels the selection of
currently listed objects
so that you can change
your selection

Reveals the lower por-
tion of the dialog box,
which contains check
boxes that control the
way specified objects
are imported

Practice

Open another Access application window,
as you did for the practice file in the previous Lesson. Then create a new database
called **Tuning Tracker** and import the two
tables from **Prac 2-12**.

Hot Tip

The Office Links button and list arrow,
available on the Database toolbar when the
Database window is active, provides
another way to get to the Office Link commands.

AC 2.25

Finding Information in a Table

Concept

Access contains a wide variety of powerful search features that enable you to find the information you are looking for in your tables quickly and accurately.

Do It!

One of Stay Fast's employees, Laura Van Pelt, has married another employee. Kyle will use Access's search capabilities to quickly find the record so that her name and address information may be updated.

1 Double-click the **Employee Roster** table icon in the objects list in the Database window to open it in Datasheet View.

2 Click the **Last Name** field selector button to select the entire column.

3 Click **Edit**, then click **Find** to open the Find and Replace dialog box, which is pictured in **Figure 2-27**. Notice that it will search only within the previously selected field.

4 Type **Van Pelt** into the Find What: text box, then click **Find Next**. Access searches for the words Van Pelt in the Last Name fields, and scrolls down to show the selected field.

5 Close the **Find and Replace** dialog box.

6 Type **Geddes** to replace Van Pelt with Laura's new last name.

7 Press [Tab] twice to select the **Street** field in Laura's record, then type in her new address to replace it, **1561 Tremont St.**

8 Press [Tab] to go to the **City** field, then type **Ardsley** to replace the previous city.

9 Press [Tab] twice to select the **Zip** field, then type **10502**.

More

Access can still search for items in a table if only a fragment is known. If you had typed **De** into the Find in field : "Last Name" dialog box and selected **Start of Field** in the **Match** drop-down list, Access would have located the record for DeBois. If the Match drop-down list was set to **Any Part of Field**, Access would also find Geddes, Adelman, and McBride, since these contain the "de" sequence in places other than the beginning of the field. The **Whole Field** option in the Match drop-down list instructs Access to search for fields that contain only what is shown in the Find What: text box. In this case, it would only find a field if the field contained "de" and nothing else. If the Match drop-down list box were set to anything other than Whole Field and the **Match Case** check box were checked, Access would find only DeBois, since the combination of uppercase and lowercase letters in the Find What: text box match those in DeBois. As you can see, these options may be used individually or in combination to fine-tune your search efforts.

You may also use wildcard characters in a search. Examples of wildcard characters are displayed in **Table 2-3**.

Table 2-3 Search Parameter wildcard characters

WILDCARD	USED FOR	EXAMPLE
*	Matching any number of characters; may be placed at the beginning, at the end, or in the middle of text	thr* finds throw, through, and thrush
?	Matching any single alphabetic character	t?n finds tan, ten, and tin, but not town
[ ]	Matching any single character within the brackets	t[ae]n finds tan and ten, but not tin
[!]	Matching any character not in the brackets	t[!ae]n finds tin and ton, but not tan or ten
[-]	Matching any one of a range of characters, specified in alphabetical order	ta[a-m] will find tab and tag, but not tan or tap
#	Matching any single numeric character	4#0 will find 410 and 420, but not 4110 or 415

Access 2000

Figure 2-27 Find and Replace dialog box

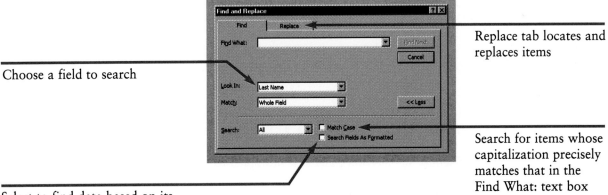

Choose a field to search

Replace tab locates and replaces items

Search for items whose capitalization precisely matches that in the Find What: text box

Select to find data based on its display format, clear to search for data based on its value; searching by format is usually slowest

Filtering and Sorting Records in a Table

Concept

Access allows you to use several filtering and sorting criteria to organize the records in your tables. Filters control what items are shown, while sorting determines the order in which they are displayed.

Do It!

Kyle wants to display the records for only those employees that live in Elmsford (a Filter by Selection).

1. Click anywhere in the City field. By default, the Sort feature will sort the field that holds the insertion point.

2. Click the Sort Ascending button ![Sort Ascending button] on the Table Datasheet toolbar. The records are displayed in a new order, listing employees by their cities of residence from Ardsley to White Plains. Now all employees from Elmsford are grouped together in the table, as shown in **Figure 2-28**.

3. To Filter by Selection, you must locate an instance of the value you want the filtered records to contain. With the table sorted, you can now easily locate and place the insertion point in one of the City fields containing the value Elmsford.

4. Click the Filter by Selection button ![Filter by Selection button] on the Table Datasheet toolbar. Access filters the table based on the contents of the selected field, the Apply Filter button on the toolbar becomes depressed and changes to the Remove Filter button ![Remove Filter button], and only the records for employees living in Elmsford are displayed, as you can see in **Figure 2-29**.

5. Now you will return the table to its original form. Click the Remove Filter button ![Remove Filter button] to show all records.

6. Click the Employee # field, then click the Sort Ascending button to sort the records in order of increasing Employee #.

7. Close the table, saving changes if prompted to do so.

More

Unlike the Filter by Selection command, the Filter Excluding Selection command (which has no button on the toolbar by default, but is located with the other filter commands on the Records menu) will display all records in the table that do not contain the specified field contents.

The Filter by Form Command displays the Filter by Form window in place of your Datasheet View. In this window, you may select several filter criteria from the fields in your table, and you may even use more than one entry for a single field by using the Or tabs at the bottom of the window. For example, you can view just the records of the female employees living in Irvington by selecting those criteria in their respective fields in the Filter by Form window. To display all female employees who live in both Irvington and Dobbs Ferry, you would select the same criteria as before, then click the Or tab, which allows you to select Dobbs Ferry as a second filtering criterion in the City field.

Figure 2-28 Table sorted in ascending order by City

Employee #	Hired	Last Name	First Name	Street	City	State	Zip	Gender
003	6/8/93	Ivanova	Harriet	264 Huntington Ave	Ardsley	NY	10502	F
050	6/5/99	Geddes	Laura	1561 Tremont St	Ardsley	NY	10502	F
008	12/17/93	Geddes	Leroy	1561 Tremont St	Ardsley	NY	10502	M
005	6/15/93	Sugarfoot	Frank	1620 Commonwealth Ave	Armonk	NY	10504	M
018	3/4/95	Nowak	Jasmine	39 Davis Ave	Briarcliff Manor	NY	10510	F
033	1/2/98	Collins	John	449 Roaring Brook Blvd	Briarcliff Manor	NY	10510	M
045	12/15/98	DeBois	Kirby	25 Springfield Ln	Bronxville	NY	10708	M
022	6/6/95	Wolff	Henryk	204 Hamilton Rd	Chappaqua	NY	10514	M
011	8/13/94	Gluggman	Richard	22 Clarendon St	Dobbs Ferry	NY	10522	M
029	5/11/96	Smith	Rhonda	11 Smith Ave	Dobbs Ferry	NY	10522	F
032	1/2/98	McDonald	John	76 Smith Ave	Dobbs Ferry	NY	10522	M
013	8/21/94	Lee	Mike	72 Charles St	Dobbs Ferry	NY	10522	M
004	6/12/93	Watanabe	Hiroshi	2268 Newbury St	Dobbs Ferry	NY	10522	M
040	7/3/98	Lee	Mike	9 Livingston Pl	Eastchester	NY	10709	M
037	4/21/98	Prakash	Dom	7 Garden Pl	Eastchester	NY	10709	M
031	10/27/97	Young	Trent	77 Silver Rd	Elmsford	NY	10523	M
002	6/5/93	Young	Tracy	665 Boylston St	Elmsford	NY	10523	F
019	4/19/95	Rosafort	Lyle	1 Upland Ln	Elmsford	NY	10523	M
023	7/2/95	James	Arthur	89 Indian Bluff Blvd	Elmsford	NY	10523	M
016	9/25/94	Collins	Elmer	17 Cornell Ave	Elmsford	NY	10523	M
041	8/1/98	Castle	Frank	51 Stone Ave	Elmsford	NY	10523	M
027	5/4/96	Rush	Francis	2122 Lincoln Rd	Elmsford	NY	10523	M
017	12/17/94	Harris	Lorna	43 Lindy Dr	Hartsdale	NY	10530	F

Record: 1 of 50

The desired records are now grouped together because of the sorting criterion that was imposed

Figure 2-29 Filter by Selection

Employee #	Hired	Last Name	First Name	Street	City	State	Zip	Gender
041	8/1/98	Castle	Frank	51 Stone Ave	Elmsford	NY	10523	M
031	10/27/97	Young	Trent	77 Silver Rd	Elmsford	NY	10523	M
027	5/4/96	Rush	Francis	2122 Lincoln Rd	Elmsford	NY	10523	M
023	7/2/95	James	Arthur	89 Indian Bluff Blvd	Elmsford	NY	10523	M
019	4/19/95	Rosafort	Lyle	1 Upland Ln	Elmsford	NY	10523	M
016	9/25/94	Collins	Elmer	17 Cornell Ave	Elmsford	NY	10523	F
002	6/5/93	Young	Tracy	665 Boylston St	Elmsford	NY	10523	
*						NY		

Record: 1 of 7 (Filtered)

Indicates that the entire table is not displayed

Practice

Sort the Customers table of the Tuning Tracker database alphabetically by Last Name, then apply a filter that will display the records for those customers that live in the 10010 zip code.

Hot Tip

When a table or form is saved, the last filter used is saved with it. You may reapply the filter when needed by clicking the Apply Filter button.

Access 2000

Using the Simple Query Wizard

Concept

A query is a set of instructions that you define and that Access uses to select and display data from tables and other queries. Queries are retained as an object within a database so that you can work with them whenever you like. The most common type of query is a select query, which retrieves data from one or more tables using criteria that you specify, and then displays them in a predetermined order. The Simple Query Wizard allows you to create simple select queries quickly and easily.

Do It!

Kyle will use the Simple Query Wizard to create a query that will contain all the relevant data from the database to run a mail merge to all employees.

1 Click the Queries button on the Objects bar in the Database window.

2 Click [New] to open the New Query dialog box, shown in **Figure 2-30**.

3 Click Simple Query Wizard to select it, then click [OK]. The Simple Query Wizard opens with the Employee Roster table selected in the Tables/Queries drop-down list box and a list of that table's fields in the Available Fields list box.

4 Click First Name in the Available Fields box, then click [>] to move it to the Selected Fields box.

5 Move the following fields, in order, to the Selected Fields box in the same way that you moved the First Name field: Last Name, Street, City, State, and Zip. When you have finished, your Simple Query Wizard window should resemble the one shown in **Figure 2-31**.

6 Click [Next >] to go to the next step of the Simple Query Wizard. The suggested query title is selected for modification.

7 Type Mail Merge to give the query a new title, then click [Finish]. Access executes the query and displays it in its own window, as shown in **Figure 2-32**. It contains all the records from the Employee Roster table, but displays only the fields that you selected. Notice that the records still appear in the original order, with Klaus Busing (Employee # 001) first.

8 Click the Close button in the upper-right corner of the Select Query window to close it. The query was automatically saved by the Wizard in the final step, so it closes without prompting you to save it first.

More

There are five kinds of queries that can be created with Access. The select query, which you created in the exercise above, is the most common type. A crosstab query performs calculations and presents data in spreadsheet format, with one type of data listed down the left side and other kinds across the top. An action query is used to select records and perform operations on them, such as deleting them or placing them in new tables. A parameter query is a flexible query that prompts you to enter the selection criteria each time it is used. An SQL query is a query created using Standard Query Language statements. SQL is the basic programming language that Access uses to create and execute query procedures.

Figure 2-30 New Query dialog box

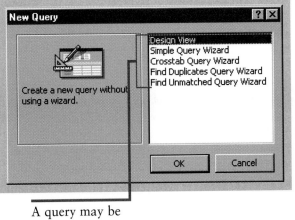

A query may be
created by any of
these methods

Moves all fields in the Selected Fields
box back to the Available Fields box,
allowing you to start over

Figure 2-31 Selected fields for simple query

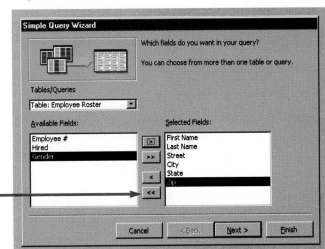

Figure 2-32 Results of Mail Merge query

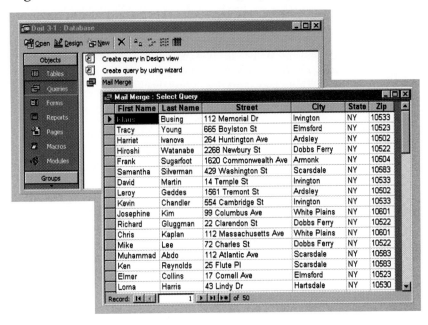

Using the Simple Query Wizard, perform a
query on the Service Records table in the
Tuning Tracker database that displays the
Customer ID # and Last Tuned fields. Name
the query **Last Tuned**.

Hot Tip

In the first step of the Simple Query
Wizard, you may add fields to the Selected
Fields box without clicking ▸ by double-
clicking the field you wish to add in the
Available fields box; double-clicking a
selected field moves it back.

Access 2000

Creating a Query in Design View

Concept	Design View offers more control over what gets included in a select query than the Simple Query Wizard.
Do It!	Kyle would like to create a query in Design View that lists Stay Fast's employees along with their employee numbers and the dates that they were hired.

1 With the Queries button on the Objects bar selected in the Employees 3 Database window, click 🗗New on the Database window toolbar to open the New Query dialog box.

2 Click ⟨ OK ⟩ to accept the default **Design View** to create a query without using a wizard. A blank Select Query window appears in the background behind the Show Table dialog box, which shows a list of the database's tables on its Tables tab.

3 Click Employee Roster if it is not already selected. Then, click ⟨ Add ⟩. A small list box appears in the Select Query window listing the fields available in the table.

4 Click ⟨ Close ⟩ to close the Show Table dialog box. The Select Query window becomes active, with the insertion point blinking in the Field row.

5 Click Employee # in the Employee Roster list box and drag it into the Field row. When dragging, the mouse pointer will appear as a miniature field cell ▦. When it is dropped, the field appears in the Field row, the table that it came from is displayed in the Table row, and the Show check box is checked, indicating that this field will appear in the final results of the query.

6 Double-click **Hired**, **Last Name**, and **First Name** from the Employee Roster field list in the upper-half of the Select Query window to add them as the remaining fields in the query. They will appear in the lower-half of the Select Query window, as shown in **Figure 2-33**.

7 To show the results of the query, click the Run button ▣ on the Query Design toolbar. The query will be displayed as a table containing all records from the Employee Roster table, but displaying only the fields that you selected. The table created by the query is pictured in **Figure 2-34**.

Figure 2-33 Select Query Design View window

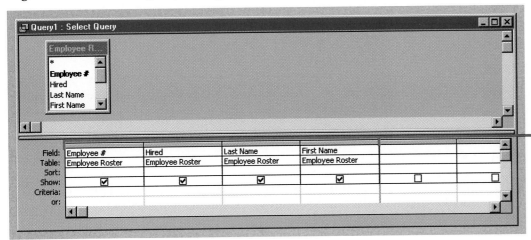

These are the fields
that will appear in
the query

Figure 2-34 Results of select query

Employee #	Hired	Last Name	First Name
001	6/5/93	Busing	Klaus
002	6/5/93	Young	Tracy
003	6/8/93	Ivanova	Harriet
004	6/12/93	Watanabe	Hiroshi
005	6/15/93	Sugarfoot	Frank
006	12/11/93	Silverman	Samantha
007	12/11/93	Martin	David
008	12/17/93	Geddes	Leroy
009	4/2/94	Chandler	Kevin
010	6/23/94	Kim	Josephine
011	8/13/94	Gluggman	Richard
012	8/21/94	Kaplan	Chris
013	8/21/94	Lee	Mike
014	8/23/94	Abdo	Muhammad
015	9/24/94	Reynolds	Ken
016	9/25/94	Collins	Elmer
017	12/17/94	Harris	Lorna
018	3/4/95	Nowak	Jasmine
019	4/19/95	Rosafort	Lyle
020	4/25/95	Wong	Carolyn

Record: 14 ◄ 1 ► ►I ►* of 50

All 50 records have been
included, though some fields
are not shown

Creating a Query in Design View (continued)

Do It!

8 Click File, then click Save As. The Save As dialog box appears, as seen in **Figure 2-35**, with the default name Query1.

9 Type Employee Roster: name and date hired to name the query, then click to save it.

10 Click the Close button at the upper-right of the Select Query window to remove it from the screen. Notice that the query's icon appears in the objects list of the Database window with the other query you created earlier.

More

As fields are added to the design grid in the Select Query window, a drop-down list arrow appears next to the currently selected field. You can click this list arrow to display a list of the table's available fields, as shown in **Figure 2-36**, which you can then use to select a different field. If you wish to remove a field from the design grid, click its selector button, which appears as a thin gray bar at the top of the field, and then select Delete from the Edit menu.

You can manipulate the tabular results of a query in much the same way that you would work with an actual table. You may select fields and perform a sort or a filter, or you can move columns and reorder the fields. Note that changes such as these that you make to the structure of the query do not affect the source table. However, a table generated by a select query, also called a dynaset, is dynamically linked to a source table. This means that any changes you make to the actual data in the dynaset will be reflected in the source table. Similarly, if you were to make a change to the Employee Roster table, the data in the dynaset would change to reflect it the next time the query was run.

Figure 2-35 Save As dialog box

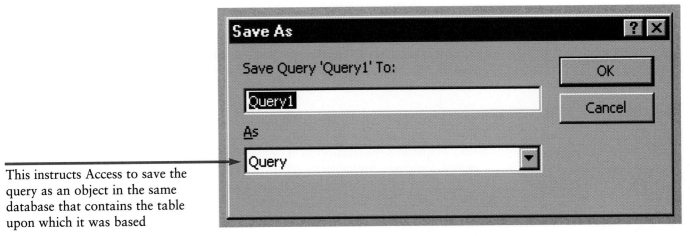

This instructs Access to save the query as an object in the same database that contains the table upon which it was based

Figure 2-36 Design grid available field drop-down list

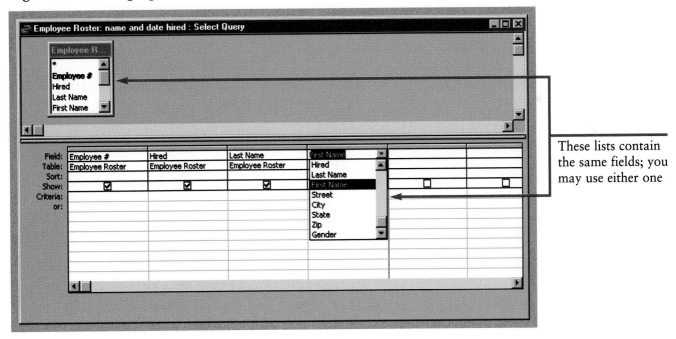

These lists contain the same fields; you may use either one

Practice

Create a query in Design View based upon the Service Records table of the Tuning Tracker database that displays the Piano Make, Piano Model, and Use fields. Name the query **Usage**.

Hot Tip

You can move and reorder fields in the Query Design window by dragging their selector buttons, just as you would in a table.

Adding Selection Criteria to a Query

Concept

After you have created a query, you may attach additional sorting and filtering criteria to it so that the table it creates shows just the data you wish to see, in the precise order in which they will be most useful.

Do It!

Kyle will now sort the query alphabetically by Last Name, move the Last Name field so that it is the leftmost field in the table, and filter the data so that only the records for those employees hired before January first of 1994 are displayed.

1. With the Employee Roster: name and date hired query selected in the objects list in the Database window, click Design. The query will open in Design View.

2. Click the Sort cell in the Last Name column. An insertion point will appear in the cell along with a drop-down list arrow.

3. Click the drop-down list arrow, then select Ascending from the three choices that appear, as shown in **Figure 2-37**. This instructs Access to sort the data in the field alphabetically from A to Z.

4. Click the Run button on the Query Design toolbar. The query will appear in Datasheet View, sorted as specified.

5. Click the Last Name selector button to select the column, then click and drag it to the left so that it is the first column in the table.

6. Move the First Name field to make it the second column in the table, at the right of the Last Name field.

7. Click the View button on the Query Datasheet toolbar to revert to Design View. Although you changed the order of the fields in the Datasheet window, this does not affect their order in the design grid. This ensures that sort criteria do not change.

8. Click the Criteria cell in the Hired field. The insertion point appears in the cell.

9. Type <1/1/94. This tell Access to display only records with dates in their Hired fields that predate January 1, 1994.

10. Click the Run button. Only those employee records that contain the specified hiring date appear, as seen in **Figure 2-38**.

11. Click the Save button to save the changes you have made, then close the Query Datasheet View window.

More

Adding selection criteria to a query requires that you know how to use special Access symbols and words. The criteria that you set to select specific records from a table are called conditions, and the symbols and words you use to set these conditions are called operators. Access provides a number of operators for use in selection criteria. They include mathematical symbols you may already be familiar with, such as the equal sign [=], the less than sign [<], the less than or equal to sign [≤], the greater than sign [>], the greater than or equal to sign [≥], and the not equal to sign [≠]. Access also has verbal operators such as **Between...And**, which selects two values and all the values between them. You can use the **In** operator, which allows you to find fields with values that match those in a list you provide. There is also the **Like** operator, which you use to find fields that match a pattern.

When you query tables, you often use a single criterion to select records. A single selection criterion is called a simple condition. For example, the simple condition "= 050" typed in the Criteria cell for the Employee # field would instruct Access to select only the record with the Employee # 050. Note that in the absence of an operator, Access assumes the equals operator, so that in this case, typing in just 050 is also acceptable.

Figure 2-37 Sort drop-down list

Select a sort order from the drop-down list

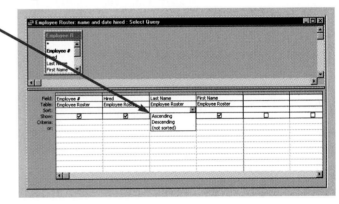

Figure 2-38 Query run with selection criteria

	Last Name	First Name	Employee #	Hired
▶	Busing	Klaus	001	6/5/93
	Geddes	Leroy	008	12/17/93
	Ivanova	Harriet	003	6/8/93
	Martin	David	007	12/11/93
	Silverman	Samantha	006	12/11/93
	Sugarfoot	Frank	005	6/15/93
	Watanabe	Hiroshi	004	6/12/93
	Young	Tracy	002	6/5/93
*				

Record: |◀ ◀ 1 ▶ ▶| ▶* of 8

Click selector button, then click and drag to move the column

Only records with Hired field values before 1/1/94 are displayed

Practice

Apply further selection criteria to the Usage query you created within the Tuning Tracker database so that only pianos with Use values greater than 3 are displayed. Save the changes you make.

Hot Tip

The **Not** operator instructs Access to select all records that do not match the criterion. For example, using the criterion Not <1/1/94 in the last exercise would have selected the records for all employees hired after the specified date instead of before.

Using Advanced Selection Criteria

Concept

Access allows you to use more than one selection criterion for a query, enabling you to select records that meet several conditions. Using more than one condition requires the use of logical operators, such as AND and OR, which allow you to connect several simple conditions together.

Do It!

To demonstrate the power of advanced selection criteria, Kyle will select all records belonging to employees who were hired before 1/1/94 and whose last names also start with the letter S. He will then modify the query to select records for employees who either have last names beginning with S or were hired before 1/1/94.

1 Select the **Employee Roster: name and date hired** query in the objects list in the Database window and click [Design]. The query opens in Design View.

2 Click the Criteria cell in the Last Name field, then type Like "S*" into the cell. The asterisk serves as a wildcard, telling Access to select all values in the field that begin with the letter S. Since this condition was placed in the same row of the grid as the condition in the Hired field, Access will perform an AND selection, finding records that meet all the conditions.

3 Click the **Run** button [!] to run the query. Access displays the two records that meet all the criteria that were set, as you can see in **Figure 2-39**.

4 Click the View button [image] to return to Design View.

5 Select the **Last Name** criteria (Like "S*"), then click the Cut button [image] to send it to the Clipboard. The Windows Clipboard is a temporary storage place for data that are being moved or copied.

6 Click the **or** cell of the **Last Name** field to place the insertion point there.

7 Click the Paste button [image] to insert the contents of the Clipboard at the insertion point, as shown in **Figure 2-40**. When you set two conditions in different rows of the design grid, Access automatically uses the OR operator to evaluate them.

8 Click the **Run** button. The query will appear with more records in its table than it had previously (**Figure 2-41**) because there are more records that match at least one of the two set conditions than meet both.

9 Click the Close button on the datasheet, but do not save changes if prompted.

More

You can further define selection queries by using combinations of AND and OR statements. For example, you could select the records for all employees who were either hired before 1/1/94 AND whose names begin with the letter S, OR who were hired after 1/1/94 AND have last names beginning with the letter R. (Refer to **Figure 2-42** to see how this would be constructed.)

Figure 2-39 Query run using a wildcard

Last Name	First Name	Employee #	Hired
Silverman	Samantha	006	12/11/93
Sugarfoot	Frank	005	6/15/93

Record: 1 of 2

Click to make the
next record active

Figure 2-40 Condition pasted into "or" cell

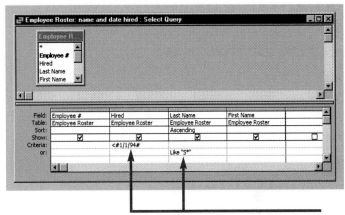

Criteria in different
rows will be applied
using the OR operator

Figure 2-41 Query run using OR operator

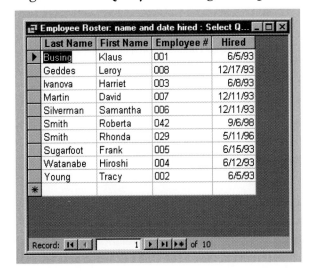

Last Name	First Name	Employee #	Hired
Busing	Klaus	001	6/5/93
Geddes	Leroy	008	12/17/93
Ivanova	Harriet	003	6/8/93
Martin	David	007	12/11/93
Silverman	Samantha	006	12/11/93
Smith	Roberta	042	9/6/98
Smith	Rhonda	029	5/11/96
Sugarfoot	Frank	005	6/15/93
Watanabe	Hiroshi	004	6/12/93
Young	Tracy	002	6/5/93

Record: 1 of 10

Access 2000

Figure 2-42 Query designed using a combination of logical operators

Field:	Employee #	Hired	Last Name	First Name
Table:	Employee Roster	Employee Roster	Employee Roster	Employee Roster
Sort:			Ascending	
Show:	☑	☑	☑	☑
Criteria:		<#1/1/94#	Like "S*"	
or:		>#1/1/94#	Like "R*"	

A combination of AND and OR statements
can be used to create more complex queries

Clearing this check box will
cause the field to be hidden
when the query is run

Establishing Table Relationships

Concept

One of Access's more powerful features is its ability to link tables together to create a relational database. Using a common field, you can define relationships between tables and effectively utilize them as if they were a single table. This is useful for selecting and correlating information from two or more tables.

Do It!

Kyle would like to define a relationship between the Employee Roster table and the Hours table in his database.

1 Click Tools, then click Relationships. The Show Table dialog box appears with the Employee Roster table selected on the Tables tab. Click Employee Roster if it is not already selected.

2 Click [Add] to add a list box containing the selected table's fields to the Relationships window.

3 Double-click the Hours table on the Tables tab to add its list box to the Relationships window as well, then click [Close] to close the Show Table dialog box.

4 Click and drag the Employee # field from the Employee Roster fields list box to the Employee # field of the Hours fields list box. The Edit Relationships dialog box appears on the screen, as shown in **Figure 2-43**. This is how a relationship between tables is established.

5 Click the Enforce Referential Integrity check box. Referential integrity ensures that relationships between records in related tables are valid. With this box checked, you cannot add records to the related table unless a matching record already exists in the primary table.

6 Click the Cascade Delete Related Records check box. With this option active, deleting a record from the primary table will automatically delete it from the related table as well.

7 Click [Create]. A line now appears between the two Employee # fields, as seen in **Figure 2-44**.

8 Click Relationships, then click Show Table. The Show Table dialog box will appear as it did before.

9 Double-click Payrates, then Position to add their field list boxes to the Relationships window, then click [Close]. The Show Table dialog box is removed from the screen.

Figure 2-43 Edit Relationships dialog box

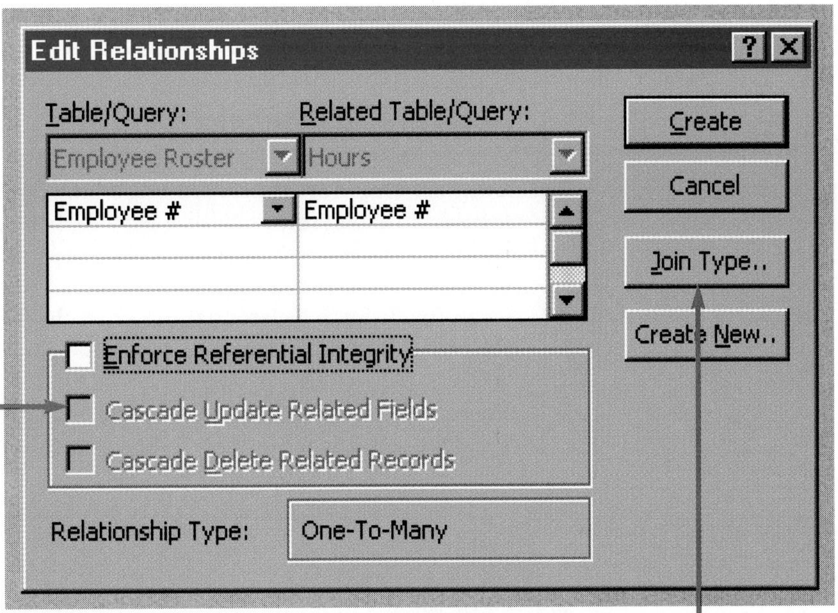

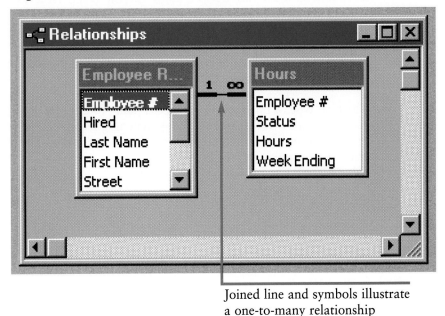

When checked, automatically updates corresponding values in a related table when they are changed in the primary table

Click to alter default join settings

Figure 2-44 Link between tables in Relationships window

Joined line and symbols illustrate a one-to-many relationship

Establishing Table Relationships

(continued)

Do It!

10 Drag the Employee # field from the Employee Roster field list box to the Employee # field of the Payrates field list box. As before, the Edit Relationships dialog box will open.

11 Click the Enforce Referential Integrity check box and the Cascade Delete Related Records check box, then click 🖫 Create .

12 Repeat the previous two steps to establish a similar relationship between the Employee Roster table and the Position table.

13 Click and drag the title bars of the list boxes to arrange them as they appear in **Figure 2-45**.

14 Close the Relationships window, saving changes when prompted to do so.

More

In Access, you can define three kinds of table relationships, depending on the data contained in each table. For example, the Employee Roster table and Position table have a common field, Employee #, the value of which is unique in each table. In fact, the Employee # field serves as the primary key for both tables. For each record in the Employee Roster table, there is one corresponding record in the Position table. The relationship between these two tables is known as one-to-one.

In contrast, the Employee Roster table and the Hours table also share the Employee # field, but its value is not unique in the Hours table. In the Hours table, the Employee number is repeated and is therefore not a primary key, but a foreign key. You can still define a relationship between the tables, with each record in the Employee Roster table corresponding to two records in the Hours table. This is known as a one-to-many relationship.

The final type of relationship is called a many-to-many relationship, where many records in both tables can have many matching records in the other. Many-to-many relationships require a third table, called a junction table, that has a one-to-many relationship with the other two tables.

Figure 2-45 Relationships defined for all tables

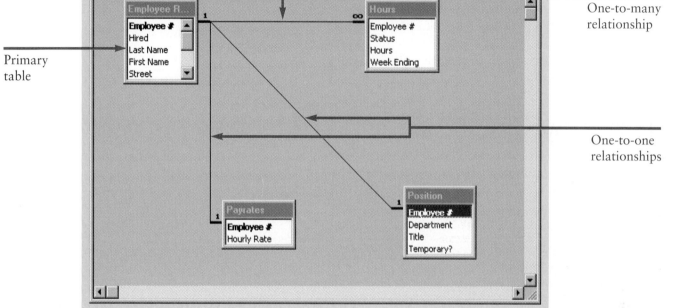

Primary table

One-to-many relationship

One-to-one relationships

Practice

Create a one-to-one relationship between the two tables in the Tuning Tracker data-base, Customers and Service Records. They should be linked by Customer ID #. Save the changes you make.

Hot Tip

To eliminate the relationships between your tables, click the **Clear Layout** button ☒. To get rid of just one relationship, right-click the line between the list boxes that repre-sents the relationship, then click Delete on the pop-up menu that appears.

Shortcuts

Function	Button/Mouse	Menu	Keyboard
Create a new database		Click File, then click New	[Ctrl]+[N]
Set Primary Key		Click Edit, then click Primary Key	
Switch to Datasheet View		Click View, then click Datasheet View	
Switch to Design View		Click View, then click Design View	
Save layout, design, or structural changes		Click File, then click Save	[Ctrl]+[S]
Undo		Click Edit, then click Undo	[Ctrl]+[Z]
Check spelling		Click Tools, then click Spelling	[F7]
Office Links		Click Tools, then high-light Office Links	
Find		Click Edit, then click Find	[Ctrl]+[F]
Cut data to the Clipboard		Click Edit, then click Cut	[Ctrl]+[X]
Paste data from the Clipboard		Click Edit, then click Paste	[Ctrl]+[V]
Show Database window		Click Window, then click name of database	[F11]

Identify Key Features

Name the items indicated by callouts in **Figures 2-46** and **2-47**.

Figure 2-46 Components of the Design View window

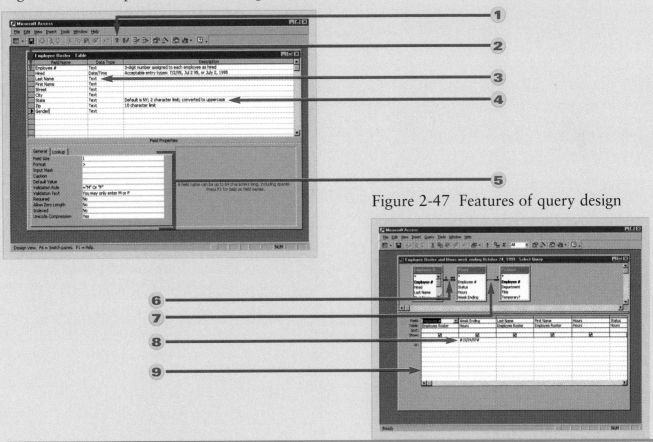

Figure 2-47 Features of query design

Select the Best Answer

10. Tells your computer what kind of information a file contains

11. Allows you to assign a field's data type and assign field properties

12. Allows you to save a database object to a new location

13. Automatically adjusts the width of a column to accommodate its widest entry

14. Restricts field entries by checking them against set conditions

15. Allows you to search for information quickly and accurately

16. Symbol used to represent unknown or unspecified data in a search or query

17. A single selection criterion

18. Expressions such as **AND** that allow you to connect several selection criteria

19. Organizes the data in a selected field from A to Z

a. Export

b. Validation Rule

c. Design View

d. File extension

e. Best Fit

f. Simple condition

g. Find command

h. Logical operators

i. Sort Ascending

j. Wildcard character

Quiz (continued)

Complete the Statement

20. All of the following are options for creating a new table except:

    a. Datasheet View

    b. Design Wizard

    c. Design View

    d. Link Table

21. To change the number of characters permitted in a field entry to a specific limit, set the:

    a. Validation Text field property

    b. Format field property

    c. Column Width field property

    d. Field Size field property

22. The character you type to instruct Access to format all entries in a field with uppercase letters is:

    a. <

    b. =

    c. >

    d. U

23. In order for a field to be used as the Primary Key, its data for each record must be:

    a. Unique and consecutive

    b. Unique and numeric

    c. Constant and numeric

    d. Constant and unique

24. Before you start working on a new database, you must first:

    a. Save it

    b. Close all other databases

    c. Import a table

    d. Export the data

25. To ensure that related tables have corresponding records, click the:

    a. Cascade Delete Related Records check box

    b. Cascade Update Related Records check box

    c. Enforce Referential Integrity check box

    d. Enforce Referential Integrity button

26. The Office Links submenu offers all of the following link options for a database except:

    a. Merge It with MS Word

    b. Analyze It with MS Excel

    c. Publish It with MS Word

    d. Merge It with MS Excel

27. To filter a table using several criteria drawn from the fields in your table, use the:

    a. Filter by Form command

    b. Filter by Selection command

    c. Filter Excluding Selection command

    d. Filter Excluding Selection button

28. A table generated by running a select query is also called a:

    a. Dynamo

    b. Related query

    c. Dynaset

    d. Parameter query

29. A table relationship can be classified as any of the following with the exception of:

    a. One-to-one

    b. One-to-many

    c. Many-to-one

    d. Many-to-many

Interactivity

Test Your Skills

1. Create a new database:

   a. Start Access from the Windows taskbar.

   b. Choose the Blank Access database option.

   c. Save the new database as Test2 in the My Access Files folder.

2. Create a new database table:

   a. Choose Design View to construct a new table.

   b. Enter the following field names to make an address book: Last Name, First Name, Street, City, State, Zip Code, Phone, Birthday.

   c. Set appropriate data types for each field.

   d. Format the Birthday field to use the Short Date form, and limit the Zip Code field size to 10 characters.

   e. Save the table as Address Book. When you are asked if you want to set a primary key, click Yes. Access will create an ID field that will be numbered automatically for you.

3. Work in Datasheet View:

   a. Toggle to Datasheet View.

   b. Enter records for at least 10 people (remember that the ID column will be numbered automatically).

   c. Use the Column Width command to Best Fit the first six columns in the table.

   d. Use the Best Fit shortcut (double-clicking) to adjust the remaining columns.

   e. Move the ID column to the end of the table so that it comes after the Birthday field.

   f. Save the changes you have made. Click No if you are asked if you want to test the existing data.

4. Create a new database and import database objects:

   a. Create a new database in the My Access Files folder called Test3.

   b. Open the Import dialog box

   c. Import the Address Book table that you created in Test2 into Test3.

   d. Design a new table that contains two fields: ID and e-mail address. Set the ID field as the primary key and make its data type AutoNumber. This table should have the same number of records as the Address Book table and they should be in the same order. If some of the people whose records you entered in the Address Book table do not have e-mail addresses, leave the field blank in the new table. Name the table e-mail.

Access 2000

Interactivity (continued)

5. Design a query:

  a. Create a new query in Design View.

  b. Choose the Address Book table from the Show Table dialog box.

  c. Design the query to display only the ID, Last Name, First Name, and Birthday fields.

  d. Run the query.

  e. Sort the resultant datasheet in ascending order by the Birthday field.

  f. Save the query as Birthdays and close it.

6. Establish a relationship between tables and query related tables:

  a. Open the Relationships window.

  b. Join the Address Book and e-mail tables using the ID field.

  c. Enforce Referential Integrity and activate the Cascade Delete Related Records feature.

  d. After you create the relationship, close the Relationships window, saving the changes to its layout.

  e. Design a query that displays the following information for all records: ID, Last Name, First Name, Phone, and E-mail address.

  f. Run the query and sort the data alphabetically by last name.

  g. Save the query as ADDRESS BOOK and E-MAIL: rapid communication.

Problem Solving

1. It is time to start building the database on magazine preferences that Ruloff and DeWitt requires. Start with a Blank Database and call it **Solved 2**. Construct each of the three tables you planned earlier in **Design View**. After you finish creating each table, save it, and then switch to Datasheet View so you can enter the data you have compiled. Once you have entered the data for a table, look over the datasheet. Adjust column widths to reduce wasted space and reveal any obscured data. Decide whether the tables need to be restructured in any way, and revert to **Design View** if necessary. Remember that you can insert and delete fields at any time. Finally, save each table with a name that accurately describes the data that it contains.

2. The next part of the Magazine project will allow you to demonstrate some impressive Access skills. The Marketing and Research manager for Ruloff and DeWitt needs the following information combined: the ID number, age, gender, occupation, number of magazine titles read regularly, favorite magazine, and hobbies of each of the people you surveyed. This information must be organized by age, with a separate datasheet for each of the following age groups: 17 and under, 18 to 34, 35 to 49, 50 to 64, and 65 and over. If an age group is not represented in your data, do not create a query for it. Next create queries so that each age group category represented in your data is divided by gender. When you are done, you should have one datasheet that shows all of the fields mentioned above for females 17 and under, males 17 and under, females 18–34, and so on. Save each query with a descriptive name.

Interactivity (continued)

Problem Solving

3. Choose one of the databases listed in Problem Solving #2 on page AC 1.22 and create a database containing at least five fields and five records. Once you have created the database, run at least two queries using the data you have created.

L E S S O N

3

CREATING FORMS

While tables may serve as the backbone of a database, they do not always provide the best representation of the data they contain. It is often much easier to view and work with data on your computer when its interface is that of a form. All of the information in a form is contained in controls. Controls are objects used in a form to display data, perform actions, or make a form easier to use. Examples of controls in a form that we will use in this Lesson are labels and text boxes.

Access offers several methods of creating a form, each giving the user a different degree of guidance and control over design. AutoForm may be the quickest, easiest way to create a form, but the Form Wizard affords the greatest balance of both guidance and control.

No matter what method you use to produce a form, you can always alter it using Design View. Design View allows you to change the format of a form and add fields, graphics, and records.

CASE STUDY
Kyle will now improve the functionality of his database by using the Form Wizard to design a form that Stay Fast employees will use instead of a table to enter and edit data. He will then format and edit the form in Design View.

Creating an AutoForm

Concept

Sometimes going through the Form Wizard can be confusing and take up a lot of time. If you don't feel the need to personally select every detail of the format of your form, then you can let Access create a standardized form for you. Access will allow you to choose from three basic formats, and automatically create a standard form with fields in the order of the database you've been working in.

Do It!

Kyle will use AutoForm to create a form directly from the database he has been working in.

1 Start Access and open the Employees 3 database. Click the Forms button on the Objects bar to display the options for creating a new form.

2 Click the New button on the Database window toolbar. The New Form dialog box will open.

3 Click AutoForm: Columnar to highlight it.

4 Click the Choose the table or query... drop-down list arrow and select Employee Roster from the list, as shown in **Figure 3-1**. This tells the computer where to get the data that will be included in the form. Click   OK   . A standard columnar form is created with all of the fields in the order specified by the Employee Roster table (see **Figure 3-2**). Close the form and do not save your changes.

More

The form you just created was in a columnar format. AutoForm allows you to choose from three different formats: Columnar, Tabular, and Datasheet. The data in AutoForm will not change as long as the data are taken from the same place. The only thing that changes is the layout of the form.

Figure 3-1 New Form dialog box

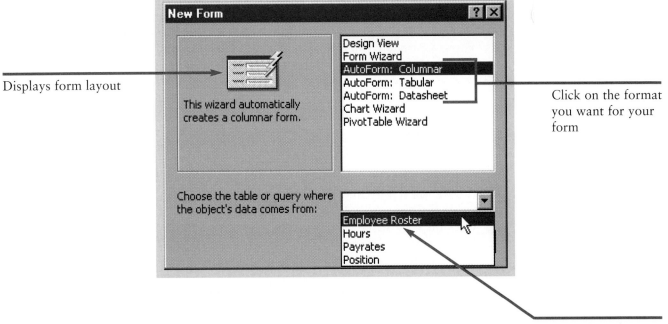

Displays form layout

Click on the format you want for your form

Drop-down list to choose what data to include in the form

Figure 3-2 Form created using AutoForm

Practice

Use AutoForm to create a tabular form that will display all fields from one of the tables in the Tuning Tracker database. Save the file under the name of the table you used.

Hot Tip

You may use only one database object to create a form using AutoForm. To create a more complex form, you must use the Form Wizard, or add the fields in Design View, two skills you will learn later in this Lesson.

Using the Form Wizard

Concept

AutoForm can limit the options you have when creating your form. If you want to change certain aspects of a form, or have more control over its creation use the Form Wizard to create your form.

Do It!

Kyle will use the Form Wizard to create a form that will make reading records in a table easier.

1. Click the Forms button on the Objects bar, then click New on the Database window toolbar. The New Form dialog box will open.

2. Click Form Wizard to highlight it.

3. Click the Choose the table or query... drop-down list arrow and select Employee Roster from the list that appears, then click [OK]. The New Form dialog box will be replaced by the Form Wizard dialog box.

4. Click the Add All Fields button [>>] to transfer all of the fields listed in the Available Fields box to the Selected Fields box. Since this will be a comprehensive form, all fields in the table should be included (see **Figure 3-3**).

5. Click [Next >] to go on to the next step of the Wizard.

6. Click the Justified radio button to select it. The preview will change to reflect the chosen layout.

7. Click [Next >] to advance to the Wizard's next step.

8. Click Stone to select it. The sample form in the preview window reflects the new style.

9. Click [Next >] to advance to the Wizard's final step.

10. Click [Finish] to accept the name Access has suggested for the form, Employee Roster, and to exit the Wizard. The form is created and saved, and appears in its own window, as shown in **Figure 3-4**.

More

The main advantage to using the Form Wizard is that you can choose fields from several tables. You don't have to choose a table or query on the drop-down list in the New Form dialog box. Instead you can choose one or more tables or queries as the record source for your form in step 5 of the Form Wizard, shown in **Figure 3-3**. You can choose the fields you want to include from as many different tables or queries as you want.

When choosing fields from several different record sources, be sure not to duplicate fields. For example, if you were creating a form for entering the hours worked each week by Stay Fast employees, you might choose fields from both the Payrates and Position tables, but you would only select the Employee # field once.

Figure 3-3 Form Wizard dialog box

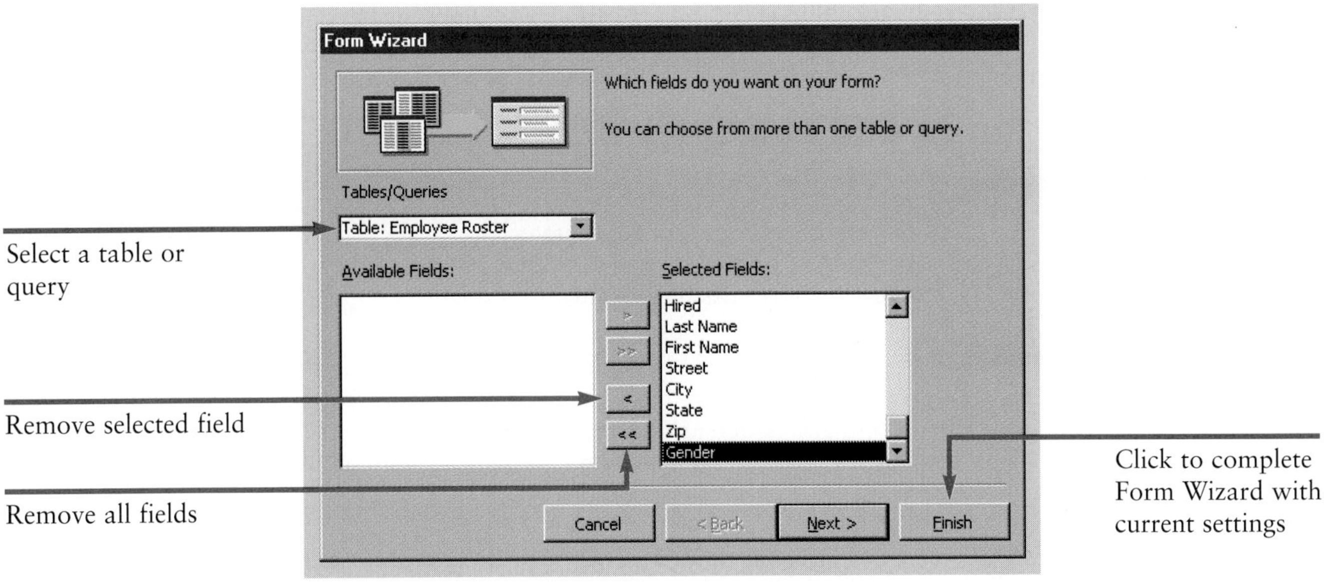

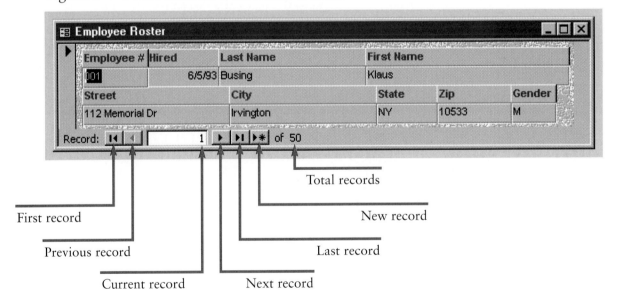

Select a table or query

Remove selected field

Remove all fields

Click to complete Form Wizard with current settings

Figure 3-4 Form created with Form Wizard

First record

Previous record

Current record

Next record

Last record

New record

Total records

Practice

Use the Form Wizard to create a columnar form that will display all fields from both tables in the Tuning Tracker database. Name the form **New Customer** and save it.

Hot Tip

You may include fields from several tables on a single form. That way, you can view all data pertaining to a single record at once, even if they are stored in more than one table. A form like this also lets you enter data into several tables at once.

AC 3.5

Formatting and Editing Form Elements

Concept

Once a form has been created, characteristics such as its field order, field size, and background style may be changed. These changes affect only the form itself, not the data that the form has been created to display.

Do It!

Kyle wants to customize the form he has created so that the Street field is large enough to accommodate its contents, then he will adjust the formatting so that the employee's last name will stand out. Finally, he will modify the background color of the form.

1. Click the View button 📑 on the Form Design toolbar to open the form in Design View. If the Toolbox toolbar appears, close it.

2. Drag the lower-right corner of the Form window downward and to the right until the entire form can be seen. As you can see in **Figure 3-5**, there are two boxes for each field. The upper box contains the label control, and will appear on the form as displayed. The lower box is a text box control, where the field's data will be entered and displayed.

3. Click the Street text box. It now appears with sizing handles. Move the pointer over the box until it turns into a hand. Click and hold the mouse and drag the Street box until the black band on the ruler at the top reaches 6⅞. The Street field and text box now appear to the right of the Gender field and text box.

4. While holding **Shift**, click the City, State, Zip, Gender, and Street field boxes. They all now appear with sizing handles. Move the pointer over the boxes until it turns into a hand. Click and hold the mouse button and drag the boxes to the left until the black marker on the ruler reaches the leftmost mark on the ruler, ⅛. Your form should match the one shown in **Figure 3-6**.

5. Click in the gray area of the Design View to clear the selections you have made.

6. Click the Street text box again.

7. Click the midpoint sizing handle on the right edge of the selected text box and drag it to the right until the black mark on the horizontal ruler reaches the 6-inch mark.

8. Click the Last Name text box to select it.

9. Click the Font/Fore Color drop-down list arrow 🅰 on the Formatting (Form/Report) toolbar, then click the blue square in the second row of the palette that appears. The placeholder text in the text box that reads "Last Name" will turn blue. Now all records on this form will display the employee's last name in blue so it will stand out from the rest of the fields.

Figure 3-5 Form in Design View

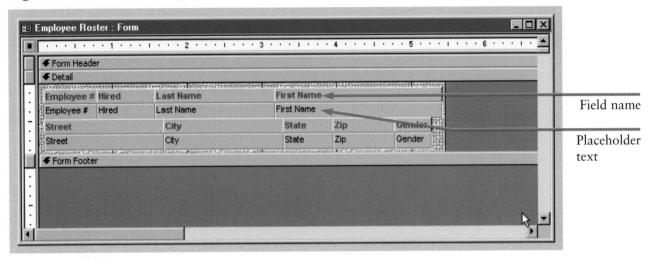

Field name

Placeholder
text

Figure 3-6 A form in progress in Design View

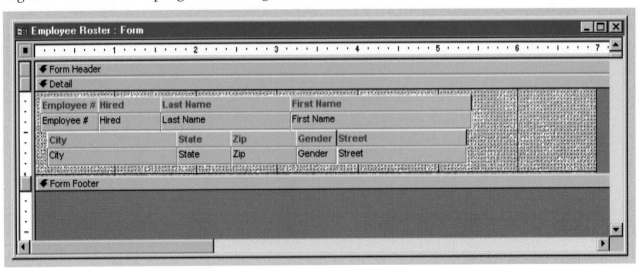

Formatting and Editing Form Elements (continued)

Do It!

10 Right-click the empty area of the record at the lower right, select Fill/Back Color from the pop-up menu that appears, and then click the pale blue square in the fourth row of the color palette. The form's background color will change to match the selected square, but you will not see the change until you return to Form View.

11 Click the View button [⊞▾] to return to Form view. Your form should look like **Figure 3-7**.

More

Once selected, every item on a form may be formatted to further enhance its appearance. The Formatting toolbar, shown in **Figure 3-8**, provides control over many aspects of your form's appearance. The Object drop-down list box at the left end of the Formatting toolbar lists every item on the form; clicking a name on the list selects the corresponding item in the window. The Font and Font Size boxes, immediately to the right of the Object box, let you adjust the typeface of selected text and the size at which it will be displayed. The Bold, Italic, and Underline buttons modify the style of selected text. The three alignment buttons, Align Left, Center, and Align Right, control the placement of text within its text box. The Formatting toolbar also contains three buttons that control the color of various form elements such as the fill or background, the text or foreground, and the lines and borders. The last two buttons on the Formatting toolbar, the Line/Border Width and Special Effects buttons, control the appearance of the lines that define a text or label box.

Figure 3-7 Formatted and edited form in Form View

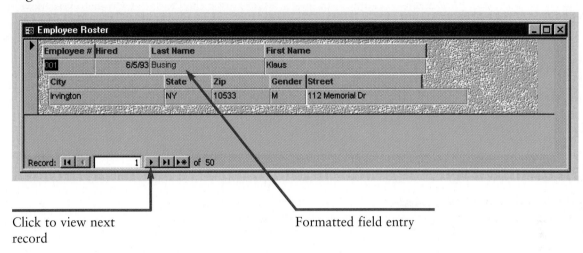

Click to view next
record

Formatted field entry

Line/Border Color

Line/Border
Width

Font/Fore Color

Figure 3-8 Formatting toolbar

Alignment buttons

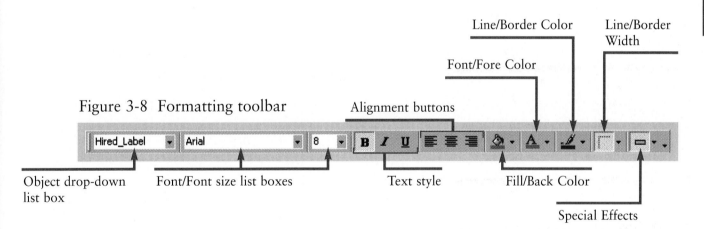

Object drop-down
list box

Font/Font size list boxes

Text style

Fill/Back Color

Special Effects

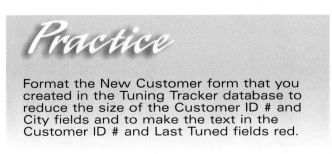

Practice

Format the New Customer form that you
created in the Tuning Tracker database to
reduce the size of the Customer ID # and
City fields and to make the text in the
Customer ID # and Last Tuned fields red.

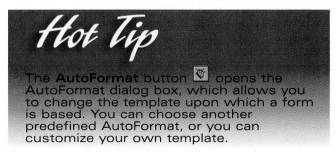

Hot Tip

The **AutoFormat** button opens the
AutoFormat dialog box, which allows you
to change the template upon which a form
is based. You can choose another
predefined AutoFormat, or you can
customize your own template.

AC 3.9

Setting Tab Order

Concept

When you enter data into a table, hitting the [Tab] key can help you move through your form more quickly and with greater accuracy than other methods. You may set the order in which the [Tab] key will bring you to the fields in your database.

Do It!

Kyle is going to set the Tab order in his form so that the Street field will appear last, as it appears in the form he just created. He also has decided to place the First Name field first in the Tab order.

1 With the Employee Roster form open in Design View, click View on the menu bar.

2 Click Tab Order. The Tab Order dialog box will open.

3 Click the Street row selector button as seen in **Figure 3-9**.

4 Holding down the mouse button, drag the Street field to the bottom of the Custom Order list, so it is the last field listed. Now when entering information, clicking [Tab] will bring you to the Street field last, as you have selected.

5 Click the First Name row selector button.

6 Holding the mouse button, click and drag the First Name field to the top of the list, so it appears first.

7 Click OK.

8 Click the View button ▦ .

9 Press the [Tab] key. The order by which Tab shows you the different fields should have changed so that the Street field is last and the First Name field is first.

More

Just changing the order of a field in a form will not change the Tab order. The Tab order can be changed to whatever order you find helpful. For example, if you find that one field is changing more than any other, you can change the Tab order so that field appears first, but stays where it is with respect to its location on the form.

Figure 3-9 Tab Order dialog box

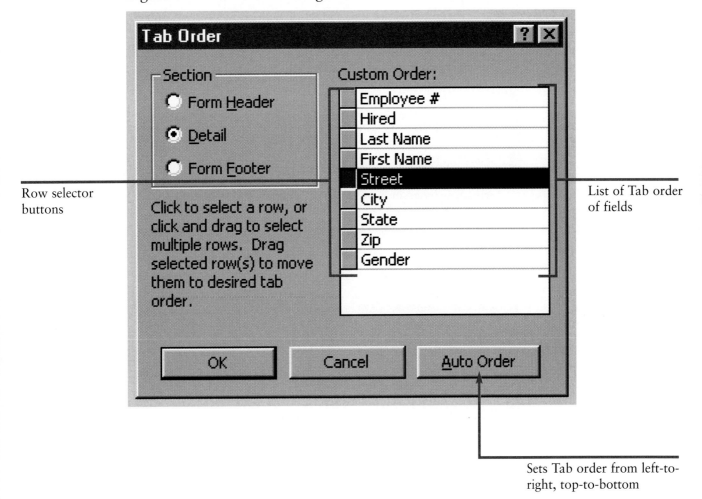

Row selector
buttons

List of Tab order
of fields

Sets Tab order from left-to-
right, top-to-bottom

Access 2000

AC 3.11

Modifying Controls with Expressions

Concept

Sometimes it is useful to modify the type of data that appears in a form. One way to do this is using an *Expression Builder*. The Expression Builder allows you to change the way data appear in a field, and what kind of data appears in a field. The data may be used to process information more efficiently.

Do It!

Kyle wants to change his form so that instead of showing the date an employee was hired, it will note the current date.

1 Open the Employee Roster form in Design View.

2 Click the Hired text box.

3 Click the Properties button [icon] on the Form Design toolbar. The property sheet for the Hired text box appears. Click the Data tab to bring the Data screen to the front, as shown in **Figure 3-10**.

4 Click the Build button [...]. The Expression Builder dialog box opens (see **Figure 3-11**).

5 Delete Hired from the Expressions text box.

6 Click the Common Expressions folder in the list on the left of the dialog box.

7 Click Current Date from the list in the middle of the dialog box.

8 Double-click Date from the list on the far right of the dialog box.

9 Click the OK button.

10 Click the Close button [X] on the Text Box: Hired dialog box.

11 Click the View button [icon]. Your screen should look like **Figure 3-12**. The Hired text box should no longer list the date hired, but instead list today's date.

More

You also may construct expressions that are mathematical in nature. Right underneath the text box in the Expression Builder dialog box there are buttons representing mathematical equations. You may use these buttons to construct a mathematical expression that will be formulated in the form you place it in.

If you construct an improper equation, the information will not show up in the form. Make sure you have selected the correct information and the correct equation before you apply it to your form.

Figure 3-10 Form dialog box

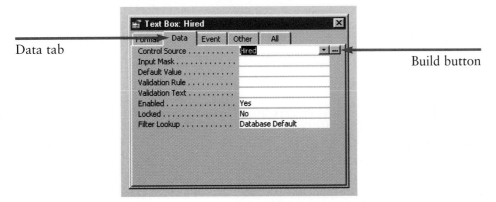

Data tab

Build button

Figure 3-11 Expression Builder dialog box

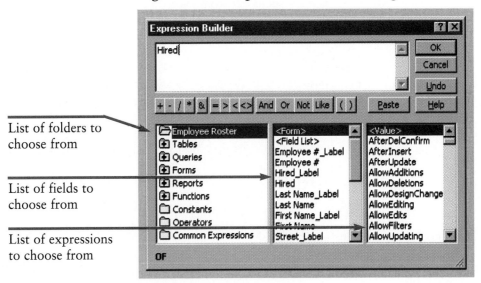

List of folders to choose from

List of fields to choose from

List of expressions to choose from

Figure 3-12 Form in Form View with expression

Expression in a form

Practice

Add an expression to the Last Tuned field in the **New Customer** form that you have saved. Make the **Last Tuned** date change to the current date when you view it in the form. Do not save this change.

Hot Tip

Similar to the phrases you can use when you run a query, some expressions may contain the phrases **And, Or, Like**, and **Not**. The buttons for these phrases are located next to the mathematical buttons in the Expression Builder dialog box.

Formatting Form Controls

Concept

You can use the same Properties options you used during the last skill to change the way data appear in a field rather than changing the actual data that appear. Instead of changing dates and numbers, you can change fonts and other formatting areas.

Do It!

Kyle has decided he wants the First Name field to stand out from the rest of the fields. He is going to change the font and change other parts of its appearance to make it stand out from everything else.

1 Open the Employee Roster form in Design View.

2 Click the First Name text box, and then click the Properties button 📇. Click the Format tab on the property sheet for the First Name text box. Your screen should be similar to **Figure 3-13**.

3 Click the down scroll arrow until you come to the Font Name text box. Click the pointer inside the text box. Click the drop-down arrow that appears.

4 Click Courier from the drop-down list that appears.

5 Scroll down again until you reach the Font Weight text box. Click the drop-down list arrow that appears when you click the text box. Choose **Heavy** from the drop-down list.

6 Click the Close button ☒ on the Text Box: First Name dialog box.

7 Click the View button 📧▾. Your final product should look like **Figure 3-14**.

More

Formatting your form in this manner is most useful when you must change minute details, like spacing in between letters and such. When very small changes need to be made, this is the better way to do them. You can still always change the font and bold text using the Formatting (Form/Report) toolbar at any time in Design View.

If you try to close the form without saving the formatting changes, you will be prompted to save the changes to the design of the form.

Figure 3-13 Format tab of Text Box: First Name dialog box

Format tab

Drop-down list arrow

Figure 3-14 Newly formatted form

Newly formatted field entry

Access 2000

Practice

Change the **Font** of the **Customer ID #** field in your **New Customer** form, using the method you just learned. Save the data when you are finished.

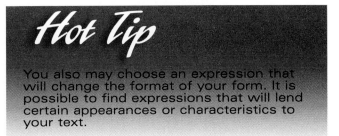

Hot Tip

You also may choose an expression that will change the format of your form. It is possible to find expressions that will lend certain appearances or characteristics to your text.

Adding a Field

Concept

Sometimes you may find it necessary to add a field after you have already created a form.

Do It!

Kyle has decided that he wants to put back the field that lists the date employees were hired. He is going to modify his report so his form will contain the current date and the date hired.

1 Open the form **Employee Roster** in Design View.

2 Click the Field List button 🔲 on the Form Design toolbar. A list of all of the fields in the form will be shown as in **Figure 3-15**.

3 Click and drag Hired from the list box to the form. When you drag this field, the pointer will turn into ⬛. Drag it to the right of the First Name label. A text box for the Hired field will appear, as well as a label that says Text 18.

4 Click once on the Text 18 label to select it, then double-click it to select the text. Type Hired. Now click the original Hired label to select it, then double-click it to select the text. Type Date.

5 Click the First Name label to bring up the resizing handles. Click the midpoint resizing handle and drag it to the left until it reaches the edge of the Hired label.

6 Click the Hired text box to bring up resizing handles. Click the left resizing handle and drag it to the left until it reaches the edge of the Hired label. Click and drag the right sizing handle and move it to the left until the black band on the horizontal ruler reaches 5½.

7 Click the View button 🔲. Your form should look like **Figure 3-16**.

More

All of the fields from the database the form was created from are available to add at any time. For example, if we had chosen not to include gender in our form, we could have added it later. It would have been available on the same field list we saw earlier.

Figure 3-15 Field list box

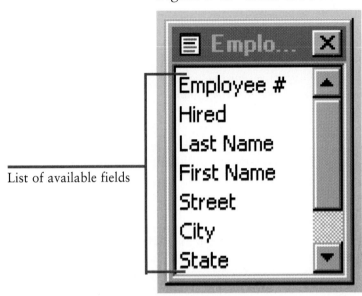

List of available fields

Figure 3-16 Form with new field

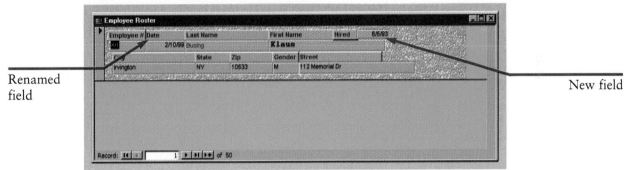

Renamed field

New field

Access 2000

Practice

From your Student files folder open the database **Prac 3-6**. Open the form that is also named **Prac 3-6** and add a field called **Odds**.

Hot Tip

The new field automatically becomes the last field in the **Tab** order, so you may find it necessary to change the **Tab** order whenever you add a new field.

Adding Graphics to a Form

Concept

Adding graphics to your form can improve its appearance. Graphics not only make forms look more attractive, but they also may help them look more professional. Graphics can make a form look less bland.

Do It!

Kyle is going to add the logo for Stay Fast Inc. to the form he created. Kyle already has the logo saved on his computer; all he has to do is open and format it to fit the form he has created.

1. Open the form **Employee Roster** in Design View.

2. Click the **Toolbox** button 🛠 on the Form Design toolbar. The Toolbox is shown in **Figure 3-17**.

3. Click the **Image** button 🖼. The pointer turns into ⁺🖼. Move the pointer underneath the bottom line of the form, underneath the City field. Click when you have the image where you want it. The **Insert Picture** dialog box (seen in **Figure 3-18**) opens.

4. Locate your **Student Files Folder** and select the image named **Stay Fast**. Click OK.

5. The image should be in place. You may use the pointer to click and drag the image if it is not where you want it to be. Your form should look like **Figure 3-19**.

6. Click the View button 🖼▾.

More

The safest way to save an image file you wish to insert into a form is as a bitmap. Other types of image files may be inserted into forms, but some, like JPEG, TIF, and others, require you to have a graphic filter installed to insert them.

If you have multiple images to insert, you can do it without clicking the same toolbox button over and over. If you double-click a button on the toolbox table, it locks it down.

Use the crosshair part of the image pointer to line up your image. Position the vertical and horizontal lines of the crosshair to line up where you want the vertical and horizontal edges of the image to begin.

Figure 3-17 Toolbox table

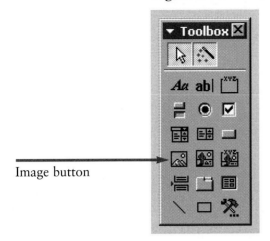

Image button

Figure 3-18 Insert Picture dialog box

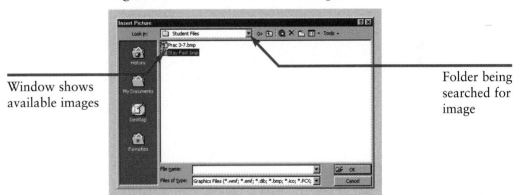

Window shows
available images

Folder being
searched for
image

Figure 3-19 Form with company logo

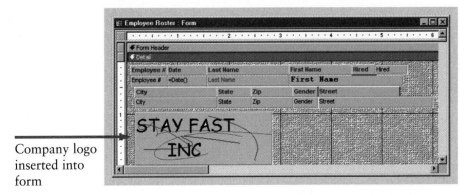

Company logo
inserted into
form

Practice

Insert the **Prac 3-7** image located in your Student Files folder into the **New Customer** form in the **Tuning Tracker** database.

Hot Tip

If you click on the image at any time, you may resize it with the resizing handles that appear. You also may move the image to any location on the form once you have inserted it.

Adding a Record to a Form

Concept

Sometimes it is necessary to update a database while you are working on a form. Access allows you to add a record to a table and database while you are working on a form.

Do It!

Stay Fast has hired someone new, and Kyle must update his form. He will do this by creating a new record in Form mode, which will also carry over to all other database modes as well.

1. Open the Employee Roster form in Form View.

2. Click the New Record button ⏭. This brings to view a blank form record. You may begin typing in the new information beginning with the new employee's first name, which is James. This is the first field in the new Tab order.

3. Then type the Employee #, which is 051. The current date is already filled in. For Last Name type Trunk. Type the name Croton for City.

4. Type in 10520, M, then 45 Wolf Rd. and 2/9/99, respectively, pressing [Tab] after each one. After all of the information has been added, your new record should look like Figure 3-20.

5. Close the form.

More

When you must create a new record, remember the way your Tab order was saved. Data will be entered in the order you set the Tab order, even if you press Enter or the arrow keys.

The new record is immediately added to the table on which the form is based. If you were to open the table on which this form was based, this new record would be added to the table.

Figure 3-20 New record in form

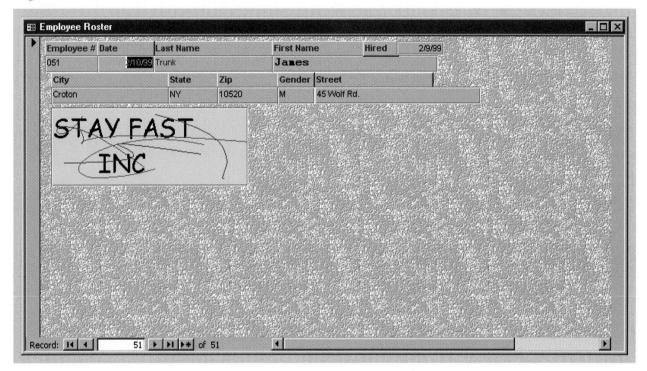

Access 2000

Practice

Open **Prac 3-6**. Add a new record for a horse named **Smokey**; the jockey, **Tom Dorn**; the trainer, **Joe Crash**; **17 wins**; **$515,089** earned; and **7:1** odds. Add this new record to that form and save it.

Hot Tip

Validation rules are still valid even if you are adding records in the form mode. Even in this mode, field entries will be matched against field property specifications.

Shortcuts

Function	Button/Mouse	Menu	Keyboard
AutoForm		Click Insert, then click AutoForm (from Database window)	
Form View		Click View, then click Form View.	
Show Toolbox/Hide Toolbox		Click View, then click Toolbox	
AutoFormat		Click Format, then click AutoFormat	
Show Field List/Hide Field List		Click View, then click Field List	
New Record		Click Insert, then click New Record	
Properties		Click View, then click Properties	

Identify Key Features

Name the items identified by callouts in **Figure 3-21**.

Figure 3-21 Features of form in Design View

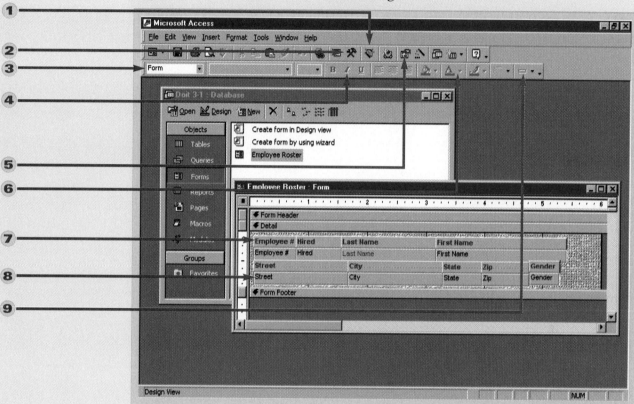

Select the Best Answer

10. Database object that commonly displays one record at a time for easy viewing and editing

11. Contains the text options Bold, Italic, and Underline

12. Creates a standardized database object with formats selected for you

13. Changes the actual data that appear in a field

14. Objects used in a form to display data, perform actions, or make a form easier to use

15. Changes the way data appear in a form

16. A set of dialog boxes that create a form specifically designed for you

17. Controls the order in which data can be entered into a form

a. AutoForm

b. Format

c. Tab Order

d. Expression Builder

e. Form Wizard

f. Control

g. Formatting toolbar

h. Form

Quiz (continued)

Complete the Statement

18. To create a form quickly with almost no input on its design use:

    a. The Form Wizard

    b. Design View

    c. QuickForm

    d. AutoForm

19. To view the name of every item on a form in Design View, use the:

    a. Object drop-down list

    b. View menu

    c. Field list

    d. Help menu

20. When you use the Form Wizard, you can choose fields from:

    a. A single table only

    b. A single query only

    c. Tables only

    d. A combination of tables and queries

21. All of the following are layout possibilities for a form created with the Form Wizard except:

    a. Datasheet

    b. Tabular

    c. Standard

    d. Justified

22. If you want to add a record to a form after the form has already been created, you may:

    a. Go back to the Database table to add the record

    b. Create a new form that includes the new record

    c. Click the New Record button

    d. Click the Record Selector button

23. To add an image to a form, you must first open:

    a. The Toolbox toolbar

    b. The View menu

    c. The Insert menu

    d. The Tools menu

24. All of the following are advantages to setting your own Tab order except:

    a. Controlling the way data are entered in a field

    b. Controlling the way data are edited in a field

    c. Quickly changing the format of certain fields

    d. Choosing to look at the most important fields first

25. Expressions are useful for:

    a. Changing the format of certain fields

    b. Modifying the data in certain fields

    c. Changing the actual fields that appear in a form

    d. Editing new records

26. The difference between AutoForm and the Form Wizard is:

    a. AutoForm allows you more control over the appearance of a form

    b. Form Wizard allows you more control over the appearance of a form

    c. AutoForm lets you make all of the decisions that affect a form

    d. Form Wizard makes all of the decisions concerning a form for you

Interactivity

Test Your Skills

1. Create a new form using the Form Wizard:

   a. Open the database you created in the previous lesson (**Test 3**).

   b. Activate the Form Wizard.

   c. In the first step of the Wizard, add all of the fields from the Address Book table and the e-mail address field from the e-mail address table.

   d. When you arrive at the last step of the Wizard, choose to open the form for viewing.

2. Format and edit a form in Design View:

   a. From Form View, toggle to Design View.

   b. Apply the AutoFormat **Stone** to the form.

   c. Manipulate the fields so that **e-mail** comes directly after **Phone**.

   d. Make sure all of the field boxes are the right size, and enlarge them if necessary so that all of the information can fit into the form.

   e. Save the form.

3. Modify the form:

   a. Use the property sheets to manipulate the size and spacing of fields in the form.

   b. Change the look of data that appear in each field by using the property sheets.

   c. Change the properties for the e-mail field so that it only appears when you print the form.

   d. Change the format of another field by manipulating the **Back Style** property.

4. Using the Expression Builder, change the data that appear in a field:

   a. Pick a field in which to change the data, and go to the Expression Builder dialog box.

   b. Choose a way to change the data. Change it to the current date, or current time, or another expression you would like to try to build.

   c. Change the Tab order of the form, to make the field you just modified with an expression the first in the Tab order.

   d. Do not save the form, and close it.

Access 2000

Interactivity (continued)

Problem Solving

1. You have done a commendable job creating a database for Ruloff and DeWitt's Marketing and Research Department. As is often the case, many people will need to access the data you have compiled. It is important, therefore, that the database has a user friendly interface, so that all members of the department are comfortable using it. Use the **Form Wizard** and Design View to create a form that will provide your colleagues with an effective way of working with your database's primary table.

2. Establish relationships between the tables and **Enforce Referential Integrity**. Program the database to automatically delete related records when a record is deleted. Create a form in the Solved2 database to facilitate data entry in all three tables so that data can be entered into the tables simultaneously. Use the Form Wizard and choose the columnar layout. Apply the **Sumi Painting** background. Name the form **Magazine Preferences**.

3. Decrease the sizes of the ID #, Age, and # of Magazines Read Regularly text boxes. Increase the size of the # of Magazines Read Regularly label so that the entire caption displays. Change the font in the Favorite Magazine text box to **Calisto MT**. Change the font color in the ID # text box to **dark blue**. Change the font weight for the Last Name text box to **semi-bold**. Save the structural changes to the form.

4. Move the # of Magazines Read Regularly field so that it is the last field on the form and adjust the **Tab order** accordingly. Move the displaced controls upward in the form and space the controls evenly. Since data entry personnel will not have to enter or edit data in the ID # field, set the **Tab Stop** property for the ID # text box to **No**. Save the changes. Use the form to add five more records to the tables.

5. Move the **Form Footer** bar downward to increase the size of the Details section of the form. Open the Toolbox. Draw an Image control in the first square of the design grid on the form underneath the Magazines Read Regularly label. Use the Look in: list box in the Insert Picture dialog box to locate your Student Files folder. Select the **Magazines** bitmap file and click the OK button. If you drew the control just within the first 1-inch square, the image will not fit in the Image control. Double-click the Image control to open the property sheet. On the Format tab, select the **Size Mode** property. Click the list arrow and select Zoom on the drop-down list. Close the property sheet. The image is fit into the Image control frame. Adjust the size of the frame. Move the Form Footer bar back up if necessary. Save the changes and switch to Form View. Close the form.

L E S S O N

4

CREATING REPORTS

Frequently, it is necessary to produce paper copies of the data contained in a table or query. For this purpose, Access includes the ability to create a report, the database object most suited for printing. As with forms, all of the information in a report is contained in controls, such as labels and text boxes. Also like forms, reports can be created with varying amounts of input from the user. No matter what method you use to produce a form or report, you can always alter it using Design View. Access also allows you to continue to sort records and data while you are working on the database in report mode.

It is important to make sure your report will look good when it is actually printed, because what you see on your monitor is not always what you will see on the printed page. You will learn how to preview a report before you print it.

CASE STUDY

Kyle will now improve the functionality of his database by using the Report Wizard to create a company directory for Stay Fast. He will format and edit the report. When he finishes formatting the report, he will utilize the Print Preview and Page Setup features to perfect the way the report will appear on paper. Finally, Kyle will print a copy of the report.

Creating an AutoReport

Concept

If you want to create a standard report, without having to decide every attribute of it, you may create a report using AutoReport. AutoReport creates a standard report with its own specifications with the layout you want. It is the quickest way to create a report.

Do It!

Kyle is going to create an AutoReport for his Employee Roster database.

1 Start Access and open the Employees 3 database. Click the Reports button on the Objects bar.

2 Click New on the Database window toolbar. The New Report dialog box appears.

3 Click AutoReport: Tabular.

4 From the drop-down list at the bottom of the dialog box choose Employee Roster, as in **Figure 4-1**.

5 Click OK. The dialog box closes and Access creates your standardized report and opens it in Print Preview mode, which you will learn about later in the Lesson, which is shown in **Figure 4-2**.

6 Close the report without saving it.

More

AutoReport is an excellent and quick way to create a clean, neat report. If you want a report that looks more stylish, or perhaps more professional, you may want to put the time in to create a report using the Report Wizard.

The major limitation of an AutoReport is that you may only use one database object to create the report. When you create a report using a Wizard, you may choose what fields from what databases you want to have included, but when you create an AutoReport, you may choose only one database, and the report contains every field from that database.

Figure 4-1 New Report dialog box

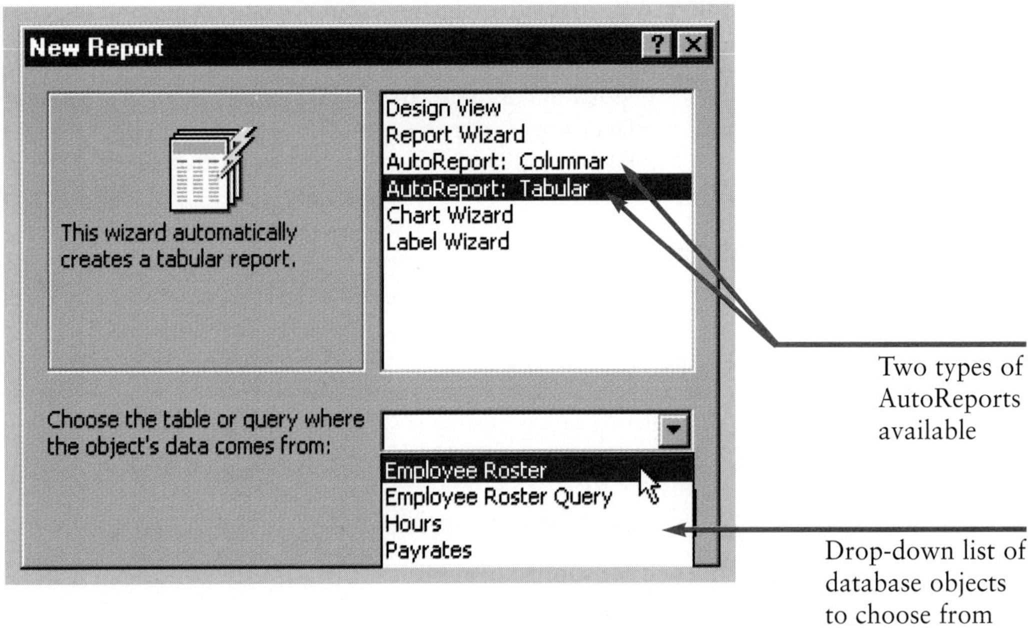

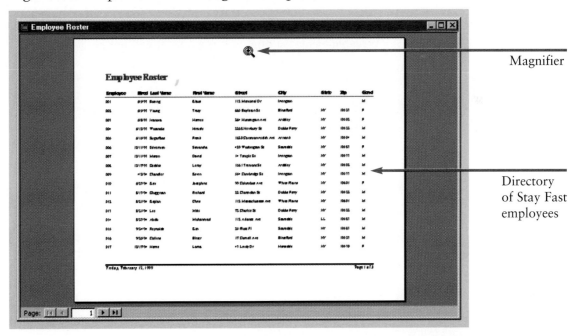

Two types of AutoReports available

Drop-down list of database objects to choose from

Figure 4-2 Report created using AutoReport

Magnifier

Directory of Stay Fast employees

Practice

Open another Access application window and the Tuning Tracker database. Use one of the tables from the Tuning Tracker database to create a columnar AutoReport. Do not save it.

Hot Tip

AutoReport is unique because when you click to create an AutoReport no dialog boxes appear, but this means your choices about your report are limited to the standard columnar or tabular report.

Using the Report Wizard

Concept

Reports are designed to effectively present your data in a printed format. Access offers control over the appearance of every item in a report to allow for design flexibility. The Report Wizard guides you through the steps necessary to create an effective report.

Do It!

Kyle will use the Report Wizard to create a company directory listing the names, addresses, and positions of all Stay Fast employees.

1 Click the **Reports** button on the Objects bar, then click [New]. The New Report dialog box appears, as shown in **Figure 4-3**.

2 Click **Report Wizard**, then click [OK]. The first step of the Report Wizard appears with the Employee Roster table's fields listed in the Available Fields list box.

3 Click the **Add All Fields** button [>>] to send all the available fields to the Selected Fields list box.

4 Scroll to the top of the **Selected Fields** list box and click Employee # to select it.

5 Click the **Remove Field** button [<] to move the Employee # field back to the Available Fields list box, ensuring that it will not be displayed on the report.

6 Repeat the previous step to remove the Hired and Gender fields from the report.

7 To add fields from another table, click the Tables/Queries drop-down list box arrow, then select Table: Position from the drop-down list that appears. The Available Fields list box now contains the names of the fields contained in the Position table.

8 Select the **Department** field in the Available Fields list box, then click the Add Field button [>] to add the Department field to the report.

9 Repeat the previous step to add the Title field to the report. Your Selected Fields list should match the one in **Figure 4-4**. Click [Next >]. The next step of the Wizard appears asking whether you wish to apply any grouping levels.

10 Click [Next >], since you will not be adding grouping levels. The next step of the Wizard asks you to determine a sort order for fields in your report.

11 Click the first drop-down list arrow and select Last Name from the list that appears. The selected field will be displayed in the box, defining it as the primary sorting criterion. The second drop-down list will become active, allowing you to choose a secondary sorting criterion if you wish.

12 Click the second drop-down list arrow and select First Name from the field list. Records in the report will now be sorted by last name and then first name, so that if several employees share the same last name, their records will appear in the correct order. Your sorting criteria should match those in **Figure 4-5**.

Figure 4-3 New Report dialog box

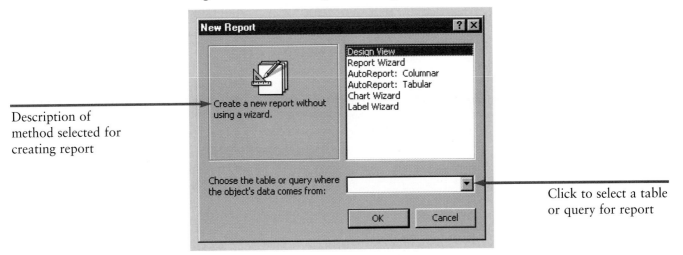

Description of
method selected for
creating report

Click to select a table
or query for report

Figure 4-4 Selected fields list

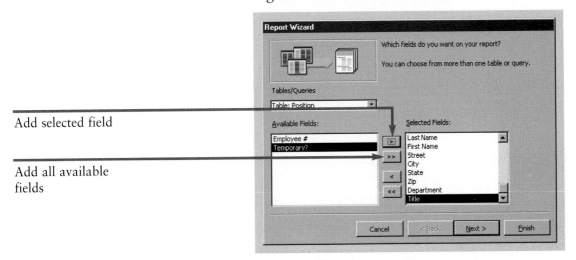

Add selected field

Add all available
fields

Figure 4-5 Choosing a sort order

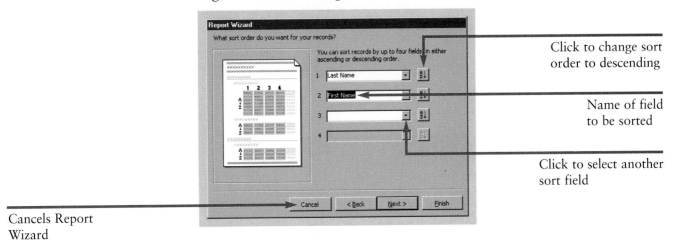

Click to change sort
order to descending

Name of field
to be sorted

Click to select another
sort field

Cancels Report
Wizard

Using the Report Wizard (continued)

Do It!

13 Click [Next >] to advance to the next step of the Wizard. This step allows you to adjust the layout of your report.

14 Click the Landscape radio button in the Orientation section. The page icon beneath the two radio buttons will change so that its width is greater than its height, indicating the way in which the report will appear on the page (see **Figure 4-6**).

15 Click [Next >]. This step of the Wizard sets the style of your report.

16 Click Bold to select the Bold style. The preview to the left of the list shows how report items will be formatted under the selected style.

17 Click [Next >] to advance to the final step of the Wizard.

18 Type Stay Fast Directory to replace the default report title, then click [Finish]. The report is saved and the Wizard closes, replaced by a window displaying the finished report in Print Preview mode, which you will learn more about later in the Lesson.

19 Click the Zoom drop-down list arrow [100% ▾] and select 75% from the list. The report is displayed at a smaller size, allowing its full width to fit within the bounds of the window, as seen in **Figure 4-7**.

More

The Report Wizard may be used to include multiple tables in a report. The same way you can when you are designing a query or a form, you may select several different tables and fields to include in your report.

The Report Wizard gives you the most options for creating a report. Its primary advantage is that you get to make all of the choices that will affect the creation of your report.

Figure 4-6 Choosing Landscape orientation

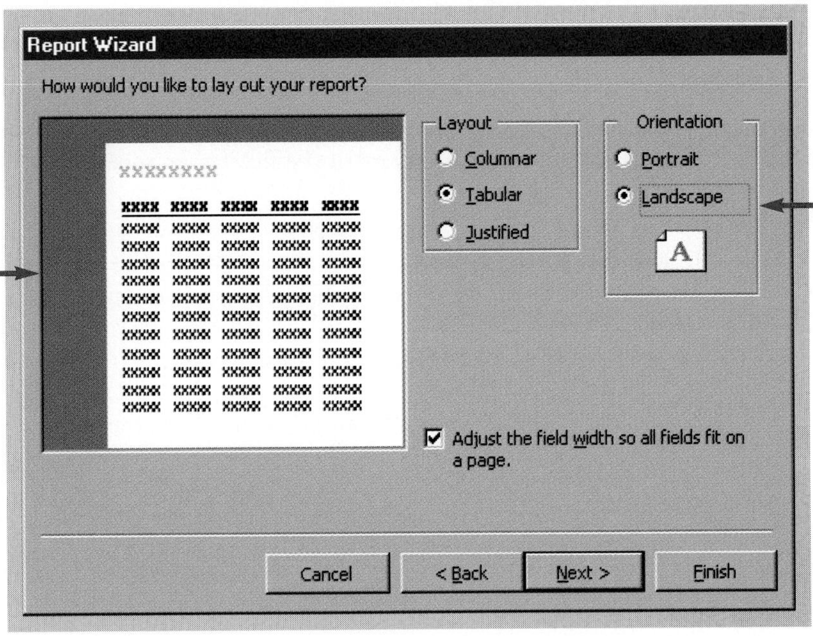

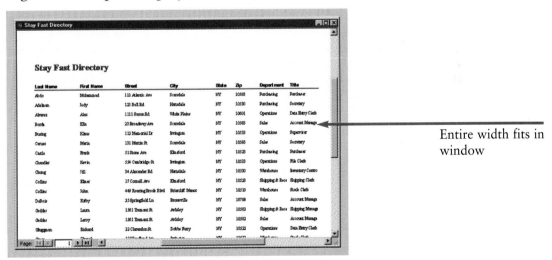

Displays preview of the selected report layout

Choose page orientation

Figure 4-7 Report displayed at 75%

Entire width fits in window

Practice

Use the Report Wizard to create a columnar report based upon the Tuning Tracker database that displays the Customer ID #, First and Last Name, Piano Make and Model, and Last Tuned fields. Name it **Customer Service Report**.

Hot Tip

You may base the report on a query instead of a table. Simply choose a query in the **Tables/Queries** drop-down list in the Report Wizard dialog box.

Sorting Records in a Report

Concept

Placing records in a particular order can prove helpful when creating a report. You may sort a report using any of the fields that appear in it.

Do It!

Kyle has been asked to sort the Stay Fast Directory by job title. He will work on the report in Design View to change the sort order.

1 Open the Stay Fast Directory in Design View.

2 Click the Sorting and Grouping button 📧 on the Report Design toolbar. The Sorting and Grouping dialog box appears.

3 Click the drop-down list arrow in the Last Name text box. Click Title from the drop-down list that appears, as shown in **Figure 4-8**. Title will replace Last Name as the first field by which the report is sorted. First Name will remain the second sorting field.

4 Close the Sorting and Grouping dialog box and return to the Print Preview view of the report. Click the right scroll arrow until the Title field is in view. Your report should look like **Figure 4-9**.

More

Changing the fields that are used to sort the records does not change the order in which the fields are displayed. Notice that although the report is sorted in ascending order of the Title of each employee, the field Title still appears as the last field, as it did before, because it was the last field chosen when you were adding fields to the report earlier.

You also may use the Sorting and Grouping dialog box to change the way the field is sorted from ascending to descending. Ascending will sort a field from A to Z or beginning with the lowest number, while descending will sort a field from Z to A or beginning with the highest number and ending with the lowest.

Figure 4-8 Sorting and Grouping dialog box

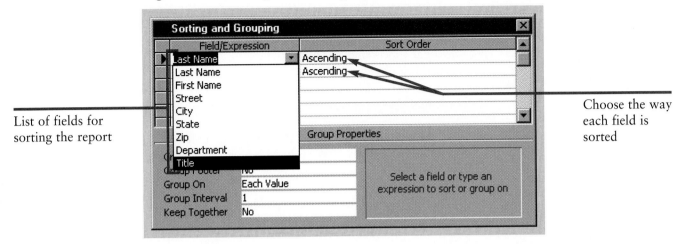

List of fields for sorting the report

Choose the way each field is sorted

Figure 4-9 Stay Fast Directory in Print Preview

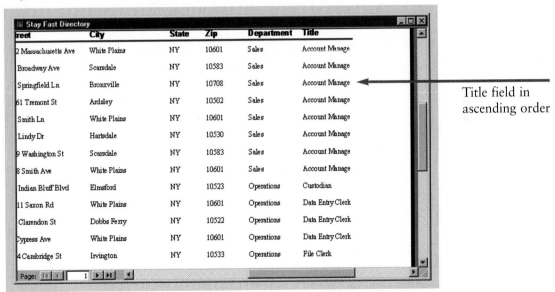

Title field in ascending order

Access 2000

Change the sort order of your **Customer Service Report** so it is sorted by the **Piano Make.**

Hot Tip

When you are prompted in the **Report Wizard** to choose a sort order, you can choose any field in the Wizard, and change that choice at any time by using the **Sorting and Grouping** dialog box.

Formatting Report Elements

Concept

Like a form, all of a report's parts may be modified to alter their appearance. In Design View, you are given complete control over the formatting factors that influence the final appearance of your report.

Do It!

Kyle will alter several aspects of his report's formatting to improve its appearance.

1 Click the View button ![icon] on the Print Preview toolbar to go to Design View and maximize the window by clicking its Maximize button ![icon] if it is not already filling the application window.

2 Click Edit, then click Select All. Every object of the report will be selected and will appear with sizing and move handles.

3 Click the Special Effects drop-down list arrow ![icon], then click the Special Effect: Etched button ![icon] from the palette that appears. The chosen effect is applied to the borders of the text boxes and will be visible in Print Preview.

4 Click the right scroll button ![icon] on the horizontal scroll bar twice to reveal the right edge of the report in the window.

5 Click in the dark gray area of the window to deselect the selected items.

6 Click the following six controls while pressing [Shift]: Zip label, Zip text box, Department label, Department text box, Title label, and Title text box. They will appear selected, as shown in **Figure 4-10**.

7 Move the mouse pointer over the selected cells until it changes to an open hand ![icon], then click and drag the selected controls to the right until the right corner of the black band in the horizontal ruler reaches the 9⅛-inch mark, which is the first mark to the right of the 9. The edge of the report expands to the right to accommodate the repositioned items. Moving these will allow you to expand the State label and text box controls so that the entire word will be visible.

8 Click the State label, then press [Shift] while clicking the State text box to select both controls.

9 Drag the midpoint sizing handle at the right edge of either control to the right until the black band in the horizontal ruler reaches the 6⅜-inch mark. The entire label can now be seen.

10 Click the Object drop-down list arrow on the Formatting toolbar, then click Label16 to select the report title, Stay Fast Directory, which appears in the header.

11 Click the midpoint sizing handle on the right edge of the selected control (which is all that currently can be seen in the window) and move it to the right until it is even with the edge of the report.

12 Click the Center button ![icon] to center the title within its box, then click the Underline button ![icon] to format it with an underline, as shown in **Figure 4-11**.

Figure 4-10 Selected report elements

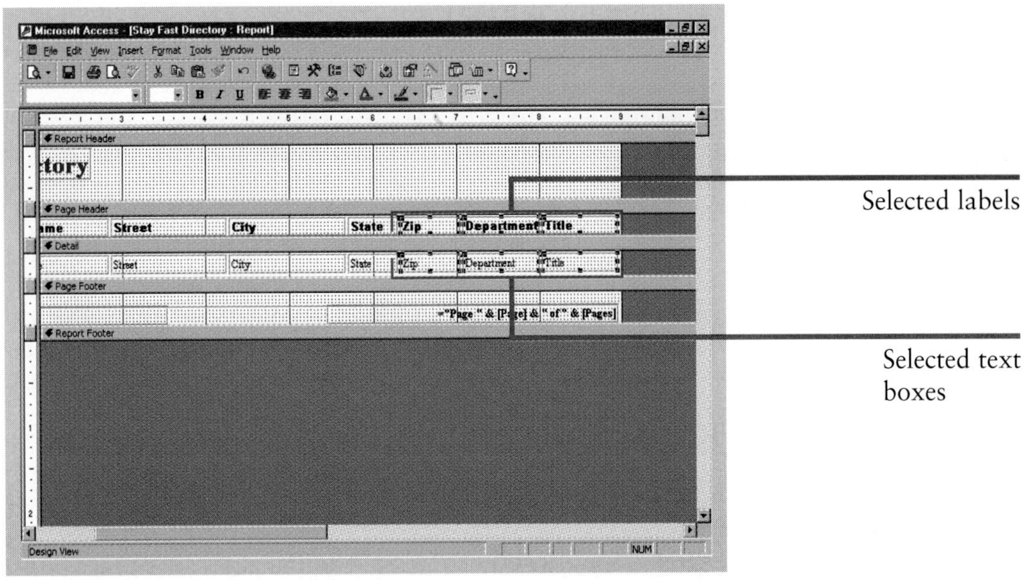

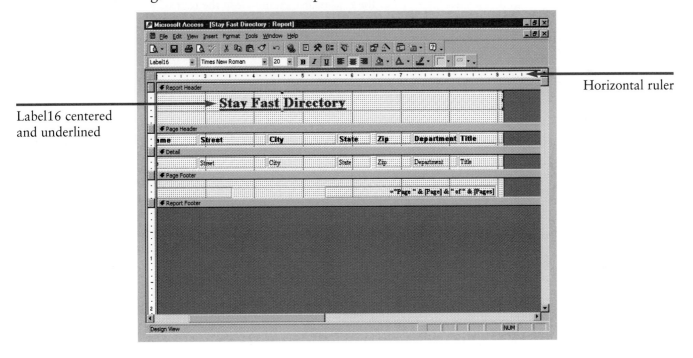

Selected labels

Selected text boxes

Figure 4-11 Formatted report label

Label16 centered and underlined

Horizontal ruler

Formatting Report Elements (continued)

Do It!

13 Use the horizontal scroll bar to scroll back to the left edge of the report.

14 Click the **Object** drop-down list, then click **Last Name** to select the Last Name text box control.

15 Click the **Font/Fore Color** drop-down list arrow [A▾], then click the blue box in the second row of the palette that appears. This will make the last names of the employees appear in blue, as they did earlier in the form you created.

16 Click the gray **Page Header Section** selector to select it, as pictured in **Figure 4-12**.

17 Click the **Fill/Back Color** drop-down list arrow [◆▾], then click the last box in the fourth row of the palette. The background color behind the labels becomes gray.

18 Click the **View** button [◻▾] to view the report in Print Preview mode.

19 Click the **Zoom** drop-down list arrow [100% ▾] and select 75% from the list to allow the entire width of the report to fit within the boundaries of the window. Your report should resemble the one shown in **Figure 4-13**.

20 Save the changes to the report design and close the report.

More

To increase the space between records in a report, you must increase the height of the detail section. To do so, position the mouse pointer over the bottom edge of the white space in the vertical ruler that corresponds with the details section. When the mouse pointer changes to a vertical movement pointer ✛, you can drag the bottom edge of the section downward. The extra space that is created will be repeated with each detail in the report.

There are a header and a footer for both the entire report and for each page. The report header appears at the top of the first page, while the report footer appears at the bottom of the last. The page header and footer appear at the top and bottom of each page, respectively. These headers and footers are added automatically when the Report Wizard creates your report. The default page footer contains the date, the page number, and the total number of pages in the report. Items can be added to a header or footer using the Text Box and Image controls in the Toolbox.

You may choose to show or hide the header and footer of the report or of each page by selecting the appropriate command on the View menu.

Figure 4-12 Page Header selected

Appears at top of first page of report

Appears at top of each page

Appears at bottom of each page

Appears at bottom of last page of report

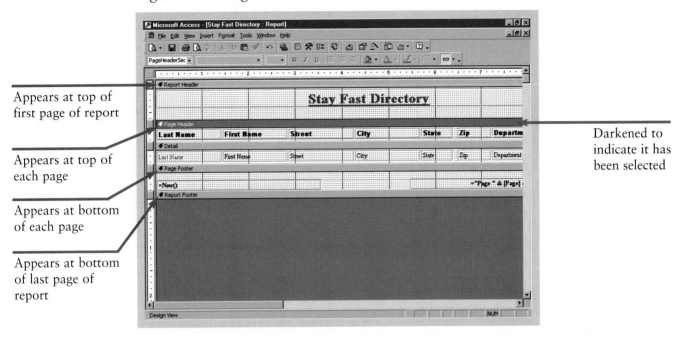

Darkened to indicate it has been selected

Figure 4-13 Formatted report in Print Preview at 75% zoom

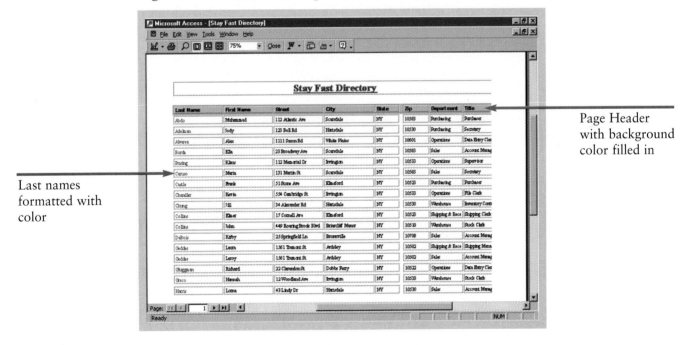

Last names formatted with color

Page Header with background color filled in

Practice

In Design View, select all the labels in the Detail section of the Customer Service Report and apply a shadowed special effect to them. Then change the background color of the Customer ID # field to yellow. Save the changes you make.

Hot Tip

In the exercise above, you used the open hand pointer to drag several selected items at once in Design View. To move just one of several selected items, grab that item's move handle at its upper-left corner with the single item pointer 👆.

Editing Report Controls

Concept

Sometimes you may find that certain controls take up more space than others and may need to be resized so the information is presented more efficiently. You can change the size of the controls in Design View.

Do It!

Kyle sees that the right edge of his report is being cut off because of the size of some of the titles in his title field. He is going to resize the controls so these titles will fit onto the page.

1 Open the Stay Fast Directory in Design View.

2 While holding [Shift], click the First Name label and text box. Move the pointer over the right midpoint resizing control on the text box, click and drag until the mark on the horizontal ruler reaches 2½, as shown in **Figure 4-14**. Click a blank area of the screen to deselect the controls.

3 Holding [Shift], click the Street, City, State, Zip, Department, and Title labels and text boxes. Move the pointer over the left-most text box, Street, until it turns into a hand. Click and drag the boxes until the left mark on the ruler reaches the first mark on the horizontal ruler after 2½, as shown in **Figure 4-15**.

4 Deselect the selected controls, then click the Title text box, located on the far right. Click and drag the right midpoint sizing control until the right edge meets the edge of the report.

5 Return the view to Print Preview. All of the letters in the titles should now fit onto the page, as shown in **Figure 4-16**.

6 Close the report and save the changes you have made.

More

If you want to change the size or placement of every control in a report, you can click Edit on the Menu toolbar, then click Select All. Once you have selected multiple controls in a report, you can use any one of those controls to make changes to all of the controls. Any changes that you make to one control also will be made to every other control you selected.

You can select multiple controls without selecting all of the controls by holding the [Shift] key while clicking the controls you want to select.

Figure 4-14 Resizing a label and text box in Design View

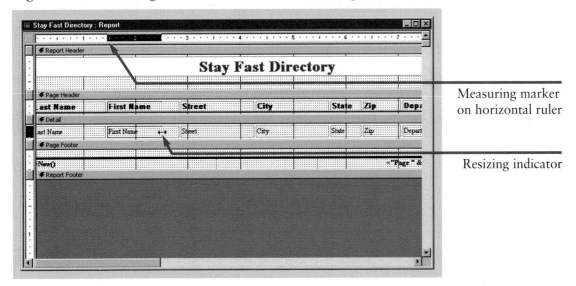

Measuring marker
on horizontal ruler

Resizing indicator

Figure 4-15 Moving elements in Design View

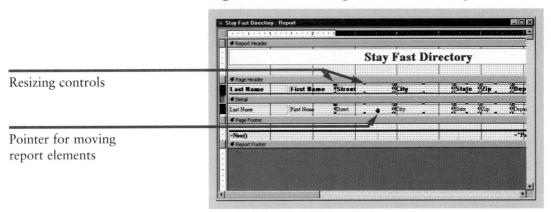

Resizing controls

Pointer for moving
report elements

Figure 4-16 Report with edited controls

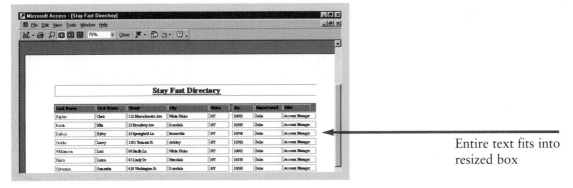

Entire text fits into
resized box

Practice

Extend the right edge of your **Customer Service Report** half an inch on the horizontal ruler. Extend all of the text boxes right edges so the extra space provided is used.

Hot Tip

If you resize or relocate the label and text boxes so the right edges run over the edge of the report, Access will automatically extend the edge of the report to fit the resized boxes.

Using an Expression in a Report

Concept

Using an expression in a report may be useful to change the type of information displayed by a report. You may use mathematical expressions to change the actual data that appear or you may use an expression that doesn't alter data but adds to the report as a whole.

Do It!

Kyle would like to add an expression so the date on the report appears in the upper-left corner as well as the lower-left corner of the report.

1 Open the Stay Fast Directory in Design View.

2 Extend the space between the Report Header and the Page Header, by moving the pointer over the Page Header Section selector until it turns into a ✛. Then click and drag down until there is enough space to fit another text box there.

3 Use the same procedure to move the Page Footer down ⅛ on the vertical ruler, to add some space throughout the report.

4 Click the Toolbox button ✸ if the Toolbox toolbar is not visible.

5 Click the Text Box button ⓐⓑ on the Toolbox menu.

6 Using the Text Box pointer ⁺ⓐⓑ, click and drag to create a new text box above the First Name label, beginning at the 1½ mark and stretching to the 4 mark on the horizontal ruler. An unbound text box and a label control are added to the report, as shown in **Figure 4-17**.

7 Deselect the two new controls. Click the label once to select it, then double-click to select the label text and type Date.

8 Click the text box, which says Unbound on the inside. Click the Properties button ⓐ .

9 Click the Data tab to bring it to the front of the Text Box dialog box that appears. Click the Build button ... . This opens the Expression Builder dialog box.

10 Click the Common Expressions folder on the left-hand side list, then double-click Current Date/Time from the middle list (shown in **Figure 4-18**).

11 Click [OK] , then close the Text Box dialog box. Toggle back to Print Preview. The current date and time will appear in the upper-left corner.

More

There is also a Build button on each of the Design toolbars ◩ . It opens a Choose Builder dialog box that allows you to choose any one of three different builders.

Figure 4-17 New text box in report

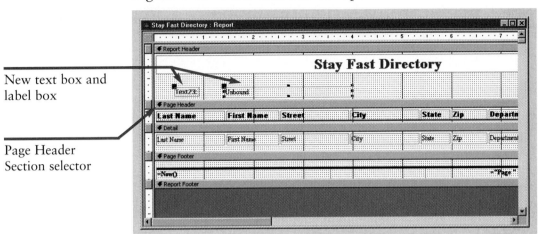

New text box and label box

Page Header Section selector

Figure 4-18 Expression Builder dialog box

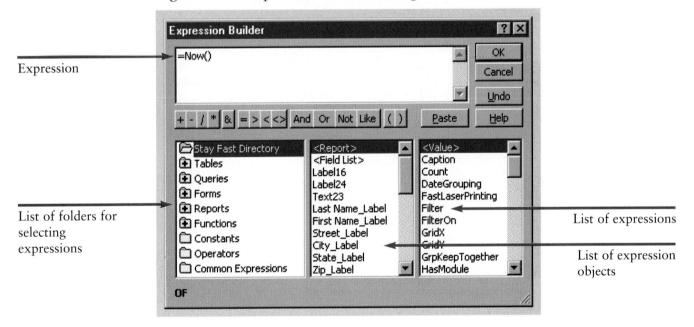

Expression

List of folders for selecting expressions

List of expressions

List of expression objects

Access 2000

Practice

Place the current date in the upper-right-hand corner of your **Customer Service Report.**

Hot Tip

If expressions are not used with the proper conjunctions and tools, the data will not compute properly. When creating an expression, make sure you know exactly how to compute the data and what tools to use.

AC 4.17

Previewing and Printing a Report

Concept

Before a document is printed, you can preview it to check for errors and to make sure it appears as you want it to. The preview shows a document exactly as it will appear on the printed page, taking into account such factors as margins, page breaks, and nonprinting items.

To create a paper or hard copy of your report, form, or other database object, it must be printed.

Do It!

Kyle wants to preview his report and fix any errors he finds. Then he will print it.

1. Click the **Multiple Pages** button ▦ to bring up a page display palette. This palette allows you to choose the number of pages you wish to view as well as the configuration in which they will be displayed.

2. Click the page icon in the lower-right of the palette that appears to view the six pages of the report in a 2*3 configuration, shown in **Figure 4-19**. The six pages of the report will be displayed together on the screen. Three of the pages seem to be mostly blank.

3. When positioned over a page in Print Preview mode, the mouse pointer appears as the magnification pointer 🔍. Click the right edge of the first page with this pointer. The clicked area is magnified, and the plus in the magnification pointer changes to a minus, as is seen in **Figure 4-20**. As you can see, Access put the remainder of what could not fit onto a separate page.

4. Click **File**, then click **Page Setup**. The Page Setup dialog box opens on the Margins tab, as shown in **Figure 4-21**.

5. Double-click the **Left:** text box to select its contents.

6. Type .75 to set the margin at three-quarters of an inch, then press [Tab]. Your entry is formatted automatically as 0.75", the Sample changes to reflect the new margin, and the Right: text box becomes selected.

Figure 4-19 Multiple Pages display palette

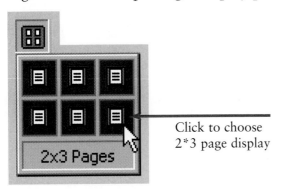

Click to choose
2*3 page display

Figure 4-20 Magnified view of pages 1 and 2

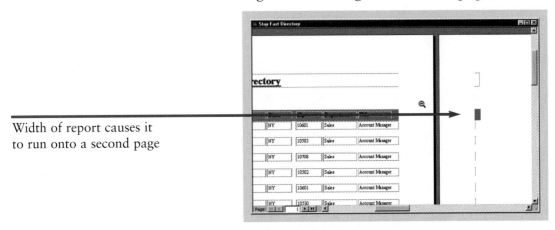

Width of report causes it
to run onto a second page

Figure 4-21 Page Setup dialog box

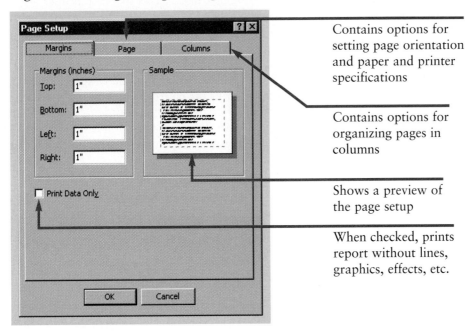

Contains options for
setting page orientation
and paper and printer
specifications

Contains options for
organizing pages in
columns

Shows a preview of
the page setup

When checked, prints
report without lines,
graphics, effects, etc.

Previewing and Printing a Report (continued)

Do It!

7 Type .75 into the **Right:** text box to adjust the margin, then click [OK]. The dialog box closes, and the new margins are applied to the document to allow each row to fit completely on each page of the report without having to spill over onto an additional page, as shown in **Figure 4-22**.

8 Click once with the demagnification pointer 🔍 to zoom out again. Notice that the report now consists of three pages instead of six, as you can see in **Figure 4-23**.

9 Click [Close] to exit Print Preview and return to Design View.

10 Click the Save button 🖫 to save the report with the changes you have made.

11 Click File, then click Print. The Print dialog box, shown in **Figure 4-24**, appears with the name of the last printer Access used selected.

12 After making sure that your computer is properly connected to a working printer (ask your instructor), click [OK]. Your document is sent to the printer.

13 Close the report, saving changes if prompted to do so.

More

The Printer section of the Print dialog box tells Access to which printer it is sending data and where it is located. The Properties button opens the Printer Properties dialog box, which contains several tabs relating to paper size and orientation, print quality, and advanced options such as two-sided printing.

The Print Range section of the Print dialog box allows you to specify what portion of the document is printed. You can print the entire document or a specific range of pages; or, if you are printing a table or query, you can choose to print only the records that you had previously selected. The Copies section defines the number of copies that will be printed and whether or not multiple copies will be collated.

Figure 4-22 Report with adjusted margins

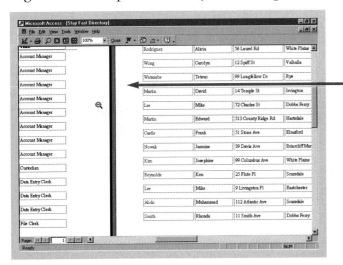

Complete records now fit on one page; page 2 now contains complete records as well

Figure 4-23 Report fit to three pages

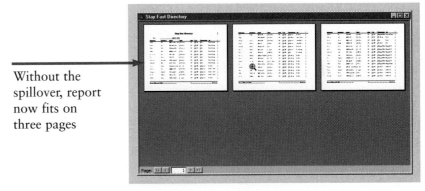

Without the spillover, report now fits on three pages

Figure 4-24 Print dialog box

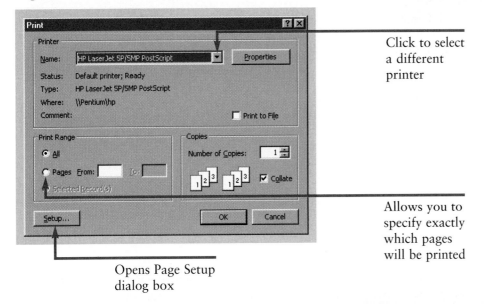

Click to select a different printer

Allows you to specify exactly which pages will be printed

Opens Page Setup dialog box

Practice

View the Customer Service Report in Print Preview, using the multiple pages button to view the report at 1x2, 2x3, and 3x4 pages. Print a copy of the Customer Service Report, then close the database, saving changes if prompted.

Hot Tip

You can quickly print a database object in its entirety by selecting it in the Database window and clicking the Print button.

Using a Query to Generate a Report

Concept

If you have already created a query that sorts and organizes the data the way you want them, it is helpful to be able to create a report directly from a query.

Do It!

Kyle is going to use a query he created earlier to create a report, which will print the exact information he needs.

1 Click the Reports button on the Objects bar.

2 Click New on the Database window toolbar, then click Report Wizard in the New Report dialog box. In the **Choose the table or query...** drop-down list, select **Mail Merge**, as shown in **Figure 4-25**.

3 Click [OK]. Then click the **Add All Fields** button [>>]. Click [Next >].

4 Click [Next >]; you don't want any grouping levels.

5 At the next step of the Wizard, choose **City** from the first drop-down list for the first sorting field, then use **Zip** as the second field for sorting, as in **Figure 4-26**.

6 Click [Next >].

7 Click the Landscape Orientation radio button, then click [Next >].

8 Click Bold, then click [Next >].

9 Type **Directory Report** to replace the default title for the report and click [Finish]. If the Enter Parameter dialog box opens, type 001-051 as the range of Employee #s from the Employee Roster table. The report from the query is now opened in Print Preview as shown in **Figure 4-27**. Close the Print Preview window when you have finished previewing the report.

More

You may create a report using as many or as few fields as you want. For example, if you needed to find out how many men and women were working at Stay Fast, you could create a report that simply shows whether an employee is male or female.

If this is run as a query, and you want to run the complete query as a report, you should choose it as the source of data in the beginning of the Wizard and add all fields.

Figure 4-25 New Report dialog box

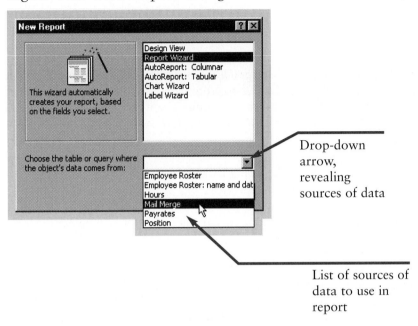

Drop-down arrow, revealing sources of data

List of sources of data to use in report

Figure 4-26 Dialog box in Report Wizard

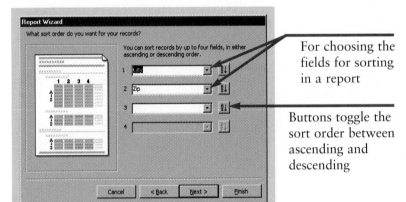

For choosing the fields for sorting in a report

Buttons toggle the sort order between ascending and descending

Figure 4-27 Report created from query

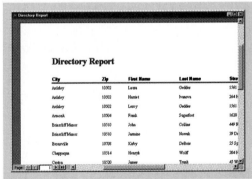

Practice

Create a report based on the query you ran in Lesson 2, **Last Tuned.** Include all of the fields from this query and save it under the title **Last Tuned Report**.

Hot Tip

You also may create an **AutoReport** from a query. When you open the New Report dialog box and choose **AutoReport**, choose to take your data from a query and your report will be created automatically.

Using the Label Wizard

Concept

Offices send out so much correspondence that one of the most productive features of Access is its ability to create labels from databases. This is particularly useful if you have a database of customers or suppliers to whom you have to send bills. You can create labels in Access by using the Label Wizard.

Do It!

Kyle is going to create a label in the Label Wizard to customize Stay Fast's correspondence with its own employees.

1. With Reports selected on the Objects bar, click New on the Database window toolbar.

2. Click Label Wizard, then click the drop-down arrow and choose Employee Roster as the table from which to get the data. Click OK.

3. Click Next > to accept the default label type. This is the first step of the Wizard, seen in Figure 4-28.

4. Click the Font Weight drop-down arrow and choose Medium from the drop-down list. Click Next >.

5. Choose Last Name and click the Add Field button ⟩. Type "," and enter a space. Then choose First Name and click the Add Field button. Type another space then choose Employee # and click the Add Field button. Press the [Enter] key.

6. Choose Street and click the Add Field button. Press [Enter].

7. Choose City and click the Add Field button. Type "," and a space, then choose State and click the Add Field button. Type a space and choose Zip and click the Add Field button. Your label prototype should look like Figure 4-29. Click Next >.

8. Choose Employee # and click the Add Field button. This sorts the labels by the Employee #. Click Next >.

9. Accept the default name for the file and click Finish. The labels you created will appear in Print Preview, sorted by the Employee # field, as in Figure 4-30.

10. Close the Print Preview window and exit Access.

More

In the beginning of the Label Wizard you can customize your own label. This allows you to choose the size and dimensions you want your label to have. You can choose from having dimensions in the Metric system or English system; you may choose the way the paper is fed into the printer and the exact dimensions of the label.

Figure 4-28 Label Wizard dialog box

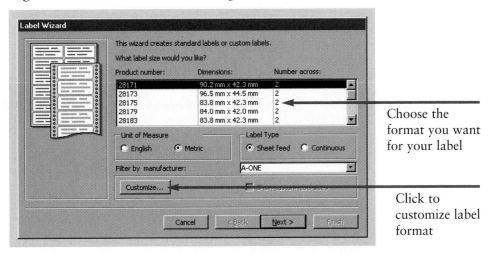

Choose the
format you want
for your label

Click to
customize label
format

Figure 4-29 Mailing label design in Label Wizard

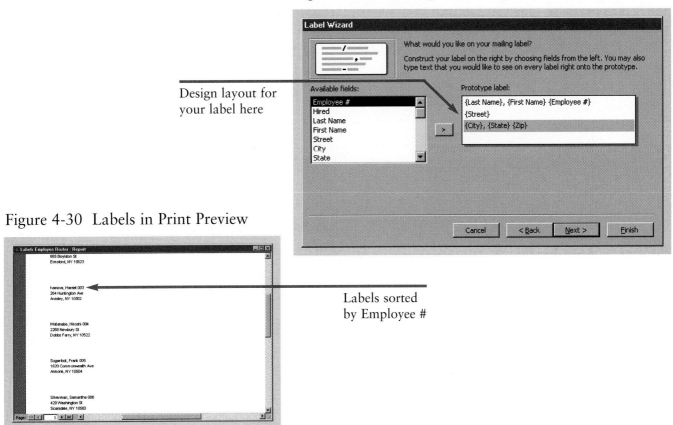

Design layout for
your label here

Figure 4-30 Labels in Print Preview

Labels sorted
by Employee #

Practice

Use one of the tables from the **Tuning Tracker** database to create a set of labels. Close Access when you are done.

Hot Tip

You also may create labels from a query. When you choose where to take the data from, before you start the Wizard, choose a query and that is how the label will be created.

Shortcuts

Function	Button/Mouse	Menu	Keyboard
Show Toolbox/Hide Toolbox	🔨 🔨	Click View, then click Toolbox	
AutoFormat	🖱	Click Format, then click AutoFormat	
Show Field List/Hide Field List	🔲 🔲	Click View, then click Field List	
Zoom (Print Preview)	100% ▾	Click View, then highlight Zoom, then click value	
Fit Print Preview to Window	🔍	Click View, then highlight Zoom, then click Fit to Window	
Zoom 100%	🔍	Click View, then highlight Zoom, then click Zoom 100%	
View one, two, or multiple pages	🔲 🔲 🔲	Click View, then highlight Pages, then click number of pages	
Print Preview	📄	Click View, then click Print Preview	
Print	🖨 (to bypass Print dialog box)	Click File, then click Print	[Ctrl]+[P] (to open Print dialog box)

Identify Key Features

Name the items indicated by callouts in **Figure 4-31**.

Figure 4-31 Features of a report in Design View

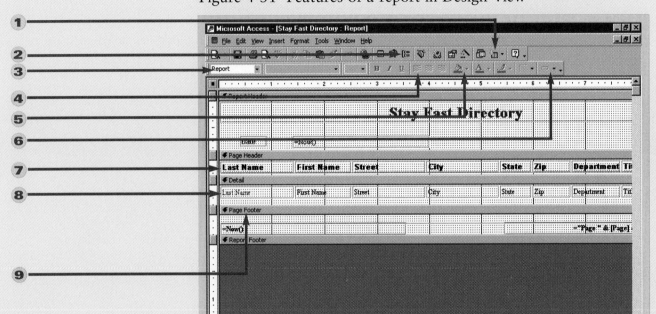

Select the Best Answer

10. Database object that formats records specifically for printing

11. Allows you to change the display size of a report for easier viewing

12. Contains the text options Bold, Italic, and Underline

13. Contains options for viewing one, two, or multiple pages

14. Controls the type of data that appears in a report

15. Changes the way in which records are presented

16. Creates labels through a series of dialog boxes that allow you to create personalized labels

17. Creates a standard report without giving you any options

a. Report

b. Label Wizard

c. Expression

d. AutoReport

e. Zoom

f. Sort Order

g. Formatting toolbar

h. Print Preview toolbar

Quiz (continued)

Complete the Statement

18. Reports created with the Report Wizard are automatically displayed in:

    a. Design View

    b. Print Preview

    c. Columnar style

    d. Justified style

19. To change the setup of a page so that its width is greater than its height, choose the orientation called:

    a. Portrait

    b. Landscape

    c. Horizontal

    d. Form View

20. To view the name of every item on a report in Design View, use the:

    a. Object drop-down list

    b. View menu

    c. Field List

    d. Help menu

21. When you use the Report Wizard, you can choose fields from:

    a. A single table only

    b. A single query only

    c. Tables only

    d. A combination of tables and queries

22. You may create a report using all of the following except:

    a. A query

    b. A table

    c. A label

    d. A form

23. When you create a report using AutoReport, you can expect:

    a. To have a lot of input into the format of the report

    b. Access to take a long time to create the report

    c. Access to create a standardized report based on the table or query you select

    d. To control every aspect of the creation of the report

24. You may sort records in a report:

    a. Only when you use the Report Wizard

    b. Only when you use AutoReport

    c. At any time by accessing the Sorting and Grouping dialog box

    d. At any time by accessing the File menu on the menu bar

25. Using AutoReport may not be the best choice for everyone because:

    a. It limits the choices you can make about the look of a report

    b. It is difficult to find on the Standard toolbar

    c. It looks unprofessional to the people who will use and evaluate it

    d. It means you are lazy

26. You can skip the process of previewing a document before you print it by:

    a. Not creating it at all

    b. Knowing the secret code

    c. Using Access's special printing program

    d. Selecting an object in the Database window and clicking the Print button

Interactivity

Test Your Skills

1. Create a new report using the Report Wizard:

   a. Start Access, open the Test 3 database, and then open the Report Wizard.

   b. Create a report using all of the fields from the query ADDRESS BOOK and E-MAIL: rapid communication.

   c. Sort the records by Last Name and then First Name, both in ascending order.

   d. When you arrive at the last step of the Wizard, choose to preview the report (if you are asked to enter a parameter value, just click OK).

2. Create a report using AutoReport:

   a. Open the New Report dialog box.

   b. Create an AutoReport using the table Address Book.

   c. Take a closer look at the report in Design View.

3. Format a report in Design View:

   a. Toggle to Design View.

   b. Choose Select All from the Edit menu.

   c. Add the special effect Sunken to the report.

4. Change the way records are sorted in a report:

   a. Open the Sorting and Grouping dialog box.

   b. Sort the report using telephone numbers.

   c. Sort the telephone numbers in descending order.

5. Print a report:

   a. Return to Print Preview.

   b. Select the Print command on the File menu

   c. Click the Setup button, and then change the margins of the page from 1 inch to .75 inch.

   d. Click OK to close the Page Setup dialog box.

   e. Print the report.

Interactivity (continued)

Problem Solving

1. Requests are already coming in at Ruloff and DeWitt for specific data from your database. Since these requests only require viewing the data and not changing it, paper reports would provide a convenient method of distributing the information. Use the Report Wizard and Design View to issue reports on the first three queries you created. Your first three queries should contain your data broken down into three different age groups. Add the fields to the reports in any order you choose. You do not need the ID # field in your reports. Experiment with different layouts and styles for your reports. You can use the **AutoFormat** button on the Report Design toolbar to change the style of a report after you have created it if you are not satisfied with your first choice in the Report Wizard. Use the **Sorting and Grouping** dialog box to experiment with different sort orders for each report. Resize and realign the controls so that all labels and field data are visible in each report in Print Preview. Then, use the Page Setup dialog box in Print Preview to finalize the appearance of the reports. Lastly, print paper copies of the three objects you just created.

2. Compare and contrast the last two reports you just created and printed.

3. Reopen one of your reports in Design View. Reformat the report title in any way you choose. You can change the font, font weight, font color, back color, border, special effect, and so on. Use both the commands on the Formatting toolbar and the property sheet to achieve a result that satisfies you. Reformat any two controls on the report. Also reformat the labels on the report. When you are satisfied with the result in Print Preview, return to Design View and click the **AutoFormat** button on the Report Design toolbar. Click the **Customize** button. Select the **Create a new AutoFormat based on the Report** (*report name*) radio button. Click **OK**. The **New Style Name** dialog box opens. Enter a name for the new format you have just created and click OK. Access will create the new AutoFormat and return you to the AutoFormat dialog box. Your new format is listed in the **Report AutoFormats** list. You can now reuse your design any time you choose. Click the **Close** button. Close the report you have opened and save the changes. Open a different report. Apply your new custom AutoForm to the report.

4. Add an Unbound text box to the report above the report title. Increase the size of the Report Header section and move the label control containing the page title down if necessary. Deselect the numbered label control and the unbound text box. Double-click the unbound text box to open the property sheet. On the **Data** tab, select the **Control Source** property. Click the **Build** button. Add the common expression **Page Number** to the expression window and close the Expression builder. Close the property sheet. Select the numbered label control. Press the **Delete** key on the keyboard to delete it. Move the page number text box to the left edge of the report. Switch to Print Preview. **Page 1** displays in the top-left corner of the report. Save the changes you have made.

L E S S O N

1

INTRODUCTION TO POWERPOINT

Microsoft PowerPoint is a computer application that helps you to create impressive and professional presentations. With PowerPoint, you can make on-screen presentations, overhead transparencies in both black and white and color, paper printouts, 35mm slides, or handouts that include notes and outlines of your presentation. You can even design a presentation to be placed on the World Wide Web. PowerPoint is an effective tool that enables you to easily organize and present information. Creating and editing text and graphics are made easy by PowerPoint's user-friendly features.

With PowerPoint you will be able to design a presentation using a premade template, or make your own starting from scratch. A quick and easy way to get started is to let PowerPoint aid you in designing a presentation by using a tool called the AutoContent Wizard. PowerPoint lets you add Clip Art, charts, photographs, video, and sound to further enhance your presentation. You can even publish a PowerPoint presentation on the World Wide Web where anyone with a Web browser can view it.

If you need advice or tips while using PowerPoint, there is an extensive Help facility built into the application, as well as the ability to access online support via the Web. PowerPoint has a feature called the Office Assistant that will offer guidance and tips and answer questions. There is also an index that can be searched by keyword.

CASE STUDY
Trista Leven is a recent college graduate who was hired by a company that grows and installs sod in a variety of markets. The president of the company has asked Trista to use PowerPoint to prepare a short presentation to be used at an upcoming residential construction conference. Trista first needs to familiarize herself with the application. To do this, she will create a short presentation using the AutoContent Wizard and use PowerPoint's many help features to obtain assistance.

Starting PowerPoint

Concept

To use PowerPoint, you must first start, or open, the application from your computer's desktop. The Windows operating system permits you to open an application in a variety of ways. You can launch PowerPoint and other programs by using the Start menu, a Quick Launch icon on the taskbar, or a desktop shortcut, or by finding the program's executable file through My Computer or Windows Explorer.

Do It!

Trista wants to begin using PowerPoint, so she will launch the application from the Start menu.

1. Click the Start button [Start] located on the Windows taskbar. The Windows Start menu will appear above the button.

2. Move the mouse pointer over Programs on the Start menu. The Programs submenu will appear.

3. Move the mouse pointer over Microsoft PowerPoint on the Programs submenu, as shown in **Figure 1-1**, and click the left mouse button. The PowerPoint application window will open with the PowerPoint dialog box displayed in the center of the window as shown in **Figure 1-2**. At this time you also may see the Office Assistant, a feature of the program that offers you help as you work. The PowerPoint dialog box contains four radio buttons that let you select one of four options for either creating or opening a presentation. There is also a list box that shows you PowerPoint files that have been opened recently. Since Trista is working with a fresh copy of the program, this box is empty and dimmed. At the bottom of the dialog box is a check box labeled Don't show this dialog box again that allows you to bypass the dialog box each time you start PowerPoint.

4. Your window may not appear exactly like the one shown here because PowerPoint can be installed in more than one way and the actions of previous users may affect the setup of your window. In the next Skill you will learn how to use the AutoContent Wizard to begin developing a presentation.

More

The PowerPoint dialog box displays four options for working with a presentation. A presentation is a file composed of PowerPoint-created slides. A slide is a single screen of your presentation. Using the AutoContent Wizard, PowerPoint's computer-assisted presentation designer, is the simplest way to make a presentation and will be discussed in detail in the next Skill. The Design Template option allows you to work with individual preformatted presentation designs. Blank Presentation is a feature that allows you to start from scratch (you will learn how to build an original presentation in Lesson 2). Finally, the Open an existing presentation option allows you to open a PowerPoint file that was saved previously.

Figure 1-1 Opening PowerPoint from the Start menu

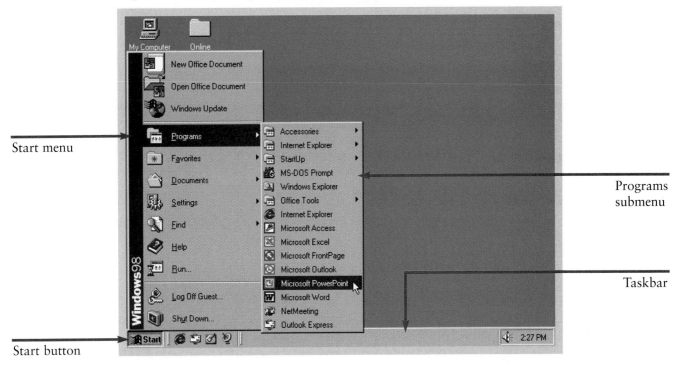

Start menu

Programs submenu

Taskbar

Start button

Figure 1-2 PowerPoint application window and dialog box

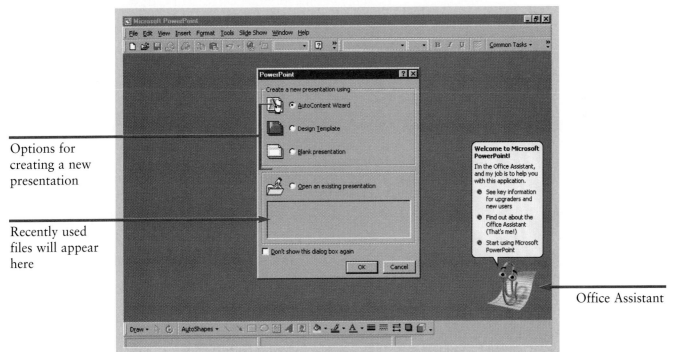

Options for creating a new presentation

Recently used files will appear here

Office Assistant

PowerPoint 2000

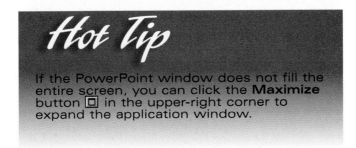

If the PowerPoint window does not fill the entire screen, you can click the **Maximize** button ▢ in the upper-right corner to expand the application window.

Using the AutoContent Wizard

Concept

The AutoContent Wizard is the easiest and quickest way to design a presentation in PowerPoint. It is a very useful tool for new users of PowerPoint and users who need to create presentations in a short amount of time. The AutoContent Wizard will assist you in basic layout design, style, and output type. All you have to do is add the content.

Do It!

Trista wants to use the AutoContent Wizard to design a presentation.

1. Click the AutoContent Wizard radio button to select it, then click ⬛ OK . The AutoContent Wizard dialog box will open as shown in **Figure 1-3**.

2. Click ⬛ at the bottom of the dialog box to summon the Office Assistant if it is not already visible. The Office Assistant offers helpful tips as you work your way through PowerPoint and will be discussed in detail later.

3. Move the pointer over the blue bullet labeled Help with this feature in the Assistant's balloon, then click the left mouse button. The Assistant will now provide you with descriptions of the AutoContent Wizard's steps as you advance.

4. Click ⬛ Next > in the AutoContent Wizard dialog box. The second step of the AutoContent Wizard (**Figure 1-4**) will be displayed requesting that you select the type of presentation you are going to give. The presentation types are divided into categories. Currently, the General category is selected and its presentation types are listed in the box to the right of the category buttons.

5. Click the All button ⬛ All to view all the presentation types at once. The first presentation type, Generic, should be selected by default.

6. Click ⬛ Next > . The next step of the Wizard asks you to choose what type of output your presentation will use.

7. Leave the On-screen presentation radio button selected and click ⬛ Next > . In the next step, Presentation options, you can add a title for your presentation and determine whether any information will appear in the footer, or bottom, of each presentation slide.

Figure 1-3 AutoContent Wizard

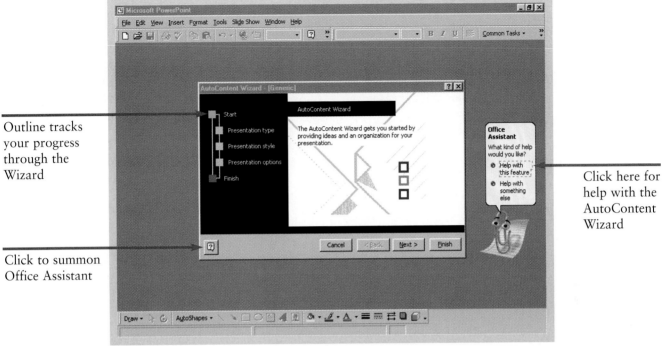

Outline tracks
your progress
through the
Wizard

Click to summon
Office Assistant

Click here for
help with the
AutoContent
Wizard

Figure 1-4 Selecting a presentation type

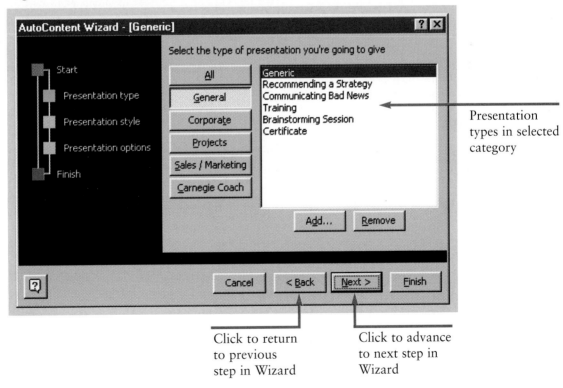

Presentation
types in selected
category

Click to return
to previous
step in Wizard

Click to advance
to next step in
Wizard

PowerPoint 2000

Using the AutoContent Wizard (continued)

Do It!

8 Move the pointer to the Presentation title: text box (it will change to an I-beam when it is in the correct position) and click the mouse button. A flashing insertion point will appear in the text box. (If there is already information in any of these text boxes, delete it by dragging the I-beam over the text to select it and then pressing [Backspace], then replace it with the following text.)

9 Type Learning PowerPoint as the title of the presentation.

10 Press [Tab] to move the insertion point into the Footer: text box.

11 Type Trista Leven. Trista's name will now appear at the bottom of each slide. Below the Footer: text box are two check boxes that allow you to include in the footer of each slide as well the date the presentation was last modified and the number of slides. Leave these boxes checked. The dialog box should resemble **Figure 1-5**.

12 Click Next >. The Wizard informs you that it has enough information to complete your presentation. You may still return to any step of the Wizard to edit the content you have provided.

13 Click the Finish button Finish. The Wizard dialog box closes and the presentation appears in the PowerPoint window in Normal View (see **Figure 1-6**). The AutoContent Wizard has created a number of slides, each with its own title and suggested discussion points. The first slide is displayed and includes Trista's name in the title. PowerPoint obtains information such as the user name during installation. You also may notice a wavy red line beneath Trista's name (or the name of the person to whom your copy of the software is registered). When PowerPoint's Check spelling as you type option is on, the program places these lines under words it does not recognize. These lines are nonprinting characters.

More

The PowerPoint AutoContent Wizard provides you with 20 of the most commonly used presentation types. The type you should choose depends on the message you are trying to convey. The AutoContent Wizard creates slides with text placeholders prompting you to insert pertinent information that will customize the presentation to fit your needs.

The Add button, located below the presentation type list box in the Presentation type step of the AutoContent Wizard, opens the Select Presentation Template dialog box from which you can choose additional presentation types. You may have to install these templates from your Office 2000 CD-ROM. You also can create your own presentation templates and make them available to the Wizard through this dialog box.

When creating a presentation with the AutoContent Wizard, you can click the Finish button at any time. The Wizard will complete the presentation with the information you have provided to that point.

Figure 1-5 Entering presentation options

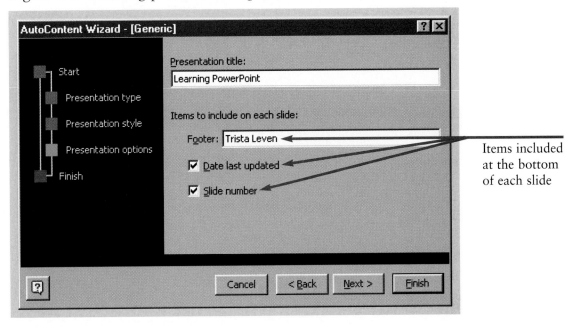

Items included
at the bottom
of each slide

Figure 1-6 AutoContent Wizard presentation in Normal View

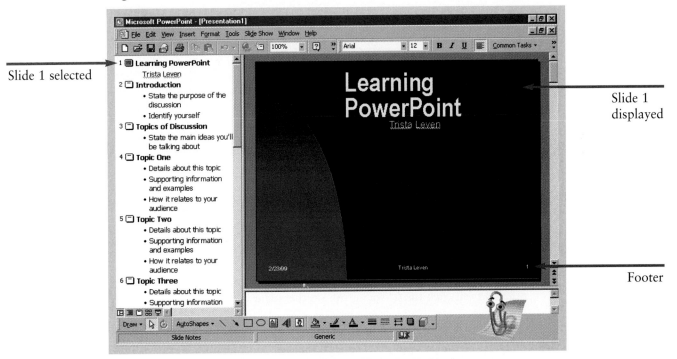

Slide 1 selected

Slide 1
displayed

Footer

PowerPoint 2000

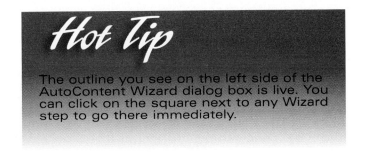

The outline you see on the left side of the
AutoContent Wizard dialog box is live. You
can click on the square next to any Wizard
step to go there immediately.

Exploring the PowerPoint Window

Concept

Exploring a program's application window is an important step in learning to use the program successfully. PowerPoint's window is made up of several user-friendly features including toolbars, icons, and window viewing controls. PowerPoint is designed so that you can perform most of the program's functions from the main window. The application window is flexible and can be customized to suit an individual user's preferences.

Do It!

Trista will familiarize herself with the PowerPoint window to gain a better understanding of its functions and features.

1. The presentation you created in the previous Skill should still be in the active window. Click the Slide View button [icon] located in the row of five buttons at the bottom-left corner of the window. Your presentation will be displayed in Slide View with the title slide in the center of the window, as in **Figure 1-7**.

2. At the top of the screen is the title bar, which shows the name of the application, PowerPoint, and the name of the active presentation. The title bar also contains three buttons: Minimize [icon], either Restore [icon] or Maximize [icon], and Close [icon]. Minimize reduces the window to a program button on the taskbar. Restore reverts the window to its original size and location. Maximize enlarges the window to fill the entire screen, and Close terminates the application. The Control menu icon [icon], located on the left side of the title bar, opens the control menu that houses commands that are similar to the sizing buttons.

3. Below the title bar is the menu bar, which contains various menus of PowerPoint commands. Click File. The File menu will open below its menu title. When you move the pointer over a command on a menu, it will become highlighted. You perform operations in PowerPoint by clicking commands on a menu. Each menu consists of a list of related commands and has two levels. The first level appears as soon as you open the menu and contains the commands you use most often. If you do not choose a command, the menu will expand after a few seconds to reveal more options. The sizing buttons on the menu bar affect the file window and act independently of the application window's sizing buttons. For example, if you want to close the presentation you are viewing, but not the entire PowerPoint application, click the Close button on the menu bar.

4. The row of icons and selection boxes below the menu bar contains two toolbars, the Standard toolbar and the Formatting toolbar. The buttons and boxes on toolbars serve as shortcuts to frequently used PowerPoint commands. The Drawing toolbar is currently active near the bottom of the window. To see a list of all toolbars available in PowerPoint, click View on the menu bar and highlight the Toolbars command. A submenu will appear with the names of all toolbars. A check will appear next to those that are currently active. Toolbars can be moved and resized, so your screen may differ slightly from the one you see on the next page. When you rest the mouse pointer over a toolbar button, a ScreenTip that identifies its function will appear.

5. The main area of the screen is known as the presentation window. This is where you view and work on your presentation slides and their content.

More

The vertical and horizontal scroll bars allow you to view data that does not fit in the window. If the full height or width of a document does fit in the window, then the corresponding scroll bar will be inactive. There are various ways to use the scroll bars. Clicking on a scroll bar arrow moves the display in small increments. Clicking in the scroll bar above or below the scroll bar box advances the presentation one screen at a time. Dragging the scroll bar box allows you to scroll to any specific point in your presentation. In Slide View, clicking scroll arrows or in the scroll bar advances the presentation one slide at a time. Below the vertical scroll bar, the Previous Slide and Next Slide buttons serve this same purpose.

The status bar at the bottom of the window gives you feedback on your current activity in PowerPoint, including which slide you are viewing and the design template being used. If you double-click the current design name in the status bar, a dialog box will appear that allows you to choose a different design.

Figure 1-7 Presentation in Slide View

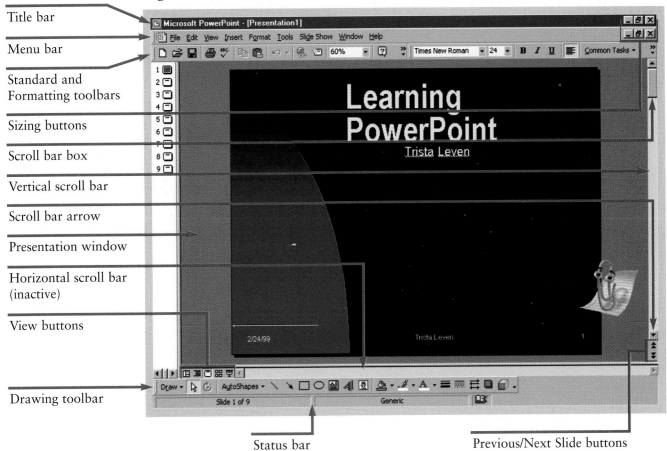

Title bar

Menu bar

Standard and Formatting toolbars

Sizing buttons

Scroll bar box

Vertical scroll bar

Scroll bar arrow

Presentation window

Horizontal scroll bar (inactive)

View buttons

Drawing toolbar

Status bar

Previous/Next Slide buttons

PowerPoint 2000

Practice

Point to each visible toolbar button with the mouse and read the ScreenTips that appear. Then use the vertical scroll bar to practice moving through the slides in the presentation. Leave the presentation on **Slide 1** when you are finished.

Hot Tip

Some menu commands have keyboard shortcuts next to them. Pressing these key combinations is equivalent to choosing the command from the menu. Clicking a command followed by an ellipsis (...) opens a dialog box for that command.

Viewing Your Presentation

Concept

PowerPoint offers several options for viewing your presentation. The different views allow you to focus on specific aspects of your presentation. The view you select will depend on the task you wish to accomplish, whether it be adding or editing text, adding graphics, organizing your slides, or previewing your presentation.

Do It!

Trista wants to see how her presentation will appear in each of PowerPoint's views.

1. The presentation is currently in Slide View. Slide View allows you to focus on one slide at a time. In this view you can add and modify your presentation's content, including text, graphics, and overall slide appearance. The list of numbered slide icons on the left side of the window offers you a quick way to display a different slide in the window. Simply click on the slide you want to view.

2. Click the Outline View button ▤. The presentation will switch to Outline View, as shown in **Figure 1-8**. This view displays the title and main topics of each slide in your presentation. It is best used for entering, editing, and arranging the text on your slides. Notice that like Normal View, Outline View has a three-pane structure. The outline occupies the large pane, while the right side of the window holds a thumbnail of the selected slide and a notes pane where you can type notes about the selected slide.

3. Click the Slide Sorter View button ▦. In Slide Sorter View, you can view thumbnails of all your presentation's slides at once in their proper order, as shown in **Figure 1-9**. This view is useful for rearranging slide order. It also is used for adding special effects and transitions to your slides.

4. Click View, then click Notes Page. In Notes Page View, each slide is presented individually accompanied by a large text box (see **Figure 1-10**). This text box is provided so that you can add your own notes for each slide in the presentation that will not appear on the slides themselves. You can then print these notes and have them available when you give your presentation. You also can add notes to a slide in Normal View and Outline View.

5. Click the Slide Show button ▣. PowerPoint runs the presentation as a full-screen slide show. Click the left mouse button to advance through each slide. When all the slides have been shown, you will be returned to the previous view.

6. Click the Normal View button ▣. Normal View is a three-pane hybrid of Outline, Slide, and Notes Page Views. Any changes you make in the outline pane will be reflected immediately in the slide pane, and vice versa.

More

PowerPoint's multiple views add significant depth to presentation design. Instead of being limited to one editing system, you have a choice of several. In each view you also have the option to zoom in and out of the page. To access this option click the Zoom drop-down list arrow 40% ▾ on the Standard toolbar. Then select a zoom percentage. You are not limited to the percentage values in the drop-down list. You can click the Zoom text box to select the current zoom percentage, and then enter any value between 10 and 400.

Figure 1-8 Outline View

Slide pane allows you to view the slide whose text you are editing

Notes pane allows you to add speaker's notes to the active slide

Figure 1-9 Slide Sorter View

Slide Sorter toolbar

Figure 1-10 Notes Page View

Type your speaker's notes here

Practice

Use the View commands and the Zoom control to examine the presentation in different views and at different magnifications.

Hot Tip

When using a view that has more than one pane, you can change the sizes of the panes to suit your needs. Place the mouse pointer over the border between any two panes, then click and drag the border to shrink one pane while expanding the other.

PowerPoint 2000

Using the Office Assistant

Concept

Even the most experienced computer users need help from time to time. The Office Assistant is a help feature that lets you ask questions related to your problems, and will reply with several help options that may be useful to you based on the question you asked. You also can configure the Office Assistant so that it senses your actions and offers relevant help tips as you work.

Do It!

Trista has questions about designing a presentation with PowerPoint. She will use the Office Assistant to obtain answers to her questions.

1 Click the Office Assistant (if the Assistant is not visible, click Help, then click Show the Office Assistant first). The Assistant's dialog balloon will appear asking what you would like to do, and its text box will instruct you to type a question.

2 Type How can I design an effective presentation?

3 Click the Search button Search . The Office Assistant scans PowerPoint's Help files and returns the topics that are relevant to the question, as in **Figure 1-11**.

4 Click on the help topic titled Computer-based slide show design guidelines. A Microsoft PowerPoint Help window like the one in **Figure 1-12** opens to display the help topic.

5 Read the topic, using the vertical scroll bar to bring the material that is not visible into view. Some Help files, like this one, contain underlined blue text. These instances of text are hyperlinks that, when clicked, take you to related Help files or other locations within the file you are reading.

6 Leave the Help window open.

More

From time to time the Assistant will offer you tips on how to use PowerPoint more efficiently. The appearance of a small light bulb, either next to the Assistant or on the Microsoft PowerPoint Help button 🔲 , indicates that there is a tip to be viewed. To see the tip, click the light bulb in whichever location it appears.

The Office Assistant can be customized. Click the Options button in its dialog balloon (refer back to **Figure 1-11**) to open the Office Assistant dialog box. This dialog box has two tabs: Gallery and Options. The Gallery tab contains different assistant characters you can install, and scrolling through the characters provides you with a preview of each one. From the Options tab, shown in **Figure 1-13**, you can control the Assistant's behavior and capabilities, and decide what kinds of tips it will show. You also can access Office Assistant commands by right-clicking the Assistant itself.

Figure 1-11 Search results

Figure 1-12 PowerPoint Help file

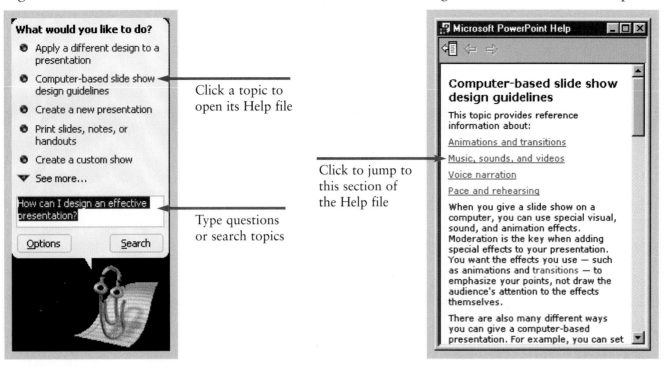

Click a topic to open its Help file

Type questions or search topics

Click to jump to this section of the Help file

Figure 1-13 Office Assistant dialog box

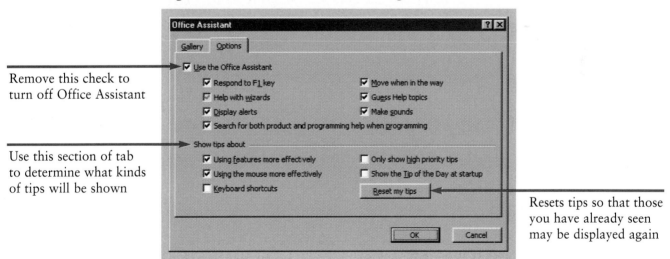

Remove this check to turn off Office Assistant

Use this section of tab to determine what kinds of tips will be shown

Resets tips so that those you have already seen may be displayed again

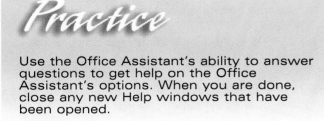

Practice

Use the Office Assistant's ability to answer questions to get help on the Office Assistant's options. When you are done, close any new Help windows that have been opened.

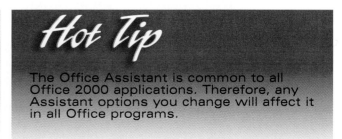

Hot Tip

The Office Assistant is common to all Office 2000 applications. Therefore, any Assistant options you change will affect it in all Office programs.

Other PowerPoint Help Features

Concept

Working with new software can be confusing and, at times, even intimidating. Fortunately, Microsoft PowerPoint offers a number of built-in help features in addition to the Office Assistant. You can use these more traditional help features when you encounter problems or just have a question about a particular aspect of the program. This method of seeking help permits you to access all of PowerPoint's Help files instead of relying on the Office Assistant to find the correct ones.

Do It!

Trista will use PowerPoint's Help tabs to find out more about presentation slide output types.

1 The Microsoft PowerPoint Help window you opened with the Office Assistant should still be on the screen. Click the Show button ⬛ near the top of the window. The window expands to a two-paneled format. The left panel consists of three tabs that organize PowerPoint's Help files in three different ways. The right panel is used to display the actual Help files.

2 Click the Index tab to bring it to the front if it is not already there. The Index presents PowerPoint's help topics in an alphabetical list of keywords.

3 Type output in the text-entry box labled 1. Type keywords. Notice that by the time you finish typing the word, the list box labeled 2. Or choose keywords has scrolled to match what you typed.

4 Double-click output in the list box. All the help topics associated with the keyword are displayed in the list box at the bottom of the tab, labeled 3. Choose a topic. The number of topics found is listed in parentheses.

5 Click the topic titled Create handouts of slides (you may have to scroll down). The Help file is displayed in the right panel for you to read, as shown in **Figure 1-14**.

6 Close the Help window. Then open the Help menu and click Hide the Office Assistant.

More

The Index tab of the Help Topics dialog box is very helpful if you know what the task you are trying to accomplish is called, or if you know the name of the feature that you want to explore. If you are unsure of exactly what you are looking for, the Contents tab may be a better option for you. The Contents tab (see **Figure 1-15**) contains every help topic that PowerPoint offers, broken down by category, and is useful if you wish to obtain a broad view of the topics available. It is organized like an outline or the table of contents you might find in a book. It begins with general topics, symbolized by book icons, each of which can be expanded to reveal more specific and focused subtopics. Once you have revealed a general topic's subtopics, you can select a subtopic in the left panel to display it in the right panel, just as on the Index tab.

The **Answer Wizard** tab replicates the Office Assistant, allowing you to request help topics by entering questions or search topics in your own words.

Once you have clicked the Show button to display the Help tabs in a Help window, the button changes to the Hide button. Click the Hide button to collapse the window back to a single panel. The Help window also includes navigation buttons so you can browse back and forth among Help files you have already displayed. You can print a Help file by clicking the Print button 🖨 near the top of the window.

For quick help on a screen item or menu command, open the Help menu and click What's This? A question mark will be attached to the mouse pointer ⊦?. When you click on the item in question with this pointer, a ScreenTip for the item will appear.

Figure 1-14 Using the Index tab

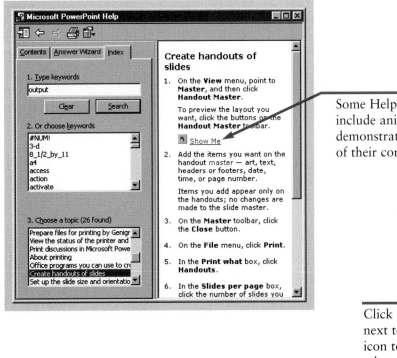

Some Help files include animated demonstrations of their content

Figure 1-15 Contents tab

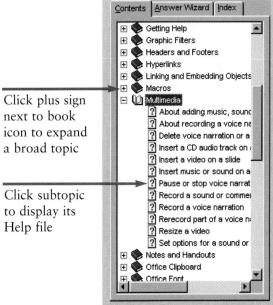

Click plus sign next to book icon to expand a broad topic

Click subtopic to display its Help file

Practice

Use the Index tab to get help on keyboard shortcuts, the Contents tab to get help on ways to get assistance while you work, and the What's This? command to get help on the Normal View button.

Hot Tip

To get help on the features of a dialog box, click the **Help** button ? inside the dialog box. A question mark will be attached to the mouse pointer just like when you use the What's This? command.

Saving and Closing a File

Concept

Saving your work properly is a crucial part of learning how to use application software. Once a file is saved, it can be reopened any time for viewing or editing. You can save your presentation to a hard drive, floppy disk, network drive, or even a Web server. Even after you save a file with a unique name, it is important to continue saving your changes to the file often. Otherwise, you could lose hours of hard work due to hardware, software, or power failures. Closing a file removes it from the screen and puts it away for later use. You can close a file while leaving the application open for use with other PowerPoint files. Or, if you are finished using PowerPoint, you can exit the application.

Do It!

Trista wants to save the presentation she created with the AutoContent Wizard in a new folder. Then she will close the file and exit PowerPoint.

1 Click File on the menu bar to open the File menu.

2 Click the Save As command. The Save As dialog box will open, as shown in **Figure 1-16**.

3 Click the drop-down arrow at the right edge of the Save in: box. A list of your available disk drives and folders will appear.

4 If you will be saving your files on a hard drive, click the drive labeled (C:). If your files are to be stored on a floppy disk, insert the disk and click the drive labeled 3½ Floppy (A:). Follow your instructor's directions if your files are to be stored elsewhere. The drive you select will appear in the Save in: box and its contents will be listed below in the contents window.

5 Click the Create New Folder button ⬜. The New Folder dialog box will open with an insertion point blinking in the Name: text box.

6 Type PowerPoint Files as the new folder's name (see **Figure 1-17**), then press [Enter]. A new folder named PowerPoint Files has been created on the drive you chose earlier and selected in the Save in: box. The contents window is blank as the folder is empty.

Figure 1-16 Save As dialog box

Click to return
to the location
you selected
previously

Use Places Bar
to choose popu-
lar storage loca-
tions quickly

Click to open
a menu of
further dialog
box options

Click to
move up one
level in the
file hierarchy

Click to change
manner in
which icons are
displayed

Click to
launch Web
browser to
search page

Click to delete
selected file or
folder

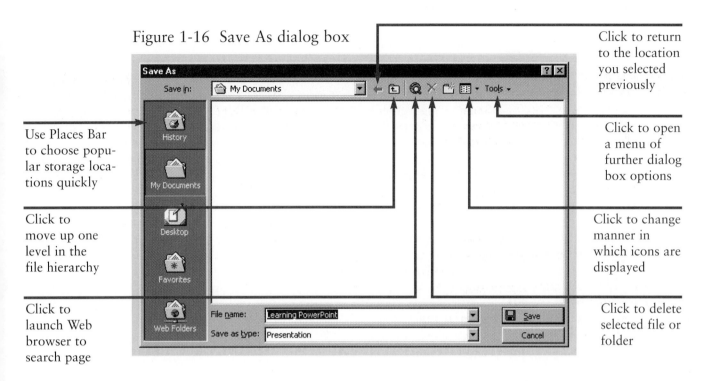

Figure 1-17 New Folder dialog box

Location where new
folder will be stored

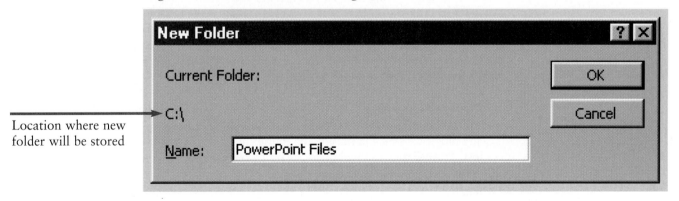

Saving and Closing a File
(continued)

Do It!

7 Now that you have chosen a storage location for your file, you must assign it a unique file name. The default name chosen by PowerPoint, **Learning PowerPoint**, should be highlighted in the **File name:** box. Depending on how your copy of Windows is configured, this name may be followed by the file extension .ppt. File extensions help an operating system associate certain file types with the appropriate applications. The extension .ppt identifies this file as a PowerPoint presentation file. You are not required to add the extension, as the program will do it for you.

8 Type **My First Presentation.ppt** to replace the default file name.

9 Click the Save button ![Save]. The file will be saved and you will be returned to the presentation window. Notice that the new file name now appears in the application window's title bar (**Figure 1-18**).

10 To close the file, click **File**, then click **Close**, as shown in **Figure 1-19**. The file will disappear from the screen, leaving a blank, gray application window.

11 To exit the application, click **File**, then click **Exit**. The PowerPoint application window closes.

More

It is important to understand the distinction between **Save** and **Save As** commands. When you use the Save command, you are telling the computer to make a copy of the current version of your file over the old version, deleting the previous copy. This is how you update a file so that it includes the latest changes you have made. The Save As command allows you to change the name and/or the location of the file you are working on. This is useful if you wish to keep multiple copies of a work in progress without overwriting an older version. If you are saving a file for the first time, PowerPoint will open the Save As dialog box regardless of whether you choose Save or Save As so you can specify a name and location for the file. Once you have saved a file, you can save your changes quickly by clicking the Save button ![] on the Standard toolbar.

If you modify a file and do not save the changes before you close it, PowerPoint will ask you if you want to save the changes you have made. If you do not save, any modifications you have made to the file since the last time it was saved will be lost. PowerPoint also will prompt you to save changes if you try to exit the program with unsaved changes in a file.

Another important distinction to make is between the application and document close buttons ![X], which are identical. The document Close button is located on the right end of the menu bar and is a shortcut to the Close command. Clicking simply closes the active presentation file. The application Close button is located on the right end of the title bar and is a shortcut to the Exit command. Clicking this button closes down the PowerPoint application.

Figure 1-18 Saved PowerPoint file

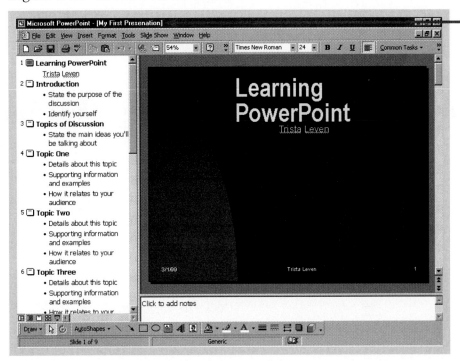

File name appears
in title bar once
file is saved

Figure 1-19 Closing a file

Click to close the
active file, leaving
PowerPoint running

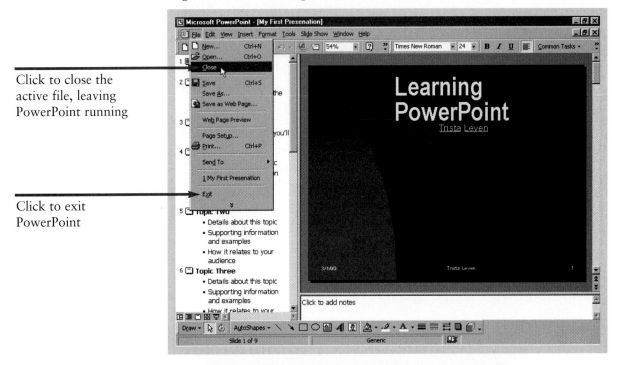

Click to exit
PowerPoint

PowerPoint 2000

Hot Tip

The File menu contains a Save as Web
Page command that allows you to save
your presentation files coded in HTML
(Hypertext Markup Language). Files saved
in this manner can be published on the
World Wide Web.

Shortcuts

Function	Button/Mouse	Menu	Keyboard
Office Assistant	?	Click Help, then Microsoft PowerPoint Help	[F1]
What's This?		Click Help, then What's This?	[Shift]+[F1]
Close a file	☒	Click File, then click Close	[Ctrl]+[W]
Exit PowerPoint	☒	Click File, then click Exit	[Alt]+[F4]
Slide View	▢		
Outline View	▤		
Notes Page View		Click View, then click Notes Page	
Slide Show	☐	Click View, then click Slide Show	[F5]
Slide Sorter View	▦	Click View, then click Slide Sorter	
Normal View	▣	Click View, then click Normal	
Save a file	💾	Click File, then click Save	[Ctrl]+[S]

Identify Key Features

Name the items indicated by callouts in **Figure 1-20**.

Figure 1-20 Features of the PowerPoint window

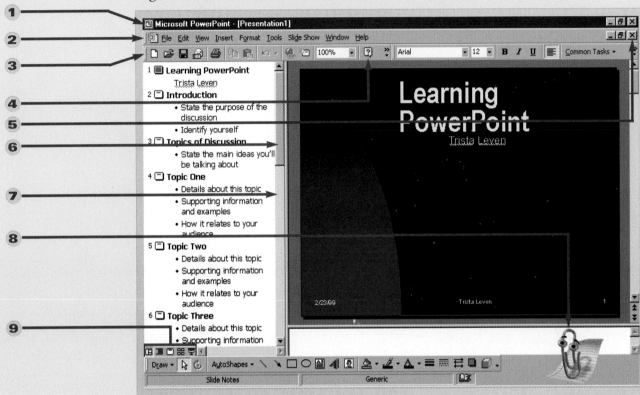

Select the Best Answer

10. A quick and easy way to design a presentation in PowerPoint

11. Allows you to set options before executing a command

12. Useful for entering, editing, and organzing text on slides

13. Increases the size of the window so that it fills the screen

14. Organizes help topics by broad categories and more specific subcategories

15. Allows you to focus on all aspects of one particular slide at a time

16. Help tab that functions like the Office Assistant

17. Permits you to choose a storage location and name for a file

a. Outline View

b. Answer Wizard tab

c. Save As dialog box

d. Contents tab

e. AutoContent Wizard

f. Maximize button

g. Slide View

h. Dialog box

Quiz (continued)

Complete the Statement

18. All of these are options for beginning a presentation except:

    a. AutoContent Wizard

    b. Open an existing presentation

    c. Design Template

    d. Finished presentation

19. To save changes to a file keeping its current name and location, click the:

    a. Save As button

    b. AutoContent Wizard

    c. Insert menu

    d. Save button

20. All of these are PowerPoint views except:

    a. Slide View

    b. 3-D View

    c. Outline View

    d. Slide Sorter View

21. Normal View consists of an outline pane, a slide pane, and a:

    a. Notes pane

    b. Slide Show pane

    c. Slide Sorter pane

    d. Help window

22. A wavy red line beneath text indicates a word that:

    a. Will appear on every slide

    b. Is part of the footer

    c. Is not recognized by PowerPoint

    d. Is a keyword

23. The best view for viewing all of your slides at once and rearranging their order is:

    a. Normal View

    b. Outline View

    c. Slide Sorter View

    d. Notes Page View

24. The toolbar at the bottom of the PowerPoint window is called the:

    a. Drawing toolbar

    b. Standard toolbar

    c. Formatting toolbar

    d. Index toolbar

25. The file extension for a PowerPoint presentation is:

    a. .pow

    b. .doc

    c. .xls

    d. .ppt

26. If you wanted to obtain a ScreenTip for a screen item, you would use the Help menu's:

    a. Microsoft PowerPoint Help command

    b. Office Assistant command

    c. What's This? command

    d. ScreenTip dialog box

Interactivity

Test Your Skills

1. Start **PowerPoint** and run the **AutoContent Wizard**:

   a. Launch the PowerPoint application from the **Start** menu.

   b. Run the AutoContent Wizard from the PowerPoint dialog box.

   c. Do not use help from the Office Assistant.

2. Use the AutoContent Wizard to create a presentation:

   a. Choose the **Projects** category of presentations.

   b. Select **Reporting Progress or Status** as the presentation type.

   c. Select **On-screen presentation** as your output type.

   d. Give your presentation the title **Test Your Skills 1**.

   e. Include **your name** and the **slide number** in the footer, but not the **date last updated**.

   f. Click the **Finish** button to display the presentation.

3. View your presentation:

   a. Put your presentation in **Outline View**.

   b. Switch to **Slide View**. Use the **vertical scroll bar** to view each slide in the presentation in Slide View.

   c. Change to **Slide Sorter View**.

   d. Run a **Slide Show** of your presentation.

   e. Return the presentation to **Normal View**.

4. Use PowerPoint's Help facilities:

   a. Show the Office Assistant if not currently visible.

   b. Ask the Office Assistant about getting **help on the Web**.

   c. Select and read a topic provided by the Office Assistant that is related to your query.

   d. Activate the Help tabs.

   e. Use the **Contents** tab to locate the same Help file you just read.

   f. Use the **Index** tab to list help topics associated with the keyword **name**. Read the Help file titled **About naming presentations**.

   g. Close the Help window and hide the Office Assistant.

   h. Use the **What's This?** command to get a **ScreenTip** for the **Save as Web Page** command on the File menu.

Interactivity (continued)

5. Save and close your presentation, then exit PowerPoint:

a. Save the presentation you created in your PowerPoint Files folder with the name TYS1.ppt.

b. Close the file TYS1.ppt.

c. Exit PowerPoint.

Problem Solving

1. Tabak, Inc., a retail book distribution company, has recently expanded its operations to eight new cities across North America. It is important that the people staffing the new office are made to feel welcome working for the company. More importantly, they must be properly motivated for the expansion to be successful. You have been asked to lay the groundwork for a motivational presentation that employees at Tabak's remote sites can view over the Web. Use the AutoContent Wizard to create this motivational Web presentation, choosing the apporiate presentation and output types. The title of the presentation should be **The Tabak Way**, and the footer should include the phrase **Beta version**. Save the presentation as **Solved1-1.ppt**. Leave the presentation open.

2. Your colleague in the Corporate Services division of Tabak, Inc., has heard about the motivational Web presentation you are creating for employees at the company's new sites. The colleague thinks the presentation would be a valuable motivational tool for her department, even though most of the employees are not new. She would like to develop a similar presentation that is constructed specifically for the Corporate Services division. First, however, she wants to examine your work so that she can use it as a building block. Save a new version of Solved1-1.ppt as **Solved1-2.ppt**. Then close both presentation files.

3. Your boss has had bad experiences with losing large chunks of important data. He wants to be sure that PowerPoint has safeguards to prevent this from happening before he decides whether to adopt the software for the company. Use the Office Assistant to find out about how to recover lost presentations. When you find the appropriate help topic, print it so that you can present the information to your boss. Then, to demonstrate PowerPoint's user-friendliness, use the Index tab to locate the same help topic.

4. You have been hired as an Assistant to the Marketing Director at **Redweb**, an Internet service provider. In the coming months, you will be attending numerous trade shows in order to increase the company's profile. Use the AutoContent Wizard's **Product/Services Overview** presentation type to create a presentation that will attract attention to your company at these conferences. Give the presentation an exciting title and include appropriate information in the footer. Do not worry about the remaining content of the presentation, as you will learn how to add it later. Save the presentation as **Solved1-4.ppt**, and then exit PowerPoint. (Note: to create a new presentation when PowerPoint is already running, click **File**, then click **New**. The **New Presentation** dialog box will open to the **General** tab. Double-click **AutoContent Wizard** on the General tab to launch the Wizard.)

LESSON

2

DESIGNING YOUR PRESENTATION

Presentation design is just as important as production. Choosing one style over another can make a big difference in how your presentation works. In PowerPoint you can design a presentation from scratch by choosing templates, colors, and object placement.

PowerPoint makes designing a project from the beginning starting with a blank presentation easy to do. Slide AutoLayouts will help you organize the content of your presentation, and the design you select will depend on the data you wish to display. AutoLayouts are preformatted slides that contain placeholders for various objects, most useful of which are text boxes. It is in the text boxes that you will enter the information to be presented to your audience.

As you have learned, PowerPoint allows you to see your presentation in several different views. Using multiple views lets you work with your presentation most effectively. In Slide View you can focus on and manipulate every element of a single slide, while Outline View is a text-oriented display. To work with all of your slides at once, in the order that they appear in the presentation, you would use Slide Sorter View. Notes Page View lets you enter text that will not appear during your slide show but that can be referred to or distributed to your audience. Normal View is a tripane hybrid that allows you to accomplish several tasks without changing views. The appropriate view will depend on the task you need to perform.

CASE STUDY
In this lesson, Trista will design a presentation for the sod company that has hired her, Green Side Up, on her own from the beginning. She will start with a blank presentation, and use PowerPoint's design features to lay the groundwork for her project. She also will begin to add content to her presentation.

Creating a New Presentation

Concept

PowerPoint allows you to create customized presentations from beginning to end. You can choose the style and layout of all features to give your presentation a personalized touch. Starting with a blank presentation gives you complete control over every aspect of the presentation's design. PowerPoint also gives you the option of beginning with a Design Template, which can give you a head start in determining the overall organization and look of a particular project.

Do It!

Trista will create a presentation on her own, starting with a blank presentation.

1 Launch the PowerPoint application from the Start menu. When the application opens, the PowerPoint dialog box should appear.

2 Click the Blank presentation radio button, then click OK. The New Slide dialog box, shown in **Figure 2-1**, will appear over a blank presentation window. The New Slide dialog box offers numerous AutoLayout slides. Each of these slides is set up differently to include places for text, pictures, and charts. The one you select will depend on how you want to present your information on a particular slide.

3 Click the slide icon named Table in the upper-right corner of the AutoLayout section. Notice that a border appears around it indicating its selection, and its name is shown in the area below the OK and Cancel buttons.

4 Click the Title Slide icon, then click OK. A blank title slide appears on the screen in Normal View.

5 Click Format, then click Apply Design Template. The Apply Design Template dialog box opens, as shown in **Figure 2-2**.

6 Click the Design Template named Nature. A preview of the design will appear to the right of the list.

7 Click the Apply button Apply. The dialog box closes and the design is applied to the Title Slide, shown in **Figure 2-3**.

8 Save the file as GSU Presentation in your PowerPoint Files folder and close the file by selecting the Close command from the File menu. Do not close the application.

More

PowerPoint offers you other ways to create a new presentation. Clicking the New button D on the Standard toolbar, or pressing [Ctrl]+[N], opens a new file and the New Slide dialog box. If you would like to browse all of the presentation style choices, click File and then select the New command. This will open the New Presentation dialog box from which you can choose a blank presentation, the AutoContent Wizard, a design template, or a specific presentation like those offered by the AutoContent Wizard. If you click the Common Tasks button Common Tasks ▾ on the Formatting toolbar, a menu will open with three frequently used commands: New Slide (adds a slide to your presentation), Slide Layout (allows you to change the AutoLayout for the current slide), and Apply Design Template.

Figure 2-1 New Slide dialog box

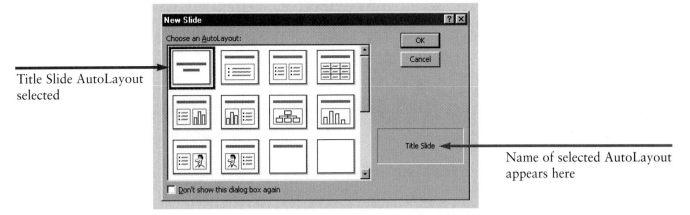

Title Slide AutoLayout
selected

Name of selected AutoLayout
appears here

Figure 2-2 Apply Design Template dialog box

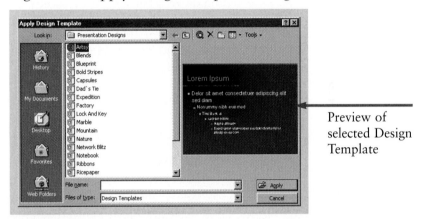

Preview of
selected Design
Template

Figure 2-3 Title Slide with Nature design

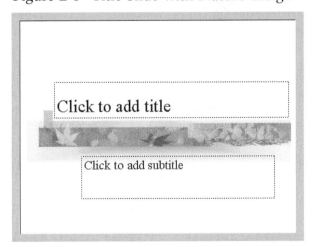

PowerPoint 2000

Practice

Click the **New** button and create a **Title Only** slide. Its icon is the third one in the third row of the New Slide dialog box. Then apply the **Notebook** design template to this slide. Save your file as **MyPrac2-1**. Close the file when you are done.

Hot Tip

Right-clicking a blank area of a slide will open a pop-up shortcut menu from which you can choose the Slide Layout and Apply Design Template commands.

Opening an Existing PowerPoint File

Concept

To view or edit a file that is saved on a hard drive or floppy disk, you first must open it. The method that you use to open a file depends on whether PowerPoint is already running, your familiarity with the software, and your personal preferences.

Do It!

Trista wants to open the GSU Presentation file she created.

1. Click File, then click the Open command. The Open dialog box will appear. The PowerPoint Files folder should be selected in the Look in: box. If not, click the drop-down arrow on the right end of the box to open a list of drives and folders available to your computer. Click the drive that contains your PowerPoint Files folder. Then, double-click the folder in the dialog box's contents window. Once the PowerPoint Files folder is selected in the Look in: box, the files it contains will be displayed in the contents window, as shown in Figure 2-4.

2. If it is not already selected (highlighted), click GSU Presentation to select it. A pre-view of the file will appear on the right side of the dialog box.

3. Click the Open button. The presentation will open on your screen in Normal View.

More

If you have just opened PowerPoint and want to work with an existing file, click the radio button labeled Open an existing presentation in the PowerPoint dialog box. The list box below the button will become active (see Figure 2-5), allowing you to select a presentation from a list of recently used PowerPoint files. Click the name of the presentation you want to open, and then click the OK button.

PowerPoint provides a powerful search facility in the event that you cannot remember the name or location of a file. Click the Tools button in the Open dialog box and then choose the Find command on the menu that appears. The Find dialog box (see Figure 2-6) will open. From the Find dialog box, you can search any drive or folder accessible from your computer. You can conduct your search using a wide variety of properties including file name, the date the file was last modified, or even the name of the file's author. Each property has its own set of conditions that you can apply to the search. For example, the File name property allows you to find a file whose name includes, begins with, or ends with a specific character or combination of characters. You submit this value in the Value: text-entry box. Use the selection and text-entry boxes at the bottom of the dialog box to set your criteria, and then click the Find Now button to initiate the search. If your search is successful, the file you requested will be selected in the Open dialog box.

The Open button in the Open dialog box includes an arrow on its right edge. Clicking this arrow opens a menu that provides commands for opening a file in a number of different ways. For example, the Open Read-Only command permits you to view a file, but prohibits you from saving changes to it. The Open Copy command creates a copy of the file you are opening and opens the copy instead. The Open in Browser command opens HTML files in your Web browser rather than in PowerPoint.

Figure 2-4 Open dialog box

Places Bar buttons allow you to open popular storage locations quickly

Click to access Find command

Preview of selected presentation

Figure 2-5 Opening a file

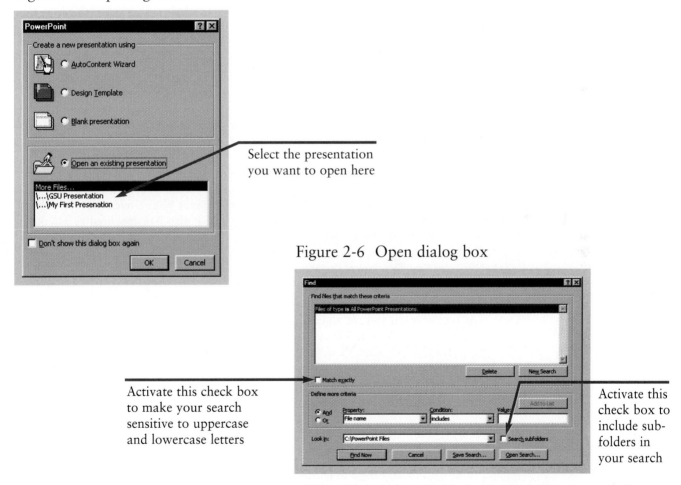

Select the presentation you want to open here

Figure 2-6 Open dialog box

Activate this check box to make your search sensitive to uppercase and lowercase letters

Activate this check box to include sub-folders in your search

Open the student file **Prac2-2**. Close the file when you are done, but be sure to leave Trista's presentation open for use in the next Skill.

Click the Views button 🔲 in the Open dialog box to open a menu of choices for displaying the items in the contents window. The available Views are List, Properties, Details, and Preview.

 # Entering Text in Normal View

Concept

Text is an essential part of a presentation. It must be informative, organized effectively, and displayed appropriately. Entering text in Normal View allows you to see how it will look on the actual slide in the slide pane, while still allowing you to view it clearly and edit it in the outline pane. Many slides come with predetermined text placeholders containing instructions for their use. These text boxes are designated by dashed borders.

Do It!

Trista will add text to her Title Slide using both the outline pane and the slide pane.

1 Click next to the dimmed slide icon ▨ labeled 1 in the outline pane (this icon represents the Title Slide). The icon will change to an active slide icon ▢ and a blinking insertion point will appear next to the icon.

2 Type the company name **Green Side Up**. Notice that as you type in the outline pane, the text also appears in the text box that contained the instruction **Click to add title** on the slide in the slide pane. The text on the slide is formatted with a font, font size, and color (see **Figure 2-7**) that are included in the Title Slide AutoLayout for the Nature Design Template.

3 Click the text box labeled **Click to add subtitle** to activate it on the slide in the slide pane. Type the company motto **Merrily We Roll a Lawn**, as shown in **Figure 2-8**. Then click a blank area of the slide to deselect the text box. Notice that the subtitle you just entered has its own set of formatting and it also has appeared below the slide title in the outline pane.

4 Click the Save ▣ button to save the changes you have made.

More

The outline pane and the slide pane in Normal View replicate the functions of **Outline View** and **Slide View**, respectively. For example, if you wanted to add text to a Title Slide in Slide View, you would click the Slide View button ▣, and then follow the same procedure that you used to enter the subtitle above. If you then switched to Outline View, you would see the new text that you added in Slide View.

Figure 2-7 Entering text in the outline pane

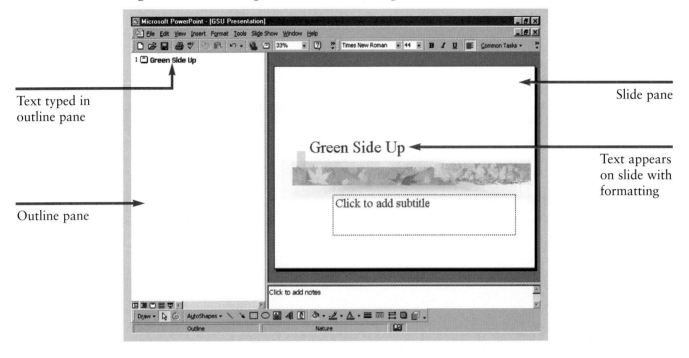

Text typed in
outline pane

Slide pane

Text appears
on slide with
formatting

Outline pane

Figure 2-8 Entering text in the slide pane

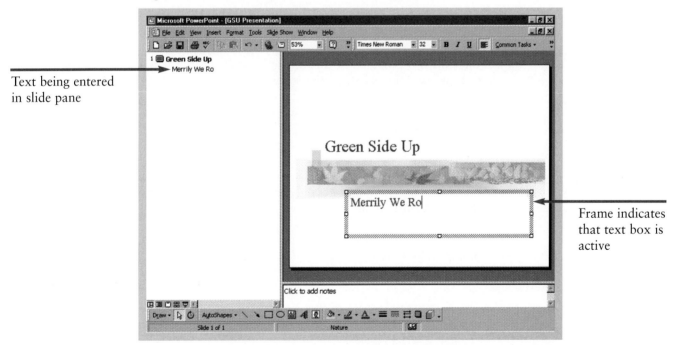

Text being entered
in slide pane

Frame indicates
that text box is
active

PowerPoint 2000

Practice

Open the file **MyPrac2-1**. In the title text box, enter the name of a fictitious company. Save your file as **MyPrac2-3** when you are done.

Hot Tip

If you want to reverse an action you have performed because you have changed your mind or made a mistake, click the Undo button on the Standard toolbar. Click the arrow to see a list of your most recent actions so you can undo several at once.

Adding a New Slide to Your Presentation

Concept

If you create your presentation without the help of the AutoContent Wizard, you will need to add each slide manually. Before adding a slide, you should have a clear idea of what kind of information it will contain and how that information will be presented. Once you have determined these factors, you can use one of several methods for adding a new slide to a presentation.

Do It!

Trista has finished her Title Slide and needs to add a second slide to her presentation.

1 Click the New Slide button 🖿 on the Standard toolbar. The New Slide dialog box will open.

2 Click the second slide icon in the top row, Bulleted List, then click ⬚ OK ⬚. A new slide will be created (see **Figure 2-9**) with the layout you just selected and the Design Template of the previous slide, Nature. The new slide is placed after the active slide (in this case after Slide 1) automatically. Notice that the status bar now indicates that the active slide is Slide 2 of 2.

3 In the slide pane, click the text box with the instruction Click to add title to activate it. Then type Growing to meet your needs as the title of Slide 2.

4 Click the text box labeled Click to add text to select it. Enter the following lines of text, pressing [Enter] after the first two entries:

> 11.2 square miles of turf laid since company was founded in 1989
> 4 varieties produced on 1217 acres
> Business has grown by an average of 21% annually

5 Notice that this text is aligned left and is displayed as a bulleted list. Click outside the slide's borders to deselect the text box. Your slide should resemble the one shown in **Figure 2-10**.

6 Click the document close button 🗙 to close the presentation. Save changes when prompted to do so.

More

There are multiple ways to create a new slide for your presentation. The Insert menu contains a New Slide command that opens the New Slide dialog box. Pressing [Ctrl]+[M] is the keyboard equivalent of this command. In addition, you can click New Slide on the Common Tasks menu.

Holding down [Shift] while clicking the New Slide button will create a new slide with the same AutoLayout as the current slide.

Figure 2-9 New Bulleted List slide

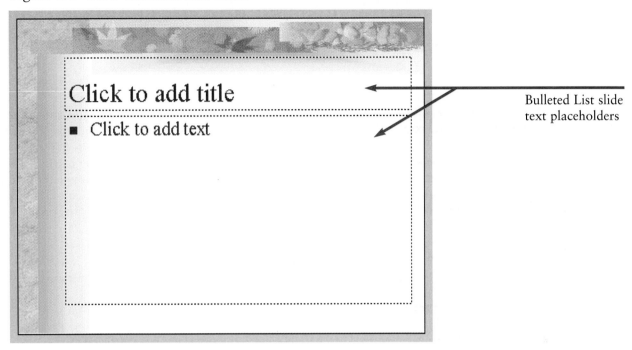

Bulleted List slide
text placeholders

Figure 2-10 Completed Bulleted List slide

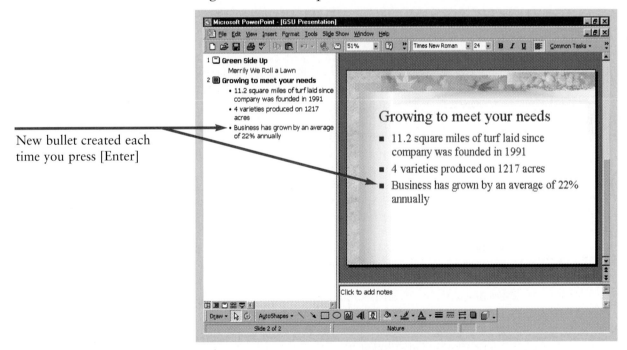

New bullet created each
time you press [Enter]

PowerPoint 2000

Practice

Open **MyPrac2-3** and add a **2 Column Text** slide. Type **Divisions** in the title text box and **Sales** and **Accounting** in the left and right column text boxes respectively. Save it as **MyPrac2-4**.

Hot Tip

If the New Slide dialog box does not offer the precise slide layout that you want to use, you can design a custom layout to present your data more effectively. You will learn how to create your own text boxes in a later Lesson.

Working with Text in Outline View

Concept

PowerPoint allows you to view all of the text in your presentation at once in a simplified outline form. In **Outline View**, text can be entered, edited, or moved about freely on newly created and existing slides. Text also can be moved or copied between different slides in the presentation. Outline View is also useful for promoting and demoting text, thereby increasing or decreasing its importance relative to the rest of the slide. While these tasks also can be accomplished in other views, Outline View gives you more space to focus exclusively on your text.

Do It!

Trista has added slides and information to her presentation. She wants to use Outline View to check the accuracy of her text and make any necessary changes.

1 Open the student file **Doit2-5**, then save it to your Student Disk as **GSU Presentation 2**.

2 Click the **Outline View** button ▦. The presentation switches to Outline View, as shown in **Figure 2-11**, showing the text of the slides that have been created in the outline pane and a thumbnail of the selected slide in the slide pane.

3 Click the down arrow on the vertical scroll bar in the outline pane until the text for **Slide 4** is visible in its entirety.

4 Move the pointer to the left of the second-to-last bullet in the text of the fourth slide, **Received the prestigious Velvet Turf award two years running**, and, with the four-arrowed movement pointer ✛, click and hold.

5 With the mouse button depressed, drag the line of text up to Slide 2, **Growing to meet your needs**, and position it at the bottom of the slide. As you drag the text, the pointer changes to a vertical double arrow ↕, and a solid horizontal line will appear. Make sure you do not drag horizontally first. The solid line shows you where the text will appear when you release the mouse button. Let go of the mouse button to drop the text into place (see **Figure 2-12**) at the end of Slide 2.

6 Place the insertion point after the item labeled **Playing Fields**, the fifth bulleted item on Slide 4, by moving the mouse pointer there and clicking.

7 Press **[Enter]** to create a new bullet, then type **Commercial**.

8 Using the same technique that you used to move text between slides, drag the **Corporate Parks** bullet on Slide 4 down four places so that it comes directly after Commercial.

Figure 2-11 Presentation in Outline View

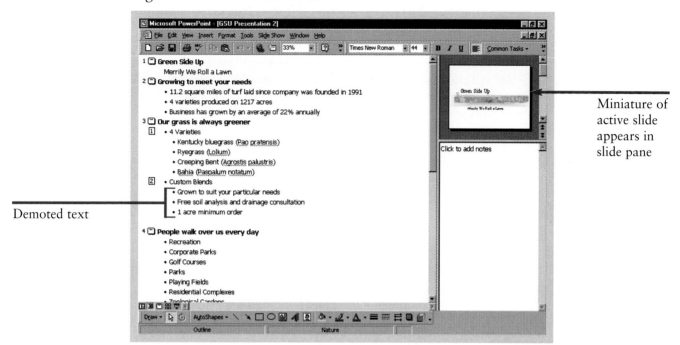

Miniature of
active slide
appears in
slide pane

Demoted text

Figure 2-12 Moving Text in Outline View

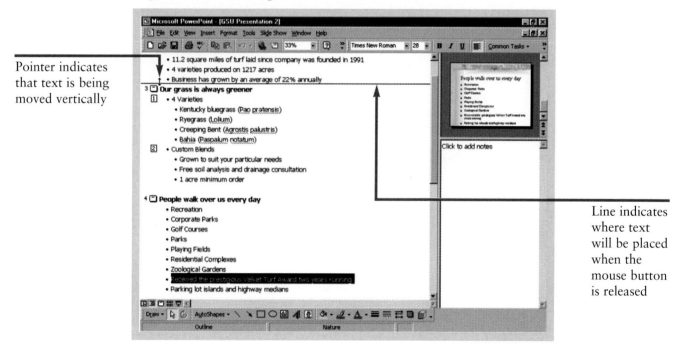

Pointer indicates
that text is being
moved vertically

Line indicates
where text
will be placed
when the
mouse button
is released

PowerPoint 2000

Working with Text in Outline View (continued)

Do It!

9 Click View, highlight Toolbars, and then click Outlining on the submenu that opens. The Outlining toolbar will appear along the left side of the PowerPoint window.

10 Click the bullet next to Golf Courses to select it. Then, hold [Shift] on the keyboard and click the bullet next to Playing Fields. This will add Playing Fields and all the items between Playing Fields and Golf Courses to the selection.

11 Click the Demote button ⬛ on the Outlining toolbar. The selected items are indented so as to be inferior to the heading above them, Recreation.

12 Select the last five bulleted items on Slide 4 using the shift-click method you used earlier. Press [Tab] on the keyboard, which is equivalent to clicking ⬛, to demote these five items.

13 Switch to Normal View. In the slide pane, click just to the left of the bullet labeled Commercial. This will activate the text box and select the bulleted item simultaneously.

14 Click the Promote button ⬛ on the Outlining toolbar to move Commercial back to the same level of the outline as Recreation. Then switch back to Outline View. Your outline should resemble the one shown in **Figure 2-13**.

15 Save the changes to your presentation.

More

Pressing [Enter] in Outline View creates a new item at the same level as the current one. If you are at the top of the hierarchy, slide level, a new slide will be created. You can then press [Tab] or [Shift]+[Tab] where the insertion point is to demote or promote the current item. Promoting a second-level item puts it on its own slide.

The Outlining toolbar provides buttons, shown in **Table 2-1**, that allow you to change the amount of information displayed with each slide. The Collapse All button reduces all of the slides to their titles only, hiding any other text. A grey line will appear under a title if there is any other text on that slide. The Expand All button can be used to view all of your presentation's text if any of the slides are collapsed. The Expand and Collapse buttons function in the same way as the Expand All and Collapse All buttons, respectively, but they act upon a single slide only. The Move Down and Move Up buttons relocate entire paragraphs or titles. Text that is moved up or down exchanges places with the next item in its path. The Demote and Promote buttons can be used to determine the level in the outline at which a particular item lies. Main points, aligned with the left margin, are at the highest level and each indentation to the right represents a drop in the outline's hierarchy. Similar items are grouped on the same level of an outline. Moving an item changes only its location, not its level. Changing an item's level with the mouse is the same as moving it by clicking buttons, but you must drag it horizontally first to get a different movement pointer ↔. A vertical line appears showing at what level the item will appear when the mouse button is released.

Figure 2-13 Rearranged outline

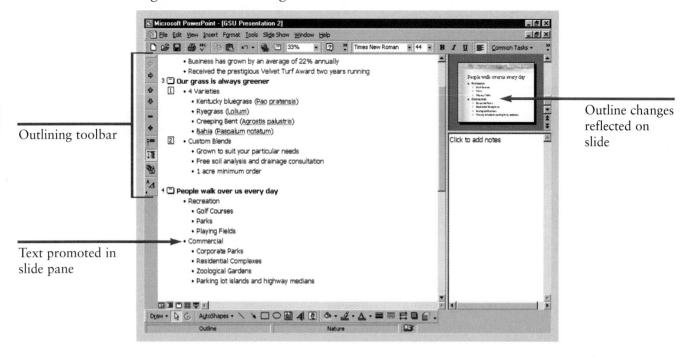

Outlining toolbar

Outline changes reflected on slide

Text promoted in slide pane

Table 2-1 Outlining toolbar buttons

BUTTON	NAME	FUNCTION
	Promote (indent less)	Moves selected item to the left, or up one level
	Demote (indent more)	Indents selected item to the right, or down one level
	Move Up	Moves the selection up in the outline by exchanging it with the previous item
	Move Down	Moves the selection down in the outline by exchanging it with the next item
	Collapse	Displays only the titles of selected slides
	Expand	Displays the titles and all of the bulleted items of selected slides
	Collapse All	Displays only the titles of all slides
	Expand All	Displays the titles and all of the bulleted items of all slides
	Summary Slide	Creates a new slide with a bulleted list of the titles of selected slides
	Show Formatting	When depressed, displays text with all its formatting, such as italics or font size; when deselected, all text appears identical on the screen to facilitate readability

Practice

Open the file **MyPrac2-4** and switch to Outline View. Insert a new slide between the two existing slides. Title it **We Produce** and then create three bullets listing three services or products supplied by your company. Save your work as **MyPrac2-5**.

Hot Tip

Double-clicking a slide's icon in Outline View collapses or expands that slide's text, depending on its current state.

Adding Speaker's Notes

Concept

When giving a presentation, it is often helpful to have precise notes that refer to each slide in the order in which it will be shown. PowerPoint allows you to create notes pages that contain presentation notes along with a small picture of the slide being referenced. These notes do not show up as part of the presentation, but can be viewed privately or printed out for rehearsal and delivery. You can enter notes in **Notes Page View** or in the **notes pane** of any tripane view.

Do It!

Trista wants to add notes to two of her slides so she can refer to them during her presentation.

1 GSU Presentation 2 should still be open in Outline View. Click anywhere in the slide title **Our grass is always greener** to make **Slide 3** the active slide.

2 Click in the notes pane, which is currently blank except for the instruction **Click to add notes**. The instruction will be replaced by a blinking insertion point.

3 Type the following text, as shown in **Figure 2-14**, to accompany Slide 3:

> As you can see, we grow four types of grass to meet a wide variety of soil and light conditions. If these sods do not meet your needs, we can create a signature turf for a slight premium.

4 Click the Next Slide 🔽 button below the vertical scroll bar in the slide pane to advance to Slide 4.

5 Click **View**, then click **Notes Page** (when the View menu opens, you may have to wait a few seconds before the Notes Page command appears). In Notes Page View, the active slide is shown on a page with a text box in which you can enter notes for that slide.

6 Click the **Zoom** box drop-down list arrow 40% ▼, then click 75%. The text box that appears beneath the slide will now be easier to read.

7 Click inside the text box (a Slide Miniature window will appear) to activate it and type the following text, as shown in **Figure 2-15**:

> We are experienced in handling both large and small jobs, laying sod on everything from exclusive 36 hole golf courses to parking lot islands measuring a mere three feet across.

8 Deselect the text box and save the changes to the presentation.

More

The image of the slide that appears at the top of the page in Notes Page View is helpful when trying to coordinate your comments with your slides during the presentation. If you need more room for your notes, the size of the image may be reduced to allow extra room for additional text; this affects only this view and has no bearing on the actual size of the slide as it appears during the presentation.

Figure 2-14 Adding speaker's notes in the notes pane

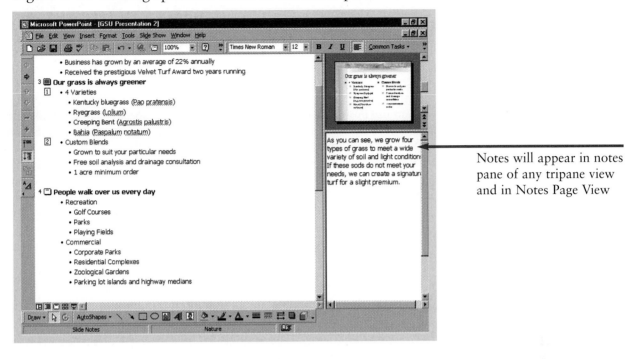

Notes will appear in notes pane of any tripane view and in Notes Page View

Figure 2-15 Notes Page View

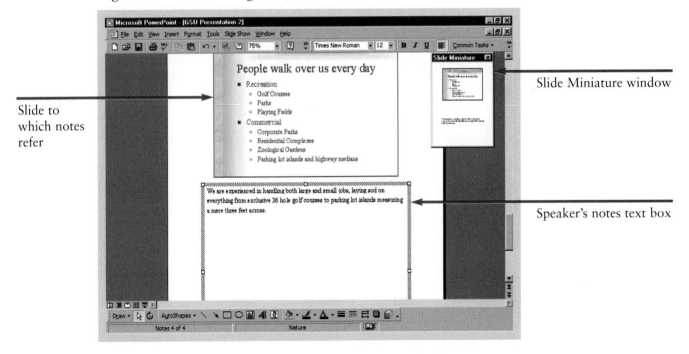

Slide to which notes refer

Slide Miniature window

Speaker's notes text box

Practice

Open the file **MyPrac2-5** and add speaker's notes to the first slide containing a brief introduction to your company for your audience. Save your work as **MyPrac2-6**.

Hot Tip

For making more complex notes that can be distributed to an audience, PowerPoint lets you export miniature images of your slides to a Microsoft Word page layout by clicking **File**, then selecting Microsoft Word from the **Send To** submenu.

Printing Slides and Notes Pages

Concept

You can use PowerPoint's Print features to produce speaker's notes, audience hand-outs, or a hard copy of your presentation. Printing a presentation can involve a single click of a button or setting numerous options to determine what elements of presentation are printed and how they are printed. You can use this output to eval-uate your own work or as part of your actual delivery. This Skill assumes that your computer is properly connected to a black-and-white printer.

Do It!

Trista wants to print hard copies of her presentations's slides and notes pages.

1 Put the presentation in Normal View and select Slide 1.

2 Click File, then click Print. The Print dialog box, shown in **Figure 2-16**, opens.

3 Make sure that the Print range is set to All, that 1 copy has been selected in the Copies section of the dialog box, and that the Print what: box is set to Slides.

4 Click [OK] to print. Your printer will produce four pages, each displaying one slide from the presentation.

5 Open the Print dialog box. Click the drop-down arrow at the right edge of the Print what: box and select Notes Pages from the drop-down list (see **Figure 2-17**).

6 In the Print range section of the dialog box, click the Slides radio button, and then type 3-4 in the text box next to it.

7 Click [OK] to print the Notes Pages you created for Slides 3 and 4.

More

The Print dialog box offers you many printing options. The upper portion of the dialog box, labeled Printer, allows you to select any of the printing devices to which your computer is properly connected. Clicking the Name: box will open a drop-down list of printers from which you can choose. As you have seen, the Print range area allows you to determine how much of your presentation will print. With the All option selected, the entire presentation will be printed. Current Slide sends only the slide that appears in the window to the printer. Selection prints the slides that you have highlighted, and the Slides option lets you enter slide numbers so you can print nonconsecutive slides and ranges of slides. You also can instruct PowerPoint to print the slides in reverse order by stating a range in reverse, such as 12-1.

In the Copies section you can determine how many times each selected slide will print. Checking the Collate box tells the computer to print one copy of the full set of slides before starting to print the next copy. If this box is not checked, your doc-ument will not be collated by the printer. For example, if you were to print three copies of a presentation without checking the collate box, three copies of the first slide will be printed before the printer goes on to the second slide. If you know the Print dialog box settings are correct, click the Print button 🖨 on the Standard tool-bar to bypass the dialog box and print immediately.

Figure 2-16 Print dialog box

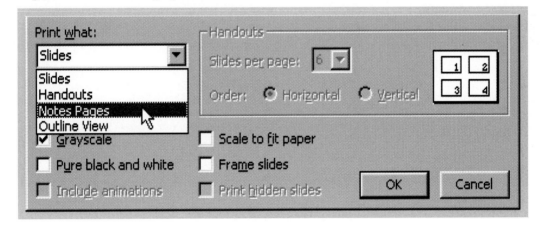

Activate to save print job as a file instead of sending it to the printer

Click arrows to increase or decrease number of copies to be printed

Click to select individual slides or a range of slides to print

Section becomes active when Handouts is selected in Print what: box

Select to print colors as shades of gray

Converts shades of gray to strictly black or white

Figure 2-17 Printing speaker's notes

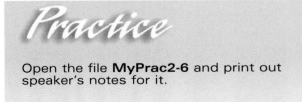

PowerPoint 2000

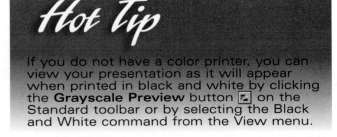

Practice

Open the file **MyPrac2-6** and print out speaker's notes for it.

Hot Tip

If you do not have a color printer, you can view your presentation as it will appear when printed in black and white by clicking the **Grayscale Preview** button on the Standard toolbar or by selecting the Black and White command from the View menu.

Shortcuts

Function	Button/Mouse	Menu	Keyboard
New file	☐	Click File, then click New	[Ctrl]+[N]
Apply Design Template	☐	Click Format or Common Tasks button, then click Apply Design Template	
New Slide	☐	Click Insert or Common Tasks button, then click New Slide	[Ctrl]+[M]
New Slide with same layout as previous slide	☐ + [Shift]	Hold [Shift] while clicking New Slide command	[Ctrl]+[Shift]+[M]
Open a file	☐	Click File, then click Open	[Ctrl]+[O]
Promote selected text	◆		[Shift]+[Tab] or [Alt]+[Shift]+[Left]
Demote text	◆		[Tab] or [Alt]+[Shift]+[Right]
Move text up	◆		[Alt]+[Shift]+[Up]
Move text down	◆		[Alt]+[Shift]+[Down]
Collapse slide text	▬		[Alt]+[Shift]+[-]
Expand slide text	✦		[Alt]+[Shift]+[+]
Collapse all slide text	☰		[Alt]+[Shift]+[1]
Expand all slide text	☰		[Alt]+[Shift]+[9]
Print	☐ To bypass Print dialog box	Click File, then click Print (opens Print dialog box)	[Ctrl]+[P] (opens Print dialog box)

Identify Key Features

Name the items indicated by callouts in **Figure 2-18**.

Figure 2-18 PowerPoint presentation in Outline View

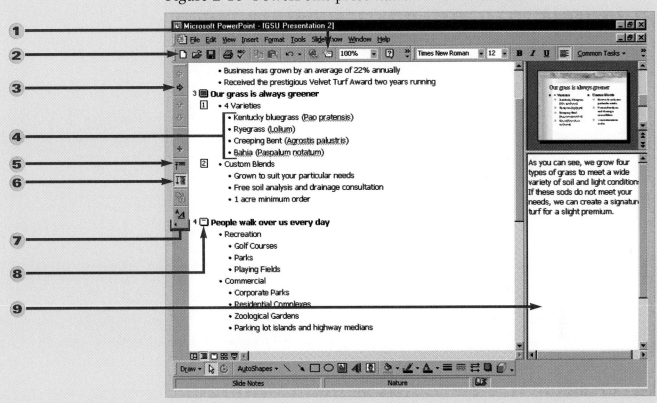

Select the Best Answer

10. Displays all text of a selected slide or slides

11. Can show both collapsed and expanded slides

12. Allows you to choose an AutoLayout slide

13. Reverses the last action performed

14. Command that lets you choose an overall design for your presentation

15. Opens a menu of frequently used commands

16. Includes a search facility for locating files

17. An example of an AutoLayout slide

18. Allows you to determine which slides will be printed

a. Undo command

b. New Slide dialog box

c. Open dialog box

d. Expand button

e. Outline View

f. Bulleted List

g. Print range

h. Apply Design Template

i. Common Tasks button

PowerPoint 2000

Quiz (continued)

Complete the Statement

19. You can insert a new slide by doing any of the following except:

    a. Clicking the New Slide button

    b. Using the Outlining toolbar

    c. Pressing [Control]+[M]

    d. Pressing [Enter] at the top level in Outline View

20. The Print dialog box allows you to print all of the following items individually except:

    a. Handouts

    b. Slides

    c. Footers

    d. Notes Pages

21. Notes that you enter in the notes pane also can be viewed:

    a. In the outline pane

    b. On the slide itself

    c. As part of the slide show

    d. In Notes Page View

22. To work more effectively in Outline View, you should activate:

    a. Grayscale Preview mode

    b. The Outlining toolbar

    c. The Drawing toolbar

    d. ScreenTips

23. Text that you place on presentation slides is contained in:

    a. Icons

    b. External files

    c. Text boxes

    d. AutoLayout slides

24. A tripane window is available in both Normal View and:

    a. Black and White View

    b. Notes Page View

    c. Slide Sorter View

    d. Outline View

25. To change the AutoLayout of a slide you have already created, select it and choose the:

    a. Apply Design Template command

    b. New Slide command

    c. AutoContent Wizard

    d. Slide Layout command

26. You can access the AutoContent Wizard, a blank presentation, or Design Templates from the:

    a. Slide pane

    b. Outline pane

    c. New Slide dialog box

    d. New Presentation dialog box

Interactivity

Test Your Skills

1. Design a presentation about your favorite musicians from scratch:

   a. Start PowerPoint.

   b. Select **Blank presentation**.

   c. Make your first slide a **Title Only** slide.

   d. Apply the Design Template **Marble** to your presentation.

   e. Enter the title **My Top 5 Musical Acts** on Slide 1.

2. Develop your presentation:

   a. Add five **Bulleted List** slides to your presentation, maintaining the Marble design.

   b. Switch to **Slide View**.

   c. Use the text box provided by the Bulleted List AutoLayout to title each of Slides 2 and 3 with the name of a favorite musical act.

   d. Switch to **Normal View**.

   e. Use the slide pane to title each of Slides 4 and 5 with the name of a favorite musical act.

   f. Use the outline pane to title Slide 6 with the name of a favorite musical act.

3. Focus on your presentation's text:

   a. Switch to **Outline View**.

   b. On Slides 2–6, type **Favorite Albums** as the first bullet point.

   c. List your three favorite albums for each musical act on the appropriate slide as bullet points demoted one level below Favorite Albums.

   d. Add a bullet point on Slides 2–6 that says **Favorite Songs** on the same level as the Favorite Albums bullet.

   e. List your three favorite songs for each musical act on the appropriate slide as bullet points demoted one level below the Favorite Songs bullet.

   f. Move the Favorite Albums section of text so that it follows the Favorite Songs section on each slide (2–6).

   g. Collapse Slides 1 and 2.

   h. Collapse all of the remaining slides.

4. Create speaker's notes for your presentation:

   a. Use the **notes pane** in Outline View to write an introduction to your presentation that will accompany Slide 1.

   b. Switch to Notes Page View.

   c. Add notes to Slides 2–6 that include any biographical information you know about each musical act and why you enjoy their music.

Interactivity (continued)

5. Create output for your presentation:

    a. Put your presentation in Normal View on Slide 1.

    b. Preview the presentation in black and white.

    c. Print a copy of each of your slides.

    d. Print your Notes Pages.

Problem Solving

1. In Lesson 1, you were asked to lay the groundwork for a motivational presentation to be used by employees at the new offices of Tabak, Inc., a retail book distributor. Now that you have started to develop your PowerPoint skills, you can begin to convert the presentation you created from a framework into a functional, customized document. Open the file you created at the end of Lesson 1, Solved1-1.ppt. Since you produced this presentation with the AutoContent Wizard, each slide contains placeholder text that serves as a guide for what information should be included. Replace these placeholders with text that is relevant to Tabak and the goals of the presentation. Add Notes Pages for at least half of the slides, including the first and last slides. Save the presentation as Solved2-1.ppt.

2. In your search for a new job, you have encountered an employment agent who encourages you to present yourself as being highly skilled in application software. Along those lines, she has suggested that you use PowerPoint to create an interactive résumé. Your résumé should include at least seven slides, beginning with a Title Slide that provides personal information such as your name, address, and telephone number. Each of the slides that follows should cover standard résumé headings such as objective, education, experience, skills, and so on. Choose a Design Template that you like, but that is also appropriate for the purpose of the presentation. When you finish the presentation, preview it in black and white, and then print out your slides. Save the project as Solved2-Resume.ppt.

3. Create a presentation that will allow you to chart your progress as you learn PowerPoint. Include a Title Slide for each Lesson in this book. Each Title Slide should be followed by individual slides for each Skill covered in that Lesson. Of course, for now you need only build the presentation through Lesson 2. Save the file as Solved2-3.ppt.

4. The Marketing Director at Redweb has approved the presentation layout that you submitted. With the first round of trade shows just a few weeks away, it is time to start developing a presentation that will attract potential clients to your company's Internet service. Open the Product/Services Overview presentation you created with the AutoContent Wizard at the end of Lesson 1 (Solved1-4.ppt). Using the placeholder text as a guide, add your own text to the presentation to make it a powerful marketing tool for Redweb. Add speaker's notes that detail exactly what the presenter should say as each slide is shown. Print your Notes Pages so you can submit them to your boss for approval. Save the new version of the presentation as Solved2-4.ppt.

L E S S O N

3

DEVELOPING YOUR PRESENTATION

During the presentation building process, you invariably will need to add, edit, and format text. PowerPoint comes equipped with an extensive collection of tools that can be used to manipulate text and text boxes. The ability to add your own text boxes at any location on a slide adds flexibility to your presentation designs. You are not limited to the preformatted and prepositioned text boxes provided by the AutoLayout slides. The placement of text on a slide can help you to accentuate the point you are making. Text boxes can be moved to any position on a slide with a simple drag of the mouse.

Editing text includes revising existing text, correcting typos, rearranging text, and checking and correcting misspellings. PowerPoint handles text much like the word processors you may have used. You can specify what font you wish your text to be in and add formatting. Text embellishments such as bolding and italics make text stand out. With PowerPoint's advanced editing tools, you can check your spelling and quickly search for and replace specific words or phrases. Each of these editing features will aid you in creating an impressive, grammatically correct presentation.

Once you have conquered the text of your presentation, you may want to enhance the presentation visually by adding drawing objects. Drawing objects can serve a functional purpose or simply be decorative.

CASE STUDY
Trista will develop her presentation by editing her existing text and adding her own custom text boxes. She will then use PowerPoint's editing tools to refine her text. Finally, she will enhance the appearance of the presentation by using PowerPoint's Drawing toolbar.

Editing and Adding Text Boxes

Concept

Text in a PowerPoint presentation appears in text boxes. You can edit text in a text box, and add new text boxes anywhere on a slide. You can create two types of text boxes with the Text Box tool: text label and word processing. In a text label box, words do not wrap to the next line when they reach the edge of the text box. This type of box is best used for single words and short phrases. If you have a longer passage of text and want it to wrap to the next line at the edge of the box, then you should create a word processing box.

Do It!

Trista has added a fifth slide to her presentation and wants to edit some of the text on it. She will then add another slide and create her own text boxes on it.

1 Open the file Doit3-1 and save it as GSU Presentation 3.

2 Advance the presentation to Slide 5, which is a 2 Column Text slide that compares Green Side Up to its competition. Notice that the slide title, We Mow Down the Competition, uses uppercase letters throughout whereas the previous slide titles use an uppercase letter only for the first word.

3 Move the mouse pointer over the title text. The pointer will change from the standard pointing arrow to an I-beam I. Position the I-beam just after the M in Mow and click the left mouse button. A hashed border will appear around the text defining the box's dimensions and indicating that it is active. A flashing insertion point also will appear where you clicked to mark the place where entered text will be inserted or deleted.

4 Press [Backspace] to delete the uppercase M, then type a lowercase m.

5 Press the right arrow key until the insertion point is just in front of the D in Down.

6 Press [Delete], which erases the character directly in front of the insertion point, and type a lowercase d.

7 Using the mouse, click and drag over the C in Competition to select it. Then type a lowercase c to replace it. The slide should now resemble **Figure 3-1**.

8 Press [Ctrl]+[M] (shortcut to the New Slide command) to open the New Slide dialog box. Select the Blank AutoLayout and click [OK] to add it as Slide 6.

9 Click 🔲 to switch to Slide View.

10 Click the **Text Box** button 🖼 on the Drawing toolbar (if you do not see the Drawing toolbar, activate it from the View menu). The mouse pointer will now appear as a text cursor ↓ when it is in the document window. The position of the pointer on the slide determines where a text box will be created when the mouse button is clicked.

11 Move the mouse pointer to the upper-left corner of the blank part of the slide and click once. An active text label text box will appear, as shown in **Figure 3-2**.

Figure 3-1 Editing text

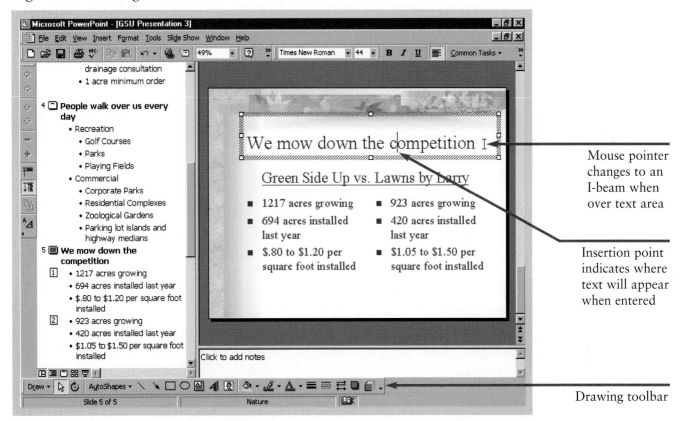

Mouse pointer changes to an I-beam when over text area

Insertion point indicates where text will appear when entered

Drawing toolbar

Figure 3-2 Creating a text label text box

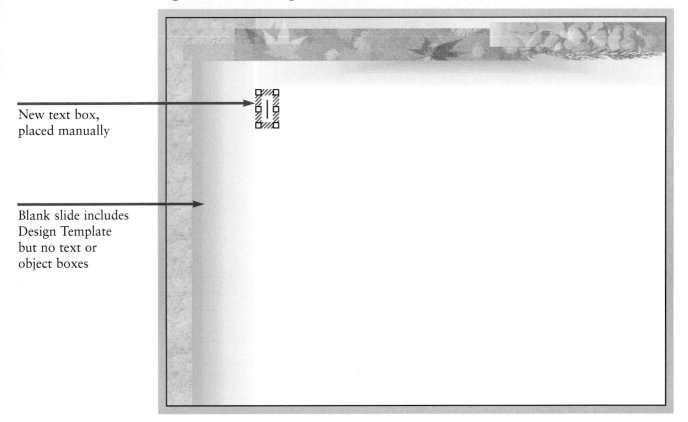

New text box, placed manually

Blank slide includes Design Template but no text or object boxes

 **Editing and Adding Text Boxes** (continued)

Do It!

12 Type We're on a roll. The text box extends as you type to accommodate the text.

13 Click the Text Box button 🖾 again.

14 Position the text cursor below the left side of the text label box you created. Then click and drag from that point down to the bottom-right corner of the slide. As you drag, the text cursor will change to a drag pointer +, and a dashed border will indicate the dimensions of the box you are creating. When you release the mouse button, the box will retain its width, but its height will be reduced to one line. The height will be determined by the amount and size of text that you enter.

15 Enter the following text (include misspellings, which you will learn how to correct later in this lesson):

Argyle County Municiple Stadium (press [Enter])
Winter Crow Golf Course and Country Club (press [Enter])
Arthur B. Milton Golden Cloud Seniors Palace, Infirmary
Care, and Recreational Facility

You may have noticed that the last line wrapped (see **Figure 3-3**), or continued on the next line, when it reached the boundary of the text box. The word processing text box that you created by dragging the text cursor allows this feature. A text label box will not wrap but will continue on the same line until [Enter] is pressed.

16 Create a text label box on the right half of the bottom of the slide.

17 Type Recently Acquired Accounts.

18 Click outside of the text box to deselect it. The slide should now approximately resemble the one shown in **Figure 3-4**.

19 Save the changes you have made.

More

The drag-and-drop method of copying and moving text is a convenient way to rearrange text in your slides. To move a section of text that you have selected, click it and drag the mouse pointer. When it is dragged, the mouse pointer will appear with a small box 🔁 indicating that text is loaded and is ready to be dropped. A dotted insertion point | moves through the text with the drag-and-drop pointer, indicating where the loaded text will be dropped when you release the mouse button. If you wish to duplicate existing text elsewhere on a slide, it can be copied in a similar fashion by pressing [Ctrl] before the text is dropped. The drag-and-drop pointer will be tagged with a plus sign 🔁, notifying you that when the text is dropped into place, the original will be left untouched.

Figure 3-3 Word processing text box

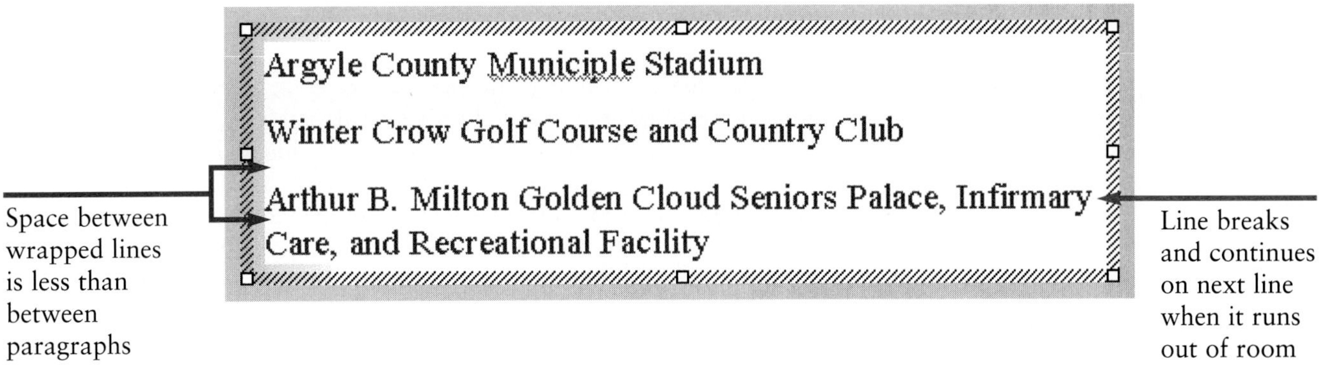

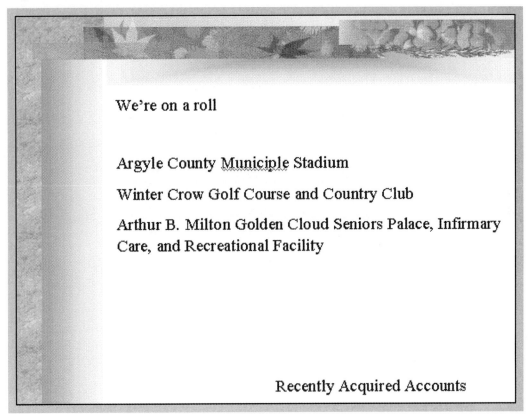

Space between wrapped lines is less than between paragraphs

Line breaks and continues on next line when it runs out of room

Figure 3-4 Slide with various text boxes added

Practice

Open the File **MyPrac2-6** and add a blank slide to the end of the presentation. Create a text label box in the upper-left corner that says **Board of Directors**, and a main text box in the body of the slide with three names in it. Save the file as **MyPrac3-1**.

Hot Tip

To position items on a slide more accurately, you can display horizontal and vertical rulers by right-clicking a blank area of the slide and selecting Ruler from the pop-up menu that appears.

Formatting Text

Concept

Most of the text you have added to your presentation so far has appeared with certain preassigned characteristics known collectively as formatting. Formatting includes the overall appearance of the text, which is determined by the font that has been applied to it. Formatting also includes font size, font color, and style. PowerPoint gives you the ability to format text as you please, even if it was preformatted as part of a Design Template. Formatting can be applied for informational, organizational, and stylistic purposes.

Do It!

Trista wants to change the formatting of the text on the last slide she created.

1. If your Standard and Formatting toolbars currently occupy the same row in the PowerPoint window, place the mouse pointer over the left edge of the Formatting toolbar so that the pointer changes to a four-headed movement pointer ✛. Click and drag the Formatting toolbar down and to the left so that it rests directly below the Standard toolbar in its own row. The full Formatting toolbar will be visible, as shown in **Figure 3-5**.

2. Click the text We're on a Roll on Slide 6 to activate the text box.

3. Click at one end of the text box and drag the I-beam across the text to the other end to select the whole title.

4. Click the drop-down list arrow on the right end of the Font Size box 24. The Font Size drop-down list will appear with the current font size highlighted.

5. Scroll down the list and click 44. The point size of the title text will increase. Points are the measurement unit used for character size and are equal to ½ of an inch.

6. Click the Font Color drop-down list arrow on the Drawing toolbar. The Font Color palette (shown in **Figure 3-6**) will appear, with a depressed button indicating the current color.

7. Click the dark blue box, fourth from the left in the row of colored boxes (when you point to it a ScreenTip saying Follow Title Text Scheme Color should appear). The color palette will disappear and the color of the slide title will be changed.

8. Click the Italic button *I*. The text will be italicized.

9. Click the Text Shadow button on the Formatting toolbar. A shadow will be added behind the title. Click anywhere outside of the text box to deselect it and view the formatting changes. The title text should resemble **Figure 3-7**.

10. Click the list of new accounts to activate their text box, and then select the three account names by dragging the I-beam from the beginning of the first line to the end of the last.

11. Click the Font drop-down list arrow Times New Roman on the Standard toolbar . A list of fonts installed on your computer will appear.

Figure 3-5 Formatting toolbar

Text alignment buttons
Increase or Decrease Font Size
Times New Roman
24
Common Tasks
Font box: shows font currently in use
Text style buttons
Convert text to numbered or bulleted list
Click to add more buttons to this toolbar
Click arrow to select a different font
Font Size box: adjusts size of text

Figure 3-6 Font Color palette

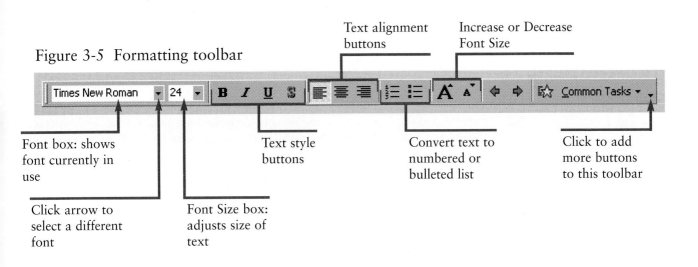

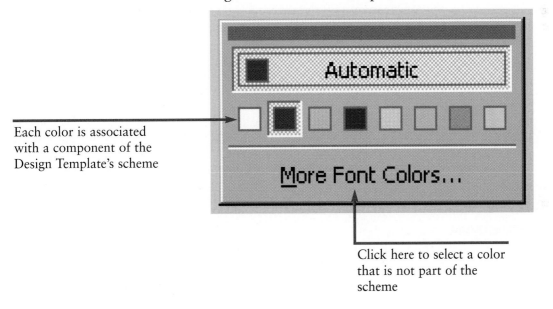

Automatic
More Font Colors...
Each color is associated with a component of the Design Template's scheme
Click here to select a color that is not part of the scheme

Figure 3-7 Formatted title text

We're on a roll

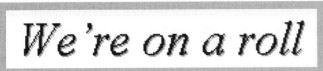

Formatting Text (continued)

Do It!

12 Scroll toward the beginning of the list and click the font named Arial. The typeface of the new accounts will change from Times New Roman to Arial.

13 Click the text label Recently Acquired Accounts to activate the text box, then triple-click the text to select the entire line.

14 Click the Increase Font Size button **A** twice. The point size will increase to 32.

15 Click the Font box (not the arrow). The current font will be highlighted.

16 Type Arial, then press [Enter]. The text will change fonts. If the text label runs off the slide, click the text box's border and drag it to the left so the entire text box is within the boundaries of the slide. The Font and Font Size boxes are text boxes. If you know exactly what typeface or size you want your text to be, you can enter this information from the keyboard; you are not limited to using the drop-down list.

17 Click the Font Color button (not the arrow). Clicking the button itself applies the last color you chose from the Font Color palette to the selected text. This color is displayed as part of the button's icon so that you know which color is loaded.

18 Click the Underline button **U**. A line will appear under the text. Whenever this text is selected, the Underline button will be indented, indicating that it is active.

19 Deselect the active text box. Your formatted slide should look like **Figure 3-8.**

20 Save your presentation.

More

If the exact point size that you want to apply to selected text is not available on the Font Size drop-down list, you can type any whole number between 1 and 4000 into the Font Size: text box. The point size of the selected text will be changed to reflect your entry.

If you need to apply several formatting changes to a selection of text, you may want to use the Font dialog box, which can be opened by choosing the Font command from the Format menu. The Font dialog box, shown in **Figure 3-9,** allows you to view all of the characteristics of the selected text at once. It also offers additional formatting options that are not available on the Formatting toolbar. These include the ability to apply an Emboss effect and to set text as subscript or superscript.

Figure 3-8 Slide with formatted text

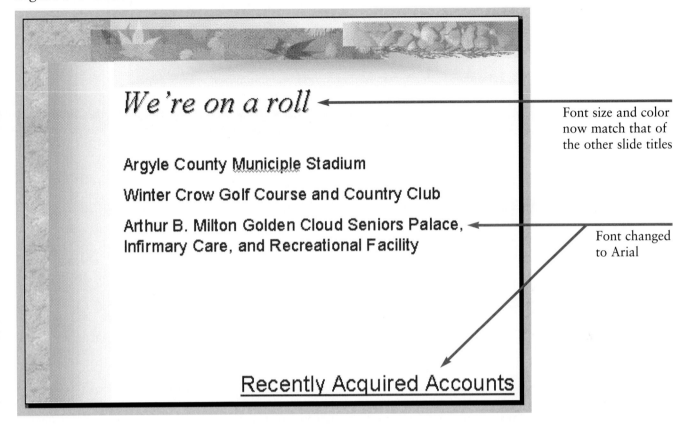

Font size and color now match that of the other slide titles

Font changed to Arial

Figure 3-9 Font dialog box

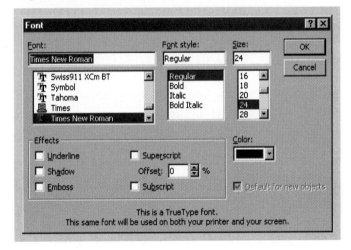

Practice

To practice formatting text, open the file **Prac3-2**. Follow the instructions on the slide, then save the file as **MyPrac3-2** and close it.

Hot Tip

You can select an entire sentence by pressing **[Ctrl]** and clicking any portion of it.

Moving Text Boxes and Aligning Text

Concept

To improve the appearance of a slide's layout, text boxes can be moved and the text inside them can be realigned. You can move text boxes easily by dragging them or by pressing the arrow keys. The four basic text alignment options are left, center, right, and justify. In addition to aligning text according to the boundaries of its text box, you can adjust the spacing between paragraphs in a text box.

Do It!

Trista wants to move the text boxes on her sixth slide and align the main text.

1. Click the title text, We're on a roll, to activate the text box. Small boxes called sizing handles will appear at the corners and at the center of each side of the frame.

2. Position the pointer over the hashed border. It will change to ⏴⏵. Then, click on the frame (not on a handle) and drag to the right until the dashed box representing the text box is centered just below the decorative band at the top of the slide. When you release the mouse button, the actual text box will relocate.

3. Click the main body text, the account names, to select its text box.

4. Click the hashed border to activate the frame instead of the text. Then press the down arrow key repeatedly to move the text box into the lower half of the slide.

5. Select the Recently Acquired Accounts text box and use the mouse to drag it to its proper place, between the title and account names, as shown in **Figure 3-10**.

6. Click the text box containing the names of the new accounts. Select all of the text by clicking before the first letter of the first line and then holding [Shift] while clicking after the last letter of the last line.

7. Click the Center button 🔲 on the Formatting toolbar. The selected text will align itself evenly between the borders of the text box.

8. Click the More Buttons 🔲 arrow at the end of the Formatting toolbar, then point to the Add or Remove Buttons command. A menu of buttons will appear. Click Increase Paragraph Spacing to add its button to the toolbar.

9. Click the Increase Paragraph Spacing button 🔲 four times. The space between each account name will increase. Click anywhere to deselect the text. Your slide should appear similar to the one shown in **Figure 3-11**.

10. Save your presentation.

More

You can resize an active text box by dragging one of its sizing handles. When you place the mouse pointer over a sizing handle, it will change to a double arrow that shows the directions in which that handle can be moved. Handles at the corners of a frame can be used to adjust the size of the box in two directions, while the handles on the sides and top and bottom only influence either the height or width.

Figure 3-10 Repositioned text boxes

Sizing handle

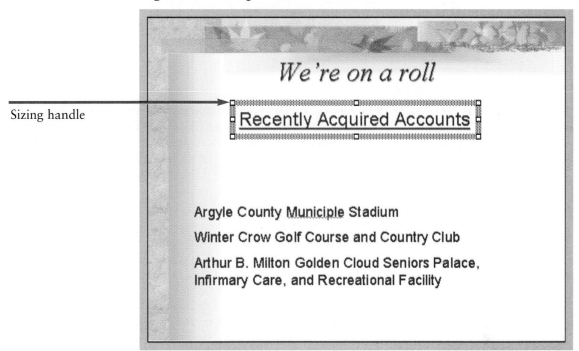

Figure 3-11 Center-aligned text

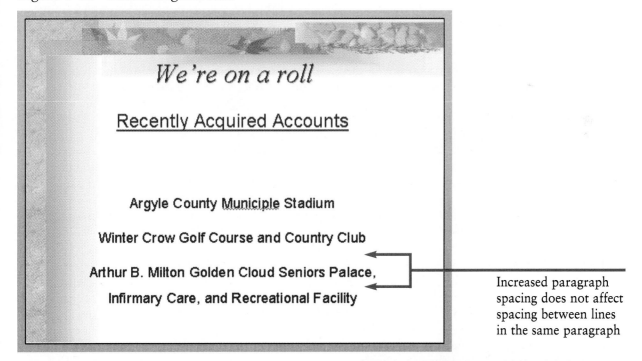

Increased paragraph spacing does not affect spacing between lines in the same paragraph

PowerPoint 2000

Practice

Open **Prac3-3** and follow the instructions on the slide. Save the file as **MyPrac3-3** when you are done.

Hot Tip

You can resize a text box while maintaining its proportions by holding **[Shift]** while you drag a corner sizing handle.

Using Spell Check

Concept

Even the most careful workers can make typing mistakes that they will not catch with their own eyes. PowerPoint has a Spell Check feature that finds spelling errors in a presentation and offers you choices for fixing them. Be aware that Spell Check cannot determine if a word has been misused, such as "there" instead of "their." Also, it will tag any words that it does not recognize, including some proper names and most words in other languages.

Do It!

Trista wants to check for misspelled words in her presentation.

1. With the presentation still on Slide 6, click the Spelling button 🔤 on the Standard toolbar. The Spelling dialog box, shown in **Figure 3-12**, appears. The first questionable word it has found, **Municiple**, is displayed in the Not in Dictionary: box. The Change to: box contains the first of the two suggested replacements for the misspelled word, which are shown in the **Suggestions:** box.

2. Click the Change button [Change] to change **Municiple** to the suggested, and correct spelling, **Municipal**. The correction is made, and the Spelling dialog box advances to the next questionable word it finds in the presentation, which is on Slide 3. The word is also highlighted on the slide itself (see **Figure 3-13**).

3. The next suspect word that appears in the Not in Dictionary: box is part of the scientific name of one of the grass varieties grown by Green Side Up. It has been flagged because PowerPoint's dictionary does not recognize the word. However, it is spelled correctly. Click the Ignore button [Ignore] to leave the word unchanged and advance to the next questionable word.

4. Click [Ignore] seven more times to ignore the remaining names that PowerPoint does not recognize. When you have finished, a dialog box will appear to inform you that the check is complete. Notice that all the red wavy lines have disappeared.

5. Click [OK] to exit the Spell Check and return to your presentation. Save the file to preserve the spelling changes.

More

Clicking [Ignore] tells PowerPoint to leave an unrecognized word unchanged and move to the next misspelled word. It will stop if it finds that same word again in the file. If you click [Ignore All], however, PowerPoint will skip any additional instances of that particular word. Likewise, the [Change All] button will change every instance of the word in question to whatever is in the Change To: text box. Ordinarily, PowerPoint places its primary suggested change directly into the Change To: box; you may click another of its suggestions or type a new word to replace the original suggestion. In the example above, PowerPoint recognized several names but failed to recognize the names of the grass varieties. If these were names that you were going to use often, you could add them to PowerPoint's custom dictionary so that they would no longer be questioned by the Spell Checker. Just click the Add button [Add] to "teach" PowerPoint the word in question. The custom dictionary is a document unique to each copy of PowerPoint that consists solely of words that have been added to it during the Spell Check process.

Figure 3-12 Spelling dialog box

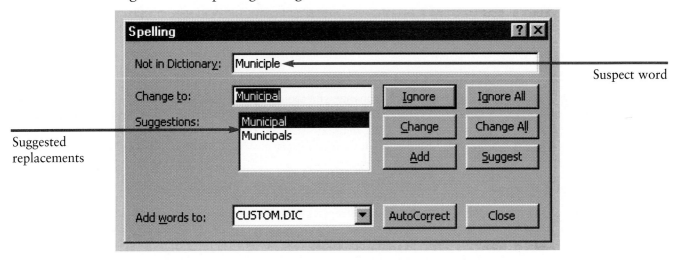

Suspect word

Suggested
replacements

Figure 3-13 Suspect word highlighted

Suspected misspelling
is highlighted so you
can see it in its proper
context

Open practice file **Prac3-4** and use
PowerPoint's Spelling dialog box to find
and correct the errors it contains. When
you have finished, close the file and save it
to your student disk as **MyPrac3-4**.

Hot Tip

You can change the language used by the
Spell Check by selecting the Language
command from the Tools menu.

Replacing Text

Concept

If there is a specific change you would like to make to a word or phrase throughout your presentation, PowerPoint offers a **Find and Replace** function that saves you from conducting long manual searches. You can view each instance of the desired item and change them individually, or instruct PowerPoint to change all instances of the item at once.

Do It!

Trista wants to find and replace a statistical error she has made in her presentation.

1 Click **Edit**, then click **Replace** (you may have to wait a moment for the Replace command to appear). The Replace dialog box opens with a blinking insertion point in the **Find what:** box.

2 Type the number 1217, and then press [Tab] to move the insertion point into the **Replace with:** box.

3 Type the number 1322, as shown in **Figure 3-14**.

4 Click the **Find Next** button [Find Next]. PowerPoint highlights the first occurrence (beginning from the active slide) of the entry in the Find what: box on the slide on which it appears, as shown in **Figure 3-15**.

5 Click the **Replace All** button [Replace All] to replace all occurrences of the number 1217 with 1322. A dialog box appears with the results of the Find and Replace operation (see **Figure 3-16**).

6 Click [OK] to continue.

7 Close the Replace dialog box and save your changes.

More

When you are working with a presentation that contains multiple slides, the Replace command can be used to search the entire presentation at once. To replace a word on a case-by-case basis, click the **Replace** button [Replace] in the Replace dialog box instead of the Replace All button. The **Find** dialog box is similar to the Replace dialog box except that it lacks the Replace function and merely searches your presentation for items you specify. This is useful if you wish to find out how many times you used certain words in your presentation, or if you need to go to a specific word or item in a presentation, but do not know the slide on which it is located. Clicking [Replace...] transforms the Find dialog box into the Replace dialog box.

Figure 3-14 Replace dialog box

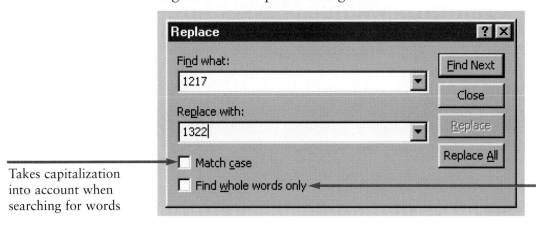

Takes capitalization into account when searching for words

Instructs PowerPoint to ignore requested word when it is part of another word

Figure 3-15 Found word highlighted

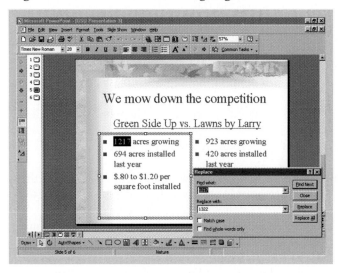

Figure 3-16 Find and Replace confirmation

Practice

Open **Prac3-5** and follow the instructions on the slide. Save the file as **MyPrac3-5** when you are done.

Hot Tip

The Find what: and Replace with: text boxes have drop-down lists that contain your previous Find and Replace entries so that you can conduct repeat searches quickly.

Using AutoCorrect

Concept

PowerPoint's AutoCorrect feature takes the idea of a Spell Check one step further. In addition to finding your spelling errors, AutoCorrect fixes them as soon as you type them. The feature recognizes a predetermined set of common typing errors such as "teh" for "the." However, you can customize AutoCorrect to act upon specific words that you frequently enter incorrectly.

Do It!

Trista wants to set AutoCorrect to automatically fix a typing mistake that she frequently makes.

1 Click the New button ⬜ to create a new file. The New Slide dialog box opens.

2 Select a Title Only slide and click ⬛ OK ⬛. The new slide appears in the document window.

3 Click Tools, then click AutoCorrect. The AutoCorrect dialog box opens with the insertion point in the Replace: box, as shown in **Figure 3-17**.

4 Type the word presentatoin. The word is misspelled here intentionally.

5 Press [Tab] to move the insertion point to the With: box.

6 Type presentation. PowerPoint will now replace the word "presentatoin" with "presentation" whenever it is entered on a PowerPoint slide.

7 Click ⬛ OK ⬛ to accept the changes you have made and to leave the AutoCorrect dialog box. The slide that you created earlier is now in the active window.

8 Click the Title text box to activate it, and type presentatoin, followed by a space. Notice that when the space bar is pressed, indicating that you have finished the word, PowerPoint automatically fixes the mistake. It also capitalizes the word, as it recognizes it to be the first word of a sentence (see **Figure 3-18**).

9 Close the file. You do not need to save it.

More

Any word following a paragraph mark ¶ or a period and a space is capitalized automatically, as PowerPoint recognizes it to be the first word of a sentence. To keep PowerPoint from capitalizing words after abbreviations, the AutoCorrect dialog box has a list of Exceptions, accessible by clicking ⬛ Exceptions... ⬛ in the AutoCorrect dialog box, that it will take into account when determining if a new sentence has been started. Entries may be added to or removed from the Exceptions list as needed. Other AutoCorrect options include automatically capitalizing days of the week and correcting the accidental use of two capital letters at the beginning of a word. To get rid of an AutoCorrect entry that you do not want, select the entry where it appears in the AutoCorrect dialog box and click ⬛ Delete ⬛.

Figure 3-17 AutoCorrect dialog box

Additional AutoCorrect options

Turns AutoCorrect on and off

AutoCorrect will convert certain
character combinations into
commonly used symbols

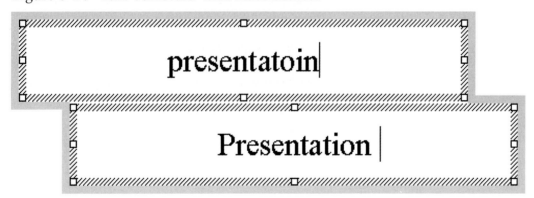

Figure 3-18 Text corrected with AutoCorrect

presentatoin

Presentation

PowerPoint 2000

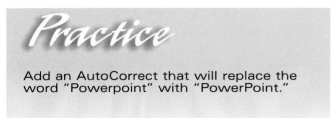

Practice

Add an AutoCorrect that will replace the
word "Powerpoint" with "PowerPoint."

Hot Tip

If you turn off AutoCorrect, you can still
use PowerPoint's Spell Check feature to
catch the common mistakes that
AutoCorrect would have corrected.

Drawing and Formatting Objects

Concept

Including drawings in your presentation helps capture the viewer's interest and imagination. PowerPoint's Drawing toolbar has tools for lines, shapes, pictures, and other graphical objects. You have complete control over where these items are placed and how much space they will occupy on a slide. Once you draw an object, you can modify virtually all aspects of it using editing and formatting techniques.

Do It!

Trista wants to create an arrow with a color gradient to enhance her presentation's Title Slide.

1. Open GSU Presentation 3 to Slide 1.

2. Click the AutoShapes button AutoShapes ▾ on the Drawing toolbar. The AutoShapes menu will appear.

3. Highlight Block Arrows, then click the Up Arrow button ⬆ on the submenu that appears (see **Figure 3-19**). The mouse pointer will change to a crosshairs pointer when you move it over the presentation window.

4. With the crosshairs, click the upper-right corner of the slide and drag down and to the left, creating an arrow that has the approximate dimensions of the one in **Figure 3-20**. When you let go of the mouse button, the arrow will appear filled, with seven sizing handles (white squares) and one adjustment handle (yellow diamond).

5. Click the Fill Color drop-down arrow 🖌▾ on the Drawing toolbar. The Fill Color palette will appear with color choices and commands that allow you to view more Fill Colors or Fill Effects.

6. Click Fill Effects. The Fill Effects dialog box will appear.

7. Click the Gradient tab to bring it to the front of the dialog box if it is not already there.

Figure 3-19 Choosing an AutoShape

Click here to view more AutoShape choices

Figure 3-20 Drawing an AutoShape

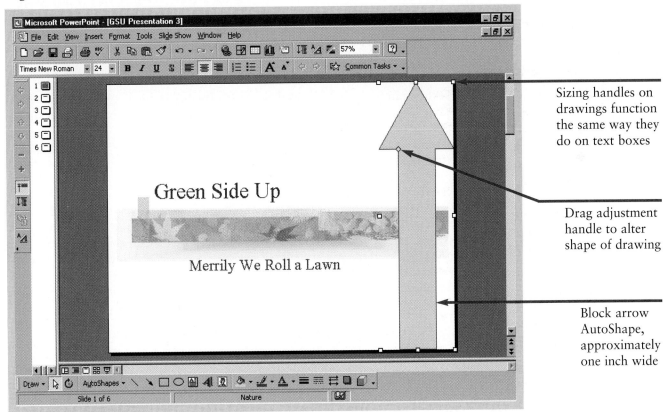

Sizing handles on drawings function the same way they do on text boxes

Drag adjustment handle to alter shape of drawing

Block arrow AutoShape, approximately one inch wide

PowerPoint 2000

Drawing and Formatting Objects
(continued)

Do It!

8 Click the **Two colors** radio button. Drop-down list boxes labeled **Color 1:** and **Color 2:** appear, as shown in **Figure 3-21**. These are used to select the two colors that will make up the Fill Color gradient.

9 Click the **Color 2:** drop-down list arrow, then select the green color box, second from the right on the color palette (its ScreenTip will say **Follow Accent and Hyperlink Scheme Color** when you point to it). Notice that the Sample: box changes to incorporate the new color into the gradient.

10 Leave the **Shading styles** and **Variants** sections set to their default options.

11 Click the **Preview** button [Preview] to see how the gradient looks when applied to the AutoShape.

12 Click [OK] to add the gradient and close the Fill Effects dialog box.

13 Click anywhere outside the slide to deselect the arrow. The slide should now resemble **Figure 3-22**.

14 Save the changes to your file.

More

The **Texture** tab in the Fill Effects dialog box provides a palette of textures, such as marble or wood, that can be applied to objects you create. The **Pattern** tab is similar to the Texture tab, but instead provides 42 simple patterns from which you can choose. The **Picture** tab allows you to fill an object with a picture or other graphic that you have on file.

You can rotate objects that you have created using the **Free Rotate** tool available on the Drawing toolbar. Simply select the object you wish to rotate, then click the Free Rotate button [C]. Green circles will appear at the corners of the selected object that you can drag to rotate it. Ordinarily, an object will rotate about its center. When [Ctrl] is pressed while rotating, however, the object will rotate about the corner opposite the one being dragged. Objects can be freely rotated to any degree you wish, or the rotation can be constrained to 15° increments by holding [Shift] while you drag.

You can rotate an object in 90° increments or flip it horizontally or vertically by using the commands on the **Rotate or Flip** submenu of the **Draw** menu, which is located at the left end of the Drawing toolbar.

Figure 3-21 Fill Effects dialog box

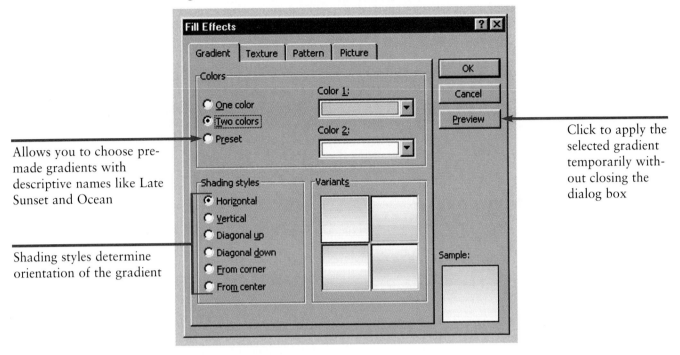

Allows you to choose pre-made gradients with descriptive names like Late Sunset and Ocean

Shading styles determine orientation of the gradient

Click to apply the selected gradient temporarily without closing the dialog box

Figure 3-22 Title Slide with finished drawing

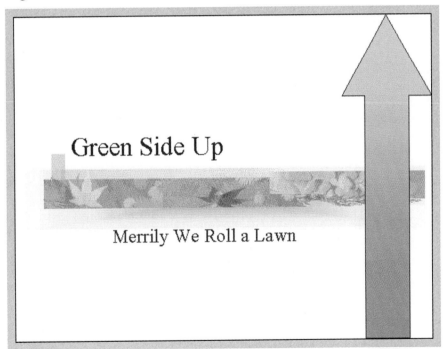

PowerPoint 2000

Practice

Open **Prac3-7** and follow the instructions on the slide. Save the file as **MyPrac3-7** when you are done.

Hot Tip

You can double-click a drawn object to open a Format dialog box tailored specifically for that object.

Modifying and Enhancing Drawn Objects

Concept

Occasionally when you add a drawn object to a presentation, it does not accomplish exactly what you had imagined it would. Fortunately, drawings such as AutoShapes can be modified so that they work better within the scheme of a slide. This includes enhancing the object itself and changing how the object interacts with the other elements on the slide.

Do It!

Trista wants to add a shadow to the AutoShape she drew on her Title Slide.

1 Click the Block Arrow on Slide 1 to select it.

2 Click the Shadow button ▣ on the Drawing toolbar. A menu of shadow types will appear.

3 Click Shadow Style 3, the third shadow in the first row. A shadow will be cast from the Block Arrow's base through the middle of the slide, as shown in **Figure 3-23**.

4 Click the Draw button ⌜Draw ▾⌝ on the Drawing toolbar to open the Draw menu.

5 Highlight the Order command on the Draw menu to open its submenu. The Order submenu contains commands that allow you to layer the objects on your slides according to your needs. Since the Block Arrow was the last object you added, it is on the top layer in the order, and its shadow is blocking the subtitle text **Merrily We Roll a Lawn**.

6 Click Send to Back on the Order submenu. The Arrow and its shadow are sent to the back of the order, revealing the text that was hidden (see **Figure 3-24**). Notice that the shadow still passes in front of the decorative band in the middle of the slide. The order of elements that are part of the Design Template cannot be changed, so they will always be behind any elements you add.

7 Deselect the Block Arrow and save your file.

More

Even though a shadow is part of the object to which it has been applied, some aspects of a shadow can be modified independently. With the object selected, click the Shadow button ▣ , and then click the Shadow Settings command. The **Shadow Settings** toolbar, shown in **Figure 3-25**, will appear. The buttons on this toolbar allow you to turn a shadow on or off; nudge it up, down, left, or right; and change its color and opacity.

The Send Backward command enables you to send an object down one place in the layering order rather than all the way to the bottom layer. The **Send to Front** and **Send Forward** commands mirror the Send to Back and Send Backward commands.

Figure 3-23 Adding a shadow to a drawing

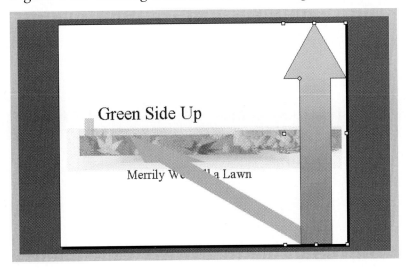

Figure 3-24 Arrow and shadow sent to back

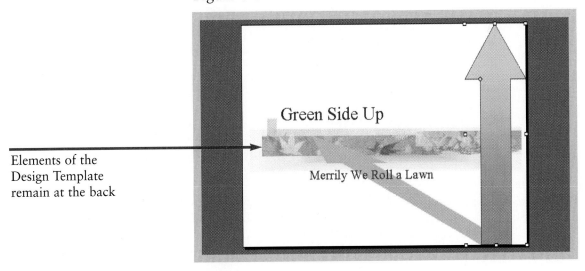

Elements of the
Design Template
remain at the back

Figure 3-25 Shadow Settings toolbar

Depressed button
indicates shadow is on

Click to change shadow color

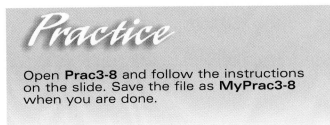

Practice

Open **Prac3-8** and follow the instructions on the slide. Save the file as **MyPrac3-8** when you are done.

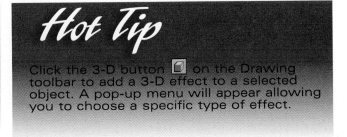

Hot Tip

Click the 3-D button on the Drawing toolbar to add a 3-D effect to a selected object. A pop-up menu will appear allowing you to choose a specific type of effect.

Shortcuts

Function	Button/Mouse	Menu	Keyboard
Bold text	B	Click Format, then Font, and select Bold	[Ctrl]+[B]
Italicize text	I	Click Format, then Font, and select Italic	[Ctrl]+[I]
Underline text	U	Click Format, then Font, and select Underline	[Ctrl]+[U]
Apply Text Shadow	S	Click Format, then Font, and select Shadow	
Center alignment		Click Format, then highlight Alignment, then click Center	[Ctrl]+[E]
Align Left		Click Format, then highlight Alignment, then click Align Left	[Ctrl]+[L]
Right alignment		Click Format, then highlight Alignment, then click Align Right	[Ctrl]+[R]
Spelling	ABC✓	Click Tools, then click Spelling	[F7]
Increase font size	A	Click Format, then click Font	[Ctrl]+[Shift]+[>]
Decrease font size	A	Click Format, then click Font	[Ctrl]+[Shift]+[<]

Identify Key Features

Name the items indicated by callout arrows in **Figure 3-26**.

Figure 3-26 Elements of the Formatting and Drawing toolbars

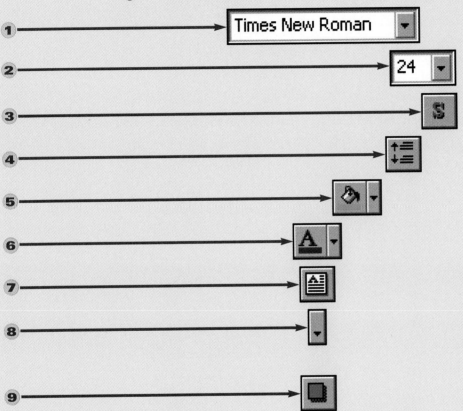

Select the Best Answer

10. Fixes spelling errors automatically as you type
11. Allows you to ignore or change a misspelled word
12. Leads to a list of abbreviations after which the next word will not be capitalized
13. Offers a full range of text formatting options
14. Allows you to teach PowerPoint words it does not know so that they will not be marked as misspelled
15. Contains options for filling an object with a gradient
16. An example of an AutoShape
17. Permits you to make global changes to a presentation's text

a. Block Arrow
b. Font dialog box
c. Replace All button
d. AutoCorrect
e. Fill Effects dialog box
f. Spelling dialog box
g. Add button
h. Exceptions button

PowerPoint 2000

Quiz (continued)

Complete the Statement

18. A text box that automatically wraps to the next line when the insertion point reaches its boundary is a:

    a. Text label text box

    b. Title text box

    c. Flex box

    d. Word processing text box

19. To move an object to the top level of a slide, choose the:

    a. Send Forward command

    b. Send Backward command

    c. Send to Front command

    d. Send to Back command

20. The Replace command is found:

    a. In the Spelling dialog box

    b. On the Edit menu

    c. On the Standard toolbar

    d. On the Editing toolbar

21. The text alignment option that is not available on the Standard toolbar is:

    a. Left

    b. Right

    c. Center

    d. Justify

22. If you are adding a single word or short phrase to a slide, it is best to use a:

    a. Text label text box

    b. Word processing text box

    c. Text shadow

    d. Bold font

23. The Rotate or Flip and Order commands are located on the:

    a. Standard toolbar

    b. Edit menu

    c. Formatting toolbar

    d. Draw menu

24. All of the following control font size except the:

    a. Font box

    b. Font Size box

    c. Increase/Decrease Font Size buttons

    d. Font dialog box

25. The yellow diamond attached to a selected object is called the:

    a. Sizing handle

    b. Adjustment handle

    c. Move handle

    d. Free Rotate tool

Interactivity

Test Your Skills

1. Practice entering and moving text:

   a. Open a new file starting with a Blank presentation.

   b. Choose a blank slide for your first slide.

   c. Apply the design **Notebook** to the presentation.

   d. Use the Text Box button to create a text label box in the middle of the slide.

   e. In the box type **My Family**.

   f. Move the text box above the solid line near the top of the slide and to the left side.

   g. Click the Text Box button again and drag a large word processing box in the area of the slide below the line.

   h. Type a brief history of your family in this text box.

2. Practice formatting text:

   a. Click the **My Family** text box to activate it.

   b. Drag the sizing handle in the middle of the right side to the right edge of the slide's light area.

   c. Center the text.

   d. Make the text **bold** and increase its size to **40** point.

   e. Click the lower text box to activate it.

   f. Increase the **paragraph spacing** slightly and *italicize* the text.

3. Build and refine your presentation:

   a. Using the **Blank Slide AutoLayout**, add a slide for each member of your family.

   b. Format each slide as you did the first one, replacing My Family with the family member's name and the brief history with a description of the family member.

   c. Format the text on each of the new slides with a different color.

   d. Use Find and Replace to replace all instances of the phrase My Family with The [Insert Last Name] Family.

   e. When you are done, Spell Check the presentation. If your last name is not in PowerPoint's dictionary, add it to the Custom dictionary.

Interactivity (continued)

4. Add, format, and modify drawing objects:

   a. Select the AutoShape **5-Point Star**.

   b. Draw the 5-Point Star on **Slide 1** of your presentation, adjusting the size and location of the slide's text boxes if necessary.

   c. Fill the star with a **Two color** gradient that uses the **Vertical** Shading style and consists of the **Fills Scheme Color** and the **Accent Scheme Color**.

   d. Apply **Shadow Style 2** to the star.

   e. Draw the **32-Point Star** AutoShape over the 5-Point Star, slightly larger.

   f. Change the color of the 32-Point Star to the Accent Scheme Color.

   g. Use the **Order** command to move the 32-Point Star behind the 5-Point Star.

Problem Solving

1. After years of toiling at an unfulfilling nine-to-five job, you have finally saved enough money to quit and realize your dream of opening a small country inn. Use PowerPoint to create an eight-slide introductory brochure that you can show to some of the investors who are helping you get your new business started. Since the inn is still in its planning stages, the presentation will consist mostly of text that describes what the inn will look like, where it will be located, the general atmosphere you hope to provide, and other kinds of information that would be important to travelers. Use text formatting, AutoShapes, and Fill Colors to make the brochure interesting and lively. Be sure to check your presentation for spelling errors. Save the presentation as **Solved3-1.ppt**.

2. Peppercorn's, a national chain of steakhouses, has hired you to do some freelance design work for their advertising department. The company is launching a print advertising campaign that will place adds in five major magazines. They want to use a different half-page ad in each of the five magazines so that the ads are geared toward specific readers. You have been asked to provide first drafts of the five ads in the form of a PowerPoint presentation so the director of advertising can preview them. The five magazines that will be running the ads are *Sports Digest*, *Women's Quarterly*, *Men Today*, *Entertainment Extract*, and *News Now*. Save your presentation as **Solved3-2.ppt**.

Interactivity (continued)

3. Use PowerPoint to recreate the slide shown in **Figure PS3a**. Then make the appropriate changes to the slide so that it resembles **Figure PS3b**. Print a copy of each slide.

Figure PS3a

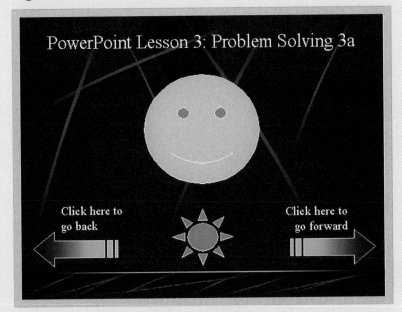

Figure PS3b

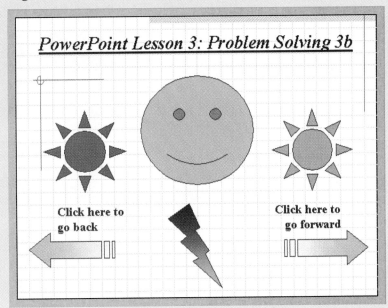

PowerPoint 2000

Interactivity (continued)

4. Use PowerPoint to recreate the slide shown in **Figure PS4a**. Then make the appropriate changes to the slide so that it resembles **Figure PS4b**. Print a copy of each slide.

Figure PS4a

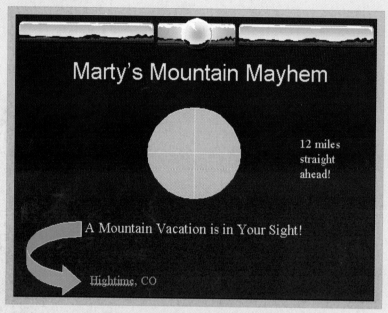

Figure PS4b

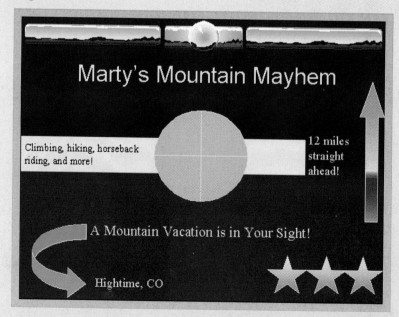

LESSON 4

STRENGTHENING YOUR PRESENTATION

A strong presentation requires more than just text and simple shapes to make it an interesting and visually stimulating slide show. You can enhance your presentation with detailed pictures provided by PowerPoint called Clip Art. Once you insert a piece of Clip Art, you will find that you can edit and format it so that it is compatible with your particular presentation. You also will learn how to insert your own image files into a presentation.

Another important visual aspect of a presentation is the manner in which data are represented. Raw statistics serve an important purpose but sometimes lack effectiveness when presented as such. PowerPoint allows you to create graphical charts to display any kind of data. Different chart types, such as line, bar, or pie, are available so you can choose the type that fits your data best. Once you have created a chart, you can control its placement on the slide, the colors and sizes of individual chart objects, its text style, and its overall size.

The end product of most PowerPoint presentations is a slide show, where the slides are displayed with all of the graphics, text, and other features that were included in their creation. Though a presentation can be created solely for the purpose of producing paper copies or overhead transparencies, PowerPoint's true strengths show through when the slides are animated and presented on a computer screen. Using the program's slide transition features, you can control exactly how each slide will make its appearance on the screen and how much time it will remain there before the presentation advances to the next slide. You also can predetermine whether slides will advance on their own or with a prompt from the presenter.

CASE STUDY
In this lesson, Trista will add pictures to her presentation, both from Microsoft's Clip Gallery and from her own file. She also will transform raw data she has accumulated into a chart, and then customize the chart to her needs and preferences. Finally, she will add transition effects to her slides and set slide timings.

Adding Clip Art

Concept

You have already seen how you can enhance your presentation by drawing objects such as AutoShapes. To take the visual aspect of your presentation a step further, you may want to use Clip Art. Clip Art is a collection of ready-made pictures that PowerPoint provides for the user. Clip Art pictures are more numerous, varied, and generally more detailed than drawings created with AutoShapes.

Do It!

Trista would like to add Clip Art to her presentation.

1 Open GSU Presentation 3 and save it as GSU Presentation 4.

2 Go to Slide 2 in the presentation, the slide titled Growing to meet your needs.

3 Click Insert, then highlight Picture, then click Clip Art. The Insert Clip Art dialog box will open. If the dialog box that appears on your screen is tall and thin and only displays one column of categories, click the Change to Full Window ⊡ button so that the dialog box looks like **Figure 4-1**. The Pictures tab contains 57 categories of pictures that you can browse by clicking their icons. You also can search for a specific type of picture.

4 Click the text in the Search for clips: text box to select it. Then type ribbons and press [Enter]. PowerPoint will search the Clip Gallery for a picture that matches the description and display its findings on the tab.

5 Place the mouse pointer over the picture of a man holding a red prize ribbon. A ScreenTip containing the picture's name and file size will appear.

6 Click the red ribbon picture. A menu will appear beside it, giving you several options (see **Figure 4-2**).

7 Click the top button on the menu, Insert clip 🖾. Then close the dialog box. The picture will appear on the slide, as shown in **Figure 4-3**.

More

If you know that a particular slide in your presentation will include Clip Art, you can choose an AutoLayout slide that is designed for that purpose. For example, if you add a Text and Clip Art slide to your presentation, it will include a placeholder for inserting Clip Art as part of its AutoLayout. When you double-click on the placeholder, the Microsoft Clip Gallery will open.

The Insert Clip Art dialog box is completely customizable. To move a clip from one category to another, select the clip, click the Copy button 🖺, select the new category, and then click the Paste button 🖺. You also can move or copy a picture file from another storage location into the Insert Clip Art dialog box by clicking the Import Clips button 🖺 Import Clips . Finally, if you have an Internet connection, you can access additional clips by clicking the Clips Online button 🌐 Clips Online . This will connect you to the Microsoft Clip Gallery Live, which allows you to download clips from Microsoft's Web site to the Insert Clip Art dialog box.

Figure 4-1 Insert Clip Art dialog box

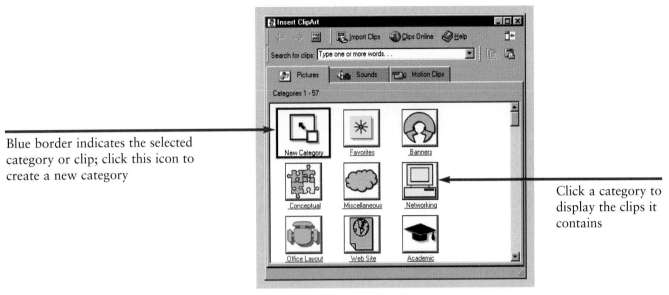

Blue border indicates the selected category or clip; click this icon to create a new category

Click a category to display the clips it contains

Figure 4-2 Inserting Clip Art

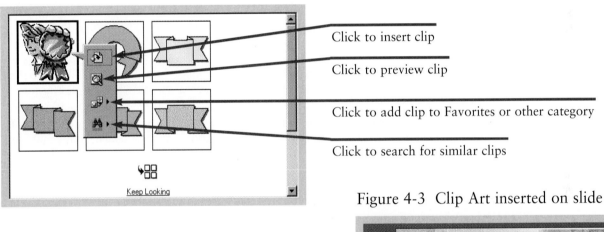

Click to insert clip

Click to preview clip

Click to add clip to Favorites or other category

Click to search for similar clips

Figure 4-3 Clip Art inserted on slide

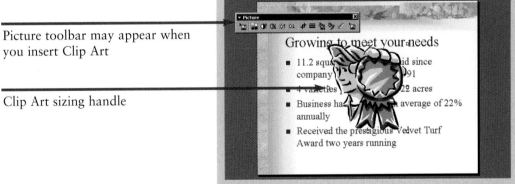

Picture toolbar may appear when you insert Clip Art

Clip Art sizing handle

PowerPoint 2000

Practice

Open the file **Prac4-1** and follow the instructions on the slide. Save the file as **MyPrac4-1**.

Hot Tip

The standard installation of PowerPoint does not provide files for the **Sounds** and **Motion Clips** tabs in the Insert Clip Art dialog box. You can add your own files or download clips from the Microsoft Clip Gallery Live.

Editing Clip Art

Concept

Clip Art files are quality, finished pictures. They have particular dimensions and colors that are part of the file. However, like other objects you insert into a PowerPoint slide, they can be repositioned, resized, and reformatted to fit the slide on which they appear. Most characteristics of a piece of Clip Art can be altered by using the Picture toolbar.

Do It!

Trista wants to resize the ribbon Clip Art she inserted and move it to its appropriate place on the slide. Then she will change the picture's color so it matches the scheme of her presentation.

1. The Clip Art you inserted in the last Skill should still be selected on Slide 2 (simply click the picture if it is not selected). If the Picture toolbar is not active, click View, then highlight Toolbars, and click Picture on the submenu.

2. Click the Format Picture ☒ button on the Picture toolbar. The Format Picture dialog box will open.

3. Click the Size tab to bring it to the front of the dialog box. The Size and rotate section of the tab allows you to adjust the height and width of the picture using linear measurements such as inches. The Scale section of the tab allows you to adjust the height and width as a percentage of the picture's original size, which is displayed at the bottom of the tab. When the Lock aspect ratio check box is checked, changing the height will alter the width in the proper proportion, and vice versa (activate this check box now if necessary).

4. Double-click the current value in the Scale section's Height: box, 100%, to select it.

5. Type the number 50 to replace the original value, as shown in Figure 4-4.

6. Click [OK] to close the dialog box and make the Scale change. Though you didn't see it change, the value in the Width: box was also changed from 100% to 50% because the aspect ratio was locked. The Clip Art picture should now appear on the slide at half its original size (see Figure 4-5).

7. Place the mouse pointer over the picture and hold down the mouse button. Then drag down and to the right until the outline of the picture is directly below the phrase Velvet Turf. Release the mouse button to drop the picture in its proper place, as shown in Figure 4-6. Notice that the picture runs over the bottom edge of the slide.

8. Click ☒ again to return to the Format Picture dialog box. In the Size tab's Size and rotate section, click the down arrow in the Height: box until the value reaches 1.49". Notice that the Width: box value and the percentages in the Scale section change as well.

9. Click [OK]. The picture now fits neatly on the slide.

Figure 4-4 Format Picture dialog box

Adjusting height changes width in the proper proportion because aspect ratio is locked

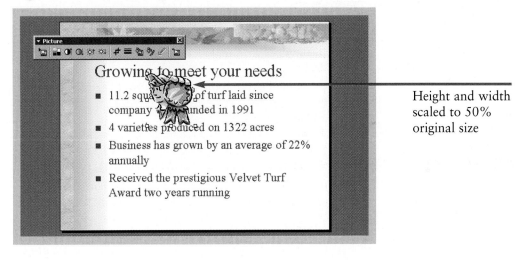

Figure 4-5 Scaled Clip Art

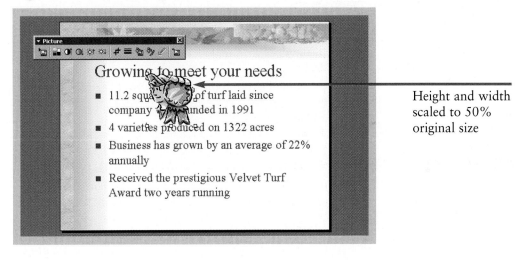

Height and width scaled to 50% original size

Figure 4-6 Moving Clip Art

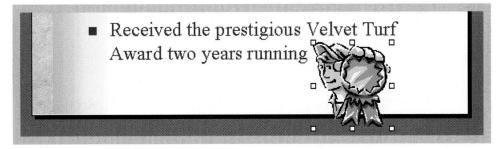

Editing Clip Art
(continued)

Do It!

10 Click the Recolor Picture button ![icon] on the Picture toolbar. The Recolor Picture dialog box will appear. The dialog box, shown in **Figure 4-7**, consists of a series of boxes that display every color used in the picture. Next to each of these boxes is a corresponding selection box that allows you to change a color everywhere that it appears in the picture. The right half of the dialog box lets you preview how your color changes will look before you actually apply them to the picture.

11 Click the Fills radio button in the Change section of the dialog box. This excludes lines from the list of items you can change, leaving only background and fill colors available for editing.

12 Click the arrow on the right end of the third color box listed in the New: column (this is the color of the ribbon itself). A color palette will appear.

13 Click Automatic to select your Design Template's Automatic Fill Color (light blue).

14 Change the fourth orignal color listed (red) to the fourth color on the palette (dark blue, Follow Title Text Scheme Color).

15 Click [OK] to make the color changes and close the dialog box.

16 Close the Picture toolbar and deselect the picture. Your slide should resemble **Figure 4-8**.

17 Save the changes you have made to your presentation.

More

In the preceding exercise, you used the Format Picture dialog box's Size tab to resize a Clip Art picture. If you are not concerned about exact measurements, you can resize Clip Art by dragging its sizing handles, just like other objects. The Crop tool ![icon] available on the Picture toolbar lets you hide part of a graphic from view. Using this tool you can adjust a picture's frame without resizing the image at the same time, and thereby use the frame to cut off portions of the graphic you do not wish to display.

Figure 4-7 Recolor Picture dialog box

Recolor Picture
Original:
New:
OK
Cancel
Preview
Change
Colors
Fills
Description
Allows you to change any color in the picture.

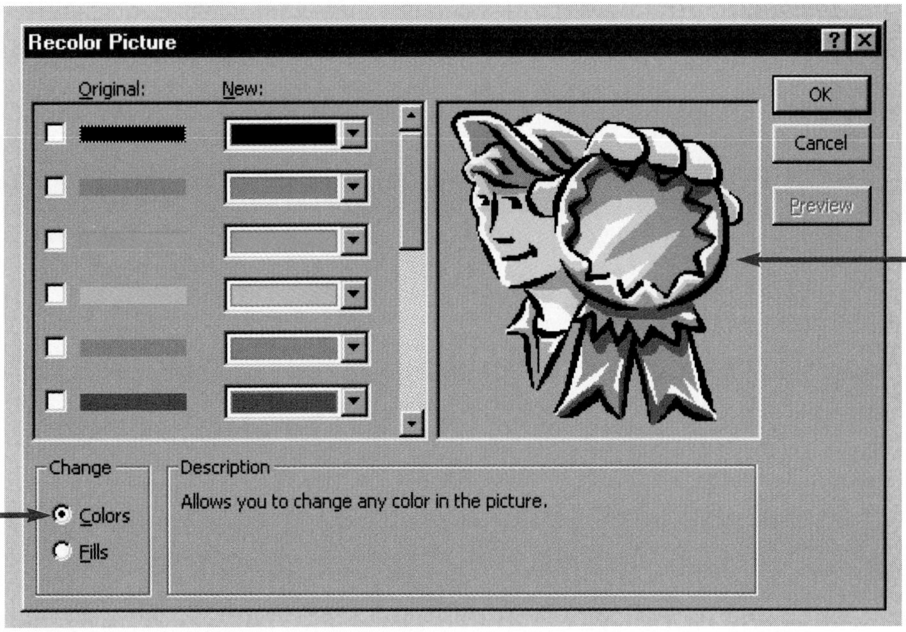

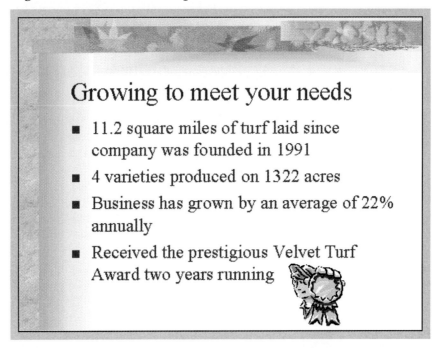

Color changes are reflected in Preview box

Allows you to change all colors including lines

Figure 4-8 Recolored Clip Art

Growing to meet your needs
11.2 square miles of turf laid since company was founded in 1991
4 varieties produced on 1322 acres
Business has grown by an average of 22% annually
Received the prestigious Velvet Turf Award two years running

PowerPoint 2000

Practice

Open the file **Prac4-2** and follow the instructions on the slide. Save the file as **MyPrac4-2**.

Hot Tip

A selected picture that has been altered can be returned to its original state by clicking the Reset Picture button on the Picture toolbar.

Inserting a Picture from a File

Concept

When adding graphics to a presentation, you are not limited to the clips found in the Insert Clip Art dialog box. If you are handy with image or drawing software, or if you have other art files available to you, you can insert your own pictures in a presentation.

Do It!

Trista wants to insert a picture she created with Windows 98's Paint program in one of her slides. Then she will crop the picture.

1 Go to Slide 6 of GSU Presentation 4.

2 Click Insert, highlight Picture, and then click From File. The Insert Picture dialog box will appear.

3 Use the Look in: box to select the drive, folder, or other location that contains your Student Files folder. Double-click the folder in the dialog box's contents window to open the folder.

4 Click the file named Check box to select it in the contents window. A preview of the picture will appear in the right half of the dialog box (see **Figure 4-9**).

5 Click the Insert button [Insert ▼]. The dialog box closes and the Check box picture appears in the middle of the slide. Use the Toolbars command on the View menu to activate the Picture toolbar.

6 Click the Crop button [⌗] on the Picture toolbar to activate the Crop tool.

7 Place the mouse pointer over the sizing handle in the middle of the picture's right side. The pointer will change to the icon on the Crop button.

8 Click the sizing handle with the Crop tool and drag to the left until the right border of the picture has completely cut off the text Check! (be careful not to cut off the top of the check mark). Then release the mouse button. The text portion of the picture disappears.

9 Use the arrow keys on the keyboard to nudge the cropped picture so that it is centered on the slide and spaced evenly between Recently Acquired Accounts and Argyle County Municipal Stadium.

10 Deselect the Crop tool and the picture and save your changes. Your slide should now look like the one shown in **Figure 4-10**.

More

PowerPoint allows you to insert a variety of image file formats into a presentation. Pictures made with the Paint program are bitmap files, represented by the file extension .bmp. The Clip Art files that come with PowerPoint are Windows metafiles, represented by the extension .wmf. In general, you can edit other image file types just like Clip Art, but there are some exceptions. For example, you would not be able to use the Recolor Picture feature on a bitmap.

Figure 4-9 Insert Picture dialog box

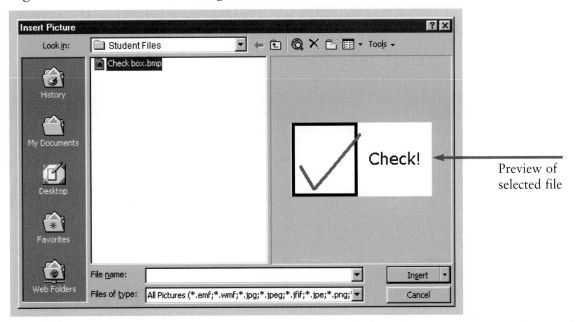

Preview of selected file

Figure 4-10 Cropped picture inserted from file

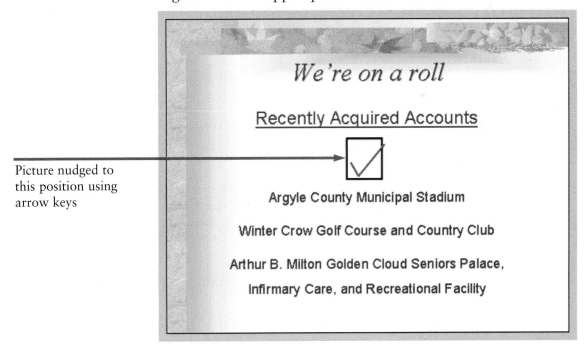

Picture nudged to this position using arrow keys

We're on a roll

Recently Acquired Accounts

Argyle County Municipal Stadium

Winter Crow Golf Course and Country Club

Arthur B. Milton Golden Cloud Seniors Palace,
Infirmary Care, and Recreational Facility

PowerPoint 2000

Practice

Create a one-slide presentation and insert the picture file **Prac4-3** from your Student Files folder. Save the new presentation as **MyPrac4-3**.

Hot Tip

If you click on the arrow on the right edge of the Insert button in the Insert Picture dialog box, you can choose to link the picture you are inserting to its source file. Then, any changes made to the source file also will be reflected in the presentation.

Inserting a Chart

Concept

As you become more skilled at designing a presentation, you will discover that certain types of information are presented best through certain media. So far, the content of your presentation has used mostly text to express its key points. Some data, such as numbers and statistics, make a greater impact on the viewer when they are displayed graphically as a chart. PowerPoint allows you to embed a chart in a slide, while still permitting you to alter its data and appearance.

Do It!

Trista has gathered some data that compare Green Side Up favorably to several competitors. She would like to present these data as a chart on a new slide.

1. With your presentation on Slide 6, click ▨ to open the New Slide dialog box. Choose the Chart AutoLayout, which includes a placeholder for a chart, and title the new Slide 7 How our sod stacks up.

2. Double-click the chart placeholder to launch **Microsoft Graph 2000**, a separate application used to create charts in Office 2000 files. A datasheet filled in with default data will appear over the slide, and a chart that corresponds to the default data will be embedded in the slide (see **Figure 4-11**). Graph 2000 inserts the default data so that the chart has structure until you enter your own data. The datasheet consists of rows, which are numbered, and columns, which are lettered. The point where a column and a row intersect is known as a cell. Cells are named by combining their column letter and row number. Thus, the first cell in the datasheet is named **A1**. The text entries in the cells in the left column and top row of the datasheet are data labels that describe the data that follow them to the right or below. The actual data that occupy a column or row are called a data series. A data series is represented in a chart by a data series marker, which is a graphical object such as a bar, line, column, or pie piece.

3. When the mouse pointer is over the datasheet, it changes to ✛, a pointer you may recognize if you have used Microsoft Excel. The active cell in a datasheet is indicated by a thick border around it, known as the cell pointer. You can change the active cell by clicking on a new cell, or by moving the cell pointer with the arrow keys on the keyboard.

4. Click cell **A2** to make it the active cell, as shown in **Figure 4-12**.

5. Click outside the chart on Slide 7 to exit Microsoft Graph. Save your presentation.

More

Inserting a chart does not require that you add a Chart AutoLayout slide to a presentation. You can add a chart to any slide by choosing the Chart command from the Insert menu, or by clicking the Insert Chart button ▥ on the Standard toolbar. Both operations launch Graph 2000 as you did above by double-clicking the chart placeholder. You will notice that the Standard toolbar transforms whenever Graph 2000 is running to include buttons related to working with charts.

Figure 4-11 Inserting chart

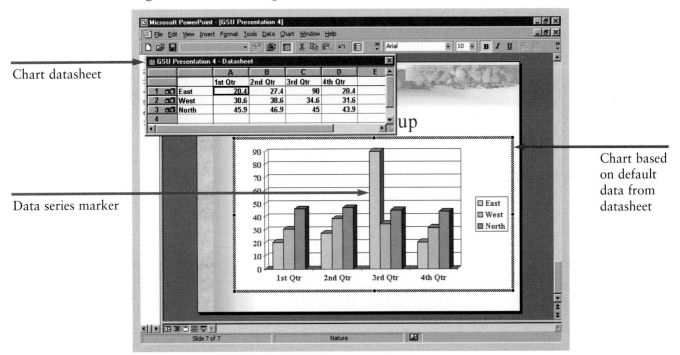

Chart datasheet

Data series marker

Chart based on default data from datasheet

Figure 4-12 Default datasheet

Columns run vertically

Rows run horizontally

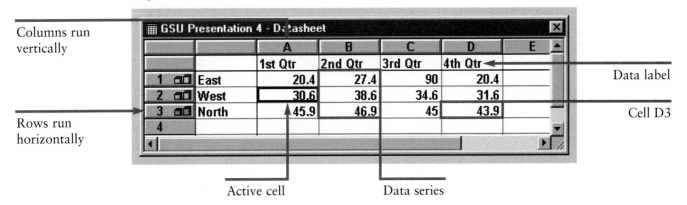

Data label

Cell D3

Active cell

Data series

PowerPoint 2000

Practice

Open file **Prac4-4** and follow the instructions on the slide. Save the file as **MyPrac4-4**.

Hot Tip

The standard PowerPoint menu commands also will be replaced by chart-related commands when Microsoft Graph 2000 is running.

Customizing the Datasheet

Concept

Once you have inserted a chart in a PowerPoint slide, you need to edit the datasheet so that the resulting chart reflects your own data and not the default data provided by the application. Otherwise, your chart will have no significance to the presentation. The datasheet window is always available to you, so you can edit a chart as often as is necessary.

Do It!

Trista will enter her comparison data in her chart's datasheet.

1 Double-click the chart on Slide 7 to open Graph 2000 and the datasheet.

2 Click the blank cell above the East data label and to the left of the 1st Qtr label.

3 Type Sod Farms and then press [Enter] to confirm the data label and select the cell below it that contains the East data label.

4 Type Green Side Up to replace the East label and press [Enter] again.

5 Type Lawns by Larry to replace the West label, press [Enter], type Marquis de Sod to replace the North label, press [Enter], type Turfin' USA in the blank cell, and press [Tab].

6 Click the cell that contains the 1st Qtr label to select it, replace the label with Acres Growing and then press [Tab]. Replace the 2nd Qtr label with Acres Installed Last Year and press [Tab] again.

7 Right-click (click with the right mouse button) the selector button [C] at the top of column C, and then click the Delete command on the pop-up menu that appears. Repeat the process to delete the data that moved into column C when you deleted it the first time.

8 Enter the following numbers to complete the datasheet:

Cell A1: 1322	Cell B1: 694
Cell A2: 923	Cell B2: 420
Cell A3: 896	Cell B3: 346
Cell A4: 890	Cell B4: 402

Your completed datasheet should now look like **Figure 4-13**.

9 Click a blank area of the presentation window to close the datasheet and Graph 2000. The chart on Slide 7 will be updated with your data, shown in **Figure 4-14**.

10 Save your presentation.

More

When you are working in Graph 2000, you can point to any data series marker with the mouse pointer to receive a ScreenTip that summarizes the marker. For example, if you pointed to the first column, the ScreenTip would say Series "Green Side Up" Point "Acres Growing" Value: 1322. These ScreenTips will appear only when the chart is selected, not when the datasheet is selected.

Figure 4-13 Completed datasheet

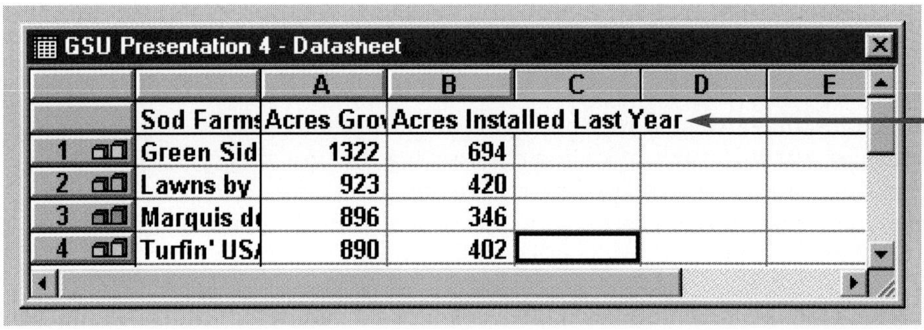

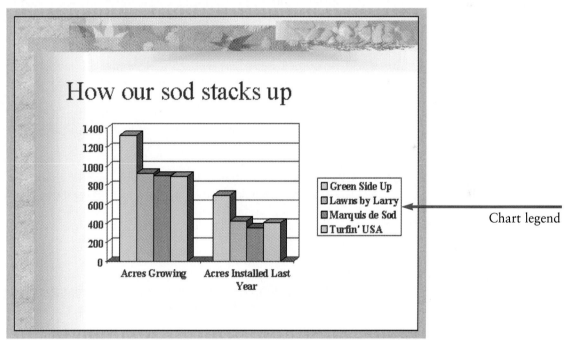

This data label is displayed fully because the cell to the right of it is empty; labels that are cut off will appear completely in the chart

Figure 4-14 Updated chart

Chart legend

Practice

Open the file **Prac4-5** and follow the instructions on the slide. Save the file as **MyPrac4-5**.

Hot Tip

If you need to work with your chart's datasheet but it does not appear when you double-click the chart, click the View Datasheet button 🔲 on the Standard toolbar.

Changing a Chart's Type

Concept

When you inserted a chart earlier in this lesson, PowerPoint's default choice for the type of chart was a Clustered Column chart with a 3-D visual effect. Even after you have finished a chart, you still can change its type. You may want to do this because you think another chart type will represent your data better, or simply because it interacts better with the other slide elements.

Do It!

Trista wants to change her chart from a Clustered Column to a Clustered Bar chart.

1. Double-click the chart on Slide 7. Close the Datasheet window if it appears.

2. Click Chart on the menu bar, and then click the Chart Type command. The Chart Type dialog box will open to its Standard Types tab. The Chart type: scrolling list box displays the basic chart types you can use in PowerPoint. The Chart sub-type: section to the right of this list box displays the sub-types available for the chart type that is selected in the list box. The sub-type highlighted in black is the one that is currently in use.

3. Click Bar in the list of chart types to select it and display its sub-types. The first sub-type, Clustered Bar, will be selected automatically.

4. Click the sub-type directly below Clustered Bar to select it. Its description, which appears below the sub-types, should read Clustered bar with a 3-D visual effect, as shown in **Figure 4-15**.

5. Click ▢OK▢ to close the dialog box and change the chart type. Deselect the chart, which should look like the one shown in **Figure 4-16**, and save your changes.

More

Table 4-1 Common chart types

CHART TYPE	DESCRIPTION	EXAMPLE
Column	Data changes over time or quantitative comparisons among items	Quarterly income projections
Bar	Similar to a column chart, but horizontal orientation places more value on the *X* value	Individual sales performance
Line	Trends in data at fixed intervals	Tracking stock trends
Pie	The percentage each value contributes to the whole. Used for a single data series	Budgets, chief exports of a country
XY (Scatter)	Comparative relationships between seemingly dissimilar data	Scientific data analysis
Surface	The range of intersections between two sets of data	Optimal fuel consumption

Figure 4-15 Chart Type dialog box

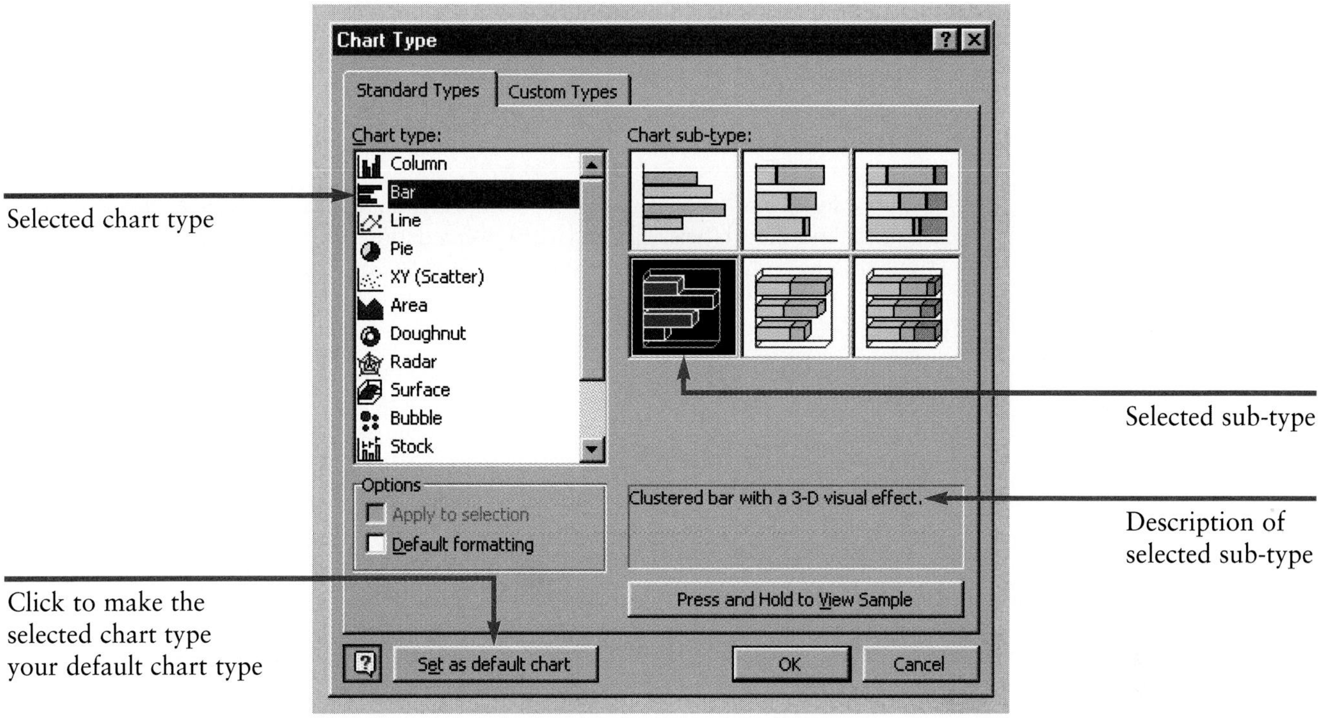

Selected chart type

Click to make the
selected chart type
your default chart type

Selected sub-type

Description of
selected sub-type

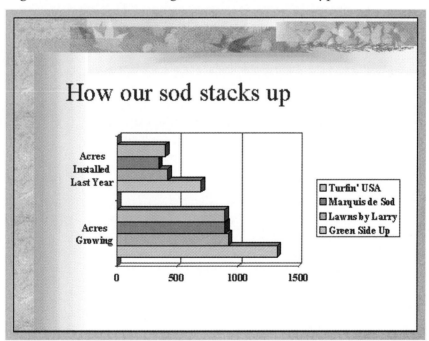

Figure 4-16 Chart changed to Clustered Bar type

Practice

Open **MyPrac4-5** and change the chart on
Slide 2 to a Line chart. Save the file as
MyPrac4-6.

Hot Tip

Click and hold the long button labeled
Press and Hold to View Sample in the
Chart Type dialog box to preview your
chart with its new type without changing
the actual chart.

Setting Chart Options

Concept

A chart can be made up of numerous components including a legend, titles, axes, gridlines, and data labels. The Chart Options dialog box allows you to determine how and where these items will appear, or if they will appear at all.

Do It!

Trista has decided to give her chart a title and reposition the chart's legend.

1. Double-click the chart on Slide 7.

2. Click Chart on the menu bar, then click Chart Options. The Chart Options dialog box opens. The dialog box contains six tabs, each of which allows you to control certain aspects of a chart. Each tab also includes a preview of the chart that reflects your changes as soon as you make them.

3. If not already in front, click the Titles tab to bring it to the front of the dialog box. Then click in the text box labeled Chart title: to place the insertion point there.

4. Type Growth Comparison for Industry Leaders. The title will appear in the text box and in the preview, as shown in **Figure 4-17**. Do not worry if the preview appears crowded as the actual chart will be displayed correctly.

5. Click the Legend tab to activate it.

6. The Placement option for the legend is currently set to Right. Click the radio button labeled Top to move the legend above the chart.

7. Click OK to accept the settings you have changed. The new Chart Options are shown on the deselected chart in **Figure 4-18**.

8. Save the changes you have made to the presentation.

More

After you alter Chart Options, you may need to adjust the size of the chart to accommodate items that you have moved or added. You can do this without working in Graph 2000. If you click on a chart once, it will be selected just like a text box or other object you have inserted. You will then be able to resize the chart by dragging one of its eight sizing handles. You also may reposition the entire chart by dragging it from its center.

Figure 4-17 Chart Options dialog box

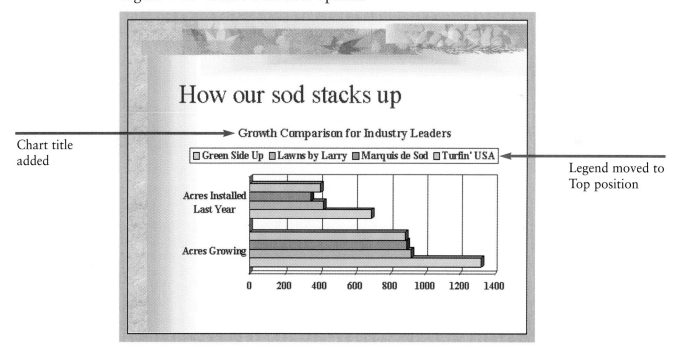

Use these text boxes to
title individual axes

Figure 4-18 Chart with new options

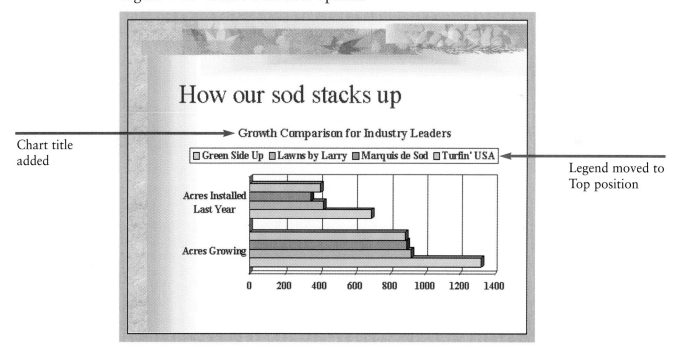

Chart title
added

Legend moved to
Top position

PowerPoint 2000

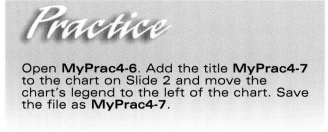

Practice

Open **MyPrac4-6**. Add the title **MyPrac4-7**
to the chart on Slide 2 and move the
chart's legend to the left of the chart. Save
the file as **MyPrac4-7**.

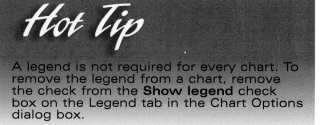

Hot Tip

A legend is not required for every chart. To
remove the legend from a chart, remove
the check from the **Show legend** check
box on the Legend tab in the Chart Options
dialog box.

Formatting Chart Elements

Concept

Now that you have learned how to convert a chart to a completely different type and modify its general structure, it is time to learn how to improve your chart by working with individual elements. You can modify many aspects of a chart including its text, colors, textures, and organization. Though the chart can be selected as a single entity, each of its components also can be selected and formatted individually. This flexibility permits you to enhance the overall appearance of the chart and call attention to specific data.

Do It!

Trista wants to italicize and change the color and font of her Category Axis labels, increase her chart depth, and add texture to one of her data series markers.

1. Double-click the chart to open Graph 2000. You do not need to view the datasheet.

2. Click the Category Axis label Acres Installed Last Year on the chart to select the entire Category Axis.

3. Click **I** on the Formatting toolbar to italicize the two Category Axis labels.

4. Click Format on the menu bar, and then click Selected Axis. The Format Axis dialog box appears.

5. Click the Font tab to bring it to the front of the dialog box. Notice that **Bold Italic** is selected in the Font style: list box, as shown in **Figure 4-19**. The Bold style formatting was applied automatically when you created the chart.

6. Click the drop-down arrow on the right end of the Color: box, which currently says Automatic. A color palette will open.

7. Click the Red color square at the beginning of the third row of the palette.

8. Click **OK** to close the dialog box and make the color change.

9. With the Category Axis still selected, use the Formatting toolbar's Font box to change the font from Times New Roman to Arial. The Category Axis labels should be formatted like those shown in **Figure 4-20**.

10. Click one of the two horizonatal bars that represent Green Side Up's data in the chart. Both Green Side Up data series markers will be selected.

11. Click Format, then click Selected Data Series. The Format Data Series dialog box will appear.

12. Click the Options tab to bring it to the front of the dialog box, as shown in **Figure 4-21**.

Figure 4-19 Font tab of Format Axis dialog box

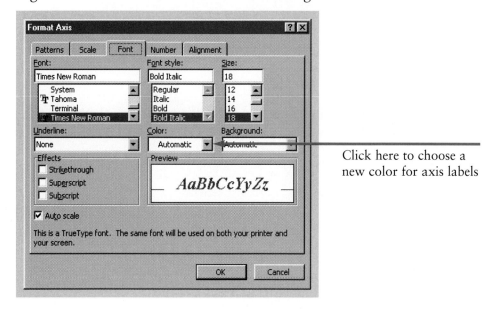

Click here to choose a
new color for axis labels

Figure 4-20 Chart with font change

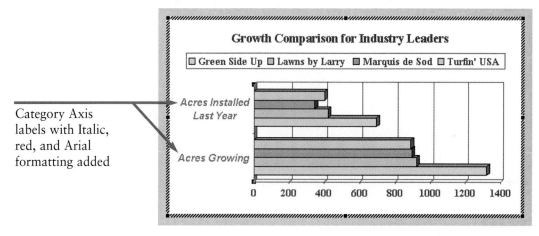

Category Axis
labels with Italic,
red, and Arial
formatting added

PowerPoint 2000

Figure 4-21 Format Data Series dialog box

Sets distance between data
markers in a 3-D chart

Sets distance between data
categories in chart

Sets depth of chart relative
to its width

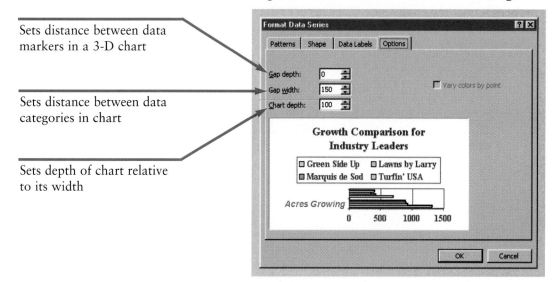

Formatting Chart Elements (continued)

Do It!

13 Double-click inside the Chart depth: box to select its current value. Type 1000 to replace the value with a new one.

14 Click [OK] to close the dialog box and confirm the depth change. Your chart should resemble **Figure 4-22**. Notice that even though only one data series marker was selected, this option affects all of the data series markers.

15 With the Green Side Up data series still selected, click the Format Data Series button [ ] on the Standard toolbar. The Format Data Series dialog box should open to the Patterns tab (click the Patterns tab if it does not).

16 Click the Fill Effects button [Fill Effects...] at the bottom of the Patterns tab's Area section. The Fill Effects dialog box appears.

17 Click the Texture tab to bring it to the front of the dialog box. The Texture tab offers a number of premade textures that you can apply to a chart object. When you click on a texture to select it, its name will appear below the Texture: box. You also can apply your own texture if you have an image file available.

18 Click the Other Texture button [Other Texture...] to apply your own texture. This opens the Select Texture dialog box, which is very similar to the Open dialog box you would use to open a PowerPoint file.

19 Use the Look in: box and the contents window to find the file **Doit 4-8,** which is a grass texture image file, in your Student Files folder. When you locate the file, double-click it in the contents window. The Select Texture dialog box will close, and the grass texture will be added to the Texture: box and be selected, as shown in **Figure 4-23**.

20 Click [OK] to close the Fill Effects dialog box. Then click [OK] to close the Format Data Series dialog box. The grass texture will be added to the Green Side Up data series markers (see **Figure 4-24**).

21 Deselect the chart and save your changes.

More

3-D charts have special formatting options available that you can access by choosing the 3-D View command from the Chart menu. The 3-D View dialog box allows you to change the elevation of the chart so that it is viewed from a different angle. You also can rotate a chart clockwise or counterclockwise, which has a different effect depending on your chart type. Other more general formatting options are available on the toolbars when you are working in Graph 2000. Some of these are highlighted in **Table 4-3**, which can be found on page PP 4.32.

Figure 4-22 Chart with depth change

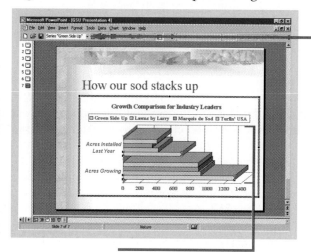

Use Chart Objects drop-down list to select any chart object from the Standard toolbar

Depth change affects
all data series markers

Figure 4-23 New texture added

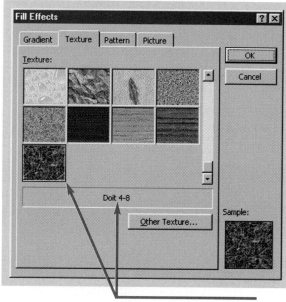

File Doit 4-8 added to
Texture tab and selected

Figure 4-24 Texture applied to data series marker

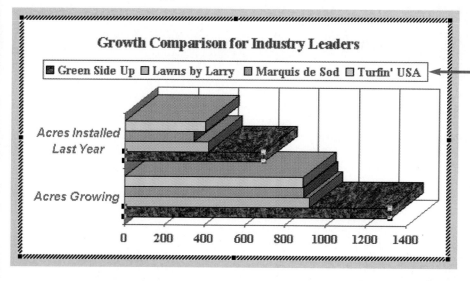

New texture also appears
in chart legend

Practice

Open the file **Prac4-8** and follow the instructions on the slide. Save the file as **MyPrac4-8**.

Hot Tip

You can open a formatting-related dialog box for any chart object by simply double-clicking the object.

Adding Transition Effects

Concept

After you have constructed your slides, it is time to think about the manner in which you will present them. Adding slide transition effects adds visual interest and emphasis to your presentation. Unlike a traditional slide show, PowerPoint's capabilities allow you to set controls that determine how a slide is displayed on the screen after the previous one is shown. You can set slides to move off the screen in different directions, to appear as if they are fading into or out of view, or even to dissolve into one another.

Do It!

Trista will now add transition effects to her presentation slides.

1 Click the Slide Sorter View button ▦. The presentation will be displayed in Slide Sorter view, which displays miniature versions of the presentation's seven slides. The slide you were viewing when you switched to Slide Sorter View will be selected (indicated by a heavy, blue border), and the **Slide Sorter** toolbar will appear (see **Figure 4-25**).

2 Click Slide 1 to select it if it is not already selected.

3 Click Slide Show on the menu bar, then select Slide Transition from the menu. The Slide Transition dialog box will open.

4 To select an effect, click the Effect drop-down list arrow to produce a list of available effects.

5 Scroll down until Uncover Up is visible in the list.

6 Click Uncover Up. It will appear in the Effect list box (see **Figure 4-26**) and a preview of the effect will run in the dialog box.

7 Click the Slow radio button to set the transition speed. A second preview of the transition effect will be shown at the new speed.

Figure 4-25 GSU Presentation 4 in Slide Sorter View

Slide Sorter
toolbar

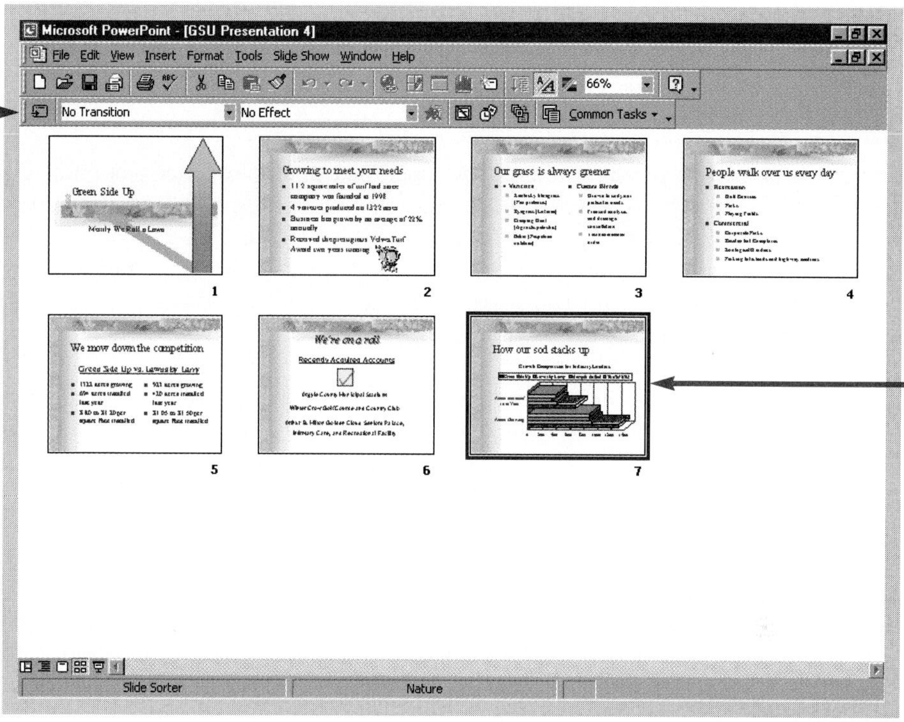

Selected slide

Figure 4-26 Slide Transition dialog box

PowerPoint 2000

Preview of selected
effects shown here

Click to apply selected
transition to selected
slide or slides

Use radio buttons to
set transition speed

Click to reveal a list of
sound effects that can
be included with the
transition effect

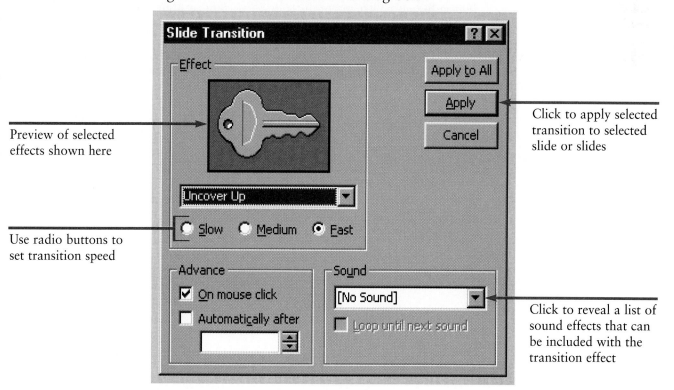

Adding Transition Effects (continued)

Do It!

8   Click the **On mouse click** check box in the **Advance** section of the dialog box to clear it. Later in the Lesson you will learn how to set automatic transition timings. Click Apply to All . The Transition Effects dialog box will close and the selected settings will be applied to every one of the slides in the presentation. A transition effect icon 🖫 will be displayed below each slide indicating that a transition effect has been applied.

9   Click the **Slide Transition Effects** drop-down arrow on the Slide Sorter toolbar, then select **Fade Through Black** from the drop-down list. A preview of the effect will be displayed on Slide 1. Applying transitions in this way affects only the selected slide, not the whole presentation.

10 Select **Slide 3** and use the Slide Transition Effects drop-down list to apply the **Wipe Down** transition effect to it.

11 Similarly apply the **Dissolve** effect to **Slide 7**. Your Slide Sorter window should look like the one shown in **Figure 4-27**.

12 Save the changes you have made to your file.

More

The Slide Transition dialog box also can be accessed by clicking the **Slide Transition** button 🖫 at the left end of the Slide Sorter toolbar, shown in **Figure 4-28**. This dialog box can be opened only if a slide is selected, even if you wish to apply a transition effect to all of the slides in a presentation. By clicking the **Apply** button rather than the Apply to All button, you can apply a transition effect to just the selected slide via this dialog box.

The Advance section of the Transition Effects dialog box lets you set the amount of time that passes before the next slide is automatically displayed. If the **On mouse click** box is checked, then clicking the left mouse button will advance the show.

Transitions also may have a sound associated with them. By choosing a sound in the Sound drop-down list, the sound will automatically play when the transition is made. Selecting **Other sound** allows you to use any sound file you have available, provided it is in a file format that PowerPoint can play.

Figure 4-27 Slides with transition effects

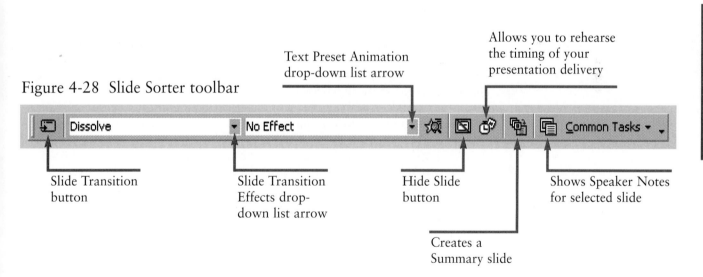

Transition effect applied to selected slide

Slide number

Transition effect icon

Text Preset Animation drop-down list arrow

Allows you to rehearse the timing of your presentation delivery

Figure 4-28 Slide Sorter toolbar

Slide Transition button

Slide Transition Effects drop-down list arrow

Hide Slide button

Shows Speaker Notes for selected slide

Creates a Summary slide

PowerPoint 2000

Practice

Open file **Prac4-9**. Apply the following transition effects: Slide 1—Wipe Left, Slow; Slide 2—Checkerboard Across, Medium; Slide 3—Cover Right, Slow. Save the file as **MyPrac4-9**.

Hot Tip

Click the Animation Preview button 🎇 on the Slide Sorter toolbar to see a preview of the transition effect that is associated with the selected slide on that slide's miniature.

Timing Slide Transitions

Concept

PowerPoint allows you to control the amount of time a slide spends on the screen before the next one appears during a slide show. Some slides require more time for the audience to absorb and for the presenter to explain, and therefore need more screen time.

Do It!

Based on the content of each slide, Trista would like to set the appropriate slide transition timings.

1 Click Slide 1 to select it in Slide Sorter View.

2 Click Slide Show on the menu bar, then click Slide Transition. The Slide Transition dialog box will open with the transition effect you selected in the previous Skill, Fade Through Black, selected.

3 Click the **Automatically after** check box in the Advance section of the dialog box to activate it. The default value, 00:00, will appear selected in the time text box.

4 Enter 5 to replace the 00:00 in the time text box (**Figure 4-29**), then click Apply . The dialog box closes and you will be returned to Slide Sorter View. The number you entered is recognized as representing seconds. Notice that Slide 1 now has :05 below it, indicating that it will advance automatically after five seconds.

5 Click Slide 2 to select it. Then hold down [Ctrl] on the keyboard and click **Slide 4, Slide 5,** and **Slide 6,** to add them to the selection.

6 The four selected slides all have the Uncover Up transition effect applied to them. Return to the Slide Transition dialog box and set these four slides to advance automatically after **15** seconds (remember to use the Apply button and not the Apply to All button).

7 Set **Slide 3** to advance automatically after **12** seconds and **Slide 7** after **10** seconds. Your Slide Sorter View should now look like **Figure 4-30**.

8 Click Slide 1 to select it, then click the Slide Show button 🖳. The slide show begins at the selected slide and runs until the last slide is shown, after which you can return to Slide Sorter View by clicking the mouse button. When you have finished watching the slide show, save the presentation.

More

When setting transition times, it is important to consider what is shown on each slide. A brief slide, such as the opening slide of Trista's presentation, does not need nearly as much time on the screen as her third slide, which contains much more information. Sounds, movies, complex animations, and other slide elements all add to the amount of time necessary for the audience to view the slide and comprehend the message that you are trying to convey. It is also necessary to take the length of the presenter's explanation, including speaker's notes, into account. If the presenter's accompanying notes are lengthy, it may be a better idea to advance a slide manually with the mouse, which will allow much more flexibility when presenting.

Figure 4-29 Setting slide timings

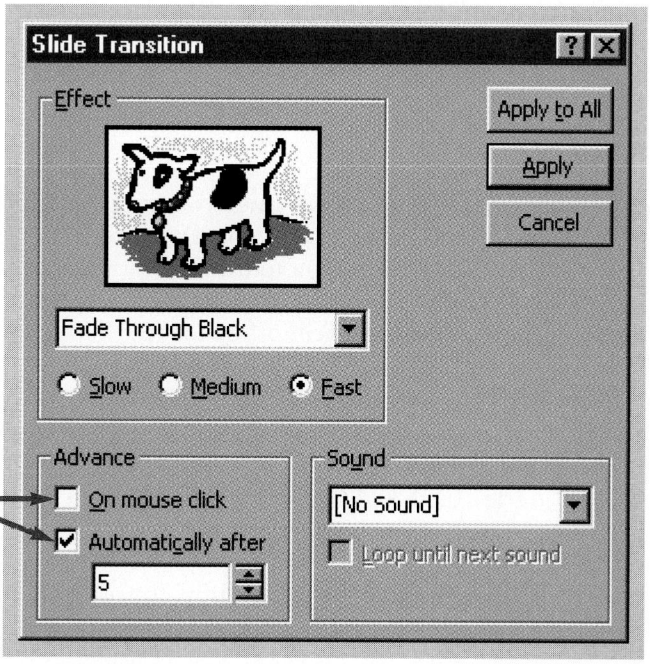

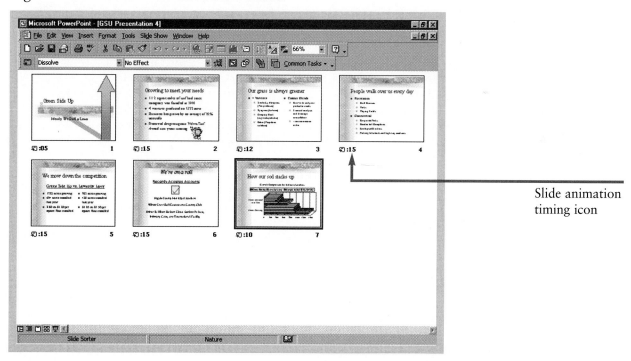

If both boxes are checked, slide will advance after set time elapses or on mouse click, whichever occurs first

Figure 4-30 Slides with transition effects

Slide animation timing icon

Practice

Open **MyPrac4-9**. Set Slide 1 to advance automatically after six seconds, Slide 2 to advance when the mouse is clicked, and Slide 3 to advance automatically after 12 seconds. Save the changes you have made to the file.

Hot Tip

If you do not wish to display a selected slide during a presentation, you can hide it by using the **Hide Slide** button 🔲 on the Slide Sorter toolbar. A gray box with a line through it will appear over the slide's number.

Annotating Slides

Concept

There are times when you might want to halt the slide show in order to explain a specific point that you are trying to make further. PowerPoint has a pen feature that allows you to draw on or annotate your slides. You can even pause your presentation to allow for more time to explain your annotations without worrying about being cut off by the next slide transition.

Do It!

Trista wants to highlight data on Slide 5 of her presentation.

1. Click Slide Show, then click Set Up Show. The Set Up Show dialog box will open, as shown in **Figure 4-31**.

2. Click the Pen color: drop-down list arrow. The Pen color palette will appear.

3. Click the sixth color square from the left (its ScreenTip will read Follow Accent Scheme Color). The Pen color palette closes and the selected color appears in the Pen color: box.

4. Click OK to close the dialog box. Then, select Slide 5 and click to begin a slide show on Slide 5.

5. When the slide show starts, move the mouse. A transparent icon will appear in the lower-left corner of the slide.

6. Click the Slide Show pop-up menu icon , highlight the Pointer Options command, and then select Pen from the submenu. The pointer will change from the standard arrow to the annotation pen pointer .

7. Circle the two numbers that represent the number of acres growing by clicking and dragging around them with the annotation pointer. The numbers will be circled in the color you chose in step 3. Your screen should resemble **Figure 4-32**.

8. Click again, and this time highlight the Screen command on the pop-up menu, and then click the Pause command on the submenu. The presentation is now paused and will not advance to the next slide.

9. Use the Pointer Options command to switch back to the standard arrow pointer, and then use the Screen command to resume your slide show.

More

When the annotation pen pointer is active, your slide show will not advance, allowing you to write or draw without interruption. Selecting Arrow from the slide show Pointer Options submenu will cause the mouse pointer to revert to an arrow, and allow the slide show to proceed if it is not on Pause. Or you can move to another slide by selecting Previous or Next from the slide show pop-up menu, which will take you out of annotation mode and return you to the slide show at the requested point. Markings that you make with the annotation pen are not permanent and are erased as soon as another slide is displayed or the show is ended. Alternatively, pressing [E] erases all annotations without having to leave the present slide.

Figure 4-31 Set Up Show dialog box

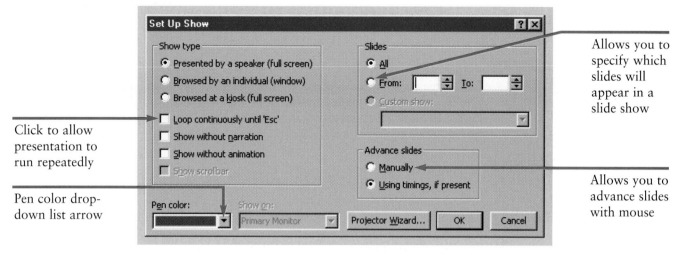

Allows you to specify which slides will appear in a slide show

Click to allow presentation to run repeatedly

Pen color drop-down list arrow

Allows you to advance slides with mouse

Figure 4-32 Annotated slide

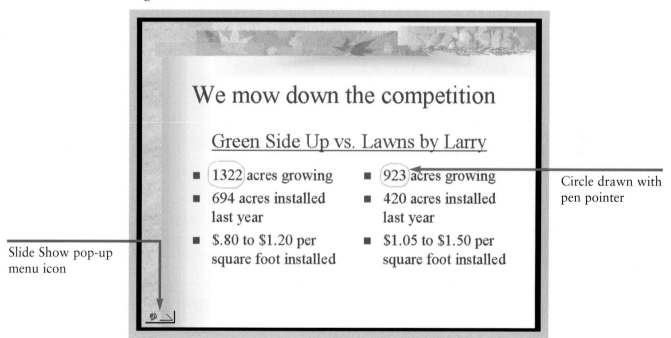

Circle drawn with pen pointer

Slide Show pop-up menu icon

PowerPoint 2000

Practice

Run GSU Presentation 4 from the beginning and practice annotating on each slide. After you mark the last slide, pause the presentation, switch back to the arrow pointer, and let the presentation conclude.

Hot Tip

To make perfect vertical or horizontal lines while using the annotation pen, press **[Shift]** while drawing. Release [Shift] to add curves again. Alternating between straight and curved lines in this way will make your drawings appear more precise.

Navigating during a Slide Show

Concept

While slide presentations generally follow a sequential order, occasions may arise when you want to display slides out of order. PowerPoint provides several ways to show any of your presentation's slides at any point during a slide show without having to end the show and restart it.

Do It!

Trista would like to explore PowerPoint's Slide Show navigation capabilities.

1. Run a Slide Show of GSU Presentation 4 starting on Slide 2.

2. When the presentation starts, right-click anywhere on the slide to open the Slide Show pop-up menu (this is the same menu that opens when you click the Slide Show pop-up menu icon).

3. Highlight the Go command on the pop-up menu, and then click the Slide Navigator command on the Go submenu. The Slide Navigator dialog box appears, as shown in **Figure 4-33**.

4. Click 7. How our sod stacks up to select Slide 7, and then click [Go To]. The slide show resumes, starting on Slide 7.

5. Right-click Slide 7 to open the pop-up menu again.

6. Highlight the Go command, and then highlight the By Title command on the Go submenu. A second submenu, consisting of all your slide titles and the Slide Navigator command, will appear as shown in **Figure 4-34**. A check mark precedes the current slide.

7. Click 1 Green Side Up on the By Title submenu to go to Slide 1. Allow the slide show to run through to the end.

More

Table 4-2 Slide Show keyboard commands

KEY	FUNCTION
[H]	Advances to the next hidden slide
[B] or [W]	Displays a blank black or white screen
[→], [N], [Enter], or [Space]	Advances to the next animation effect or slide
[←], [P], or [Backspace]	Goes to the previous animation effect or slide
[Slide Number] + [Enter]	Goes to a specific slide
[S]	Pauses a slide show or restarts a paused slide show
[Esc]	Exits the slide show

Figure 4-33 Slide Navigator dialog box

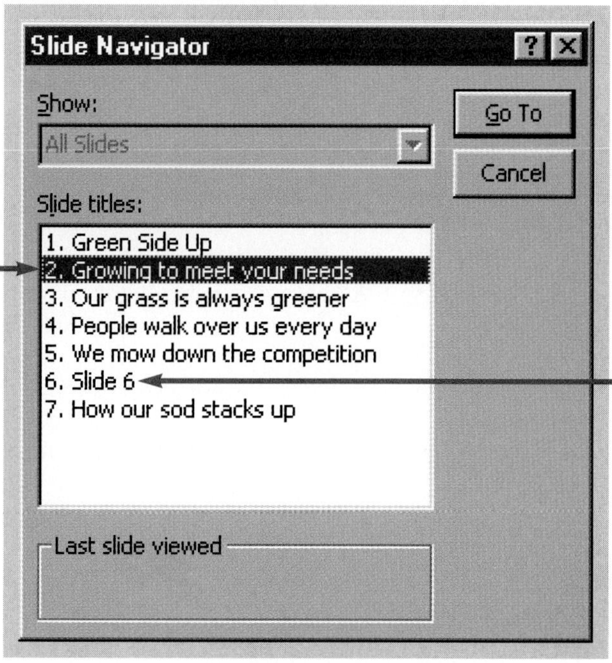

Current slide is highlighted when dialog box opens

Title for Slide 6 is not displayed because it was not entered in an AutoLayout slide title text box

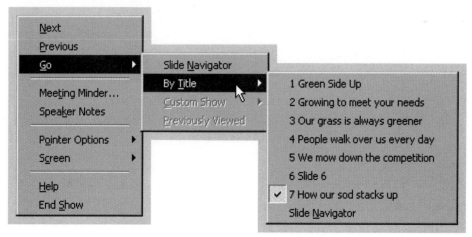

Figure 4-34 Navigating with By Title submenu

Practice

Open **Prac4-12** and start a slide show on Slide 5. Open the Slide Navigator and go to Slide 8. Then use the By Title command to go to Slide 1. Exit the slide show and close the file without saving changes.

Hot Tip

Pressing [F1] during a slide show or clicking the Help command on the Slide Show pop-up menu displays a comprehensive list of slide show controls.

Shortcuts

Function	Button/Mouse	Menu	Keyboard
Insert Clip Art	🖼	Click Insert, then highlight Picture, then click Clip Art	
Format data series (or other selected chart object)	🖼	Click Format, then click Selected Data Series (or other object)	[Ctrl]+[1]
Run slide show	🖥	Click Slide Show, then click View Show	[F5]
Get help during slide show/view keyboard shortcuts	Right-click, then click Help on pop-up menu		[F1]
End slide show	Right-click, then click End Show		[Esc]

Table 4-3 Graph 2000 formatting tools

BUTTON	COMMAND	FUNCTION
🖱	Import File	Opens the Import File dialog box, allowing you to import a file, an entire sheet of data, or a selected range into a chart
🔲	View Datasheet	Displays the datasheet window, or hides it if it is currently showing
🔲 or 🔲	By Row or By Column	Plots chart data series from data across rows or down columns
🔲	Data Table	Displays the values for each data series in a grid below the chart
🔲 or 🔲	Category Axis Gridlines or Value Axis Gridlines	Shows or hides category axis or value axis gridlines in charts
🔲 or 🔲	Angle Text Downward or Angle Text Upward	Rotates selected text down or up at a 45-degree angle to more efficiently utilize the available space on a chart

Identify Key Features

Name the items identified by callouts in the figures below.

Figure 4-35 Elements of Slide Sorter View

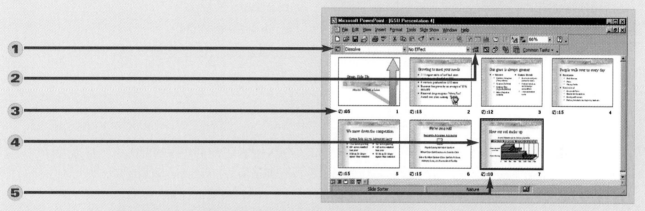

Figure 4-36 Elements of Graph 2000

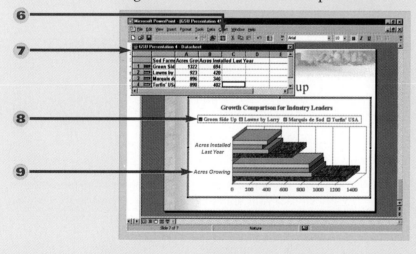

PowerPoint 2000

Select the Best Answer

10. Provides pictures that you can add to your presentation

11. Allows you to mark a slide temporarily during a slide show

12. Controls the manner in which slides appear on the screen

13. An example of a slide transition effect

14. Stores the information that drives a chart in tabular form

15. The intersection of a column and a row

16. Allows you to jump to any slide during the delivery of a presentation

17. Includes the Pointer Options command

a. Cell

b. Wipe Down

c. Slide Navigator

d. Insert Clip Art dialog box

e. Slide Show pop-up menu

f. Pen pointer

g. Datasheet

h. Slide Transition dialog box

Quiz (continued)

Complete the Statement

18. You can add texture to a chart object using an option on the:
    a. Patterns tab
    b. Fill Effects tab
    c. Font tab
    d. Chart toolbar

19. You can edit and format Clip Art by using the:
    a. Standard toolbar
    b. Picture toolbar
    c. Microsoft Clip Gallery
    d. Slide Navigator

20. A column is an example of a:
    a. Data series marker
    b. Data label
    c. Category axis
    d. Value axis

21. When working in a datasheet, pressing [Enter] moves the cell pointer:
    a. One cell to the right
    b. One cell to the left
    c. To the next row in the same column
    d. To the next column in the same row

22. Chart titles and legends can be added in the:
    a. Chart Type dialog box
    b. Notes pane
    c. Datasheet window
    d. Chart Options dialog box

23. Adding transition effects and slide timings is best accomplished in:
    a. Normal View
    b. Slide Sorter View
    c. Microsoft Graph 2000
    d. Slide Show mode

24. You can change the elevation of a chart in the:
    a. Chart Options dialog box
    b. Format Data Series dialog box
    c. 3-D View dialog box
    d. Presentation window

25. To change a Bar chart to a Pie chart, use the:
    a. Chart Options dialog box
    b. Formatting toolbar
    c. Datasheet
    d. Chart Type command

26. To maintain precise control over your presentation, set your slides to advance:
    a. Automatically
    b. Automatically after 10 seconds
    c. On mouse click
    d. With sound effects

Interactivity

Test Your Skills

1. Insert pictures into a slide:

   a. Open the PowerPoint file **TYS4-1** from your Student Files folder.

   b. Insert the Clip Art file named **summer** into the Title Slide.

   c. Resize and reposition the image so that it fits between the slide's subtitle and the dotted line below it.

   d. Insert the picture file named **TYS4 Image** from your Student Files folder.

   e. Position the image above the title text and resize it so that it covers most of the top of the slide.

2. Format a picture:

   a. Select the summer Clip Art picture you added in step 1 and activate the Picture toolbar.

   b. Open the Recolor Picture dialog box.

   c. Replace the color black with the color whose ScreenTip is **Follow Shadows Scheme Color**.

   d. Save the presentation as **TYS4-1-Complete** and close the file.

3. Add a chart to a presentation and format it:

   a. Start a new blank presentation. Make the first slide a **Title Only** slide.

   b. Insert a chart. You will be using the dummy data that appear in the datasheet.

   c. Close the Datasheet window, then drag the chart's border down so that it does not obscure the title box.

   d. Add the title **Accounts Acquired by Region** to the slide.

   e. Move the chart's legend to the left side.

   f. Create another title slide.

   g. Insert another chart. This time, delete rows 2 and 3 (West and North) from the datasheet.

   h. Close the datasheet.

   i. Change the chart type to **Exploded pie with a 3-D visual** effect.

   j. Title the slide **East Accounts by Quarter**.

   k. Create similar slides with charts for the West and North data. Make the West chart a plain pie chart and the North chart a Doughnut chart.

   l. Select a data series from the doughnut chart and add texture to it.

   m. **Underline** the titles of each chart you created.

   n. Save the presentation as **Accounts** and close the file

PowerPoint 2000

Interactivity (continued)

4. Add transition effects and advance timings to a presentation:

   a. Open the PowerPoint file TYS4-4 from your Student Files folder.

   b. Apply the Box In transition effect at Slow speed to Slide 1, and set it to advance automatically after five seconds.

   c. Apply the Horizontal Blinds transition effect at Medium speed to Slide 2, and set it to advance after 10 seconds.

   d. Use the Slide Sorter toolbar to apply the Random Bars Vertical transition effect to Slide 3. Then set the slide to advance when you click the mouse.

5. Practice running a slide show:

   a. Run a slide show for TYS4-4 that starts on Slide 2.

   b. When you get to Slide 3, use the Pen pointer to underline the word Congratulations! on the screen.

   c. Use the Slide Navigator to go to Slide 1.

   d. Use the By Title command to go back to Slide 3.

   e. End the slide show and save the presentation as TYS4-4-Complete. Close the file.

Problem Solving

1. Open the file Solved3-1.ppt, which is the brochure you created at the end of Lesson 3 for the country inn you are planning to open. Use PowerPoint's gallery of Clip Art to enliven the brochure. Each slide in the brochure should contain at least one example of Clip Art. Recolor the Clip Art pictures you add so that they match the Template Design scheme used in the presentation. Add a new slide to the presentation that compares your projected rates to those of other local inns in the form of a chart. Save the presentation as Solved4-1.ppt.

2. Using the PowerPoint skills you have learned, create a five-slide comic strip using Clip Art pictures for your characters. The first slide should serve as an introductory panel that shows the comic strip's name and introduces the characters. Use the other four slides for the actual strip dialogue. Program this presentation so that each slide advances after 20 seconds or on a mouse click, whichever comes first. Also use exciting transition effects, appropriate for a comic. Save the presentation as Solved4-2.ppt.

3. Create a new blank presentation. On a Title Only slide, insert a chart. Edit the datasheet so that the chart will display the name of each of the four Lessons you have completed in this book and the number of Skills each lesson contains. Once the chart is created, change it to a Pie chart. Format the pie slices so that one is black, one is red, one is blue, and one has texture. Place the chart's legend at the bottom of the chart. Save the file as Solved4-3.ppt.

4. Your consulting firm has been hired by a large market all-news radio station to perform a demographic study of its listeners. You will be presenting your findings with PowerPoint. The data you have found (fictional) should be presented both as text and in chart form. Your study includes the following: separate breakdowns of the total audience by age group and gender; average number of hours listening per week; overall satisfaction with station's performance. Each of these statistical areas and the methods used to gather their data should be explained thoroughly in the presentation. Your work also should make full use of a Design Template, Clip Art, AutoShapes, slide transitions, slide timings, and all types of formatting. Save the finished project as Solved4-4.ppt.

L E S S O N

1

OFFICE INTEGRATION AND WEB FEATURES

Once you have mastered the individual tools that make up the Office 2000 suite, you may find it useful to use these tools together. Word, Excel, Access, and PowerPoint are programmed to work together seamlessly. You have already seen how some features, like the Office Assistant and the Office Clipboard, are shared by all four applications. The documents and data you produce with these programs can be shared among them as well. For example, you may have produced a chart on an Excel worksheet that you want to include in a PowerPoint presentation. Or you may need to convert a presentation into a Word document. You can even use an Access database to drive a mail merge that will create documents such as mailing labels in Word. Transferring data between two Office applications can be accomplished with a variety of techniques, the most common of which are pasting, linking, and embedding.

Another feature that Office 2000 applications share is their Web capabilities. Each Office program allows you to save a file as a Web page, which allows you to publish it on the World Wide Web without losing formatting, structure, or functionality. Once this is done, anyone with a Web browser can view your Office documents. You can, in turn, "round-trip" your Web documents back into their original Office applications for editing, and then publish them again. Publishing documents has been made easier, as you can save a file directly to a Web server.

CASE STUDY:
The hot, new company Fix Brothers has become one of the leaders in online catalog clothes shopping. The company's headquarters has adopted Microsoft Office 2000 to run its daily operations. Different departments use different tools, but all employees are required to be proficient with the entire suite. This way, they have no difficulty collaborating on projects or sharing data.

Using an Excel Chart in a PowerPoint Slide

Concept

The strength of the PowerPoint application is its ability to present information in an informative and appealing manner. While you also can use PowerPoint to produce the information you present, it is sometimes easier to generate your data in another application that is better suited for a particular task. You then can insert the data from the second application into PowerPoint as an object.

Do It!

Alan Riley works in the sales department and realizes that two types of clothing dominate Fix Brothers' sales data. He thinks this information will be useful in a presentation he must deliver to his department, so he will embed an Excel chart that contains the data in one of his PowerPoint slides.

1. Open the PowerPoint presentation Doit1-1a from your Student Files folder's Office directory.

2. Go to Slide 5 in the presentation.

3. Click the Common Tasks button, and then click New Slide. The New Slide dialog box opens, as shown in **Figure 1-1**.

4. Click the Large Object AutoLayout slide to select it, and then click [OK]. The Large Object slide will be added to the presentation after Slide 5.

5. Double-click the slide as per its instruction to open the Insert Object dialog box.

6. Click the Create from file radio button, and then click [Browse...].

7. Use the Browse dialog box's Look in: drop-down list to find and select the Excel file Doit1-1b in the same folder as above and then click [OK].

8. Click [OK] in the Insert Object dialog box.

9. The Excel chart from Doit1-1b appears on the PowerPoint slide as in **Figure 1-2**.

More

In this Skill you learned how to embed an object from one Office tool in another. There is a difference between embedding an object and linking an object. When you embed an object, it becomes part of the file to which you have moved it. All connections to the original, or source, file are broken. Linked objects retain their connections to the source file. Any changes you make to the source file will be updated in the linked object the next time its file is opened. To link an object, activate the Link check box in the Insert Object dialog box before you insert an object.

Figure 1-1 New Slide dialog box

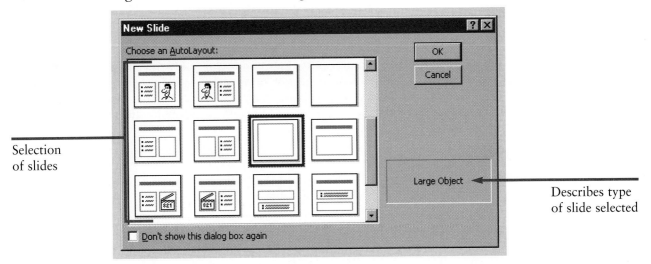

Selection of slides

Describes type of slide selected

Figure 1-2 Slide with Excel chart in it

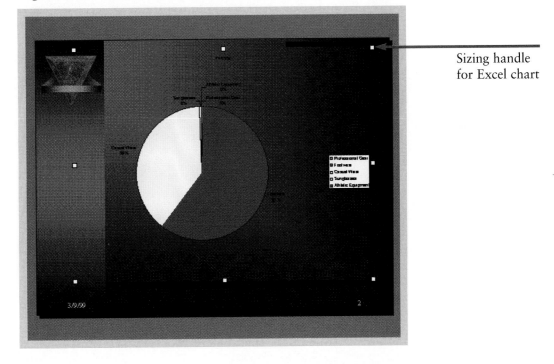

Sizing handle for Excel chart

Office 2000

Practice

Open **Prac1-1a**, a **PowerPoint** presentation, from your Student Files **Office** folder and insert the **Excel** chart from **Prac1-1b** into the presentation.

Hot Tip

You also may copy an object in one tool's file to the Clipboard, and then paste the object to embed it in a file created with another tool.

Linking Excel and Word Files

Concept

Sometimes it is more appropriate and useful to link documents rather than embed them. For example, if you know that the source file for an inserted object changes frequently, and you want those changes to be reflected in the object automatically, it makes sense to link the object. Linking saves you the time it would take to edit or update two files.

Do It!

Alan decides it also will be useful if he links his Excel data to a memo he will send to other departments in the company.

1 Open the Excel file Doit1-2a and view Sheet 1.

2 Open the Word File Doit1-2b.

3 Right-click the Windows taskbar and click Tile Windows Vertically. Both documents appear on the screen, side by side.

4 Click in the Excel window to activate it and select the range A11 to E18 by clicking and dragging.

5 Click Edit, then click Copy. An animated box appears around the cells you copied.

6 Click inside the Word window to activate it. Then click after the initials of the author at the bottom of the memo to place the insertion point there.

7 Press [Enter] to move the insertion point to a new line.

8 Click Edit then click Paste Special. The Paste Special dialog box opens, as shown in **Figure 1-3**.

9 Click the Paste Link radio button, and select Microsoft Excel Worksheet Object in the As: list box. Click ⊏ OK ⊐.

10 The selected cells you copied from the worksheet appear in the Word document, as shown in **Figure 1-4**. Once you save the memo, the data you pasted as a link will be updated in accordance with its source worksheet whenever you open the Word file.

11 Close both files, saving the changes you have made to the Word file Doit1-2b.

More

The process for linking a chart to a word document is the same, although you could also use the Object command on the Insert menu to accomplish the task. If you do not use Paste Special, but simply Paste, then you are simply embedding a copy of the object rather than linking it. By using the Insert Object command, you also can embed or link an entire worksheet in a Word document or PowerPoint slide instead of just a chart or cell range.

Figure 1-3 Paste Special dialog box

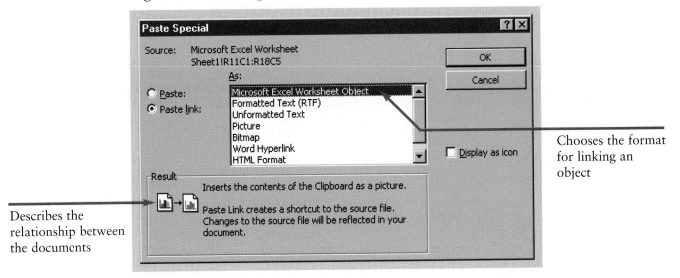

Chooses the format
for linking an
object

Describes the
relationship between
the documents

Figure 1-4 Windows tiled vertically next to each other

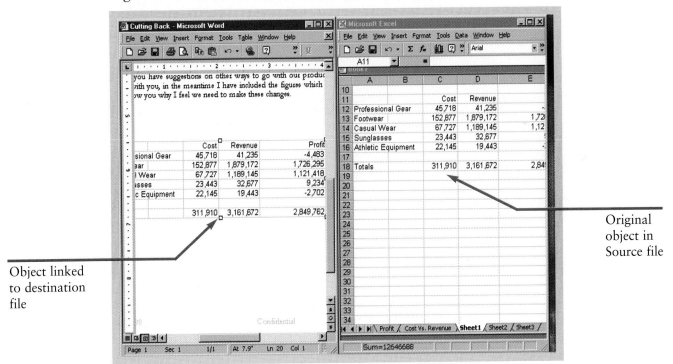

Original
object in
Source file

Object linked
to destination
file

Open a blank **Word** document and link the
spreadsheet from the **Excel** file **Prac1-1b** to
this blank **Word** document.

Hot Tip

The Paste Special command is part of the
advanced section of the **Edit** menu. If it
does not appear right away, wait for a few
seconds for the menu to expand or click
the arrow at the bottom of the menu to
expand it immediately.

Editing Linked Excel Data

Concept

The advantage of linking data rather than inserting them is that any changes you make to a source file are reflected automatically in any files that are linked to it. Editing linked data does not require any special procedures. You can use the same simple editing techniques you have already learned to update your linked files.

Do It!

Alan realizes that he made a typing error in his Excel Worksheet, which has also appeared in his Word memo because it is linked. He will edit the worksheet, and the changes will be reflected in the memo.

1 Open the Word file Doit1-2b.

2 Double-click the linked Excel data that you inserted at the bottom of the memo. Its source file, the Excel workbook Doit1-2a, will open in Excel (see **Figure 1-5**).

3 Double-click in cell **A12**, which contains the misspelled label **Proffessional Gear**.

4 Place the mouse pointer, which will be an I-beam, after the second f in Proffessional and click to place the insertion point there.

5 Press [Backspace] on the keyboard to erase the second f.

6 Click another cell in the worksheet to confirm the change to cell A12. The extra f in Proffessional will be removed from the linked worksheet in Doit1-2b, as shown in **Figure 1-6**.

7 Close both applications, saving the changes you have made in both documents.

More

It is possible for you to change a linked object into an embedded object once you have already linked it from one file to another. To make this change, click the object that is linked in the destination file to select it. Then click Edit and select the Links command on the Edit menu. In the Links dialog box there is an option to Break Link. Once you select this option, the linked object becomes an embedded object and changes no longer reflect on the source file, and vice versa. The Links dialog box also allows you to change other aspects of a link, including its source file and whether it is updated automatically or manually. If your file contains more than one linked object, each link will be listed in the Links dialog box. Click the link you wish to work with to select it before making changes to it.

Figure 1-5 Editing a linked object

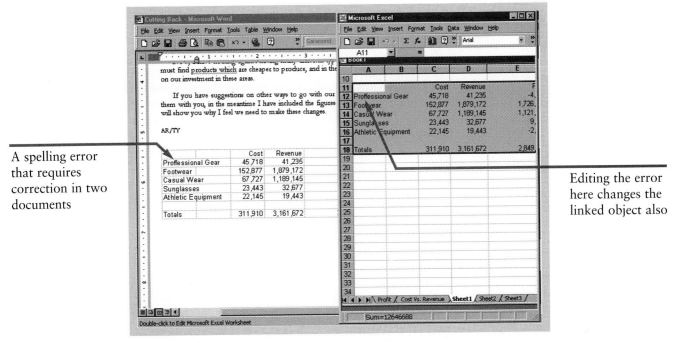

A spelling error that requires correction in two documents

Editing the error here changes the linked object also

Figure 1-6 Corrected and updated linked object

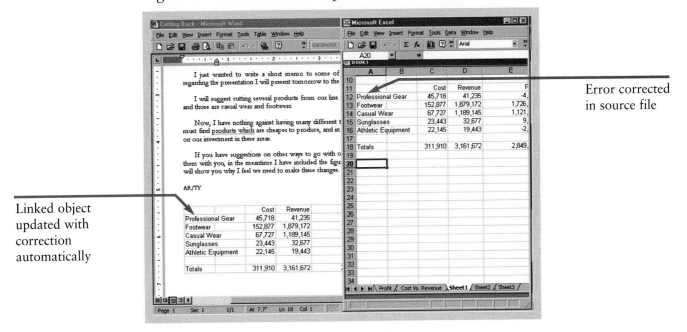

Linked object updated with correction automatically

Error corrected in source file

Practice

Delete the final row of cells from the **Excel** spreadsheet you linked to the **Word** document. Check to see that both documents are updated.

Hot Tip

The Edit menu also contains a command for working with the selected linked object. The name of the command changes to reflect the type of linked object that is selected. The command's submenu allows you to open, edit, or convert the link.

Converting a Presentation into a Word Document

Concept

Converting an existing Office document to another type of Office file can be useful for completing certain tasks or for simply increasing your own comfort level. For example, you may be a novice PowerPoint user who needs to edit and revise the text that accompanies a presentation. Since you are experienced with Word, a program that is designed for working with electronic text, you could export the PowerPoint presentation to Word in order to write your notes.

Do It!

Alan has decided to export his PowerPoint presentation to Word, which he will use to compose Speaker's Notes for his presentation. He also knows that he may use some of these notes in his Word memo, and having the text in Word will make the transfer smoother.

1 Open the PowerPoint presentation Doit1-1a.

2 Click File, then highlight Send To.

3 When the Send To submenu appears, click Microsoft Word. The Write-Up dialog box opens, as shown in **Figure 1-7**. The top section of the dialog box, labeled Page layout in Microsoft Word, lets you choose how the presentation will be organized in Word.

4 Click Notes below slides, a layout that places each presentation slide on its own page and includes an area below each slide for typing notes.

5 Click OK . The Word application launches and creates a document with the layout described above (see **Figure 1-8**).

6 Close both documents. You do not need to save the changes.

More

The bottom section of the Write-Up dialog box determines whether the Word document you create will include your actual slides or just links to them. If you are concerned about the size of the file created when you send a presentation to Word, choose the Paste link option instead of the Paste option.

It is also possible to create PowerPoint presentation text in Word. You can create an outline of a presentation in Word by using heading styles from Word, such as Heading 1 for slide titles, Heading 2 for secondary text, and so on. When you open PowerPoint, click Insert, then click Slides from Outline. Choose the proper Word file and PowerPoint will produce a presentation based on the Word outline.

Figure 1-7 Write-Up dialog box

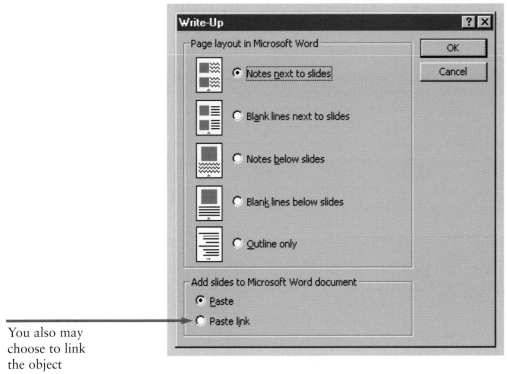

You also may
choose to link
the object

Figure 1-8 PowerPoint slide in Word

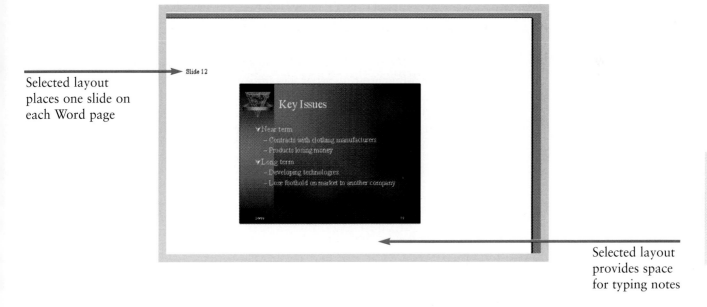

Selected layout
places one slide on
each Word page

Selected layout
provides space
for typing notes

Office 2000

Practice

Export the **PowerPoint** presentation
Prac1-1a to **Microsoft Word**.

Hot Tip

If you added Notes Pages to your slides in
PowerPoint, these notes will be transferred
to the new Word document as well if you
export the presentation to Word using a
layout that includes notes.

Adding a Word File to a Word Document

Concept

Word makes it easy to combine two files into one. You can add the text of one file to another without even having to open the file being inserted. This allows for quick collaborations while minimizing the possibility of errors.

Do It!

Alan is going to add data from another memo written by someone in his department to his memo.

1. Open the Word file Doit1-2b.

2. Click Insert, then click File. The Insert File dialog box appears, as shown in **Figure 1-9**.

3. Use the Look in: box to select the Word file **Money Management** from the **Student Files** folder's Office directory and then click ⎙ Insert ▾.

4. The text of the Money Management file appears at the top of the active document, as shown in **Figure 1-10**. Note that when you insert a file, it will be placed where the insertion point is currently located.

5. Save the file as Combined Memo so that you have both versions of the memo on file.

6. Close the file.

More

You can import numerous types of files into Word documents. At the bottom of the Insert File dialog box there is a drop-down list box labeled Files of type:. Click the drop-down arrow and you can choose the type of file you want to insert in your Word document. The possibilities range from other Office documents to sound and image files and even Web pages.

Figure 1-9 Insert File dialog box

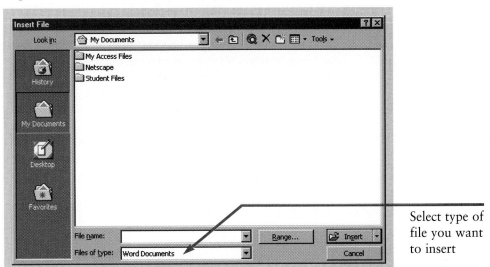

Select type of
file you want
to insert

Figure 1-10 Two Word documents combined

Position of
inserted file is
determined by
location of the
insertion point

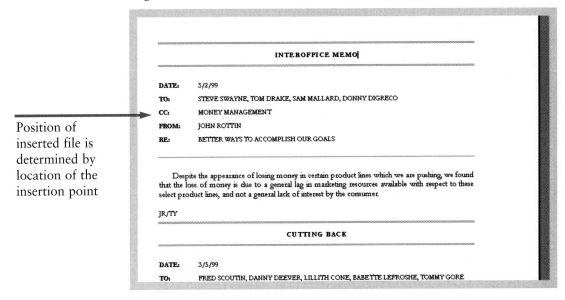

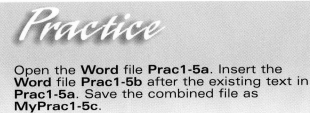

Merging Access Data with a Word Document

Concept

Databases that generate mailing lists, inventory reports, and statistical reports are a key component to many businesses. Using databases for practical purposes can be as challenging as it is imperative. Using them efficiently can be the greatest challenge of all. With Office 2000, you can merge Access data fields with a Word document to create a powerful data management and output tool.

Do It!

Alan wants to generate a catalog of Fix Brothers' products in Word by merging an existing Access database table with a new Word document.

1 Open a new blank Word document.

2 Click Tools, then click Mail Merge. The Mail Merge Helper dialog box appears, as shown in **Figure 1-11**.

3 Click [Create ▾]. A list of document types drops down.

4 Click Catalog from the list. A pop-up window appears that asks you to use the open document or create a new one. Click Active Window [Active Window].

5 Click [Get Data ▾] in the second step of the Mail Merge Helper dialog box to choose the source for your merge data.

6 Click Open Data Source from the list that drops down, meaning the data will come from an existing file. The Open Data Source dialog box opens, as shown in **Figure 1-12**.

7 Click the Files of type: drop-down list arrow and select MS Access Databases as the file type.

8 Select the Access file Doit1-6 in your Student Files folder's Office directory.

9 Click [🖼 Open].

10 A dialog box titled Microsoft Access will open to its Tables tab with the Products table already selected. This dialog box lists all of the objects in the database you opened that can be used as a data source. Click [OK] to accept the Products table as your data source.

Figure 1-11 Mail Merge Helper dialog box

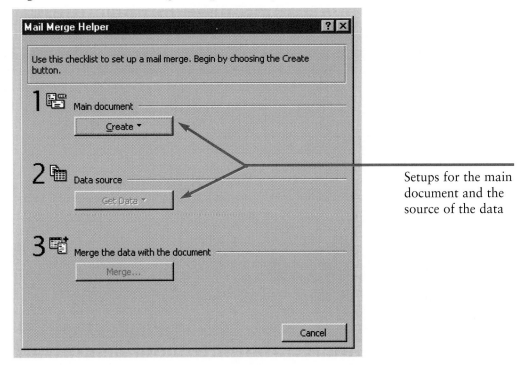

Setups for the main document and the source of the data

Figure 1-12 Open Data Source dialog box

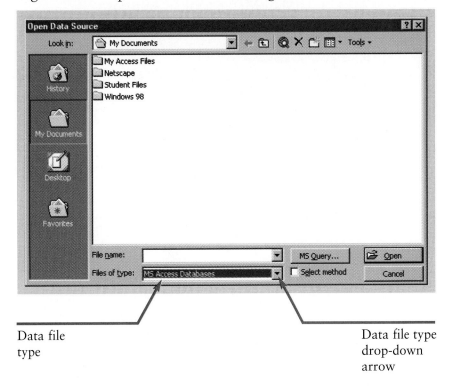

Data file type

Data file type drop-down arrow

Merging Access Data with a Word Document (continued)

Do It!

11 An alert box will appear to inform you that Word found no merge fields in your Word document, which of course is blank. Follow the instructions to click the Edit Main Document button so you can add merge fields. You will notice that the Mail Merge toolbar has appeared (see **Table 1-1**).

12 Click the Insert Merge Field button `Insert Merge Field ▾` on the Mail Merge toolbar. A list of the field names from the selected Access database appears. Click the ID field to add it to the document as a merge field.

13 Repeat step 12 to add ProductName, Description, Stock, Order, and Price as merge fields (see **Figure 1-13**). Press the [Enter] key at the end of the line.

14 Click the View Merged Data button 〈〈〉〉. The first record from the Access Products table is shown merged in the Word document. Click the button again to display the merge fields again.

15 Click the Merge to New Document button. The Mail Merge runs and creates a new document in Word that includes the data in all of the merge fields you selected for all of the records in the Products table, as shown in **Figure 1-14**.

16 Save the merge fields document as Products merge and the document generated by the merge as Products catalog.

More

Table 1-1 Mail Merge toolbar buttons

FUNCTION	BUTTON	LETS YOU
Record Navigation buttons	⏮ ◀ ▶ ⏭	View specific records
View Merged Data	〈〈〉〉	Preview the data that will be merged
Mail Merge Helper		Opens the Mail Merge Helper dialog box
Merge to New Document		Creates the Mail Merged document
Merge to Printer		Prints the Mail Merge
Mail Merge	Merge...	Starts Mail Merge
Find Record		Finds specified record
Edit Data Source		Allows you to edit data source

Figure 1-13 Merge fields chosen from Access table

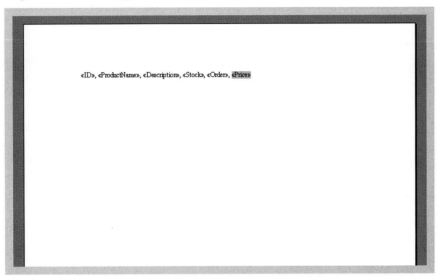

Figure 1-14 Access table merged with Word document

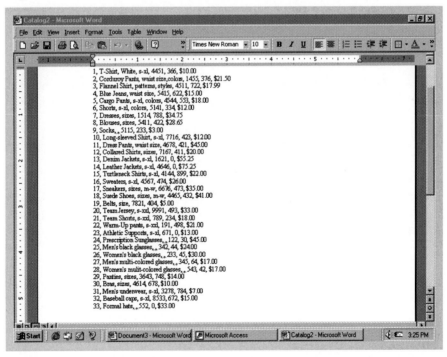

Practice

Open a new **Word** document and use Mail Merge to create a form letter that uses merge fields from the **Contacts** table in the **Access** database **Prac1-6**. Be sure to set up the merge fields properly on the page to create the structure of a form letter.

Hot Tip

If you use mail merge commands frequently, click **View**, then highlight **Toolbars**, and finally click **Customize**. You can then add the required **Mail Merge** buttons to your Standard toolbar.

Creating Hyperlinks and Web Pages

Concept

The rapid growth of the Internet has increased the individual's ability to share information with others around the world almost immeasurably. By publishing documents on the World Wide Web, posting information in newsgroups, and sending messages and files via e-mail, you can reach previously unavailable audiences with remarkable speed and ease. To assist you in taking advantage of this technology, Office 2000 allows you to insert hyperlinks in a document and to save your documents as Web pages. Saving a document as a Web page converts it to HTML, or HyperText Markup Language, the current standard for Web page authoring.

Do It!

Alan has designed a departmental directory for Fix Brothers using Microsoft Word. He would like to add the directory to the company's Web site. First he needs to insert one final hyperlink. Then he will save the document as a Web page.

1. Open the Word document named Directory from your Student Files folder's Office directory. Scroll to the second page of the document so that the last entry in the directory, Technical services, is visible.

2. Click and drag over the text Technical Services to select it, and then click the Insert Hyperlink button 🔗 on the Standard toolbar. The Insert Hyperlink dialog box will open with a blinking insertion point in the Type the file or Web page name: box.

3. Type http://www.domain.com/fixbros/techserv.html as shown in **Figure 1-15**. This is the Internet address (fictional) to which the text you selected will be linked.

4. Click ⬜ OK ⬜. The dialog box closes to reveal that the text you selected has been converted to a hyperlink. Once this page is published on the Web, clicking on this link will take the user to the Technical services page on Fix Brothers' Web site.

5. Click File, then click Web Page Preview. Your default Web browser will be launched so that you can view your document as it will appear on the Web (see **Figure 1-16**).

6. Close the Web browser.

7. Click File, then click Save as Web Page. The Save As dialog box opens.

8. Use the Save in: box to choose a storage location and click 💾 Save . Your document is now saved as a Web page and can be published on the World Wide Web.

More

If you have access to your organization's Web server, and it supports Web folders (shortcuts to the Web server), you can save your Web pages directly to a Web folder to publish them. To create a Web folder, select Web Folders from the Save As dialog box's Save in: drop-down list and then click the Create New Folder button 📁 . This will activate the Add Web Folder Wizard. You should consult your system administrator before attempting to save any documents directly to a Web server.

Figure 1-15 Inserting a hyperlink

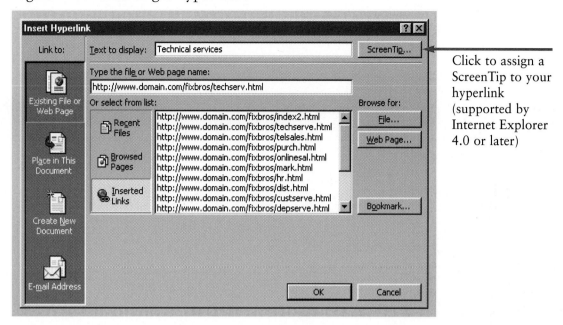

Click to assign a ScreenTip to your hyperlink (supported by Internet Explorer 4.0 or later)

Figure 1-16 Previewing a Web page

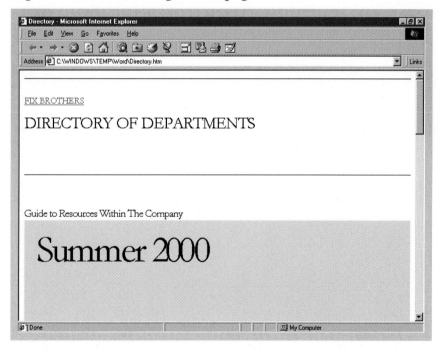

Practice

Create a Web page using the **Mail Merge** catalog you created earlier in this Lesson.

Hot Tip

The **Save as Web page** command is also available in **Excel** and **PowerPoint**. To prepare **Access** data for the Web, use the **Pages** object button in the **Access** database window.

Shortcuts

Function	Button/Mouse	Menu	Keyboard
Insert Hyperlink		Click Insert, then click Hyperlink	[Ctrl] + [K]
Save as Web Page		Click File, then click Save as Web Page	
Search the Web			
Web Layout		Click View, then click Web Layout	
Stop current jump			
Start Page			
Show only Web toolbar			

Identify Key Features

Identify the items indicated by callouts in Figure 1-17.

Figure 1-17 Two Office tools being used together

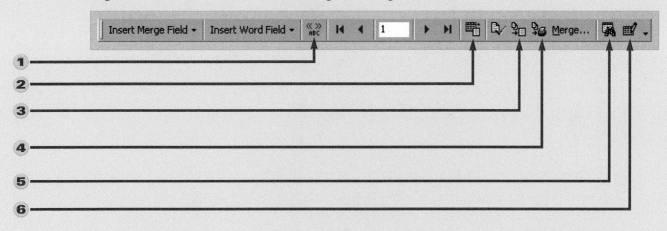

1
2
3
4
5
6

Select the Best Answer

7. An alternate method of embedding an object from one Office program in another

8. Traditional path of inserting an object into a PowerPoint presentation

9. Where an object originates

10. Where an object is inserted

11. An object that is updated automatically whenever its source file is changed

12. An object that originated in one file, but maintains no ties to its source

13. Allows you to combine data and fields from one program in another

14. Programming language used in Web pages

15. Text that connects you to another data source when you click it

a. Destination file

b. Insert Object slide

c. Hyperlink

d. Embedded object

e. Data source

f. Linked Object

g. Copy and paste

h. Mail Merge

i. HTML

Office 2000

Quiz (continued)

Complete the Statement

16. To see the first merged record after you have completed the setup of a mail merge, click the:

    a. Merge to Printer button

    b. Merge to New Document button

    c. Mail Merge Helper button

    d. View Merged Data button

17. Office 2000 allows documents to be saved and viewed as Web pages by:

    a. Eliminating all complicated objects

    b. Changing the format of the document

    c. Saving them in HTML

    d. Adding Web servers

18. You can unlink an object:

    a. By accessing the Links dialog box

    b. By clicking the Unlink command on the toolbar

    c. By accessing the Chart Tools dialog box

    d. By right-clicking it in the destination file

19. Office 2000 makes it easy to move a PowerPoint presentation to Word by:

    a. Cutting and pasting notes and slides from the presentation.

    b. Accessing the Write-Up dialog box from the File menu

    c. Clicking Insert, then clicking Presentation File

    d. Clicking File, then Import From, then PowerPoint presentation.

20. You can create a presentation in Word and import it into PowerPoint by:

    a. The exact same process needed to move a PowerPoint presentation into Word

    b. Writing the outline in Word, then opening the Insert menu in PowerPoint

    c. By creating the presentation in Word, then clicking Save as PowerPoint presentation

    d. Clicking Insert, then clicking PowerPoint Slides

21. Office 2000 allows you to combine two Microsoft Word documents easily by:

    a. Clicking Edit, then Cut, then Paste, to open the Paste Special dialog box

    b. By clicking Paste Special from the File menu and pasting the second file

    c. Clicking Tools, then clicking Mail Merge, to open the Mail Merge Helper dialog box

    d. Clicking Insert, then File, and then choosing the file you want to combine

22. The Paste Special dialog box is useful when you are trying to:

    a. Break a link

    b. Paste data as a link

    c. Both a and b

    d. Neither a nor b

Interactivity

Test Your Skills

1. Using PowerPoint with other Microsoft Office 2000 programs:

   a. Open the PowerPoint presentation Test1-1.

   b. Insert the chart in the Excel file Test 1-2 into the PowerPoint presentation.

   c. Export PowerPoint presentation Test 1 to Word.

2. Using Excel with other Microsoft Office 2000 programs:

   a. Paste the Excel chart as a link at the end of the Word document Test1-3.

   b. There is a spelling error in the chart that you just linked. Edit the chart so that both versions of it are correct.

3. Using Access with other Microsoft Office 2000 programs:

   a. Create a Mail Merge using Access file Test 1-4 and a new Word document.

   b. First, add the fields from the Access file.

   c. Then, merge the data from Access with the fields you have added to Word.

4. Use Word to create a Web page:

   a. Create a Web page using the Word document you created above.

   b. Preview the page with your Web browser.

Problem Solving

1. You work for the company Randolph & Mortimer. You have been assigned the task of making a proposition to save the company money, while at the same time increasing revenue. You will be preparing a presentation to the Board of Directors in just a few days, and you must be prepared for their interests, concerns, and worries. The most important part of this presentation will be PowerPoint and using PowerPoint to create the presentation. In the presentation you also may be required to present charts, worksheets, and perhaps other objects that display financial information that may be relevant to this particular presentation. For the Excel worksheet you will want to create a sheet that represents the six different departments in the company: Sales, Bonds, Investment Services, Accounts, Online Investing, and Equity. Three of the departments are losing money: Equity, Accounts, and Sales. You must create a spreadsheet and chart that represent the profits and losses of all six departments and insert this chart into a PowerPoint slide for your presentation. Sales loses $10,125, Accounts loses $3,562, and Equity loses $22,876 per year. Online Investing just broke $31,000 in profits, Bonds makes $14,212 in profits, and Investment Services brings roughly $1 million per year in profits alone. The spreadsheet should compare the success of each department as part of the whole, which is the total profit per year. Insert this chart into your PowerPoint presentation.

Interactivity (continued)

2. Create a Word document describing exactly what your proposal is. You are going to propose that you cut Equity and Sales from the company because they are losing too much money and other departments are carrying them. Describe the reasons why you think it would be a good idea to get rid of these failing departments, and back it up by inserting the numbers from the spreadsheet and/or chart you created in Excel.

3. Create an Access Database. Call the database Services Offered. Your fields will be services and departments. There will be 12 records. All of the services fall into the three money-losing departments because the database is tracking how you can redistribute these services. The services are checking, savings, cd's, and investment services in Accounts; mortgages, auto loans, school loans, and scholarships in Equity; and customer service, gift certificates, warranties, and credit cards in Sales. Create a Mail Merge between this database and a new Word document.

4. Take the Mail Merge and the other Word document you created earlier and combine them into one document. Once you have finished, take the Word documents you have created for your presentation so far and save them as Web pages. First, view them to make sure the format is correct. Remember, you can view your document in your browser before actually saving it as a Web page.

A

Absolute cell reference
A cell reference that will remain fixed, even if the formula containing the reference is moved. To make a cell reference absolute, place a dollar sign ($) before both the column letter and row number.

Action Query
A query that is used to select records and perform operations on them, such as deleting them or placing them in new tables.

Active cell
The currently selected cell on a worksheet or chart datasheet, indicated by the cell pointer.

Adjustment handle
A small yellow diamond that appears when certain objects are selected. Dragging the handle allows you to alter the shape of the object.

Alignment
The horizontal position of text within a line or between tab stops. Word's alignment options are right, left, centered, and justified. Also the horizontal position of values or labels within a cell (for example, left, right, or center).

Anchor cells
The first and last cells in a cell range; the cells used to express a range address (for example, B9:E9).

Animated border
Indicates that a cell's contents have been sent to the Clipboard.

Annotation pen pointer
A tool that enables you to draw freely on slides during a slide show.

Answer Wizard tab
Help tab that replicates the Office Assistant by allowing you to ask questions or enter search topics in your own words.

Application
A software program that performs specific tasks, such as Microsoft PowerPoint.

Argument
Information such as a cell address, range, or value, enclosed in parentheses, used by a function or macro to produce a result.

Arithmetic operators
Symbols used by Excel to perform formula calculations such as +, -, *, and /.

Arrow keys
Used to move the insertion point, to select from a menu or a list of options, or in combination with other keys to execute specific commands.

Assumption
A variable factor that is useful for conducting What-If analysis in a worksheet.

AutoCalculate box
Automatically displays the total of the values in a selected group of cells in the status bar.

AutoComplete
Automatically finishes entering a label when its first letter(s) match that of a label used previously in the column.

AutoContent Wizard
A feature that assists you in designing a PowerPoint presentation quickly and easily. The AutoContent Wizard guides you through the steps of choosing basic layout design, style, and output type.

AutoCorrect
A feature that corrects common typing errors automatically as you type. AutoCorrect can be customized to correct specific mistakes that you frequently make.

AutoFill
Automatically fills a range with series information such as the days of the week when the range after the first value is selected using the fill handle.

AutoForm
Creates an Access form automatically from the table or query that you select. You can use AutoForm by selecting it from the New Form dialog box or by clicking the drop-down arrow on the New Object toolbar button.

AutoFormat
A feature that improves the appearance of a document by applying consistent formatting and styles based on a default document template or a document template that you specify. The AutoFormat feature also can add bullets or numbers to lists and symbols for trademarks and copyrights where necessary.

AutoLayout

Any of 24 predesigned slides set up to accommodate different combinations of text, pictures, charts, and other objects.

Automatic save

A feature that automatically saves document changes in a temporary file at specified intervals. If power to the computer is interrupted, the changes in effect from the last save are retained. Enabled by default, you can turn off this feature from the Save tab of the Options dialog box on the Tools menu.

AutoReport

Creates an Access report automatically from the table or query that you select. You can use AutoReport by selecting it from the New Report dialog box or by clicking the drop-down arrow on the New Object toolbar button.

AutoShape

One of numerous figures that can be drawn by simply selecting a shape from the Drawing toolbar and dragging the mouse. The user determines the dimensions and the location of an AutoShape.

AutoSum

A function that automatically adds the values in the cells directly above or to the left of the active cell.

AutoText

Text that Word is programmed to recognize. When you begin to type a word or phrase that Word recognizes, the program offers to complete it for you.

B

Best Fit

Resizes the width of a column so that it can accommodate the widest entry in the column, including the field name. You also can apply Best Fit by double-clicking the right border of a column's field name.

Black and White View

Shows how your presentation will appear when printed in black and white in case you do not have a color printer.

Browser

An application that allows you to find and view information on the World Wide Web. Major browsers include Netscape Navigator and Microsoft Internet Explorer.

Bullet

A small graphic, usually a round or square dot, that is commonly used to designate items in a list.

C

Cancel button

Removes the contents of a cell and restores the cell's previous contents if there were any; marked by an X on the Formula bar.

Cascade Delete Related Records

A command that, when active, ensures that deleting a record from the primary table will automatically delete it from the related table as well.

Case

Refers to whether or not a letter is capitalized. Some search features are case-sensitive; that is, they will differentiate between words that are spelled the same but have different capitalization.

Cell

The basic unit of a table, worksheet, or datasheet where you enter data, formed by the intersection of a row and a column.

Cell address

A cell's identification code, composed of the letter and number of the column and row that intersect to form the cell (for example, B22).

Cell pointer

The black rectangle that outlines the active cell.

Cell reference

A cell address used to refer to a cell in a formula. Cell references can be relative or absolute.

Character style

A combination of character formats from the Font dialog box that is identified by a style name. Changing an element (such as the font size) of a character style changes all text that has been formatted with that style.

Chart

A graphic representation of data values and their relationships, used to identify trends and contrasts in data.

Chart elements

The objects that represent information in a chart such as bars, columns, or text labels.

Chart type

Determines the style in which a chart graphically interprets data.

Chart Wizard

A series of specialized dialog boxes that guide you through the creation or modification of a chart.

Check box

A small square box that allows you to turn a dialog box option on or off by clicking it.

Clear Layout button
Allows you to eliminate relationships between tables, but does not eliminate just one relationship.

Click
To press and release a mouse button in one motion; usually refers to the left mouse button.

Clip Art
A precreated, usually copyright-free, graphic image that can be inserted into a document to illustrate a point or to add visual interest. Clip Art often comes in large collections.

Clip Gallery
A Microsoft Office facility that acts as a library of Clip Art, pictures, sounds, and videos. It allows you to import, store, and reuse these objects in Office documents.

Clipboard
A temporary storage area for cut or copied text or graphics. You can paste the contents of the Clipboard into any Office document or into a file of another Microsoft Windows program. The Office Clipboard differs from the Windows Clipboard in that it can hold up to 12 items at once instead of just one. You can view the contents of the Office Clipboard by activating its toolbar from the View menu.

Close
To quit an application and remove its window from the screen. You also can close a file while leaving the application open. The Close button appears in the upper-right corner of the application or document window.

Close button
A button at the top-right corner of every window and box that appears in Microsoft Office, it automatically closes that particular window or box.

Collapse
In PowerPoint's Outline View, reduces the selected slide to its title only, hiding all other text.

Collapse All
In PowerPoint's Outline View, reduces all slides to their titles only, hiding all other text.

Collate
A printing option that instructs your computer to print one complete copy of a document before beginning the first page of the next copy.

Color scheme
The default colors assigned to basic aspects of a presentation such as text, background, and fill color.

Column
A vertical grouping of cells that contains the values for a single field in a database table. Also part of the basic structure of a worksheet or datasheet.

Column selector button
The grey rectangle that appears above each column in a worksheet and/or datasheet and displays its column letter.

Comment
An electronic note that can be attached to a cell. Similar to a text box, but can be hidden from view.

Common Tasks button
In PowerPoint, clicking this button opens a menu that offers three frequently used commands: New Slide, Slide Layout, and Apply Design Template.

Contents tab
A comprehensive Help facility that organizes information by broad categories and subtopics.

Control menu
Contains commands relating to resizing, moving, and closing a window.

Controls
The functions in databases that control the data that are presented. Editing these controls changes the way data functions are performed and the way data are represented.

Copy
To place a duplicate of a file, or portion thereof, on the Clipboard to be pasted in another location.

Criteria
Conditions you set that instruct Access to select certain records for a query or filter.

Crop
To cut off portions of a graphic that you do not wish to display.

Crosstab Query
Query that performs calculations and presents data in a spreadsheet format. It displays one type of data listed down the left side and other types of data across the top.

Custom Animation
A text or object movement, sometimes accompanied by sound, that animates a slide element in order to call attention to it or simply add to the overall effectiveness of the presentation.

Custom dictionary
A document containing all the words that have been "learned" by Word's spell checker. More than one custom dictionary can be created and referenced by a single copy of an Office application.

Cut
To remove selected text or a graphic from a document to the Clipboard so that it may be reinserted elsewhere in the document or in another document.

D

Data
The fields, values, records, and other information entered and stored in a database.

Data series
Data taken from a row or column of a worksheet or datasheet.

Data type
Allows you to specify and limit what kinds of data Access will accept in a particular field.

Database
A system for storing, organizing, and retrieving information.

Database management system (DBMS)
Permits you to create a database, and then edit and manipulate its elements.

Database toolbar
Contains graphical buttons that execute specific commands when clicked.

Database window
The main control center for building and working with an Access database. Displays the database object buttons.

Datasheet
A table of information that serves as a data source for creating a graphical chart. In Access, displays the data from a table, form, or query in tabular form.

Datasheet View
Displays an Access table as it was created in Design View.

Default value
A field property that automatically enters an assigned value into a field for every record in a database.

Defaults
Predefined settings for variable items such as page margins, tab spacing, and shortcut key assignments; these can be changed when necessary.

Demote
To indent a line of text so that it is moved down a level in an outline hierarchy.

Design grid
The Design View grid in which you create a query or advanced filter.

Design Templates
Prepared designs you can apply to presentation slides that include organizational patterns, formatting, and color schemes.

Design View
The window in which you create and edit a database object.

Dialog box
A box that offers additional command options for you to review or change before executing the command.

Document window
The window on the screen in which a document is viewed and edited. When the document window is maximized, it shares its borders and title bar with the application window.

Documentation
The first section of a worksheet. It contains important information such as the spreadsheet's author, purpose, date of creation, file name, macros, and ranges.

Drag
To hold down the mouse button while moving the mouse.

Draw Table tool
Allows you to create the borders and gridlines of a table freehand.

Drawing toolbar
Contains tools for creating and formatting shapes, text boxes, and WordArt.

Drive
The mechanism in a computer that reads recordable media (such as a disk or tape cartridge) to retrieve and store information. Personal computers often have one hard disk drive labeled C, a drive that reads floppy disks labeled A, and a drive that reads CDs labeled D.

Dummy row/column
A blank row or column at the end of a defined range that holds a place so that Excel can recalculate formulas correctly if a new row or column is added to the range.

Dynaset
A table that is generated from a select query; it is dynamically linked to a source table.

E

Edit
To add, delete, or modify text, cell contents, or other elements of a file.

Effects
Text formats such as small caps, all caps, hidden text, strikethrough, subscript, or superscript.

Electronic spreadsheet application
A computer program designed to organize information in columns and rows on a worksheet and facilitate performing rapid and accurate calculations on groups of interrelated numbers.

Elevation
An option that allows you to change the angle at which you view a 3-D chart.

Ellipsis
Three dots (...) after a command that indicate a dialog box will follow with options for executing the command.

Embedded object
An object created in one file and then inserted in another. Embedded objects can be linked to their original source for automatic updating.

Enforce Referential Integrity
A command that ensures that for each record in the primary table, there is at least one corresponding record in the related table.

Enter button
Confirms cell entries in Excel. The Enter button is located on the Formula bar and is symbolized by a check mark.

Expand
In PowerPoint's Outline View, reveals all of the selected slide's text if it has been collapsed previously.

Expand All
In PowerPoint's Outline View, reveals all text on all slides if any of them have been collapsed previously.

Exploded pie slice
A pie chart slice that has been dragged away from the rest of the pie to emphasize it.

Export
Allows you to save database objects into other databases to be used there.

Expression
A mathematical equation or other form of data control that makes data entry more efficient.

Expression Builder
A dialog box offering you the option of creating a preselected expression or putting an expression together yourself using the values presented.

F

Field
The place in a main document where a specific portion of a record, such as a postal code, will be inserted when the document is merged. Also known as a merge field. Also, a column of information in a database table that contains a specific type of data.

Field list box
In Access, the small window appearing in such places as query Design View and the Relationships window that displays the fields contained in a particular table.

Field properties
Characteristics that control how a field appears, what kinds of data will be accepted in a field, and how these data will be formatted.

Field selector
The gray bar at the top of each Access datasheet column that contains the field name. Clicking the field selector selects the entire field.

Field size
A field property that limits the number of characters you can enter in a field.

File
A document that has been created and saved under a unique file name.

Fill handle
The small black square at the bottom-right corner of the cell pointer. Dragging the fill handle copies a cell's contents to adjacent cells or fills a range with series information.

Filter
Criteria you set that Access uses to find and display certain records.

Filter by Form
Command that allows you to select several different criteria from different tables to use to filter your table.

Filter Excluding Selection command
A filter that, when applied, searches for every record that does not include the data you have specified.

Find

Allows you to locate specific types of data or specific records in a database by searching for criteria that you specify.

Find and Replace

Allows you to locate and edit specific instances of text without having to conduct a manual search.

Floating toolbar

A toolbar housed in its own window rather than along an edge of a window. All toolbars in Office 2000 can be dragged to a floating position.

Folders

Subdivisions of a disk that function as a filing system to help you organize files.

Font

A name given to a collection of text characters at a specific size, weight, and style. Font has become synonymous with typeface. Arial and Times New Roman are examples of font names.

Font size

Refers to the physical size of text, measured in points (pts).

Font style

Refers to whether text appears as bold, italicized, underlined, or any combination of these and other formats.

Form

A database object that often serves as the main user interface for a database. It organizes records so that they are easy to work with.

Form View

The view in which you work with a form, entering and editing records.

Format

The way information appears on a page. To format means to change the appearance of data without changing their content.

Formula

A combination of cell addresses and operators that instructs Excel to perform calculations such as adding, subtracting, multiplying, or averaging. Formulas also can be used to perform calculations in Word tables.

Formula bar

The area below the Formatting toolbar that displays cell contents whether they are labels, values, or formulas. You may enter and edit cell contents in the formula bar rather than in the cell itself.

Freeze Columns command

Lets you freeze one or more columns on a datasheet so that they become the leftmost columns of your table.

Function

A built-in formula included in Excel that makes it easy for you to perform common calculations.

G

Gallery tab

An option available from the Office Assistant that allows you to choose a new Office Assistant character.

Get External Data submenu

Appears on the File menu under Import, allowing you to bring data from an external source into your Access database.

Global template

In Word, a template named NORMAL.DOT that contains default menus, AutoCorrect entries, styles, and page setup settings. Documents use the global template unless a custom template is specified. See also Template.

Go To

A useful command for moving great distances across a worksheet.

Graph 2000

The application used to create charts in Office documents.

Grayscale Preview button

Converts a presentation to shades of gray so you can see how it will appear when printed with a black-and-white printer.

Gridlines

The lines that separate cells in a table or worksheet.

H

Hanging indent

A paragraph format in which the first line of a paragraph extends farther to the left than subsequent lines.

Header/footer

A header is an item or group of items that appears at the top of every page in a section. A footer appears at the bottom of every page. Headers and footers often contain page numbers, chapter titles, dates, and author names.

Hidden text

A character format that allows you to show or hide designated text. Word indicates hidden text by underlining it with a dotted line. You can select or clear the Hidden Text option with the Options command on the Tools menu. Hidden text may be omitted when printing.

Hide/Unhide columns

Command that allows you to view the contents of a table without viewing the borders of the columns; it literally hides, or unhides, the actual columns.

Horizontal ruler

A bar displayed across the top of the document window in all Word views. The ruler can be used to indent paragraphs, set tab stops, adjust left and right paragraph margins, and change column widths in a table. You can hide this ruler by clicking View, then clicking Ruler.

HTML

An acronym for HyperText Markup Language, which is the language that defines the way information is presented on a Web page. Word can automatically convert the formatting you have given a document into HTML, which functionally turns your document into a Web page.

http

An acronym for HyperText Transfer Protocol; appears at the beginning of a URL to notify the browser that the following information is a hypertext Web document.

Hyperlink

Originated as an element of Web page design; usually text, clicking a hyperlink brings you directly to a predefined location within a document or to a specific page or file on the World Wide Web.

I

Icon

A small graphic that identifies a button or an object.

Import

Allows you to select database objects from other databases and bring them into a new one.

Indent

The distance between text boundaries and page margins. Positive indents make the text area narrower than the space between margins. Negative indents allow text to extend into the margins. A paragraph can have left, right, and first-line indents.

Index tab

Organizes help topics in an alphabetical list.

Input

The data you enter into a worksheet and work with to produce results.

Insertion point

A vertical blinking line on the screen that indicates where text and graphics will be inserted. The insertion point also indicates where an action will begin.

J

Junction table

A table that has a one-to-many relationship with two other tables, it is required when creating a many-to-many relationship with a third table.

L

Label

A box describing the data of the text box attached to it in Access form or report. In Excel, text that describes the data in neighboring cells.

Label prefix

A typed character that marks an entry as a label. For example, if you type an apostrophe before a number, it will be treated as label rather than as a value.

Label Wizard

A set of dialog boxes that lead you through a series of steps ending in the creation of a prototypical label for your personal or business correspondence.

Landscape orientation

A particular style of page orientation that creates a report on a page so that the horizontal width is greater than the height; opposite of portrait, or vertical, orientation.

Launch

To start a program so you can work with it.

Legend

Part of a chart that explains what each of the various data series markers represents.

Line break

A mark inserted where you want to end one line and start another without starting a new paragraph. A line break may be inserted by pressing [Shift]+[Enter].

Line spacing
The height of a line of text, often measured in lines or points.

List box
A box from which you can choose a number of options.

Logical operators
Operators that allow you to connect multiple simple conditions in a select query.

M

Macro
A set of instructions that automates a specific multi-step task that you perform frequently, reducing the process to one command.

Magnifier tool
Allows you to take a closer look at a page in Print Preview; it is controlled by the mouse and acts as the mouse pointer when in Print Preview mode.

Mail Merge
A function that allows you to combine the fields and data from an Access database with a Microsoft Word document.

Margin
The distance between the edge of the text in the document and the top, bottom, or side edges of the page.

Match Case
An option used with the Find command; forces a search to be sensitive to uppercase and lowercase letters.

Maximize
To enlarge a window to its maximum size. Maximizing an application window causes it to fill the screen; maximizing a document window causes it to fill the application window.

Menu
A list of related application commands.

Menu bar
Lists the names of menus containing commands for an application. Click a menu name on the menu bar to display a list of commands.

Merge and Center command
Combines two or more adjacent cells into a single cell and places the contents of the upper-left-most cell at the center of the new cell.

Merge cells
Command that combines two or more cells in a table into one cell.

Microsoft Clip Gallery
An index that contains tabs for storing Clip Art, pictures, sounds, and videos that you can insert into files.

Microsoft Clip Gallery Live
A Microsoft Web page that provides additional clips that you can download to your computer. Your computer must be connected to the Internet to access this gallery.

Microsoft Organization Chart
The application you use to create an organization chart for a PowerPoint presentation slide.

Minimize
To shrink a window to its minimum size. Minimizing a window reduces it to a button on the taskbar.

More Buttons arrow
Permits you to add buttons to a particular toolbar.

Mouse pointer
The arrow-shaped cursor on the screen that you control by guiding the mouse on your desk. You use the mouse to select and drag items, choose commands, and start or exit programs. The shape of the mouse pointer can change depending on the task being executed.

Move handle
In Access's Design View, the large black square in the upper-left corner of a selected item. Drag the move handle to place the object in a new location.

Multiple Pages display
A mode of Print Preview that allows you to view your document as it will be seen on multiple pages.

N

Name box
The box at the left end of the Formula bar that displays the address of the active cell or the name of a selected range that has been defined and named. You also can use the drop-down arrow in the Name box to select a named range.

Nonprinting characters
Marks displayed on the screen to indicate characters that do not print, such as paragraph marks or spaces. You can control the display of these characters with the Options command on the Tools menu and the Show/Hide ¶ button on the Standard toolbar.

Normal View

In PowerPoint, a tripane view that includes an out-line pane, a slide pane, and a notes pane, allowing you to work with different aspects of a presentation in the same window. In Word, used for most editing and formatting tasks. Normal View shows text formatting but simplifies the layout of the page so that you can type and edit quickly.

Note pane

A special window in which the text of all the footnotes in a Word document appear. The note pane can be accessed by double-clicking a note reference mark.

Notes Page View

A PowerPoint view option that allows you to insert reference notes that you can use during a presentation or print out for the audience.

O

Object

An item such as a chart or graphic that can be relocated and resized independently of the structure of a document. In Access, one of the seven main components of a database. Tables, queries, forms, reports, macros, modules, and pages are all database objects.

Office Assistant

An animated representation of the Microsoft Office 2000 Help facility. The Office Assistant provides hints, instructions, and a convenient interface between the user and Office's various help features.

Office Links submenu

An Access feature that allows you to publish parts of or whole database objects in Microsoft Word, or create a mail merge.

Open

Command used to access a file that has already been created and saved on disk.

Open Copy

Command that opens a copy of the file you want to work with instead of the original file.

Open in Browser

Command that allows you to open a file in your Web browser rather than in the application that created it.

Open Read-Only

Command that allows you to view a file, but not to make any permanent changes to it.

Operators

Symbols and words used to express conditions for selection criteria in a query.

Options

The choices available in a dialog box.

Order command

Controls the order in which objects on the same PowerPoint slide are layered.

Order of operations

The order Excel follows when calculating formulas with multiple operations: (1) exponents, (2) multiplication and division from left to right, (3) addition and subtraction from left to right. In addition, operations inside parentheses are calculated first, using the above order.

Outline View

A PowerPoint view option that facilitates entering, editing, and arranging text that will appear on slides.

Outlining toolbar

A PowerPoint toolbar that contains shortcuts to commands for promoting and demoting lines of text as well as for controlling what is visible in Outline View.

Output

The results produced by calculations done on the input data of a worksheet.

Overtype

An option for replacing existing characters one by one as you type. You can select overtype by selecting the Overtype option on the Edit tab with the Options command on the Tools menu. When you select the Overtype option, the letters "OVR" appear in the status bar at the bottom of the Word window. You also can double-click these letters in the status bar to activate or deactivate overtype mode.

P

Page Break

The point at which one page ends and another begins. A break you insert is called a hard break; a break determined by the page layout is called a soft break. In Word's Normal View, a hard break appears as a dotted line and is labeled Page Break, while a soft break appears as a dotted line without a label.

Paragraph style

A stored set of paragraph format settings.

Parameter Query
A query that is flexible and will prompt you to enter selection criteria every time the query is used.

Paste
To insert cut or copied data into a new location.

Paste Function command
Command that allows you to choose and perform a calculation without entering its formula on the keyboard.

Paste Special command
Allows you to paste the contents of the Clipboard using formatting and behavioral characteristics that you specify.

Path
The address of a file's location. It contains the drive, folder and subfolders, and file name. For example, the complete path for Microsoft Word might be C:\Program Files\Microsoft\Office\Winword.exe.

Personal Macro Workbook
Allows you to store macros so that they will be available to all Excel workbooks.

Placeholder
A dashed border that designates where to insert specific objects.

Point size
A measurement used for the size of text characters and row height. There are 72 points in one inch.

Portrait
A term used to refer to vertical page orientation; opposite of "landscape," or horizontal, orientation.

Presentation window
The main area of the PowerPoint window where you create, view, and edit your presentation.

Primary key
A field that contains a unique and constant value for each record and can therefore be used as the common field in linked tables.

Print Layout View
A view of a Word document as it will appear when you print it. Items such as headers, footnotes, and framed objects appear in their actual positions, and you can drag them to new positions.

Print Preview
A view that shows how a document will appear when printed on paper. Useful for evaluating the layout of the document before printing it. Includes a magnifier tool and the ability to view multiple pages at once.

Program
A software application that performs specific tasks, such as Microsoft Word or Microsoft Excel.

Program window
A window that contains the running program. The window displays the menus and provides the workspace for any document used within the application. The application window shares its borders and title bar with maximized document windows.

Programs menu
A menu on the Windows 95, 98, or 2000 Start menu that lists the applications on your computer.

Promote
To move a line of text up a level in an outline hierarchy.

Properties button
In Access, a button on the Formatting toolbar that allows you to add an expression to a form and change formats of the form.

Q

Query
A database object that uses a set of criteria to retrieve records.

R

Radio button
A small circular button in a dialog box that allows you to turn options on or off.

RAM (random access memory)
The memory that programs use to function while the computer is on. When you shut down the computer, all information in RAM is lost.

Range
A group of two or more cells, usually, but not necessarily, adjacent.

Range name
A name chosen for a selected group of cells that describes the data they contain.

Read-Only
A file setting that allows a file to be opened and read, but not modified.

Record
A row in an Access datasheet composed of all the field data for an individual entry.

Record selector
Clicking this gray box at the left edge of a datasheet record highlights the entire record.

Redo
Counteracts the Undo command by repeating previously reversed actions or changes, usually editing or formatting commands. Only actions that have been undone can be reversed with the Redo command.

Relational database
A database that contains multiple tables that can be linked to one another.

Relationship
The join created between two or more tables using common fields.

Relative cell reference
Allows a formula to be moved to a new location on a worksheet. The formula will then follow the same directional instructions from the new starting point using new cell references.

Remove Filter button
Undoes the filter that had previously been applied to your table, and shows all the records that appear in the table.

Repeat command
Performs your previous action again.

Report
A database object that arranges and formats data specifically for printing.

Resize
To change the size of an object (such as a text box, window, or graphic) by dragging the sizing handles located on its border. You also can adjust the dimensions of many objects from a dialog box.

Restore button
Replaces the Maximize button when a window is maximized. Clicking this button returns the window to its size before being maximized.

Reviewing toolbar
Contains commands for inserting, deleting, displaying, and navigating among comments.

Right-click
To click the right mouse button; often used to access specialized shortcut menus. The designated right and left mouse buttons may be reversed with the Mouse control panel to accommodate user preferences.

Row
The horizontal grouping of data fields that forms a record in an Access datasheet. Also one of the major structural components of an Excel worksheet.

Row height
The measurement of a cell from top to bottom.

Row selector button
The gray rectangle that appears to the left of each row in a worksheet or datasheet that displays its row number.

Run
Command that activates a query in Access. Also refers to starting an application and initiating the steps of a macro.

S

Sans serif font
A font whose characters do not include serifs, the small strokes at the ends of the characters. Arial and Helvetica are sans serif fonts.

Save
Stores changes you have made to a file maintaining the file's current name and location.

Save As
Command used to save a new file for the first time or to create a different version of a file that has already been saved.

ScreenTip
A brief explanation of a button or object that appears when the mouse pointer is paused over it. Other ScreenTips are accessed by using the What's This? feature on the Help menu or by clicking the question mark button in a dialog box.

Scroll arrows
Appear at either end of the scroll bar. Click them to scroll through a window in small increments.

Scroll bar
A graphical device for moving vertically or horizontally through a document. Scroll bars are generally located along the right and bottom edges of the application window.

Scroll bar box
A small gray box located inside a scroll bar that indicates your current position relative to the rest of the window. You can advance a scroll bar box by dragging it, clicking the scroll bar on either side of it, or clicking the scroll arrows.

Section
A part of a document separated from the rest of the document by a section break. By separating a document into sections, you can use different page and column formatting in different parts of the same document.

Select All button

The gray rectangle in the upper-left corner of an Excel worksheet where the row and column headings meet. Clicking the Select All button highlights the entire worksheet.

Select query

The most common type of query, used to extract and associate fields from tables and other queries, and present the data in datasheet form.

Selection bar

An invisible column at the left edge of a document to select sections of text. In a table, each cell has its own Selection bar at the left edge of the cell.

Series of labels

A range of incremental labels created by entering the first label in the series and then dragging the fill handle the number of cells desired. Excel automatically enters the remaining labels in order.

Serif font

A font that has small strokes at the ends of the characters. Times New Roman and Palatino are serif fonts.

Sheet

The term Excel uses to refer to an individual worksheet (Sheet1, Sheet2, etc.).

Sheet tab scrolling buttons

Allow you to access Sheet tabs that are not visible in the spreadsheet window. An Excel workbook opens with only 3 worksheets, but you may use 255 per workbook.

Shortcut key

A keyboard equivalent of a menu command such as [Ctrl]+[S] for Save.

Shortcut menu

A pop-up menu accessed by right-clicking the mouse. The contents of the menu depend on your current activity.

Simple Condition

A single selection criterion that is used to sort records in a query.

Simple Query Wizard

A wizard that allows you to create a simple, select query quickly and easily, by helping you with a series of dialog boxes.

Sizing handle

A small square on the frame of an object that you can drag to resize the object. Sizing handles are generally located on the corners of a frame and at the midpoint of each of its sides.

Slide icon

A small rectangular symbol that rests next to the title of each presentation slide in Outline View.

Slide Navigator

Allows you to go to any slide in a presentation quickly during a slide show.

Slide Show

Runs your slides as they would appear during a presentation.

Slide Show pop-up menu

Menu that offers commands for working with a slide show. Can be opened by clicking the Slide Show pop-up menu icon or by right-clicking a slide.

Slide Sorter View

A PowerPoint view option that displays all slides simultaneously in miniature form. In Slide Sorter View you can rearrange slide order by dragging the miniatures and apply special effects to individual slides or groups of slides.

Slide Transition effect

A special effect that controls how a slide makes its appearance during a slide show. Slide transition timings also can be set.

Slide Transition icon

A small slide symbol that appears beneath a slide in Slide Sorter view to indicate that a slide transition has been applied to that slide. Clicking the icon runs a preview of the transition effect.

Slide View

A PowerPoint view option that facilitates creating, modifying, and enhancing individual slides.

Soft return

A line break created by pressing [Shift]+[Enter]. This creates a new line without creating a new paragraph.

Sort order

The direction in which data are organized (i.e., ascending or descending).

Sorting and Grouping dialog box

Allows you to change the direction in which a database field is sorted.

Specific record box

The box in the bottom-left corner of a datasheet or form that indicates the number of the active record.

Spreadsheet program

A software program used for calculations and financial analysis.

SQL query

A query created using the Standard Query Language, the basic programming language Access uses to create and perform queries.

Standard Query Language (SQL)

Programming language used by Access to create and execute queries.

Standard toolbar

The row of buttons just below the menu bar that performs the most basic and most commonly used commands in an application.

Start

To open an application for use.

Start button

A button on the taskbar that accesses a special menu that you use to start programs, find files, access Windows Help and more.

Status bar

The grey bar at the bottom of the window that provides information about your current activity in a program.

Style

A group of formatting instructions that you name and store, and are able to modify. When you apply a style to selected characters and paragraphs, all the formatting instructions of that style are applied at once.

Style Checker

A PowerPoint feature that checks your presentation for visual clarity, case, and end punctuation.

Style dialog box

A feature that allows you to examine the overall formatting and styles used in a document template. You also can preview your document formatted in the styles from a selected template.

Summary slide

A slide that summarizes an entire presentation by presenting all of the presentation's slide titles as a bulleted list.

T

Tab Order

The direction in which the insertion point will move through the fields of a database object when the [Tab] key is struck.

Tab stop

A measured position for placing and aligning text at a specific distance along a line. Word has four basic kinds of tab stops: left-aligned (the default), centered, right-aligned, and decimal. Tab stops are shown on the horizontal ruler.

Table

One or more rows of cells commonly used to display numbers and other data for quick reference and analysis. Items in a table are organized into rows and columns. You can convert text into a table with the Insert Table command on the Table menu. Also, the object that gives a database its basic structure, storing its records and fields in tabular form.

Taskbar

A bar, usually located at the bottom of the screen, that contains the Start button, shows which programs are running by displaying their program buttons, and shows the current time.

Text box

A rectangular area in which text is added so that it may be manipulated independently. Also can refer to a box inside a dialog box where you enter information necessary to execute a command.

Text label box

A text box created by clicking once with the Text Box tool. Text in this type of box does not wrap to the next line when it reaches the edge of the box. Text label boxes are best used for single words or short phrases.

Text wrap

Automatic placement of a word on the next line when there is not enough room for it on the current line.

Timing

The amount of time a slide remains in view before a slide show advances to the next slide. Animation effects also have timings to control when they occur.

Timing icon

In Slide Sorter View, displays the amount of time a slide will remain on the screen before the presentation advances to the next slide.

Title bar

The horizontal bar at the top of the window that displays the name of the document and application that appears in the window.

Title Slide

A slide AutoLayout, generally used for the first slide in a presentation.

Toolbar
> A graphical bar containing buttons that act as shortcuts for common commands.

Toolbox
> An Access toolbar that contains items you can add to a form or report in Design View.

U

Undo command
> Reverses the last action you performed. The Undo button includes a drop-down list of all your recent actions so that you may undo multiple operations.

URL
> An acronym for Uniform Resource Locator; an address specifying where a particular piece of information can be found. A Web address is a kind of URL.

V

Validation Rule
> A rule that modifies the type of data that are acceptable in a database field.

Validation Text
> Lets the user know that the Validation Rule has been violated, and what type of data will be accepted into the database.

Values
> The numbers, formulas, and functions that Excel uses to perform calculations. Also, the data you place in a database field.

Vertical alignment
> The placement of text on a page in relation to the top, bottom, or center of the page.

Vertical ruler
> A graphical bar displayed at the left edge of the document window in Print Preview view. You can use this ruler to adjust the top and bottom page margins and change row height in a table.

View
> A display that shows certain aspects of the document. Word has seven views: Normal, Print Layout, Outline, Web Layout, Master Document, Full Screen, and Print Preview. PowerPoint views include Normal, Slide, Outline, Slide Sorter, and Notes Page.

View buttons
> Appear in the horizontal scroll bar in Word. Allow you to display the document in one of four views: Normal, Print Layout, Web Layout, and Outline.

View Datasheet button
> Toggles the Datasheet window on and off when you are working in Microsoft Graph 2000.

W

What's This?
> A help feature that allows you to click on a screen item in order to receive a ScreenTip that explains the item.

What-If analysis
> Technique by which you change certain conditions in a worksheet to see how the changes affect the results of your spreadsheet output.

Wildcard characters
> Symbols that represent unknown letters or numbers when using the Find feature.

Window
> A rectangular area on the screen in which you view and work on files.

Wizard
> A series of specialized dialog boxes that walk you through the completion of certain tasks.

Word processing program
> Software used to create documents efficiently. Usually includes features beyond simple editing, such as formatting and arranging text and graphics to create attractive documents.

Word processing text box
> A text box created by clicking and dragging with the Text Box tool. A word processing box allows text to wrap to the next line when it reaches the edge of the box and is useful for longer sentences and passages of text.

Workbook
> An Excel file made up of related worksheets. An individual workbook may contain up to 255 worksheets.

Worksheet
> The workspace made up of columns and rows where you enter data to create an electronic spreadsheet.

Worksheet tab

The markers near the bottom of the window that identify which worksheet is currently active. To open a different worksheet, click its tab. Worksheet tabs can be named to reflect their contents.

World Wide Web

A major component of the Internet, which is a vast global network of smaller networks. The Web is a network of server and client computers that exchange information via Web pages. Web pages include hyperlinks and present information in a graphical format that can incorporate text, graphics, sounds, and digital movies.

WYSIWYG

An acronym for What You See Is What You Get; indicates that a document will print out with the same formatting that is displayed in the document window.

X

X-axis label

A label summarizing the horizontal (*x*-axis) data on a chart.

Y

Y-axis label

A label summarizing the vertical (*y*-axis) data on a chart.

Z

Zoom

A command used in Print Preview mode while the cursor appears in the shape of a magnifying glass; allows you to take a closer look at the document in Print Preview mode.

Zoom box

Allows you to "zoom in" on your work for easier viewing by entering a magnification value.

Index